THE BIBLICAL WORLD

——•◆•——

The Biblical World is a comprehensive guide to the contents, historical setting and social context of the Bible. It presents the fruits of years of specialist study in accessible form, and is essential reading for anyone who reads the Bible and would like to know more about how and why it came to be.

Volume I begins with an overview of the full range of Biblical material (Old Testament, Apocrypha and New Testament), before going on to more detailed discussion of the major genres of biblical literature – from myth and prophecy to poetry and proverbs. The contributors also consider the ways in which the texts have been transmitted, the significance of parallel and related versions, and past interpretations of the Bible.

Explorations of the historical background are complemented by the findings of archaeology, and discussion of matters such as language, law, administration, social life and the arts offer a fuller understanding of the social and cultural setting of ancient Israel and the early Christian churches. Major figures in the Bible – including Abraham, Jesus and Paul – are studied in detail, as are its central religious concepts, such as salvation and purity. Volume II concludes with a survey of how the Bible is studied and seen today.

Written by an international collection of acknowledged experts, this monumental work will be an invaluable resource for students, academics and clergy, and for all to whom the Bible is important as a religious or cultural document.

John Barton is Oriel and Laing Professor of the Interpretation of Holy Scripture, University of Oxford, and Fellow of Oriel College, Oxford. He is the author of numerous books and articles on biblical texts, and is also the editor of *The Cambridge Companion to Biblical Interpretation* (1998) and (with John Muddiman) of *The Oxford Bible Commentary* (2001).

THE BIBLICAL WORLD

Volume II

Edited by

John Barton

London and New York

First published 2002
by Routledge
11 New Fetter Lane, London EC4P 4EE

Simultaneously published in the USA and Canada
by Routledge
29 West 35th Street, New York, NY 10001

Routledge is an imprint of the Taylor & Francis Group

© 2002 John Barton selection and editorial matter; individual chapters, the contributors

Typeset in Garamond 3 by
Florence Production Ltd, Stoodleigh, Devon
Printed and bound in Great Britain by
TJ International Ltd, Padstow, Cornwall

British Library Cataloguing in Publication Data
A catalogue record for this book is available from the British Library

Library of Congress Cataloging in Publication Data
Barton, John, 1948–
The biblical world / John Barton.
p. cm.
Includes bibliographical references and index.
1. Bible—Introductions.
BS475.3 .B37 2002
220. 6′1–dc 21   2001045714

ISBN 0–415–16105–3 (2 vol. set)
ISBN 0–415–27573–3 (Vol. 1)
ISBN 0–415–27574–1 (Vol. 2)

CONTENTS

———•◆•———

— Contents —

ILLUSTRATIONS

———·◆·———

PART V

INSTITUTIONS

CHAPTER TWENTY-SEVEN

THE HEBREW AND ARAMAIC LANGUAGES

——— .◆. ———

John Huehnergard and Jo Ann Hackett

LINGUISTIC CONTEXT

Hebrew and Aramaic are members of the Semitic family of languages, which is attested from the mid-third millennium BCE up to the present day. The Semitic family itself is part of a still larger language group, the Afro-Asiatic family (also called Hamito-Semitic), which also includes ancient Egyptian and Coptic, and several modern branches: Berber, spoken in pockets across northern Africa; Cushitic, spoken in northeastern Africa (Eritrea, Ethiopia, Kenya, Somalia); Omotic, in western Ethiopia; and Chadic, in western Africa.

It is interesting as well as useful to review the languages of the Semitic family according to their genetic relationships to one another, that is, according to subgroups of languages within the family that are more closely related to each other than to other members of the family, and that therefore share a more recent common ancestor. The ancestor of all Semitic languages, called Common Semitic, was probably spoken until some time in the fourth millennium; since writing had not yet been invented, there are no written records of this early ancestral form of Semitic. In the fourth millennium, Common Semitic split into two branches, East Semitic and West Semitic.

East Semitic consists of only two languages, Akkadian and Eblaite. Akkadian is the language of ancient Mesopotamia, which is the earliest-recorded Semitic language, first attested in cuneiform tablets from the twenty-sixth century BCE. (Another ancient Mesopotamian language, Sumerian, which is the world's first written tongue, is not part of the Semitic family, or, indeed, of any known linguistic group.) Akkadian itself split into two branches that begin to be recognizable about the end of the third millennium, Babylonian in the south and Assyrian in the north. It continued to be spoken until some time in the mid-first millennium BCE, and was written for several centuries after that, until the first century CE. Eblaite, which is very closely related to Akkadian, was the language of the city of Ebla, about 60 km south of Aleppo in modern Syria; also written in cuneiform script, it is known from several thousand clay tablets, all of which date to about the twenty-fourth century BCE.

The West Semitic branch comprises all other Semitic languages. It split very early into two subbranches, called South Semitic and Central Semitic. Most of the South

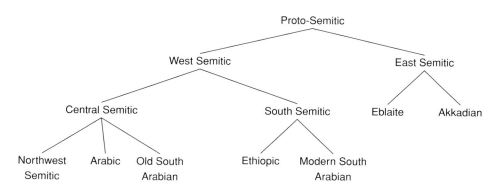

Figure 27.1 The Semitic language family.

Semitic languages are found in Eritrea and Ethiopia, including Geʿez (or Classical Ethiopic, or simply Ethiopic), the language of the Ethiopian Christian church since the fourth century CE, not spoken (except by priests) since about the tenth century; Amharic, the national language of modern Ethiopia; Tigrinya, the national language of modern Eritrea; and more than a dozen other modern languages. Another group of South Semitic languages is spoken by a very small number of people (roughly fifty thousand, and declining) in modern Yemen and Oman, on the southern coast of the Arabian peninsula.

Central Semitic has three subbranches. The Old South Arabian (or Epigraphic South Arabian, or Sayhadic) languages are attested from about the sixth century BCE until the sixth century CE in thousands of monumental building and other inscriptions carved into rock, as well as in recently deciphered documents incised on palm-leaf petioles. The best-attested of these languages is Sabaean, the language of Sabaʾ, the biblical kingdom of Sheba. A second subbranch of Central Semitic consists solely of Arabic, from pre-Islamic inscriptional dialects beginning at least as early as the sixth century BCE to the classical language of the Koran, to the plethora of modern dialects spoken today by nearly 200 million people in Africa and Asia.

At last we come to the third subbranch of Central Semitic, called Northwest Semitic, where Hebrew and Aramaic are situated. Evidence for Northwest Semitic appears as early as the beginning of the second millennium, in Akkadian (and also a few Egyptian) texts in the names of individuals who are called Amorites (whose relationship to the later Amorites of the Bible is a subject of scholarly debate). Ancient Semitic names were usually recognizable words, phrases, or sentences in the language of the name-bearer's culture. Thus, for example, the name *Rɔḥel*, Rachel, means 'ewe' in Hebrew; *ʾăḇimɛlɛḵ*, Abimelech, means 'my father is king' and *Yonɔṯɔn*, Jonathan, means 'Yahweh has given.' Now, the names of Amorites, although they appear in Akkadian texts, are not composed of elements of the Akkadian language, but of a language that is clearly more closely related to Aramaic and Hebrew. (It is also interesting that a few of the Amorite names are very similar to Hebrew names of the patriarchal stories; thus, for example, *Abī-rām*, 'my father is exalted,' is comparable to Hebrew *ʾAḇrɔm*, Abram ['the father is exalted'];

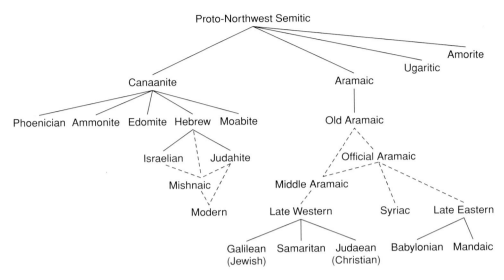

Figure 27.2 The Northwest Semitic languages.

Ya'qub-'il, 'the god has protected,' is comparable to Hebrew *Ya'aqoḇ,* Jacob ['he has protected'].)

Clay tablets inscribed with a unique cuneiform alphabet, discovered on a Syrian tell on the Mediterranean coast in 1929, revealed a hitherto-unknown Northwest Semitic language, now called Ugaritic after the ancient name of the town, Ugarit (modern Ras Shamra). Ugaritic turned out to be very close linguistically to Hebrew and Aramaic, but the texts are from the fourteenth to thirteenth centuries BCE, and thus earlier than Hebrew or Aramaic are first attested. Because of the close linguistic kinship, Ugaritic was for the most part deciphered, and its grammar understood, on the basis of Hebrew and Aramaic. But in turn, because of its greater antiquity and the similarity of many constructions and even phrases in Ugaritic and Hebrew, especially in poetic texts, Ugaritic has elucidated the grammar and meaning of a good number of previously obscure Hebrew biblical passages.

The rest of Northwest Semitic, with one or two exceptions, is divided into two large branches: Aramaic, which will be considered in detail further below; and Canaanite, the best-attested member of which is Hebrew. Thus, Hebrew and Aramaic are fairly close cousins within the Semitic language family. Canaanite comprises a very closely knit group of languages and dialects, many of which may have been mutually intelligible. The term 'Canaanite' is based on the ancient geographical term 'Canaan,' where its member languages were spoken. After Hebrew, the most important member of the Canaanite branch is Phoenician, the language of the important Phoenician cities of Byblos, Beirut, Tyre, Sidon, and others, and their colonies, such as Carthage (Phoenician *qart-ḥadašt,* 'new town'; the Phoenician dialect of Carthage is traditionally called Punic). Also Canaanite were the languages of other of Israel's neighbors: Ammonite, known from a few small inscriptions and seals; Edomite, still more sparsely attested; and Moabite, known especially from a long mid-ninth-century BCE inscription of the Moabite king Mesha (2 Kings 3:4), an inscription that in mentioning the Israelite king Omri furnishes the earliest extra-biblical attestation of a person mentioned in the Bible (although mention should be made of a ninth-century Aramaic inscription discovered recently at Tel Dan in Israel that refers to the kingdom of Judah as 'the house of David').

The earliest evidence for the Canaanite branch comes, surprisingly, from a group of texts written in Akkadian. These are cuneiform tablets dating to the early four-teenth century BCE, found in Egypt at the site of el-Amarna, which was the capital of the heretic pharaoh Akhenaton (Amenophis IV). The el-Amarna archive of nearly four hundred texts is part of the diplomatic correspondence of that pharaoh and his immediate predecessor and successors. Some of the letters are to other great powers of the period, such as Babylonia and Hatti, but the majority are letters from and to Egypt's vassal cities in Syria–Palestine, such as Ashkelon, Beirut, Byblos, Gezer, Jerusalem, and Shechem. The letters from the vassals in Canaan exhibit a very pecu-liar form of language: most of the vocabulary is Akkadian, but the morphology and the syntax, that is, the grammar, of the tablets is Canaanite. For example, for 'I wrote,' the Akkadian was normally *ašpur*, whereas the Canaanite of this period was *katabtī*; but in the el-Amarna letters from Canaan the scribes usually wrote the Akkadian verb in the Canaanite pattern, that is, *šapartī*. There are also a few purely

Figure 27.3 An Amarna tablet from Jerusalem. Copyright British Museum.

Canaanite words sprinkled among the texts. Thus a significant amount of information about early Canaanite, several centuries before the earliest known truly Canaanite document, can be extracted from these texts.

Recently excavations at the site of Ashkelon uncovered a small cuneiform fragment, from about the same period as the el-Amarna letters, that turned out to be part of a lexical (dictionary) tablet. Such lexical texts in Mesopotamia normally have two columns, a Sumerian column and an Akkadian column that provides glosses for the Sumerian words. The Ashkelon fragment, however, has an extra column giving translations also into a local Canaanite dialect.

HEBREW

The name of the language

It was noted above that in modern usage the word 'Canaanite' as a linguistic term refers to the close-knit subgroup of Northwest Semitic that consists of Hebrew and the other languages of ancient Canaan. In the Bible, what is now called 'Hebrew' is similarly referred to as 'the speech of Canaan' (*śfat knaʿan*; Isaiah 19:18). In the biblical passage concerning the Assyrian siege of Jerusalem in 701 BCE, the Hebrew of the kingdom of Judah is termed 'Judahite' (*yhudit*; 2 Kings 18:26, 28 = Isaiah 36:11, 13). Interestingly, the term 'Hebrew' (*ʿibrit*) is not used of the language in the biblical text.

Hebrew texts

The overwhelming majority of our knowledge of ancient Hebrew is based on the text of the Hebrew Bible. While it is notoriously difficult to date the composition of biblical texts, there is a consensus that the earliest poems in the Bible, such as the Song of Deborah in Judges 5 and the Song of the Sea in Exodus 15, go back to the twelfth century. The latest biblical text, the book of Daniel, was composed about 135 BCE. During this thousand-year period the language underwent many changes. While many of these changes were smoothed over by repeated editorial processes, nevertheless enough distinctive characteristics remain that scholars refer to chronological phases of the biblical language: Archaic Biblical Hebrew, the language of the earliest poetry; Standard Biblical Hebrew, in the period of the monarchy; and Late Biblical Hebrew, in the post-exilic period.

Although it is likely that parts of the Hebrew Bible were first composed as early as the twelfth century, the earliest extant copies of parts of the biblical text are from much later, thus far not before the third century BCE, which is the dating assigned to the oldest manuscripts among the Dead Sea Scrolls (such as a manuscript of the books of Samuel). A dazzling exception has recently come to light on small silver scrolls found in a burial at the site of Ketef Hinnom near the Old City of Jerusalem, in an archaeological context of the mid-seventh to early sixth century BCE; written on the silver surface is the lovely benediction of Numbers 6:24–6.

The inscribed benediction from Ketef Hinnom is but one of over three hundred objects with (usually quite short) inscriptions written in Hebrew that have been

Figure 27.4 An eighth-century BCE ostracon from Samaria with a Hebrew inscription. Photo courtesy of the Harvard Semitic Museum and the West Semitic Research Project.

found in archaeological excavations of biblical-period sites in Israel. The earliest known Hebrew inscription that is not simply a list of the letters of the alphabet is an eight-line farmer's almanac from Gezer that dates to the late tenth century. Many inscriptions, written in ink on potsherds, are letters, such as those found at Arad, written to a certain individual concerning delivery of staples such as bread and wine; or that to an official from a reaper whose cloak had been stolen; or those from a garrison commander in Lachish. Other inscriptions are receipts, such as a number of ostraca from Samaria, for jars of wine and oil. Still other inscriptions are simply one-word labels, or the name of an individual on a seal.

The language of the inscriptions is essentially the same as that of the Hebrew of the Bible, a fact that ensures that Biblical Hebrew is not a relatively late, invented language, as has sometimes been claimed. The inscriptions do, however, provide evidence of small but interesting differences between the dialect of the northern kingdom of Israel (sometimes called Israelian) and that of the southern kingdom of Judah (Judahite). In Judahite, for example, as in the Hebrew of the biblical text, 'house' and 'wine' are written *byt* and *yyn*, respectively, indicating a pronunciation with a diphthong *-ay-* in the middle of the words, *bayt* and *yayn* (biblical Hebrew *bayit* and *yayin*), whereas in Israelian the middle *y* does not appear, thus *bt* and *yn*, indicating that the diphthong *-ay-* has conracted to a single vowel, so that the words were probably pronounced *bêt* and *yên* in the northern kingdom. In biblical Hebrew the word 'year' is written *šnh* and pronounced *šɔnɔ*, but in Israelian inscriptions it is written *št*, and was probably pronounced *šatt*.

Hebrew is written from right to left in an alphabet of twenty-three characters. The alphabet, including the shapes of the letters, was borrowed from the Phoenicians to the north of Israel. Developments in the shapes of the letters occurred, so that the writing of Hebrew inscriptions has a discrete appearance that distinguishes it from the alphabetic writing of Israel's neighbors. After the fall of Jerusalem, however, the Hebrew script slowly died out and was replaced by a script used to write Aramaic. Thus the letters that are traditionally considered to be 'Hebrew' are in fact Aramaic shapes.

Figure 27.5 A page of the Leningrad Codex of the Hebrew Bible (fol. 6v = Genesis 11:6–12:1). Photo Bruce and Kenneth Zuckerman, in collaboration with the Ancient Biblical Manuscript Center. Courtesy the Russian National Library (Saltykov-Shchedrin).

The characters of the Hebrew alphabet represent consonants, some of which, however, are also used to indicate vowels, namely, *w* for the vowels *o* and *u*, *y* for the vowels *i* and *e*, and *h* at the end of a word for the vowels ɔ, ɛ, and *e*. In the earliest inscriptions, vowels were indicated only when at the ends of words. Later, long vowels were also sometimes indicated within words. But during the biblical period and for many centuries thereafter, most vowels were not normally indicated; they were easily supplied by the reader from his or her knowledge of the language. As Hebrew died out as a spoken language, to be replaced by Aramaic during the last centuries BCE, knowledge of the pronunciation of Hebrew among the laymen, who were expected to read aloud biblical passages during the weekly synagogue services, became more and more precarious. Thus a means had to be found to denote the vowels along with the consonants. Since the consonantal text of the Bible had by then been fixed, and was regarded as unchangeable, the vowels were indicated by diacritical marks, called points, that were placed below and above the consonants after which they were to be pronounced. Several such vowel pointing systems are known. The earliest, called the Palestinian, is known from a large number of manuscript fragments, the earliest of which date to the sixth century CE. Another system was used by Babylonian Jews beginning in the seventh century. In the end, however, only one system prevailed, a complex, comprehensive system devised by scribes in and around Tiberias in Galilee, and therefore known as the Tiberian vocalization, which is first attested at the end of the eighth century, and with which the biblical text has been adorned almost exclusively since the tenth century.

Between the writing down of the first biblical texts in the consonantal alphabet and the appearance of the vocalization systems, then, many centuries had elapsed, during which time the pronunciation of Hebrew, like that of any other language, continued to change. Thus, the vowel system of Tiberian Hebrew does not reflect the pronunciation of the biblical texts at the times they were written. A few sources provide some evidence for the pronunciation of Hebrew some centuries earlier than the vowel systems. These are transcriptions of Hebrew words, and sometimes even whole verses, into the Greek and Latin alphabets. The earliest such transcriptions are found in the Septuagint, the Greek translation of the Hebrew Bible begun in the third century BCE; in the Septuagint, place names and personal names, which, as was noted above, were usually meaningful Hebrew words and phrases, were simply transcribed, so that at least an indication of their pronunciation at that time has been preserved.

Summary of Biblical Hebrew grammar

Hebrew has twenty-three consonants. Six of these have two pronunciations each, a hard (stop) pronunciation (indicated by a dot in the letter, called *dagesh*) and a soft (spirant). Five of the letters have special forms that are used when they are the last letter in a word.

Consonant	Trans-literation	Pronunciation
א	ʾ	glottal stop, as in 'uh-oh'
ב	b	b
בַ	ḇ	v
ג	g	g as in 'get'
ג	ḡ	as in French r
ד	d	d
ד	ḏ	as th in 'then'
ה	h	h
ו	w	w
ז	z	z (originally, dz)
ח	ḥ	like ch in Scottish *loch*, German *Bach* (originally, a voiceless h pronounced in the pharynx of the throat)
ט	ṭ	t (originally, t plus glottal stop)
י	y	y
כ, final ך	k	k
כ, final ך	ḵ	like ch in Scottish *loch*, German *Bach*
ל	l	l
מ, final ם	m	m
נ, final ן	n	n
ס	s	s (originally, ts)
ע	ʿ	originally, a voiced counterpart to ח (ḥ)
פ	p	p
פ, final ף	p̄	f
צ, final ץ	ṣ	ts (originally, ts plus glottal stop)
ק	q	k (originally, k plus glottal stop)
ר	r	r
ש	ś	s (originally, an 's'-sound pronounced with air flowing through the side of the mouth, as in Welsh *ll*)
ש	š	sh (originally, s)
ת	t	t
ת	ṯ	th as in 'thin'

There are seven vowels, indicated by diacritics above and below the consonantal letters. There is also a sign, called *shewa*, indicating the lack of a vowel (within words; not usually used at the end of a word).

Vowel sign	Transliteration	Pronunciation	Example
◌ָ	*a*	as in 'b*a*ck'	שַׁעַר (*šaʿar*) 'gate'
◌ָ	*ɔ*	as in 'c*o*t'	מָטָר *mɔṭɔr* 'rain'
◌ֶ	*ɛ*	as in 'b*e*t'	לֶחֶם (*lɛḥɛm*) 'bread'
◌ֵ (also ◌ֵי)	*e*	as in 'th*ey*'	גֵּר (*ger*) 'sojourner'
◌ִ (also ◌ִי)	*i*	as in 'pol*i*ce'	בִּתִּי (*bitti*) 'my daughter'
◌ֹ (also ◌וֹ)	*o*	as in 'n*o*te'	קֹל or קוֹל (*qol*) 'voice'
◌ֻ (also ◌וּ)	*u*	as in 's*ou*p'	יָקֻמוּ or יָקוּמוּ (*yɔqumu*) 'they will arise'
◌ְ	—	—	סִפְרִי (*sipri*) 'my book'

There are also three ultrashort vowels indicated by a combination of the last sign (*shewa*) and one of the first three vowel signs above.

Doubled consonants are indicated by a *dagesh* (the same dot that marks certain of the consonants as stops or spirants), for example, עַמִּי *ʿammi* 'my people.'

The accent or word stress normally falls on the last syllable of a word, as in כָּתַב דָּבָר *kɔṯáḇ dɔḇár* 'he wrote a word.' Exceptions, such as certain types of nouns and certain verb forms, have the accent on the second-last syllable, as in לֶחֶם *léḥɛm* 'bread,' יָקֻמוּ *yɔqúmu* 'they will arise.'

As in other Semitic languages, most nouns and verbs in Hebrew are based on a root of three consonants. The root denotes a basic meaning. Meaningful forms are derived from roots by means of vowel patterns, preformatives, sufformatives, and other devices. An example is the root שׁמר *š-m-r*, which has to do with 'keeping, watching'; the following forms, among many others, are derived from this root:

שָׁמַר	*šɔmar*	'he watched'
יִשְׁמֹר	*yišmor*	'he will watch'
שֹׁמֵר	*šomer*	'watching, watcher'
הִשָּׁמְרִי	*hiššɔmri*	'watch yourself!'
מִשְׁמָר	*mišmɔr*	'prison, watch'
מִשְׁמֶרֶת	*mišmɛrɛṯ*	'guard, watch'

Nouns occur in two genders, masculine and feminine. Masculine nouns bear no special mark, while most feminine nouns end either in *-ɔ* or in *-t*; examples are

מֶלֶךְ *mɛlɛk* 'king' and מַלְכָּה *malkɔ* 'queen,' יֹשֵׁב *yošeḇ* 'male inhabitant' and יֹשֶׁבֶת *yošeḇet* 'female inhabitant.' In the plural, masculine nouns usually end in ־ים *-im* and feminine nouns in ־וֹת *-ot*: סוּס *sus* 'horse,' סוּסִים *susim* 'horses'; פָּרָה *pɔrɔ* 'cow,' פָּרוֹת *pɔrot* 'cows.' A dual form, used for precisely two of something, occurs with certain substantives that occur naturally in pairs and certain time words; the dual is indicated by the ending ־יִם *-ayim*, as in יָד *yɔd* 'hand', יָדַיִם *yɔdayim* '(two) hands'; יוֹם *yom* 'day,' יוֹמַיִם *yomayim* 'two days.'

The definite article, 'the,' has the form of a prefix, ־הַ *ha-*, plus the doubling of first consonant of the noun to which it is attached, as in מֶלֶךְ *mɛlɛk* 'king' and הַמֶּלֶךְ *hammɛlɛk* 'the king.'

Adjectives follow the substantives they modify and agree with them in gender and number; attributive adjectives also agree in definiteness: סוּס טוֹב *sus ṭoḇ* 'good horse,' הַסּוּסִים הַטּוֹבִים *hassusim haṭṭoḇim* 'the good horses.'

A characteristic feature of the Semitic languages, including Hebrew, is the juxtaposition of two nouns to express a genitive relationship, as in סוּס הַמֶּלֶךְ *sus hammɛlɛk* 'the horse of the king.' Such a juxtaposition is called a 'construct chain,' and the first word is said to be 'in construct' with the second. Many Hebrew nouns undergo sound changes when in construct, since construct forms are unaccented; for example, דָּבָר *dɔḇɔr* 'word' becomes דְּבַר *dḇar* when in construct, as in דְּבַר הַמֶּלֶךְ *dḇar hammɛlɛk* 'word of the king.'

Hebrew personal pronouns exhibit a variety of forms, depending on whether they are independent subjects of their sentence (as in 'I am king'), possessive (as in 'my book'), or objects of verbs (as in 'the scribe saw me'). Unlike English, Hebrew distinguishes four forms for the second person ('you'): masculine singular, feminine singular, masculine plural, and feminine plural. Below are the independent forms of the pronouns:

'I'	אֲנִי or אָנֹכִי	*ɔnoki* or *ˀani*	'we'	אֲנַחְנוּ	*ˀanaḥnu*
'you' masc. sg.	אַתָּ(ה)	*ˀattɔ*	'you' masc. pl.	אַתֶּם	*ˀattɛm*
'you' fem. sg.	אַתְּ	*ˀatt*	'you' fem. pl.	אַתֵּנָה	*ˀattenɔ*
'he'	הוּא	*huˀ*	'they' masc.	הֵם, הֵמָּה	*hem, hemmɔ*
'she'	הִיא	*hiˀ*	'they' fem.	הֵנָּה	*hennɔ*

Possessive pronouns are suffixes attached to nouns, as in סוּס *sus* 'horse,' סוּסִי *susi* 'my horse,' סוּסָהּ *susɔh* 'her horse,' סוּסֵנוּ *susenu* 'our horse.' As in the construct chain, many nouns undergo sound changes when possessive pronoun suffixes are added to them: סֵפֶר *seḓer* 'book,' סִפְרִי *siḓri* 'my book'; דָּבָר *dɔḇɔr* 'word,' דְּבָרוֹ *dḇɔro* 'his word,' דְּבַרְכֶן *dḇarkɛn* 'your (fem. pl.) word.'

The forms of the verb constitute easily the most complex part of Hebrew morphology. Each verbal root may occur in several finite and non-finite forms, and in a range of conjugational types.

The basic form of the verb, and the form under which verbal roots are listed in dictionaries of Biblical Hebrew, is the third person, masculine, singular of the finite form traditionally known as the Perfect, which is used to express completed action (usually in the past). For the root שָׁמַר 'watch, keep,' which was cited as an example above, this form is שָׁמַר *šɔmar* 'he watched.' The paradigm of the Perfect of שָׁמַר *šɔmar* is as follows:

שָׁמַר	*šɔmar*	'he watched'	שָׁמְרוּ	*šɔmru*	'they watched'
שָׁמְרָה	*šɔmrɔ*	'she watched'			
שָׁמַרְתָּ	*šɔmartɔ*	'you (masc. sg.) watched'	שְׁמַרְתֶּם	*šmartem*	'you (masc. pl.) watched'
שָׁמַרְתְּ	*šɔmart*	'you (fem. sg.) watched'	שְׁמַרְתֶּן	*šmarten*	'you (fem. pl.) watched'
שָׁמַרְתִּי	*šɔmarti*	'I watched'	שָׁמַרְנוּ	*šɔmarnu*	'we watched'

The form traditionally called the Imperfect is used for action that is not necessarily completed (present, future, past continuous, various modal nuances):

יִשְׁמֹר	*yišmor*	'he watches'	יִשְׁמְרוּ	*yišmru*	'they (masc.) watch'
תִּשְׁמֹר	*tišmor*	'she watches'	תִּשְׁמֹרְן	*tišmornɔ*	'they (fem.) watch'
תִּשְׁמֹר	*tišmor*	'you (masc. sg.) watch'	תִּשְׁמְרוּ	*tišmru*	'you (masc. pl.) watch'
תִּשְׁמְרִי	*tišmri*	'you (fem. sg.) watch'	תִּשְׁמֹרְן	*tišmornɔ*	'you (fem. pl.) watch'
אֶשְׁמֹר	*'ešmor*	'I watch'	נִשְׁמֹר	*nišmor*	'we watch'

In addition to the Perfect and the Imperfect, other finite forms of the verb are the Imperative ('watch!'), the Cohortative (first person only, as in 'let me/us watch,' 'I/we would watch'), and Jussive ('may he watch,' 'let him watch'). When a special form of the conjunction –וְ *w-* 'and', namely, –וַ *wa-* (plus doubling of the following consonant), is added to the Jussive, a narrative preterite is formed, as in יִבֶן *yiben* 'let him build,' וַיִּבֶן *wayyiben* 'and he built'; this is the most common type of finite verb in the biblical text. Nonfinite forms of verbal roots include the participle, as in שֹׁמֵר *šomer* 'watching, watcher'; two infinitives, שְׁמֹר *šmor* 'to watch' and שָׁמוֹר *šɔmor* (the latter used mostly adverbially to emphasize a finite verb).

The verbal forms listed in the preceding paragraphs are said to be in the *Qal*, or simple, conjugation, because, apart from the vowels and afformatives that indicate person and aspect or tense, no other augmentation of the root occurs. Most verbs, however, also occur in other conjugations that are denoted by specific augments;

these conjugations alter the meaning of the verb in fairly well-defined ways. The main conjugations, besides the *Qal*, are the following:

Conjugation	Characteristic	Meaning	Example
Niphal	prefixed –נ *n-*	passive, reflexive	*Qal* שָׁמַר 'watch,' *Niphal* נִשְׁמַר 'be watched, watch oneself'
Piel	doubling of middle consonant	factitive and others	*Qal* שָׁלֵם *šɔlem* 'be whole,' *Piel* שִׁלֵּם *šillem* 'make whole'
Pual	*Piel* with vowels *u–a*	passive of *Piel*	שֻׁלַּם *šullam* 'be made whole'
Hiphil	prefixed –ה *h-*	causative	*Qal* מָלַךְ *mɔlak* 'rule,' *Hiphil* הִמְלִיךְ *himlik* 'cause to rule, make king'
Hophal	*Hiphil* with vowels *ɔ–a*	passive of *Hiphil*	הָמְלַךְ *hɔmlak* 'be caused to rule'
Hithpael	prefixed –הת *hit-*	reflexive and others	*Qal* נָשָׂא *nɔśɔ'* 'raise,' *Hithpael* הִתְנַשֵּׂא *hitnaśśe'* 'raise, exalt oneself'

The morphology of the verb is further complicated by the existence of many so-called 'weak roots,' roots in which one or more of the three consonants undergo sound changes.

The normal word order of a Hebrew sentence is Verb–Subject–Adjunct (the latter being an object, an adverb, or a prepositional phrase). A few biblical sentences conclude this very brief overview of Hebrew grammar.

Genesis 11:7:

הָבָה נֵרְדָה וְנָבְלָה שָׁם שְׂפָתָם אֲשֶׁר לֹא יִשְׁמְעוּ אִישׁ שְׂפַת רֵעֵהוּ:

hɔbɔ nerdɔ wnɔblɔ šɔm śpɔtɔm 'ašɛr lo' yišm'u 'iš śpat re'ehu

come (literally, give) let-us-descend and-let-us-confuse there speech-their which not they-will-hear man speech-of companion-his

'Come, let us descend and confuse their speech there, so that they will not understand each other's speech.'

Numbers 6:24–6:

24 יְבָרֶכְךָ יהוה וְיִשְׁמְרֶךָ:

yḇɔrɛkkɔ yahwɛ wyišmrɛkɔ

may-he-bless-you Yahweh and-may-he-keep-you

25 יָאֵר יהוה פָּנָיו אֵלֶיךָ וִיחֻנֶּךָ:

yɔ'er yahwɛ pɔnɔw 'elɛkɔ wihunnɛkkɔ

may-he-make-shine Yahweh face-his toward-you and-may-he-favor-you

26 יִשָּׂא יהוה פָּנָיו אֵלֶיךָ וְיָשֵׂם לְךָ שָׁלוֹם:

yiśśɔ' yahwɛ pɔnɔw 'elɛkɔ wyɔśem lkɔ šɔlom

may-he-raise Yahweh face-his toward-you and may-he-set for-you peace

'May Yahweh bless and keep you; may he shine his face upon you and favor you; may he look upon you and give you peace.'

2 Kings 18:26:

וַיֹּאמֶר אֶלְיָקִים בֶּן־חִלְקִיָּהוּ וְשֶׁבְנָה וְיוֹאָח אֶל־רַב־שָׁקֵה דַּבֶּר־נָא אֶל־עֲבָדֶיךָ אֲרָמִית
כִּי שֹׁמְעִים אֲנָחְנוּ וְאַל־תְּדַבֵּר עִמָּנוּ יְהוּדִית בְּאָזְנֵי הָעָם אֲשֶׁר עַל־הַחֹמָה:

wayyoʼmɛr 'elyɔqim bɛn-ḥilqiyɔhu wšɛḇnɔ wyoʼɔḥ 'el-raḇ-šɔqe dabbɛr-nɔʼ 'el-ʽaḇɔdɛkɔ ʼarɔmit ki šomʽim ʼanɔḥnu wal-tdabbɛr ʽimmɔnu yhudiṯ bʼɔzne hɔʽɔm ʼašɛr ʽal-haḥomɔ

and-he-said Eliakim son-of-Hilkiah and-Shebnah and-Joah to-(the)-Rab-shakeh speak-then to-servants-your Aramaic for hearing we and-not-you-speak with-us Judahite in-ears-of the-people which on-the-wall

'Eliakim, the son of Hilkiah, and Shebnah and Joah said to the Rab-shakeh, "Speak to your servants in Aramaic, for we understand (it); do not speak with us in Judahite within the hearing of the people on the wall."'

Isaiah 19:18:

בַּיּוֹם הַהוּא יִהְיוּ חָמֵשׁ עָרִים בְּאֶרֶץ מִצְרַיִם מְדַבְּרוֹת שְׂפַת כְּנַעַן וְנִשְׁבָּעוֹת לַיהוה
צְבָאוֹת עִיר הַהֶרֶס יֵאָמֵר לְאֶחָת:

bayyom hahuʼ yihyu ḥɔmeš ʽɔrim bʼɛrɛṣ miṣrayim mḏabbroṯ śfaṭ knaʽan wnišbɔʽoṯ lyahwɛ ṣḇɔʼoṯ ʽir hahɛrɛs yeʼɔmer lʼɛḥɔṯ

in-the-day the-that they-will-be five cities in-land-of Egypt speaking speech-of Canaan and-swearing to-Yahweh (of) hosts city-of the-destruction it-will-be-said for-one

'On that day there will be five cities in the land of Egypt speaking Canaanite and swearing themselves to Yahweh of hosts; one of them will be called "the City of Destruction."'

Post-biblical forms of Hebrew

In addition to the chronological developments mentioned above, Hebrew as spoken in the biblical period undoubtedly comprised a number of regional dialects as well, one of which is revealed in the inscriptions written in the northern kingdom of Israel. A few dialectal peculiarities are also attested in the biblical text itself, although most of these were smoothed over by later editors to conform to a standard dialect, probably that of Jerusalem. In the post-biblical period, Hebrew was also the language in which the Mishnah was written. Mishnaic (or Rabbinic) Hebrew exhibits a number of significant differences from the standard biblical language, and is probably not a direct linguistic continuation of the latter, but rather reflects a different dialect, the origins of which are not yet entirely clear. On the other hand, the Hebrew of the Dead Sea Scrolls, including that of the nonbiblical manuscripts, is relatively close

Figure 27.6 A fragment of a text from Qumran (4Q109 Qohelet a = Ecclesiastes). Photo Bruce and Kenneth Zuckerman, West Semitic Research, Courtesy Department of Antiquities.

to biblical Hebrew, and probably reflects a deliberate attempt to reproduce the latter in a time when it was no longer spoken. Another form of Hebrew was written, in a descendant of the original Hebrew script, by the Samaritans. In the Middle Ages Hebrew continued to be used in the Near East and in Europe as the written language of an extensive literature. Modern Israeli Hebrew was created in the late nineteenth century on the basis of both Biblical and later dialects, with vocabulary drawn from all periods of the language; this revival of a language that had died out as a native tongue is unique in the world's history.

ARAMAIC

The vast majority of the 'Hebrew Bible' is indeed written in Hebrew. There are, however, a very small number of passages that are written instead in Aramaic; these are Ezra 4:8–6:18 and 7:12–26; Daniel 2:4–7:28; Jeremiah 10:11; and two words in Genesis 31:47. The reason or reasons for the presence of Aramaic in the biblical text have been the subject of scholarly debate. In the book of Ezra it is likely that the author, in using the correspondence of the royal Persian court as source material, retained the original Aramaic of the latter, and also employed Aramaic between the letters to lend an air of authenticity to the narration. In the book of Daniel, too, the use of Aramaic probably reflects an attempt at authenticity in the presentation of the speech of foreigners.

In our review of the Semitic languages above, it was seen that Aramaic is a member of the Northwest Semitic branch, and thus a relatively close cousin of Hebrew. Aramaic first appears in inscriptions from the early first millennium BCE, and it continues to be spoken to the present day. In this long period, a wide range of dialects is attested. The earliest inscription discovered thus far is a long bilingual text (the other language being Akkadian) on a statue of a Syrian potentate dating to the mid-ninth century BCE. This and a number of other inscriptions from the ninth through the sixth centuries are referred to collectively as Old Aramaic, although already dialectal differences are evident. When the Persian king Cyrus conquered the Near East in the latter half of the sixth century, Aramaic was already widely spoken across much of his realm. (Note the plea of the Jerusalem officials to the Assyrian Rab-shakeh in 2 Kings 18:26, cited above, that he speak Aramaic with them.) Recognizing this, Cyrus and his successors made Aramaic one of the official languages of their empire. This official status had two significant effects on Aramaic: first, a fairly standardized form of the language came to be used throughout the empire; and, second, the language, especially in this standardized form, called variously Imperial or Official Aramaic, came to be even more commonly spoken and written. Many Official Aramaic texts written on papyrus have been found in Palestine and Egypt. The Biblical Aramaic of the passages of Ezra is also an example of Official Aramaic.

Following the fall of the Persian Empire to Alexander, Aramaic continued to be widely spoken and written throughout the Near East. The period from the third century BCE through the second century CE is the Middle Aramaic stage. Many texts in a number of distinct dialects are attested from this time, including the texts and dialects of Hatra, of Palmyra, and of the Nabataeans. The dialect of the city of Edessa

(Urfa), which came to be known as Syriac, also first appears in this period. In addition, a Standard Literary Aramaic, based largely on the earlier Official dialect, is attested in a large number of writings, including the Biblical Aramaic of the book of Daniel, the Aramaic of the Dead Sea Scrolls, and the early Aramaic Targums (translations of the Bible). Other Aramaic documents from this time have been found from Egypt to Afghanistan.

From the third century CE on is the period called Late Aramaic, which exhibits enough linguistic variation to be classified into three branches: Late Eastern Aramaic, Syriac, and Late Western Aramaic. Late Eastern Aramaic comprises Mandaic, the language of the Mandaeans of southern Mesopotamia and adjacent Iran, a very small group of whom continue to speak Mandaic as a native language to the present day; and Babylonian Jewish Aramaic, the language of the large corpus of the Babylonian Talmud. Syriac, which was, as noted above, based on the Aramaic dialect of Edessa, is the language of the eastern church; a vast Syriac literature is preserved, dating from the fourth through the thirteenth centuries. The descendants of dialects akin to Syriac continued to be spoken in the vicinity of Kurdistan until the twentieth century; most of the roughly two hundred thousand speakers have now dispersed to other countries, including Armenia, Georgia, Germany, Israel, Russia, Sweden, and the United States. Late Western Aramaic is known from a number of dialects: Galilean (or Jewish) Palestinian Aramaic, in which are written the Palestinian Talmud, Midrashim, and Targums; the Aramaic dialect of the Samaritans; and Judaean Aramaic (also known as Christian Palestinian Aramaic, Syro-Palestinian, or Palestinian Syriac), the dialect of the early Palestinian Christians, and probably the dialect of Jesus and that reflected in the few Aramaic forms preserved in the New Testament (for example, two words spoken by Jesus in Mark 5:41, Greek ταλιθὰ κουμι for Aramaic טַלִיתָא קוּמִי *ṭalyṯɔ qumi* 'young girl, arise'; an invocation at the end of one of Paul's letters, 1 Corinthians 16:22, Greek μαραναθά for Aramaic מָרַן אֱתָא *mɔran ᵃtɔ* 'our lord, come'). A remnant of Late Western Aramaic continues to be spoken in three small villages near Damascus.

Aramaic differs from Hebrew in a number of significant features. In its phonology, for example, Aramaic is characterized by the reduction of Proto-Semitic short vowels in open syllables, whereas in Hebrew these are frequently preserved and modified. Aramaic has preserved the Proto-Semitic long vowel *ā* essentially unchanged while in Hebrew it has become *o*. While Hebrew and Aramaic have roughly the same consonants, some of the consonants in both languages reflect the merging of two or more Proto-Semitic consonants; those mergings were quite different in the two languages, however. These differences may be illustrated by a few examples. Because of the limited corpus and vocabulary of Biblical Aramaic, the Aramaic forms have been taken from Syriac:

	Aramaic	Hebrew
'three'	*tlāṯ*	*šɔloš* (שָׁלֹשׁ)
'my land'	*ʾar ͨ i*	*ʾarṣi* (אַרְצִי)
'gold'	*dhaḇ*	*zɔhɔḇ* (זָהָב)

Naturally there are many other differences between Hebrew and Aramaic, including the forms of pronouns, the declension of the noun, and the types of conjugation in which verbs may occur.

It was noted above that the Aramaic of Ezra is a form of Official Aramaic. Indeed, some of the Aramaic passages, such as the correspondence with king Artaxerxes, read as though they are nearly verbatim copies of ancient Aramaic letters to and from the Persian court. A sample passage concludes this section:

Ezra 4:17:

פִּתְגָמָא שְׁלַח מַלְכָּא עַל־רְחוּם בְּעֵל־טְעֵם וְשִׁמְשַׁי סָפְרָא וּשְׁאָר כְּנָוָתְהוֹן דִּי יָתְבִין
בְּשָׁמְרָיִן וּשְׁאָר עֲבַר־נַהֲרָה שְׁלָם וּכְעֶת:

*piṯgɔmɔ šlaḥ malkɔ ʿal-rḥum bʿel-ṭʿem wšimšay sɔfrɔ ušʾɔr knɔwɔṯhon di yɔṯḇin
bšɔmrɔyin ušʾɔr ʿaḇar-nahªrɔ šlɔm ukʿɛt*

message-the he-sent king-the to-Rehum lord-of-decree and-Shimshai scribe-the and-rest-of associates-their which living in-Samaria and-rest-of beyond-river peace and-now

'The king sent a message: "To Rehum the commander and Shimshai the scribe and the rest of their associates living in Samaria and the rest of Beyond-the-River: Greetings. Now . . ."'

WRITING AND THE ALPHABET

Hebrew and Aramaic use a form of the alphabet that they borrowed from the Phoenicians. We know that both borrowed the alphabet from elsewhere because the alphabet they use is not an exact match for the consonant repertoire in either Hebrew or early Aramaic; further, the letter names that we know from Hebrew and Aramaic actually correspond to the pronunciation of those words in Phoenician, another clue that the source script was Phoenician.

The earliest inscriptions using this alphabet date from about 1800 BCE, but the earliest extensive body of material comes from Serabit al-Khadem in the Sinai peninsula, written by Canaanite-speaking miners working the Egyptian turquoise mines there. These 'Proto-Sinaitic inscriptions' date from about 1500; they are largely religious in nature – votive inscriptions or prayers – and include, for instance, *lbʿlt* 'for the lady' (presumably the Egyptian goddess Hathor, since some of the inscriptions were found on objects in the Hathor temple), and *hnḏ ʾḫtʾ* [*m*]*tn nt*[*n*] [*l*] *ʾl* 'this is what 'Aḥta' has given as a gift [to] El.'

When we speak of the 'alphabet' that was invented in the second millennium, we are referring to consonants only. The alphabet operated according to the acrophonic principle: drawing a picture to represent the first consonant of the word the picture represents, as in rebus writing (drawing a door to represent /d/ and a bee to represent /b/, and so on). In this alphabet the original *b* was a picture of a house because the Canaanite word for house, *bayt*, begins with the *b*-sound; '(palm of) hand'

Pictograph	Object Depicted	Name	Sound Value	Early Phoenician Form	Hebrew/Aramaic Form	Hebrew Name
ඌ	house	*bêt*	*b*	⤸	ב	*beṯ*
⌐	throwstick	*gaml*	*g*	⅂	ג	*gimel*
⌐	forearm	*yad*	*y*	⅂	י	*yoḏ*
ᗐ	palm of hand	*kapp*	*k*	⌵	כ	*kap̄*
 ∿∿	water	*mêm*	*m*	⅗	מ	*mem*
ᕯ	head	*raʾš*	*r*	ⴱ	ר	*reš*
+	mark	*taww*	*t*	×	ת	*tɔw*

Figure 27.7 Examples of early alphabetic pictographs, illustrating the acrophonic principle.

is *kapp*, a word that begins with the *k*-sound, and so the *k* is a picture of a hand. Some speaker(s) of a Canaanite language probably adapted a principle similar to the one at use in one group of Egyptian hieroglyphs – those that represent one consonant only. These Canaanites would have been familiar with Egyptian writing, but they realized what the Egyptians did not: that there was no need for the more complicated Egyptian syllable-signs or word-signs. Instead, each of the original 27 or 28 symbols represented a distinct consonantal phoneme. The result was revolutionary: completely pictographic writing requires a picture for every word (or group of words similar in meaning); syllabic writing uses one sign for /bi/ and a different sign for /ib/, and still another for /bib/, so that hundreds of signs are needed to spell out all the words of a language; this early alphabet, however, consisted of 27–28 letters only, easy enough to learn in a day for anyone with a need for writing.

Between 1600 and 1000 the alphabet continued to develop. Whereas the Proto-Sinaitic inscriptions were written both vertically and horizontally, very shortly the horizontal came to predominate. A given early inscription could be written from right to left or from left to right, and some were even written *boustrophedon*, or 'as the ox ploughs' (that is, alternating left-to-right and right-to-left), but by 1000 the direction of writing had stabilized right-to-left. Since several of the pictographs changed stance to reflect the direction of writing, when the latter stabilized, so did the stance of the letters.

Already by the eleventh century, virtually all of the pictograph forms had developed into stylized 'linear' descendants. This linear Phoenician script is used through the first millennium to write Phoenician and Punic, and even neo-Punic (post-146 BCE) inscriptions, but the Hebrew and Aramaic scripts had begun to follow separate paths by the tenth century. The first inscription we have in a clearly Hebrew script is from Kuntillet Ajrud in the far south, dating around 900. In the Aramaic realm, the Tell Fakhariya inscription of the mid-ninth century from northern Syria is written

21

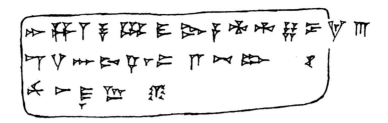

Figure 27.8 A Ugaritic abecedary.

The letters are in the following order:
first row: ʾa b g ḫ d h w z ḥ ṭ y k š l;
second row: m ḏ n ẓ s ʿ p ṣ q r ṯ;
third row: ǵ t ʾi ʾu s̀

in a peculiar script, somewhat unlike later Aramaic inscriptions, but the contemporary Tel Dan inscription, from much farther south (Dan in northern Israel), is written in a script that is identifiably Aramaic.

Alongside this Canaanite–Phoenician alphabet there was also in use in the same general area a cuneiform alphabet, the 'Ugaritic' or 'Canaanite' cuneiform alphabet. Found at Ugarit and elsewhere and dating from the fourteenth to twelfth centuries, it consists of the consonants in the Ugaritic language represented not by pictographs but in simple cuneiform ('wedge-shaped') characters, impressed left-to-right with a stylus on wet clay tablets. It seems that at least some of the letters in this cuneiform alphabet were drawn to resemble the Canaanite alphabet we have been discussing, which indicates that the cuneiform alphabet is an adaptation of the alphabet 'idea' to the clay tablet and cuneiform writing that were very much in use at Ugarit for international correspondence (in the lingua franca, Akkadian).

Archaeologists have also found abecedaries at Ugarit (an abecedary – pronounced 'a-b-c-dary' – is a writing of the alphabet in the order in which it is learned and memorized), and they show us the order of the Ugaritic alphabet: *ʾa, b, g, ḫ, d, h, w, z, ḥ, ṭ, y, k, š, l, m, ḏ, n, ẓ, s, ʿ, p, ṣ, q, r, ṯ, ǵ, t, ʾi, ʾu, s̀.*

This order is familiar to us from the Hebrew and Aramaic alphabets, but with more signs interspersed since Ugaritic used 27 different consonants, more than Hebrew or Aramaic. (The last three letters are add-ons.) A simplified cuneiform writing system – and a reduced consonant repertoire of 22 – is also known to us from a very few inscriptions, written right-to-left, from such Canaanite sites as Taanach, Sarepta, and Beth Shemesh, and three from Ugarit itself. An unexpected find at Ugarit, however, has been copies of Ugaritic cuneiform abecedaries with a radically different letter order: *h, l, ḥ, m, q, w, ṭ, r, b, t, ḏ, š, k, n, ḫ, ṣ, s, p, ʾ, ʿ, ẓ, g, d, ǵ, ṭ, z, y.* Remarkably, this is the order of the alphabet in Old South Arabian and in Ethiopic, the so-called *South* Semitic order. Those who developed the South Semitic script clearly borrowed this alternative ordering of the alphabet along with the alphabet itself.

The Phoenician alphabet was, of course, the source of the Greek and Latin alphabets. It was the Greeks who developed the first full system of vowel signs, by utilizing some of the earlier alphabetic signs for consonants that were not part of Greek (*ʿayin,* for instance – first an eye with pupil, then a circle with a dot, then a plain circle – is not pronounced in Greek, but was used for Greek *omicron* instead). There are Greek alphabetic inscriptions by the eighth century, but the antiquity of some Greek letter forms and the amount of development beyond Phoenician forms suggest a long period of contact between Phoenicians and the West before the final form of the Greek alphabet emerged. There is, for instance, a fragment of a Phoenician inscription found in Nora on Sardinia that dates to the eleventh century, and another Nora inscription from the ninth century. So there is no doubt the Phoenicians and the Greek world had an extended period of contact, at least three centuries, in fact, before the date of the first-known Greek inscriptions. All of these features argue for a complicated and extended process of the Greeks borrowing their alphabet from the Phoenicians, rather than one date that can be proposed as the moment of transmission.

BIBLIOGRAPHY AND FURTHER READING

The linguistic context

Garr, W. R. 1985. *Dialect Geography of Syria–Palestine, 1000–586 BCE*. Philadelphia: University of Pennsylvania Press.

Gelb, Ignace J., et al. 1980. *Computer-Aided Analysis of Amorite*. Chicago: The Oriental Institute.

Ginsberg, H. L. 1970. The Northwest Semitic Languages. Pp. 102–24 in B. Mazar, ed., *The World History of the Jewish People*. Givatayim: Jewish History Publications. Vol. 2.

Hetzron, Robert, ed. 1997. *The Semitic Languages*. London: Routledge.

Moran, William L. 1961. The Hebrew Language in its Northwest Semitic Background. Pp. 53–72 in G. Ernest Wright, ed., *The Bible and the Ancient Near East: Essays in Honor of William Foxwell Albright*. New York: Doubleday.

Moran, William L. 1992. *The Amarna Letters*. Baltimore: The Johns Hopkins University Press.

Rainey, A. F. 1996. *Canaanite in the Amarna Tablets*. 4 vols. Leiden: E. J. Brill.

Sivan, Daniel. 1997. *A Grammar of the Ugaritic Language*. Leiden: E. J. Brill.

Watson, W. G. E. and Wyatt, N., ed. 1999. *Handbook of Ugaritic Studies*. Leiden: E. J. Brill.

Hebrew

Barkay, Gabriel. 1992. The Priestly Benediction on Silver Plaques from Ketef Hinnom in Jerusalem. *Tel Aviv* 19: 139–92.

Gogel, Sandra Landis. 1998. *A Grammar of Epigraphic Hebrew*. Atlanta: Scholars Press.

Joüon, Paul. 1991. *A Grammar of Biblical Hebrew*. 2 vols. Trans. and rev. T. Muraoka. Rome: Pontifical Biblical Institute.

Kautzsch, E., ed. 1910. *Gesenius' Hebrew Grammar*. Trans. A. E. Cowley. 2nd edn. Oxford: Clarendon Press.

Kutscher, Eduard Yechezkel. 1982. *A History of the Hebrew Language*. Jerusalem: Magnes/Leiden: E. J. Brill.

Pérez Fernández, Miguel. 1997. *An Introductory Grammar of Rabbinic Hebrew*. Trans. John Elwolde. Leiden: E. J. Brill.

Polzin, Robert. 1976. *Late Biblical Hebrew: Toward an Historical Typology of Biblical Hebrew Prose*. Missoula: Scholars Press.

Qimron, Elisha. 1986. *The Hebrew of the Dead Sea Scrolls*. Atlanta: Scholars Press.

Sáenz-Badillos, Angel. 1993. *A History of the Hebrew Language*. Trans. J. Elwolde. Cambridge: Cambridge University Press.

Aramaic

Arnold, B. T. 1996. The Use of Aramaic in the Hebrew Bible: Another Look at Bilingualism in Ezra and Daniel. *Journal of Northwest Semitic Languages* 22: 1–16.

Beyer, K. 1986. *The Aramaic Language: Its Distribution and Subdivisions*. Trans. J. F. Healey. Göttingen: Vandenhoeck & Ruprecht.

Fitzmyer, Joseph. 1979. *A Wandering Aramean: Collected Aramaic Essays*. Chico: Scholars Press.

Huehnergard, John. 1995. What is Aramaic? *Aram* 7: 265–86.

Rosenthal, Franz. 1995. *A Grammar of Biblical Aramaic*. 6th edn. Wiesbaden: Harrassowitz.

Snell, Daniel. 1980. Why is There Aramaic in the Bible? *Journal for the Study of the Old Testament* 18: 32–51.

Writing and the Alphabet

Albright, William Foxwell. 1969. *The Proto-Sinaitic Inscriptions and their Development*. Cambridge, Mass.: Harvard University Press.

Cross, Frank Moore. 1989. The Invention and Development of the Alphabet. Pp. 77–90 in Wayne M. Senner, ed. *The Origins of Writing*. Lincoln: University of Nebraska Press.

Hackett, Jo Ann. 1996. Canaanites. Pp. 409–14, in Eric Meyers, ed., *Oxford Encyclopedia of Archaeology in the Near East*. Vol. 1.

McCarter, P. Kyle. 1996. *Ancient Inscriptions: Voices from the Biblical World*. Washington, D.C.: Biblical Archaeology Society.

Naveh, Joseph. 1982. *Early History of the Alphabet*. Jerusalem: Magnes.

CHAPTER TWENTY-EIGHT

THE GREEK LANGUAGE

——— •◆• ———

John Muddiman

INTRODUCTION

Alexander the Great constructed his vast empire on the force of Greek arms and the power of the Greek language. The linguistic dominion lasted much longer than the military one, for armies capture only territory: language colonizes the mind. It is appropriate therefore in this section, devoted to the institutions of the biblical world, that the chapter on biblical languages should precede the one on warfare.

Greek belongs to the great swathe of Indo-European languages and is one of the oldest for which documentary evidence survives. *Ancient* (Mycenaean) Greek was written in a syllabic script (known to scholarship as Linear B), with some ninety-odd characters. That complicated system, and with it literacy itself, disappeared with the fall of Mycenae in the twelfth century BCE. Four hundred years later the Greek language was encoded afresh in a very different sort of alphabet, borrowed from the Phoenicians. It had, like Hebrew, signs for each consonant, but extra symbols for vowels as well. This modification of the writing system was a dramatic improvement. Having lost the art of writing for so long, Greek culture recovered it in a flexible and efficient form that was to contribute significantly to the promotion of literacy, education, science and literature in the ancient and modern worlds.

In the following four hundred years, *Classical* Greek, though written in the same alphabet, was spoken in a variety of different accents and dialects: principally Doric, spoken in Southern Greece; Aeolic, spoken in Boeotia and Thessaly; and Ionic, which was used along the Eastern coast of the Aegean. Closely related to the latter was Attic, the dialect spoken in the territory of Athens. Colonization by the Greek city-states spread these different dialects in a patchwork across the Mediterranean world, from Southern France, across Italy, and Sicily and to the East into Turkey. But the cultural and political hegemony of fifth-century Athens made Attic the gold-standard of educated speech. It was adopted by the court of Philip of Macedon to underline his imperial pretensions, and spread by his son's whirlwind military successes. Greek unified the chain of command in army and government. It facilitated trade and stimulated local economies. Greek-speaking cities, with all the outward appurtenances of Greek culture, theatre, temples and gymnasia, sprouted across the conquered territories, including Syria–Palestine. The effect of this expansion on the Greek language was to reverse, in part, the natural tendency of language to diversify, and to bring about convergence, simplification and clarity at the cost of subtlety and grandeur. A new form of Greek was beginning to evolve.

HELLENISTIC GREEK

Greeks defined non-Greeks on linguistic rather than other grounds: they called them barbarians; that is, those who babble (see Homer, *Iliad* 2.867: the word only gained the sense it has in English of 'uncivilized and aggressive' after the Persian War). Language was felt to be a more significant factor in Greek identity than either ethnicity or political association. The verb from which the adjective 'Hellenistic' derives (*hellēnizō*) means literally 'I speak Greek'. This linguistic sense is reflected in New Testament usage: at Acts 6.1 'Hellenists' means Greek-speaking Jewish Christians living in Jerusalem; and at Acts 9.29 it refers to Greek-speaking Jewish opponents of Paul. The latter reference clearly indicates that no other supposed characteristic of 'Hellenistic' Judaism, for example, less strict observance of Torah or reservations about the Temple cult, is implied.

Hellenistic Greek is common (*koinē*) Greek in both senses of the word: universal and vulgar. It merges with classical Attic at the upper end of the scale of literary composition and reaches down to a subliterate level at which all the rules of grammar may be ignorantly violated. But in between lies a spectrum of broadly homogeneous or at least mutually comprehensible forms of the language, within which are to be found at different points the books of the Greek Bible. Hellenistic Greek is also a language in rapid evolution slowed only (for the educated) by the pull of classical masterpieces like the works of Plato or Demosthenes. Its main characteristics may be summarized briefly, as long as it is remembered that they encroached upon earlier forms only gradually and unevenly.

Koine eroded the differences between the dialects, with Attic forms usually predominating except where its forms were notably eccentric: 'Hellenistic language is thus by and large a compromise between the claim of the strongest and that of the majority' (BDF s.3). Because the literature of classical Athens continued to exercise enormous influence among the intelligentsia in the Hellenistic age, its forms did not disappear altogether and they were periodically revived. There was a distinct 'atticizing' movement in the late second century CE and another in the fourth. When atticisms occur among the variant readings of the Greek Bible, therefore, we have to ask whether they are residual, or secondary 'improvements' introduced by the scribes (Kilpatrick 1963).

The need for unambiguous communication between speakers for one or both of whom Greek was a second language produced simplification. Literary refinements in style or vocabulary that make no difference to the intended sense would have been a waste of effort. So, for example, the dual and optative forms of the verb fall out of regular use. Periphrastic formulations (i.e. auxiliary plus participle) begin to encroach on proper inflection. Particles, indicating the precise logical connection between one sentence and the next – the glory of classical Greek – are substituted by simple 'and' or 'but', and parataxis increases at the expense of subordinate clauses. Direct speech is preferred to indirect. The varied ways of expressing purpose are reduced to one standard idiom. Irregular nouns and verbs are forced to conform, and there is a steady decline in the use of the superlative adjective and of prepositions that govern the dative and genitive cases.

At the same time, the drive for clarity also produces redundancy for the sake of emphasis. Compound verbs (with prepositional prefixes) are preferred to their simple forms. Similar but subtly differentiated words become mere synonyms and are doubled up to ensure the message gets across. Pronouns are added even though they are strictly unnecessary since that information is already conveyed in the inflected form of the verb. Even the increased preference for diminutive forms can be seen as a form of emphasis, by understatement.

The pronunciation of koine varied significantly between speakers of different native tongues. Josephus, the Jewish historian, who wrote in a refined atticizing style, nevertheless confessed that he never managed to rid himself of his Semitic accent (*Antiquities* 20.263). One result of change in pronunciation was the reduction in the subtle differences between vowels and diphthongs in spoken koine. This can be traced by confusions in the textual tradition (since manuscripts were often copied from dictation); for example the pronouns we (*hēmeis*) and you (*hymeis*) would have been indistinguishable when spoken.

As a living language of international communication, Hellenistic Greek is not straightforwardly recoverable from literary remains. Most of the literature of the period is more conservative and 'classicizing'. But there are exceptions, like the discourses of the Stoic philosopher Epictetus, and indeed the New Testament itself, which come closer to the forms of koine as it was spoken. This conclusion was confirmed when a stock of non-literary Egyptian papyri came to light towards the end of the nineteenth century (Deissmann 1927; see further below).

THE SEPTUAGINT

The translation of the books of the Hebrew Bible into Greek was a long process that began in the third century BCE with the Pentateuch and continued into the early Christian period. The large Jewish community in Alexandria had been 'Hellenized' to such an extent that many were no longer able to understand their sacred writings in the original. For purposes of worship, exegesis and legal debate they needed a full translation, and not just an *ad hoc* rendering (or *targum*) of the Hebrew.

The translation that resulted is known as the Septuagint (LXX) because of the legendary account of its origins given in the so-called *Letter of Aristeas* (Charlesworth 1983). That book purports to have been written by a Gentile in the court of Ptolemy Philadelphus II (285–247 BCE) and tells how the king ordered a translation of the laws of the Jews to be made for the Royal Library, by bringing seventy (or seventy-two) learned elders from Jerusalem who completed the work faultlessly in as many days. Later tradition added the detail that each of these scholars worked independently on the whole text of the Bible, and their translations turned out, miraculously, to be identical.

The Aristeas romance is clearly a piece of Jewish propaganda for the authority of the Septuagint, quashing any doubts on that score that arise from its frequent omissions, variations and additions *vis-à-vis* the Hebrew. By the end of the second century BCE (Sirach, Prologue) the prophetic and other books had been added to the growing corpus.

The translation Greek of the LXX is quite varied even within the Pentateuch itself. In some instances (2 Kings) it is slavishly literal, in others (parts of 1 Kings) it is free to the point of paraphrase. Certain books, like Proverbs and Job, achieve a degree of literary artistry that even improves on their originals. With translations, some grammatical structures and specialized vocabulary from the originating language are likely to enter the bloodstream of the receiving language. This is especially so when the translation itself goes on to acquire scriptural authority. (Compare the effect of the English Bible in this respect.) Yet, at the same time its sacred 'classic' character is retained by a certain distancing. Thus, in the New Testament, there are both 'domesticated' Septuagintalisms and also, when the Old Testament is actually cited, its 'archaic' idiom and style especially in regard to word-order are deliberately retained.

BIBLICAL GREEK?

Judged by the standards of classical Greek many parts of the Greek Bible, above all perhaps Jeremiah in the Old Testament and Revelation in the New, leave a lot to be desired. Towards the end of the second century CE, with the idea of the plenary inspiration of the sacred text gaining ground, the nature of biblical Greek itself became a topic of theological debate. The apparent infelicities in the text might be explained (Origen, *Against Celsus* 1.62) as God's way of shaming the wisdom of the wise. Or they could be flatly denied and the authoritative scriptures be taken as the arbiter of good taste (Ambrose, *Epistles* 8).

As the first grammars and dictionaries of the Greek Bible were being compiled in the late sixteenth and seventeenth centuries, the debate broke out afresh between those who emphasized the importance of Hebraic idioms and the unity of the two Testaments, and those who claimed that the language of inspired scripture must be the purest form of Greek and attempted to adduce parallels to biblical diction from classical sources (see Voetz 1982–8: 897–906).

The breakthrough came in the late nineteenth century with the discovery of koine. The insights of Adolf Deissmann (1909, 1927) were vindicated by the full analysis of the vocabulary (Moulton and Milligan 1930) and syntax (Moulton 1908) of the Greek New Testament compared with non-literary papyri, and new grammars and dictionaries were produced that have become standard (BAG; BDF). While, on the one hand, the number of 'Jewish peculiarities' admitted in biblical Greek has continued to reduce, on the other, the Aramaisms and Semitisms, especially of the Gospels and Acts (Wilcox 1965; Black 1967) have been intensively studied. The historians of the language are still debating the question: Is the Greek of the Bible just koine at various stages of its evolution and at various levels of literariness with distortions caused by elements of translationese, or was there a distinctive and relatively unified biblical (or Jewish) Greek as a variant form of koine in which Semitic idioms had become firmly indigenized?

The most recent research, under the impact of modern linguistic theory and semantics, has begun to challenge the historical diachronic approach to biblical Greek and to ask the synchronic question about how it operates as a language system. One area of current enquiry is the attempt to produce an accurate description of verbal aspect in Greek. Is it correct to describe this in terms of tenses (past, present, future) since in non-indicative moods (infinitive, imperative, etc.) the distinction between the present, aorist and perfect forms has to do, not with time, but with the type of action involved (i.e. completed or incomplete, etc; see Porter and Carson 1993). Similar work on a range of other issues may well eventually result in the need to rewrite yet again the grammars and dictionaries of biblical Greek.

THE GREEK OF THE NEW TESTAMENT

Very few books of the Greek Old Testament were originally composed in Greek, but it is nearly certain that all the New Testament books were. (If the early Christian movement produced any literature in Aramaic, it is now lost; probably it did not.) Their Greek ranges from a near-literary koine to a moderately educated popular form of the language.

The Greek of Mark's Gospel is strong if unsophisticated. Its meaning is rarely in any doubt, even without the help of particles and subordinate clauses. The high incidence of the historic present and of 'immediately' (*euthys*) or 'again' (*palin*) in a sense subjective to the narrator (viz. 'moving quickly on' and 'here's another point') adds pace and directness to the tale; everything appears to be happening before the very eyes of the audience's imagination with a kind of narrative inevitability that corresponds to Mark's providential view of history. His Gospel bears the stamp of its origins in oral performance and was probably intended to be itself orally performed.

Mark's style provided the model and set the standard for the later evangelists. Luke in particular must be deliberately imitating the idiom, as we can tell from the fact that his own stylistic range is much greater: the elegant preface (Luke 1.1–4), the Septuagintal ring of the infancy story (esp. Luke 1.46–55, 68–79), the eloquence of Paul's speech on the Areopagus (Acts 17.22–31) and the accurately detailed account of his shipwreck (Acts 27). John's Gospel, while the most complex theologically, is the simplest in terms of its Greek. Its vocabulary is more limited and its syntax, apart from the more frequent use of conditional clauses, undemanding. Certain idiosyncrasies are apparent, such as the overuse of the perfect tense, as though the action of the Gospel story is ongoing in its present effects and the overuse of 'therefore' (*oun*) as an all-purpose connective, for everything follows on logically in John's powerful apologetic.

Paul's Greek is a lively, contemporary koine, far less coloured by Semitic forms than most of the rest of the New Testament, though in places that influence is noticeable (e.g. in the tendency to position verbs at the beginning of sentences). Paul adopts and adapts the conventions of Greek letter-writing; for example in his opening greetings and in the formula 'I beseech you, brethren' to introduce passages of moral exhortation. He also has some acquaintance with the conventions of rhetoric, in particular the Stoic–Cynic debate form known as diatribe (e.g. Rom. 2.1–6, 17–34), which he has blended with his own preaching style that makes his letters sound in places more like sermons. This is even more the case with the other New Testament epistles, 1 John, for instance; and, at a higher level of literary competence, 1 Peter and Hebrews.

Of all the books of the New Testament only the Apocalypse of John sinks below the normal range of what is grammatically acceptable. This can only partly be explained by the interference of Semitic speech forms: the author also seems to lack certain basic competencies in the language, so that, for example, indicative verbs are made to do duty for participles (Rev. 1.4). We may suspect that the author of this text was much more comfortable in some other language (probably Aramaic) than in koine (Mussies 1971).

The Semitisms in the New Testament arise from several sources. They are partly due to the use of the LXX. Partly, they are to be explained by the fact that the authors, especially the evangelists, are retailing traditions that originated in Aramaic. Yet other Semitisms belong to the local colouring of Greek as spoken in Egypt and Syria–Palestine; that is, loan words like Amen and grammatical usages which, though rare in Greek, are frequent in the New Testament because they coincide with Semitic usage. With these exceptions, the Aramaic words in the Gospels are always translated; this probably indicates that their intended audiences knew little or nothing of the language.

Secondly, there are a number of Latin loan words, in the Gospels and Acts particularly; for example transliterations of 'praetorium', 'legion', 'centurion', 'census', 'whip' (*flagellum*), 'executioner' (*speculator*), words for weights and measures, like 'pound' (*litra*) or 'pint' (*sixtarius*), and for coinage, like *denarius* and *quadrans*. It is a mistake to think that such terms point to Rome as the provenance of the documents in which they occur (e.g. Mark). They simply reflect the all-pervasive presence of the Roman army, of commerce and administration in the provinces of the Empire. The Greek of the New Testament is a genuine vernacular, interacting with local circumstances and open to external influences.

LINGUISTIC INNOVATION IN EARLY CHRISTIANITY

Jesus of Nazareth proclaimed a message of salvation and hope that was couched in the terms and images of rural Palestinian Aramaic-speaking culture. That within half a century it had spread to all the major urban centres of the Roman world is an indication of the linguistic power and adaptability of the early Christian movement. The New Testament follows the syntactical conventions of a middle-brow koine with a strong Semitic colouring; it is in its specialized vocabulary that it becomes more distinctive.

Simple terms in daily use such as 'way', 'word', 'brother', 'the breaking of bread' were loaded with new, deeper meaning to refer to the movement itself (Acts 24.14), its basic message (Acts 4.4), the relationship of its adherents (Acts 11.1), and its central rite (Acts 2.42) respectively. New words were coined to refer to important institutions. For example, Apostle (*apostolos*) in ordinary Greek is a collective noun used to denote an embassy, a party of colonists or the crew of a ship. In the New Testament it becomes a singular title for a delegate sent from one church to another (2 Cor. 8.23), or, more importantly, for someone like Paul sent by the Christ to proclaim the gospel (1 Cor. 1.17). Eventually the word would be identified with membership of the Twelve as the founding fathers of the Church and the irreplaceable historic witnesses to Jesus (Acts 1.21–2). In a similar way, the word 'gospel' (*euangelion*) appears in a peculiarly singular usage (Greek, like English, normally uses the plural) to refer to the only really 'good news', namely the offer of salvation in Christ.

The Christian movement also created its own technical vocabulary. For example baptism (*baptisma*) became the term for the Christian rite of initiation; the normal Greek word is *baptismos*, 'immersion' or 'ablution' without any ritual connotation. Or again, words like 'rising up' (*anastasis*) or 'I keep awake' (*grēgoreō*) in ordinary Greek would require contextual specification if they were to gain the technical meaning they have in many New Testament passages, of resurrection from the dead (esp. John 11.25) and eschatological expectancy (Mark 13.37).

Words with Semitic backgrounds provided another source of linguistic innovation. In standard Greek, the son of the man (*ho huios tou anthrōpou*) is a phrase that would have very limited and unexceptional applicability. In the Gospels, under the influence of its Hebrew (*ben adam*) and Aramaic equivalents, it describes the vocation to suffer like the prophets of old (Mark 9.12) and the certainty of vindication and appointment as judge in the age to come (Mark 8.38). Paul brilliantly translates this fuller sense by the equally Semitic but linguistically more immediately comprehensible title, the Last Adam (1 Cor. 15.45). Similarly repentance (*metanoia*, literally 'a change of mind') would not have had such a prominent role in the Gospels and Acts without the deeper meaning of its Semitic underlay, 'return'; that is, return to the gracious God of the covenant. Paul's use of the word righteousness (*dikaiosunē*) as God's gracious act of forgiveness in Christ (justification) embracing Gentiles as well as Jews is very strange when compared with secular Greek usage, but it makes much more sense when the Hebrew idiom, God's righteousness as his 'self-vindication' before Israel and the nations, is taken into account (Hill 1967).

Koine Greek, like good Roman roads, no doubt facilitated the rapid spread of the Christian gospel. But Greek as one of the institutions of the biblical world provided more than just an efficient medium of mass communication. It provided also the vocabulary and grammar for expressing a new way of believing in the one God. Concepts like 'grace', 'faith' and 'love', by constant repetition and emphasis, were filled with an evocative meaning they lacked before. Prophecy was reborn in the outpouring of the Holy Spirit. The narrative form of God's dealings with Israel was refocused on the simple but poignant story of Jesus' life, death and resurrection, as one who not only uttered the unutterable Word of God, but enacted and even embodied it (John 1.14).

BIBLIOGRAPHY

BAG = Bauer, W., Arndt, W. F. and Gingrich, F. W. 1957. *A Greek–English Lexicon of the New Testament and Other Early Christian Literature.* Chicago: University of Chicago Press.

BDF = Blass, F., Debrunner, A. and Funk, R. W. 1961. *A Greek Grammar of the New Testament and Other Early Christian Literature.* Chicago: University of Chicago Press.

Black, M. 1967. *An Aramaic Approach to the Gospels and Acts.* Oxford: OUP.

Charlesworth, J. H. 1983. *The Old Testament Pseudepigrapha.* Vol. 1. London: Darton, Longman & Todd.

Deissmann, A. 1909. *Bible Studies: Contributions Chiefly from Papyri and Inscriptions to the History of the Language, the Literature, and the Religion of Hellenistic Judaism and Primitive Christianity.* Edinburgh: T. & T. Clark.

—— 1927. *Light from the Ancient East: The New Testament Illustrated by Recently Discovered Texts of the Graeco-Roman World.* 2nd edn. London: Hodder & Stoughton.

Hill, D. 1967. *Greek Words and Hebrew Meanings* (SNTSMS 5). Cambridge: CUP.

Kilpatrick, G. D. 1963. 'Atticism and the Text of the Greek New Testament', in *Neutestamentliche Aufsätze: Festschrift für Joseph Schmid zum 70 Geburtstag.* J. Blinzler, O. Kuss, F. Mussner, eds. Regensburg: F. Pustet.

Moulton, J. H. 1908. *A Grammar of New Testament Greek.* Vol. 1: *Prolegomena.* Edinburgh: T&T Clark.

Moulton, J. H. and Milligan, G. 1930. *The Vocabulary of the Greek Testament Illustrated from the Papyri and Other Non-literary Sources.* Grand Rapids: Eerdmans.

Mussies, G. 1971. *The Morphology of Koine Greek as Used by the Apocalypse of St John: A Study in Bilingualism.* Leiden: Brill.

Porter, S. E. and Carson, D. A. 1993. *Biblical Greek Language and Linguistics: Open Questions in Current Research.* Sheffield: JSOT Press.

Voetz, J. 1982–8. 'The Language of the New Testament', in *Aufstieg und Niedergang der römischen Welt.* 2.25.2. Berlin: de Gruyter.

Wilcox, M. 1965. *The Semitisms of Acts.* Oxford: OUP.

CHAPTER TWENTY-NINE

WARFARE

———•◆•———

Thomas M. Bolin

Because many of its texts deal with the history of the Iron Age states of Israel and Judah, the Hebrew Bible (HB) is replete with material concerning warfare and its accouterments. Palestine was the arena for many military actions on the part of the great powers that ruled antiquity. Its strategic location as a landbridge between Asia and Africa, and its coastline with ports allowing access to the Mediterranean, made Palestine a highly prized goal in the political and commercial designs of Egypt and Mesopotamia. Rulers in both regions glorified their military exploits in the region with large and elaborate monuments in their home countries, such as the account of the battle of Megiddo in 1468 BCE inscribed by Pharaoh Thutmosis III at the Temple of Amon-Re in Karnak, and the detailed reliefs erected by Sennacherib in his palace at Nineveh depicting the siege of Lachish in 701 BCE. Palestine's widely diverse geography prohibited large-scale political unification and, as a result, left it vulnerable to foreign domination. Given these factors, it is hardly surprising that much of the region's history for over a millennium comprises a list of the foreign powers that dominated it. Beginning in the mid-second millennium BCE, and with only partial interruption, the Egyptians, Hittites, Assyrians, Babylonians, Persians, Ptolemies, Seleucids, and Romans each in turn exercised political control over all or part of Palestine, including ancient Israel. Practically all of the contemporaneous extrabiblical references to ancient Israel are in the military annals of her neighbors. In fact, the earliest known occurrence of the name 'Israel' is in a list of conquered regions and peoples on a victory stele of the Pharaoh Merneptah (1207 BCE; Hasel 1994). Consequently any discussion of warfare in the HB must deal with archeological and literary data from the larger context of the ancient Near East.

WARFARE IN ISRAEL AND THE ANCIENT NEAR EAST

Weapons

The vast majority of information concerning ancient weaponry comes from pictorial representations on monuments and tombs. Many of these are collected and illustrated in the work of Yadin (1963; see also Fretz 1992). Those parts of weapons made from wood have not survived except in the dry climate of Egypt. Weapons unearthed in Palestine consist mainly of those parts made of bone, metal, or stone, which resist decay. By the transition from the Late Bronze to Early Iron Ages in Palestine (ca 1400–1150 BCE) – the earliest historical period that might pertain to ancient Israel – technological advances in the design and manufacture of weapons and fortifications had reached a point that would remain relatively unchanged until innovations were introduced by the Romans (Chapman 1997: 338). Offensive weapons were basically of two types: stabbing or cutting for hand-to-hand combat, and launching for fighting from a distance. Among the former were the sword, ax, mace, and heavy spear. Swords had been for centuries crescent-shaped, with the edge on the outside of the crescent and hence used mainly for cutting. By the Iron Age long, straight, dual-edged swords were introduced, which allowed for both cutting and stabbing. This is the kind of sword, 'with two edges, a cubit in length' (Judg 3:16), that figures prominently in the story of Ehud, who uses one to stab Eglon, driving the blade straight into the large man. Axes were also crescent-shaped, and fitted onto the haft either by a socket or tang. As armor, shields, and helmets became stronger, ax-blades were narrowed and made thicker in order to give them greater force upon impact. Spears were long and heavy, with broad heads. The base of the shaft was also fitted with a metal point so that the spear could be planted upright in the ground (1 Sam 26:7). Because of their size, spears were used mainly for stabbing and possessed a great deal of force, as illustrated in Numbers 25:6–9, where Phinehas impales two people on a single spear. While weapons made of iron were not considerably stronger than those made of bronze, the advent of iron technology in Palestine meant that swords, axes, and spears could be made in greater abundance due to the more plentiful resources of iron ore in the region (Mcnutt 1991; Chapman 1997: 337). Weapons used for long-range fighting were the bow, javelin, and sling. The bow was by far the most effective of these, allowing for greatest range and accuracy. In the second millennium BCE the compound bow was introduced, so named because it is made by combining wood, gut, and horn. The result was a bow that allowed for much greater tension on the string and, hence, greater distance and force. Arrowheads were made of metal or bone and were either leaf-shaped or barbed; these have been found in abundance, many inscribed (De Vaux 1961: 243). Javelins were shorter than spears and often thrown by means of a rope coiled around the shaft. The person throwing the javelin would hold the end of this rope and use it to launch the weapon; this method allowed for greater distance and force. Slings were pouches attached to long ropes; a stone was placed in the pouch and then swung over the thrower's head. Stones could be as large as grapefruit and could be hurled a considerable distance with some force, as the famous story of the duel between David and Goliath in 1 Samuel 17 portrays.

To protect against these weapons soldiers utilized helmets, shields, and armor/mail coats. Helmets and shields varied in size and material. Egyptian and Assyrian shields were for the most part rectangular and almost the height of the bearer. Smaller round shields (bucklers) were introduced by the Sea Peoples, groups who came to Palestine after the collapse of the Mycenaean civilization in the thirteenth–twelfth centuries BCE (Yadin 1963: 65). Mail coats were fashioned of small, thin bits of metal resembling scales. Each bit was pierced and then sewn to an undergarment of cloth or leather. According to some ancient texts, there could be as many as 1,000 scales on a single mail coat. Fragments of an Assyrian mail coat from the siege of Lachish in 701 BCE have been found (Shanks 1984: 54). The Sea Peoples also introduced armor consisting of metal or leather bands attached to an undergarment. While these different kinds of armor offered some protection against assault, they were often cumbersome and impeded movement. Weapons were made stronger and heavier in order to pierce mail and helmets. The seams or joins of the sleeves to the torso in mail coats were also a weakness. This is how King Ahab of Israel met his end in battle with the Arameans: 'But a certain man drew his bow and unknowingly struck the king of Israel between the scale armor and the breastplate' (1 Kgs 22:34).

By far one of the most crucial military tools available to ancient armies was the chariot. For centuries it was unmatched in its quick maneuverability and striking capability. Solomon was reputed to have at his disposal 1,400 chariots and 12,000 horses quartered in cities throughout his kingdom (1 Kgs 10:26). In a victory inscription of the Assyrian king Shalmanessar III (858–824 BCE) commemorating the battle of Qarqar, King Ahab of Israel is said to have fielded 2,000 chariots in a losing effort (Pritchard 1969: 279). Drawn by two or, sometimes, three horses, the chariot served as a mobile platform for archers and javelin throwers. The standard chariot team consisted of two men, a driver and an attacker, although occasionally a third man was added as shield-bearer. Armies sought a delicate balance between the chariot's protection and firepower and its speed and mobility. Consequently, developing technology in regards to the chariot involved a constant trade-off between strength and velocity. The presence of a second or third rider, in addition to shields, armor and spare weapons, greatly decreased the vehicle's mobility. Moving the axle back on the body as far as possible allowed for sharper turns but put more strain on the horses. The introduction by the Assyrians of infantry armed with long, heavy spears greatly reduced the effectiveness of chariotry. The vehicle's speed often proved lethal to its passengers when they were impaled on the spears. By the middle of the first millenium chariots were relegated to roles of transport. Mobile assault units were then fielded as cavalry, although their full potential would not be exploited for centuries, until the invention of the stirrup allowed the rider to steer the horse with his feet and freed his hands for use of a weapon (Littauer and Crouwel 1979; Drews 1989: 19; Chapman 1997: 338).

Fortifications and siegeworks

In looking at the development of fortifications in the ancient Levant one must bear in mind that it goes hand in hand with the growth of the city as a social reality. This is made clear at Jericho, the oldest walled town on earth. Excavators there discovered in one of the earliest strata (ca 7000 BCE) a large stone tower attached to a massive wall, which they interpreted to be part of defensive fortifications (see Figure 29.1; Yadin 1963: 32–5; but for an alternative interpretation see Herzog 1992: 845). In Palestine the presence of large fortified cities on tells – artificial mounds containing the ruins of previous sites – occurs in several archeological periods often with long gaps in between where cities were destroyed and/or abandoned. Such gaps appear between the Early and Middle Bronze Ages (ca 2300–1800 BCE) and

Figure 29.1   Stone tower, Jericho, ca 7000 BCE. Photo Thomas M. Bolin.

the Late Bronze and Early Iron Ages (ca 1400–1150 BCE). By Iron II (1000–539 BCE) many fortified cities are present in Palestine. With few notable exceptions, the kinds of fortifications devised during the Bronze Age were used in successive periods, although at certain times and locales some tactics were favored more than others.

Most cities were surrounded by walls that could vary in thickness, being as wide as 10 meters (see Figure 29.2). They were made of mudbricks, fieldstones, or ashlars placed on foundations of earth or stone (see Herzog 1992 and Fritz 1995: 33–5). No walls have survived to their original height, but based on the size of their foundations and information from pictorial scenes, they rose to a height of several stories.

Figure 29.2 Iron Age wall, Jerusalem, eighth century BCE. Photo Thomas M. Bolin.

The ramparts were topped with a crenelated parapet that often jutted out over the face of the wall. One type of wall used in the region (e.g., at Hazor, Samaria, and Beer-Sheba) during the early Iron Age was the casemate, which consisted of two parallel walls placed a few meters apart and joined by supporting perpendicular walls. The resulting structure had a series of chambers that could function as dwellings, guardhouses, or storerooms and were filled with earth and debris during a siege for added protection (Fritz 1995: 137–8). The harlot Rahab who aids the Israelites in the capture of Jericho is said to have lived in a house 'on the outer side of the city wall, within the wall itself' (Josh 2:15). Additionally cities often had a ring of earthen ramparts outside the perimeter of the walls. One specific type of rampart is the glacis, which rises at a steep angle up to the base of the walls. The surface could be coated with plaster or stones and during a siege wetted. This created a slippery, steep surface that prevented both frontal assault and mining operations by a besieging force. There were several means by which fortifications provided their defenders with an angle to fire upon an enemy and repulse an attack. Walls could be outfitted at regular intervals with towers, redans, that is, angular or semicircular protuberances, or with a jagged outline resembling the teeth in the blade of a circular saw (offset–inset walls). The Iron II stratum of Megiddo is a good example of this last type. Each kind of fortification allowed defenders to fire at the flanks of enemy soldiers and siegeworks, thus exposing the attackers beyond the protection of their shields.

Because they constituted by their very nature the weakest component of urban fortifications, gates were equipped with several key defensive features. After the Early Bronze Age most cities possessed a single gate, although posterns and underground passages were also used. Gates were flanked on both sides by large towers, often constructed of large ashlars. These towers would have passages that led from chambers inside them and opened onto the gate's passageway. By the Iron Age these passages and chambers had been broadened to such an extent as to create anywhere from one to three pairs of large chambers on either side of the passageway that opened directly onto the gate (see Figure 29.3; Herzog 1992: 847, 849–51; Fritz 1995: 36, 139). Chambered gates built according to a similar layout at Megiddo, Hazor, and Gezer were long dated to the tenth-century BCE and attributed to Solomon's building program mentioned in 1 Kings 9:15. However, after further investigation they have since been dated to the succeeding century (Ussishkin 1992: 673–7). Approaches to gates were often from the right (looking from the outside) and ran parallel to the walls before making a sharp right turn into the gate proper. This would require those entering the gate to slow in order to negotiate the turn. One can still see a variation of this kind of defensive feature in the Damascus Gate,

Figure 29.3   City gate, Megiddo, ninth century BCE. Photo Thomas M. Bolin.

built by Suleiman the Magnificent in 1537 CE into the northern wall of the Old City of Jerusalem. One approaches the gate head-on, but must then make sharp left- and right-hand turns in rapid succession inside the gate before emerging into the city. The direction of approach of ancient gates would expose the unprotected right sides of attackers (because most people are right-handed, shields would be carried in the left) to fire from the walls. Some cities (e.g., Iron Age Dan, Megiddo, Beer-Sheva, and Lachish) were equipped with double gates, the second gate being placed farther down the tell perpendicular to the main city gate. Deuteronomy 3:5 talks of the fortified cities of King Og of Bashan in the Transjordan, 'with high walls, double gates, and bars' captured by the Israelites.

One crucial component of a city's defenses concerned its access to drinking water during a protracted siege. For obvious reasons many cities were built near natural springs. However, the springs would usually be located in a ravine, whereas the city would continually occupy rising ground as the successive layers of its tell grew. This often placed the spring outside the city walls and presented the dilemma of getting water inside the city during a siege when the gate could not be opened. To address this problem three different solutions were devised in the Iron Age, each requiring that tunnels be dug through many meters of prior debris and solid rock (Mazar 1990: 478–85; Fritz 1995: 151–60). Some tunnels tapped into subterranean sources of groundwater inside the city and allowed inhabitants to descend by means of stairs to draw water. At Gibeon a spiral staircase was carved into a shaft 10 meters in diameter that descended 25 meters down a flight of 172 steps to the groundwater (Fritz 1995: 152–3). Alternatively, an underground tunnel could be cut to provide direct access to the spring outside the city, which was then camouflaged to prevent detection from besiegers. A well-preserved example of this type of water system is at Megiddo. Other rock-cut channels brought water from an outside source into the city where the water collected in a pool. There are two examples of this system in Jerusalem: Warren's Shaft and Hezekiah's Tunnel. The former brought water inside the city to collect in a pool, and it could then be drawn up through a vertical shaft reached by subterranean stairs. The latter was dug by Hezekiah, most likely in preparation for the Assyrian siege of 701 BCE (2 Kgs 20:20; Sir 48:17). An inscription found in the shaft and now in a museum in Istanbul records the dramatic moment where quarrymen, digging from both sides, met and joined both halves of the tunnel. 'While there were still three cubits to be cut through, there was heard the voice of a man calling to his fellow' (Pritchard 1969: 321). Another reference to Hezekiah's tunnel in the HB could be in an anachronism that occurs in the story of David's purported capture of the city, set two centuries before Hezekiah. There David states that if a person wants to capture Jerusalem, 'let him get up the water shaft' (2 Sam 5:8, although the text is dubious). No water system resembling that mentioned by David is known to exist from that time. While the Warren Shaft is dated earlier than Hezekiah's Tunnel, one cannot use it to gain entry into the city. However, the Hezekiah Tunnel will allow a person access from the external spring into the city at the Siloam pool. One call still walk the length of the tunnel and exit at the pool, as tourists do to this day.

We know a great deal about siegeworks in ancient Palestine from Egyptian and Assyrian reliefs (illustrations in Yadin 1963; Ussishkin 1980; 1982; Shanks 1984;

Russell 1991). The biblical text mentions in several places the horrors brought about by protracted siege, the most notable being famine. 2 Kings 6:24–32 tells of the populace of Samaria devouring its own children during a siege by the Arameans. Attackers would throw up a ramp against a vulnerable part of the city's defenses, most often the gate. The Assyrian siege ramp of 701 BCE is visible at Lachish (Figure 29.4). Certainly the most impressive and well-known ramp in the region is that erected by the Romans at Masada in 73 CE, which rises nearly 150 meters above the desert floor and reaches almost to the top of the mountain fortress (see Figure 29.5). Defenders inside the city could counter with a defense ramp in an attempt to maintain the advantage of higher ground; this strategy was employed by the inhabitants of Lachish against the Assyrians in 701 BCE (Ussishkin 1984). Battering rams would be sent up the ramp, supported by archers and slingers who could be positioned on movable siege towers to place them higher than the defenders in the city. Ezekiel is commanded by God to symbolize the siege of Jerusalem by the Babylonians by taking a brick and placing 'a ramp . . . and battering rams against it all around' (Ezek 4:2). The most potent rams were those of the Assyrians, which were placed on mobile carts covered with leather and metal armor. A long pole with a large head was suspended by ropes inside the cart. The pole was swung back on the ropes and released in an attempt to lodge it between stones or bricks in the wall. Once the pole was inserted into the wall the ram's operators would jiggle it in an attempt to loosen bricks or stones. Defenders would hurl torches on the rams

Figure 29.4 Assyrian siege ramp, Lachish, 701 BCE. Photo Thomas M. Bolin.

Figure 29.5 Roman siege ramp, Masada, 73 CE. Photo Thomas M. Bolin.

in order to set them alight. The attackers, in turn, would pour water on the poles and carts. In addition to torches, the besieged would also rain arrows and stones down upon the attackers and occasionally engage in sorties outside the city walls. The attackers would often attempt to negotiate a parley with the city before beginning a siege, such as the Assyrians did under Sennacherib at Jerusalem in 2 Kings 18–9. In fact, Deuteronomy 20, which is the HB's 'code of conduct' for warfare, advises Israelite armies to attempt a peaceful resolution of a siege before taking a city. Occasionally a city would capitulate, as in the case of David's siege of Abel Beth-Maacah (2 Sam 20:14–22) where the inhabitants accede to the request of David's commander to turn over the traitor Sheba by lobbing his head over the wall to the besiegers. Often the parleys would not avert a siege. In 1 Kings 20 Ben-Hadad of Aram camps his army before Samaria and sends a threatening message to King Ahab. Ahab responds with a martial proverb – 'One who puts on armor should not brag like one who takes it off' (v. 11) – that does little to appease the Aramean king. Finally, cities could be taken by ruse or betrayal. The best known subterfuge used in the taking of a city comes not from the Bible but mythology, where the Trojan

Horse of the Greeks brings about the fall of Troy. However, there are instances in the HB of cities falling both to ruse and betrayal. In Judges 1:22–6 Bethel is taken when one of its inhabitants shows the invading Israelites the way into the city.

The fates of the defeated were varied, but rarely ever good. Noncombatants, especially women, were considered spoil and often taken into slavery (for the role of women in biblical warfare, see Niditch 1993: 78–89). In Judges 5, as the mother of Sisera wonders to herself why her son delays in returning from battle, she offers the following explanation: 'Are they not finding and dividing the spoil? A girl or two for every man' (v. 30). The irony of her words is clear to the reader, who knows that Sisera will never come home from the battle because he has fallen by the hand of a woman. Many captives were executed. Deuteronomy 20:13–14 states that when the Israelites capture a town they must kill every man but may take women and children as booty. Assyrian reliefs portray the killings of captives with graphic cruelty, depicting men being impaled or flayed. In a relief from his palace in Nineveh, the Assyrian king Ashurbanipal (668–33 BCE) is shown dining while the head of a conquered enemy hangs from a nearby tree. Assyrian ruthlessness was legendary in antiquity and thus it is that the prophet Nahum can say to them, 'Who has ever escaped your endless cruelty?' (Nah 3:19).

Victorious armies did not always spare their enemies. In an inscription dating from ca 830 BCE the Moabite king Mesha tells of capturing the cities of Atarot and Nebo in the Transjordan and killing their entire populations (7,000 men, women, and children in the case of Nebo) as an offering for his god, Chemosh (Smelik 1991: 29–50). This practice is parallel to the so-called 'ban' (חרם) in the HB, where certain peoples are set aside for total destruction because of their status before God as abominable. This is Yahweh's decree concerning the fate of the entire population of Canaan, and the Israelites' continued favor from God is contingent upon the total extermination of the Canaanites (Deut 20:16–17). The HB speaks repeatedly of certain cities captured by the Israelites being 'put to the ban', that is, exterminated, on divine command (e.g., Num 21:34–5; Josh 6:17–18). Saul's violation of the order to annihilate the Amalekites and their livestock is what leads to his rejection by Yahweh (1 Sam 15). It remains for the prophet Samuel to fulfill the ban on the Amalekites: 'And Samuel hewed Agag in pieces before Yahweh in Gilgal' (v. 33). This biblical mandate for genocide has caused exegetes much consternation, exerting a profound influence on scholarship that has until only recently gone unnoticed (Niditch 1993; Whitelam 1996: 79–87).

One strategy utilized in the first millennium by the Assyrians, Babylonians, and Persians in regards to conquered peoples was deportation. Under the auspices of these three military powers thousands of people were moved great distances. This tactic figures prominently in the HB since the capital cities of both Israel and Judah were captured and their inhabitants deported by the Assyrians (721 BCE) and Babylonians (597, 587 BCE) respectively (2 Kgs 17; 24:8–17; 25:1–21). Archeological evidence bears out the dramatic impact both deportations had on the population of Palestine (Jamieson-Drake 1991: 48–80; Younger 1998: 211–19). Deportation afforded many advantages to regimes seeking hegemony over vast populations and territories. Deportees would be relocated to an unfamiliar region, which contributed to deterring revolt. More importantly after the passage of time, usually no more than three or four generations, deported peoples begin to lose a sense of their past and, hence, their identity as they become assimilated into the structures created by their conquerors. Deportation was often presented as the establishment of order or the rectification of flawed political relationships. This is related to the worldview of the ancient Near Eastern powers, which understood areas beyond their borders or sphere of influence to be chaotic and uncivilized (Liverani 1990: 33–112, 135–43; Younger 1990). Consequently, military conquest and deportation are viewed as re-establishing the proper state of affairs in a region. In his account of the destruction of Samaria in 721 BCE, Sargon II of Assyria notes that 'I led away as prisoners 27,790 inhabitants . . . the town I rebuilt better than it was before and settled therein people from countries which I myself had conquered' (Pritchard 1969: 284; see also Oded 1979; Younger 1998). In the HB the spokesman of Sennacherib makes a strong propagandistic ploy to Jerusalem during the siege of 701 BCE by painting deportation under the Assyrians as a blessing:

> Thus says the king of Assyria: 'Make your peace with me and come out to me; then every one of you will eat from your own vine and your own fig tree, and drink water from your own cistern, until I come and take you away to a land like your own land, a land of grain and wine, a land of bread and vineyards, a land of olive oil and honey, that you may live and not die.'
>
> (2 Kgs 18:31–2 NRSV)

Nebuchadnezzar II of Babylon (605–562 BCE) describes his conquest of Lebanon and resettlement of its inhabitants thus: 'I made that country [Lebanon] happy by eradicating its enemy everywhere. All its scattered inhabitants I collected and reinstalled' (Pritchard 1969: 307). Nebuchadnezzar's portrayal of deportation as the restoration of displaced peoples to their rightful homes is a propagandistic tool used to great success also by Cyrus the Great of Persia (Mullen 1997). Cyrus's self-aggrandizement is taken up by the HB, where he is lauded for restoring the Judean exiles to their homeland.

The ideology of war in the ancient Near East

Like so many other aspects of ancient Near Eastern culture, religion was intricately bound up with the waging of war and the rationale behind it. Kings were seen as the chosen representatives of the national god and went to war as the god's champion. Most ancient texts that deal with battles are highly tendentious because they serve mainly to magnify the king by telling of his power and bravery (Liverani 1990: 115–25; De Odorico 1995). It was understood that a war between two peoples was also a war between their gods. Battle then was not only a military matter, but possessed cultural and theological components as well, and the victory of one people over another represented the triumph of one god over another. Again, the words of the Assyrian envoy to Jerusalem clearly show this:

> Do not listen to Hezekiah when he misleads you by saying 'Yahweh will deliver us.' Has any of the gods of the nations ever delivered its land out

of the hand of the king of Assyria? . . . Who among all the gods of the countries has delivered their countries out of my hand, that Yahweh should deliver Jerusalem out of my hand? (2 Kgs 18:33–5 NRSV, adapted)

When a city was taken its temples would be destroyed and its gods taken into captivity, a symbolic act that underscored the complete conquest of the vanquished. In light of the important role of the gods in warfare, their favor was necessary for an army to be victorious. Prophets and oracles were consulted and sacrifices performed to insure providential regard by the divine powers (Kang 1989: 11–110). With few exceptions, every battle in the HB is either undertaken at Yahweh's command or preceded by consultation of an oracle or means of divination. It is against this backdrop of the regular consultation of prophets before battle that King Ahab complains of the prophet Micaiah that 'he never prophesies anything favorable about me, but only disaster' (1 Kgs 22:8). Outside of the Bible there is the famous case of Croesus, who is given an oracle stating that if he goes to war against the Persians he will destroy a great kingdom (Herodotus *Ana.* 1.53). Thinking this an auspicious omen, Croesus undertakes the campaign and in the process destroys his own realm. According to 2 Kings 3:21–37, the Moabite king Mesha (mentioned above) sacrificed his eldest son as a burnt offering to his god in an attempt to turn the tide of battle against the Israelites (cf. Levenson 1993: 3–52).

In addition to the portrayal of the king as the favored son of his god, some texts make the claim that the king and his armies had been chosen by the god of the conquered peoples to restore order. So Sennacherib claims to the inhabitants of Jerusalem, 'Yahweh said to me, "Go up against this land and destroy it"' (2 Kgs 18:25). Cyrus of Persia makes use of this assertion in an inscription dealing with his conquest of Babylon. The text paints a picture of chaos throughout Babylon. Proper worship of the gods has been neglected by the Babylonian king: 'Daily he did blabber incorrect prayers. He furthermore interrupted in a fiendish way the regular offerings, . . . The worship of Marduk, the king of the gods, he changed into an abomination' (Pritchard 1969: 315). Many gods have been taken to Babylon against their will. In search of a champion to redress their grievances, Marduk, the god of Babylon, 'scanned and looked through all the countries, searching for a righteous ruler . . . Then he pronounced the name of Cyrus' (Pritchard 1969: 315). Cyrus, acting in accordance with the will of the Babylonians' god, restores the rites and returns the other gods to their proper homes. This portrayal of Cyrus as the savior of the vanquished people chosen by their god figures prominently in the HB where Cyrus is understood as the elect instrument of Yahweh and designated as the 'anointed,' or 'messiah' (משיח ; Isa 45:1; c.f. Thompson 1992: 348–51). This attempt to make sense of a political reality – in this instance Cyrus's conquest – by means of a theological explanation that understands the foreign conqueror as the instrument of Yahweh is one of the favorite strategies of the biblical authors.

WARFARE AND THE HEBREW BIBLE

Biblical narrative and history

Battle narratives in the HB can be grouped into two categories. First are those found in Numbers–Judges that describe the conquest and settlement of Canaan by the Israelites. Next are those in 1 Samuel–2 Kings that tell of the campaigns undertaken by the kings of Judah and Israel. The enemies of the Israelites in these latter accounts are mainly neighboring small city- or nation-states such as Ammon, Edom, Moab and additionally are the Philistines along the Palestinian coast and the Arameans in Syria. With the exception of the Exodus story, the great powers of Egypt and Mesopotamia appear in the Bible as conquerors who either put the Israelites into vassalage or defeat them.

The question of the historicity of the conquest narratives has been one of the most hotly debated problems in twentieth-century biblical scholarship. For a time archeological data were thought to support the biblical account of the military incursion of the Israelites into Palestine from the Transjordan. However further excavations revealed that not only was there no supporting external evidence for the conquest, but that the archeological record speaks directly against any such event (Ramsey 1981: 65–98; Finkelstein 1988: 295–314). Sites such as Arad, Jarmuth, Ai, and Jericho were shown to have been abandoned for centuries prior to and/or during the putative time of the Israelites' conquest of them described in the book of Joshua. Also, many sites showed no evidence of occupation – Israelite or otherwise – in Iron I. In addition to throwing open the question of Israelite origins in Palestine, this development also led to a reevaluation of the literary nature of the conquest accounts. It is now understood that the picture portrayed in the book of Joshua of a unified Israel capturing the entire land of Canaan and exterminating its inhabitants is an idealized fiction. Many scholars believed the alternative scenario in the book of Judges to be more realistic and hence, historical, because it depicts the tribes working separately and sometimes against each other in a partial and piecemeal conquest of the land. Plausibility, however, should not be confused with history. It has been known for a long time that the texts acquired their present form centuries after the events they purport to relate, and that their authors subsumed the matter of recording history to theological and rhetorical concerns. Uppermost among the latter is the repeated understanding that the Israelites' military success is due solely to the intercession of Yahweh, whose assistance is contingent upon his people's rejection of alien worship. The most obvious example of this is the schematized structure of the book of Judges, which repeats *ad nauseam* the pattern of Israelite apostasy from Yahweh, followed in turn by Yahweh's rejection in the form of foreign oppression.

With the material concerning the Israelite and Judean kings, the issue of historicity is mixed. Recently skepticism has been voiced concerning the historical worth of the texts dealing with Saul, David, and Solomon. Analogous to the case of the conquest, certain archeological data thought to demonstrate the existence of a highly structured nation-state as portrayed in the Bible have been reexamined. Much of the monumental architecture and fortifications excavated at many sites and dated to the reign of Solomon (e.g., at Hazor, Gezer, and Megiddo) have now been redated to the following century (Finkelstein 1996). Moreover, survey results indicate that settlement sizes and distributions were not large enough to support the bureaucracy a monarchy would require (Jamieson-Drake 1991). To this is added the curious fact that to date, no reference to the alleged vast kingdom of David and Solomon (with the possible exception of a stele from Tel Dan, but several key issues surrounding this text have yet to be established) has been discovered in the records of other countries with which the Bible says these kings dealt. Of the many histories of Palestine/Israel published, two of the most recent take opposing sides on the issue of the historicity of the United Monarchy of David and Solomon (Thompson 1992: 108–16, 146–57; Ahlström 1993: 421–542). Many scholars, however, use the same methodology in historical analysis of the materials in Joshua–Judges in regard to 1 Samuel–1 Kings, that is, remove the miraculous or exaggerated elements from the text and use the remainder to reconstruct Israelite history.

Concerning the kings after Solomon we are on much firmer ground. Many of them, for example, Omri, Ahab, Jehu, and Hezekiah, are mentioned in contemporaneous extrabiblical documents, most of which deal with the military defeat of these kings. Yet despite the independent attestation of these biblical figures, caution should be exercised in assessing the historical worth of the stories in which they figure. There is hardly a better illustration of this need for care than the state of affairs presented by the independent accounts of the siege of Jerusalem by Sennacherib in 701 BCE. Here is the Assyrian version inscribed on a clay prism:

> As to Hezekiah, the Jew, he did not submit to my yoke, I laid siege to 46 of his strong cities . . . Himself I made a prisoner in Jerusalem, his royal residence, like a bird in a cage. I surrounded him . . . I increased the tribute . . . due to me as his overlord . . . Hezekiah himself, whom the terror-inspiring splendor of my lordship had overwhelmed . . . did send me, later, to Nineveh, my lordly city . . . all kinds of valuable treasures, his own daughters, concubines, male and female musicians. (Pritchard 1969: 288)

This report is similar to many others in the Assyrian annals. The vassal state foolishly chooses to rebel against Assyrian hegemony. The great king, led by his god, brings his military power to bear on the transgressor, who either capitulates or is destroyed. In this instance Hezekiah resubmits to Sennacherib's yoke and is assessed additional tribute as his punishment. The biblical account, portions of which have already been quoted, describes some of the events in the same way as the Assyrian version: Sennacherib captures many Judean cities and Hezekiah pays him tribute. However the biblical text resolves the conflict in a significantly different way, by means of a prophecy of Isaiah and its fulfilment:

> Therefore thus says Yahweh concerning the King of Assyria: 'He shall not come into this city, shoot an arrow there, come before it with a shield, or cast up a siege-ramp against it. By the way that he came, the same way he will return; he shall not come into this city', says Yahweh . . . That very night the angel of Yahweh set out and struck down 185,000 in the camp

of the Assyrians; when morning dawned, they were all dead bodies. Then King Sennacherib of Assyria left, went home, and lived at Nineveh. (2 Kgs 19:32–3, 35–6 NRSV, adapted)

Both accounts are guided by their respective ideologies. For the Assyrians, the issue is Hezekiah's abrogation of his duties as vassal. The military expedition is cast in light of a redress of grievances; the aggressor is depicted as a wronged party in a contract dispute. Once Sennacherib has reasserted his authority and meted out proper punishment, he returns home and collects tribute from his chastised servant. Order and right relations are restored. In 2 Kings, the Assyrians are portrayed as the villains. In a key difference from the Assyrian account, Hezekiah begs for forgiveness and, in an attempt to buy him off, offers gold and silver to Sennacherib *before* he lays siege to Jerusalem. Accepting the tribute and then carrying out the siege regardless makes Sennacherib the scoundrel, necessitating the intervention of Yahweh in the form of a fantastic fairytale rescue. In this instance, because of the presence of an independent account of the same event, scholars are able to separate rhetoric, ideology, and miracle from both accounts in an attempt to glean historical knowledge. However, in the case of the narratives about the conquest and the United Monarchy, absence of corroborating textual and archeological evidence, presence of discordant data, and knowledge of the ideologically tendentious nature of ancient narrative combine to advise against too facile a reading.

Yahweh as warrior and the idea of holy war in the Hebrew Bible

Of the many metaphors used of God in the HB, that of divine warrior is one of the most prevalent, appearing in the historical books (Gen–2 Kings), prophetic writings, and the Psalter. God is frequently referred to as 'Yahweh of hosts' (יהוה צבאת) or 'Yahweh, the god of hosts' (יהוה אלהי צבאת). Thus David says to Goliath, 'I come to you in the name of Yahweh of hosts, the god of the armies of Israel' (1 Sam 17:45) and the prophetic texts are replete with the phrase 'Yahweh, the God of hosts is his name' (e.g., Isa 47:4; Jer 10:16; Amos 4:13). For weapons, God has recourse to the mighty power of storms, with their wind and lightning bolts (Judg 5; Ps 68). Some connection has been made between Yahweh's characterization as a storm god and the etymological derivation of his name (van der Toorn 1995). Creation was understood as God's cosmic, primeval battle against creatures symbolic of chaos. Certain texts that celebrate Yahweh's victory over the monstrous brutes Behemoth and Leviathan before the creation of the world (Ps 74; Job 39–41) have parallels with other cosmogonic texts from the ancient Near East (Miller 1973: 8–63). Thus, in the same way that war propaganda understood conquest as the institution of order, so too Israelite creation mythology viewed the cosmos as an ordered whole under the sovereignty of Yahweh its conqueror.

God is often portrayed as assisting the Israelites in their military endeavors (list of examples in von Rad [1958] 1991: 42–9). This is certainly the most common understanding of the divine role in warfare throughout the ancient Near East; gods were understood to go into battle with armies and were given credit for victories

(Kang 1989; Hiebert 1992: 877). In some biblical texts Yahweh concretely accompanies the Israelites into war in the form of the Ark that is carried by the Israelites (1 Sam 4). A variant of this theme of divine assistance appears in texts where it is clear that God's aid not merely supplements military force, but supplies it with necessary power or even replaces it entirely. The story of Gideon makes this point explicit. There Yahweh commands Gideon to reduce the size of his army before battling the Midianites, for otherwise 'Israel would only take the credit away from me' (Judg 7:2). Even more drastic is the account of the crossing of the Red Sea in Exodus 14. There the Israelites do nothing and it is Yahweh alone who fights and destroys the Egyptians. Moses promises the Israelites, 'Yahweh will fight for you, and you have only to keep still' (v. 14). This is echoed in the words of the Egyptians when their chariot wheels are clogged: 'Let us flee from the Israelites, for Yahweh is fighting for them against Egypt' (v. 25). After the 'battle' is over and the Israelites survey the Egyptian casualties, their victory song acclaims Yahweh as a warrior with prowess in battle (Exod 15:1–10; cf. 2 Chron 20). This emphasis on human passivity in military endeavors is taken up in the prophetic literature and made obligatory, so that true faith in Yahweh requires the abnegation of recourse to military action. Isaiah chastises his king for seeking help from Egypt in meeting the Assyrians: 'Woe to those who go down to Egypt for help and who rely on horses, who trust in chariots because they are many and in horsemen because they are strong, but do not look to the Holy One of Israel or consult Yahweh' (Isa 31:1).

This theme is also taken up in the Psalms, which declare that

> A king is not saved by his great army;
> a warrior is not delivered by his great strength.
> The war horse is a vain hope for victory,
> and by its great might it cannot save. (Ps 33:16–17 NRSV; cf. also Ps 44:6)

One should be careful not to confuse pacifism with this mandate against taking up arms. The authors are not speaking against the immorality of war, as an examination of the numerous oracles against foreign nations in Isaiah, Ezekiel, and Amos shows (cf. Weisman 1998: 55–100). Rather they are urging the Israelites to let Yahweh exact the reckoning from their enemies since he can do it much more effectively than they (cf. Niditch 1993: 148). Such an ideology, which speaks against military involvement but hopes for divine recompense upon the foe, is appropriate for the small states of Israel and Judah in their encounters with the larger powers of Egypt and Mesopotamia in the first millennium. This hoped-for vengeance that is to come at some point in the indeterminate future is occasionally referred to in the prophetic texts as 'the day of Yahweh' (although this phrase has other meanings in the HB). The motif of God vindicating the righteous and punishing the wicked takes on an eschatological cast, and its pairing with the imagery of the divine cosmic battle describing this drama of divine justice at the end of the present age plays a role in the doctrines of apocalyptic groups in ancient Israel and early Judaism. It is by means of apocalyptic that a portion of the theological views about war in the HB leave their most influential mark in the New Testament (Hanson 1984: 359–61).

Closely related to the understanding of God's role in warfare is that which views the armies of Israel's enemies as tools with which Yahweh punishes Israel. This theme is prevalent in the prophecies of Jeremiah and Ezekiel in reference to the invading Babylonians. Similarly, in telling of the defeat and exile of Samaria at the hands of the Assyrians, the biblical author notes, 'This occurred because the people of Israel had sinned against Yahweh their god' (2 Kgs 17:7). So too the account of the exile of the Jerusalem elite by the Babylonians is accompanied by the editorial remark that 'surely this came upon Judah at the command of Yahweh, to remove them out of his sight, for the sins of Manasseh' (2 Kgs 24:3). In Isaiah, God reminds the Assyrians that they are his tool, and as such are not to act contrary to his intentions.

> Ah, Assyria, the rod of my anger –
>   the club in their hands is my fury!
> Against a godless nation [Israel] I send him,
>   and against the people of my wrath I command him . . .
> But this is not what he intends,
>   nor does he have this in mind [. . .]
> Shall the axe vaunt itself over the one who wields it,
>   or the saw magnify itself against the one who handles it?
>
>   (Isa 10:5–7, 15 NRSV)

As mentioned already, the HB understands the return of deportees from Babylon to Jerusalem under Cyrus as an act of God by means of his chosen agent. Although the idea that God will one day fight in place of the Israelites against their enemies appears to contradict the belief that these conquering enemies are the instruments of the very same god, these two notions should be seen as differing methods the biblical authors employed to make sense of repeated Israelite domination at the hands of the great Near Eastern powers. When one always loses, hopes are nursed that either the oppressors will eventually receive their just deserts or that such calamities must happen 'for a reason' and that things are under the control of a just and benevolent God.

In light of the major role played by Yahweh in biblical warfare, scholars have attempted to discern a holy war theology in the religion of the ancient Israelites. The name most associated with the idea of holy war in the HB is Gerhard von Rad. In a small but influential study ([1958] 1991) von Rad argued that from its earliest days as a loose tribal confederation in Palestine prior to the establishment of the monarchy, Israel had a doctrine of holy war. It was part of the Israelite religious cultus and involved certain rites in which Yahweh's aid was invoked before battle and praised afterward. Behind these external practices lay the faith of the Israelites, unique among their neighbors, that Yahweh was a god who intervened decisively in their history. Von Rad's book traces the historical vicissitudes of this tenet through Israelite history which he constructed from the Bible. Little of von Rad's thesis has escaped criticism. Most importantly, further examination of the battle reports from countries surrounding ancient Israel show the Bible's understanding of the divine as an active participant in battle (and history in general) to be part and parcel of ancient Near Eastern belief (Albrektson 1967; Weippert 1972; Jones 1975; 1989: 299–302; Kang 1989). Put another way, one expects the Israelite battle accounts to claim that their god fights for them because that is the norm for such accounts from that region and epoch. To attempt to claim uniqueness (and invariably, superiority) for biblical practices against that of their neighbors in this instance amounts to special pleading. Additionally there has been little agreement about what exactly is understood by the phrase 'holy war.' Does it imply war against 'unbelievers'? Does it require only the belief that the god fights alongside his armies? Are there specific practices that distinguish it from secular war? Given the fundamental role in antiquity of religion in international relations, especially warfare, the search for a distinct category, 'holy war,' is perhaps a case of losing sight of the forest for the trees. Nevertheless the history of this concept in modern scholarship is illuminating (survey in Lind 1980: 23–34; Ollengburger's Introduction to von Rad [1958] 1991: 1–33). The perception that the HB contained a doctrine of holy war has been used to advance nationalist, bellicose aims (Gunkel 1916; discussion in Mitchell 1995). More recently it has confounded Jewish and Christian exegetes and theologians who argue for the renunciation of violence on biblical grounds (Craigie 1978; Lind 1980; Walzer 1992).

Although those for whom the Bible represents divine revelation should no longer have to contend with the idea that it advocates a doctrine of holy war, many of its narratives are shocking in their brutality and glorification of violent conquest. As this chapter hopes to have demonstrated, however, this aspect of the HB is due to a vast network of beliefs that created and sustained the cultural milieux of the ancient Near East. In antiquity cities, peoples, and nations owed their inception and continued survival to military success. So it is that the oft-quoted opening to Virgil's *Aeneid*, the epic account of the birth of Rome, begins *Arma virumque cano* – 'I sing of arms and the man.' As a collection whose aim in part is to tell of the origin of the people of Israel, the HB likewise extols the military prowess of great figures (real or imagined) who through their struggles helped to create Israel. The nascent Israelite nation wandering in the desert between Egypt and Canaan for a generation is portrayed in the biblical text as a vast mobile army, organized in groups of descending size (De Vaux 1961: 214). That is not to say that the HB never exhibits a pacifist stance. In addition to several prophetic texts that foretell a utopia free from the horrors of war (e.g., the famous passage in Isa 2 carved in stone at the United Nations building) there is the lesser-known but provocative story in 2 Kings 6:8–23. There Yahweh strikes an entire Aramean army blind at the request of Elisha. The prophet then leads the helpless force to Samaria, where it is at the mercy of the Israelite king. When the king asks Elisha whether he should destroy the enemy army, he is told 'No . . . set food and water before them . . . and let them go to their master' (v. 22). However texts such as these (here one might also add the antiwar satire of Aristophanes's *Lysistrata*) are the exception rather than the rule in ancient literature. Yet despite this pessimistic observation, one may take comfort in the fact that through their writings the Israelites have had greater influence on history than their more powerful contemporaries did with their armies, proving perhaps that the pen is indeed mightier than the sword.

BIBLIOGRAPHY

Ahlström, G. (1993) *The History of Ancient Palestine*, Philadelphia: Fortress.

Albrektson, B. (1967) *History and the Gods: An Essay on the Idea of Historical Events as Divine Manifestations in the Ancient Near East and Israel*, Lund: Gleerup.

Brettler, M. (1993) 'Images of YHWH the Warrior in Psalms', *Semeia* 61: 135–66.

Carroll, R. (1989) 'War', in M. Smith and J. Hoffman (eds) *What the Bible Really Says*, San Francisco: HarperCollins.

Chapman, R. (1997) 'Weapons and Warfare', in E. Meyers (ed.) *The Oxford Encyclopedia of Archaeology in the Near East*, New York: Oxford University Press.

Collins, J. (1998) *The Apocalyptic Imagination: An Introduction to Jewish Apocalyptic Literature*, 2nd edn, Grand Rapids: Eerdmans.

Craigie, P. (1978) *The Problem of War in the Old Testament*, Grand Rapids: Eerdmans.

De Odorico, M. (1995) *The Use of Numbers and Quantifications in the Assyrian Royal Inscriptions*, Helsinki: Neo-Assyrian Text Corpus Project.

De Vaux, R. (1961) *Ancient Israel: Its Life and Institutions*, repr. 1997, Grand Rapids: Eerdmans.

Drews, R. (1989) 'The "Chariots of Iron" of Joshua and Judges', *Journal for the Study of the Old Testament* 45: 15–23.

Finkelstein, I. (1988) *The Archaeology of the Israelite Settlement*, Jerusalem: Israel Exploration Society.

—— (1996) 'The Archeology of the United Monarchy: An Alternative View', *Levant* 28: 177–87.

Fretz, M. (1992) 'Weapons and Implements of Warfare', in D.N. Freedman (ed.) *The Anchor Bible Dictionary*, New York: Doubleday.

Fritz V. (1995) *The City in Ancient Israel*, Sheffield: Sheffield Academic Press.

Gunkel, H. (1916) *Israelitisches Heldentum und Kriegsfrömmigkeit im Alten Testament*, Göttingen: Vandenhoeck & Ruprecht.

Hanson, P. (1984) 'War and Peace in the Hebrew Bible', *Interpretation* 38, 10: 341–62.

Hasel, M. (1994) '*Israel* in the Merneptah Stele', *Bulletin of the American Schools of Oriental Research* 296: 45–61.

Herzog, C. and Gichon, M. (1978) *Battles of the Bible*, Jerusalem: Steimatzky.

Herzog, Z. (1992) 'Fortifications (Levant)', in D. N. Freedman (ed.) *The Anchor Bible Dictionary*, New York: Doubleday.

Hiebert, T. (1992) 'Warrior, Divine', in D.N. Freedman (ed.) *The Anchor Bible Dictionary*, New York: Doubleday.

Jamieson-Drake, D. (1991) *Scribes and Schools in Monarchic Judah: A Socio-Archeological Approach*, Sheffield: Almond Press.

Jones, G. (1975) '"Holy War" or "Yahweh War"'? *Vetus Testamentum* 25: 642–58.

—— (1989) 'The Concept of Holy War', in R. Clements (ed.) *The World of Ancient Israel*, Cambridge: Cambridge University Press.

Kang, S.-A. (1989) *Divine War in the Old Testament and in the Ancient Near East*, Berlin: de Gruyter.

Levenson, J. (1993) *The Death and Resurrection of the Beloved Son: The Transformation of Child Sacrifice in Judaism and Christianity*, New Haven: Yale University Press.

Lind, M. (1980) *Yahweh Is a Warrior: The Theology of Warfare in Ancient Israel*, Scottdale, Pennsylvania: Herald.

Littauer, M. and Crouwel, J. (1979) *Wheeled Vehicles and Ridden Animals in the Ancient Near East*, Leiden: Brill.

Liverani, M. (1990) *Prestige and Interest: International Relations in the Near East ca. 1600–1100 B.C.*, Padua: Sargon.

Mazar, A. (1990) *Archaeology of the Land of the Bible: 10,000–586 B.C.E.*, New York: Doubleday.

Mcnutt, P. (1991) *The Forging of Israel: Iron Technology, Symbolism and Tradition in Ancient Society*, Sheffield: Sheffield Academic Press.

Miller, P. (1973) *The Divine Warrior in Early Israel*, Cambridge, Mass.: Harvard University Press.

Mitchell, G. (1995) 'War, Folklore and the Mystery of a Disappearing Book', *Journal for the Study of the Old Testament* 68: 113–19.

Mullen, E. (1997) *Ethnic Myths and Pentateuchal Foundations: A New Approach to the Formation of the Pentateuch*, Atlanta: Scholars Press.

Niditch, S. (1993) *War in the Hebrew Bible*, New York: Oxford University Press.

Oded, B. (1979) *Mass Deportations and Deportees in the Neo-Assyrian Empire*, Wiesbaden: Harrassowitz.

Pritchard, J. (1969) *Ancient Near Eastern Texts Relating to the Old Testament*, Princeton: Princeton University Press.

Rad, G. von (1958) *Holy War in Ancient Israel*, repr. 1991, Grand Rapids: Eerdmans.

Ramsey, G. (1981) *The Quest for the Historical Israel*, Atlanta: John Knox.

Rofé, A. (1985) 'The Laws of Warfare in the Book of Deuteronomy: Their Origins, Intent and Positivity', *Journal for the Study of the Old Testament* 32: 23–44.

Russell, J. (1991) *Sennacherib's 'Palace Without Rival' at Nineveh*, Chicago: University of Chicago Press.

Shanks, H. (1984) 'Destruction of a Judean Fortress Portrayed in Dramatic Eighth-Century B.C. Pictures', *Biblical Archeology Review* 10/2: 48–65.

Smelik, K. (1991) *Writings from Ancient Israel: A Handbook of Historical and Religious Documents*, Edinburgh: T. & T. Clark.

Smend, R. (1970) *Yahweh War and Tribal Confederation*, 2nd edn, Nashville: Abingdon.

Thompson, T. (1992) *Early History of the Israelite People: From the Written and Archaeological Sources*, Leiden: Brill.

Toorn, K. van der (1995) 'Yahweh', in K. van der Toorn (ed.) *Dictionary of Deities and Demons in the Bible*, Leiden: Brill.

Ussishkin, D. (1980) 'The "Lachish Reliefs" and the City of Lachish', *Israel Exploration Journal* 30: 174–95.

—— (1982) *The Conquest of Lachish by Sennacherib*, Tel Aviv: Tel Aviv University Publications.

—— (1984) 'Defensive Judean Counter-Ramp Found at Lachish in the 1983 Season', *Biblical Archaeology Review* 10/2: 66–73.

—— (1992) 'Megiddo', in D. N. Freedman (ed.) *The Anchor Bible Dictionary*, New York: Doubleday.

Walzer, M. (1992) 'The Idea of Holy War in Ancient Israel', *Journal of Religious Ethics* 20: 215–28.

Weippert, M. (1972) '"Heliger Krieg" in Israel und Assyrien: Kritische Anmerkungen zu Gerhard von Rads Konzept des "Heiligen Krieges im Alten Israel"', *Zeitschrift für die alttestamentliche Wissenschaft* 84: 460–93.

Weisman, Z. (1998) *Political Satire in the Bible*, Atlanta: Scholars Press.

Wevers, J. (1962a) 'War, Methods of', in G. Buttrick (ed.) *The Interpreter's Dictionary of the Bible*, New York: Abingdon.

—— (1962b) 'Weapons and Implements of War', in G. Buttrick (ed.) *The Interpreter's Dictionary of the Bible*, New York: Abingdon.

Whitelam, K. (1996) *The Invention of Ancient Israel: The Silencing of Palestinian History*, London: Routledge.

Wiseman, D. (1989) 'The Assyrians', in J. Hackett (ed.) *Warfare in the Ancient World*, New York: Facts on File.

Yadin, Y. (1963) *The Art of Warfare in Biblical Lands in the Light of Archaeological Study*, Jerusalem: International Publishing.

Younger, K. (1990) *Ancient Conquest Accounts: A Study of Ancient Near Eastern and Biblical History Writing*, Sheffield: Sheffield Academic Press.

—— (1998) 'The Deportation of the Israelites', *Journal of Biblical Literature* 117: 201–27.

CHAPTER THIRTY

THE ARTS
Architecture, music, poetry, psalmody

———— •◆• ————

Susan Gillingham

What counted as 'the arts' in the biblical world? An equivalent Hebrew word, *maʿaśeh*, occurs only twice in the Old Testament, referring to skill or craftsmanship (in this case, of perfumers: see Exodus 30:35 and 2 Chronicles 16:4). An equivalent Greek word, *technē*, occurs just once in the New Testament, and here it refers to the representative art of pagan cultures (see Acts 17:29). So given this limited framework of reference, it is clear that any attempt to discover the significance of 'the arts' in the Bible is going to be difficult. If we mean *representational arts* – figurative and iconographic art especially – then the evidence within the biblical tradition itself is surprisingly slim. If we mean *performing arts* – music, drama and song – then even here the actual evidence is not overwhelming. But if we mean *literary arts* – poetry, psalmody, narrative – then because the Bible as a collection of literature is full of poems and stories, we shall of course find a wealth of such material.

How are we to assess the evidence? Archeological studies are inevitably fragmentary and inconclusive, and the relevant descriptions in the Bible itself are selective and often biased. It is quite clear that orthodoxy in both the Jewish and Christian biblical tradition was expressed not so much through visual art forms as through words – through preaching, writing, collecting, editing and preserving ancient texts. The essence of these traditions is more ethical than aesthetic: the Torah and the Sermon on the Mount exemplify well the core belief that an obedient life surrendered to God is closer to true faith than anything evoked by artistic endeavour. Furthermore, creative expression was somewhat crippled by the teaching in the second of the Ten Commandments: 'You shall not make for yourself a graven image, or any likeness of anything that is in heaven above, or that is in the earth beneath, or that is in the water under the earth . . .' (Exodus 20:4 RSV). Just how much this is the case will be seen in the following section.

REPRESENTATIONAL ARTS AND THE BIBLE: AN ASSESSMENT OF ARCHITECTURE AND ARTEFACTS

Within the Bible, representational art falls into two categories: popular artefacts, in terms of personal items such as pottery, textiles, seals, jewellery and amulets; and,

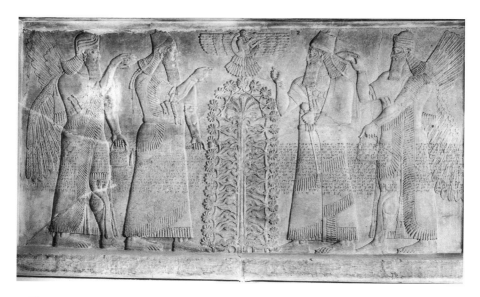

Figure 30.1   The king and the sacred tree: relief from Ashurnasirpal's throneroom, Nimrud, ninth century BCE. Copyright British Museum.

on a more public level, monumental architecture (such as palaces, defences, temples, and official dwellings). In ancient times, Israel borrowed much from the surrounding cultures; yet, because of her distinctive beliefs, she also adapted much as well.

Excavations at royal palaces offer an interesting example of this phenomenon. Throughout palaces in the ancient Near East, representational artwork – whether on reliefs, ivory carvings, victory steles, and sculptures and official seals – is a predominant feature. The military and domestic concerns of particular religions and cultures are all skilfully portrayed in decorative human figures and deities, depicting national pride and public grandeur. Outside Israel, important examples are as various as the Hittite palaces at Bogazkoy (Hattusha) in Anatolia; the Egyptian palace of Akenaten, the worshipper of the sun-god Re, at Tell-el-Amarna, on the river Nile; the Ugaritic palace at Ras Shamra, in Syria; the Assyrian palaces of Ashurnasirpal II at Nimrud, of Sargon II at Khorsabad, and of Sennacherib and Ashurbanipal at Nineveh; and the Persian palaces of Darius I and Xerxes at Persepolis. Of these, the Assyrian sculptures and basalt reliefs of sacred trees, the winged disk of the sun, and attendant priests offer a striking illustration (see Figure 30.1).

Israelite monumental architecture, by contrast, is somewhat different. Figurative art is minimal, with a handful of exceptions. For example, at the Samaritan palace of Omri, king of Israel (ninth century BCE), plaques of carved ivory have been found, produced in Syria, and yet also suggesting Egyptian and Canaanite influence: one of these is a relief of a carved cherub set amid palm trees (see Figure 30.2). Other notable examples include a well-preserved wall carving of a roaring lion at a sanctuary called Hazor, and ivory plaques depicting bulls, lions and eagles from a fortress town called Lachish. But these are very much the exceptions: the most common decoration is floral, and occasionally geometric, whether using examples as various

Figure 30.2   Cherub and 'palmette' on ivory: from Samaria, ninth–eighth century BCE.
Copyright Israel Antiquities Authority.

as decorations found on defence works (gates, towers and walls) at Megiddo and
Mizpah, from the ninth to seventh centuries BCE, and carvings on rock-cut tombs
in Jerusalem, dating from the fifth to third centuries BCE.

The above examples are all from Old Testament times. From the first century BCE
to the first century CE, the same reserved style, borrowing yet adapting the artwork
of other cultures, is still in evidence at the Herodian palaces at Caesarea, Sebaste
(Samaria) and Masada. Fragments of frescos and mosaics found at these palaces
certainly reflect the influence of Graeco-Roman art, but there is undoubtedly a
distinctive Jewish adaptation. Again we find several examples of intricate decoration, but it is floral and geometric art; given the Graeco-Roman milieu, the lack of
figurative art is remarkable.

In terms of more popular artefacts from everyday life, the most signficant discoveries in Syro-Palestine are from Canaanite culture (c. 1600–1200 BCE), of which the
best-known examples have been found at Ugarit (Ras Shamra) in Syria, dating from
1400 to 1300 BCE. These offer some insights into the way that Canaanite art
combined several different cultures. For example, a golden embossed plate found
close to the temple mount depicts the king of Ugarit hunting: the animals, chariots,
hunting-games and the sacred tree all suggest Babylonian and Akkadian influence,

Figure 30.3 Golden embossed bowl showing the king of Ugarit hunting: from Ugarit, fifteenth–fourteenth century BCE. From *The Cuneiform Texts of Ras Shamra-Ugarit* by C. F. A. Schaeffer (Schweich Lectures of the British Academy, London: Oxford University Press 1936). Copyright British Academy.

while the dress and posture of the figures reveals Egyptian borrowing (see Figure 30.3). On a more domestic level, countless clay figurines, and innumerable seals, amulets and painted pottery have been found, not only at Ugarit but throughout Syro-Palestine – at Jerusalem, Samaria, Megiddo, Beth-Shean and Tell el Farʿah – which further illustrate the cultural influence of Canaanite art combined with a mix of other cultures. At Beth-Shean, dating from the Late Bronze Age, at the time when the city served as a stronghold for Egyptian administration, basalt reliefs of fighting animals (lions, bulls) bear the mark of both Canaanite and Egyptian art, although the sanctuary later came under Solomonic (i.e. Israelite) rule. In Canaanite and Egyptian culture, the most popular art form is figurative – animal designs, fertility cult objects and various types of figurine – although decorative floral and geometric art is evident as well. Another good example, because it is so intricately decorated and well preserved, is a cultic stand dating from the tenth century BCE found at Tell Taanach in 1968 (see Figure 30.4).

However, were these artefacts used not only in Egyptian and Canaanite culture, but also, in later times, by the Israelites as well? This is more than likely, for at least two reasons. First, the references to skilled craftsmen in, for example, Exodus 31:3–4, whose work was 'to devise artistic designs, to work in gold, silver and bronze, in cutting stones for setting, and in carving wood, for work in every craft' suggests

Figure 30.4 Front view of decorated cultic stand, showing fertility figures and sun disk: from Tell Taanach, tenth century BCE. Copyright Israel Antiquities Authority.

that what may have been a skill in purely decorative art in more orthodox circles could well have developed into the figurative art more akin to that of Israel's neighbours in popular practice. And second, the laws against figurative craftmanship (e.g. Deuteronomy 16:21–2 and Leviticus 26:1, on not making idols or images or figured stones) suggests that in popular religion such artwork, which inspired fertility practices, was common; for if such art forms could be depicted on public monuments at places such as Samaria, Hazor and Lachish – even though they went against the grain of the teaching of the law and the prophets – they would undoubtedly have been used in more familial, popular life as well.

The most convincing example of the influence of Canaanite and multicultural art in Israel is in fact in the early Solomonic Temple, dating from the tenth century BCE. Given that Zion (Jerusalem), the city of David, took over the ancient Canaanite site of the Jebusites, and given that the Temple itself was built close to the Canaanite sanctuary, it would be more surprising if some Canaanite artistic influence had not left its mark here. Even the descriptions of the Temple in 1 Kings 5–10, written by those inclined elsewhere to despise foreign influence, depict a good deal of foreign borrowing, both in material goods, in the cedars from Lebanon, and in skilled labour, in the preparation of timber, stone and bronzework by craftsmen from Tyre (see 1 Kings 5:6, 18 and 7:13–14). In architectural design, the Temple had much in common with Canaanite, Syrian and Phoenician prototypes, with its outer and inner courts, and its inner covered sanctuary and the Holy of Holies (see 1 Kings 6). The description of the inner walls, doors and passages covered with sculptured panels of wood with gold inlays, and geometric designs of flowers, gourds, and palm trees certainly points in this direction.

The adaptation of Canaanite art is perhaps most clear in the description of the cherubim in the Holy of Holies; these were figures with human faces and wings – also found in the ivories from Samaria – akin to the winged figures guarding temples in Syria, Mesopotamia and Egypt. Furthermore, in the outer court, the capitals of the two standing pillars, Jachan and Boaz – themselves akin to Canaanite phallic symbols called standing stones – are depicted as adorned with pomegranates, lilies, palm trees, flowers, and gourds, and these too suggest typically Canaanite influence, as do also the fertility figures of the twelve oxen supporting the huge bronze laver for sacrifice nearby.

It is somewhat ironic that the Temple provides the best illustration of all kinds of art, including figurative and symbolic art; or at least, so the texts tell us, for there is no real archeological evidence to support it. And given that so little artwork like it has been found in ancient Israel – either in the texts or from archeological evidence – our observations are necessarily conjectural. But given that the writers were not prone to accept such influence in Israel themselves, there is no reason to suspect their account.

Turning to the New Testament, the archeological evidence for any sort of representational art is minimal, and to make matters worse, even the texts give us very little information. It is more than likely that the second Temple, built in the sixth century BCE and reconstructed by Herod some five hundred years later, had many features in common with the first Solomonic Temple. But the relevant biblical texts have little interest in what it looked like; other than one or two passing comments (see Matthew 23:16–22, on not swearing by 'the gold of the temple' and Mark 13:1–2, on its wonderful stones and buildings) there is little to go on.

Excavations at various synagogues have produced some examples of representational art; but again, the mosaics, relief works and frescoes at Masada, Herodium and Gamla, for example, offer no examples of figurative or animal images, such as one would expect to find in contemporary Graeco-Roman culture. The synagogue at Capernaum probably goes further than most: there we find plenty of floral patterns

Figure 30.5 The Ark of the Law: from one of the lintels of the first century (or fourth century) CE synagogue at Capernaum. From *Recovering Capernaum* by S. Loffreda (Jerusalem: Edizioni Custodia Terra Santa, 1985). By permission of the Franciscan Printing Press, Jerusalem.

decorating several lintels, and even a relief of the Ark of the covenant on wheels as part of the same decoration (see Figure 30.5). On a capital of one of the pillars, a seven-branched candlestick, an incense shovel and a ram's horn are all set within an intricate design of palm trees; in addition, the painted plaster stuccos all have different patterns of fruits and flowers, suggesting fertility imagery adapted from pagan art forms.

It is not until the post-biblical tradition that one finds the real flowering of the representational arts, where figures and theological symbols are used with less

Figure 30.6   Wall painting; the wilderness encampment and the miraculous well of Be'er.
Dura-Europos Collection, Yale University Art Gallery.

restraint. One of the first Jewish illustrations dates from the third century CE. In a synagogue in a small Roman town called Dura-Europos, on the river Euphrates, a number of scenes from the entire Old Testament have been found painted on the walls. One of these is of Moses striking water from the rock (see Figure 30.6). Its larger than life representation of Moses, and the symbolic interpretation of the story (e.g. the addition of the seven-branched candlestick, and the twelve tribal representatives, each in his booth, being apportioned their share of the miraculous water) reveal how far Jewish art had by now progressed. Its ultimate purpose was in fact more didactic than aesthetic. Adorning a synagogue – a place of instruction – the Dura-Europos paintings served to teach the congregation about God's provision at a time of need.

Christian works of art from the same period suggest the same concerns. Some of the earliest are wall-paintings from the Roman catacombs; one striking example is of Daniel's three friends in the fiery furnace. Again the figures are simply and crudely drawn, for their purpose is again hardly aesthetic. Symbolic additions may be seen in the sign of the dove, representing God's ever-present Spirit, and in the classical poses of prayer. Their lesson is that, even at times of intense suffering and persecution, God has the power to redeem and save.

From the third century onwards, figurative art began to develop, and the diffidence at employing pagan art forms began to disappear: even the signs of the zodiac are to be found in fourth-century CE synagogues at Hammath Tiberias and Beth 'Alpha. It may be that a less negative view of Graeco-Roman culture influenced this development; it may also be that the developing Christian artistic tradition also encouraged Jewish creativity along the way. For from the third century onwards, Christian symbols such as the dove, fish, bread, grapes, olive branch, ship and anchor all became popular signs of faith (many of these having been found in the catacombs).

By the Middle Ages a most innovative tradition developed in both Jewish and Christian traditions – the illumination of biblical manuscripts. Whereas previously the text alone was seen as the most vital resource for faith, that very same text is now presented alongside decorative illustrations, many of which are purely figurative art. This was quite a change from biblical times when artistic expression – at least in orthodox circles – was reserved for decorative art alone.

PERFORMING ARTS AND THE BIBLE: AN ASSESSMENT OF MUSIC AND DRAMATIC RITUAL

One quite early text gives us a clue about the importance of music in the life of ancient Israel. Genesis 4:20–2, written as ancient aetiological explanation of the three basic 'skills' (the first smith, Tubal-cain, the first cattlebreeder, Jabal, and the first musician, Jubal) has some correspondences with an early Sumerian myth entitled *Tagtug and Dilmun*. The Genesis passage shows that music was considered among the most ancient of occupations in Israel, even more so before the advent of poetry and song. Whether in percussive sounds (such as beating with a stick on stone, wood, or animal skin) or in sounds made by the breath (using mouths and lips with leaves, animal horns, hollowed wood) or in sounds created by crudely made stringed instruments (using animal gut from hunting bows to create instruments like the harp and lyre), music was a fundamental performative art throughout the ancient world; hence it would be surprising to find Israel exceptional in this respect. If, in spite of the teaching in the Ten Commandments, Israel could adapt (albeit selectively) some of the forms of the decorative arts, there was surely scope to adapt some of the performing arts as well.

It is unclear whether music was used as an accompaniment to secular songs. Certainly battle songs (e.g. Exodus 15:21 and 17:16) and working songs (e.g. Numbers 21:17–18) and love songs (e.g. Song of Songs) were in popular use, but there are few suggestions of any musical accompaniment in such references. It is more probable that the essential place for music was in accompanying liturgy. Certainly the importance of music in worship is evidenced by drawings in other ancient cultures, such as in Syro-Palestine, Egypt and Babylon. The lack of graphic illustration in the biblical tradition makes us dependent upon these other cultures for our knowledge of which instruments were probably used in Israel's worship. For example, the trumpet was probably brought to Israel from Egypt (as depicted on a relief on a stele from Ramases II in the thirteenth century BCE), and the horn was

Figure 30.7 An Assyrian military band with tambourines, lyres and cymbals: alabaster relief from Assurbinipal's palace at Nineveh, seventh century BCE. From *The Symbolism of the Biblical World* by Othmar Keel (ET of original German edn; London: SPCK, 1978). By permission of Othmar Keel.

first used in Egypt, Assyria and Babylon. Tambourines, lyres and cymbols were also borrowed from other cultures (see Figure 30.7).

Within the biblical tradition, the psalms offer us the best examples of the use of music in worship The word *šîr*, meaning 'song', is used almost forty times in the Psalter. The word 'psalm' is taken from the Greek word *psalmos*, which is a translation of the Hebrew *mizmôr*, meaning 'a song to a stringed instrument'. The word *lamᵉnaṣṣeʾaḥ*, meaning 'to the choirmaster', is used in the headings of fifty-five psalms. Asaph (a heading for Psalms 50, 73–83) and Korah (heading Psalms 42, 44–9, 84–5, 87–8) are probably guilds of Levitical musicians. Phrases in superscriptions such as 'Do Not Destroy' (Psalms 57–9, 75) and 'Dove of the Far-Off Terebinths' (Psalm 56) and 'Hind of the Dawn' (Psalm 22) and 'Lilies' (Psalms 45, 69, 80) and 'Gittith' (Psalms 8, 81, 84) and 'Shushan Eduth' (Psalm 60) almost certainly suggest the tunes – whether originally popular profane tunes is unclear – to which the psalms should be sung. Musical instruments are of course evident: these include the 'flute' (Psalm 5), the 'pipes' (Psalm 150), the 'trumpet' (Psalm 47), the 'sheminith' – probably an eight-stringed instrument – (Psalms 6, 12), 'stringed instruments' (Psalms 4, 6, 54, 55, 67, 76), the 'lyre' (Psalm 33), the 'harp' (Psalms 57 and 150), the 'cymbals' (Psalm 150) and the 'timbrels' (Psalms 81, 149 and 150). There are even possible references to male and female voices: the expression *ʿal-mûṯ labēn* in Psalm 9 may indicate a male soprano, and the term *ʿal-ʿalāmôṯ* in Psalm 46 could suggest the accompanying voices of women. The term *selāh* used seventy-one times in thirty-nine psalms, is also probably a musical term. It always occurs in the middle or at the end of a verse, often following a refrain. This suggests it is a music notation, occurring at the end of a phrase: it could be from the word s-l-l, meaning 'raise' (hands, voice, eyes) or the root s-l-h, meaning 'bow down' or 'prostrate oneself' in worship, or the noun *sal*, meaning basket or drum, indicating the rhythmic beat of the psalm. The Greek translates this word as *diapsalma* – meaning 'pause' – that is, an interlude in the performance of the psalm. Whichever meaning is preferred, it is hard to interpret *selāh* in any other way than as a musical term.

However, with regard to the rituals and dramatic enactments that would accompany music and psalmody in liturgy, very little can be known with any certainty. The psalms are compositions without any of the rubrics we might find in a more modern prayer book: the absence of any explanation of the ritual activities accompanying the words thus means it is extremely difficult to reconstruct the liturgical performances. We can try to reconstruct some form of drama by way of reading into the contents of various psalms – for example, ritual processions of the Ark paraded into Jerusalem (see 2 Samuel 5–6 for the narrative, and Psalms 24, 68 and 132); different coronation rites involving the king (Psalms 2, 72 and 110); special festal activities that took place at the turn of a new year (Psalms 50 and 81); national celebrations at times of victory in war (Psalms 21, 46 and 48); and sacrifices and oblations accompanying more individual psalms (Psalm 134). But all we really can say is that because ritual and drama were very much part of ancient Near Eastern liturgy, what happened elsewhere almost certainly would have happened in Israel as well. For example, the use of processions, involving the king and his cultic officials, with the men, women and children following behind, is documented on other ancient Near Eastern reliefs and steles (see Figure 30.8). It is impossible to deny that, alongside music and song, ritualized and dramatized liturgy from other cultures would have been adopted in Israel as well.

Within the New Testament, there is very little explicit evidence of *any* performing art, be it music, drama or song. In part, this may be due to a negative reaction to the pagan grandeur of Roman culture; in part it may be due to the growing importance of synagogue worship, for these were not so much places of music as of the reading and recitation of Scripture. Luke 7:32 and Matthew 11:7 refer to the performance of flutes and dances, but even these refer more to secular music, and so give no evidence of the wider use of music and ritual in liturgy. Ephesians 5:19 speaks of the importance of Christian songs and melodies; and parts of Revelation (4:11, 5:9–11, 7:15–17 and 11: 17–18) are imitations of psalmody, as also are parts of Luke 1–2 (from which come the *Nunc Dimittis* and the *Magnificat*). Together these fragments certainly imply the use of hymnody in liturgy; nevertheless, although they demonstrate the importance of singing, they do not give any details of musical or dramatic accompaniment.

However, when we look at the post-biblical tradition, as we did with regard to the figurative arts, we again see that the performing arts – especially those concerned with music – became more conspicuous by the time of Constantine (fourth century CE) onwards. From this time on, there is more evidence to show how music made a distinctive contribution to early Jewish and Christian liturgy, where (rather like the illumination of manuscripts some time later) the syntax was brought to life through musical accompaniment.

For example, in Jewish tradition, it seems that the use of certain *sigla* in the copied texts of the Hebrew Bible suggests some commonly acknowledged musical

Figure 30.8 'The solemn processions of my God, into the sanctuary – the singers in front, the minstrels last' (Ps. 68). Stele from Ramases II, Abydos, thirteenth century BCE. From *The Symbolism of the Biblical World* by Othmar Keel (ET of original German edn; London: SPCK, 1978). By permission of Othmar Keel.

notation, describing pitches and tones for singing, and these may be dated from at least the second century CE onwards. The fact that these are used in a distinctive way in poetic books such as Psalms, Proverbs and Job might well suggest that this sort of poetry was most suitable for musical adaptation. The rise in Palestine of a group of Jewish singers in the fourth to fifth centuries called *piyyutîm* – composers and singers of new liturgical prayers and hymns for sabbaths and holy days – also shows that the musical tradition of the Old Testament continued to progress; and by the medieval period, musical notation in Jewish liturgy had developed into a most complicated system of performing art.

In Christian tradition, musical interpretation through melodic and tonal singing of psalms probably began as early as the second century CE. The tradition of the fourteen canticles (e.g. Exodus 15; Deuteronomy 32; 1 Samuel 2; Habakkuk 3; Isaiah 26; Jonah 2; Daniel 3, and two apocryphal additions, namely the Prayer of Azariah and the Song of the Three Young Men; Isaiah 38; the apocryphal Prayer of Manasseh; Luke 1:68–79 and 46–55; Luke 2:29–32; and the Gloria) is attested by the time of Pope Gregory the Great (590–604 CE), and these canticles, along with the Psalms, were performed as *plainsong*, or 'sung-speech'. The language used was of course Latin; but the flexible line-forms of the poetry, allowing an 'ascent' (the first recit and cadence) a pause (the mediant) and a 'descent' (the second recit and cadence) made plainsong particularly evocative.

Our conclusions follow those of our earlier section. It seems that during its earliest stages, Jewish and Christian culture was essentially word-based and text-based. Within the biblical tradition itself, the world of music, like the world of art, though implicitly important, is very difficult to ascertain in detail, but in the post-biblical tradition music, like art, became a vital means of bringing the text to life.

LITERARY ARTS AND THE BIBLE: AN ASSESSMENT OF POETRY AND PSALMODY

One problem in assessing the importance of poetry in the literature of the Old Testament is deciding what may be classified as poetry and what as prose, for the boundaries between the two are blurred. In part, it is the performative quality of poetry that distinguishes it from prose: one has only to compare the poetic account celebrating the victory over the Egyptians in Exodus 15:1, 4–6 (the so-called 'Song of the Sea') with the parallel narrative account in Exodus 14:26–9 to recognize this difference; similarly, the poetic victory song in Judges 5:24–7 ('Deborah's Song') and the parallel narrative account in Judges 4:18–21 illustrates this well.

But this only works in part, for reading prose may be a performing art as well (e.g. the reading from the Torah as synagaogue practice). Hebrew poetry has some distinctive features, such as a terser style, more figurative imagery, phonetic devices, archaisms, word-pairing (balancing phrases by way of repetition or by contrast) and a clearer division of the material into line-forms, although the difference between prose and poetry is more one of degree than of kind.

There are in fact two essential characteristics that mark out Semitic poetry from prose. One lies in the *sense*, or the presentation of the ideas in parallel, corresponding line-forms. The other lies in the *sound*, or in the rhythmic way in which those ideas are heard. Together these suggest that biblical poetry was composed to be performed: the words are the 'performing art'. The terse style beomes an aid to memory, and this is reinforced by the ways in which the words are spoken (or sung) and heard.

Characteristically, the ancient Israelites adapted a good deal from the ancient Near Eastern cultures around them. In the cases of the representational and performative arts, we have seen that one early influence was Canaanite culture; it should be no surprise, therefore, to find that this influence is also found in Israelite poetry, both in terms of sense and of sound.

In terms of the sense, the brief binary line-forms have many correspondences with Canaanite poetry. Epic poems written in Ugaritic, dating from between the fourteenth and twelfth centuries BCE, found at Ras Shamra in Syria, suggest many associations with the later poems of the Hebrew Bible, not only in their contrasting word pairs (such as light / darkness; sea / river; earth / deep; death / life; tent / dwelling; justice / righteousness) but also in their accentual stresses (2:2, 3:3; and so on) in the line-forms. One intriguing example, taken from a poem called *Ba'al and 'Anat Cycle* (CTA 2.iv.8–9) , has close links with Psalm 92:9, in terms of line-forms, its 3:3 stress, and even its language.

now,	thine enemies	O Ba'l
ht	ibk	b'lm
now,	thine enemies	thou shalt smite
ht	ibk	tmḥṣ
now,	thou shalt destroy	thy foes . . .
ht	tṣmt	ṣrtk

(Ba'al and 'Anat Cycle)

For lo,	thy enemies,	O Lord,
for lo,	thy enemies	shall perish
all evil-	doers	shall be scattered.

(Psalm 92:9)

As well as the form, the contents of several Old Testament poems reveal many of the themes found in Ugaritic poetry. Various psalms borrow their creation imagery from earlier Canaanite mythology, whether depicting God as the rider of the clouds (Psalm 104:3), as the king or judge in a heavenly council (Psalms 89:6–7; 82:1), as the one enthroned above the floods (Psalm 93:1–4), as the Lord dwelling on a mountain (Psalm 68:16), as the judge of the nations (Psalm 2:1–3, 10–11; 46:8–10), as the Most High God (Psalms 46:4 and 47:2) or as the God of the storm. In this latter respect, Psalm 29 as a whole is very much like a Canaanite hymn to Ba'al-Hadad, the storm-god. The sevenfold voice of God, the appearance of God through the clouds, the references to the cedars of Lebanon and Syrion (from which Ba'al's temple was built) all echo similar motifs in the Canaanite hymn. This is not to presume any exclusive relationship between the biblical poets and the poets of Canaan: much of this imagery (e.g. lightning as fire and the thunder as the voice of

God) was commonly used throughout the ancient world, as can be seen on a seal as early as the eighteenth century BCE from Syria.

Ideas found in other hymns have much in common with other ancient Near Eastern hymns, particularly those from Egypt and Babylon, illustrating a shared cultural milieu. For example, a common ancient Near Eastern myth about the creation of the world being linked to the deity's fight with a dragon of the sea, known to the Babylonians and the Canaanites, is referred to explicitly in Psalms 74:12–17 and 89:5–10. The first part of Psalm 19A is a hymn to God as the creator of the sun. Not only in form but also in content it has many affinities in its imagery with a Babylonian hymn to the sun-god, Shamesh: the sun emerges as a bridegroom coming out of his 'tent', circling the earth through the daylight hours, and is personified as a 'strong man' (see Psalm 19:4c–6). Again, that this is part of a much larger culture is clear: the same scene is depicted on a cylinder seal from Mesopotamia, dating between 2350 and 2150 BCE.

Psalm 104, like 19A, is a hymn to God as creator of the sun: as well as having some Canaanite correspondences, verses 20–30 have several striking affinities with the Egyptian Hymn to Aton, found at Tell el-Amarna:

> Thou settest every man in his place,
> Thou suppliest their necessities:
> Everyone has his food, and his time of life is reckoned . . .
> The world came into being by thy hand,
> According as thou hast made them.
> When thou hast risen they live,
> When thou settest they die.
> Thou art lifetime thy own self,
> For one lives [only] through thee.
>> (from *Ancient Near Eastern Texts Relating to the Old Testament*
>> [3rd edn with Supplement], ed. J. B. Pritchard, Princeton
>> University Press, Princeton N.J., 1969, pp. 370–1)

> These all look to thee,
>> to give them their food in due season.
> When thou givest to them, they gather it up;
> When thou openest thy hand,
>> they are filled with good things.
> When thou hidest thy face, they are dismayed;
> When thou takest away their breath, they die and return to their dust.
> When thou sendest forth thy Spirit, they are created;
>> and thou renewest the face of the ground.
>> (Psalm 104:27–30 RSV)

Laments also have much in common, not only in terms of form but also of substance, with those from Egypt and Babylon. The terror of destructive forces, often personified (Psalm 102:3–11), the imagery of being near death, and being trapped in a pit or grave (Psalm 143:7), the sense of drowning in deep waters (Psalm 69:1–3), of being parched as in the desert (Psalms 63:1 and 42:1–2) – all these are descriptions of distress commonly used in laments throughout the ancient Near East. A cylinder seal from Babylon, dating from about 1800 BCE, illustrates figuratively this common perception of being in the grip of chaotic forces.

With regard to Israelite poetry in its own setting, as we have already noted, much Old Testament poetry was performed on special liturgical occasions, whether at local sanctuaries or at the Jerusalem Temple. This is the case even with poetry outside the Psalter. A good example is the so-called 'Aaronic Blessing' found in Numbers 6:24–6 (RSV):

> 'The LORD bless you and keep you:
> The LORD make his face to shine
>   upon you, and be gracious to you:
> The LORD lift up his countenance
>   upon you, and give you peace.

Although this is described as a blessing offered by the priests, its early use in popular piety is illustrated by a seventh-century amulet, found in 1979 in a seventh-century tomb in S.W. Jerusalem, bearing some of the words of this blessing.

But what were the characteristics of literary poetry? The following examples (all from the RSV) illustrate 'parallelism' – the balance of sense in the line-forms, whereby repeated or contrasting images in a second line reinforce, positively or negatively, the idea expressed in the first line. Where straightforward repetition occurs, we may term it A + A, B + B, and so on. An example from Amos 8:9–10 illustrates this point:

[. . . and on that day, says the Lord GOD]	
'I will make the sun go down at noon,	A
and darken the earth in broad daylight.	A
I will turn your feasts into mourning,	B
and all your songs into lamentation . . .'	B

Psalm 33:10–11 is another good illustration of this:

The LORD brings to nought the counsel of the nations;	A
he frustrates the plans of the peoples.	A
The counsel of the LORD stands for ever,	B
the thoughts of his heart to all generations.	B

Where contrasting ideas are presented, we may term this A + B, C + D, and so on. One example is found in Proverbs 3:33:

The LORD's curse is on the house of the wicked,	A
but he blesses the abode of the righteous.	B

Similarly Psalm 30:5:

For his anger is but for a moment,	A
and his favour for a lifetime.	B
Weeping may tarry for the night,	C
but joy comes with the morning.	D

Obviously there are many more permutations of this basic model, and not every line-form corresponds as closely as do the above examples. One development is the partial statement of an idea in one line, with the completion of it taking place in the next (A>B) – what some have called 'staircase parallelism'. The call to praise in Psalm 29:1–2, a creation psalm, is a good illustration, with the third line being a repetition of the second, and the fourth a development of it:

Ascribe to the LORD, O heavenly beings,	A>
ascribe to the LORD glory and strength:	B
Ascribe to the LORD the glory of his name;	B>
worship the LORD in holy array.	C

As far as sound in Hebrew poetry is concerned, phonetic devices consist of assonance, alliteration, rhyme and word-play. For example, 'â' 'î' and 'û' sounds – usually found at the ends of words – are an important technique in creating the impression of wailing in laments; a good example is found in Jeremiah 9:19:

For a sound of wailing is heard from Zion:
　'How we are ruined (*'êk šuddād^enû*)!
　We are utterly shamed (*bōšnû m^eōd*),
because we have left the land (*kî-'azabnû 'āreṣ*),
　because they have cast down our dwellings (*kî-hišlîkû mišk^enôtênû*).'

Sharp consonants such as 'š' and' b̲' and ''k and 't̲' are also used for dramatic purposes. In Psalm 140:3 they illustrate the hissing and spitting of the serpents:

They make their tongue sharp	as a serpent's
šān^anû l^ešônām	*k^emô-nāḥāš*
and under their lips	is the poison of vipers
ḥ^amat 'akšûb̲	*taḥat ś^ep̲ātêmô.*

Onomatopoeia is used in some of the poems about God's creative power. Psalm 93:4 illustrates this, with the use of 'îm' and 'ām' and 'ôt̲' suggesting the sound of the floods and seas:

Mightier than	the thunders of many waters
miqqōlôt̲	*mayim rabbîm*
Mightier than	the waves of the sea
'addîrîm	*mišb^erê yām.*

Word-play, another phonetic device, is used mainly by the prophets; Isaiah 5:7 is a good example:

. . . and he looked for justice	(*l ᵉ mišpāṭ*),
but behold, bloodshed	(*miśpāḥ*):
for righteousness	(*liṣᵉdāqâ*)
but behold, a cry!	(*ṣᵉᵉāqâ*)

Despite the importance of the sound of Hebrew poetry, it is extremely difficult to find any clear evidence of *metrical* patterns. Scholars who have proposed a regular metre have not only been up against uncertainty about the original pronunciation of Hebrew poetry, but have postulated such contradictory hypothetical theories (some counting syllables, others forcing the rhythm into iambic metre, with the stress falling on the second syllable) that it is best to speak instead of a free accentual rhythm, created mainly by the intensification of the binary ideas. No absolute metre exists, although usually some sort of regular rhythm is detectable: for example, hymnic poetry often can be read in terms of a 3:3 or a 2:2 accentual beat, while by contrast poems of lament often have a more halting 3:2 accentual beat. Nevertheless, this is rhythm, not metre, because it is so fluid and flexible. For example, a 2:2 beat (not metre) is evident in Psalm 29. The hymn is to Yahweh, as God of the storm, and here the beat is intended to suggest the relentless noise of the storm; for example, verse 3:

The voice	of the LORD
qôl-	ʾᵃdōnay
is upon	the waters
ʿal-	hammāyim
The God of	glory
ēl-	hākkābôd
thun	ders
hir	ʿîm
The LORD is	above
ʾᵃdōnay	ʿal-
many	waters
mayim	rabbîm.

The halting beat 3:2 is more characteristic of laments. Psalm 5 is a good example; taking the English without the transliterated Hebrew, using verses 1–2, the beat would appear as follows:

Give ear to	my words, O LORD
give heed	to my groaning.
Hearken	to the sound of my cry
my King	and my God.

---

1. **Hymns**

General Hymns: 8, 29; 33; 100; 103; 104; 111; 113; 114; 117; 135; 136; 145; 146;
   147; 148; 149; 150

Also: 78, 105.

Zion Hymns: 46; 48; 76; 87; 122.

Kingship Hymns: 47; 93; 96; 97; 98; 99.

2. **Laments**

Individual Laments: 3; 5; 6; 7; 12; 13; 17; 22; 25; 26; 28; 31; 35; 36; 38; 39; 42–3;
   51; 54; 55; 56; 57; 59; 61; 63; 64; 69; 70; 71; 86; 102; 109; 120; 130; 140;
   141; 142; 143.

Communal Laments: 44; 60; 74; 77; 79; 80; 82; 83; 85; 90; 94; 106; 108; 123; 126;
   137.

3. **Miscellaneous Forms**

Royal Psalms: 2; 18; 20; 21; 45; 72; 89; 101; 110; 132; 144.

Individual Thanksgiving: 9–10; 30; 32; 34; 40; 41; 92; 107; 116; 138.

Communal Thanksgiving: 65; 66; 67; 68; 118; 124.

Individual Psalms of Confidence: 4; 11; 16; 23; 27; 61; 84; 91; 121; 131.

Communal Psalms of Confidence: 115; 125; 129; 133.

Liturgies: 15; 24; 134.

Prophetic Exhortations: 14; 50; 52; 53; 58; 75; 81; 95.

Didactic Psalms: 1; 19; 37; 49; 73; 112; 119; 127; 128; 139.

Figure 30.9   The forms of the Psalter. From *The Poems and Psalms of the Hebrew Bible* by S. E. Gillingham (Oxford: Oxford University Press, 1994). By permission of Oxford University Press.

Many scholars who presume there is some regular metre in Hebrew poetry also work on the assumption that it follows the same rules as those of classical verse. But Hebrew and Greek poetry are very different. Hebrew poetry is more terse and economical, yet also impassioned and irregular in its expression of ideas, while on the whole Greek poetry is more flowing, controlled and harmonious, with a more copious and consistent metrical pattern.

In biblical poetry, then, the sound brings the sense to life. The fact that 'parallelism of sense' is the most important characteristic has an interesting consequence: Hebrew poetry does not altogether lose its essence even when it is translated into non-Semitic languages such as Greek, Latin and English.

One of the other features about Hebrew poetry that we find especially in the Psalter is the use of *conventional forms* (see Figure 30.9). Hymns and laments dominate just as they do within the poetry of other ancient Near Eastern cultures, such as in Egypt and Babylon. The *hymns* fall into three categories: general praise, hymns celebrating God's presence in Zion, and hymns celebrating the kingship of God in the heavens and on the earth. These all follow a broadly similar pattern: a call to praise, a description of the reasons for praise, and a final call to praise. The *laments* fall into two categories of individual and communal petitions, although it is clear that the 'I' form is used in both categories and the dividing-line between prayers of the individual and prayers of the community is somewhat blurred. Most laments also follow a similar pattern: a cry for help, the reasons for the distress, and a vow of confidence that God will act. The most common *miscellaneous forms* fall into two basic types: individual and communal *thanksgivings* (thanking God for specific acts of restoration, these are more particular adaptations of the general hymns of praise) and individual and communal psalms of *confidence* (which are prayers as yet unanswered). The prophetic exhortations are essentially didactic poems using oracular teaching typical of the prophets. Prophetic oracles are also found in several royal psalms (see Psalms 2:7–9; 89:19–37; 110:4) but overall royal psalms are an unusual category, for they are classified according to their content (their subject matter pertains to the affairs of king and people) rather than because they share any special form. The liturgies are composite works, suggesting various rituals. The didactic psalms suggest the later influence of those sages and scribes who were gifted in writing didactic, reflective poetry: in contrast to the royal psalms and liturgies, whose concerns are more public and formal, these didactic psalms are more meditative and personal in their tone.

There is plenty of evidence of these forms elsewhere in the Hebrew Bible, showing this to be an established part of Israel's literary heritage. Psalmic poetry influenced other writers; and other biblical writers influenced the composers of the psalms. For example, hymns and thanksgivings are prominent in Isaiah 40–55, where they are used to evoke hope in God's restoration of his people. The lament form is used to great effect in the book of Jeremiah, where it dramatizes the sufferings of the people. Poems that speak of a coming royal deliverer develop the language and style of the royal psalms (see Isaiah 9:2–7 and 11:1–9). Hymns and laments are further used together for dramatic purposes, to highlight a particular message, in books with interests as diverse as prophecy (Amos) and wisdom (Job). The didactic psalms have some correspondences with the poetry in Proverbs, and especially in the much later book of Ecclesiasticus.

When we come to apply these observations to the New Testament, the results are very different because, by contrast, there is far more narrative and very little poetry, and the medium is Greek, not Hebrew. Narrative form predominates in the Gospels and Acts (one exception already noted being Luke 1–2, where the poetry imitates the psalmody). Although the more hortatory style of the Epistles is interspersed with some poetic fragments, many of these are simply quotations from the Greek translation of the Old Testament (the Septuagint) as seen, for example, in Romans 8:36, taken from Psalm 44:22; in Romans 9:25–6, from Hosea 2:23 and 1:10; and in Romans 10:19–21, taken from Deuteronomy 32:21 and Isaiah 65:1–2. In these cases the style is hardly continuously poetic. What fragments of Greek poetry there are come from quotations of Greek philosophers – for example, Epimenides and Aratus in Acts 17:28.

The really clear evidence of New Testament poetry is found in some of the poetic aphorisms in the Gospels; these may be part of an oral tradition going back to the sayings of Jesus, and so, if they were originally spoken, they would not have been in Greek, but in vernacular Aramaic – a language closely related to Hebrew and hence possibly like Hebrew poetry as well. The terse style, the word-pairing, the balance of particular phrases, the possible division of the material into line-forms, their performative, hortatory nature, rather like the preaching of some of the earlier Old Testament prophets – all these suggest the characteristics of poetry, not prose. Most of these sayings have clear ethical concerns; taking Luke as a source (for the Gospel of Luke has more interest in poetry, as seen in the psalmic imitations in Luke 1–2) three examples (all from the RSV) must suffice. First, the appeal to love one's enemies in Luke 6:27, set out in appropriate parallelism:

Love your enemies,	A
do good to those who hate you,	A
Bless those who curse you,	B
pray for those who abuse you.	B

Second, the injunction not to judge in Luke 6:37–8 (Matthew 7:1–2):

Judge not, and you will not be judged;	A
condemn not, and you will not be condemned;	A
forgive, and you will be forgiven;	B
give, and it will be given to you.	B

Third, the exhortation to lose one's life for Christ's sake, in Luke 9:24 (Matthew 16:25; Mark 8:35), which uses contrasting parallelism:

For whoever would save his life will lose it;	A
and whoever loses his life for my sake, he will save it.	B

Just as we saw with representational and performative art, the post-biblical tradition offers many examples of poetry and in this case is in more continuity with the already established biblical tradition. The imitations of poetry and psalmody found in the so-called *Hôdayôt* at Qumran offer good examples of this in the Jewish tradition; and in the Christian tradition, examples are found in the ways in which poets as diverse as Herbert, Wesley, Watts, Wyatt, Vaughan, Milton, Lyte, Keble, and Tate and Brady have developed the Psalms in English to create new forms of hymnody. This of course relates to what was said earlier about the importance in the biblical period of communication through texts and words, and so this art form perpetuates the biblical tradition itself.

CONCLUSION

From the limited textual and archeological evidence, the *representational arts* were apparently less important in biblical times than they were in the post-biblical period, particularly with regard to figurative and symbolic art. The most evidence comes from the earlier period before the exile; there is much less actual evidence of any artwork beyond the exile itself. By contrast, there is a little more textual evidence – mainly from the references to music and liturgy in the Psalms – that the *performative arts* were important (at least, they were so in the Temple) throughout the biblical period. But the only clear and compelling evidence within the Bible itself is from the *literary arts*, in terms of a clearly established tradition of poetry, and even here the Old Testament has more of this than the New.

By post-biblical times we have innumerable examples of the different ways in which artistic expression served to bring the texts to life. This may be in part due to the element of the numinous inherent in the message of the Bible, which ultimately required another form of expression than that by word of mouth and word of text. Given that the purpose of religious language is to describe other-worldly realities in temporal and spatial terms – realities that can never be contained by words alone – there is always an element of mystery in communicating the story of God revealing himself to humankind, and other art forms are an essential reminder of the importance of communication of religious mysteries in symbols beyond words alone. This recognition was of course evident in biblical times, but it was notably constrained, because the spoken and written words were paramount. Interestingly, it was only after the literature had been compiled, collected and recognized by different communities of faith that Jews and Christians started to borrow more boldly from the 'pagan' forms of arts – using more freely the music, drama, sculpture, painting and iconography of surrounding cultures. It was as if in biblical times the ban on such borrowing (as exemplified in the Second Commandment) was to ensure the survival of faith; and, paradoxically, it was as if in post-biblical times such a ban had to be lifted for that very same reason – the survival of faith.

CHAPTER THIRTY-ONE

LAW AND ADMINISTRATION IN THE NEW TESTAMENT WORLD

——————

J. Duncan M. Derrett

INTRODUCTION

Modern Western readers, understanding the New Testament to be about behaviour, its amelioration, and God, would ask how far it reflects their expectations. The authors (e.g. Paul) presupposed both Graeco-Roman and Jewish ideas of sin, civil wrong, crime, punishment, and reprieve – all foreign to us; though any who have lived in territories ruled by Muslims will feel at home in the New Testament. A democratic state takes for granted schools of law and administration, verifiable collections of statutes, treatises on them, and advocacy as a profession. The application and amendment of law follows a due process, and the Rule of Law prevails. The New Testament world knew little of this, though admittedly Greeks and Romans had statutes and knew the use and abuse of advocacy; codes of *parts* of Greek laws in Egypt were framed; and Egyptian priests produced one manual of legal solutions. Jews knew what non-Israelite judges did; but while pagans were familiar with 'rights' Jews emphasized 'duties', hoping thereby to perform the divine 'commandments'. God had done their legislating for them.

Nevertheless in public they relied on patrons. One succeeded less by appealing to rights than by petitioning those who wielded extra-legal pressure. Legal entitlement was proverbially insecure. The widow and orphan had reason to fear oppression. Moreover Jews did not rely on contractual rights as Romans did. The modern concept of the Rule of Law, too, was foreign to them. Solidarity and reciprocity were more meaningful. The non-Israelite (pagan) world was 'profane' to Jews, so that it was a serious question whether people should return to a pagan property he had lost. If the panoply of law meant more in Greece and Rome, 'equality before the law' existed nowhere. Law, best avoided, was a lottery everywhere.

About AD 200 R. Judah the Prince began the compilation of the Mishnah, which contains very many legal and extra-legal precepts, loosely based on the Written Torah (the Pentateuch) and the Oral Law, traditions of various ages: some Mishnaic rules already existed in our period. The Mishnah was intended to inculcate a more scrupulous Judaism, a 'way of life' (*halakha*) surviving the loss of the Temple in AD 70 and the despoiling of the country by the Romans, thus rescuing the image of an ideal theocracy from oblivion and rejecting tendencies to assimilate to the pagan world. In the 'order' *Nezîqîn* (Damages) and elsewhere true legal problems are handled, along with many outside any court's scope, for example impurity by reason of contiguity to a corpse, circumcision, and ritual immersions. The preferences of the '(ignorant) People of the Land', who opted not to be too scrupulous, were ignored. Few of the now traditional 613 Commandments came before courts. However, though sons could seldom be compelled to 'Honour Father and Mother', one could be flogged for cursing a parent in an Israelite if not in a Greek court; and blasphemy was a criminal offence. Pagans and Jews alike valued jurists, who studied legal theory as an adjunct to justice. A Jewish jurist would ask whether a rule was derived from scripture, and how. Since worship of an idol was forbidden, might an Israelite sit in the shade of a sacred grove? This illustrates a jurist's, not a judge's, problem. The 'replies' of jurists were at best a possible source of law, for judges could decline to follow them. Unlike Greeks, Israelites, who had God's commandments supplemented by the legendary arrangements of Moses and Joshua, saw no point in statutes, for their Torah was perfect. Rabbis (or their first-century predecessors) knew what 'was done', and what not. Political authority was powerless to develop *halakha*, whatever orders might be circulated to state judges.

SOURCES OF POWER

To both Greeks and Israelites 'power' meant 'the unconstrained capacity to do (something)'. The emperor (Nerva was a good example), the principal power-holder, his delegates, governors of Roman provinces (e.g. the proconsul of Achaea), and tetrarchs (e.g. Herod Antipas of Galilee) exercised legal power constitutionally. Pontius Pilate was *praefectus* (governor) of Judaea AD 26–36. Greeks and Romans operated a chain of command in civil and military affairs such as Jews could only envy. Greek cities were decaying democracies; decision by majority hovered in Roman and Greek politics, and figured in some law trials; but Jews eschewed majority decision except in Alexandria, and (one is told) important trials. It was also a means of terminating a juristic controversy, but it was an exotic expedient. To them 'power' was *de facto* control, autocratic and irresponsible, even if Roman officials might have to answer to the emperor. Rule in Palestine was visualized as arbitrary and opportunistic: rulers were thought to have much in common with demons. The fantasy that God ruled Israel through a king descended from David inspired would-be revolutionaries: but even supernatural leadership would not be democratic.

Jewish families obeyed the senior most active male, who answered for females (see Gen 18:13), and villages were run by 'elders'. The real leaders were 'notables', the most competent, therefore the richest, who represented none but themselves. The 'powerful', once in possession of a district, might summon matrons, not to speak of virgins, to their beds, and were 'righteous' if they abstained. Under Rome the significant ruler was the High Priest, whom Rome, following Herod the Great, appointed or deposed. He represented the state *vis-à-vis* foreigners and attempted to maintain order at home. Chief priests could nominate even generals through nepotism. Without a true personal authority (such as the emperor had) Israelites were virtually acephalous. The hereditary priesthood, often maligned, held a prestige derived from their monopoly of the Temple service. In the diarchy between High Priests and Romans, Caiaphas, High Priest AD 18–36, proved it could succeed. Inhabitants of Jerusalem (if Jewish) were respected as sophisticates.

No 'elder', 'ruler', or 'notable', even in the supreme court (Sanhedrin), was elected, or appointed under a discoverable system. Expediency and bargaining facilitated coalescence. The bureaucracy of Egypt, even imperial censuses, will have had counterparts in Judaea, but apart from the Bar Kokhba letters we lack archives. In general, consensus was desired, preferences being traded for influence. Sheer force restrained protests, and the rich fed on the poor (cf. Am 8:4–7). Sacred scripture continually pleads for the oppressed. It depicts abuse of powers even by Saul and David. It tenders Ahab and Jezebel as a royal pair. First-century Israelites expected no better. The story of Eli and his sons (1 Sam 2) already asks how one controls priestly corruption.

Romans, for their part, could 'divide and rule'. In AD 41 Rome decided against Jewish pretensions in Alexandria and later destroyed Jewish rights in Egypt. Rome taxed all Jews as such between AD 70 and c. 150. Israelites hated Samaritans, and demanded equal treatment with Greeks wherever they were coresident, to the latter's annoyance. Apart from Jews abandoning the *halakha* to serve government, a pool of collaborators existed to help put down Jewish revolutionary fervour. This erupted throughout the imperial procurators' time (AD 44–66), after Herod Agrippa I, whose calm reign (AD 41–4) owed something to his respect both for Israelite scrupulosity and pagan broadmindedness.

LEGAL SYSTEMS

Let Roman and the various Greek constitutions differ, Jewish and non-Jewish laws diverged in point of sources, content, and administration. Despite the reputation of Rhodes and Priene, the whole world was short of reliable arbiters. In Palestine all classes were subject to foreign rule; the governor kept turbulent mobs in order with foreign troops and tried to settle disputes, political and legal. Granted, a tendency intensified after AD 70 and the collapse of Israelite autonomy in 135, to ape Westerners' ways, separate living and endogamy encouraged the promulgators of the Mishnah to consolidate Israelite rules, whether these, and these alone, would be applied to Jews, or not. There was no Roman colony in Palestine. Roman private law was not at hand to study or imitate, even if Herod the Great found a Roman to sit along with Jews at a show trial. Israelite effort was put into defining the *halakha*. Roman citizens could appeal to the emperor in private-law cases.

In modern colonial territories a 'dominant' legal system countenances and encourages one or more 'servient' systems (e.g. the Islamic *shari'a* and customs) – a practical arrangement. Procurators of Judaea maintained Jewish law and custom under imperial policy, and natives took judicial responsibility. Romans could seldom make anything of a Jewish law claiming divine origin (an idea foreign to both Greece and Rome). Matters of Israelite religion were outside their jurisdiction, though it might interfere sharply with Roman plans. Small wonder if a royal Ptolemy desired the Hebrew Bible in Greek: what rules ('Torah') *ought* Jews to obey? Meanwhile natives could bamboozle foreign judges.

Under Jewish self-government there had already been servient systems: the law applicable in and to the Temple enclave, diverging in places from the general *halakha*; Noachide law applied by Jews to their resident aliens; and sectarian law (about which see below). Where a dominant legal system utilizes servient systems anomalies will arise. Natives entitled to litigate before their own courts may have recourse to the dominant system, especially if official judges are more easily bribed (Ex 23:8; Mishnah, *Peah* 8:9). Important criminal and fiscal cases would be heard by state tribunals. Greeks in Egypt would be sued only in Greek courts; their tenures were not subject to native law. A troublesome soldier billeted on natives would not appear before a native court: a petition to government was required. So a disappointed litigant in Judaea might challenge the elders' jurisdiction, allege that a possible breach of the peace loomed, and alert an appointed official. Then only pleas, evidence, and remedies the latter would recognize could operate, Jewish principles being disregarded. Hence private transactions could be framed and engrossed in Greek as well as Aramaic so that they might be valid internationally in either type of court. Some said the law of the land was the law.

Potential litigants claimed membership of a community and chose a court appropriate to the remedy sought or to the balance of power. However, if one went to a district governor over, say, a boundary, he would recommend a compromise, or refer the case to local arbitration, thus combining native justice, the best evidence, and an effective execution procedure. A servient system is hampered if the loser obtains an order to halt process: a suit in which more than one court has concurrent jurisdictions is a nightmare. On the other hand in Palestine as in Egypt litigation was a form of entertainment. If God was the true fountain of justice, did not the Israelite mind revel in juridical arguments which, by definition, were also religious? To carry one's complaint to any court rescued one from anonymity, and might enhance the influence of one's group or faction.

SUBSTANTIVE AND ADJECTIVAL LAWS

Laws are no better than their administration, which depends on the skill and honesty of judges and their decrees' being implemented. The mosaic of jurisdictions was indescribable. An international law of the sea was emerging while Rome mistakenly fancied she perceived a much wider 'law of nations', applicable to foreigners in Rome. Each Greek city had its own laws, procedures, and system of law revision. No doubt there was a *climate* of Greek law and jurisprudence; but citizens could normally sue only in their own city, where aliens must depend on patrons. There was no intercity reciprocity apart from treaties; even on one island (Crete) treaties were required to secure mutual recognition of public laws and select areas of private law (e.g. intermarriage). In Corinth Roman law applied to Roman citizens. City committees might handle local affairs: defence, markets, sewers, aqueducts, the mint, temples, and (one thinks of Tyre and Ephesus) the 'asylum'. Each city had elected its inferior magistracy. The poor were disregarded, and fared badly in litigation; mass protests produced reprisals.

Failure to digest laws left the public at the mercy of manipulators. When a temporarily independent Jerusalem sent a governor to an outlying province he appointed 70 local judges and kept capital cases in his and his assessors' hands (Josephus, *Life*, 79). The Sanhedrin, presided over by the High Priest or his deputy, had some original criminal and civil jurisdiction and some revisional powers. It could formulate directions in Torah matters; but how all these powers were employed is uncertain. Its decrees had high persuasive value in Israelite communities, but they would not impress dissentients. Many held that the king (and therefore his agents?) could neither sue nor be sued in an Israelite court.

The Mishnah suggests the Sanhedrin observed regularity, members voting in a specific order, with a quorum ensuring verdicts by a clear majority. Did this obtain in our period? Some rules were applied that did not find a place in the Mishnah. No Jewish court could decide a matter outside the *halakha*, for example the impressment of labour or services. Judicial torture was unknown, unless Jewish rulers adopted Roman practices, torturing slaves and defaulters. Should one sue for slander in a Greek or a Jewish court? Where could insolvent debtors be condemned to be sold? Could Jewish courts adminster a testator's estate, familiar as Jews were with gifts before death? The Torah was notoriously weak in dealing with theft and robbery. Pagan and Jewish laws were said to be simply incompatible.[1] Jews insisted on two competent witnesses for judicial proof, more interested, as they were, in the admissibility of testimony than its cogency. A Jewish court might quail at the amount of relevant law. If they placed custom first, customs differed from region to region, and towns' customs could differ from their hinterlands'. A principle of *halakha* could be included by reference in an imperial decree (e.g. freedom from process on the Sabbath); but Torah experts might differ as to its compass. The emperor could issue decrees regarding a crime (e.g. tomb-robbery). Above all laws and regulations stood unrepealed Seleucid and Ptolemaic statutes, especially concerning the economy.

Court-hearings were not adversarial; judges, both state appointees and 'elders', interrogated witnesses. Notabilities sometimes interceded for prisoners. A few of the latter conducted their own cases, appealing for mercy with abject confessions. Some Torah experts, unable to move any judge, would pray to God to help widows and orphans, his own protégés. Could justice come from such a medley? An Israelite must pursue justice (Dt 16:20), but the royal duty to administer it (cf. 2 Sam 8:15) was elusive. When Philip, tetrarch of Gaulanitis (d. AD 34), went on progress hearing cases he thereby proved local methods insufficient. Jewish fundamentalist zealots stood out against all rule save their own, claiming they along could enforce the Torah. No problem lacked an answer if their biblical blueprint was inerrant and exhaustive. They could quote chapter and verse, while their pagan neighbours hardly knew their own laws.

JEWISH LAW

Under the Romans Jewish law (*halakha*) was not dominant but servient (following Alexander the Great's model), nevertheless only a few Israelite judgements, for example that X was 'worthy of death', required the ruler's endorsement. Israelites were an agricultural people and became adept at commerce. Fictions, needed in all legal systems, flourished among them. If at the approach of a Sabbatical Year people avoided lending for fear of not being repaid (Dt 15: 1–2, 7–10), means were invented whereby money could be recovered notwithstanding the Year. Accommodation loans and investments, hampered by the Torah's prohibition of 'increase' (usury), were eased by ingenious expedients. A Ptolemy fixed legal interest at 25 per cent, but the *halakha* would have none of that. The 'stubborn and rebellious son' (Dt 21:18–21) escaped death by rabbis' construing the text shamelessly strictly; and when adulteries increased the archaic ordeal of the 'bitter waters' (Num 5:11–31) was declared obsolete.

Testaments and adoptions were unknown. *Halakha* does not allow a wife to divorce her husband, though it permits him to divorce her without restriction. Marriage under Greek-style contracts permitted her to free herself in stated circumstances, and eventually rabbis could force a husband to divorce her if he became insufferable.[2] So contracts could modify general rules. They did not bind without at least a token of present possession (cf. Lk 10:35). Bargains could be annulled for 'overreaching'. Borrowers automatically insured the objects borrowed. Moveables could be acquired only by lifting or drawing, unless taken simultaneously with immoveables. Land would be lost by three years' adverse possession; and chattels became ownerless if the owners 'gave up hope of recovery'. To become a partner each must become a servant of the other(s); and agents represented their principals without liability for fraud. Greeks would find such rules archaic.

Jews prized documents above witnesses, and a confession could settle a civil, though not a criminal action. Money cases were distinguished from capital cases, which required a fuller court: the standard of proof being lighter in the former class, where the decision depended, in some cases, on a party's oath. Seizure of debtors was facilitated by contracts allowing the lender to proceed 'as if by decree of the court'. The custom whereby *A* could vow to the Temple any benefit *B* might have had from *A* could defeat the spirit of biblical protection of parents.[3] Rabbis offered to annul such a vow if *A* repented – but no one compelled him to repent. A proselyte from paganism entered Israel (by immersion, with circumcision if male) as if newly born, without property or relations.

Matrimonial law, too, was peculiar. Though marriages were usually 'arranged' with a dowry, intercourse alone could make a marriage; but *halakha* regarded marriage with a pagan as a concubinage. The levirate, known to 'primitive' peoples, was strange to Greeks and Romans. A wife's barrenness would excuse the surviving practice of polygamy (*sc.* Polygyny). A wife had an assured sum at her husband's death or divorce without fault on her part; but she was not his heir, and stepchildren might neglect her. Adultery was a crime, but not fornication. Inheritance was patrilineal and agnatic, males preferred to females. *Talio*, making punishment fit the crime, had divine approval; but a compensation procedure developed to meet claims more logically. There were five mandatory sentences according to the crime: flogging (the 39 lashes),[4] stoning, burning (he who has intercourse with a woman and her daughter), beheading, and strangling. Anyone preparing to commit a very grave crime, for example buggery, could be killed by a passer-by. Extra-halakhic punishments included amputation of hands, casting over a precipice, and drowning. The executed criminal was exposed on a pole till sunset (Dt 21:22–3): the foreign penalty of hanging up alive (impalement/crucifixion) was recognized as compatible with the text, and suitable for blasphemers. A 'plotting' witness incurred the penalty he intended for his victim (Susannah 61–2). Witnesses were the executioners. 'Strange worship' was a capital crime, provided actual idolatry was proved. Bestiality (known among pagans and readily imputed to them) was criminal, an 'abomination' like homosexuality, itself forbidden even to all the descendants of Noah.

Halakha was immune to amendment. No ruler could change it or dispense from observance of it. Contracts in favour of the Temple were exempt from some restrictions applicable in transactions between individuals. The High Priest was supreme judge there and priests might apply lynch-law to protect the place's holiness. A non-priest serving in the Temple was subject to a severe but unknown punishment (Mishnah, *Sanh.* 9:6), but it was a remote contingency. Priests were subject to extra restrictions in marriage. Rome allowed pagans to be warned off entering the inner enclosure; but until the High Priest ended the practice sacrifices were offered on behalf of the emperor. No Jewish king, or common priest, could interfere with the Temple, while the general *halakha* could be expounded to the public by priests and later by rabbis through interpretation. Useful principles guided those interpreters: no law must be imposed on people beyond their strength; the door of repentance must be left open; no untrained persons could attain halakhic soundness; nevertheless ordinary presumptions served God's purposes (e.g. when is a witness presumed to lie?); and reason supplied useful canons of textual interpretation (e.g. scripture does not contradict itself). In dire emergencies departure from the Torah was allowed to a Jewish court.

Experts, giving the Torah an imperative voice to those Israelites who were presumed to be observant, surely held a power all their own. Jurists in Rome related what reason had made of the Twelve Tables and old practices; in Greece laws new and old were collected in archives and sometimes carved in stone; but the *halakha* represented Jewish adepts' estimate for the time being of what God commanded Moses. One who doubted Moses risked being swallowed up by the earth,[5] if he had not been coerced already!

RELIGION AND LAW

God selected, as his people, the descendants of Abraham through Isaac. At Mount Sinai they accepted the Covenant, to be binding on their issue for ever. If they obeyed him they would prosper in the Land, otherwise they would incur curses (Dt 28). The 'nations' rejected such an offer and served as instruments of his vengeance. If Jews were subject to them God's mercy had not prevailed over his justice. Secularly-minded Romans wondered at Jews' social exclusiveness, glorifying their Torah. If jurists settled an abstruse point of *halakha* or elders dealt with some farming practice, the court on earth knew its decree was binding in heaven, for the Torah was on earth, not in heaven. Yet the judges' scope was imperfect: what did 'cutting off from the people' mean (Lev 17: 10, 14)? Did such divine displeasure require excommunication, or the death penalty? The thought-world is illustrated by the following:

> The False Prophet (Dt 18:20) prophesies what he has not heard or has not been told to him [by God] – his death is by the hands of man [strangulation]. But he that suppresses his prophecy, or disregards the words of another prophet, or transgresses his own words, his death is at the hands of heaven [mysteriously]. (Mishnah, *Sanh.* 11:5).

Gaps left by the *halakha* are noticed in heaven. One who repudiated his contract for want of present consideration would suffer in the World to Come (Bab. Talmud, Baba Meṣiʿa 49a; cf. Ps 73:11); and he who caused a conflagration by means of a deaf-mute or a minor was liable (only) in the Court of Heaven (Mishnah, *Baba Qamma* VI.4).

Since righteousness won blessings from the Lord (Ps 24:3–6), a greater scrupulosity was propitious. On the other hand for a scholar to retract was not shameful. One tried to 'do justice and righteousness' even when not obligated to do so (cf. Lk 16:5–8), and to keep to the *halakha* even when one's failure would pass undetected. Righteous kings were expected to free cities from taxation, redeem captives and free slaves and prisoners. Subjects aimed to do 'deeds of kindness', helping the 'poor and needy'. Since God redeemed the Israelites from Egypt they must be generous (Dt 15:1, 15; 24:17, 22). Very scrupulous people, unorganized yet identifiable, the *ḥasîdîm* (God's beloved), would, for example, bury objects endangering the unwary, and pay the heirs of deceased persons to whom they *might* have owed money.

Israelites valued some rules, for example the Temple's sanctity, so highly that they would give their lives to maintain them, though no court compelled them. The 'nations' could be incredulous.[6] Meanwhile troublemakers would accuse even kings of unrighteous behaviour, and claim that the Torah required objectors to remedy matters. Herod the Great made short work of such protests, but Agrippa I, keen to appear observant, was more understanding. Religion can be a cloak for self-interest;[7] but it could also be an immovable object in the way of Roman force. Whose master would win?

Some Sadducees, associated with the priesthood, construed the law strictly, while Pharisees ('Separatists') were more inventive and more scrupulous. Among these were groups of different levels of observance: Greeks thought they were schools of philosophy. None of these rules was false (who could prove it?); and Greeks understood them to be *nomoi*, 'laws'. A Pharisaic rule could be enforced if their faction was in power. Sadducees respected Pharisaic rules in the Temple to avoid popular demonstrations (cf. Josephus, *Antiquities* 13:372). Could a Pharisaic majority sway a judicial decision? Who could tell? Mere indifference towards an alleged rule of *halakha* would excuse no accused. On the other hand Jews could extract testimony from a reluctant witness by appealing to God's injunction to speak out (Lev 5:1).

A Galilean must be aware of five 'laws': the various forms of Israelite *halakha*; the *halakha* of the Samaritans, with their sanctuary on Mount Gerizim and their own priesthood; that of *ḥasîdîm*; the laws of Greek cities and cosmopolitan cities like Tiberias; and the Roman law with its ultimate sanctions, which did not always respect the privileges of Roman citizens. Did obedience to the Torah really exempt one from care about state law (so R. Nehunya, c.AD 70–130)? Could one even organize a discussion at an inn between individuals subject to those laws? At least three would not eat with each other nor with any of the remainder. If a Jew pontificated in the name of a 'strange god' he must be put to death, even if he had always conformed to the *halakha* himself, declaring 'unclean' or 'forbidden' what was indeed so (Dt 18:20; Mishnah, *Sanh.* 11:6).

THE INNOVATOR

A jurist might opt for greater severity, or he could change his mind. With law unpredictable and chaotic and administration arbitrary innovation could be welcomed; but originality was suspect. Jews were collective, hierarchical, and chauvinistic. A disloyal son was an abomination whatever his arguments. Israel was supple in her joints because she was firmly joined. Apostates could be ignored; 'false' prophets could not. Hebrew did not distinguish 'dependant' from 'slave': the independent person was unknown. Despair of improvement, granted the confidence of interpreters of scripture, appears from two current fantasies: an immortal Elijah who would eventually right secret wrongs; and one or more coming Messiah(s), who would implement justice as no other person could (cf. Jer 23:5).

A leader citing scripture could collect a mob and challenge Rome. A religious maniac (e.g. Jesus son of Ananias, AD 62) might be handed over by Jews to the Romans. A desert-dwelling ascetic, such as the Baptist, could form a school of righteousness from disciples who 'repented' (Mt 3:8, 11). If he actually censured a tetrarch's marital life he incurred martyrdom. Rome did not object to sects, only to threats to imperial rule; but Jerusalem was alert to preachers seducing people to 'strange worship' or disbelief in Moses as she understood him. A threat to the solidarity of Israel was criminal. But a powerful genius, despising the High Priest, might devise a *halakha*, with a new calendar, a new vision of Jerusalem and the Temple, a new edition of the Pentateuch, and, with supporters who condoned his 'overvalued idea', found a community with its constitution. So the Essenes, who had great patrons, came to cultivate holiness within the 'world', while a branch sought sanctuary in the Judaean desert. The documents found near Qumran, a library of a sect that perished about AD 71, show they once included married couples, and later adapted their constitution to a celibate, coenobitic establishment.

Their 'Temple Scroll' shows that the Pentateuch could be simplified. We have their disciplinary code and a penal law (another servient system); those that deserved death would be handed over to the Romans. Slandering the community, lying knowingly about money, insulting a member, falling asleep during a session of the Many, murmuring: all these were crimes even though not specified in the Pentateuch. A revised law of evidence was needed, and they insisted on the biblical duty to rebuke offenders (Lev 19:17). One could be excluded from sacred meals for various periods, locked up, and even expelled. One could not argue with the leaders' judgements.

The innovator might have stimulated, over time, a halakhic reform within Israel. But the Many inducted newcomers subject to severe tests of sincerity, shunning outsiders, not even asking after their welfare. Pious Israelites already shunned disreputable people, including Rome's fellow-travellers. The Qumran sectaries followed the pious in refusing anything tainted by 'wickedness'. Even gifts from strangers were rejected; so the Essenes operated a kind of community (at any rate a sharing) of untainted property without seeming to be a 'race' apart.

In spite of their hostility to Pharisees and Sadducees, Qumran sectaries found no new way of discovering *halakha*. They studied the same sources with similar methods (permitting quaint interpretations, e.g. Mic 7:2 at CD 16: 14–15), and obtained results distinct from Pharisees'. The 'replies' in 4QMMT prove that, anterior to the

Mishnah, many problems of those who 'separate themselves from the multitude' could be settled by experts' interpretation, the results packaged in a mini-code. These 'Deeds of the Law' (distinct from behaviour without Torah significance) are a conglomeration. They relate to the calendar, Temple offerings (those by pagans now forbidden), the Red Heifer (a rare ritual), sin offerings, ritual slaughter, illicit marriages, tithes, lepers and numerous topics that, whoredom apart, have nothing to do with what we call 'law'. Characteristically, dietary restrictions and sexual relations appeared to be kindred topics.

Such 'replies' would bind only those who asked for them. Another separation to practise holiness was attempted by the Therapeutae, another desert group, about whom little is known. A feature of such experiments in 'separation' was that though they withdrew from 'lax' Israelite life they would constitute no real threat to it.

THE TRIAL OF CHRIST

Christians believe that Christ must die to redeem many from their sins. He was the Righteous Sufferer of the Hebrew scriptures and the Suffering Servant depicted in Isaiah 53, which with Psalm 22 was among passages allowed to 'explain' the so-called trial(s) of Jesus and his crucifixion. This process, noticeable in Matthew and in John, can have distorted the story beyond hope of historical reconstruction. One must use the New Testament accounts, only slightly corroborated by Talmudic fragments showing that Jews later believed Israelites were justifiably responsible for Jesus' death.[8] We may ask how did the High Priest and his colleagues reach the fatal decision; why did Jews demand that Jesus die by crucifixion; why did Pilate gratify them; and why did they desire his death in the first place?

The Sanhedrin had no ordinary right to inflict a death penalty, which Roman law would reserve to the prefect. In religious riots a lynch-mob might defy the restriction; but if Jesus had been regularly condemned on a court day the Sanhedrin would have the odium of destroying a reputed holy man and prophet. But at Passover the Torah prohibited preparations for an execution, and all judicial proceedings were suspended. One could, however, investigate Jesus, leaving any sequel to the one person uninhibited from taking action, though he was confined to Roman forms of coercion. Granted that Jesus posed a problem, a formal investigation was desired (not tied to Mishnaic trial rules), where testimony could be tendered ('He said he could destroy the Temple and rebuild it'), and tested – we are told it failed as self-contradictory.

Jesus then admitted (no doubt under some pressure) that he was the Messiah and gratuitously prophesied, as if he were God's confidant, the Son of Man's coming in the sight of his own inquisitors. This was taken as blasphemous (he did not challenge that ruling), and he was declared 'worthy of death'. No one could stone him because of the Feast.

Pilate, activating a recognized 'extraordinary' procedure, perceived the priests had grounds for invoking his aid, without presuming to act in revision of their sentence (they had passed none). He did not query whether they had acted within their jurisdiction. He was not negligent, for he was not bound to go behind their certificate that Jesus was 'worthy of death'. Whether Pilate went over the priests' and elders' heads to appeal to the bystanders, offering them a chance to rescue Jesus, is doubtful but not unthinkable. Pilate had the shortest of exchanges with Jesus. Was he a king (*sc.* the king Messiah)? He got no more out of him. He then acted as governor, since for him to reject the application of the High Priest would mar his ongoing collaboration with him. It seemed to be a public order matter (so Lk 23:2, 13), and Jesus was crucified between brigands. Pilate knew that Judaism could have political implications, and here he is supporting the limited self-government of Israel in a matter of religion.

But whence came the *prima facie* case against Jesus, the most interesting of our enquiries? His violent demonstration within the Temple; his scepticism of authority-bearing characters of all types; his proclamation of the Kingdom of God as 'at hand' and his followers its only subjects – all showed him a potential rabble rouser. His reputation as a miraculous healer, a broker of divine patronage, intensified alarm. He was not condemned as a false prophet, a rebellious elder, a seducer to idolatry, or otherwise under the Pentateuch; but two intelligible allegations seem to have been relevant. Jesus led ('seduced') people out of the beaten path of their ancestors; and he claimed a nearer relationship with God than God's priestly agents and practitioners of piety (including the rare miracle worker) had ever claimed for themselves. This combination, repugnant to the Prophets,[9] was ultimately fatal. Pilate, however reluctantly, acted as the priests' and elders' implement, as the emperor's interests and good sense required.

THE POPULACE AND IDEALS

The crowd, no negligible force, did not save Jesus and he did not rely on them to do so. Israelites traditionally expected the poor to be righteous, the rich wicked, and government a form of exploitation. Roman taxation capped it all. The mob reacted violently to disrespect for their faith: a collective thrives on common fears. Religious zeal, widely tolerated, fostered antagonism to non-Jews. No police force prevented aggressive or subversive activities. A prudent governor convened not the council only but also popular leaders.[10] In the New Testament 'mob' signifies a potential support for Jesus. He might well have proved their hero – but there were contrary indications. His healings encouraged belief in him, while he aimed sarcasms against hoarders and other power-holders, sparing only those ready to 'repent'. Some of these disgorged ill-gotten gains. He encouraged women to think, not a pointless eccentricity. The story of the conspiracy against Jesus indeed shows the High Priest concerned that the crowd might prevent Jesus' arrest.

But how single-mindedly could the populace support him? Whichever interpretations of Torah gained currency depended ultimately on popular recognition. Pharisaic or other notions became authoritative as the public adopted them. Jesus' lack of influential disciples could not escape notice. A popular movement, antagonistic to the priests, could indeed have insisted on Jesus' innocence; but the High Priest must be supported in any confrontation with Rome – and a moment had arrived to be realistic. The evangelists have chosen to dramatize the crowd's unfortunate participation since, just as Israel had accepted the Covenant at Mount Sinai for their issue, so an agreement between High Priest and people could offer Jesus as if he were a scapegoat on behalf of sinners. So he was sent away to death, while the heart-searchings that allowed this 'fulfilment' of scripture remain conjectural. Judas' role remains a puzzle.

For the governor to appeal to the people was not un-Roman. But if his powers owed nothing to bystanders, their reactions must throw light on the case. A significant proportion of the public had wanted God to reign at last in fact. Scripture had supported them. Justice and judgement would flourish and the disadvantaged would get their deserts; obnoxious foreign rule would be ousted; and for all this personal and public purity were indispensable. John the Baptist preached repentance and many had listened. True to God, crowds would respond to a conversionist movement within Israel. But what would it cost?

Jesus' message had been simple. The work of Sadducees and various schools of Pharisaism had been founded on presuppositions that tolerated or even fostered abuses. They concentrated pedantically on God's commandments (Mt 23:23), rather than on the disposition that he implicitly, or through Prophets explicitly, required. All could turn to God, ignoring expediency and mere opportunism. Personal piety would take biblical rules in its stride, a solution within the scope of the uneducated and those with little to lose. Could pagans accept such a doctrine? The populace would be indifferent to this, but Jesus' teaching incidentally threatened differentials. And there was more.

Who can forgive every debtor, turn the other cheek, love enemies, practise humility, and yet retain the protection of a respectable group? Jesus' answer raises doubts: one would have associates as unworldly as oneself (Mk 10:30). Love of God enables one to reach a high spiritual standard: but many wanted recognition here and now, for shame went with low status. To disregard differentials and legal distinctions fits an ascetic;[11] but even *ḥasîdîm* behaved as if they stood before the bar of heaven, not as if commandments were symbolic. Moreover if the Messiah comes, who can 'abide his coming' (cf. Mal 3:2)? Only those who have nothing to fear will await that Kingdom. Such reservations, impressive even to the simplest, will have served *a fortiori* to impel Jewish rulers to crush this movement.

CONCLUSION

In a society where democracy, and representative and responsible government are unknown 'justice' and 'judgement' must be chimerical. What legal criteria could usefully be invoked? What 'law' is 'right'? Rabbis say that all responsible legal opinions are 'words of the Living God', even if contradictory (Jerusalem Talmud, *Yebamot* I, 6 (3b)). What can that mean in practice? Who will settle one's case? The corruption of judges was proverbial (Babylonian Talmud, *Šabbat* 116b). Does one need an intercessor? Would self-help be cheaper and more effective? Israelites' doubts about Greek judgements are severe: even if they are factually unexceptionable they should be ignored.[12]

Jesus' own formula appears from Luke 12:13–21, where, as at Luke 18:2–6, a justiciable right is denied its remedy in practice. In the former passage Jesus neither recommends going before a judge (a deplorable experience: Mt 5:26) nor offers to act as arbitrator. Attention is distracted from a hypothetical right towards the litigants' subjective condition. Once the parties begin to seek each other's welfare their problem melts. In marriage each spouse must keep the other from adultery; and when Caesar claims revenue, what matters is that one should not begrudge him what one really owes him.

Confusion of rights and duties could arise from studying both *halakha* and state laws without eliminating covetousness and pride. However, in the second passage one sees how the oppressed must not give up; they must not make a present to the wrongdoer and so subsidize vice. God, for his part, had cursed oppressors time out of mind through Moses and the Prophets (cf. Lk 16:31). One must concentrate on the moral state of the actor, rather than the book-norm or custom the judge must consult.

If this formula applies universally an Israelitish version of righteousness could at last commend Israel herself to a sceptical world. It would take advantage of Roman broadmindedness and Greek curiosity, proceeding as it does not as a moral philosophy but as a deduction from scripture. Individuals' responsibility is enhanced, and likewise their sense of self-worth, while halakhic texts remain to be construed as moral guidelines. This, then, is not a religious law, but a call for a subjective disposition. There is no code, memory is not burdened, scrupulosity is channelled, ethnic peculiarities become symbolical (Mt 12:7; 15:18–20), and one ends with a prescription for the soul's health. Yet where law is a lottery the legally minded still object that a list of duties is more manageable, and can be propounded with more confidence, than an amorphous change of heart. The populace of Jesus' day might well suspect, let Torah-specialists argue for ever, their own pedestrian aspirations were more sound. When non-Jews became Christians the result was a separate 'race' who were prepared to go back to Noah's progeny for their 'law'.

NOTES

1 Josephus, *Antiquities* 18:371.
2 Riskin 1989. For divorce in Qumran see G. Brin in Bernstein 1997: 231–44.
3 See Ex 20:12; 21:17; also Dt 27:16.
4 By a neat interpretation of Dt 25:2–3 Pharisees reduced the biblical 40 lashes to 39 (Mishnah, *Makk.* 3:10; 2 Cor 11:24).
5 Num 16:32; 26:10; Ps 106:17.
6 Josephus, *Against Apion* 1:208–12.
7 Josephus, *Jewish War* 2:517; *Antiquities* 18:319, 323; *Life* 65–7.
8 Babylonian Talmud, *Sanh.* 43a.
9 See Is 3:12; 14:14; 46:5; Ezek 13:8–16; 28:2–10; Am 2:4; 1 Kgs 14:16; 2 Kgs 21:9, 12–16; Mt 27:63–4; 24:3–5, 24; Jn 5:18; 7:12, 47; 10:36.
10 Josephus, *Life* 284, 301.
11 Derrett 1995.
12 Elon 1994, 1: 16–18 (the ban on forcing Jews before a non-Israelite court endured for long).

BIBLIOGRAPHY

Bammel, E. and Moule, C. F. D. (eds) (1984) *Jesus and the Politics of His Day*, Cambridge: Cambridge University Press.
Bernstein, M. et al. (eds) (1997) *Legal Texts and Legal Issues: Proceedings of the Second Meeting of the International Organisation of Qumran Studies, Cambridge 1995*, Leiden: Brill.

Betz, O. (1982) 'Probleme des Prozesses Jesu', *ANRW* II 25,1: 565–647.

Blinzler, J. (1969) *Der Prozess Jesu*, 4th edn, Regensburg: Pustet.

Bloch, M. (1893) *Der Vertrag nach Mosaisch-talmudischem Recht*, Budapest.

Bockmuehl, M. (2000) *Jewish Law in Gentile Churches*, Edinburgh: T. & T. Clark.

Brown, Raymond (1994) *The Death of the Messiah: from Gethsemane to Grave: A Commentary on the Passion Narrative in the Fourth Gospel*, New York: Doubleday.

Carroll, J. T. et al. (1995) *The Death of Jesus in Early Christianity*, Peabody: Hendrickson.

Danby, H. (trans.) (1933) *The Mishnah*, London: Oxford University Press.

Davies, W. D. (1962) 'Law in the New Testament [nomos, TORAH]', *Interpreter's Dictionary of the Bible*, Nashville: Abingdon Press; repr. in (1984) *Jewish and Pauline Studies*, London: SPCK, 227–42.

Derrett, J. D. M. (1970) *Law in the New Testament*, London: Darton, Longman & Todd.

—— (1982) 'Law and society in Jesus' world', *ANRW* II 25,1: 477–564.

—— (1995) 'Primitive Christianity as an ascetic movement', in V. L. Wimbush and R. Valantasis (eds) *Asceticism*, New York: Oxford University Press, 88–107.

Elon, M. (1994) *Jewish Law: History, Sources, Principles*, 4 vols, Philadelphia & Jerusalem: Jewish Publication Society.

Falk, Z. W. (1972–8) *Introduction to Jewish Law of the Second Commonwealth*, 2 vols, Leiden: Brill.

Fitzmyer, J. A. (1976) 'The Matthean divorce texts and some new Palestinian evidence', *TS* 37: 197–226.

Garnsey, P. (1970) *Social Studies and Legal Privilege in the Roman Empire*, Oxford: Clarendon Press.

Grabbe, L. L. (1992) *Judaism from Cyrus to Hadrian. Vol. 2: The Roman Period*, Minneapolis: Fortress Press.

Hempel, C. (1997) 'The penal code reconsidered', in F. G. Martínez (ed.) *Texts from Qumran 4: The Cambridge Conference of 1995*, Leiden: Brill.

Herzog, I. (1965–7) *The Main Institutions of Jewish Law*, 2 vols, London: Soncino Press.

Horowitz, G. (1973) *The Spirit of Jewish Law*, New York: Central Book (original edn, 1953).

Jackson, B. S. (1979) 'The concept of religious law in Judaism', *ANRW* II 19,1: 33–52.

Kelly, J. M. (1966) *Roman Litigation*, Oxford: Clarendon Press.

Kertelge, K. (ed.) (1989) *Der Prozess gegen Jesus: Historische Rückfrage und theologische Deutung*, Freiburg: Herder.

Kuhn, H.-W. (1982) 'Die Kreuzesstrafe während der frühen Kaiserzeit: Ihre Wirklichkeit und Wertung in der Umwelt der Urchristentums', *ANRW* II 25,1: 648–793.

Lewis, N. (1986) *Greeks in Ptolemaic Egypt: Case Studies in the Social History of the Hellenistic World*, Oxford: Clarendon Press.

Lewis, N. et al. (eds) (1989) *The Documents of the Bar-Kokhba Period in the Cave of Letters*, Jerusalem: Y. Yadin Memorial Fund.

McLaren, J. S. (1992) *Powers and Politics in Palestine*, Sheffield: Academic Press.

Malina, B. J. (1996) *The Social World of Jesus and the Gospels*, London & New York: Routledge.

Mantel, H. (1961) *Studies in the History of the Sanhedrin*, Cambridge, Mass.: Harvard University Press.

Martínez, F. G. (1994) *The Dead Sea Scrolls Translated: The Qumran Texts in English*, Leiden: Brill.

Modrzejewski, J. M. (1995) *The Jews of Egypt from Rameses II to Emperor Hadrian*, Edinburgh: T. & T. Clark.

Rakover, N. (1994) *A Guide to the Sources of Jewish Law*, Jerusalem: Jewish Legal Heritage Society.

Riskin, S. (1989) *Women and Jewish Divorce*, Hoboken, N.J.: Ktav.

Safrai, S. and Stern, M. (eds) (1974–6) *The Jewish People in the First Century*, 2 vols, Assen: Van Gorcum.

Sanders, E. P. (1992) 'Law in Judaism of the New Testament period', *ABD* 4: 254–65.

Schalit, A. (1969) *König Herodes: Der Mann und sein Werk*, Berlin: de Gruyter.

Schiffman, L. H. (1975) *The Halakhah at Qumran*, Leiden: Brill.

—— (1983) *Sectarian Law in the Dead Sea Scrolls: Courts, Testimony, and the Penal Code*, Chico: Scholars Press.

Schneider, G. (1972) 'Die Verhaftung Jesu: Traditionsgeschichte von Mk 14, 52–53', *ZNW* 63: 188–209.

Schürer, E. (1973–86) *The History of the Jewish People in the Age of Jesus Christ (175 BC–AD 135): New English Version, rev. edn*, G. Vermes and F. Millar, 3 vols, Edinburgh: T. & T. Clark.

Segal, P. (1989) 'The penalty of the warning inscription from the Temple of Jerusalem', *IEJ* 39: 79–84.

Sherwin-White, A. N. (1963) *Roman Society and Roman Law in the New Testament*, Oxford: Clarendon Press (rev. edn 2000, Oxford: Clarendon Press).

Sugranyes de Franch, R. (1946) *Études sur le droit palestinien à l'époque évangélique*, Fribourg: Librairie de l'Université.

Taubenschlag, R. (1944) *The Law of Greco-Roman Egypt in the Light of the Papyri 332 BC – 640 AD*, New York: Herald Square Press (2nd edn, 1955).

Tcherikover, V. (1959) *Hellenistic Civilization and the Jews*, Philadelphia: Jewish Publication Society; Jerusalem: Magnes Press.

Tosato, A. (1990) 'Il problema del potere politico per gli Israeliti del tempo di Gesù', *EstBíb* 48: 461–87.

Vliet, H. van (1958) *No Single Testimony: A Study on the Adoption of the Law of Deut. 19:15 par. into the New Testament*, Utrecht: Kemink & Zoon.

Weinfeld, M. (1995) *Social Justice in Ancient Israel and in the Ancient Near East*, Jerusalem: Magnes Press; Minneapolis: Fortress Press.

Wolff, H.-J. (1960) 'Plurality of laws in Ptolemaic Egypt', *RIDA*, 3rd series, 7: 191–223.

—— (1962) *Das Justizwesen der Ptolemäer*, Munich (MBPF 44).

RELIGION IN PRE-EXILIC ISRAEL

—•◆•—

Rainer Albertz
Translated by Hazel Harvey

The Hebrew Bible presents matters as if Moses revealed to Israel on Sinai its entire religion, fully developed (Exodus, Deuteronomy). But the Bible narrative then has to assume that a great part of the Torah of Moses was subsequently forgotten or ignored, in order to explain the very different reality of Israel's pre-exilic religion. According to 2 Kings 22f., the ancient religion of Moses was rediscovered only by King Josiah towards the end of the pre-exilic period (622 BC) and it was not until about 400 BC in the post-exilic period that Israel was pledged to the 'Law of the God of Heaven' by Ezra (Ezra 7–10).

Whereas earlier scholars have been content to accept (with certain modifications) the Bible's presentation of the situation, it is now often argued that the religion of Israel in the pre-exilic period was nothing but a variant of Canaanite polytheism; and it was not until the exile and the succeeding period that it developed into the exclusive monotheistic belief in Yahweh attributed to Moses. This view is based, first, on the recognition that almost all the documentation of the early days of Israel originated at a much later date. Also, the findings of modern archaeology have revealed that pre-exilic Israel had much closer cultural and religious ties to its Near Eastern neighbours than was previously realized.

But however much we are justified in assuming that Israel's religion, like any religion, had to grow and develop into its final form, the question remains of why it began to differentiate itself from the other religions of the Near East. I shall follow a middle way in attempting to reconstruct this process, starting from the belief that what arose in the early days of Moses was not the entire religion, but nevertheless surely some important impulses towards its further development.

ISRAEL'S RELIGION IN THE PERIOD BEFORE THE STATE

It is difficult to find any documentary evidence for the origins of Israel's religion, but there are three starting points that help us to construct a history.

The first is the flight from slavery in Egypt of a fairly large Semitic group, led by Moses, in the second half of the thirteenth century BC (Exodus). The god Yahweh had commanded Moses to organize this flight, and had also promised to provide a new homeland for the refugees (Exod. 3f.). At this time Yahweh was a mountain god of the Midianites in the north Arabian desert, without a pantheon; his attributes were those of a weather god. Moses knew of him from his father-in-law (Exod. 2:15ff.; 18). The successful escape and the survival of the Red Sea crossing (Exod. 14f.) and the experience of theophany on Sinai (Exod. 19f.) helped to create a personal link between the god Yahweh and the group led by Moses. The special circumstances that gave rise to Israel's religion help to explain three of its characteristics that would later become important: (1) Yahweh's personal relationship to a whole group of people – cf. the epithets 'God of the Hebrews' (Exod. 5:3); 'God of Israel' (Judg. 5:3, 5). The gods of the Near East were usually attached to cities or regions and had no personal relationship except with kings and single individuals. (2) The extreme experience of escaping from an alien power influenced this personal relationship with God, giving it an inward solidarity and an outward exclusivity. Later, this would become a most prominent feature (cf. Deut.). (3) Having originated in a process of social revolution, the Yahweh religion continued to express frequent criticism of rulers and of society.

The second starting point is the Canaanite religion of the farmers and herdsmen of Palestine. When the culture of the late Bronze Age collapsed towards the end of the thirteenth century BC these people freed themselves from the Canaanite city-states and founded family communities in villages in the mountains. They united in a defensive league called 'Isra-'el' (recorded on the stele of Merneptah, 1219 BC), placing themselves under the protection of the god El ('May El reign'), who had stood at the head of a Pantheon in Ugarit as 'king of the gods', but who now, in the altered social circumstances, had developed on the one hand into a Most High God (as El-Elyon Deut. 32:8) and on the other hand into a personal god (cf. personal names). El was venerated at various locations in the area (Beth-El Gen. 31:13, Shechem Gen. 33:20; El-Olam in Beersheba Gen. 21:33). Also the many place names formed from *Baal* indicate that this god was venerated in the area. When the group led by Moses came upon the tribes fighting for their freedom, it gave them the opportunity of combining with El their own god Yahweh (who had already proved his effectiveness in an act of liberation) and of making him the patron lord of the league. This transformed Yahweh into a regular war god (cf. Exod. 15:3; 1 Sam. 18:17; 25:28), with whose help charismatic leaders defended the freedom of the tribes against the attacks of their neighbours (Judg. 15:19f., 23; 7:18). As long as Yahweh occupied the position of ruler no permanent political power could develop within the group (Judg. 8:22f.). In this way Yahweh preserved the liberty and the relative equality of all the families of the tribal society which existed before the development of a state.

In this period the unique position of Yahweh gave rise to exclusivity only on a political level. As for religion, other gods and goddesses were venerated besides Yahweh/El, without giving rise to any conflicts (Judg. 6:25–32 refers to a later period). It was probably a remnant of Canaanite religiosity that caused Yahweh to be given the company of a goddess. The secondary veneration of 'his Asherah' at his side, which is attested from Kuntillet Ajrud and Khirbet el-Qôm for the ninth and eighth centuries, probably harks back to the early syncretism of El/Yahweh, from which Yahweh inherited the consort of El. With an Assyrian overlay this became, in the seventh to sixth centuries, veneration of the 'Queen of Heaven', probably an Ishtar figure (Jer. 44:15ff.).

The Bronze Age practice of erecting temples in cities was mostly discontinued by the Israelites. The only temple buildings used by them were the ones at Shiloh and Shechem. The typical holy place before the state was established was a 'Height', an open space set apart on a rise outside a settlement, such as has been excavated in Dothan ('Bull site'), in Arad and perhaps also in Dan. Next to the altar, Massebe and Asherah symbolized the divine presence, probably as a male–female duality. Typical celebrations at these simple, decentralized cult locations were agricultural festivals at the start of the harvesting of the barley fields (Mazzot), wheat fields (Shavu'ot) and orchards and vineyards (Sukkot, Judg. 21:19), with acts of thanks-giving for blessings received and prayers for fruitfulness to come. There was feasting and drinking and merrymaking (Hos. 4:11–14). It is still common to differentiate between the Yahweh religion and the 'Canaanite fertility religion', but it must be emphasized that the aspect of fertility was firmly integrated into the religion of Israel in the times before the state. That was not incompatible with the festival of Mazzot also being used for remembrance of the flight from Egypt (Exod. 23:15).

The third starting point is family religion, which forms a widespread substratum under the historical religions of the Near East. The Israelite families chose a god from their region as their personal family god (the father's god) and expected him to help, protect, support and bless their members. Beside him, they could also venerate a family goddess (Asherah, later 'Queen of Heaven'). Family gods of the early period included El, Baal, Shadday, Gad, Shalem, and so on, as can be seen from personal names that incorporate the name of a god. On the other hand, it was not until late in the time of the kings that the national god Yahweh also became the favourite family god. Whereas Israel's relationship with Yahweh had a historical basis, each individual based his or her trust in the personal family god on his creation at the time of birth (Ps. 22:10f.). House cults, in which the family god could be invoked, are attested by texts (Judg. 17f.) and by archaeological finds (e.g. at Megiddo). In addition to the veneration of the family god there was also a certain amount of ancestor-worship.

RELIGION IN THE EARLY MONARCHIC PERIOD

Saul and David established the monarchy; David and Solomon oversaw the development of Israel into a territorial state, ruled from the centre, with a surrounding ring of vassal states. This led to a thoroughgoing transformation of the Israelite religion. In the early monarchic period the need to legitimize the newly won political power, for which the Yahweh religion had no ready answers, forced the addition of major features borrowed from other religions. The court theologians of David and Solomon used Egyptian and Meopotamian precedents to develop a new theology of kingship, according to which the king, as the incarnate son of Yahweh, was commissioned by him to bring the whole world to bow down to him (Ps. 2:7f.). At the same time the king claimed for himself, as the son of God, to be the channel of blessings, preserver of justice (Ps. 72) and high priest (Ps. 110:4).

Closely connected with this theology was the theology of the Temple at Jerusalem, which David and Solomon built as a splendid cult centre for their realm. Jerusalem was presented as the city of God, identical with the mountain of the gods in the north and therefore the centre of the world (Ps. 48:2f.). Yahweh was present there (Ps. 46:6); that is why the city could not be overrun by the threatening forces of chaos or men (Ps. 46:4f, 7). Rather, from Zion Yahweh would conquer every nation (46:10f.).

In the theology of Jerusalem, Yahweh himself became a king of gods with a royal consort; he became El-Elyon ('highest El') and Yahweh-Zebaoth ('Yahweh of the armies'). He was enthroned in and above the Holy of Holies in the Temple at Jerusalem, where cherubim guarded a gigantic throne made of olive-wood and covered with gold leaf. The small ark beneath was intended to maintain continuity with the old religion of Yahweh. But as God of the state of David and Solomon, Yahweh had grown far beyond the god of Israel and had become ruler of the universe, as befitted David's imperial policies. Within the state, David's young monarchy used Yahweh as guarantor of its permanence (2 Sam. 7).

It is peculiar to Israel that these 'normal' political and religious changes never found general acceptance. Among the disempowered tribal authorities there was widespread resistance throughout the kingdom to the autocratic regime and its annexation of Yahweh. The protest led to several uprisings against David and Solomon, during which the slogan 'Yahweh is king' (cf. 1 Sam. 8:7; 12:12) was used against the monarchy. When Solomon repeatedly compelled Israelites to labour on his ambitious building-works, Jeroboam led a rebellion (1 Kgs 11:26–8; 12), calling upon the god who had delivered them from slavery in Egypt (12:28). The golden images of calves (which Jeroboam dedicated to Yahweh after the uprising had proved successful) were originally intended only as receptacles for the invisible god, symbolizing his power.

In the rebellion, which led to the separation of the northern kingdom, the liberation ideals of the Yahweh religion, which predated the state, made further inroads against the monarchy. Jeroboam tried to find a form of government better suited to the religion; to this end he refrained from establishing a permanent residence, and decentralized the state cult, establishing it in Bethel and Dan. However, as the northern kingdom continued to lose stability, Omri provided a fixed residence for the northern kingdom in Samaria. Unfortunately there is no documentation for the theology of kingship in the north. But it does seem that the greater significance attached to the Exodus tradition in the north made the institution of the monarchy much less stable there (frequent usurpations 1Kgs 15:27f.; 16:15–22; 2 Kgs 15:10, 14, 25, 30).

OPPOSITION FROM THE PROPHETS IN THE NINTH AND EIGHTH CENTURIES

From the ninth century the opposition to the monarchy shifted to prophetic groups. This began with the social encroachment (1 Kgs 21) and the religious politics of the Omrides, who provoked the protest by the prophets Elijah and Elisha. In the course of the politics of alliance Ahab had provided for his Phoenician wife and her followers a temple in Samaria for Baal, god of Sidon. Ahab no doubt intended a subsidiary veneration of Baal next to Yahweh, the national god. However, this diplomatic syncretism aroused a bitter backlash from conservative prophetic circles. It began with a public contest about which god, Baal or Yahweh, could better bring rain (1 Kgs 18) and ended in 845 BC in a bloody revolution. A follower of Elisha anointed the officer Jehu as king. He put to death all the sons of Omri, together with the detested Jezebel, and destroyed the temple of Baal and all its worshippers (2 Kgs 9f.). It was in this confrontation that the Yahweh religion first displayed religious intolerance and cruelty in a political context.

The prophetic opposition became more radical in the eighth century, shortly before and during the period in which both northern and southern kingdoms came under pressure from the military expansion of the Assyrians towards the west. Now single prophets arose, proclaiming in the name of Yahweh the downfall of both Israel and Judah. Also Amos in the northern kingdom and Isaiah in the southern pitilessly exposed the deplorable social conditions. The expulsion of small landholders from their plots (Mic. 2:1–3), the cruel application of the laws of credit forcing them into debt-bondage (Amos 2:6), a legal system that gave lesser folk no recourse to the law (Is. 10: 1–4) – they attacked all this as sins against Yahweh. At the same time they condemned the life of luxury led by the upper classes (Amos 6: 1–6) and denied legitimacy to worship that was not matched by righteousness in daily life (Is. 1:10–1).

Isaiah in the south and Hosea in the north exposed the ruinous foreign policies by which each new ruler believed he could win benefits from holding the balance of power between his larger neighbours, Assyria and Egypt (Hos. 5:12–14). To put one's trust in an ally and his superior chariot capacity seemed to Isaiah to show a lack of trust in God and was therefore doomed to fail (Is. 7:9; 31:1–3).

Finally, in the north, Hosea condemned Israel's religious rites in the rural areas and in the capital city as neglect of Yahweh, being a regular 'cult of Baal'. The merrymaking on the heights sometimes degenerated into obscenity (Hos. 4:11–14) and no longer expressed the reverence that was due to Yahweh. Israel believed that it could ensure fertility and political stability by means of sacrifices, images of gods and many rituals, but meanwhile Yahweh was neglected, he who had lovingly bound himself to Israel in its early days, like a man to a woman (Hos. 2:4ff.) or parents to their child (11:1ff.). He had once delivered them from Egypt, he alone had cared for them in the desert and given them their fruitful land (Hos. 13:1–8). That is why Yahweh would take back from Israel all the cultivated fields (2:11–15) and send the people back to Egypt or Assyria (11:5, 11). Only when the process of delivery had been completely undone could the failed love story of Yahweh and his people make a fresh start in the waste places of exile (2:11–17).

The prophets of divine judgment in the eighth century, and then also those of the seventh and sixth centuries (Jeremiah, Ezekiel), found little acceptance during their lifetimes for their radical message. On the contrary, they were sent away (Amos 7:10–17), denounced as traitors (Is. 8:11–15), tortured (Jer. 20:1–6) and declared insane (Hos. 9:7). Nevertheless their significance for the history of Israel's religion can hardly be overestimated. The prophets of judgment made Israel aware, in a completely new way, of the strong emotionality and high ethical demands of its god. Yahweh had bound himself closely in great love to this one people, Israel. But, for this very reason, he also made special demands on Israel, to be faithful to him, and to administer justice (Amos 3:1f.; Is. 5:1–7). If Israel did not fulfil these justified demands, but instead trod Yahweh's love underfoot, he was capable, as lord of the universe, of turning his might against his own people and sending Assyria to destroy them. In saying this, the prophets showed Israel for the first time a new possibility of defining itself primarily in religious terms, from its peculiar relationship to God.

THE REFORM MOVEMENTS OF THE EIGHTH AND SEVENTH CENTURIES

The collapse of the northern kingdom in 722 BC (when the Assyrians conquered Samaria) caused profound dislocation among the communities. The prophets Amos and Hosea had been right, although no one had believed them! The followers of Hosea, who came with the refugees from the north as far as Jerusalem, were particularly active in stirring up reform movements in the southern kingdom at the end of the eighth century under King Hezekiah, and at the end of the seventh century under King Josiah. The reformers were anxious to learn the causes of the catastrophe that had befallen the northern kingdom, in order to save Judah from a similar fate.

'Hezekiah's reform' was a reform of the cult and probably also a social reform. Hezekiah purged the Jerusalem cult of ambiguous symbols for God, removing Nehustan, a snake symbol, from the temple, although the tradition was said to go back to Moses; he also closed down sanctuaries on hill tops, where statues of Massebe and Asherah had allowed syncretistic abuses to arise (2 Kgs 18:4). Evidence of provincial sanctuaries being closed down in this period has also been found by archaeologists in Arad and Beersheba.

If we may associate this reform with the so-called 'Book of the Covenant' (Ex. 20:22–3, 19), then this is where we see for the first time an effort to forbid the use of images of God and the subsidiary veneration of other gods within the cult of Yahweh (Ex. 20:23; 22:19; 23:13). In order to avoid syncretism, Yahweh must be worshipped only at sites officially declared sacred to him (20:24). These measures were intended to remove from Judah the cultic abuses Hosea believed had brought God's judgment upon Israel.

At the same time there was an attempt to mitigate the social inequities Amos and others had denounced. Thus debt-bondage was limited to a maximum of six years (Ex. 21:2–6), the courts of justice were to stop favouring the wealthy (23:1–8) and it was forbidden to oppress the poor, strangers, widows and orphans, for Yahweh was a merciful god (ss:20–6). The sacred institutions of a weekly day of rest and a system of leaving fields fallow in turn provided a basis for the development of an early system of poor-relief (23:10–12).

The new aspect of this reform of the laws was that each new religious and social reform was announced in the name of Yahweh as being directly authorized by him, Yahweh came personally to Israel, bringing his commandments and laws, and expected them to reform their religion and society in the way he wished, as an integral part of their worship. In the rest of the Near East – and in Israel too in earlier times – the gods were the guardians of the law only in a general sense, and it was the king who dispensed the law, usually without any religious aspect, or the law courts that passed judgment; but now things changed. The reform movement of the eighth century led Israel for the first time towards a directly theologized law and, as time went on, this became ever more central to its relationship with God.

Hezekiah's reform was probably not very successful, for the uprising he led against the Assyrians in 701 was a failure, and during the long reign of King Manasseh in the seventh century Judah continued to suffer massively under the political and cultural yoke of the Assyrians.

But scarcely had the Assyrian empire begun to weaken, from 640 on, than there came together in Judah a broad reform coalition composed of sections of the bureaucracy of Jerusalem (Shaphan) and the priesthood (Hilkiah) as well as the Judaean rural nobility ('People of the Land') and also some prophets (Huldah, the young Jeremiah). They put Josiah on the throne, although he was only 8 years old, and were determined that the new chance of independence he represented should be used for a thoroughgoing reform of Judah. The so-called reform of Josiah that, after long preparations came into force in 622, was a national, religious and social reform. Its legislation probably forms the nucleus of the book of Deuteronomy (Deut. 12–26).

Josiah had perceived that the withdrawal of Assyrian power from Palestine had provided the great opportunity for the nation to re-establish the empire of David. He therefore marched into the territory of the former northern kingdom and destroyed the ancient sanctuary of Bethel (2 Kgs 23:15–18), in order to force his brothers in the north to worship Yahweh in Jerusalem, with no syncretistic additions. The young Jeremiah also preached to them, calling upon them to reject all syncretism and false alliance and to return to the religion and cult of Yahweh on Zion (Jer. 2:4–4:3; 31:2–6).

However, the main thing was the reform of the cult. In the light of their experience of political collapse and foreign domination (by the Assyrians) the reformers saw the need to follow the path preached by the prophets and to create a new identity for Israel based on its religion. That is why they made every effort to establish the exclusive worship of Yahweh (monolatry) in all sections of society. Their slogan was 'Hear, O Israel, Yahweh is our God; there is one God, Yahweh' (Shema Yisrael, Deut. 6:4).

This entailed, first, ridding the Temple at Jerusalem of all the subsidiary cults of other divinities (e.g. the cult of Asherah, 2 Kgs 23:6f.) and the influence of foreign religions, which had become established during the Assyrian occupation (worship of the constellations, horses for the sun god Shamash 23:4, 11).

Secondly, it meant centralization of the cult; in other words, in order to increase control and to strengthen the unity of the state, the legitimate cult of Yahweh was restricted to Jerusalem. All provincial shrines were obliterated (Deut. 12), the once so popular hill-shrines lost their symbols of God since Massebe and Asherah were banned (Deut. 16:21f.). This not only destroyed the basis of all local differentiation in Israel's religion (the Yahwehs of Bethlehem, Samaria or Hebron: poly-yahwism) but it also robbed the family cults of their independence; from now on, family sacrifices were allowed only during the pilgrimage festivals in Jerusalem, which the priests controlled. In order to stop uncontrolled private sacrifices, the reformers even sanctioned profane slaughter (Deut. 12:13ff.).

This leads on to the third aspect – the reformers' interest in integrating more decisively into the worship of Yahweh the Israelite family religion, which had been practised until then in a largely independent and unnoticed way within the Yahweh religion. During the long years of Assyrian occupation, family religion had provided an open door for foreign religious influences. People were fascinated by Babylonian rooftop rituals (Zeph. 1:5), they made use of foreign fortune-telling methods, baked crescent cakes for the 'Queen of Heaven' (Jer. 7:18), and enthusiastically embraced the cult of Moloch (Jer. 7:31; Ezek. 16:20f.) (in which children were most likely not sacrificed but merely underwent a ritual of dedication).

Jeremiah had already pointed out the inconsistency of calling upon Yahweh in times of national distress but turning to one's family god and goddess during everyday upsets (Jer. 2:27–8a; cf. 44:15ff.). If the reformers did not want to lose the half-won battle they needed to have greater control over family religion. They therefore banned all foreign auguries and conjuring rites (Deut. 18:10b–14) together with the related 'cult of the stars' (17:2–7) and the Moloch cult (18:10a). Nor, in their opinion, could the family god be any other than Yahweh; they therefore required every family member to forget bonds of blood or friendship and to report any worship of any other god in the household (Deut. 13:7–12). On the other hand, they seem to have regarded ancestor-worship as less harmful, forbidding only the use at the meal for the dead of food that had been dedicated as a tithe to Yahweh (26:14). However, necromancy (consulting the spirits of the dead) was strictly forbidden (18:11).

In order to integrate family religion and state religion it was decreed that when heads of families performed sacrifices they should include an acknowledgment of the history of Yahweh's relationship with the whole nation of Israel (Deut. 26:1–11) and tell it to their children (6:20–5). The reformers gave them a ready-made catechism in the form of the decalogue, combining the most important things demanded of every head of family (to worship no other god, to make no images) with remembrance of the fact that Yahweh had delivered every individual Israelite from slavery in Egypt and had become his or her personal God (Deut. 5:6–10). They were consciously welding together national and the individual destiny. On the other hand, when they called upon Israel to love Yahweh 'with all your heart' (Deut. 6:5) they were trying to imbue the personal relationship of God and his people with the warmth of a personal devotion.

Finally, 'Josiah's reform' was a far-reaching social reform. The legislator required an end to be put to the devastating effects of the harsh credit laws, by a remission of debts every seven years (Deut. 15:1–3, 7–11), and debt-slaves were to be given start-up capital on release (15:12–18). Poor-relief was greatly extended: the tithe was to be given every third year to the needy (14:28f.). Moreover, families were to invite the local poor to share their pilgrim feasts when they travelled to Jerusalem for the festivals of Pesach-Mazzot, Shavu'ot and Sukkot (16:1–17). The strict external exclusivity set up by the reformers in the field of religion was to be matched by an internal solidarity that would unite the whole nation under Yahweh.

In the course of their reform the Deuteronomic authors created for the first time a consistent theology for Israel. What is most noticeable about it is their emphasis (like Hosea's previously) on the religious traditions of the early days: the exodus,

Sinai and the occupation of the land, and the considerable reduction of the importance assigned to the state tradition: the theology of king and Temple. They did say that the Temple had been chosen by Yahweh, but he wanted only his name to reside there (Deut. 12:11). Likewise, while the king was chosen by God, he was forbidden to raise himself above his 'brothers'; the king was no longer the law-giver; indeed he himself became subject to the law (Deut. 17). Instead, the reformers had recourse to the authority of Moses, issuing their laws in his name. Because Josiah's reform regarded itself as a return to Israel's beginnings, the idea arose of a Book of Law proclaimed by Moses in early times, written down and then forgotten (2 Kgs 22:8ff.). The fact that not only Temple and kingship but now for the first time a book was given a central religious role in Israel's relationship with its God was to prove vital for the survival of Israel's religion.

It is very probable that the two central theological concepts of the Old Testament, 'chosen people' and 'covenant', derive from the Deuteronomic authors. According to them, Yahweh, universal creator of the world, lord of all things, had made Israel (alone of all the nations) his 'chosen people' by delivering them from Egypt (Deut. 7:6–8; 10:14f.), and not because of any special virtue among the Israelites but from his divine love. Thus Israel's peculiar relationship with God in early times and Yahweh's universality, which had come to be attributed to him in the time of the kings, were not incompatible. But Israel could not match the expectations of its God by accommodating itself among its neighbours. On the contrary, Israel's destiny was to cut itself off from all other nations. God's attention, and the requirement, which went along with being chosen, was summed up by the Deuteronomic theologians in the concept of 'covenant', which they borrowed from the political terminology of Assyrian vassalage treaties. Yahweh was said to have promised their forefathers that he would give Israel the fruitful land they now occupied (Deut. 7:8f.). Israel owed a debt of gratitude and was therefore required to keep Yahweh's laws and commandments (7:12ff). If Israel lived up to Yahweh's expectations it would dwell happily in the land with Yahweh's blessing, but if it ignored his laws and commandments it would be cursed by God and would lose the land (Deut. 28). From the viewpoint of Deuteronomy a formal covenant had been entered into between Yahweh and Israel in the early days, on Horeb (= Sinai, Deut. 5) and again after Moses' proclamation of the reformed laws shortly before the entry into the Promised Land (Deut. 29). These became the model for the new covenant between Josiah and the nation in which he solemnly pledged himself to carry out the legislation of Deuteronomy (2 Kgs 23:1–3).

There is no general agreement about whether it was actually possible to enforce this extreme reform in the way in which it was conceived. The reform legislation in Deuteronomy is partly utopian in character, and many scholars have doubted whether it could be put into practice. However, it is possible to start from the fact that at least parts of the Deuteronomic laws became state law in Judah in 622–609 BC. It is clear that the reform of the cult was carried through to a large extent; it is the social reform that can hardly have been achieved in every detail. However, the theology of Deuteronomy was of enormous importance in the years to come, and would form the essential basis for the theology of the time of exile.

THE RELIGIOUS ARGUMENTS AT THE END
OF THE MONARCHICAL PERIOD

With the early death of Josiah in 609 BC, when he fell in Megiddo fighting against Pharaoh Necho, Judah became once more a vassal state, first of the Egyptian empire and then from 603 of the new Babylonian empire. This brought the reform to a standstill. We can see from Jeremiah's criticism of society that there was another serious social crisis in Judah (Jer. 5:26–8; 6:6f.); the protective dams set up in the cause of religiously motivated internal solidarity were too weak to restrain the force of the economic interests of the upper classes. In the arguments about the validity of the social aspects of Josiah's reform the coalition of its supporters fell apart: the priesthood of Jerusalem had seen their interests fulfilled with the centralization and purification of the cult. They believed that Judah would survive because the Temple at Jerusalem had been purified (Jer. 7:4). The officials around the Saphan family, who had been the chief supporters of the reform, went over to the opposition during the reign of King Jehoiakim (cf. Jer. 36) and were no longer in a position to supervise enactment of the legislation for social reform. And Jeremiah himself became disillusioned and left the reform campaign. In his view Yahweh's law had been betrayed by the upper classes (Jer. 5:4f.) and falsified by the scribes (8:8). Instead, he now foretold, in the name of Yahweh, destruction for this society so riddled with violence, injustice, hypocrisy and falsehood (9:1–10); Yahweh himself would destroy his own Temple, which they had turned into a robbers' cave (7:1–15).

After Jehoiakim's vacillating policy of contracting alliances had led to Nebuchadnezzar's siege of Jerusalem in 597, and the first Judaean deportation, which sent into exile, among others, the young King Jehoiachin and the prophet Ezekiel, the political and religious elite split into two parties, which clashed violently with each other. On the one side stood the 'Nationalists' led by the Hilkiah family (who provided the high priest for the Temple in Jerusalem). They believed that an alliance with Egypt would enable them to shake off the Babylonian yoke; they argued against Jeremiah's message and, with the support of such prophets of salvation as Hananiah, disseminated comprehensive religious propaganda, saying that those in exile would soon return home (Jer. 28:2–4), and that Yahweh – as in the theology of Zion – would always prevent any capture of Jerusalem.

Opposed to this party stood the officials who had been supervising reform under the leadership of the Shaphan family. They were pro-Babylon and supported Jeremiah, who was counselling submission to Babylonian rule in order to survive (Jer. 27). His letter to those in exile, advising them to settle and even to pray for their enemies, called forth an angry protest from the Nationalist (Jer. 29). Close to this party was the priest–prophet Ezekiel, who, among the exiled, argued against the Nationalists' hopes of salvation (Ezek. 17). He proclaimed that Yahweh's glory had left the Temple, which meant that Jerusalem was doomed to destruction (Ezek. 7–11).

When the Nationalists succeeded in winning over the vacillating vassal-king Zedekiah and persuaded him to begin a risky policy of rebellion, Nebuchadnezzar was provoked into further reprisals. This time he did not temper justice with mercy; Jerusalem was put to the torch in 587. The Temple, which provided the theological basis for resistance to Babylon, was laid waste, and Zedekiah and the leaders of the Nationalists were severely punished (2 Kgs 56:6f., 18–21). Now the state of Judah had also fallen, as predicted by Jeremiah and Ezekiel, and by Isaiah and Micah before them.

CHAPTER THIRTY-THREE

RELIGION IN ISRAEL DURING AND AFTER THE EXILE

Rainer Albertz
Translated by Hazel Harvey

Whereas earlier research into the history of Israel's religion concentrated on the pre-exilic epoch, it has recently become increasingly clear that the formative period of the Israelite–Jewish religion was the time of exile and the years immediately following.

THE SIGNIFICANCE OF THE EXILE FOR THE HISTORY OF ISRAEL'S RELIGION

For the further history of Israel's religion the significance of the fall of the state of Judah in 598–587 BC and the resulting deportation can hardly be overestimated. The northern kingdom had already collapsed, and now with this new political catastrophe it seemed that Yahweh had finally cancelled all His historical promises of salvation. Was Yahweh inferior to Marduk, the god of the victorious new Babylonian empire? With the exile, Israel's religion fell into its worst every crisis; nevertheless, it was in the exile that the foundation for its comprehensive renewal was laid. However, not all the constituent parts of Israel's religion were affected by the crisis to the same extent.

The destruction of the sanctuary at Jerusalem and the fall of David's monarchy shattered the old-style theology of Temple and kingship, with its unconditional guarantee of salvation. This greatly damaged the theological basis of the 'Nationalistic' party.

However, what remained unaffected was the Deuteronomic reform theology that (shortly before the exile) had already been emphasizing the pre-state tradition of salvation rather than the state traditions. It is true that the loss of the land made some of the population question the Deuteronomic concept of having been given the land after the exodus, but this could be explained theologically by linking God's promises to the obedience to His laws that was required in return. Thus the theology of Deuteronomy was able to provide the decisive basis for various groups (which we group together under the term 'Deuteronomists') to overcome the crisis of exile.

The exile confirmed the message of the radical prophets who had preached divine judgment. They had foretold the catastrophe as Yahweh's judgment on His unfaithful people. Most of the inhabitants of Judah had previously rejected their message, but it now provided an important key for interpreting the political catastrophe as Yahweh's punishment, and accepting it in that sense. In this way the theology of the prophets, which had previously been the voice of the opposition, became during the exile the decisive basis for the general religion of Yahweh.

The exile had not completely extinguished the piety of Israelite families. During all the difficulties that many of them had to bear, their piety remained firmly based on God's activity as Creator, which would be unaffected by any historical catastrophe. And the survivors soon experienced for themselves Yahweh's protection and blessing, albeit in exile. Thus family religion became in the exile an essential basis for Israel's general religion.

Thus the crisis brought about by the exile led to a far-reaching shift within Israel's religion. With the destruction of the Temple and the end of the monarchy the religious traditions lost most of their connections with institutions. Instead, informal groups of theologians grew up around leading families, prophets and priests, or else around their writings, and there was a great increase in literary activity. Thus, in the time of exile, there was an astonishing blossoming of theology, although this carried with it the danger of losing touch with reality, and introducing divisions in the religion of Yahweh.

HOW THE THEOLOGIANS OVERCAME THE CATASTROPHE OF THE EXILE

For those living at the time of the political catastrophe of 587 BC its significance was by no means as clear as it is for us today. For the 'Nationalists', who had continued until the last minute to hope that Yahweh would intervene to save Zion, it was a crushing blow that destroyed the entire structure of their belief. But the 'Reformers' also had to face difficult questions: how could the catastrophe have happened despite Josiah's reform? Indeed, might the reform itself even possibly have caused the catastrophe, by establishing monolatry, which may have angered the gods who were rejected, causing them to withdraw their protection from the people of Judah? In any case, women who had fled to Egypt early in the time of exile reproached Jeremiah, saying that the disaster befell them and their families only when they ceased venerating the Queen of Heaven (Jer. 44:15–19). Thus it entailed a great effort, among both those left at home and those in exile, to come to terms with the catastrophe and to establish the correct theological interpretation of it.

One area where this was achieved was in exilic liturgies. The major cult of the time of exile consisted mainly of liturgies of lament, which were not linked to any holy site. In remembrance of the fall of the state of Judah, four great holy fasts were celebrated every year (Zech. 7:2ff; 8:18f.) either in the ruins of the Temple of Jerusalem (Jer. 41:5) or in exile in Babylon facing in the direction of Jerusalem (1 Kgs 8:46–51). It can be seen from the so-called Lamentations (Lam. 1–5) and the psalms of national lament (Pss 44; 60; 74; 89; Is. 63:7–64, 11) that it was usual in these services to recognize (under the cover of the Babylonian aggressor) Yahweh himself as the author of the catastrophe (Lam. 2:1–10; 4:11–16) and to acknowledge the people's own guilt, be it the failed policy of vacillating between the great powers (4:17) or the false guarantee of salvation preached by the Temple prophets and priests (2:14; 4:13), and to beg Yahweh, despite his apparent ineffectiveness, to pour down forgiveness and restitution on them and retribution on their enemies.

It is probable that these services included readings from those prophets who had proclaimed God's judgment, and that special collections of their utterances were made for this very purpose (Jer. 8:4–10, 25*) or even composed especially (Amos 4:6–13). Their provocative and hurtful words, which had once been heard only on the streets, now received, for the first time, the respect accorded to the Word of God by the entire congregation. The purpose of these readings was to bring the survivors to a recognition of the prophets' message, which they had previously largely rejected. Hearing once more the accusations of the prophets they were intended to realize what had caused the catastrophe, and hearing the prophets' proclamation of judgment they were intended to understand that the catastrophe was God's right-eous judgment, which they could have avoided if they had paid attention the first time they heard it.

In addition to the incorporation of the prophetic messages into the cult, there was during the time of exile a widespread concern outside the cult with the legacy of the prophets of judgment, which can be seen in the production or the revision of many of the books of the prophets. Of these, the Deuteronomistic book of Jeremiah (Jer. 1–45* = Jer. D) is particularly interesting.

The term 'Deuteronomistic' is used to designate the groups that modelled their theological thinking and literary style on Deuteronomy, and developed it further. The anonymous Deuteronomistic editors of Jeremiah D probably included the descendants of the reform party, which had been led by the Shaphan family. Their efforts were directed at taking the message of the prophet who had been close to their parents and grandparents and bringing it to the people of Judah who had stayed at home; it was proclaimed in the modernized form in order to avoid further disasters and to provide a direction for a new beginning. Their book of Jeremiah, which they rewrote in about 550 BC, is the literary distillation of a long period of missionary work, trying to educate the populace, during which they preached publicly about Jeremiah's message (Jer. 7:1–8, 3) and involved their contemporaries in discussions (9:11–15). They regarded themselves as direct descendants of Jeremiah.

The means used to integrate Jeremiah and the other prophets of judgment into the Deuteronomistic theology was the concept of a unified Word of God. This concept had appeared during the making of the Covenant in Egypt, in the procla-mation of the Decalogue and the Deuteronomic Law (Jer. 11:3f. 6f.; 34:13f.). On the other hand, the Word had also been proclaimed by the prophets sent continu-ally by God ever since Israel had been unfaithful at the very time of their rescue from Egypt, prophets sent to call the Israelites to convert and to follow the Law (26:3f.; 34:12ff.) With that, Jeremiah became a preacher of the Law in the tradi-tion of Moses (cf. Jer. 1:7b, 9, 17 and Deut. 18:18b). It was only when they wanted to silence him that the covenant became invalid (Jer. 11:10) and Yahweh was forced to send down upon his people the disaster that had already been announced in Deut. 28.

In the view of his Deuteronomistic interpreters, Jeremiah's main demand was obedience to the first and second commandments. They believed that the worship of alien gods and veneration of images had been the main causes of the catastrophe

(Jer. 5:19; 9:13). That is why they saw it as their task to clear away the syncretism that had regained its hold (8:2f.; 19:12f.) in order to avert the continuing effects of God's judgment. But the Deuteronomistic editors of Jeremiah also emphasized Jeremiah's social criticism and made a connection with the Deuteronomic social commandments (Jer. 34; cf. Deut. 15). They believed that a new start was possible only if the people of Judah made far-reaching changes in religious and social areas (Jer. 7:3, 5ff.). Like Jeremiah, they argued against putting one's trust in the Temple (7:4), and expecting its reconstruction to bring security and well-being to the land. Nor did they put their hope in the last king, Jehoiachin, who had been deported to Babylon. He and his family were rejected and should never reign again in Judah (22:24–30). That is, instead of a restoration of state and cult imposed from above on the model of Josiah's reform, the descendants of the reformers led by the Shephan family canvassed for a broad renewal of the whole populace, a renewal that should surge up from beneath. They preached that in fact it would be Yahweh himself who would bring the new age of salvation when, after three generations (27:7) or 70 years (29:10) the universal rule (27:5f.) of his 'servant' Nebuchadnezzar would be over. Then Yahweh would make a new covenant with his people, which would be kept by everybody of their own free will and would therefore last for ever (31:31–4).

In an attempt to overcome the catastrophe of the exile, there was, first, the effort described above to make the populace accept the judgment prophecies and realize their contemporary validity, and to use them to interpret past events and to provide guidance for the future. What was also needed was a new interpretation of Israel's history, the history that had led to the catastrophe. This challenge was taken up by another party of Deuteronomists, who were at work most probably in Babylon, possibly in the circle around the exiled families of Jehoiachin and Hilkiah, who had once been figureheads of the 'Nationalistic' party. They were at work soon after 560 BC, using older traditions to create the Deuteronomistic historical account (Dtr. H), which, after a recapitulation of the events of the exodus and on Sinai, begins with Moses' proclamation of the Deuteronomic Law, narrates the seizure of land by Joshua, the wars waged by the Judges and the establishment of the monarchy, and ends with the downfall of both kingdoms (Deut. 1–2 Kgs 25*). In exactly the same way as their colleagues who were revising the book of Jeremiah they believed that the main reason for Israel's collapse was its failure to observe the first and second commandments; the northern kingdom when it erected imaged of calves at Bethel (1 Kgs 14:4–18; 2 Kgs 17:7ff.), the southern kingdom when alien gods were venerated by King Manasseh (2 Kgs 21).

The downfall was brought about not by Yahweh but by Israel itself, who was continually unfaithful to him despite all his warnings. To this extent their work was a huge act of penitence, composed in exile. Nevertheless, in contrast to Jeremiah the historians were careful not to let the entire history of Israel amount to the relentless decline of Israel. They believed that there had also been periods in Israel's history when their religion had been godly and uncontaminated by syncretism. The first such period was the time of arrival, when Yahweh gave Israel (through Moses) the gift of salvation, which is the Ten Commandments, and gave Israel (through Joshua) the gift of salvation, which was the Promised Land (Deut. 5 to Josh. 23).

All this fitted in exactly with the Deuteronomic theology. But it also went beyond it: the Deuteronomists also regarded the early monarchic period as a time of grace, during which Yahweh had granted Israel David's kingship and the Temple at Jerusalem. (1 Sam. 7:3–1; Kgs 9:9). It was not until the ageing Solomon began to venerate alien gods that David's empire began to crumble and fall (1 Kgs 11f.). But the Deuteronomistic theologians pointed out that history showed again and again that it was God's promises linked to the Temple and to David's line (1 Kgs 2:4; 8:16, 25; 9:5; 11:12f, 32, 36; 15:4; 2 Kgs 8:19; 19:34) that safeguarded the survival of the southern kingdom for a long period from great catastrophes. It is true that they regarded God's promises as conditional upon the obedience of his people – to this extent they had learned from the prophets' criticism – but they refused to abandon the theology of king and Temple in which their 'Nationalistic' predecessors had put their trust. Despite the fall of the state they believed that the state tradition of salvation was still meaningful.

The Deuteronomistic historians presented Josiah's Reform as the splendid zenith of the history of the southern kingdom (2 Kgs 22f.) while reducing it to nothing but a reform of the cult, making no mention of the social reforms, and they thereby made the purified Temple at Jerusalem the decisive option for the future. They believed that the only reason why the cultic reform had not prevented the catastrophe was the abominable syncretism of King Manasseh, who had provoked Yahweh to an irrevocable abandonment of Jerusalem (23:26f.). Basically, Josiah had shown that the right path was the exclusive veneration of Yahweh. When the Deuteronomistic historians ended their historical account (25:27–30) with a note about Jehoiachin's rehabilitation by a Babylonian king, Evil-Marduk (662 BC), they were indicating that they still put their hopes in the descendants of David. While the Deuteronomistic revisers of the book of Jeremiah were calling for a comprehensive grassroots renewal, the Deuteronomistic authors of the historical account regarded the need for a royal cultic reform imposed from above as the lesson to be learned from the catastrophes.

The crisis of the exile was overcome by the messages of the prophets, by the Deuteronomistic theologians and also by the continuing piety of families. Josiah's Reform had incorporated their beliefs more firmly into the official Yahweh religion, and now family religion provided its basis and representative functions.

Since the downfall of the state, the family was the only element of the social structure that remained more or less intact. It is therefore hardly surprising that in the time of exile hope for the defeated nation depended on individual religious experiences and beliefs within families. If, despite the catastrophe, Yahweh had rescued certain individuals, then the community did not need to abandon trust in his saving power (Lam. 3). The personal avowal of belief that God had created every individual (Ps. 22:10f.) was increasingly applied to Israel as a whole (Is. 64:7) in order to pass beyond Yahweh's historical promises, which were open to question, and to find an indisputable basis for belief in the Creator. The Deutero-Isaiah group would also adopt this approach in order to provide credibility for its unbelievable message of salvation (Is. 43:1; 44:2, 21, 24.). Also, the descendants of those families who had been part of a small nation but had survived in exile and even become a great nation (Is. 51:1f.) were presented as the recipients of unconditional promises from God and as a precedent for the move back into Palestine (Gen. 11:27–12:3), in order to strengthen the will of the exiled to survive and to return. Finally, ancient family customs, such as circumcision, which had proably been an apotropaic rite of manhood until then (Ex. 4:25; Gen. 34), and certain rituals to do with diet and the preparation of food (Deut. 14:3–21; Lev. 11) now, during the exile in Babylon, took on the function of indicating membership of Israel and the Yahweh religion (Gen. 17:10f.). In addition, the festival of the Sabbath, which before the exile had been a Temple festival on the day of the full moon (cf. Lam. 2:6), was reshaped into a family festival (Deut. 5:12–15) during which the head of each family could publicly express his loyalty to Yahweh (in the face of the pressure to conform to surrounding custom) by honouring Yahweh, not with a sacrifice, but by a day of rest and therefore loss of income. Also Pesach became once more a family festival in the time of exile (Ex. 12:1–14). Thus the family by celebrating the Sabbath and Pesach, commemorating the deliverance from Egypt, turned into an important carrier for the entire religion of Yahweh. The situation of being in exile among strangers gave it the function of preserving the unity of the nation through rituals that defined it.

THE START OF A NEW BEGINNING, LATER IN THE TIME OF EXILE

Options for a possible new beginning had been considered during the efforts to come to terms with the past, but the impulse to make a new start came during the exile, from the prophets of salvation.

With the fall of Judah in 587–586 BC the unconditional and all-embracing prophecies of judgment had come to an end. After the catastrophe what was heard instead – hesitantly at first – was a mostly anonymous message of salvation, heard most clearly in Deutero-Isaiah (Is. 40–55) and in the book of Ezekiel (Ezek. 33–48).

'Deutero-Isaiah' was proably composed by a group of former cultic prophets and temple singers who had gathered in Babylon around the writings of the prophet Isaiah. Impressed by the spectacular conquest by young Cyrus of the Medes in 550 BC, and of Asia Minor in 546, the group came to the electrifying perception that none other than Yahweh had aroused the Persian king (Is. 41:2ff.), in order to deliver his people from captivity in Babylon (43:14f.) The time of judgment Isaiah had announced (Is. 6) was finally over, Jerusalem's guilt was absolved, Yahweh would bring in a new age of salvation (40:1–8).

The group of prophets took their message to the resigned people in exile and found disbelief and scepticism. The very suggestion that Yahweh would call an alien ruler to be his 'anointed' was contrary to all their religious traditions. This forced the group to find arguments to defend their incredible message. While doing this they arrived at insights that not only went far beyond the earlier national religion but also developed completely new dimensions for the concept of Yahweh's nature: Yahweh was not only Creator of the world and Lord of history, as had been sung in the hymns in the Temple at Jerusalem (as the group of prophets remembered (40:12–31) but he was altogether the only effective god. Only he could announce future happenings that came to pass, and had already done this in earlier times (Is. 41:22f, 26f.; 46:9f.). The way in which Yahweh had planned events in history would now not only be seen in his announcement that Cyrus would conquer Babylon but had been seen long before in Israel's history, not least in the prophecy of judgment that had indeed come to pass. But that meant that in the very moment of his apparent defeat, the fall of Jerusalem, Yahweh was in fact demonstrating that he was in control. The group described in terms of a fictitious court of law in heaven how all the other gods melted away in the face of Yahweh's monopoly of power over history (41:1–5, 21–9; 43:8–13). They predicted the fall of the two Babylonian gods who seemed so powerful, Marduk and Nebo (46:1f.). But, by doing this, for the first time in the history of Israel's religion they arrived at the idea of absolute monotheism.

This belief that there was only one god was closely bound up with making the Yahweh religion available to the whole world. If Yahweh as the only god could commission an alien king to upset the balance of political power in the Near East, his works of salvation could not longer be limited exclusively to Israel. Thus when Babylon fell the 'Survivors of the Nations' were invited to let themselves be rescued by Yahweh and to turn to him (Is. 45:20–5). In proclaiming this the prophets did not relinquish Israel's peculiar relationship with God, but clearly entered a new stage when the Yahweh religion was no longer merely the national religion: in the eyes of this group of prophets Israel now had the function of being a witness to Yahweh in the forum of the nations (43:10–12; 44:8; 55:4). Members of other nations were given the opportunity to join Israel's religion (44:5; 55:5). But this laid the foundation for the later Jewish mission.

The elevation of Yahweh to the one true God did not, in the opinion of the group of prophets, entail Israel having any particular political powers or status. The amalgamation of God's power and political power, which had been built up by monarchic theology, was now dissolved. Israel's foreign policy was no longer to rule the world. Israel was now 'Yahweh's servant', commissioned to bring righteousness to the nations (Is. 42:1–4), and to bring them Yahweh's salvation as 'a light for the nations' (49:6). And when the group of prophets described how the kings and the nations would be amazed to recognize that this humiliated 'servant of Yahweh' would carry their sins, then they went as far as to give a universal scapegoat function to Israel's humiliation in exile (52:13–53 :12). Within the state, the group expected that Yahweh would lead the exiled people home and then he himself would take over the role of king in Zion (52:7–10). That sounded utopian, but in real terms it excluded the possibility of an earthly monarch for Israel; instead, the everlasting Covenant with the line of David was transferred to Israel as a whole (55:1–5). By establishing his own kingdom on earth, Yahweh prevented any mortal attempt at seizing power, be it by Babylon (47) or by the kings of Israel.

While the Deutero-Isaiah group recruited adherents from the non-priestly personnel of the Temple of Jerusalem, the members of the group that formed around the priest–prophet Ezekiel in Babylon were of priestly origin; from 573 until about 520 BC they were at work, following his insights, but also went beyond his thinking in a broad vision that developed their concept of rebuilding the Temple once more (Ezek. 40–8).

The main interest of these reforming priests was to defend their own independence by every means, an independence they had acquired when the Temple and the monarchy collapsed. Before the exile, the Temple had been accommodated in the same building as the royal palace. They planned a new Temple that would be completely separate from the king, architecturally and institutionally. The glory of Yahweh that would inhabit the new Temple was not to be contaminated by amalgamation with political power (Ezek. 43:1–12). That is why the Temple was to have massive walls and gates, so that entry could be controlled by the priests alone. Before the exile, the king had been in control (44:4ff.). In the future only the priests would be allowed to enter the inner court and to serve at the altar. At the same time they removed from the king his ancient privilege (as son of God) of functioning as highest priest. He would be allowed only a place of honour in the outer court as foremost of the lay people, and from there he would be able to watch from afar as his sacrifice was offered (46:2–8).

The theological lever the reforming priests used to attack, for the first time, the concept universal in the East, that the monarchy was sacred, was the priestly distinction between sacred and profane, that is, the differentiation of areas of varying degrees of sacredness. This argument would only guarantee to the priests their cultic freedom at the price of demanding greater degrees of holiness for their own group, and a complete separation from non-priestly life. However, in order to provide the cult's necessary interaction between lay and priest, they would introduce a grade of lower priesthood, the 'Levites'. The Zadokite priests of Jerusalem understood by 'Levites' the priests of all other sanctuaries, because they belied that they bore the responsibility for the worship of idols in pre-exilic times and their descendants must accept being downgraded (44:9–14). This division into priests and Levites, later backdated to early times, was to cause considerable conflict when the exile was over (Num. 16:8ff.).

Finally, the reforming priests also used their scheme of separate areas to achieve their aim of creating a new political arrangement of society as a whole (45:1–89; 47:13–48:29): the capital city was to be separate from the Temple and was to be ruled no longer by the king's officials but by representatives of the tribes. They and the priests were to be given estates so that they could maintain themselves and would not need to raise taxes. Only the cultic gifts to the Temple should continue; this would represent a great reduction compared to the previous tithe (45:13–15). Each tribe was to be given an equal allotment of land so that all might live undisturbed at the same level of prosperity. But the king would receive land apart from the land of the tribes. And when the king made gifts of land to members of his family or his servants he would be required to do it from his share (46:16–18); this meant that the populace would be permanently protected from the monarchy's insatiable demand for land. Thus in the reform scheme made by the school of Ezekiel it was clear that the intention was to use the new beginning after the exile to correct the failed social developments of the monarchic period and to hark back in an almost utopian way to the times before the state.

THE FAILURE TO ACHIEVE A RESTORATION AFTER THE EXILE

Compared with the high expectations of the prophets of salvation, the real opportunities opened up for the Jews by Cyrus' conquest of the new Babylonian empire in 539 BC were disappointing. It is true that Cyrus probably gave permission for the Temple at Jerusalem to be rebuilt, and retrieved gold and silver vessels that the Babylonians had taken from the Temple (Ezra 5:13ff.). But the rebuilding did not get under way, not least because of warnings voiced by the supporters of Jeremiah and Deuteronomy among those who had remained. Moreover, the prospect of living in Palestine under Persian rule instead of under Babylonian rule seemed so un-attractive to those settled in exile in Babylon that there were no significant returns under Cyrus and Cambyses.

But when Darius usurped the Persian throne in 522 BC he faced uprisings in every part of his empire, which forced him to make greater concessions to the Jews in order to win their loyalty. He appointed Zerubbabel, grandson of Jehoiachin, as regent of Judah (Ezra 6:7; Hag. 1:1), commissioned him and Joshua, grandson of the last high priest of Jerusalem, to lead a large group of willing returnees back to their former homeland (Ezra 2) and apparently offered the prospect of a generous partial autonomy of the province of Judah under Davidic leadership. When this group returned to Judah from exile they rebuilt the Temple as the start of the new beginning, in complete accordance with the plan for the state cult outlined by the Deuteronomistic history in 520 BC.

In view of the desolate economic situation, Zerubbabel needed the support of the prophets Haggai and Zechariah to mobilize the population (Ezra 5:1f.). They invested the rebuilding of the Temple with high hopes of salvation: Haggai expected it to bring about not only the start of a new age of blessings (Hag. 1:2–11; 2:15–19) but also an imminent shake-up of the world of nations, which would cause the wealth of the nations to flow into the new Temple (2:6–9). Zechariah predicted a great upheaveal in world politics in 517 BC, which Yahweh would bring about to Jerusalem's advantage, using his heavenly messengers (Zech. 1:8–15; 6:1–8), and saw in a vision how the horns of the nations would be thrown down (2:1–4). At the same time, both prophets invested Zerubbabel of David's line with bright hopes for the nation. Haggai expressly lifted the curse that Jeremiah and his Deuteronomistic followers had laid upon the family of Jehoiachin (Jer. 22:24–30) and transferred to him for the time after the upheaval Yahweh's mandate to rule (Hag. 2:20–3). Zechariah took into account the aspirations of the priests to be independent and even prepared a coronation of Zerubbabel and Joshua (Zech. 6:9–14), who as Yahweh's 'anointed sons' were to exercise his universal hegemony (Zech. 4:1–6, 10–14). In this undertaking he was even supported by 'Nationalist' circles among the exiles in Babylon who sent gifts of silver and gold.

But these avid hopes, which dreamt of the restoration of an independent Davidic empire and even more beside, were not fulfilled. Even as late as 519 BC Darius was well able to put down the last rebellion in the Persian empire. He sat firmly in the saddle. The developments in Judah must have seemed to him like early signs of further rebellion. There are indications that the Persians intervened over the head of their satrap Tattenai (Ezra 5:3–17): it is true that the rebuilding of the Temple was permitted, but Zerubbabel vanished; Haggai and Zechariah were silenced. At any rate, they were not present when the Temple was dedicated in 515 BC. Thus the attempt by leading promoters of return (such as the families of David and Hilkiah) to restore both the monarchy and the state cult, with Persian permission, came to nothing because of the impatience of the nationalistic utopians.

What happened next can be explained only by the fact that among those who had stayed and those who had returned there were groups who wanted no such restoration, and they had their way. Among the former we should name the descendants of the reformers around the Shaphan family, who are known to have refused a return to Davidic rule; among the latter were the reformer priests who followed Ezekiel and strove for independence from the monarchy.

The form of social organization they introduced in Persian times was modelled rather on the pre-state situation. Under the supervision of the Persian satrap and his administrators two independent councils directed Judah's fortunes: the Elders and the College of Priests. They were assisted by an assembly of the people. All the councils were organized strictly according to family groups, and anyone wanting to participate had to be enrolled in the lists (Neh. 7:5ff.). The two main councils enjoyed a wide autonomy in the areas of religion, culture and local politics. The cult and the Temple were run and controlled by the priests, under the high priest, although the Persian king gave donations to the Temple and expected prayers of intercession in return (Ezra 6:8–10; 7:21–3). This situation, Jewish self-rule under the Persian umbrella, provided the leading families, both lay and priestly, with a greater share in decision-making than their own kings had ever allowed them. This may be one reason why later attempts to restore the monarchy were also blocked (Neh. 6:6–14) and why the Persians are the only world power never criticized in the Bible (apart from much later apocalyptic).

However, the loyalty shown to the Persians, which the majority favoured and found fruitful, had a high price to pay: the people were subjected to rigid Persian tax policies, which brought renewed misery to a section of the population.

The fiasco of the prophecies of salvation by Haggai and Zechariah had far-reaching consequences for post-exilic prophecy. Whereas the prophecies during the time of exile had generally been acknowledged and had been particularly effective and stimulating while the Temple was being rebuilt, they now fell into discredit again among most of the population. The writings of Haggai and Zechariah had to suffer modifications and revision (cf. the Deuteronomistic changes in Zech. 1:1–6; 7:4–14; 8:14–17, 19b). Groups who, despite all their disappointment when the time of blessings failed to appear, continued to mass around the prophetic traditions, for example the Trito-Isaiah circle around the Deutero-Isaiah prophecy (Is. 60–2), were marginalized by the pro-Persian majority in society (66:5). It was in this situation that post-exilic prophecy lost its relevance to concrete politics and concentrated instead on a distant change of fortunes that would overturn the entire present miserable reality (e.g. Is. 65:17–25).

CREATING A RELIGIOUS IDENTITY UNDER THE PERSIANS: THE SECOND TEMPLE AND THE CANONIZATION OF THE TORAH

The hesitant and fragmented resettlements from Babylon had already shown that Israel could no longer be expected to return to being one nation united in one land. Since the diaspora would continue, there was a need to provide a clear identity for the Jewish groups dispersed in scattered locations within the Persian empire. Because there was no unified state this identity would have to be expressed in religious or cult terms. The way that was chosen was the one already indicated by the Deuteronomic reformers: a sense of unity could be based on respect for one Temple and one holy book to which all Jews were subject.

The second Temple, completed in 515 BC, was not only the centrepiece for the small local Jewish community but became the unifying reference point for many sections of the Jews of the diaspora who were obedient to the Deuteronomistic centralization of the cult and refrained from erecting their own altars. As far as we know, it was only the Jewish military colony in Egypt that failed to support this consensus; before 525 BC it had already built itself a Temple on the island of Elephantine in the Nile (see Elephantine Papyri 30, 12). Even though the Jews of the diaspora seldom had the opportunity to undertake a pilgrimage to Jerusalem, the Temple there remained for them a place of religious nostalgia; they undertook a kind of 'spiritual pilgrimage' that consisted of reciting psalms (cf. Pss 42–83). This development is directly connected with the end of the state cult. The Temple, controlled by the reformer priests, no longer belonged to the king but to the whole nation. Everybody had to contribute to the upkeep of the fabric and of the cult. Everybody had to pay the priests for sacrifices, pay the tithe for the Levites and also pay a Temple tax (Ex. 30:11–16). In the course of the post-exilic period the amount of taxes rose to about a third of income; this meant that the Temple became the most important economic factor for the Jewish community.

Even if the structure of the second Temple was basically similar to the first, it was very different in the cult it housed and in what it symbolized. The sublimated theology of holiness developed by the reformer priests meant that the Holiest of Holies remained empty; at the most a golden mark set into the pavement could symbolize the divine presence. And as befitted its claim to supreme holiness, the cult began to emphasize its function of atonement. In order to cleanse the sanctuary of pollution, and the whole population of their sins, an annual festival was introduced in the form of a Day of Atonement (Lev. 16). A popular image was adopted: the sins of Israel were transferred to a scapegoat and eliminated by chasing it into the wilderness (vv. 7–9, 20–22, 26). According to the theological thinking of the reform priests, purification and atonement were effected by the high priest sprinkling some drops of blood in the direction of the place that marked the presence of Yahweh in the Holy of Holies. In the same way, the newly created institutions of sin-offering and guilt-offering would repeatedly achieve atonement for individuals and for the whole community (Lev. 4; 5:14ff.) so that a catastrophe such as that of 587 BC might never happen again.

But precisely because their own troubled history had taught them the extent to which Israel's fate depended on the behaviour of all, the Temple alone was seen not to be enough, despite its function as a unifying religious bond and a centre for atonement. Those responsible for Israel's future had to take steps to regulate the thoughts and actions of all members of the nation, wherever they lived, in order to protect Israel from further judgment by Yahweh.

The means to achieve this was provided by the Persians' readiness, not only to respect the local laws of the nations under their yoke, but even to help publish them and to underwrite their local application with the authority of the Persian state itself (cf. Ezra 7:25f.). The two governing councils of the Jews, the Elders and the College of Priests, were thus given the opportunity to create a document containing all the binding obligations and laws of Israel's religion, in order to obtain the Persian government's authorization of them for all the Jews in the empire. This is the background for the literary process of the creation and canonization of the Torah, which began during the fifth century BC and was probably completed towards the end of that century with the book of Ezra (Ezra 7).

When politics provided this opportunity to regulate the religion, the situation forced the two leading councils, lay and priestly, to come to a compromise. As a result, the Pentateuch they commissioned shows signs of compromise, because it had to respect the attitudes and interests of both the lay people and the priest–theologians. Recent research allows us to distinguish a pre-priestly contribution that follows Deuteronomistic theology (KD) from a somewhat later priestly one (KP).

The most important decision made by the lay theologians was to create a foundation history of Israel's beginnings, using older traditions, beginning with the patriarchs (Gen. 12), reaching a high point in Exodus (Exod. 1–15) and the gift of the Commandments on Sinai (Ex. 19ff.) and ending with the delivery of the Mosaic Law shortly before the conquest of the Promised Land (Deut.). In this way Deuteronomy but not the extra material Deuteromistic History (the conquest of the Promised Land and the time of kings) was incorporated into the foundation history. This meant that Israel's religion was presented according to the tradition of the Jeremiah Deuteronomists, that is, it omitted most of the theology of king and Temple. Also, the fulfilment of the claim to the whole of Palestine was postponed to an indefinite future date, proably out of regard for Persian interests.

By including tales of the patriarchs, who wandered between Mesopotamia, Egypt and Palestine, the lay theologians created for the Jews of the diaspora their own place and identity, but at the same time insisted that they should regard Palestine as the homeland assigned to them by God (Gen. 12, 15). Placed centrally in their work was the covenant made between Yahweh and Israel on Sinai, which delivered God's guidance to his people in the form of the Ten Commandments and the Book of the Covenant and the Deuteronomic Law. As the elders understood it, Israelites would serve God through the conduct of their daily life. This was exactly how the prophets and the Deuteronomic reformers thought things should be.

Here, in the heart of Israel's religion, the lay theologians attempted to correct the insidious clericalization. They believed that the fact that Yahweh had made a covenant and called Israel his 'Chosen People' had made it not only (as the Deuteronomic reformers had believed) the 'holy nation' (Exod. 19:6; cf. Deut. 7:6; 14:21; 26:19), which should remain separate from all other nations, but had given it the distinction of becoming a 'kingdom of priests' (Ex. 19:6). The view of the lay theologians was that this made the whole of Israel into a competent priesthood. The sacrifice made at the time of the Covenant was carried out by both Moses and laypeople (24:5f.). It was only after the worship of the golden calf (Ex. 32), which symbolically prefigured Israel's fall and Yahweh's judgment, that (the lay theologians believed) it became necessary to have recourse to cult personnel and cult objects (Ex. 32:26–9; 33:7–11). But, they said, Israel owed its survival of God's judgment not to the cult but only to God's faithful adherence to his promises (Ex. 32:13; 33:1) and his generosity, which tempered his anger and caused him to renew his covenant (Ex. 34).

Since the time of exile prophecies had been accepted, but were not without risk. The theologians of the Council of Elders gave them due respect in their account of the foundation; for example, they designated Moses as a prophet (Ex. 3f.; Deut. 34:10), but far greater emphasis was laid on his supreme authority in revealing God's will and establishing the Law (Num. 12:6–8). Those who were directly descended from Moses and could lead Israel as he intended were not the prophets but the Seventy Elders (Num. 11:11ff.). By saying this, the lay theologians provided, for the post-exilic Council of Elders, for whom they were working, an explicit legitimization, in the foundation history.

Naturally, the College of Priests could not accept such an effacement of the cult. Their theologians therefore built up the theophany of Sinai (Ex. 24:15b–18) into a comprehensive foundation for the cult. In their presentation, Yahweh had given precise instructions (Ex. 25–31) for the whole people, led by Moses, to construct a portable sanctuary even in the wilderness (35–9), the equivalent of the Temple at Jerusalem. Yahweh himself in all his glory had dedicated the sanctuary (Ex. 40) and legitimized the first rites (Lev. 9). They also portrayed the rituals of sacrifice and the investiture of priests as regulated by God down to the smallest detail (Lev. 1–7, 8). And when the priest–theologians placed their version of the construction of the sanctuary (Ex. 25, 31:35–40) each side of the report of the lapse from faith and the renewal of the Covenant (32–4) they were underlining that it was the cult that had overcome the crisis of the lapse, and would help to prevent its recurrence.

It is true that the form of sanctuary and divine service that the reform priests invented was free from any reminders or symbols of the royal state cult. The newly created office of high priest, for example, was intended to take over the role of the king in the cult in the long run (Ex. 28f.). In this matter they were in full agreement with their lay colleagues. On the other hand they completely rejected the claim of laymen and Levites to priestly dignity; they believed that only the acts of atonement by Aaron and his sons, that is, the Zadokite priests, could avert Yahweh's anger from his people (Num. 16–18).

The priest–theologians went beyond the particularistic conception of the lay theologians when they inserted a creation history before the history of Israel's foundation (Gen. 1–11). By doing this they set the story of Yahweh's special relationship with Israel into the larger perspective of the history of the world and of humanity. This allowed a place for the universalizing tendencies that had become attached to Israel during the time of exile: Yahweh was no longer merely the God of Israel – he was Creator of humankind and of the whole world (Gen. 1), he had made a covenant not only with Abraham (17) but also with Noah and the whole of creation, a covenant that guaranteed the continuation of the world after the catastrophe of the flood (9). But it was only to Israel that Yahweh had revealed himself by name (Ex. 6:2), in order to build a direct relationship with Israel that would be expressed in its worship (Gen. 17:7; Ex. 6:3, 7; 25:8), the relationship that had been broken when creation went astray before the flood. This meant that Israel had a positive function for the world and could work together with other nations and other religions. Thus the priest–theologians contributed significantly to the success of the initiative to draw up, with the approval of the Persian authorities, a religious and legal code for all the Jews of the empire.

SOCIAL AND RELIGIOUS SCHISMS UNDER THE PERSIANS

The efforts to standardize the religion could not prevent another social crisis in the Jewish community, in the fifth century BC. The catalyst was the harsh Persian tax system, which continually forced smallholders into bankruptcy, while the money-lenders, members of the Jewish upper class, profited from pawnbroking and debt-slavery (Neh. 5:1–5).

This new crisis resembled the one in the pre-exilic period. But this time it was more disturbing because members of the Jewish aristocracy were gathering taxes for a foreign power. Also, because in the interim an ethos of mutual help had been written definitively into the Torah, this cold and calculating concentration on money making was regarded as contrary to the spirit of the Yahweh religion.

For this reason the social crisis of the fifth century caused the upper class to split into two camps: on the one side were those members who were intent on winning economic advantage regardless of the religious obligation to help one another; their opponents called them 'sinners' and 'godless' and implied that their behaviour had cast them outside Israel's relationship with God. On the other side were the members of the upper class who were willing to embrace the social obligations of the Torah and to alleviate the distress of the bankrupt by making donations from their own wealth. They referred to themselves as the 'pious' or the 'righteous'.

The party that advocated mutual help carried on a hard-hitting theological debate with their opponents, which has left its imprint on many sections of the post-exilic literature, in Proverbs, Psalms and in the books of the Prophets. In the many proverbs referring to sinners and righteous people, for example, the aim is to give a strong message to the young that the actions of an apparently thriving sinner will never-theless bring him to a bad end (Prov. 10:11, 16, 22). Didactic psalms sung in the Temple openly attacked the seductive position of the sinners (Pss 37, 49, 52, 62, 73, 94, 112). When the sinners went so far as to make wealth into their god (Pss 49:7; 52:9) and to exploit the weak (94:5f.) then – in the strong terms employed by their opponents – they were virtually denying the God of Israel and leaving the ranks of the people of God (Ps. 94:5, 14f.). The members of their own group were warned that they should put their trust in God and not in extorted wealth (Ps. 62:9, 11). It was thus that in the post-exilic period the monotheistic argument was first used against the practice of making a god of riches (Job 31:24–8), and religion, not ethnicity, became the criterion for belonging to the nation of Israel.

At the same time the pious section of the upper class developed a comprehensive system of pastoral care within their own group (Job 4:3–5). They had to contend with the tempting economic success enjoyed by the 'sinners' (Ps. 73:2ff.). Also, as shown by the book of Job, they had to deal with the more worrying problem that members of their own group, however pious and tireless in helping the poor (cf. Job 29, 31), could themselves fall from grace. This social crisis under the Persians let loose in Israel's religion the vexed question of theodicy (Job 9:21–4).

A second theological disagreement caused rifts between the impoverished lower classes and the two factions of the upper class. Socially marginalized, the poor joined the outsiders who kept alive the legacy of the prophets and sought salvation in social revolution, which they believed Yahweh himself would bring about. There are, at least, texts in post-exilic prophecy that allow us to surmise that there were sects within the lower classes who were inspired by the prophets (Malachi; Is. 29:17–24; 56:9 – 57:21).

Also, the poor regarded themselves as the righteous, because they put their trust only in Yahweh to rescue them from their misery. They hoped that he would make haste to strike down their oppressors, so that they, 'the most wretched of people', would break out in joy and jubilation (Is. 29:19f.). Then even the 'blind' and the 'sullen' who now mocked the prophetic expectations, would perceive their truth (vv. 18–24). This probably referred to the supporters among the pious section of the upper class, who helped the poor with alms but feared that a social revolution would threaten their own interests. The poor foresaw a limited place for them in God's future nature; the sinners, they believed, would be cast out.

THE THEOLOGIZATION AND SPLITTING OF PERSONAL PIETY

The depth of the split, both social and religious, in the Jewish community, can be seen from the fact that it even reached the level of personal piety. The Deuteronomic reformers had already assimilated the religion of the family to the official Yahweh religion; during the exile it had taken over vital representative religious functions. In the post-exilic period, because of the smallness of the Jewish communities in Palestine and in the diaspora, there was even closer assimilation of these two levels of Israel's religion.

On the one hand, in private prayer, some included intercessions for the nation and for Zion (Pss 3:9; 25:22; 28:8f.) and referred to the history of the nation (22:5f.) or the promises relating to Zion (102:13–22). On the other hand the community increasingly linked their prayers of lamentation and praise to the religious experiences of individuals (cf. Pss 90, 123, 125, 126, 128; 8, 103, 107, 124), since there was little evidence now of any political intervention in history by Yahweh. In this context, personal piety was reflected in the theology; their direct relationship of trust in God – in contrast to the alternatives practised by the 'sinners' – was problematized and made the subject of a conscious decision (Pss 118:8f.; 115:9–11; 125:1). The distance between God and man increased; out of the recognition of sinfulness, which Israel as a whole had had to embrace since the exile, even individual piety had to admit a deep consciousness of sin (Pss 32:2–6; 51:9–11; 130:4).

In the course of this theologization, with the pressure caused by the fifth-century social crisis, personal piety developed in two different ways, according to class: there was the personal theology of the pious upper class, and the 'piety of the poor', the personal piety of the oppressed underclass.

The members of the pious upper class wished to impose a personal piety on all, a complete and totally ethical piety. This would not only satisfy the increased ethical demands of the Yahweh religion but would also ward off the danger of clashes between piety and the rational practices of the blatant 'sinners'. If every individual could simply claim protection form his Creator, without having to moderate his behaviour, then the grace of God could be misused all too easily to cover unrighteous deeds. In order to exclude this possibility, the pious wealthy declared that 'fear of God' and 'a complete change in behaviour' were signs of a genuine personal relationship with God (Job 4:6). It was only those who tried to change their lives to ones pleasing to God (in which not the least important element was compassion and practical help for the poor [29:12–17; 31:13–27]) who could safely hope for God's support and reward (29:18–20).

The book of Job is evidence of how this ambitious personal theology of the upper class was subjected to severe testing under the pressure of the social crisis. In the face of the depressing reality that their great piety often failed to bring them any reward – indeed that several of them, despite their selfless support of the poor, were themselves in danger of losing their position in society (cf. Job 30:1ff.) – many pious rich men asked themselves the hard question of whether their piety was any use (Mal. 3:14f.; Ps. 73:13). The composer of the moral tale of the rich and pious Job (Job 1:1–2, 13; 42:7–17) countered this question with another: should not true piety (which aspires to being more than a good bargain) be prepared to renounce all reward (1:9)? The writer, describing how Job withstood God's terrible testing, to the extent that even in deepest distress he was able to praise God (1:21f.; 2:10), is arguing for a new ideal of an independent piety, which went far beyond the piety of Israel's usual family religion.

On the other hand, the author of the dialogue (Job 3:1–42:6) found it more realistic to have Job screaming in his anger and disappointment. This moral drama puts the theology of wisdom in the mouth of Job's friends: sorrow is God's way of teaching you, it should be accepted humbly (5:17; 22:22); loud lament was a foolish thing (5:2–5), God would listen only to humble prayer (5:8; 22:21; 35:10); finally, man is born a sinner and so can never lay claims against God (4:17–21; 15:14). It is true that the writer of the book of Job described how this ambitious personal theology crumbled in the face of Job's real suffering. But he was by no means prepared to let Job win the argument with his wild laments, in which he even cursed God as a selfwilled tyrant and sinner (9:11–24). When he showed how Job was harshly put in his place by God (38ff.) when he made the mistake of challenging him to a legal battle (31:35–7), he was making it clear to his upper-class colleagues that their demand for a fair return for their service would put God's universal jurisdiction out of joint (40:8–14). He shows Job, confronted with the power of the Creator and Lord of History, regretting his wild laments by the end (42:1–6).

Even the author of the book of Job could not supply the members of the pious upper class with an answer to the question of theodicy, which had become an urgent one. Himself a member of the upper class, he could not share the hopes nurtured in prophetic circles that God would bring about a fairer society. But he did indicate that it was possible that after Job's death he would become reconciled with God and his merits would be recognized (Job 14:13–17; 16:18–22; 19:23–7a). This was a new idea inasmuch as the older Israelites had believed that a person's relationship with God ended at death. In the theology of wisdom in late Persian times, under pressure to cling to the idea of God's justice in the face of massive social injustices, the possibility was raised that the relationship of trust with one's personal God must survive death, in order for the pious sufferer to be rewarded. This was the beginning of the latter hope of a personal resurrection (Is. 25:8; 26:19; Dan. 12:2).

In the piety of the poor the question of God's fairness was also fiercely debated. But in contrast to their rich patrons in the upper class the bankrupt smallholders could not point to good deeds of their own; they concentrated on the unrighteousness of the sinners, which was not merely an abstract matter for them since it affected their own survival. Thus in their prayers they could do nothing but commend their own poverty and misery to God, hoping to move him to mercy (Pss 10:12; 69:30; 70:6; 109:22). Powerless themselves, they put their hopes for vengeance in appeals to Yahweh, asking him to display his great power as Judge and King of the world (Pss 7:8f.; 10:16; 75:3) to set up a great court of judgment (9:20; 12:6; 14:5), to destroy the powerful sinners and their foreign allies, so that the oppressed might be set free and might once again rejoice before God (9:6, 18; 109:6–20). In this the poor were harking back to elements of the old Temple theology, but converting them now to a call for social revolution.

There are indications that the poor gathered in small religious groups and held services in their homes or in synagogues. In doing this they associated themselves with old practices of the family cult, such as the ceremony of individual lament or a ritual of thanksgiving (Pss 6f., 22). Here they were fighting back against the oppression of their small community and showing that God had not forgotten or abandoned them (22:25). A particular way to ensure salvation was to proclaim a slogan for their group, or a curse upon their enemies (Pss 12:6; 14:5f.; 75:3–9; 82:1–7). While the lower-class participants in such rituals looked for future salvation, they were drawing strength from religion that preserved the self-respect of the socially disadvantaged. And while the poor regarded themselves as the pious ones (Pss 12:2; 14:5; 69:29) they were using religious means to defend themselves against social marginalization.

THE SAMARITANS BREAK AWAY FROM THE CULT

To this social conflict was added in the fifth century a political battle, which – if we may believe Josephus (*Ant.* XI:302–47) – led at the end of the Persian period to a split within the cult and the erection of a Yahweh sanctuary on Mount Gerizim at Shechem.

Since the conquest of the northern kingdom in 722 BC there had again and again been worshippers of Yahweh in mid- and northern Palestine who oriented themselves in worship either towards Bethel (2 Kgs 17:28) or towards Jerusalem (Jer. 41:5). It even seems that the sanctuary at Bethel, unaffected by having been shut down by Josiah, came back into use after the destruction of the Temple at Jerusalem, and in the time of exile was used by the Judaeans who stayed at home; this can be the only explanation for the harsh polemics of the Deuteronomistic History, composed in exile, which said that Bethel was a syncretistic mongrel cult cobbled together from the Yahweh religion and the religions of other nations brought in as settlers by the Assyrians (2 Kgs 17:24–34a).

When the Temple at Jerusalem had been rebuilt after the exile, those faithful to Yahweh in the north were invited (2 Kgs 17:34b–40) and participated in its cult. That was not a problem as long as Judaea was still part of the Persian province of Samaria. It was only when the south began to strive for political independence that the leaders of the Samaritans began to resist and to use every possible means to prevent the reconstruction of the walls of Jerusalem (Ezra 4:6, 7–22; Neh. 4–6). When Judaea gained political independence, at the latest after Nehemiah around 450 BC, the province of Samaria no longer had a Yahweh sanctuary, and its worshippers of Yahweh, who by then included even the family of the satrap Sanballat, threatened to lose all influence on the Temple at Jerusalem. The tribal–ethnic organization of the Jewish community, which admitted as members only those who could prove descent from Judah or Benjamin (Neh. 7:5ff.), meant that nobody could gain admission to their self-rule councils except by marrying in. The family of Sanballat attempted this several times, marrying into the family of the high priest (Neh. 13:28; *Ant.* XI.209f.). Also a majority of the priests apparently pleaded for the incorporation of their religious brothers from Samaria, who had long forsworn all syncretism and recognized the obligations of the Torah. But this attempt was blocked for political reasons by Nehemiah or perhaps by the Council of Elders, who suspected a danger of political infiltration; the sons of the high priest who had married Samaritan women were both expelled (Neh. 13:28; *Ant.* XI:306–8).

After it had proved impossible to open up the Jewish cult community to all Israel, Sanballat III conceived the plan of providing his expelled sons with their own sanctuary on the territory of his province. This did not contravene the Deuteronomic law of centralization (Deut. 12). He could argue that in the Torah the name of the sanctuary Yahweh would choose was not named. But if Jerusalem was not mentioned in the foundation document of Israel's religion, whereas the old sanctuaries of the northern kingdom such as Bethel, Shechem and Mount Gerizim were mentioned (Gen. 28:10–22; 33:18ff.; Deut. 27:11f.), then the Samaritans could justifiably claim that they were supported by holy tradition, if they wanted their own cult centre in Shechem and on Mount Gerizim. The Persian authorities seem to have hesitated for a long time before they allowed such an interpretation, since they were interested in maintaining good relations with the people of Jerusalem. But when Darius III was unexpectedly killed at Issus in 333 BC, Alexander gave Sanballat permission to build the temple on Mount Gerizim, in recognition of his military support.

When the Samaritans gained independence for their cult it by no means represented a religious schism. Both in Jerusalem and on Mount Gerizim the rites were performed by Zadokite priests. Both communities regarded the same Torah as the basis of their religion and of daily life. It was only much later, in the course of the expansion of the new state of Judaea after John Hyrcanus had destroyed the temple on Mount Gerizim in 128 BC and Shechem in 107 BC that the Samaritan sect split off in anger from Judaism.

THE EARLY JEWISH RELIGION UNDER HELLENISM

After the chaos of the battles between the Diadochoi ('successors'), Alexander's victory over the Persians in 333 BC brought Judaea under the rule first of the Ptolemies and then of the Seleucids, but did not bring marked changes in politics or religion. Politically, Judaea kept its partly autonomous self-rule, although it was exercised by the high priest, who extended his authority to include not just the College of Priests but also the Council of Elders. As for the politics of religion, the Macedonians allowed Judaeans to live according to the laws of their fathers.

Nevertheless, the Hellenistic period was a time of transition. There were hardly any more developments influencing the form of Israel's religion; the last scriptures to be incorporated into the Hebrew Bible stem from this time (third–second century BC). But new developments that would shape Judaism and Christianity began in this time, for example piety based on the Torah, apocalypticism, or the creating of religious sects such as in Qumran. After the brothers of the former northern kingdom of Israel had split their cult off from Jerusalem one can justifiably speak for the first time of a specific 'Jewish Religion'.

Apart from with the Samaritans, rivalry was above all being taken into the sphere of Hellenism, which represented the greatest challenge for the early Jewish religion of the third and second centuries BC. In the face of this fascinating culture that embraced east and west, the question of Jewish identity arose again: the strict religious apartness that had been cultivated when the Jews were a threatened minority during the exile and the early post-exilic period was a considerable hindrance to the now much larger ethnic group who wished to participate in international intellectual and economic life. But (apart from a few initiatives) the meeting of Greek and Jew was not fruitful. Those who promoted an opening out of the Jewish religion in the direction of Hellenism were mostly Jewish aristocrats, following their own economic interest regardless, and they had been quick to deny their religion according to the pious of both upper and lower classes. The notorious social and religious split was now made worse by a cultural split. The Jews of the Hellenistic period were chiefly concerned with maintaining the religion of their fathers and opposing the influence of Hellenism.

The books of Chronicles, which probably date from the first half of the third century BC, are consciously non-Hellenistic. The leaders of the Jewish community were obsessed with the problem within Israel of the rival Samaritan sect. In order to refute their claim to legitimacy based on the Torah they decided that the foundation history should incorporate the texts that laid emphasis on the Temple at Jerusalem and David's monarchy, that is, above all the books of Samuel, Kings and the Prophets. It is true that this presented a problem; when the Judaic councils had canonized the Torah they had excised the history of the monarchy because of anti-monarchic reservations, and had not been keen on the writings of the prophets for fear they might arouse enthusiasm. This is why they ordered the revision of Dtr. H. so that on the one hand their reservations might be lifted, and on the other it might provide a clearer justification for their leadership as opposed to the Samaritans. The work that resulted from these efforts is a great harmonizing synthesis. It is so crammed with quotations and references to other texts that it probably came from the pen of a new type of professional, a Bible scholar, who since the canonization of the Torah had supervised the transmission of the text.

Beside the foundation epoch of early times, which they reduced to the genealogical framework important for the creation of a Jewish identity after the exile (1 Chr. 1–9), the Bible scholars placed emphasis on a second foundation epoch in the reigns of David and Solomon, making it take up nearly half of their composition (1 Chr. 11 – 2 Chr. 9). This identified as the purpose and high point of the history of Israel and of God's choosing of his people the construction and furnishing of the Temple at Jerusalem. However, the scholars revised the account in Dtr. H: they acknowledged that the model for David's Temple – like Moses' Ark of long ago – had been revealed by Yahweh (1 Chr. 28:11ff.; cf. Ex. 35:9) and built by Solomon to Yahweh's exact specifications, but it was no longer a royal possession, being mostly financed by the people (1 Chr. 29:1–9, 14, 17). It is true that the personnel of the cult had been decided by David down to the smallest detail. However, the priests and the Levites were no longer the king's officials, but received an independent maintenance grant from the people (2 Chr. 31:2ff.; cf. Num. 18). In other words, the scholars took from Dtr. H. the proof that only the Temple at Jerusalem was the sanctuary chosen by Yahweh, but at the same time they excluded the option of its being a state cult. As they presented it, the cult at Jerusalem was in no way heretical (as the Samaritans claimed) but everything in it was ordered exactly according to the prescriptions of the Torah.

It was more difficult to deal with the monarchy. The scholars strove to dispel the problems this presented by, on the one hand, referring to Nathan's promise to Solomon, that the line of David would rule for ever, but restricting it to apply only as far as Solomon (1 Chr. 17:11ff.); on the other hand making it clear that the monarchy was subservient to Yahweh's kingship over Israel (1 Chr. 17:14; 28:5; 29:23; 2 Chr. 9:8; 13:8). They presented the harmonious image of an ideal monarchy, always consulting this people and caring tirelessly for them (2 Chr. 20:21; 19:4–11). In doing this they were trying to ward off aspirations from the line of David and to open the way for the long-desired constitutional monarchy.

Apart from this, the Bible scholars introduced the Psalms and the prophetic tradition into their work of history. They countered the gloomy view of history given by Dtr. H with the certainty often expressed in the cult, that Yahweh's mercy would last for ever (2 Chr. 20:21; cf. Ps. 117). Since salvation was present in the cult at Jerusalem, there could not be any fateful entanglements in its history. Instead, they gathered from their readings of the prophets Isaiah and Jeremiah (2 Chr. 20:20; 15:2; cf. Is. 7:9; Jer. 29:13f.) that each generation would be punished only for its own transgressions (cf. 2 Chr. 36) and that God gave each generation a new opportunity for salvation, if they turned honestly towards him. In this view of history there was no longer a 'too late', of which the prophets of judgment had so emphatically warned. Therefore even the brothers in Samaria who had been led astray could be invited to convert and to join the cult of Jerusalem (2 Chr. 30).

Such a view reduced the message of the prophets to an individual optimistic teaching of fair reward, reminiscent of the wisdom of the pious. The prophets pointed the way to a righteous life, and that was all. This consciously negated the eschatological interpretation of the prophecies by the lower class. The harmonious picture of history built up by members of the middle class left no place for social upheavals.

The interpretative work of the Chronicles was intended to be nothing less than a revision of the canon. Its broad but harmonizing syntheses led the way to the canonization of the minor prophets (Joshua to 2 Kings) and the major prophets (Isaiah, Jeremiah, Ezekiel, book of the Twelve), completed by at the latest the end of the third century BC. It was also the first step towards a specially Jewish canon that was not approved by the Samaritans.

Also on the level of personal piety there began in the Hellenistic period a specially Jewish form of personal theology, 'Torah piety' (Pss 1, 19, 119). It, too, probably derives from the position of the Bible scholars. Once the Torah had been canonized as the basis of the official Yahweh religion this professional group was also concerned with making it the basis of an individual's relationship with God. They set at the centre of this new piety a strongly emotional, even erotic, relationship to the scriptures (Pss 119:47, 97, 131). It was no longer merely general maxims of wisdom as in the personal theology of the pious upper class but the commandments of the Torah that should pervade the ethical relationship of trust in God (119:1–16, 73). No longer would general experiences of God, but intensive meditation on the scriptures (1:2), reveal God's merciful presence (119:18, 105). 'Acting according to the Torah' and 'Learning from the Torah' were (for the first time) declared to be a demanding Jewish *praxis pietatis*, which required every layperson to become a 'little theologian'.

But this ideal of Jewish piety met with resistance. In the upper class at Jerusalem there were also groups who oriented their philosophy of life rather more towards the international currents of the Hellenistic world around them. They are exemplified in the figure of the teacher of wisdom Qoheleth, active in Jerusalem around the middle of the third century BC.

Drawing on sceptic philosophical traditions, Qoheleth subjected the wisdom of piety to a pitiless critique. Its teaching of two kinds of retribution, that would reward the pious and punish the sinner, could easily be refuted (7:15–18; 8:12–14) from the harsh reality of the Ptolemaic economic system, built upon personal advantage and competition (Eccles. 4:4). Further, all its optimistic belief that one could arrange one's life in a way wise and pleasing to God seemed to Qoheleth an illusion, since humans are subject to an unchangeable destiny and cannot understand God's intentions (Eccles. 3:1–11). Death is inevitable and wipes out all differences between wise person and fool (2:12–17; 9:11f.). In the face of the meaninglessness of all happenings the only possibility for people is to enjoy life to the full as best they can (2:24; 3:12f., 22; 5:17; 8:15; 9:7–9).

In saying this, Qoheleth was probably recognizing that the harmonizing piety of his time had lost touch with reality; he gave a pitiless analysis of the social fragmentation in his community (Eccles. 4:1; 5:7f.; 10:5f.) but unlike the pious upper-class circles behind the book of Job he did not intervene in the conflicts. He merely saw them as the expression of the basic absurdity of human life. But the result was that Qoheleth saw God as a distant, unapproachable dispenser of destiny. He could hardly be reached by human prayer (5:1f.); it was madness to accuse him as Job had done (6:10f.). Qoheleth was certainly not one of the sinners who pretended to be pious but showed by their ungenerous behaviour that they had stepped outside

Israel's relationship with God (8:11f.), but in the face of his critical rationality the personal piety in Israel, which until then had been characterized by a particularly close and living relationship with God, mostly melted away.

Thus it is no surprise that at the beginning of the second century BC a conservative teacher of wisdom and Bible scholar from Jerusalem, Jesus Sirach, began to attempt to create a personal Jewish theology of wisdom that would satisfy even the demands of high philosophy. In his opinion, the universal wisdom that functions as a means of revelation between the Creator and the whole world (cf. Prov. 8) had, by God's command, found a permanent resting place in Israel (Jes. Sir. 24:1–12). This meant that it was especially effective in Israel in the services in Jerusalem and in the Torah (24:10, 23). By saying this, Jesus Sirach transferred Yahweh's choosing of Israel over into the theology of wisdom, and made it possible to unite universality and particularity even at the level of a personal philosophy of life. All other people might orientate themselves to the international currents of Hellenistic philosophy, but for Jews the orientation for their lives could be found only in the Temple cult and in the Torah. A wisdom divorced from the Torah, as represented by Qoheleth, could not exist for Israel in the opinion of Jesus Sirach; on the contrary, when each Jew bathed in the fountain of wisdom that sprang from the Torah thanks to its exposition by scholars, he was enjoying an unusually large share of universal divine wisdom (24:23–34). When Jesus Sirach revealed that God had made all creation with differences and opposites, giving humankind freedom of choice, he was promoting the idea that Israel's peculiar position with regard to the personal laws of daily life could be seen as part of God's wisdom (33:7–18). With this, Jesus Sirach created a theological and philosophical basis that allowed a specifically Jewish personal theology of wisdom to coexist confidently with the Hellenistic world.

The actual battle against integration in Hellenism was fought increasingly on the ground not of personal piety but of eschatological prophecy and the new apocalypticism. After the downfall of the Persian empire and Alexander's campaign of 332 BC had not brought the great switch to salvation expected since Deutero-Isaiah (Zech. 9:1–8), but on the contrary the battles between the Diadochoi that followed (321–301 BC) could be regarded only as the fall of the great power and a sign of divine anger (11:4–16), prophetic groups among the opposition and in the lower class became convinced that there would have to be a terrible Day of Judgment, with God judging the world and Jerusalem, before Yahweh could set up his kingdom in Zion (Zech. 12–14; Is. 24–6). The entire sinful world with its proud Hellenistic city culture would have to pass away (Is. 24:1–6, 10ff.; 25:1–5), the kings would have to be put in prison and the sinners destroyed (24:21f.; 25:4f.) before Yahweh would prepare a feast for the hungry and oppressed poor and set aside all their sorrows (25:6–9). In their worship, the prophetic circles in the lower class pleaded for God's liberating court of justice to come (26:7–18) and firmly believed that even the pious dead would share in the future salvation (26:19). This brought them for the first time to a genuine belief in resurrection: when their deliverance came, then even death, which now separated them from God, would be set aside (25:8).

This eschatological prophecy, which was developed in groups of outsiders, became more relevant to the mainstream when Judaea, after a long period of stable Ptolemaic rule, fell, from 221 BC, between the fronts of the Seleucids (Antiochus III [223–187

BC]) and the Ptolemies, and in 198 BC were added to the Seleucid empire. During the political and military disputes, the conflicts between the conservatives and the Hellenists (who were radical to a greater or lesser degree) split the Judaean upper class, reaching a critical intensity and giving a new edge to the underlying social conflict with the lower class (who mostly remained faithful followers of Yahweh). This explosive situation erupted for the first time at the end of the third century BC in a rising against the Ptolemies, which failed (Dan. 11:14), but then after a short time of consolidation broke out again more strongly from 167 BC in the Maccabean civil war, after the radical Hellenists, supported by Antiochus IV (175–164 BC) had attempted to turn Jerusalem, in its politics and its cult, into a Hellenistic community.

These anti-Hellenistic revolts were regarded from the beginning through the eschatological perspective of the prophet-oriented groups of the lower class as the arrival of God's Day of Judgment before the great turnaround to salvation. This perspective was accepted by the population because of a new eschatological theology that had been developed by scholars among the opposition; they appear in the Maccabean rebellion as Ḥasidim ('Group of the Pious') (1 Macc. 2:42; 7:13). Their work was based on the eschatological prophecies that had been voiced from the middle of the third century and was called 'apocalyptic'.

Typical of this apocalyptic theology was a systematization of eschatological expectations in a clear sequence of events, the concept of an end of history and a new 'Thereafter' brought in by God, and the synchronization of their own time with the drama of the end of time, that is, shortly before the expected transformation.

In the sense of this apocalyptic concept, the author of the Aramaic book of Daniel (Dan. 2–7*), writing during the first phase of the rebellion, at the end of the third century BC, produced an anti-Hellenistic theology of political resistance; using ancient legendary tales about Daniel, the famous interpreter of dreams from the Babylonian and Persian periods, he pointed out that God's kingship had prevailed previously against the emperors, and that their empires had lasted only so long as they acknowledged Yahweh's rule (Dan. 3:31f.; 4:31f.; 5:17–30; 6:26–8). Borrowing Greek concepts of four empires and epochs declining in quality, he created a theory of the political history of the world, which after the empires of Babylon, the Medes and then the Persians had reached an absolute nadir with the all-destroying Hellenistic empire. He demonstrated the similarity and the sequence of the four empires in the dream-vision of Nebuchadnezzar (2:31ff.) of an imposing giant statue shattered by a falling rock that symbolizes God's kingship (2:34ff.). This collapse of world history would come about without any human intervention, but all pious people were called to resist (to the point of martydom [Dan. 3:6]) the totalitarian claims of the Hellenistic rulers expressed in the latter's ruler-cult. The author depicted Daniel seeing in his final vision that after the destruction of the increasingly bestial empires the authority of God would be given to a 'son of man' (7:1–15); this cheered the community of the pious (vv. 18, 27), hearing that after their severe sufferings under the murderous self-idolizing Hellenistic rulers they would soon participate in a completely new and humane form of government.

In the second, much more violent, phase of the rebellion, sparked off by brutal measures intended to enforce Hellenism on worshippers of Yahweh under Antiochus

IV in 167 BC, including the erection of an altar for Baal-Shamem/Zeus Olympios in the Temple at Jerusalem, the Aramaic book of Daniel was extended with a Hebrew framework (Dan. 1:8–12) and made more relevant. The author of the Hebrew book regarded the impertinent desecration of the Temple as the beginning of the Last Days. He even tried to use learned calculations, interpreting Jeremiah's reference to the 70 years of exile (Jer. 29:10) as 70 × 7 (490 years) (Dan. 9) in order to find the exact time from then (probably 165 BC) to the end, coming to varying results (9:27: 3.5 years; 8:14: 1,150 days; 12:11: 1,290 days; 12:12: 1,335 days). And he tried to increase confidence in the accuracy of his prediction of the events of the Last Days by making Daniel predict the entire history of the Hellenistic empire in the guise of a vision (Dan. 10–12). But unlike the Maccabees, who wanted to use force of arms to overcome Antiochus and the radical Hellenists who were his allies, and unlike the apocalyptic teachers who interpreted this battle as the divine battle at the end of time before the advent of salvation (*1 Enoch* 89f.), the author of the Hebrew book of Daniel believed that it was the archangel Michael alone who would rescue the pious (Dan. 12:1). The difficult times before the end he interpreted as a testing time of probation that would decide whether the pious and their apocalyptic teachers would share in the final salvation (11:32–5; 12:10). He expected a resurrection of two kinds, to external life or to eternal shame (12:2), from which only the apocalyptic teachers who had unerringly shown others the way to righteousness would proceed in glory (12:3). Thus, unlike the author of the Aramaic book of Daniel, the author of the Hebrew parts was concerned that there should be a purely religious, passive, non-violent resistance in the turbulent situation of the civil war. Instead of an alternative model of the political government of the future (Dan. 7) he gave an individual view of salvation consisting of resurrection and Day of Judgment.

The apocalyptic theology contributed greatly to the success of the fight to preserve Jewish identity in the face of the pressure to conform to Hellenism in the first half of the second century BC. The prophesying that had long been officially marginalized – even in its eschatological version – became a widely accepted constituent of Israel's religion. Even if the immediate expectations of the apocalyptic writings inspired by the Maccabean crisis were not fulfilled precisely – it was possible to cleanse the Temple of Hellenistic syncretism in 164 BC, but the hoped-for arrival of Yahweh's reign did not occur; instead, the Maccabean war of liberation led to the beginning of the Hasmonaean monarchy – yet the new viewpoint, looking for an apocalypse at the end of time, became an important element of both early Judaism and (to an even greater degree) of Christianity. Israel's religion originated as a historical religion of deliverance. With the idea of apocalyptic it developed into an eschatological religion of salvation.

JUDAISM AT THE TURN
OF THE ERA

—— •◆• ——

Jarl Fossum

To describe Judaism and Jewishness at the turn of the era is no easy task. What was the common denominator of the Jewish religion? Who was a Jew? Today we identify a person as Jewish on the basis of her or his adherence to Judaism and/or on the basis of the person's filiation. Even if a person is of non-Jewish extraction, he or she has to be considered Jewish if having converted to Judaism. When considering the filial aspect, it must be borne in mind that the Jewish family is matrilinear. One is Jewish if one's mother is Jewish: the actual religion of one's parents or oneself does not matter.

These circumstances cause problems in Israel today. Civil law does not accept a Jew as ʿoleh, someone who has the right to immigrate to Israel under the Law of Return of 1949, if he or she has embraced, say, Christianity. The religious authorities, on the other hand, build on the Rabbinic rulings which laid down that even a person who has lapsed from Judaism remains a Jew.[1]

PHARISAIC RABBINISM

How was the situation at the turn of the era? The rabbinic interpretations of the Torah, the Mosaic Law, and its applications to everyday situations in a society far removed from that of the time of its writing, are set down in the Mishnah, 'Teaching'.[2] The Mishnah was written around 200 CE, but its promulgators obviously had forebears: they are apparently the Pharisees, a group well known from the Gospels.[3] In the Gospels we often find the junction 'Scribes and Pharisees' (e.g. Matt 15.1; 23.2, 13–15; Mark 7.1, 5; Luke 6.7), but this should not mislead us to think that the names are more or less synonymous. More than one group had scribes, that is, men trained in the interpretation of the Bible.[4] Mark's expression 'Scribes of the Pharisees' (2.16) seems to be a pointer in the right direction. There can be no denying the fact that the 'Scribes of the Pharisees' were the main forerunners of the rabbis.

Who were the Pharisees? 'Rabbi' simply means 'master' or 'teacher'. As is the case with the term 'scribe', not each and every rabbi was a Pharisee. Jesus was addressed as a 'rabbi' (Mark 10.51; John 20.16),[5] but he is never called a Pharisee; the New Testament portrays the Pharisees as the opponents of Jesus.[6] The name 'Pharisee' is probably derived from the word *Perushim*, 'separatists'. The Pharisees constituted a party of lay people who were very serious about the injunctions in the Torah that *all* Israel should be a holy people and a nation of priests.[7] The Pharisees took the priestly purity rules to be incumbent upon the entire people. Moreover, the priests had deserted Israel and her God; therefore, penance had to be done by the people.

Now the priestly purity regulations were extremely difficult to practise for people at large, and the Pharisees distinguished themselves from the ʿAm ha-Aretz, the 'people of the land'. As time went by, however, the climate became somewhat milder: the ʿAm ha-Aretz remained despised but not rejected.[8]

The Pharisees got together in clubs of *Ḥaberim*, 'Associates', which developed into veritable schools where the Law was studied and new rules formulated so that it could be made applicable to everyday situations in society. The most famous schools at the turn of the era were *Beth* Hillel and *Beth* Shammai, named after two teachers who lived in the first century BCE. Hillel is attributed with seven rules for scriptural interpretation, so-called *middoth*. At the beginning of the second century CE, Rabbi Ishmael increased the number of *middoth* to thirteen. Later we hear about no less than thirty-two *middoth*.[9]

The rabbis distinguished carefully between the biblical books, the written Law, and their own writings, called the 'oral Law'. The biblical period was regarded as a closed chapter, and the rabbis deliberately abandoned the literary forms and language of the Bible.[10] The Holy Spirit, the prophetical inspiration, had departed from Israel.[11] The expert decisions of the rabbis, reached by means of the various *middoth*, replaced pronouncements in the name of God.

On the other hand, the rabbis distinguished carefully between the written Law and the oral Law on the one hand and the 'extraneous books' on the other. Although the rabbinic writings (the oral Law) are full of arguments and discussions, the rabbis claimed to be keepers of a tradition reaching back to the revelation given to Moses on Mount Sinai.[12] The oral Law as well as the written Law was believed to be God's revelation. The rabbis were the successors of Moses, and everything produced outside rabbinic circles was simply the work of fallible human minds. Working out a program of ritual and legal practice according to their conceptions of what was central in their religion, the rabbis frowned upon other topics.[13]

AN ANACHRONISTIC UNDERSTANDING OF JUDAISM AT THE TURN OF THE ERA

Pharisaic Rabbinism is usually what we today understand by the term 'Judaism'. This is a religion that is led by rabbis, teachers of the Law and conductors of the synagogue worship. The term is acceptable when applied to the present-day situation, but it is rather misleading when being used of Israelite religion at the turn of the era, for such a usage implies that what we know about Judaism today is a measure for what Jews or at least 'orthodox' Jews believed and practised about 2,000 years ago.

An example from one of Jacob Neusner's numerous books on Judaism may illustrate this point. In his 'Glossary' to *An Introduction to Judaism*, Neusner brushes the Sadducees away with two lines – he describes them as a 'sect'. The Pharisees, on the other hand, get ten positive lives without any sect label.[14]

THE SADDUCEES

Like the Pharisees, the Sadducees are often mentioned in the New Testament. Like the Pharisees, they quarrelled with Jesus. But the Pharisees and the Sadducees did not agree, and the description of the Sadducees as a sect goes back to the Pharisaic rabbis – we find it already in the Mishnah.[15] Now we ought to consider that the spiritual head of the Jews before the fall of the temple in 70 CE was a Sadducee, namely the high priest. The Jerusalem temple, the religious centre for the majority of Jews, was managed by the Sadducees. It ought to be clear that the Sadducees cannot be written off as a 'sect'.

On the other hand, the Sadducean party had several facets. The name of the party probably derives from that of Ṣadoq, the priest of David and Solomon. Now the last legitimate Ṣadoqite high priest, Onias III, was deposed by the Seleucid ruler, Antiochus IV Epiphanes, in 175 BCE. Although the high priesthood became a prize in the troubled politics of the time, the Sadducean party remained in control of the temple. It is true that the Sadducees at the turn of the era cannot be described as a strictly priestly party, for lay people from the new money aristocracy had made their way into the Sanhedrin, the 'Great Assembly', the highest judicial and religious organ of the Jews, which traditionally had been dominated by the priests. The priestly Sadducees and the new lay Sadducees joined forces in a law-and-order policy: they worked together with the Romans who had occupied Palestine since 64 BCE; by their cooperation with the occupying power, the Sadducees could profit from temple taxes and trade.[16]

This does not mean that it is right to describe the Sadducees as a 'sect' in a derogatory sense. Josephus, a first century CE historian (with a Sadducean ancestry), sided with the Romans and fought Jewish insurrectionists. Still, Josephus is regarded by most as a good Jew, apparently because he fought the Romans to begin with and wrote positively on Jewish history even after he had changed side.[17]

THE ZEALOTS

There were other groups than the Pharisees and the Sadducees. One of them was that of the Zealots, whose movement appears to have been made up of people from different social strands, the majority probably being Galilean tenants. The Zealots killed Jews they did not trust as well as Romans, thereby breaking the commandment of Exodus 20.13 ('Thou shalt not kill' – by which members of the People of Israel of course are indicated). Still, the Zealots are reckoned as belonging to the Jewish fold: they fought against the Romans, and the Jews they killed (before they started to fight among themselves) were Sadducees.[18]

THE ESSENES

The Essenes constitute the Jewish party about which we are best informed (the Christians being excluded). This is due to the fact that we have obtained so much Essene text material. We do not possess Sadducean or Zealot texts, and – as mentioned above – the first Pharisaic–rabbinic writings date from about 200 CE. Until the discovery of the Dead Sea Scrolls we were dependent upon the descriptions of the Essenes made by Josephus, the Jewish philosopher Philo of Alexandria, who lived in the same century as Josephus, and the Roman author Pliny the Elder, also of the same century.[19] Right after World War II, however, a huge library of Essene writings was discovered at Qumran at the north-west bank of the Dead Sea. Thus we speak of the Qumran-Essenes being a branch of the wider Essene movement.[20]

The Essenes, whose name proably derives from *Ḥasidim*, the 'Pious Ones', took an evasive attitude to society at large. In this they were similar to the Pharisees, but the Qumran-Essenes at least took this attitude to its extreme by isolating themselves in the wilderness well removed from Jerusalem and its temple.[21] The Qumran-Essenes were not against the temple *per se*, but against the priesthood, which – in their opinion – had desecrated the temple. The high priest in Jerusalem was not a true descendant of Ṣadoq; the leaders of the Qumran society were the true 'Sons of Ṣadoq' (1Q S 5.2, 8).[22]

The Essenes do not seem to have been closer to the Pharisees than to the Sadducees. The Qumran writings criticize those who 'seek after smooth things' (4Q p Nah 1.2,7; 2.2, 4; 3.3, 7), a characterization that may very well be applied to the Pharisees, who did not adhere to a literal interpretation of the Law but tried to adapt the Torah to suit life in a society different from that of ancient Israel.[23]

In rejecting the oral tradition, the Essenes were at one with the Sadducees. It is true that the Sadducees did not believe in the resurrection of the dead and predestination,[24] whereas these tenets are found in Essene writings,[25] but it must be kept in mind that the Essenes – in contrast to the Sadducees – did not have a closed canon. The book of Daniel, cherished by the Qumran-Essenes, teaches that the resurrection of the righteous is part of the consummation of God's plan.[26] The canon of the Sadducees was the Pentateuch alone.

Moreover, in contrast to the Pharisees as well as the Sadducees, the Essenes lived in the world of the Bible. Continuing the prophetic tradition, the Essenes subjected the life of their community to the guidance of men such as the 'Legitimate Teacher',[27] who possessed the divine spirit. Being prophetically inspired, the Teacher could issue decisions beyond questioning. This is seen in the document designated as 4Q MMT, where the Teacher's rulings are handed down like biblical ordinances.

JESUS AND THE FIRST CHRISTIANS

It has become theologically correct to say that Jesus was a Jew and that primitive Christianity was a form of Judaism. This is all true, but the view cannot be upheld if we take Pharisaic rabbinism as a criterion for what was Judaism at the turn of the era.

G. Vermes has in a couple of books sought to bring Jesus into harmony with Jewish teachers on the Law. Thus, Vermes attempts to bring Jesus' healings on the Sabbath in line with the rabbinic dictum that it is permissible to do work on the seventh day if the purpose is to save life.[28] But now there is no discussion about the likelihood that the man with a withered hand was in danger of losing his life.

In legal matters Jesus was similar to the Essenes in that he referred directly to the Law and not to the 'tradition of men' (Mark 7.7–9). In the Sermon on the Mount

Matthew portrays Jesus as the, or at least *a*, prophet like Moses who gives the right interpretation of the Law at the same time as he breaks down the expostion based on oral tradition: 'You have heard that it was said to the ancients . . . But I say to you . . .' (5.21; etc.). Although the community may be responsible for the antitheses, we may assume that the core of the teaching goes back to Jesus himself. This appears to be quite evident in the case of the prohibition of divorce, where Jesus' commandment supersedes even the written Law.[29]

Employing scriptural proof-texts for his activity to a rather limited extent,[30] Jesus stood forth as a charismatic figure by his own *fiat*.[31] He was different from the 'scribes'.

What about Paul, the most productive author in the New Testament? Paul was a Pharisaic rabbi who kept the Law.[32] Paul is in fact the Pharisee who is best known to us. Now how many descriptions of Pharisaism reckon with Paul? Paradoxically, it might be quite right to exclude a discussion of Paul when considering Pharisaism. Paul said that Christ was the end of the Law and that, although the Law was good,[33] it could not effect salvation.[34] No Pharisaic rabbi said anything similar.

There were other forms of Judaism at the turn of the era than those surveyed above. A text in the Talmud – a huge collection of rabbinic traditions consisting of elaborations upon the Mishnah – says that there were as many as twenty-four *minim*, 'sects' or 'heresies', at the time of the destruction of the temple.[35] Christian sources usually speak about seven sects.[36] The numbers should not be taken literally but seen as conventional (e.g. the number of tribes multipled by two, or the number of priestly classes; the number of days in the week, or the seven planets), but the picture emerging from these categories is that Judaism at the turn of the era was highly complex.

THE TERRITORIES

We also have to consider Galilee and the Galileans, Samaria and the Samaritans, Idumaea and the Idumaeans, and finally the Jewish diaspora. Galilee had a bad reputation. Already Isaiah 9.1 speaks of 'Galilee of the Gentiles'. At the turn of our era John 1.46 repeats the Judaean view that 'nothing good' can come from Galilee. The province was separated from Judaea by Samaria and lay open to Gentile influence from the west, north and east. The most concrete example of such an influence appears to be found in the mosaic depictions of the sun-god Helios in Galilean synagogues. Here the very beginning of the Ten Commandments is torpedoed.

The Galileans were not the only Jews who venerated the material manifestation of the deity under the image of the sun; there are indications to the effect that the Essenes did the same.[37] Moreover, illustrations are not lacking at religious sites in Judaea.[38]

What about Samaria and the Samaritans? Traditionally the origin of the Samaritans is found in 2 Kings 17. This chapter relates that the Israelites in the northern kingdom of Israel were deported by the Assyrian king, who turned the country into one of his provinces (Samaria, the name of the capital, being extended to the entire land). Foreigners being brought into the country grafted a superficial Yahweh cult upon their own religion and continued the worship on the high places made by the

Shomronim, an anachronistic term designating the people in the northern kingdom of Israel.

It has now become clear that the account in 2 Kings 17, being part of the Deuteronomistic centralization programme, is a strong Judaean polemic against the Israelite cult at Bethel.[39] It has been known for a long time that only a small percentage of the population in the northern kingdom was carried away; the colonists who arrived were in a minority and adopted the cult of Yahweh. The Samaritans as they have been known throughout the centuries are devout Yahweh worshippers, sacrificing lambs at Passover on their holy mountain, Mount Gerizim, every year until this date.

Josephus's representation of the Samaritans is highly polemical, and he is just as critical of the Idumaeans. Idumaea was originally a kingdom south of Judaea. The male part of the population had been forcibly circumcised during the Jewish campaign led by the Hasmoneans against the Syrian rulers of Israel in the second century BCE. The Idumaeans had become adherents to the Jerusalem cult, and Herod the Great, an Idumaean, who became the client king of the Romans when they occupied Palestine in 64 BCE, made the Jerusalem temple into a magnificent compound. Still, Josephus (at least in his later works) carefully distinguishes the Idumaeans from the Jews, using the latter term to refer to people of Judaea proper and characterizing Herod the Great as a 'half-Jew'.[40]

What about the Jewish diaspora, the Jews who lived beyond the borders of Palestine? We know that there were temples in other places than Jerusalem. In Palestine itself there was a sanctuary for the biblical God in another place than Jerusalem, for the Samaritans continued to worship God on Mount Gerizim even after their temple had been destroyed.[41]

We also know that there were at least two Jewish temples in Egypt, one in Transjordania, and perhaps even one in Babylonia.[42] The erection of these temples contravenes the stipulation in Deuteronomy that the cult of Yahweh should be centralized in Palestine.[43]

It must also be mentioned that the synagogues in the diaspora had pictures. The synagogue in Dura-Europos in Mesopotamia is particularly famous because of its many magnificent illustrations of biblical scenes.[44]

THE VENERATION OF YAHWEH

It appears that it is not easy to decide what constituted Judaism and Jewish identity at the turn of the era. As far as I know, no one was labelled as a Jew on the basis of physical characteristics (Egyptians and Arabs were also circumcised). Probably the only criterion we can work by is the answer to the question: Who venerated the god known by the biblical names Yahweh (Greek, *Iaō*), El, Elohim, Sabaoth, and so on? The answer may surprise us, for the god designated by these names was worshipped by Greek and Roman authors, by those who produced the Egyptian magical papyri, by those who made and wore certain amulets, and by some of the Gnostics.

Macrobius, a Platonic philosopher who wrote at the beginning of the fifth century CE, says, 'I declare Iaō to be the highest God of all' (*Saturnalia* I.18).[45] In the magical papyri – written in Greek, Demotic and Coptic – we time and again come across adjurations of 'Lord Iaō', 'Iaō Sabaoth', and the like.[46] In like manner, the divine name 'Iaō' is very popular on magical amulets, where the deity often is depicted as a monstrous figure, for example with the head of a cock, the torso of a man, and a serpentine lower body.[47]

The Gnostics, so called because they stressed the importance of revealed 'knowledge' (*gnōsis*) instead of faith, often spoke derogatorily about the biblical God, whom the Gnostics held to be the god of those who had faith but no *gnōsis*. However, this rule was not one without exceptions. The Church Father and heresiologist Irenaeus (ca. 180) quotes a cultic formula of some Gnostics belonging to the school of Valentinus, an Egyptian Gnostic who lived ca. 140 CE: 'I am redeemed; I am established; and I redeem my soul from this age and from all that comes from it in (or: through) the name of Iaō . . .' (*Against All Heresies* I.21.3). Clearly, Iaō is here the name of a redeeming power.

The same is the case of the Gnostic work *Pistis Sophia* (literally, 'Faith-Wisdom') from the third or fourth century CE. Here we find the 'Little Sabaoth' and the 'Great Sabaoth' as well as the 'Little Iaō' and the 'Great Iaō'.[48] These are all designations of beneficial powers.[49]

The cult of the biblical God had become so diversified – through adoption, adaptation, conversion and intermarriage – that it could no longer be seen as the religion of one single nation. After the conquest of the Near East by Alexander the Great, the national religions disintegrated. The cult of the gods was no longer bound to a particular place and a particular people. This was also the case with the religion of the Jews. The close relationship between the Jewish religion and the Jewish nation is often emphasized,[50] but – as has been pointed out above – the idea of what constituted Judaism and Jewishness varied from group to group. The Law, including the Commandments, was interpreted differently. There were different Jewish sanctuaries, even beyond the borders of the Holy Land. The idea of Jewish nationality was not an invariable one.

Now it must be kept in mind that there were signs of universalism in ancient Israelite religion. The post-exilic prophets looked forward to a time when all peoples would worship in Jerusalem.[51] There was even the idea that Yahweh would be worshipped in other countries.[52]

What about the Jewish sanctuaries outside Palestine? Did non-Jews join in the cult at these places? During the period under Syrian rule in the second century BCE, the 'Highest God of Heavens', identical with the Phoenician Baʿal Shamem and the Greek Zeus Olympios, was worshipped in the Jerusalem temple. Undoubtedly some Jews, finding the biblical God in this theocracy, partook in the cult.[53]

CANONICITY

If Macrobius, the magical texts and gems, and the Gnostics may be seen as representatives of the cult of the biblical God, what are we to make out of the concept of canonicity? There is no indication that Macrobius, the magicians and the Gnostics had a canon similar to the Jewish one. But how are we to understand the concept of canon at the turn of the era? The Writings, the third and last part of the Jewish canon, after the Law and the Prophets, were not clearly defined at that time.

There were also other Jewish writings at the turn of the era – what status did they have? These writings are referred to as apocrypha and pseudepigrapha. Apocryphal books (literally, 'hidden' or 'secret' books) are works that were 'hidden away' because they were found in the Greek translation of the Jewish Bible, which was the version used by the Christians. This group of writings includes important works such as the *Wisdom of Solomon* and *Ecclesiasticus* (the *Wisdom of Jesus ben Sirach*).[54] Now the Greek version of the Jewish Bible (the 'Old Testament' according to the Christians) was the product of Jewish translators working in Alexandria in pre-Christian times. It is anachronistic to call some of the books in this translation 'apocryphal' in a derogatory sense.

Pseudepigrapha are works written under a pseudonym, the name of a famous figure from the history of Israel. Thus, we have books of Adam, books of Enoch, the *Apocalypse of Abraham*, the *Apocalypse of Moses*, and so on. Now the Jewish canon itself contains pseudepigrapha. The book of Daniel is a classic example because it is not written by a prophet who lived at the time of the Babylonian exile, as is claimed in the book itself, but by a Jew who lived under the Hasmonean insurrection against Syrian supremacy in the second century BCE. Even the Torah, the fundamental part of the Jewish canon, is a pseudepigraphic work, for it was not written by Moses.[55]

It appears that there were Jewish groups who held non-biblical works in higher esteem than the books traditionally reckoned as canonical. Thus, there is no indication to the effect that the Qumran-Essenes took Genesis to be more sacred than the book of *Jubilees*, a pseudepigraphic work said to have been written by Moses.

The so-called *Temple Scroll* of the Qumran-Essenes is a kind of deutero-Deuteronomy, but with the significant difference that God himself, and not Moses, addresses the People of Israel. Presumably the *Temple Scroll* had more authority than Deuteronomy.

The revision of Genesis that we find in the book of *Jubilees* and *1 Enoch* may be compared to what is seen in some Gnostic writings. In the *Apocryphon of John* we often come across a flat rejection of 'what Moses said'. This in itself does not mean that the Gnostic apocryphon is non-Jewish: the writing reveals intimate knowledge of the first chapters of Genesis and often offers a counter-interpretation of the actual scriptural passage by referring to another place in the Bible.[56] This is not dissimilar to Jesus' interpretation of the law of divorce: Jesus distinguishes between the fundamental will of God, indicated by Genesis 1.27 and 2.24, on the one hand, and the will of God as expressed by the law-giver Moses, as found in Deuteronomy 24.1, on the other.

We should also bear in mind that there were stages of transition in the history of Gnosticism. In the so-called book of Baruch by a Gnostic called Justin,[57] we find a revision of the first chapters of Genesis, but here the gist of the biblical narrative has been maintained. Justin the Gnostic teaches that the creator god, Elohim by name, was originally separated from the highest God, the 'Good', but was no evil figure. Elohim is the first to be let into heaven, from where he sends out saviours to humankind so that others can make the same ascent as he did. The serpent is no incarnation of the saviour, as is the case in the *Apocryphon of John*. The eating from the Tree of Knowledge is still seen as a sin, not as a means of obtaining *gnōsis*, as is the case in the *Apocryphon of John*.

TERMINOLOGICAL QUESTIONS; CONCLUSION

It ought to be clear that we are in need of a terminology that is able to distinguish between the multifaceted Judaism at the turn of the era and the form of Jewish religion today. The term 'Late Judaism' (*Spätjudentum*) used for Judaism at the turn of the era is ridiculous. Judaism cannot be said to have been in throes for the last 2,000 years. Moreover, the term implies that Israelite religion *before* the turn of the era is to be called 'Judaism', but this is not appropriate if we compare that form of religion to modern Judaism.

A somewhat better term is 'Ancient Judaism', but this implies that there is a close relationship to Jewish religion in our times. Pharisaic rabbinism is taken as a gauge for the identification of Judaism and seen as the legitimate heir of 'Ancient Judaism'.[58]

The elaborate term 'Israelite religion during the time of the second temple' focuses too strongly on the destruction of the temple in 70 CE as a watershed. There were Jewish groups who did not assign much significance to the temple.

The term 'Late Israelite Religion' is fortunate in so far as it implies a connection with the ancient Hebrew religion and suggests that the stage is set for something new. However, the adjective 'Israelite' is somewhat unfortunate because of its ethnic connotations. It has been shown above that people of the Hebrew tribe were not the only ones who worshipped the biblical God. The best term for Judaism at the turn of the era is 'Yahwism at the turn of the era'.

NOTES

1 On the problem of Jewish identity, see R. Posner, 'Halakhic Definitions', in 'Jew', *Encyclopaedia Judaica* (Jerusalem 1971), 10.23ff.
2 See H. Danby (trans.), *The Mishnah* (Oxford 1933 and reprints).
3 Scholars have questioned if there runs a direct line from the Pharisees to the later rabbis. It is true that the rabbis never refer to their forerunners as 'Pharisees', but by names such as *Haberim*, 'Associates', and *Hakamim*, 'Sages'. However, it would be wrong to conclude that there was no connection whatsoever between the Pharisees mentioned in the New Testament and the later rabbis. On this question, see J. Neusner, *The Rabbinic Traditions about the Pharisees* (Leiden 1971); E. Rivkin, *The Hidden Revolution* (London 1975).
4 See Matt 13.52; Luke 11.45–6.
5 The term 'rabbi' is obviously at the root of the frequent Synoptic term *didaskalos*, 'teacher', used of Jesus. See the article by K. H. Rengstorft in *TDNT* 4.421ff., 429ff.; R. Riesner, *Jesus als Lehrer* (Tübingen 1981).
6 On this question, see J. W. Bowker, *Jesus and the Pharisees* (Cambridge 1973).
7 The linchpins were Exod 19.6 and Lev 19.2. The party of the Pharisees took its beginning from the ranks of the *Hasidim*, the 'Pious Ones', who supported the Hasmoneans (Maccabees) in the insurrection against Syrian rule in the second century BCE; see 1 Macc 2.42–3. Later, however, the 'Pious Ones' turned against the Hasmonean rulers who usurped the high priestly office; see Josephus, *Antiquitates* 13.171ff., 288ff. See the discussion by R. Meyer, 'Tradition und Neuschöpfung im antiken Judentum', *Berichte über die Verhandlungen der Sächsischen Akademie . . . zu Leipzig* 110/2 (1965), 18ff., 44ff. Cf. below, n. 21.
8 See E. P. Sanders, *Paul and Palestinian Judaism* (London 1977), 152ff.
9 For the *middoth*, see C. K. Barrett, *The New Testament Background: Selected Documents* (2nd edn, San Francisco 1989).

10 See *b. 'Abod Zar.* 58b; *b. Menah.* 65a.

11 See *b. Sota* 48b; *b. Sanh.* 11a.

12 See *m. Abot* 1.1.

13 On the work of the rabbis, see J. Neusner, *The Oral Torah* (San Francisco 1986).

14 See J. Neusner, *An Introduction to Judaism* (Louisville 1991), 462 on the Pharisees and 464 on the Sadducees.

15 See *Berakhot* 9.5 (variant); *Erubin* 6.2; *Hagigah* 1.4; *Makkoth* 1.6; *Yadaim* 4.6, 7; etc.

16 It was of importance to the Sadducees that Jerusalem should obtain the status of a *polis*, an autonomous city state. A *polis* was exempt from paying taxes to the central government and supplying military troops. Situated at the crossroads where trading routes met, the *poleis* became prosperous cities. The priestly as well as the lay Sadducees would profit if Jerusalem became a *polis*: if the city became an autonomous state (as actually was the case for a short time), non-Jewish people would worship their God in Jerusalem and pay taxes to the temple. On Sadduceeism, see W. Buehler, *The Pre-Herodian War and Social Debate* (Basel 1974).

17 Josephus described himself as one 'skilled in divining the meaning of the ambiguous utterances of the Diety' (*Bellum* 3.352). Perhaps he was reaching back to Jeremiah; see M. Hadas-Lebel, *Flavius Josephus* (New York 1989), 105, 175–8.

18 On the Zealots, see M. Hengel, *Die Zeloten* (Leiden 1961).

19 See especially T. S. Peall, *Josephus' Description of the Essenes Illustrated by the Dead Sea Scrolls* (Cambridge 1988).

20 For the scholarly consensus that the Qumran people were Essenes, see J. H. Charlesworth, 'Qumran Scrolls and a Critical Consensus', in *Jesus and the Dead Sea Scrolls* (ed. J. H. Charlesworth, New York 1993), xxxi–vii.

21 The Essenes thus had basically the same origin as the party of the Pharisees (cf. above, n. 7). See already F. M. Cross, Jr, *The Ancient Library of Qumran and Modern Biblical Studies* (London 1958), 107 n. 66; J. Carmignac, 'Les éléments historiques des "Hymnes" de Qumran', *Revue Qumran* 2 (1959/60), 20–1. The Qumran-Essenes, however, said that they had 'separated' (*parashnu*) from the people at large (4Q MMT, C7; cf. the interpretation of Isa 40.3 in 1Q S 8.13–14; 9.20; and see also 4Q p Ps 37.3, 1).

  There was perhaps an Essene enclave in Jerusalem; see R. Riesner, 'Jesus, the Primitive Community and the Essene Quarter of Jerusalem', in *Jesus and the Dead Sea Scrolls* (ed. Charlesworth), 198–234. The Jerusalem Essenes may be identified with the 'Herodians' mentioned in Mark 3.6 and 12.13. Josephus (*Ant.* 15.373ff.) relates that the Essenes were favoured by Herod the Great, during whose reign Qumran was not inhabited. See R. de Vaux, *Archaeology of the Dead Sea Scrolls* (London 1973), 21–3.

22 The leaders of the Qumran-Essenes would seem to have been priests who would not support the Hasmoneans (Maccabees) when the latter usurped the high priestly office. For the expectation of the restoration of the temple cult under a just priesthood, see 1Q M 2.1ff.; 11Q Temple. Cf. 4Q MMT, B12.26–7, describing the present priesthood as unrighteous.

23 Cf. 4Q MMT, B77 and C10–12: only the written Law is to be invoked; there is no collection comparable to the rabbinic *halakoth*, which were arrived at by oral tradition and majority vote.

24 See Mark 12.18–27; Acts 23.8; Josephus, *Ant.* 13.173; 18.17. Josephus uses the term *heimarmené* to denote the Essene belief that God has foreordained everything. The word, meaning 'fate', is not a happy one, but it was well known in the Hellenistic world.

  According to Acts 23.8, the Sadducees also said that there is neither angel nor spirit. This is quite incomprehensible if taken to mean that they denied the belief in angels, for the Sadducees accepted the Pentateuch. D. Daube, 'On Acts 23: Sadducees and Angels', *JBL* 109 (1990), 493–7, has suggested that the Sadducees only denied the attested belief that a good person spent the span between death and resurrection in the mode of angel of spirit.

25 See 1Q S 4.2ff.; 3.15–16; 4Q MMT, C32–3.

26 See 12.3, 10.

27 The common translation 'the Teacher of Righteousness' is a misnomer.

28 See Vermes, *The Religion of Jesus the Jew* (London 1993), 22–3, discussing Mark 3.1–6, etc.

29 See Deut 24.1. Vermes, 33, discussing Jesus' view on the law of divorce. Now Mark 10.6–12 and 1 Cor 7.10 show clearly that divorce in itself and not 'remarriage following divorce'

fundamentally conflicts with Jesus' view on marriage. Matt 5.32 does not say anything else than that the man cannot be blamed for driving the woman to adultery by divorcing her in the case where she already has been unfaithful. However, even this is an addition to Jesus' words, as is seen from the parallel in Luke 16.18. Matt 19.9 goes further and allows for divorce and remarriage in the case of unfaithfulness. There is no allowance for this in Matthew's source, Mark 10.11–12.

30 See Mark 2.25–6.

31 See Mark 1.21–2, 27; 10.37; etc.

32 See e.g. Phil 3.3–6. Cf. Acts 21.24–6; 23.6.

33 See Rom 7.12.

34 See e.g. Rom 10.4 and, above all, the letter to the Galatians, especially ch. 3. On Paul's view of the Law, see E. P. Sanders, *Paul, the Law and the Jewish People* (Philadelphia 1983); H. Hübner, *Law in Paul's Thought* (Edinburgh 1983).

35 See *p. Sanh.* 10.5.

36 See the survey by J. Fossum, 'Social and Institutional Conditions for Early Jewish and Christian Interpretation of the Hebrew Bible with Special Regard to Religious Groups and Sects', in *Hebrew Bible/Old Testament: The History of Its Interpretation* (ed. M. Sæbø et al.; 1/1 Göttingen 1996), 240–3.

37 Josephus (*Bell.* 2.128–9) avers that the Essenes prayed at dawn, as if entreating the sun to rise. On Jewish sun worship at the turn of the era, see M. Smith, 'Helios in Palestine', *ErIsr* 16 (1982), 199–214.

38 See S. L. Y. Rahmani et al., 'The Tomb of Jason', *'Atiqot* 4 (1964), 1–40. The tomb of Jason, probably a Sadducee, dates from about 80 BCE and contains depictions of ships.

39 On the origin of the Samaritans and their religion, see F. Dexinger, 'Der Ursprung der Samaritaner im Spiegel der frühen Quellen', in *Die Samaritaner* (ed. F. Dexinger and R. Pummer, Darmstadt 1992), 67–140.

40 Josephus characterizes Herod in *Ant.* 14.152. The people of Iturea north of Galilee would also seem to have been coerced to convert under the Hasmonean ruler John Hyrcanus; see Josephus, *Bell.* 1.68–9 and *Ant.* 13.299, and further E. Bammel, Ἀρχιερεὺς προφητεύων *TLZ* 79 (1954), 351–6.

41 We might ask if the Samaritans really had a temple on Mount Gerizim; their sanctum may have been a 'high place'.

42 About the temple and religion of the Jews on the island of Elephantine in the Nile, see A. Vincent, *La Religion des Judéo-Araméens d'Eléphantine* (Paris 1937); and B. Porten, *The Archives from Elephantine: The Life of an Ancient Jewish Military Colony* (Berkeley 1968). About the temple at Leontopolis in Egypt, see C. T. R. Hayward, 'The Jewish Temple at Leontopolis: A Reconsideration ', *JJS* 33 (1982), 429 ff. On the existence of a Jewish temple in Transjordanian Ammanitis, see L. H. Vincent, 'La Palestine dans les papyrus Ptolémaïques de Gerza', *RB* 29 (1920), 198–202, and especially P. W. Lapp, 'The Second and Third Campaigns at ʿArâq el-ʾEmir', *BASOR* 171 (1963), 8–39. On the possibility of the existence of a Jewish temple in Babylonia, see L. E. Browne, 'A Jewish Sanctuary in Babylonia', *JTS* 17 (1916), 400ff.

Isa 19.19 may allude to the existence of an early Jewish temple in Egypt, probably in Thmuis; see J. Harmatta, 'Irano-Aramaica, zur Geschichte des frühhellenistischen Judentums in Ägypten', *Acta antiqua* 7 (1959), 404–9. There may even have been some kind of Jewish temple at Antioch; see Josephus, *Bell.* 7.44–5.

43 On the question whether the actual place was Gerizim or Zion, see Fossum 1996: 244f.

44 On the Dura-Europos synagogue, see J. Guttmann (ed.), *The Dura-Europos Synagogue: A Re-Evaluation (1932–72)* (Missoula 1973).

45 Similar declarations often occur in texts of a syncretistic character where the proper name of the highest god is of no importance; see M. Hengel, *Judentum und Hellenismus* (3rd edn, Tübingen 1988), 473ff. Still, the fact that the name of Iaō does occur in such texts cannot be considered insignificant.

46 See H. D. Betz (ed.), *The Greek Magical Papyri in Translation* (2nd edn, Chicago 1992); M. Meyer and R. Smith (eds), *Ancient Christian Magic: Coptic Texts of Ritual Power* (San Francisco 1994).

47 On the name of Iaō in magic, see R. Ganschinietz, 'Iaō', *Pauly-Wissowa Realencyklopädie der classischen Altertumswissenschaft* 9 (2nd edn, Stuttgart 1914), 698–721. On amulets, see especially C. W. King, *The Gnostics and Their Remains* (London 1864 and reprints).

48 On the 'Little Iaō', see ch.7. On the 'Little Sabaoth', see especially chs 137 and 147. On the 'Great Iaō' and the 'Great Sabaoth', see chs 63 and 140. For the work *Pistis Sophia*, see C. Schmidt and V. MacDermot (trans.), *The Pistis Sophia* (Leiden 1978).

49 The name 'Little Iaō' derives from the Jewish term, the 'Little Yahweh', the special angel who was given God's own name and sent to lead the Hebrews from Egypt to the Promised Land; see Exod 23.21 and further H. Odeberg (ed. and trans.), *3 Enoch* (Cambridge 1928, repr. New York 1973), Part I, 33–4, and J. Fossum, 'Kyrios Jesus as the Angel of the Lord in Jude 5–7', *NTS* 33 (1987), 226–43.

50 See Hengel 1988, *passim*, especially the summary on 560.

51 See e.g. Isa 56.7; Micah 4.1–2; 7.12.

52 See Zeph 2.11. Cf. already Isa 19.19.

53 See Hengel 1988: 486ff., 503ff., and especially 515ff., 555f. As an early remarkable example of Israelite universalism we may cite Isa 45.1, where the prophet hails the Persian king Cyrus as the Messiah on account of the fact that Cyrus had conquered Babylon and allowed the exiled Judaeans to return home. Traditionally the Messiah was seen as an anointed Israelite king who would rule from Jerusalem.

54 They are part of the Catholic canon, while the Protestants follow the Jews.

55 See e.g. the claim in Deut 31.24.

56 For the *Apocryphon of John*, see B. Layton (trans. with introductions and annotations), *The Gnostic Scriptures* (Garden City 1987), 23–51. On the Gnostic interpretation of scripture, see B. Pearson, 'Use, Authority and Exegesis of Mikra in Gnostic Literature', in *Mikra* (Assen 1988), 635–52.

57 See Hippolytus, *Refutations of All Heresies* V.26.1–27.5 (introduced and trans. E. Haenchen, in W. Foerster (ed.), *Gnosis 1*; ET ed. R. McL. Wilson, Oxford 1972), 48–58.

58 A desperate attempt to establish a new terminology is made by G. Boccaccini, *Middle Judaism: Jewish Thought 300 B.C.E. to 200 C.E.* (Minneapolis 1991). The title implies that there was a Judaism before 300 BCE that was continued after 200 CE. The mistakes of 'Late Judaism' and 'Ancient Judaism' are combined. Confusingly, Boccaccini also speaks of Christianity as one of the 'Judaisms of *modern* times' (15 *et passim*; italics mine). When Paul said that the observance of the Law had been abrogated by the sacrifical death of Christ, he was not simply expressing a 'different way of understanding the Law' (Boccaccini 1991: 17).

CHAPTER THIRTY-FIVE

THE FIRST CHURCHES
Social life

—— •◆• ——

Justin J. Meggitt

PROBLEMS

The social life of the first churches has been the subject of considerable debate over the last few decades (see Horrell 1999). Its study raises an array of problems, primarily of definition, interpretation and context, that have proved difficult to resolve. It is tempting to bypass these and go straight to the more concrete business of describing this aspect of early Christian existence but to do so involves making a host of implicit assumptions, which, if left unexamined, invalidate any reconstructions we might offer. Although attending to such critical preoccupations might seem to distance us from the past everyday reality that is the object of our study, nonetheless we must begin by addressing these initial difficulties, however abstract.

Firstly, we are faced with the problem of definition. How should we define 'social life' and what limitations does our definition impose? In what follows I shall assume that the 'social life' of the early Christians consists of their major interactions, both with their co-religionists and with others, and more specifically, those recurrent interactions that they considered significant, such as those between wives and husbands, or children and parents, or between one church member and another. But, while such a simple definition will do for our purposes, it will appear unhelpfully narrow to some and we should not forget that such social interactions shaped, and were shaped by, additional aspects of human life (such as those essentially biological, economic, legal, cultural or religious).

Secondly, there is the problem of translation, though not so much of words but of concepts. There is nothing self-evident, ahistorical or universal about how human beings organize themselves socially. Consequently, it is not immediately obvious how we should go about describing the interactions of the early Christians. Even using the term 'family' to describe the central domestic unit common at the time, and within which most significant interactions took place, is fraught with problems (see Moxnes 1997) given that primary social relationships in this period included those with individuals not connected by descent or marriage (see below). So how can we interpret the social interactions that took place in the first churches in a way that retains, as far as possible, the meanings and associations that they had within the original contexts and yet still makes some sense to us today? How do we prevent ourselves falling victim to anachronism or ethnocentrism in our analysis? Of too readily interpreting the social realities of the first Christians in the light of our own?

One means of avoiding these perils that has become particularly influential among some New Testament scholars today, largely as a consequence of the work of Malina (see esp. Malina 1981), is to develop generic models from cross-cultural readings of other comparable societies (in particular, the contemporary or near-contemporary Mediterranean). These then provide ways of ordering social data, explaining the operation of social processes, and the presence of certain social forms, and can be applied to the disparate evidence we can glean from the New Testament texts to allow us to make sense of the limited information we possess.

Such an approach has its advantages, perhaps the greatest being that its practitioners put their cards clearly on the table, and seek to stop their interpretations being plagued by implicit assumptions (Esler 1994: 12–13). However, such generic model-making also has significant weakness (for criticisms, see Garrett 1992; Meggitt 1998; Horrell 1999). It ignores or downplays the diverse and distinctive social forms and practices of inhabitants of different cultures within the eastern Mediterranean (the region within which Christianity first emerged), skating over significant differences (such as those between the permissible sexual activity of married men or the legal capacity of women – see below). Such an approach is also predicated upon a misplaced belief in the essential continuity between ancient and contemporary Mediterranean social life, ignoring, for example, evidence of striking discontinuity, such as that afforded by slavery, a complicated and complicating social phenomenon unknown in the region today but prominent in the early Roman Empire in which the first Christians lived. In addition, such model-making encourages a rather narrow perception of the nature of social life *per se*, as something primarily fixed and uncontested, with, as it were, all ancient Mediterranean people, whatever their geographical, ethnic, religious or class differences, reading from the same script and acting accordingly, with no room for conflict, change, nor the 'moments and processes that bring surprise, uncertainty, ambiguity, and paradox', which are characteristic features of human social existence (Fenn 1987: 98). The reassuring fit between the models created and early Christian data, something often held to justify the validity of the approach by its practitioners, is often, unfortunately, misleading, and regularly achieved by either applying a Procrustean bed to the evidence or treating it in the manner of a Rorschach ink blot.

A more fruitful way of dealing with these interpretative problems is to engage in a critical, inductive method, which seeks a dialogue between the past and present, and attempts a dialectical relationship between descriptions and explanations of social life that are given by the actors themselves (sometimes termed 'emic' explanations) and those given by modern interpreters (referred to as 'etic'). Such an approach runs the risk of appearing epistemologically naïve, particularly in the current pessimistic intellectual climate (usefully demonstrated by the recent debate between Evans (1997) and Jenkins [1995]). And at its best, its constructions are ultimately provisional, open to constant review and criticism. But, nonetheless, it remains the most helpful way to approach the subject (and is later used to construct the descriptions).

Thirdly, we are faced with the problem of context. Interpreting the evidence demands that we know something about the original context within which it initially made sense and yet we have only a severely restricted knowledge of this: much of our evidence for social practices in this period comes from a very limited range of unrepresentative literary sources of one kind or another, produced by a small elite who were largely unconcerned with life outside their rarefied circles and whose descriptions of social reality are of only limited value given their peculiar ideological and rhetorical preoccupations. This failing is all the more acute because almost all the early Christians came from the undocumented dead, the great mass of non-elite inhabitants of the Eastern Roman Empire (about 99 per cent of the total population; see Meggitt 1998), despite the recent popularity of attempts to argue the contrary (Theissen 1982; Meeks 1983). Consequently we know little about the context within which the first Christians lived. The value of neglected, more representative sources is gradually being recognized and new approaches that can help us construct appropriate, popular contexts within which to make sense of the limited pertinent data (Meggitt 1998) are being developed, but this work is still in its infancy. We should also bear in mind the salutary observation of Garnsey and Saller: what evidence we have 'is limited in quantity and quality. While these deficiencies should not be allowed to determine what historical questions are asked, they do circumscribe the field of questions to which convincing answers can be given' (Garnsey and Saller 1987: 108).

Finally we are faced with a host of more specific problems that need to be addressed if we are to make some sense of early Christian social life. Some of these are familiar to anyone engaged in the critical exegesis of the New Testament. For example, if we are to avoid using the New Testament in a simplistic and homogenizing way we have to make decisions about a host of often interrelated issues, such as the textual and chronological relationships of the documents that make up the New Testament, and their respective authors, genres, sources, redactions, and places of origin. And, as any critical introduction to the New Testament will indicate (e.g. Duling and Perrin 1994), these are not simple decisions to make, particularly as some of the assured results of previous generations of scholars become rather less so. Other problems are perhaps less familiar and are more specific to the subject of this study. For example, when faced with apparent inconsistencies in the social behaviour prescribed by an early Christian text, should we assume that such material comes from different communities, or even different stages in the development of one community (see, e.g., Theissen 1978)? Or is such an argument hopelessly anachronistic (something that may seem inconsistent to us might not have done so to early Christians; indeed it did not do so to the final redactors of the texts). What is the significance of the symbolic language of the first Christians for understanding the social life of the churches? Do the metaphors and analogies drawn from, for example, the household, market or other areas of social life, provide a fruitful source of data for determining their social practices and experiences, or do they reflect literary or oral conventions independent of social realities? Do the central symbols of the new communities (such as their various Christologies) allow us to determine, for example, their social integration or alienation (see, e.g., Meeks 1972), or is it wrong to assume such a fundamental correlation between the symbolic and social (for a useful discussion see Holmberg 1990)? Having touched on a few of the major problems inherent in the subject of our study (and there are, needless to say, plenty more) let us move on to the business of actually describing early Christian social life.

DESCRIPTION

It is helpful to distinguish between the 'public' and 'private' social lives of the members of the first churches, to differentiate between, for example, those interactions they had with the governing authorities of their day or at markets or festivals or games, and those that occurred within their households or their churches. Although, having said this, we should also be aware that there was a variety of ways that 'public' and 'private' could be conceptualized within the Empire (in fact some of these were themselves in a process of transition in this period; Wallace-Hadrill 1998). None coincide very closely with modern assumptions (e.g. some rooms within private houses could be considered public spaces, open to the uninvited; see, Vitruvius, *On Architecture* 6.5; Mk 14:3–9 and par.; 1 Cor. 14:23; Veyne 1987; Wallace-Hadrill 1988; Grahame 1997).

Social life: public

Authorities

The authorities encountered by the earliest Christians were essentially of two kinds: imperial and Jewish. Christian interactions with both are not easy to characterize.

Although the author of Revelation is unreservedly hostile towards the Roman authorities (Rev. 13 and 17), and suggests that relations with them were limited to persecutions of one kind or another (Rev. 1:9; 2:13; 6:9–11), most other New Testament texts are rather more equivocal and seem to evidence a rather more complicated state of affairs. For example, Paul could call on Christians to *submit* to the Roman authorities (Rom. 13; cf. also 1 Pet. 2:13–14; 1 Tim. 2:1–2; Tit. 3:1), and yet it is evident, from the punishments he suffered at the hands of their representatives (2 Cor. 11:25 – the beating with rods was a specifically Roman punishment), he did not *obey* them, nor, from his language elsewhere (1 Cor. 2:8; 6:1–8; 1 Thess. 5:3; Elliott 1994), did he think very much of them. Likewise the author of Acts of the Apostles depicts Roman rule to be both fair (Acts 25:12) and corrupt (Acts 24:25–6), capable of protecting the early Christians (Acts 27:43) and also of cruelly persecuting them (Acts 16:22). While interactions with the Jewish authorities are portrayed more consistently in a negative light (Mt 10:17; 23:34; Mk 13:9; Lk 12:11; 21:12; Jn 9:22; 12:42; 16.2; Acts 6:12ff.; 1 Cor. 12:24; Gal. 6:12; 1 Thess. 2:14; Rev. 2:9; 3:9) a number of positive depictions of Jewish leaders and institutions (Mk 5:22ff.; 15:43; Lk 2:22ff.; 24:53; John 19.39; Acts 2:46; 3:1; 5:34; 6:7) make it clear that early Christian relationships with these were not always quite so hostile. Indeed difficulties in determining who actually constituted the 'authorities' within Jewish communities at this time and the extent to which the first churches considered themselves part of these communities, make this relationship a particularly difficult one to determine.

But, despite the diversity of different positions articulated in the New Testament nevertheless we can discern a unifying feature to all the interactions between Christians and the authorities of their day, whether imperial or Jewish. The new allegiance of Christians to Jesus and their new or transformed allegiance to God relativized and qualified their former obligations to those in traditional positions of authority. As Acts informs us, Christians could be seen to be proclaiming a different king to Caesar (Acts 17:6–7; cf. Jn 19:12–15) and evidently believed themselves to be obeying 'God rather than men' (Acts 5:29).

Festivals and games

Religious festivals, whether Jewish or pagan, were central to the lives of inhabitants of the eastern Empire, wherever they lived (Sanders 1992; Beard 1998a; Price 1999) as were often closely associated leisure activities, whether Greek (athletics or the theatre) or more distinctively Roman (spectacles or the baths). Palestine was no exception in this respect (Gardiner 1930; Feldman 1993; Toner 1995; Weiss 1999). The part the first Christians played in these public, collective events is difficult to ascertain. However, given that at least some church members took part in regular Jewish and pagan worship (Lk 24:53; Acts 2:46; 3:1; 1 Cor. 10:21; Col. 2:16) it is probably the case that at least a few also participated in festivals in one way of another. A number may also have attended athletic competitions and spectacles. Indeed, athletics provided a rich source of similes and metaphors for early Christian authors (1 Cor. 9:24–7; Phil. 2:16; 3:13–14; Gal. 2:2; 2 Tim. 2:5; 4:8; Heb. 12:1; 1 Pet. 5:4; Pfitzner 1967) although, admittedly, such language had become commonplace by the first century. Attendance at the games may be rather more surprising

Figure 35.1 Seat from the theatre at Miletus. The inscription indicates that this section was reserved for Jews and/or proselytes. Photo Justin J. Meggitt.

Figure 35.2 The entrance of the synagogue at Sardis. Although from a later period, it demonstrates the public prominence of some Jewish communities in the Roman Empire. Photo courtesy of Melanie Wright.

given the part they played in later Christian persecutions and the fact that they were not only extremely violent but regularly presented as re-enactments of pagan myths (as Christians were to become painfully aware when they found themselves starring in such charades before being martyred; Coleman 1990). Yet some Christians, even if a minority, probably watched such events in this early period, given what we can glean from later Christian writers (Tertullian, *On the Spectacles*) and the fact that we know that some Jews, who shared similar religious and moral objections to such activities, certainly did so at this time (see Claudius's letter to the Jews of Alexandria, CPJ 2, n. 153).

Commerce

Although the economies of the eastern Empire were rudimentary and largely unintegrated (Meggitt 1998), nonetheless markets and other collective forms of economic interaction were also a prominent feature of public life in the period. The degree of participation by Christians in these seems to have varied significantly. Some communities preserved teaching in which work was regarded as evidence of a lack of faith (Mt 6:25–33), and something that should be abandoned by those who responded to Jesus' call (Mk 1:19–20), while other churches seem to have had prominent members who played a full part in the economic life of their day and assumed that others should do likewise (1 Cor. 9:6; Eph. 4:28; Acts 16:14; 18:3; cf. Rev. 13:17).

However, all New Testament traditions, despite their considerable differences, make relative the importance of material possessions (Mt 6:19–21; Lk 12:13–21; 1 Tim. 6:10; Heb. 13:5), and consequently the importance of commercial interactions (1 Cor. 7:30–1; Jas 4:13–17). A few communities also radically critiqued economic behaviour of the time (Mk 10:17–31; and par.; Jas 5:1–6; Rev. 17–19:5), and initiated new models of economic interactions, rooted in the mutualism of the Christian gospel (Meggitt 1998; Swartley 1998).

None of the earliest Christian communities existed in literal seclusion from wider society, although psychologically many may have felt considerable distance from their non-Christian neighbours (e.g. Rev. 6:15; 19:18). Although the degree to which Christians interacted with those outside no doubt varied from location to location (Barclay 1992), and between different groups within churches, it seems that in day-to-day terms, early Christians continued to live within society, taking an active, if critical and sometimes limited, part in its public life in its various manifestations.

Social life: private

The household

A wide variety of ways of conceptualizing and defining the primary social unit existed in the world in which Christianity emerged, and it is important, as we have already noted, to stress that none coincides with modern notations of the family (see, e.g., Peskowitz 1993; Saller 1994). Indeed, it is largely misleading to use the term 'family' for this period. 'Household' is a more useful label to employ because, despite the significant differences between the cultures of the eastern Empire, the primary domestic unit was considered to consist not only of those individuals related to one another by descent, marriage or adoption but also others united by common residence and consumption. The near-universal practice of slavery, common to virtually every ethnic and economic group within the Empire (see, e.g., Martin 1993; Garnsey 1996; Meggitt 1998) was the major cause of this unusual feature of ancient domestic life. However, other categories of individuals were included within the primary social unit, in addition to slaves, such as hired workers, freed slaves, friends, lodgers and others.

Not all households were, by any means, the same. What evidence we have seems to point to a diversity of potential configurations, a consequence of a variety of factors including different ethnic, religious, economic and demographic influences. They could be as limited in size as one or two people (as we see in the Pseudo-Virgilian poem *Moretum*) or as extensive as the household of Herod the Great or a Roman emperor. Households could include families of one kind or another, whether nuclear, lone parent, extended, multiple or reconstituted (though it should be noted that the limitations of mortality and fertility meant that these could consist of only one or two generations; Bagnall and Frier 1994). But some did not (in the *Moretum* the household consists of one free and one enslaved person). Power could, at one extreme, be monopolized by a male patriarch, the oldest living male ascendent, such as the Roman *paterfamilias*, while at the other it was not unknown for a single autonomous woman to have fundamental authority within the unit (Lydia [Acts 16:15], Nympha

[Col. 4:15], Chloe [1 Cor. 1:11] and Mary [Mk 6:3] provide examples of this phenomenon) and there was also a myriad of variations in between.

This diversity, which appears to have been common throughout the Empire, has become clear from recent studies of documentary papyri and epigraphic sources. It has also become evident as we recognize the limitations on actual, as opposed to idealized, household forms imposed by such demographic variables as age at marriage, life expectancy and the prevalence of divorce, in addition to cultural, social and legal constraints (see Saller and Shaw 1984; Lewis 1989; Bagnall and Frier 1994; Martin 1996; Scheidel 1996).

Despite the almost bewildering array of permutations we can discern a couple of characteristics common to most households at the time. Popular literature and epigraphic sources for the period, both Greek, Roman and Jewish (see, e.g., Lattimore 1942; Horbury and Noy 1992; Noy 1993, 1995; Hansen 1998) indicate, perhaps unsurprisingly, that a male dominated most households, though his authority did not equate with that of the all-powerful patriarch, which was of such ideological significance for many elite authors in the Empire (Gaius, *Institutes* 1.55; Dionysius of Halicarnassus 2:26–7; Josephus, *Against Apion* 2. 199–208). They also, perhaps more surprisingly, show that kinship relationships, much beyond the most immediate, were of marginal consequence to most people (Garnsey and Saller 1987: 129). There was little real concern for clans, tribes or other broader associations based on kinship (genealogies were associated with only a small number of untypical individuals, and often fabricated *a posterioi* to legitimate their authority (as was probably the case with Jesus, e.g. Mt 1 and Lk 3). Instead the same limited number of household relationships preoccupied individuals in the early Empire: those between husbands and wives, parents and children, masters and slaves.

Given the significant interest in this triad of primary relationships in the household, which were also, as we shall see, of major concern to early Christians, these will be the focus or our study. But before we examine these in detail it is important to make some general remarks about the household in earliest Christianity, so that by concentrating on the parts, we do not overlook the unusual features of the whole.

The household in early Christianity

GENERAL REMARKS

There are significant differences within the New Testament over attitudes towards the primary social unit, as has been noted in a number of recent studies (e.g. Barton 1994; Carter 1994; Osiek and Balch 1997). On the one hand, the household is given a special place in early Christian life. Traditional household obligations were confirmed (see, e.g., the affirmation of the fifth commandment [Ex. 20:12 / Deut. 5:16] in Mk 7:10; 10:19 and par.) and careful attention is paid to its core relationships, as is particularly evident in the units of ethical parenesis termed 'houselists' (Eph. 5:22 – 6:9; Col. 3:18 – 4:1; 1 Pet. 2:18 – 3:7; cf. also 1 Tim. 2:8–15; 6:1–2; Tit. 2:1–10; *Didache* 4:9–11; *Barnabas* 19:5–7; *1 Clem.* 21:6–9; Ignatius, *Pol.* 4:1 – 5:2; Polycarp, *Phil.* 4:2–3; Dunn 1996). Indeed, the traditional household was the social unit from which the first churches were constructed and the primary means by which the new faith was transmitted (Rom. 16:10–11; 1 Cor. 1:16; 16:15, 19; Col. 4:15; 2 Tim. 1:16; 4:19; Philm; Acts 2:46; 5:42; cf. also Acts 10:24ff.; 16:15; 16:33; 18:8) and it is not unsurprising that the churches could even refer to themselves as the household of God (Gal. 6:10; Eph. 2:19; 1 Tim. 3:15; Heb. 3:2–6; 1 Pet. 4:17), albeit following precedents in the Jewish Bible (e.g. Num. 12:7).

However, the significance of the conventional household was also made radically relative and some traditions even called for the destruction of its primary relationships (e.g. Mt 10:35–7; Lk 12:53; 14:26; cf. also Mt 19:29; Mk 10:29–30; Lk 18:29; Mt 8:22; Lk 9:60; Mt 10:21; Mk 13:12–13) and their replacement by relationships built solely upon common faith (Mt 12:46–50; Mk 3:31–5; Lk 8:19–21). Indeed, in Luke Christians are actually told to *hate* their families (14:26).

This hostility towards the household was not in itself distinctive at the time (e.g. Josephus, *War* 2.120–1; Barton 1997) and even some of the most negative language had its precedents (the demand to hate one's family echoes traditional calls to arms; Klassen 1999: 387). However, the justification provided by the early Christians for such behaviour, the primacy of allegiance to Jesus and the gospel over all other earthly ties (Mk 1:16–20; 2:13–14 and par.), was most certainly unique. The critique of the power of the leading male within the household, implicit in the vision, ascribed to Jesus, of a future in which fathers no longer had a role (Mk 10:29–30; cf. also Mt 23:9–10; Francis 1996), was also striking.

With these observations in mind, and while paying attention to the original contexts against which these domestic interactions were played out, let us now examine the major relationships within early Christian households.

WIFE AND HUSBAND

The relationship between a wife and a husband was understood very differently in various cultures in the early Empire (however one wishes to distinguish them). Nonetheless, as is clear from a host of evidence from the period, epigraphic, architectural, legal, literary and other, it was almost universally perceived to be an unequal one in which the wife was expected to be subordinate to the husband. However, the degree of inequality varied significantly in different cultures and classes. For example, most Roman wives had significantly more legal, social and financial autonomy than elite Greek wives, at least on mainland Greece, though rather less than most in Egypt (Henry 1989; Gardner 1991; Rowlandson 1998). The wife–husband relationship was also essentially a contractual relationship that was often viewed as provisional, even though the notion of a single partner throughout life became something of an ideal in the first century (Dixon 1992).

The emotional lives of the married are difficult to reconstruct in any epoch (Anderson 1980), particularly in such a poorly documented one, but there are enough literary and epigraphic remains, however formulaic, to demonstrate that mutual affection was not unusual or unexpected within marriage (see, e.g., Apuleius's *Apologia* or Pliny the Younger's remarks in his *Epistles* about his wife Calpurnia); indeed, if Veyne (1978) is correct it was becoming an increasingly common feature of such relationships in this period. There also seems to have been considerable congruence in the qualities expected in a partner in different cultures within the Eastern Empire. For example, piety, fidelity, fecundity, self-sacrifice, and prudence are almost universally praised in the epitaphs of wives, Greek, Roman, Jewish or other, throughout the region (Lattimore 1942).

Although Jews had much in common with their neighbours when it came to their understanding of marriage, they were distinctive in a number of ways. They were, for example, unusual in the restrictions they placed on the permitted sexual activity of husbands (compare, e.g., Artemidorus, *Oneirocritica* 1.78, with Josephus, *Against Apion* 2.199) and their practice of endogamy (Deut. 7:3; Num. 25:1–9; Josephus, *Antiquities* 4.131–55). The fact that Jews at the time were only allowed to initiate divorce if they were male (following Deut 24:1–4) was also distinctive (women could, e.g., initiate divorce under Roman law) as was their practice of polygamy, which seems to have continued to be practised by at least some Jews in this period, and not just untypical individuals such as Herod the Great (Josephus, *War* 1.477ff.; Kokkinos 1998), as has become clear from the recently published second-century Babatha archives (Lewis et al. 1989). (Being a wife in such a polygamous marriage did not necessarily cause a woman to lose all economic or social power. Babatha was a second wife in a polygamous second marriage but seems to have exercised considerable economic independence, loaning money, in her own right, to her new husband.)

Against this background relationships between spouses in the first churches appear unusual in a number of ways. Perhaps most obviously, the hostility to divorce, a feature of the ethical praxis of most early churches (Mt 5:31–2; 19:3–9; Mk 10:2–12; Lk 16:18; 1 Cor. 7:10–11), was striking in the context of the first century. This took two slightly different forms in the earliest material (although both replace the biblical law of divorce (Deut. 24:1–4) with an argument for monogamy based on the depiction of marriage in Genesis 2:24 (Keener 1991)). In the Markan form (Mk 10:2–12, which also seems to be found in Lk 16:18 and 1 Cor. 7:10–11) divorce is not allowed under any circumstances (an unusual position in the context of the day, though not completely unparalleled). While in Matthew divorce is allowed but solely on the grounds of the wife's adultery (Mt 5:32; 19:3–9) and remarriage is prohibited (divorced men were to become 'eunuchs for the kingdom', Mt 19:12). Although both forms are not unparalleled in literature of the time (the former resembles the position found in some Qumran literature, 11Q 19 and CD 4.20–1, the latter that ascribed to the rabbi Shammai) this would have appeared a very distinctive position for the churches to hold. Paul's addition to the tradition he received in this area, allowing divorce but only if it is instigated by an unbelieving spouse (1 Cor. 7:12–16), or perhaps a believing wife (1 Cor. 7:11a) as long as she did not seek to have a subsequent marriage until the death of the first partner (1 Cor. 7:39), would have done little to diminish this.

The practice of endogamy, only entering into marriage with other believers (1 Cor. 7:39; 2 Cor. 6:14 – 7:1), and the limitation of permissible sexual activity to marriage (1 Cor. 7:2–9, 36–8; 1 Thess. 4:3–8; Heb. 13:4; cf. 1 Cor. 6:12–20), were rather less unusual and had clear parallels in mainstream Judaism, although to gentiles they would have appeared somewhat strange. Monogamy (1 Tim. 3:2, 12) would have appeared less so as it was the norm within the Empire. The fact that

Christianity encouraged affection between spouses (Eph. 5:33) was not, as is clear from the above, an innovation; it was unusual in the justification given for such sentiments (the work and experience of Christ, e.g. Eph. 5:21–33) and in its mutual quality, at least in the earliest period (something particularly evident in 1 Cor. 7), which is unprecedented in the extent to which it addresses both partners in the marriage relationship and gives them the same obligations.

As with all the core relationships in the household, the bond between the married couple was also made radically relative in early Christian communities. Indeed, it could be discouraged in some, though such hostility was not predicated upon a negative view of sexual relations in this early period but was maintained for more pragmatic reasons: the need to attend to the concerns of a spouse, it was argued, could distract a believer from wholehearted service to the gospel (1 Cor. 7: 32–4; though cf. 1 Tim. 5:14). The possibility of opting out of marriage could present an attractive opportunity to many church members, particularly women, for whom marriage often resulted in the loss of a significant degree of autonomy, as can be seen, for example, in later apocryphal traditions such as the popular *Acts of Paul and Thecla*.

CHILD AND PARENT

There was significant diversity in the relationship between children and parents in the Roman Empire during this period. There was also considerable paradox. For example, Romans, Greeks and most other inhabitants of the eastern Empire practised exposure, infanticide and abortion as a means of limiting family size (see esp. Harris 1982, 1994). Jews were almost unique in not doing this (Tacitus, *Histories* 5.5, Josephus, *Against Apion* 2.202; Ex. 21:22–5; cf. also Diodorus Siculus 1.80). Such acts were carried out with a casualness and callousness that is at times chilling (e.g. a romantic letter includes the following admonition to a wife from a husband: 'If you chance to bear a child, and it is a boy, let it be; if it is a girl, cast it out' [POxy 4.744]). For those who were lucky enough to survive infancy, a significant degree of violence accompanied their rearing, whatever their status, meted out by parents, guardians, owners or their representatives. Offspring in antiquity were understood as inferiors in a strongly authoritarian, and often brutal, relationship (Shaw 1987) in which adults sought to tame children. In modern Western societies, which understand 'childhood' as a distinct, vulnerable stage in the psychological and social development of a human being (a recent perspective, Kleijwegt 1991), such behaviour is shocking and difficult to comprehend. It is all the more bewildering when it is observed that many parents and children nonetheless forged relationships characterized by deep affection (Hallett 1984; Golden 1988; Currie 1993).

The early Christians, despite affirming traditional, autocratic relationships between parents and children (Mk 7:10; 10.17 and par; 14.36; Rom. 1:30; Eph. 6:1; Col. 3:20; 2 Tim. 3:2; Heb. 5:8; 12:9), gave a new status to children, including them, along with other powerless groups in society, such as the sick and the poor, at the centre of the new faith. This unusual concern probably originated with the historical Jesus whose interest in children was obviously considered striking by his contemporaries (Mt 19:13–15; Mk 10:13–16; Lk 18: 15–17) but also appears to have been sustained in later traditions. For example, rather surprisingly, children are included in the ethical advice found in Colossians 3:20 and Ephesians 6:1–4, where they are valued as active moral agents and the parent–child relationship itself is perceived as one of mutual submission. It is also evident in the wide use made of similes, metaphors and forms of address drawn from the world of childhood in early Christian literature (Mt 7:9–11; 11:16–19, 25; 18:1–7; 19:13–15; Mk 9:33–7, 42; 10:13–16; Lk 7:31–5; 9:46–8; 11:11–13; 17:1–2; 18:15–17; Jn 1:12; 12:26; 13:33; Rom. 8:12–19; 9:7–8; 26–7; 1 Cor. 3:1; 4:14; 13:11; 14:20; 2 Cor. 12:14; Gal. 4:7, 19; 1 Thess. 2:11; 1 Tim. 1:2; 2 Tim. 1:2; Tit. 1:4; Philm 10; Heb. 12:7–8; 1 Jn 2:1, 18, 28; 3:7, 18, 5:1, 21). The fact that, like Jews, the early Christians objected to exposure, infanticide and abortion (*Didache* 2.2; *Barnabas* 19.5; *To Diognetus* 5:6; Justin, *Apology* 1:27–9; Boswell 1988) may also indicate this special status, as might the practice of infant baptism (Wiedemann 1989; cf. also Eyben 1993), although this is almost certainly a later development.

But while the new status afforded to children in some early communities is undeniable, in later New Testament literature it is noticeable by its absence. Parent–child relations, for example, do not merit inclusion in the houselist found in Titus 2:1–10, and elsewhere in the pastoral epistles children only appear as objects of parental control and are no longer addressed in their own right (1 Tim. 3:4, 12; Tit. 1:6). As Strange accurately remarks, 'After Colossians and Ephesians, children were occasionally spoken about, but never to' (Strange 1996: 7). Nor did Christianity lead to any noticeable changes in the method of child-rearing (corporal punishment remained an accepted feature of Christian parenting; Heb. 12:7; *Didache* 4.9; *Barnabas* 19.5) and there is no evidence, despite some recent claims to the contrary (Stark 1996), that the new faith led to increased numbers of children in the early communities, as one might expect. It is also important to bear in mind that even in the earliest strata of Christian tradition, the child–parent bond was not always understood as a positive thing. It could also be depicted as negative, as a hindrance to the proclamation of the gospel (Lk 14:26), something perhaps evident in Jesus' own rather ambiguous relationship with his own mother (Mk 3:21 and par.).

SLAVE AND MASTER

Although we have little evidence from the point of view of slaves or ex-slaves in the Empire in this period (with notable exceptions such as the *Life of Aesop* or the writings of Epictetus), and so our knowledge of relationships between slaves and their owners is unavoidably one-sided, we can sketch a few of their general characteristics. Perhaps unsurprisingly, as something predicated upon the legal ownership of one person by another, slave–master relationships were typified by abuse of a physical, sexual, social and psychological kind (Bradley 1984, 1994). While some slaves in the Roman Empire could achieve significant autonomy, and even establish households of their own (indeed, they could even own other slaves), the experiences of the few should not distract us from the misery of the many: the most slaves could reasonably hope for was that the owner would provide them with at least the necessities of food, clothing and shelter required to remain a functioning part of the household and, if they were fortunate enough, the opportunity to be manumitted in a good enough physical condition that they could provide for themselves (elderly or sick slaves were often freed to starve). Although some of the famished free poor might sell themselves into servitude to secure food at times of crisis (Ramin and Veyne 1981) or to raise capital to help others (*1 Clem.* 55.2), the situation seems to have been barely tolerable for most, and a significant minority sought release through flight, suicide or murder when the opportunity arose (see Augustus, *Res Gestae* 25) and small-scale acts of resistance and insubordination (of which Aesop was the fictional slave hero *par excellence*) remained a common feature of slave behaviour. Although a few, such as Philo (*Special Laws* 3.137–43) censured its excesses, none subjected the institution of slavery to any sustained critique (Garnsey 1996), and virtually none, except the Jewish sectarian Essenes and Therapeutae, believed it should not exist at all.

The slave–master relationship was, however, significantly altered within the first churches, both in a positive and negative manner. At least among the earliest communities it was expected to be functionally, if not officially, at an end between fellow Christians, who were expected to forge a new relationship characterized by equality and mutual submission (official manumission was something tightly restricted in the early Empire, and probably not an option in most cases). This is most clear from Paul's letter to Philemon (if it is, as is traditionally thought, a letter concerning a runaway slave, something recently unconvincingly contested; see Barclay 1991; Nordling 1991; Callahan 1997). In this the apostle makes it clear that he considers the relationship between Philemon and Onesimus to be completely transformed, physically as well as spiritually, by virtue of their common faith. The master and slave are now brothers 'in the flesh and in the Lord' (Phlm 16), an idea which echoes that found in the egalitarian baptismal formulas of the Pauline churches (1 Cor. 12:13; Gal. 3:28; Col. 3:11). The early houselists similarly depict the relationship between the Christian owner and slave as fundamentally different from that found in the outside world, as one of reciprocal submission and mutual concern (Eph. 5:21; 6:5–9; Col. 3:22 – 4:1), although these also include an additional innovation in dignifying the enslaved person as a moral agent within the relationship (the later list found in 1 Pet. 2:18–25 addresses enslaved Christians but says nothing of the responsibilities of masters, and appears to justify a far more conservative, one-sided, ethic; cf. also Tit. 2:9–10). However, there was obviously some tension about how practically this relationship should be transformed, and it is clear, at least in some of the later literature, that the expectations of some Christian slaves were not met (1 Tim. 6:1–2).

However, the effect of the new faith appears to have been less positive where a slave was a Christian and the owner was not, and consequently self-sacrifice was not reciprocated (not all Christians lived in Christian households: 1 Cor. 7:12–16; 1 Pet. 3:1–2). Slaves became an active, diligent agent in their own suffering, with no visible, this-worldly, compensation, even if the suffering was given a theological significance, which it had not had before (1 Pet. 2:20–1). Indeed, early Christian teaching could have the consequence (even if this was not the intention) of reinforcing and legitimizing the institution of slavery in a way not previously seen in antiquity (Bradley 1994: 145–53; de Ste Croix 1975) as the subsequent history of the application of these texts indicates.

But all traditions of Christianity in the New Testament, however radical or conservative, had one tangible effect on the master–slave relationship, perhaps too easily overlooked but that, at least for many of those enslaved in non-Jewish households, would have, if implemented, led to one significant change in the experience of slaves: early Christian concern to limit sexual activity to marriage meant that a slave was no longer the sexual property of the owner, and no longer exposed to the sexual abuse that so often accompanied this.

THE CHURCH

The social relationships that operated when believers assembled as a church (1 Cor. 11:18) have been the subject of much study in recent decades (publications in this area have been legion but notable among them are Theissen 1982; Meeks 1983; Schüssler Fiorenza 1983; MacDonald 1988; Horrell 1996). In particular, scholarship has been interested in two aspects of these. On the one hand the processes of routinization, institutionalization and legitimization have attracted considerable attention. How, for example, did authority became associated with offices rather than specific individuals (Acts 6:1–6; Eph. 4:11; 1 Tim. 3:1–13) and what were the consequences of this for the position of women within the communities (Schüssler Fiorenza 1983; MacDonald 1988; Wire 1990)? Secondly, studies have tried to discern the extent to which conflicts in the first churches were primarily social in their origins. What role, for instance, did different religious or class-based perceptions of appropriate forms of social behaviour play in these disagreements?

Such work has been instructive. For example, disputes over the consumption of food, which appear regularly in early Christian literature (e.g. Acts 10:1 – 11:18; 15:1–35; 15:20, 29; 21:25; Rom. 14:1–23; 1 Cor. 5:11, 8–11; Gal. 2:11–14; Rev. 2:14, 20), and that are not just concerned with *what* one should eat but *with whom* one should eat, provide evidence that social factors were undeniably important in some arguments that divided believers. (Jesus' innovative behaviour in this area probably lay behind some of these later difficulties: see, e.g., Mt 9:10–13; 11:19; Mk 2:15–17; Lk 5:29–33; 7:34; Crossan 1991.) Nevertheless, such scholarship has also had significant faults. It is impossible, for instance, to describe structural developments of any kind in formative Christianity because we know so little for certain about the relationships between the documents and traditions that constitute the New Testament (although, in broad terms, increasing institutionalization over time appears to be undeniable). In noting the social origins of conflicts between Christians studies have also exaggerated the part played by alleged absolute socio-economic differences, such as those between the 'strong' and the 'weak' of Corinth (Theissen 1982). These differences, especially when viewed against the non-elite context of the day, appear rather less than certain (Meggitt 1998). Too much has also been made of a small number of social practices and conventions erroneously assumed to be universal and widespread at the time. Patronage provides a good example of this. Far from this social practice having a significant explanatory role to play in understanding tensions within some of the first churches (e.g. Chow 1992; Clarke 1993) it actually had little significance within the world in which the early Christians lived, barely affecting the lives of the non-elite in the eastern Empire at all (it is only explicitly referred to once in the entire New Testament – Rom. 16:1–2; though cf. also Lk 22:25).

But perhaps the biggest problem with current scholarship is that its preoccupations have led us to underestimate the distinctive social character of the first churches, something visible in a mass of telling but incidental detail common to all early Christian traditions. Although to some degree these communities resembled pre-existing social forms, such as the household, synagogue, club or philosophical school (Meeks 1983; Ascough 1998), they also constituted a radical departure from what had gone before, creating an environment in which unprecedented forms of social interaction took place.

For example, within the first churches members of diverse gender, status and ethnic groups (women and men; slaves, the freed and the free; Jews, Greeks, Romans, Samaritans, Syrians and others) created relationships unparalleled in the period. Although we can discern that this was the case from various key descriptive and programmatic statements about the constitution of the churches (such as the 'baptismal' formulas; e.g. 1 Cor. 12:13; Gal. 3:28; Col. 3:11; or the evangelistic commissions found in Mt 24:14; 28:19; Mk 13:10), it is only by close analysis of indirect data, such as the list of individuals found in the concluding section of Paul's letter to the Romans (Lampe 1991), that we can confirm this picture and see their variegated form more clearly. It is through analysis of such apparently peripheral material that we discover, for example, the crucial role played in the early communities by such prominent women as Phoebe or Junia (Rom. 16:1–2, 7; cf. 1 Cor. 14:34 and 1 Tim. 2:12–15). Only the initial Jerusalem church appears to have been somewhat less heterogeneous, and represents a partial exception to this picture, though even this was, if Acts is accurate, composed of a diverse, cosmopolitan group of Jews (Acts 2:1–47; 6:1–6; 15:5).

The members were bound together in a web of mutual obligations that, again, were highly unusual. These were expressed in a variety of ways, but perhaps most visibly in an ethic of interdependence that saturated early Christian literature – what Lohfink (1985) terms a 'praxis of togetherness', in which concern, indeed love, for 'one another' was its dominant, consistent hallmark (e.g. Jn 13:34–5; 15:12, 17; Rom. 12:10; 13:8; 16:16; 1 Cor. 11:33; 12:25; Gal. 5:13; 6:2; Eph. 4:2, 32; 5:21; Col. 3:13; 1 Thess. 5:15; 2 Thess. 1:3; Jas 5:16; 1 Pet. 1:22; 4:9; 5:5; 1 Jn 1:7; 3:11). This expressed itself more specifically in new patterns of commensality (Lk 14:12–14; Acts 2:46; Gal. 2:11–14), hospitality (Mk 6:8–11; Acts 16:15; 18:3; Rom. 12:13; 2 Jn 10), economic activity (Acts 2:44–5; 4:34–5; Rom. 15:26; 1 Cor. 16:1–4; 2 Cor. 8–9; Gal. 2:10), authority (Mk 10:42–5; Mt 23:8; 2 Cor. 1:24; 4:10–12), care for the socially and materially powerless (Acts 6:1; 9:36–43; 1 Tim. 5:3–16) and in a general concern for the mutual upbuilding of the community (1 Cor. 14:26; 1 Thess. 5:11). These new relationships were regarded as having precedence over those already established, and reshaping the norms of social interaction between believers (e.g. 1 Cor. 6:1–8). They were thought to result from a shared experience and identity that ultimately owed itself to the activity and authority of Jesus (through, e.g., the presence of the Spirit-Acts 2:17–19; Rom. 8; 1 Cor. 12–14; Jn 14–16; etc.), although they were also enforced by the churches themselves (Mt 16:17; 18:15; 1 Cor. 5:1–13; 6:1–8; Gal. 6:1) and ultimately, of course, by God (1 Cor. 11:27–32; Acts 4:33 – 5:11).

It is no surprise that the strong, mutual relationships between Christians were both a source of pride for early apologists (Aristides, *Apology*, 15) and ridiculed by the first critics of the new faith (Lucian, *Peregrinus* 13).

But as well as being tightly bound together, not only by distinctive praxis but by such things as participation in common rites, knowledge of common central myths and the use of emotive terms to describe believers and non-believers, such as those associated with kinship and purity (e.g. Rom. 1:7, 13; 7:1; 10:1; 12:1; 15:25, 26; 16:2, 15; etc.), most communities also remained open to those outside. They clearly believed that they had responsibilities towards those not in their churches, primarily of an ethical and evangelistic kind (Mt 5:44; 19:19; 22:39; 28:19; Mk 12:31 {16:15}; Lk 6:27–8; 24:47; Rom. 12:17–21; 3:9; 15:15, 1 Cor. 19:19–24; Gal. 6:9–10; 1 Thess. 5:15; 1 Pet. 3:9). Although they considered themselves contrast societies (Lohfink 1985), in critical opposition to the world about them and its values (Mt 5:14; Phil. 2:14–15), they continued to interact with their neighbours. Even the gospel of John, so often interpreted as the work of an anti-social community, withdrawn into itself as a result of persecution (Jn 9:22 and 16:2), was produced by a church in active dialogue with various groups outside its fold (Rensberger 1988).

CONCLUSIONS

As observed at the outset, a diversity of problems, of both method and data, make the business of describing the social life of the first churches a particularly difficult undertaking and one that has spawned a plurality of different reconstructions. My sketch, like all others by students of this field, must remain partial and provisional. Although it cannot be otherwise as the difficulties are so intractable, nonetheless, until scholars take seriously the popular cultures of the early Empire within which early Christianity arose, all work in this area will remain vulnerable to criticism, even at the most fundamental level.

Despite the provisional nature of these findings, it seems likely that two characteristics of early Christian social life, which have surfaced a number of times in this analysis, will be enduring features of any future descriptions. Firstly, early Christian social life was clearly one of considerable diversity. However one views the evidence, it seems that some churches did not share the same ideas about such social issues as, for example, the treatment of children, or the institution of slavery. Striking innovations among some communities appear to be unknown, forgotten or perhaps repressed in others. Conversely, early Christian social life also possessed a surprising degree of uniformity, too readily overlooked. It is especially evident in the way that all the traditions seem to assume that pre-existing social relationships of whatever kind were fundamentally reconfigured and made relative by the new allegiance and experience of Christ. But it can also be seen in the common expectation that interactions between members of the communities founded in his name were to have a discernible, distinctive quality characterized by mutual concern and interdependence. While we shall undoubtedly learn a great deal more about the social life of the first churches in the near future, as considerable scholarly energy continues to be expended on its study, these two general features, diversity and uniformity, will remain key in any future constructions.

BIBLIOGRAPHY

Anderson, M. (1980) *Approaches to the History of the Western Family, 1500–1914*. London: Macmillan.

Aries, P. (1973) *Centuries of Childhood*. Harmondsworth: Penguin.

Ascough, Richard S. (1998) *What Are They Saying about the Formation of the Pauline Churches?* Mahwah, N.J.: Paulist Press.

Bagnall, R. S. and B. W. Frier (1994) *The Demography of Roman Egypt*. Cambridge: Cambridge University Press.

Barclay, J. M. (1991) 'Paul, Philemon, and the Dilemma of Christian Slave Ownership.' *New Testament Studies*, 37: 161–86.

—— (1992) 'Thessalonica and Corinth: Social Contrasts in Pauline Christianity.' *Journal for the Study of the New Testament*, 47: 49–74.

Barton, S. C. (1994) *Discipleship and Family Ties in Mark and Matthew*. Cambridge: Cambridge University Press.

—— (1997) 'The Relativisation of Family Ties in the Jewish and Graeco-Roman Traditions.' *Constructing Early Christian Families: Family as Social Reality and Metaphor*. Ed. H. Moxnes. London: Routledge, 81–100.

Beard, M., J. North and S. Price (1998a) *Religions of Rome: A History*. Cambridge: Cambridge University Press.

Boswell, J. (1988) *The Kindness of Strangers: The Abandonment of Children in Western Europe from Late Antiquity to the Renaissance*. London: Penguin.

Bradley, K. R. (1984) *Slaves and Masters in the Roman Empire*. Bruxelles: Latomus.

—— (1994) *Slavery and Society at Rome*. Cambridge: Cambridge University Press.

Branick, Vincent (1989) *The House Church in Paul*. Wilmington: Michael Glazier.

Callahan, Allen (1997) *Embassy of Onesimus: The Letters of Paul to Philemon*. Valley Forge: Trinity Press International.

Carter, W. (1994) *Households and Discipleship: A Study of Matthew 19–20*. Sheffield: JSOT Press.

Chow, J. K. (1992) *Patronage and Power*. Sheffield: JSOT Press.

Clarke, Andrew D. (1993) *Secular and Christian Leadership in Corinth: A Socio-Historical and Exegetical Study of 1 Corinthians 1–6*. Leiden: E. J. Brill.

Clark, E. (1995) 'Antifamilial Tendencies in Ancient Christianity.' *Journal of the History of Sexuality*, 5: 356–80.

Coleman, K. M. (1990) 'Fatal Charades: Roman Executions Staged as Mythological Enactments.' *Journal of Roman Studies*, 80: 44–73.

Crossan, J. D. (1991) *The Historical Jesus: The Life of a Mediterranean Jewish Peasant*. Edinburgh: T&T Clark.

Currie, Sarah (1993) 'Childhood and Christianity from Paul to the Council of Chalcedon.' Unpublished PhD: Cambridge University.

Dixon, S. (1992) *The Roman Family*. Baltimore: The Johns Hopkins University Press.

Duling, Dennis C. and Norman Perrin (1994) *The New Testament: Proclamation and Parenesis*. 3rd edn. London: Harcourt Brace.

Dunn, J. D. G. (1996) 'The Household Rules in the New Testament.' *The Family in Theological Perspective*. Ed. Stephen C. Barton. Edinburgh: T&T Clark, 43–63.

Elliot, Neil (1994) *Liberating Paul: The Justice of God and the Politics of the Apostle*. Sheffield: Sheffield Academic Press.

Esler, P. (1994) *The First Christians in their Social Worlds: Social-Scientific Approaches to New Testament Interpretation*. London: Routledge.

Evans, Richard (1997) *In Defence of History*. London: Granta.

Eyben, E. (1993) *Restless Youth in Ancient Rome*. London: Routledge.

Feldman, Louis H. (1993) *Jew and Gentile in the Ancient World*. Princeton: Princeton University Press.

Fenn, Richard K. (1987) 'Sociology and Social History: A Preface to a Sociology of the New Testament.' *Journal for the Study of the Pseudepigrapha*, 1: 95–114.

Francis, James (1996) 'Children and Childhood in the New Testament.' *The Family in Theological Perspective*. Ed. Stephen C. Barton. Edinburgh: T&T Clark, 65–85.

Gardiner, E. N. (1930) *Athletics in the Ancient World*. Oxford: Clarendon.

Gardner, Jane F. (1991) *Women in Roman Law and Society*. London: Routledge.

Gardner, Jane F. and Thomas Widemann (1991) *The Roman Household*. London: Routledge.

Garnsey, Peter (1996) *Ideas of Slavery from Aristotle to Augustine*. Cambridge: Cambridge University Press.

Garnsey, Peter, and R. Saller (1987) *The Roman Empire: Economy, Society, and Culture*. London: Duckworth.

Garrett, S. (1992) 'Sociology (Early Christianity).' *Anchor Bible Dictionary*, Vol. 6. Ed. D. N. Freedman. New York: Doubleday, 89–99.

Golden, M. (1988) 'Did Ancients Care When Their Child Died?' *Greece and Rome*, 35: 152–63.

Grahame, Mark (1997) 'Public and Private in the Roman House: Investigating the Social Order of the Casa del Fauno.' *Domestic Space in the Roman World: Pompeii and Beyond*. Ed. R. Laurence and A. Wallace-Hadrill. Portsmouth: Journal of Roman Archaeology, 137–64.

Hallet, Judith P. (1984) *Fathers and Daughters in Roman Society: Women and the Elite Family*. Princeton: Princeton University Press.

Hansen, William (1998) *Ancient Greek Popular Literature*. Indiana: Indiana University Press.

Harris, W. V. (1982) 'The Theoretical Possibility of Extensive Infanticide in the Graeco-Roman World.' *Classical Quarterly*, 32: 114–16.

—— (1994) 'Child Exposure in the Roman Empire.' *Journal of Roman Studies*, 84: 1–22.

Henry, M. (1989) 'Review Essays: Some Recent Work on Women and the Family in Greek and Roman Antiquity.' *Journal of Family History*, 14: 63–77.

Holmberg, Bengt (1990) *Sociology and the New Testament: An Appraisal*. Philadelphia: Fortress.

Horbury, William and David Noy (1992) *Jewish Inscriptions of Graeco-Roman Egypt*. Cambridge: Cambridge University Press.

Horrell, D. (1999) *Social-Scientific Approach to New Testament Interpretation*. Edinburgh: T&T Clark.

Jenkins, Keith (1995) *On 'What Is History?' From Carr and Elton to Rorty and White*. London: Routledge, 1995.

Keener, C. S. (1991) *And Marries Another: Divorce and Remarriage in the Teaching of the New Testament*. Peabody: Hendrickson.

Klassen, William (1999) 'The Authenticity of the Command: "Love Your Enemies".' *Authenticating the Words of Jesus*. Eds. Bruce Chilton and Craig Evans. Leiden: Brill, 385–407.

Kleijwegt, M. (1991) *Ancient Youth: The Ambiguity of Youth and the Absence of Adolescence in Greco-Roman Society*. Amsterdam: Gieben.

Kokkinos, Nikos (1998) *The Herodian Dynasty: Origins, Role in Society and Eclipse*. Sheffield: Sheffield Academic Press.

Lampe, Peter (1991) 'The Roman Christians of Romans 16.' *The Romans Debate*. Ed. Karl P. Donfried. 2nd edn. Edinburgh: T&T Clark, 216–30.

Lattimore, Richmond (1942) *Themes in Greek and Latin Epitaphs*. Urbana: University of Illinois Press.

Lewis, N., Y. Yadin and J. Greenfield (1989) *The Documents from the Bar Kokhba Period in the Cave of Letters*. Jerusalem: Israel Exploration Society.

Lohfink, Gerhard (1985) *Jesus and Community*. London: SPCK.

MacDonald, Margaret (1988) *The Pauline Churches: A Socio-Historical Study of Institutionalisation in the Pauline and Deutero-Pauline Writings*. Cambridge: Cambridge University Press.

MacMullen, Ramsey (1982) 'The Epigraphic Habit in the Roman Empire.' *American Journal of Philology*, 103: 233–46.

Malina, Bruce J. (1981) *The New Testament World: Insights from Cultural Anthropology*. London: SCM.

Martin, Dale (1993) 'Slavery and the Ancient Jewish Family.' *The Jewish Family in Antiquity*. Ed. S. J. D. Cohen. Atlanta: Scholars Press, 113–29.

—— (1996) 'The Construction of the Ancient Family: Methodological Considerations.' *Journal of Roman Studies*, 86: 100–38.

Mayer, Herbert T. (1970) 'Family Relationships in the New Testament.' *Family Relationships and the Church: A Sociological, Historical, and Theological Study of Family Structures, Roles, and Relationships*. Ed. O. E. Feucht. Saint Louis: Concordia, 57–75.

Meeks, Wayne. (1983). *The First Urban Christians*. New Haven: Yale University Press.

Meggitt, J. (1998) 'Review of Bruce Malina, *The Social World of Jesus and the Gosples*, London: Routledge, 1996.' *JTS* 49: 215–19.

Moxnes, H. (1997) 'What Is Family? Problems in Constructing Early Christian Families.' *Constructing Early Christian Families: Family as Social Reality and Metaphor*. Ed. H. Laxnes. London: Routledge, 13–41.

Nordling, John (1991) 'Onesimus Fugitivus: A Defense of the Runaway Slave Hypothesis in Philemon.' *Journal for the Study of the New Testament*, 41: 97–119.

Noy, David (1993) *Jewish Inscriptions of Western Europe*. I. *Italy*. Cambridge: Cambridge University Press.

—— (1995). *Jewish Inscriptions of Western Europe*. II. *The City of Rome*. Cambridge: Cambridge University Press.

Osiek, Carolyn and David L. Balch (1997) *Families in the New Testament World: Households and House Churches*. Louisville: Westminster John Knox.

Peskowitz, Miriam (1993) '"Family/ies" in Antiquity: Evidence from Tannaitic Literature and Roman Galilean Architecture.' *The Jewish Family in Antiquity*. Ed. S. J. D. Cohen. Atlanta: Scholars Press, 9–36.

Pfitzner, V. C. (1967) *Paul and the Agon Motif: Traditional Athletic Imagery in the Pauline Literature*. Leiden: Brill, 1967.

Price, Simon (1999) *Religions of the Ancient Greeks*. Cambridge: Cambridge University Press.

Rensberger, D. (1988) *Overcoming the World: Politics and Community in the Gospel of John*. London: SPCK.

Rohrbaugh, R. (1996) *The Social Sciences and New Testament Interpretation*. Peabody: Hendrickson.

Rowlandson, Jane (1998). *Women and Society in Greek and Roman Egypt*. Cambridge: Cambridge University Press.

Saller, Richard P. (1994) 'Familia, Domus, and the Roman Conception of the Family.' *Phoenix*, 38: 336–55.

Saller, Richard P. and B. Shaw (1984) 'Tombstones and Roman Family Relations in the Principate: Civilians, Soldiers and Slaves.' *Journal of Roman Studies*, 74: 124–56.

Sanders, E. P. (1992) *Judaism: Practice and Belief 63 BCE – 66 CE*. London: SCM.

Scheidel, Walter (1996) *Measuring Sex, Age and Death in the Roman Empire: Explorations in Ancient Demography*. Ann Arbor: Journal of Roman Archaeology.

Schüssler Fiorenza, E. (1983) *In Memory of Her: A Feminist Reconstruction of Christian Origins*. London: SCM.

Shaw, Brent D. (1987) 'The Family in Late Antiquity: The Experience of Augustine.' *Past & Present*, 115: 3–51.

Stark, Rodney (1996) *The Rise of Christianity: A Sociologist Reconsiders History*. Princeton: Princeton University Press.

Ste Croix, G. E. M. de (1975) 'Early Christian Attitudes to Property and Slavery.' *Church, Society and Politics*. Ed. D. Baker. Oxford: Clarendon, 1–38.

Strange, W. A. (1996) *Children in the Early Church: Children in the Ancient World, the New Testament and the Early Church*. Carlisle: Paternoster.

Swartley, W. (1998) 'Mutual Aid Based on Jesus and Early Christianity.' *Building Communities of Compassion*. Eds W. Swartley and D. Kraybill. Scottdale: Herald Press, 21–39.

Theissen, G. (1978) *Sociology of Early Palestinian Christianity*. Philadelphia: Fortress.

—— (1982). *The Social Setting of Pauline Christianity*. Philadelphia: Fortress Press.

Toner, J. P. (1995) *Leisure and Ancient Rome*. Cambridge: Polity Press.

Veyne, P. (1978) 'La famille et l'amour sous le Haut-Empire romaine.' *Annales ESC*, 33: 35–63.

—— (1987) *A History of Private Life*. I. *From Pagan Rome to Byzantium*. London: Harvard University Press.

Wallace-Hadrill, A. (1988) 'The Social Structure of the Roman House.' *Papers of the British School at Rome*, 56: 43–97.

—— (1998) *Pompeii: Public and Private Life*. Cambridge, Mass.: Harvard University Press.

Weiss, Zeev (1999) 'Adopting a Novelty: The Jews and Roman Games in Palestine.' *The Roman and Byzantine Near East: Some Recent Archaeological Research*. Ed. J. H. Humphrey. Portsmouth: Journal of Roman Archaeology, 23–49.

Wiedemann, T. (1981) *Greek and Roman Slavery*. London: Routledge.

—— (1989) *Adults and Children in the Roman Empire*. London: Routledge.

Wire, Antionette Clark (1990) *The Corinthian Women Prophets*. Minneapolis: Fortress.

THE FIRST CHURCHES
Religious practice

———•◆•———

Justin J. Meggitt

PROBLEMS

In order to examine the religious practices of the early Christians a number of problems need to be addressed from the outset. This is necessary if we are to avoid constructing a picture that is nothing more than an articulation of our presuppositions or, indeed, for some of us, our own practices.

The first and most obvious difficulty we face is one posed by the nature of the evidence itself: none of the writings contained in the New Testament were composed in order to give a detailed record of what took place when the first believers came together to worship. In fact, the New Testament gives us frustratingly little information about this aspect of their lives. It tells us nothing about many important practices (e.g. what rites, if any, accompanied early Christian weddings?) and what sparse information it gives us about others is often baffling (what, e.g., was the 'baptism on behalf of the dead' to which Paul refers in 1 Cor. 15:29 and which is not mentioned elsewhere?). The closest we have to a description of early Christian worship in the New Testament is found in 1 Corinthians 11–14, and any study must make a great deal of use of this material, but it comes from a highly polemical letter in which Paul is preoccupied with certain practices that had become problematic among the Corinthians, and consequently it gives us little information about those that had not. Early sources from outside the New Testament, such as the *Didache*, Justin Martyr's *First Apology* (especially 61–7), the *Shepherd of Hermas*, and Pliny the Younger's *Letter to Trajan* (10:96) can give us some help but are of only limited value: we cannot be certain how well they reflect the behaviour of the New Testament churches, a few of which flourished nearly a century before some of these writings were composed.

The problems involved in making sense of what little pertinent evidence we have are compounded by a series of errors common to much scholarship in this area. Many studies have, for example, fallen victim to what can be called *panliturgicalism*, a failing that consists of seeing fragments of early liturgy buried throughout the New Testament (Moule 1961). In fact, few such fragments can be confidently distinguished by any agreed criteria. Others have imposed a uniformity on the evidence that it does not *a priori* possess (it is not, for instance, obvious that all references to

157

baptism are to a ritual involving water nor that the rites practised in Corinth were practised in the same way, if at all, in other early churches, such as those of Rome or Jerusalem). A number have unthinkingly interpreted the evidence using evolutionary models, and have assumed, for example, that the religious practices of the earliest churches became more complex over time. This may be right but is not necessarily so. A considerable body of studies has displayed symptoms of *parallelomania* (Sandmel 1962) and has drawn unwarranted conclusions about the relationship between various Christian and non-Christian practices on the basis of alleged resemblances of one kind or another (resemblances that often turn out to exist only in the eye of the beholder). There has also been a widespread tendency to focus upon practices that have been capable of liturgical formulation, and consequently have had an afterlife in the church (e.g. the Lord's Supper) to the exclusion of others, which have played little part in formal Christian worship throughout the last two millennia of its history (e.g. glossolalia).

Nor, of course, is it self-evident what practices can be accurately labelled 'religious', given that the idea of 'religion' held by most moderns is quite different from that of inhabitants of the first century. Although there were significant differences between the various cultures from which the first Christians were drawn, 'religion' was conceived of as something embedded in most areas of human life, not the discrete and autonomous phenomenon it is often characterized as today. As a result we must be careful not to limit our analysis to those activities that seem to us to be clearly 'religious', such as the rituals associated with the Lord's Supper or water baptism, and omit or downplay those that do not (such as the holy kiss or the collection for the Jerusalem congregation).

We must also be wary of recent, functionalist readings of specific worship practices that claim to explain their role in the social construction of the formative communities. Different practices undoubtedly helped to create and maintain new identities, solidarities, and even shared cosmologies, among the first Christians, and it might even be useful, as some have argued, to make distinctions between, for example, irregular rituals of transformation and regular ceremonies of consolidation in explaining how they did this (Neyrey 1990; Horrell 1999). But, while some general remarks in this area are valid, we must be careful of pushing the evidence too far and of too quickly providing neat, functionalist readings, that seem all the more compelling with the benefit of hindsight, of specific practices that, in this early phase of Christian history, were inchoate and had not yet become the highly stylized, formalized activities they were to become (see, e.g., 1 Cor. 11:17–34). Indeed, it is quite possible that many of the rites were not even as significant (1 Cor. 1:14–17) for the original practitioners as they are for their modern interpreters and so it is all the more dangerous to make too much of their role in this respect.

But perhaps the largest problem we face in examining the religious practices of the first Christians is the most difficult to resolve: how can we do justice to the fact that they were not originally understood in isolation from each other, nor, more importantly, from the wider religious experience of the individuals and communities. How, as it were, can we see the wood for the trees? This may seem an obvious point to make but it has been a missing dimension in New Testament studies, as Luke T. Johnson (1997) has recently observed. If we concentrate solely on categorizing or describing what the early Christians *did* and not what they *meant* by what they did, we run the risk of misunderstanding their worship life completely. The analogy made famous by the philosopher Gilbert Ryle is perhaps the best way to emphasize the significance of this: a twitch and a wink can appear identical but they are not: the meanings underlying both are completely different (Pals 1996). It is difficult to uncover these meanings and perhaps the best we can do is try to describe the dominant recurring motifs present in the descriptions of worship we are given; but we should be conscious that the ideas and experiences embodied in these practices, and not their form, should be the focus of any serious attempt to understand this aspect of early Christian life.

PRACTICES

Before we begin to look at religious practices undertaken by members of the first churches that were distinctively 'Christian' it is important, in order to gain a comprehensive understanding, to look at those that were not: to examine the specifically Jewish and pagan practices within the first communities.

Jewish and pagan practices of the first Christians

It is quite clear that members of the first churches continued to participate in the religious lives of other groups, both Jewish and pagan, in addition to their own. We know for example, at least according to Luke–Acts, that many remained observant Jews, attending synagogues and the temple in Jerusalem (Lk 24:53; Acts 2:46; 3:1; Acts 18:26; 21:26; 22:17; Barrett 1991), and that they did not do so entirely for polemical or evangelistic reasons (though some may have; e.g. Paul in Acts 13:5, 14; 14:1; etc.). In the earliest period Christians seem to have been indistinguishable from Jews (Acts 18:2; 18:15; Suetonius, *Life of Claudius* 25.4). This should not come as a surprise. Despite the clear antagonism between the two groups in some New Testament writings (e.g. Jn 9:22; 12:42; 16:2; Gal. 1:13; 1 Thess. 2:14) the thoroughgoing separation of the two religions did not occur in the period they cover. Indeed, it took some time for 'Christians' to acquire a separate identity (the term 'Christian' is a late invention and is only used three times in the New Testament – Acts 11:26; 26:28; 1 Pet. 4:16). The diffuse nature of authority in Judaism, particularly before the revolt of Bar Kochba (132–5 CE), and its stress upon right action rather than right belief, meant that many Christians who were also Jews could be expected to be left largely untroubled if they did not abandon central Jewish practices, such as dietary laws and circumcision. The ability to sustain such a dual identity was problematic and by the second century proved largely impossible (*Epistle of Barnabas* 4.13–14; Justin, *Dialogue with Trypho* 16.4; 93.4; 95.4) but at least in this early period, it remained, to a greater or lesser extent, a real possibility for some.

We also know that some members continued to take part in the religious practices of paganism, even though this was regarded as scandalous by others, notably Paul (1 Cor. 10:21: 'You cannot drink the cup of the Lord and the cup of demons; you cannot partake of the table of the Lord and the table of demons'). Again, this is unsurprising as pagan religiosity, in its numerous forms, saturated the public and private lives of individuals within the Empire (Beard et al. 1998a, 1998b), and its essentially tolerant nature (Garnsey 1984) meant that becoming a Christian did not, at least from a pagan point of view, preclude a person from taking some part in its worship.

It is difficult to ascertain the meaning that these practices, Jewish and pagan, possessed for the members of the earliest churches who continued to observe them (or even perhaps adopted them; Gal. 6:12), but it is obvious that, at least for some, they were of far from marginal significance and cannot be ignored.

Christian practices

Context

Before we detail the specific practices of the communities, it is important to recognize the contexts in which they took place. The primary place at which worship was undertaken was at gatherings at which all the members of the church came together (1 Cor. 14:23, 26), most probably held on the first day of the week (Sunday) (1 Cor. 16:2; Acts 20:7; Justin, *Apology* 1.67.7) and most often in private dwellings of one kind or another (Acts 2:46; Rom. 16:5; 1 Cor. 16:19). In later centuries, as churches grew in size and attracted individuals of a higher social status, large domestic structures were adapted for congregations (White 1996, 1997) but it seems probable that, in the New Testament period, Christian worship normally took place in more modest locations, such as the rented rooms, workshops, or lean-tos, that were 'home' for most people in the first century (Jewett 1993; Meggitt 1998). Given the public nature of a great deal of what we would now think of as 'private' space it is no surprise that the meetings seem to have been open, with unbelievers having access to the proceedings (1 Cor. 14:23).

In the earliest period the worship lacked any formal leadership or structure, with all members, men and women, participating in different ways, and the different practices being undertaken in any order (1 Cor. 14:26). At times, it appears to have been rather anarchic (1 Cor. 14:40). However, later New Testament writings provide evidence that distinct offices emerged in the church (Eph. 4:11; 1 Tim. 3) and that worship became noticeably more structured. These offices became occupied solely by men (1 Tim. 3), and the participation of women appears to have become restricted (contrast 1 Cor. 11:5 and 1 Tim. 2:11–15), although this correlation between the growth in authority structures and the marginalization of the role of women in worship is by no means certain (see, e.g., 1 Cor. 14:34–5 and Rom. 16:1–2; Schüssler Fiorenza 1996).

General practices

PRAYER

Prayer was obviously central to the life of the first churches and their individual members (Mt 6:6; Acts 1:14; 2:42; 6:4; 12:5; Rom. 12:12; 1 Cor. 7:5; Col. 4:2; Cullmann 1995). Prayers could be of various kinds: thanksgiving (Lk 2:38; Col. 4:2;

Heb. 13:15; Rev. 11:17–18); benediction (Lk 1:68; 2 Cor. 1:3; Eph. 1:3; 1 Pet. 1:3); and petition (e.g. Mt 6:11; Lk 11:3), particularly intercessionary petition (e.g. Mt 5:44; Jn 17:9; 2 Cor. 1:11; 4:3; Jas 5:16; Wiles 1974). They could be both extempore (Acts 4:24ff.) or prescribed (*Didache* 8.3, e.g., requires that the Lord's Prayer be said three times a day).

Early Christians mostly prayed out loud, following the practice of their contemporaries (van der Horst 1994), although inaudible prayer was not unknown in the period (e.g. Seneca, *Letters* 10.5; Philo, *Special Laws* 1.272) and there is evidence that

Figure 36.1 The Nash Papyrus. A second century BCE liturgical fragment containing the *Shema* (Deut. 6:4–5) and the Decalogue. Reproduced by permission of the Syndics of Cambridge University Library.

some Christians prayed silently on occasion (1 Thess. 5:17). The posture for prayer seems to have varied. Prayers could be delivered standing, kneeling, and even prostrate (Mt 26:39; Mk 11:25; 14:35; Lk 22:41; Acts 7:60; 9:40; 20:36; 21:5; Eph. 3:14; Rev. 4:10; 7:11; 11:16; 19:4, 10; 22:9).

The form and, to a large extent, the character of Christian prayer would have been familiar to Jews and others (Kiley 1997). Prayer was, for example, a significant component in Jewish worship in the Temple and elsewhere (the *Shema* of Deut. 6:4–5, was probably said by most observant Jews twice a day; Sanders 1992). Indeed, it seems to have become more important with the emergence of synagogues and prayer halls just prior to the birth of the new religion (Falk 1995). However, Christianity was unusual in the way that prayer emerged as a partial replacement for sacrifice (Tertullian, *On Prayer* 27–8), something not unknown among Jewish sectarians before the destruction of the temple in 70 CE but not true for Judaism as a whole until after this date (Chazon and Bernstein 1997).

More striking, however, was the place given to Jesus, a man, in whose name Christian prayers were spoken and who functioned as the intermediary through whom prayers to God were made (Jn 14:13f.; 15:16; 16:24, 26; Rom. 1:8; 7:25; Heb. 13:21; Jude 1:25). Even more unusually, Jesus could at times be not just the mediator but also the object of such prayers (Jn 14:13; Acts 7:59). Jesus' position as the exemplar, *par excellence*, of prayer (Mt 6:9; Lk 11:2) was also, of course, unique, as was the model prayer ascribed to him (Mt 6:9–13; Lk 11:1–4) despite evident parallels with various Jewish traditions of the time (Davies and Allison 1988).

The place of the Spirit as enabler of Christian prayers and intercessor (Rom. 8:26; 1 Cor. 14:14; Eph. 6:18; Jude 20) was also innovative. However, some Jews believed in angelic intercessors (Job 33:23–8; Tob. 12.15; 1 *Enoch* 9.3; 15.2; 99.3; 104.1; *T. Levi* 3.5; 5.6–7; *T. Dan.* 6.2) and could view angels and spirits as virtually synonymous (1 *Enoch* 15.4, 7; *Jub.* 1.25; 1 QH 1.11) so it probably is best not to see this aspect of Christian prayer as completely unprecedented.

SINGING

Singing was a prominent feature of worship in many, if not all, the early communities (1 Cor. 14:15, 26; Eph. 5:19; Col. 3:16; Jas 5:13; Acts 16:25; Pliny, *Letter to Trajan* 10.96.7) and had probably been an aspect of the devotional life of the Jesus movement from the outset (Mk 14:26; Mt 26:30).

Although we do not possess any early Christian hymns, it seems likely, on stylistic and linguistic grounds (see. e.g., Stauffer 1955; Barth 1974) that some hymnic material can be discerned in the New Testament. (The most probable fragments are Lk 1:46–55 [the Magnificat]; 1:67–79 [the Benedictus]; 2:29–32 [Nunc Dimittis]; Jn 1:1–18; Eph. 2:14–16; Phil. 2:6–11; Col. 1:15–20; 1 Tim. 3:16; Heb. 1:3–4; 1 Pet. 3:18–22; and Rev. 5:9–14). It is also likely that some Christian singing was extempore as this is the best explanation for the distinction made in the New Testament between psalms, hymns and 'spiritual songs' (Col. 3:16; Eph. 5:19; cf. 1 Cor. 14:15). As a consequence, much of it is now irretrievably lost to us.

Of course there was nothing unusual in the place given to singing by Christians. Nor, as far as we can tell, in the forms that it took. Psalms and hymns were a feature of Jewish worship, both in the temple and in other settings (e.g. the *Hymns Scroll* of Qumran; Phil, *On the Contemplative Life* 80; *T. Job* 14; Falk 1995) and pagans too used singing as part of their religious devotions (Bremmer 1981). However, one distinctive element of Christian behaviour, at least for non-Jews, would be the fact that singing appears not to have been accompanied by dancing, a stable of most forms of pagan worship, and in particular the types of piety associated with mystery cults such as Cybele, Isis and Atargatis (Apuleius, *Golden Ass* 8.27).

The content of the songs also appears to have been distinctive in one obvious way. As with the prayers, the prominence given to Jesus and the soteriological narrative of his pre-existence, descent, life, death and exaltation, was, of course, unique, as was the emphasis on its implications for the present and future experience of the believer. Although this seems to have developed from the use by early Christians of certain scriptural psalms that leant themselves to Christological interpretation (such as 2, 8, 22, 110, 118) in combination with, among other things, the speculations about Wisdom found in Proverbs 8, Sirach 24, Wisdom 2–5 (Karris 1996), it was, nonetheless, an original and unusual development.

READING

It is likely that the Jewish scriptures were regularly read as part of the public worship life of the earliest churches (1 Tim. 4:13). The programmatic statement found in 2 Timothy 3:16 ('All scripture is inspired by God and is useful for teaching, for reproof, for correction, and for training in righteousness') is indicative of its central significance and authority in the lives of the first congregations, and the quotations and allusions present throughout the New Testament confirm this. But as there is no clear reference to the public reading of the Jewish scriptures by Christians until the middle of the second century (Justin, *Apology* 1.67.3) we should perhaps be wary of assuming that this was definitely the case. It is unlikely that scripture reading played much of a direct role in private worship life given the high cost of book and scroll ownership in the Empire (Fantham 1996; though see Acts 8:28). Some may have been able to access collections of scripture excerpts (testimonia) but evidence for these is scanty for this early period (see 4 QTestimonia for a possible example from Qumran).

In addition to scripture, letters written by leaders of the churches were also read (Acts 15:31; Col. 4:16; 1 Thess. 5:27; 2 Pet. 3:16; Rev 1:3). Indeed, it is sometimes argued that these letters were deliberately composed to fit the structure of worship in these communities (Bornkamm 1969; Cuming 1975) though given the scant state of our knowledge such speculations remain unverifiable. Other types of literature produced by the new movement, such as the memoirs of the apostles (Justin, *Apology* 1.67 – probably forms of the gospels) and books of prophecy (Rev. 22:18; cf. 1 Cor. 14:26) also appear to have been recited.

The central part reading played in worship mirrored its role in the Judaism of the time (Lk 4:16–20; Acts 13:15; Josephus, *Against Apion* 2.175; *Antiquities* 16.43; Levine 1987). But it would have been unusual for non-Jews. Most forms of paganism in the period were not textually orientated to any notable extent (though there were exceptions, most notably Orphism).

Once again, however, the explicit Christological content of many of the materials read in worship would have been distinctive: a cursory reading of the different forms of literature contained in the New Testament confirms this prominent characteristic. Indeed, the Jewish scriptures themselves would have been read in such a way that they too would have appeared to early Christians to be, in some sense, a Christological document (something that seems clear from the hermeneutical principles articulated, e.g., in Acts 7:52; Rom. 16:25–7; 2 Cor. 3:12–16; Hanson 1983; cf. Acts 8:28ff.). It is no surprise that what preaching there was appears to have been primarily exegetical (something that seems to have developed from synagogue practice; Acts 13:15ff.; Sanders 1992), attempting to demonstrate the status of Jesus with reference to the Jewish scriptures (Acts 18:28; cf. Acts 2:25ff.).

LORD'S SUPPER

The practice of Christians collectively consuming bread and wine was a central feature of the worship life of most early churches (Mt 26:26–30; Mk 14:22–6; Lk 22:15–20; 1 Cor. 11:17–34), though not necessarily all (John's gospel makes no overt reference to it, despite the apparent sacramentalism often detected in that gospel; Cullmann 1953). Its importance is evident from the role it appears to have had in shaping the traditions about Jesus as they were recounted in the early churches, more specifically in the accounts of the feeding miracles (Mt 14:14–21; 15:32–9; Mk 6:35–44; 8:1–10; Lk 9:12–17; Jn 6:5–13) and some of the resurrection narratives (Lk 24:30; Jn 21:9; Acts 10:41).

The details of the rite remain elusive, although it seems that, at least at the earliest stage, no one presided over it (1 Cor. 11:17–34), in clear contrast to later practice (Ignatius, *To the Smyrnaeans* 8; Justin, *Apology* 1.65). Various theories abound as to whether the Lord's Supper was originally a part of a proper meal (perhaps indicated by 1 Cor. 11:25), took place at the conclusion of a meal (perhaps indicated by 1 Cor. 11:21ff.), or was undertaken on its own without any accompanying meal (Meggitt 1998). Indeed, all these alternative practices may represent stages in the development of the rite (Dunn 1977) or may have existed at the same time in different communities. Its relationship with the so-called love feast referred to in Jude 12 (cf. also 2 Pet. 2:13b; Acts 2:42, 46; 20:7; 27:35) and subsequent literature is also difficult to determine.

The Lord's Supper was understood by the early church as instituted by Jesus during his last meal with his disciples, as we can see from Paul's words in 1 Corinthians 11:23–6 and in the accounts of the Last Supper in the synoptic gospels (Mt 26:26–30; Mk 14:22–6; Lk 22:15–20). This historical event evidently provided the aetiological justification for the practice, though the fellowship meals, which were a striking feature of Jesus' ministry (e.g. Mt 11:19), may well have contributed to its establishment. These fellowship meals appear to have been given a particular eschatological significance by Jesus (Mt 22:1–14; 25:10; Mk 2:19; 10:35–40; Lk 14:16–24; 22:30; cf. Isa. 25:6; 65:13; 1 *Enoch* 62:14; 2 *Baruch* 29:8; 1 QSa 2.11–22), something also present in the accounts of the Lord's Supper (Mt 26:29; Mk 14:25; Lk 22:18; 1 Cor. 11:26; *Didache* 10; Wainwright 1971). Cultic meals were well known in other traditions, both Jewish and pagan (Lev. 6:29; 7:6; Josephus,

Antiquities 3.231; 4.75; 1 QS 6.4–5; Slater 1991; Garnsey 1999) and these too may have had a part to play in its inception. However, despite the fact that the Last Supper is described as a Passover meal (Mt 26:17; Mk 14:12; Lk 22:8; though see Jn 18:28 for a different tradition) it certainly was not, as many New Testament scholars seem to assume (Jeremias 1964), the *seder* meal we know from later rabbinic sources (e.g. *m. Pesahim* 10) and that is found in modern Judaism. The *seder* developed as a response to the destruction of the temple in 70 CE (Bokser 1984) and the resultant need for different foci of religious observance among Jews. There is no clear evidence that any elements of the *seder* predate this cataclysmic event (Hilton 1994).

There were some obvious differences in the interpretation of the Lord's Supper according to the material we possess (see Jeremias 1964; Marshall 1980). Matthew's account, for example, is unique in emphasizing its efficacy in the forgiveness of sins (Mt 26:28) and Luke and Paul are distinctive in the stress they lay on its commemorative nature (Lk 22:19; 1 Cor. 11:25). But a key feature common to all traditions is the figure of Jesus himself: the ritual was first and foremost a celebration of the new covenant with God inaugurated by his death (Mt 26:28; Mk 14:24; Lk 22:20; 1 Cor. 11:25). For early Christians Jesus both initiated the rite and was its fundamental focus, and as such it was probably a symbolic affirmation of the central 'myth' of the community, the life, death and exaltation of Jesus (if by 'myth' we mean a story that explains the nature of the cosmos and worshippers' place in it) although such an interpretation is uncertain at this early stage when opinions obviously varied among worshippers as to its meaning (1 Cor. 11:17–34).

The rite itself clearly perturbed contemporaries of the early Christians. The emphasis on consuming Jesus' blood (stressed in all four accounts of the Last Supper), however figuratively understood, would have been particularly disturbing for Jews of the time (Lev. 17:10–14; cf. Acts 15:20, 29; Jn 6:52–9) and the practice undoubtedly lay behind the accusations of cannibalism often made against the early Christians (Benko 1985; Edwards 1992).

BAPTISM

Baptism was another central feature in the early church and is visible in a number of traditions that make up the New Testament (Mt 28:19; Jn 3:4–5, 22; 4:1f.; Acts 2:38; 10:47–8; Rom. 6:3ff.; 1 Cor. 1:13–17; 12:13; 15.29; Gal. 3:27; Col. 2:12; Tit. 3:5; Heb. 6:2; 1 Pet. 3:21). Little is known about its form but it is probable that immersion in water was a common feature of many of its manifestations (Mt 3:11; Mk 1:8; Lk 3:16; Jn 1:33; 3:5; 1 Pet. 3:20). Baptism became understood as an initiation rite for entry into the new community (1 Cor. 1:13–17; Acts 2:38) something particularly visible in Acts where baptism functions in the narrative at crucial moments in the expansion of the gospel as the means by which entrance to the church is confirmed (Acts 2:38–41; 8:12, 35–9; 9:18; 10:44–8; 16:14–15, 30–4; 18:8; 19:5). In this respect it could be regarded as analogous to circumcision among Jews (Col. 2:11–12; cf. Gen. 17:10–11) although circumcision of the heart, rather than the rite of baptism, was understood as the replacement for this prominent Jewish rite among the early Christians (Rom. 2:28f.; Phil. 3:3; Col. 2:11–12; cf. Deut 10:16; 30:6). Water baptism seems to have been administered quite quickly in these early years without the lengthy catechumenate that characterized later church practice (Dunn 1975; Dujarier 1979).

The most obvious origin of this rite was the baptism of John the Baptist, which the gospel writers depict Jesus undergoing at outset of his ministry (Mt 3:13–17; Mk 1:9–11; Lk 3:21–2; Jn 1:32–4). This seems to have been a baptism of repentance, which was deeply eschatological in its content (Mt 3:1ff.; Mk 1:4ff; Lk 3:2ff.; Jn 1:15, 19ff.; Acts 19:4; cf. Josephus, *Antiquities* 18.116ff.). However, the baptism of John cannot fully explain the occurrence of the rite among the early Christian as it was not an initiation rite and was considered, by various New Testament writers, as inadequate in some way (Mt 3:11; Mk 1:8; Lk 3:16; Acts 19:3–7). So it seems likely that other forms of Jewish ritual washing also had a part to play. Proselyte baptism may well have been the most significant additional influence (*b. Yebamot* 46a, b; *Bekorot* 47a; Epictetus, *Discourses* 2.9.20) though the ritual ablutions of the impure (Lev. 11:28; 13:6; 15:6; etc.), priests (e.g. Ex. 30:19), sinners (1 QS 3:5–9, *Sibylline Oracles* 4.165) or ascetics (Josephus, *Life* 11) were probably not unimportant in baptism's genesis. Pagan worship, particularly the worship of the mystery cults (Apuleius, *Golden Ass* 11.23), also included rites of immersion and ritual ablution, as early Christian apologists were only too aware (Tertullian, *On Baptism* 5), but the significance of these should not be exaggerated as the resemblances between them and Christian baptism are not particularly close (Wedderburn 1987).

Baptism was interpreted in a number of ways. Early Christians appear to have retained John the Baptist's association of baptism with the forgiveness of sins (1 Cor. 1:13; 6:11; Acts 2:38; 10:43ff.; 22:16; *Epistle of Barnabas* 11:1; *Acts of Thomas* 132) and the coming eschaton (Acts 2:38–40; Jn 3:5; Rom. 6:4–5; Tit. 3:5–7; Hartman 1997). It also seems to have been understood as leading to rebirth (Jn 3:5; Tit. 3:5; Justin, *Apology* 1.61.3); as a means of acquiring salvation (1 Pet. 3:21; Acts 2:40; 11:14; 16:30–3); as a means of purification (Heb. 10:22); and also as God's seal on Christians (2 Cor. 1:21–2; Eph 1:13–14; 4:30; *Shepherd of Hermas*, Similitudes 9.16.1–4; though it not necessarily the case that water baptism is being spoken of on all these occasions).

Once again the figure of Jesus was central to the way this rite was performed and understood. Baptism, from the outset, was accompanied by a regular form of words in which the believers were described as baptized into Jesus' 'name' (Acts 2:38; 10:48), 'in the name of the Lord Jesus' (Acts 8:16; 19:5 – cf. also Rom. 6:3; 1 Cor. 1:13; Gal. 3:27; Jas 2:7; Justin, *Apology* 1.61.10–13), or, probably somewhat later, 'in the name of the Father, and of the Son and of the Holy Spirit' (Mt 28:19; *Didache* 7:1; Justin, *Apology* 1.61.3, 13; Hartman 1997). Baptism somehow united the believer with Christ (1 Cor. 1:12; Gal. 3:27–8), but given the richness of language employed to describe this union, it is hard to see exactly how this was affected. Nevertheless, it was perceived to be a tangible relationship of some kind as we can see from the part it played in the articulation of early Christian ethics: baptism had a significant role in reconstituting the ethical life of the believer (Rom. 6:12; 1 Cor. 6:9–11; cf. also Col. 3:1–17) and in creating new bonds of solidarity with others who were also 'in Christ' (Gal. 3:27–9). Although, in expressing baptism's significance, New Testament writers also drew on stories of redemption from the Jewish scriptures (1 Pet. 3:20–2; cf. also 1 Cor 10:1–5), the narrative of Jesus was intrinsic to the way this rite was conceptualized. This is most evident in Paul's description of baptism as participation in the death and resurrection of Christ (Rom. 6:3–11; Col. 2:12, 20; cf. also 1 Cor. 1:13; Eph. 2:4ff.) but it is also spoken of in different ways elsewhere (e.g. Mk 10:38; Lk 12:50).

Indeed, this might in some sense explain one of the other notable features of Christian baptism: the role of the Spirit. The Spirit played a prominent part in gospel accounts of Jesus' own baptism (Mt 3:16; Mk 1:10; Lk 3:22; Jn 1:32) and was also central to descriptions of the baptism of believers in a number of early traditions (e.g. Acts 2:38; 8:14–17; 9:17–18; 10:47–8; 19:1–6; 1 Cor. 6:11; 12:13). However, there is no clear causal relationship between the rite of water baptism and the reception of the Spirit in early Christian literature: the Spirit could be received by a believer both before baptism (Acts 10:44–8) or after it (Acts 2:38; 8:14–17; 19:1–7). Indeed, it seems quite likely that when baptism is spoken of in the New Testament it often refers to a spiritual event, independent of water baptism, something not necessarily a rite at all but a metaphor for a common form of religious experience (Acts 1:5; 11:16; 1 Cor. 12:13; Dunn 1970; Fee 1987), which was thought to owe its origins, ultimately, to the activity of Jesus (Mt 3:11; Mk 1:8; Lk 3:16; Jn 1:33).

Other aspects of this phenomenon have remained elusive, especially the baptism on behalf of the dead mentioned in 1 Corinthians 15:29, a practice Paul takes for granted as occurring in the Corinthian community. We have no idea who was being baptized on behalf of whom, and what was the expected result.

Charismatic practices

A group of distinctive religious practices, usually termed 'charismatic', deserve to be discussed together. These practices are usually given this label because they are included among the 'gifts' (*charistmata*) of the Spirit mentioned in 1 Corinthians 12:8–10 (cf. also 12:28–30; 13:1–3, 8; 14:6, 26; Rom. 12:4–8; Eph 4:11) and are usually said to consist of utterances of wisdom and knowledge, gifts of healing, working of miracles, prophecy, discernment of spirits, speaking in tongues (glossolalia), and the interpretation of tongues. (Although it should be noted that not all *charismata* can be thought of as practices of one kind or another; e.g. 'faith' in 1 Cor. 12:9 can hardly be regarded as a specific activity.)

The form that some of these activities took is unclear. We have no idea how a person went about 'discerning between spirits' (1 Cor. 12:10) and we can do little more than guess, from narratives elsewhere in the New Testament, what exactly a person with the gift of 'working miracles' or the person described as having the gift of 'healing' (1 Cor. 12:9) *did*. However, we can say a little more about a couple of practices that receive attention from Paul in 1 Corinthians and also appear in other parts of the New Testament in a similar, if slightly different, form: the gift of prophecy (1 Cor. 11:4–5; 12:10, 29; 13:2; 14:1ff.; cf. Rom. 12:6; 1 Thess. 5:20; Acts 11:27; 13:1; 15:32; 21:9) and that of glossolalia (1 Cor. 12:10, 30; 13:1; 14:2ff.; cf. Acts 2:1–13; 10:46; 19:6; Mk 16:17). The former appears to have involved an individual delivering an intelligible, inspired message, aimed primarily at believers (1 Cor. 14:4) though also capable of affecting unbelievers (1 Cor. 14:24). The latter seems to have been quite different. Glossolalia involved speaking an unknown (1 Cor. 14:2), possibly angelic (1 Cor. 13:1), language, incomprehensible to its hearers, requiring interpretation by someone thought to possess another, distinct, gift (1 Cor. 12:10; 14:27; contrary to the phenomenon described in Acts 2:1–13).

It is clear that some of these 'charismatic' practices were rather shocking to outsiders and capable of misinterpretation (1 Cor. 14:23; Acts 2:13). This is unsurprising. Although there were no precise ancient analogies for most of them, particularly glossolalia (Forbes 1997), and such behaviour was not truly ecstatic as worshippers appear to have remained in control of their actions (1 Cor. 14:29ff.), to an undiscerning outsider the activities could have resembled the kind of enthusiastic worship practised by adherents of the mystery cults and that what often stigmatized as mad by more sober contemporaries (Apuleius, *Golden Ass* 8.27).

The Spirit was understood as the inspiration of these forms of worship (e.g. 1 Cor. 12:4; 14:12; etc) and something available to all believers, at least for the earliest Christians, because of its profoundly eschatological character (Dunn 1975). The use, by the author of Acts, of an adapted form of Joel 2:28–32 (which describes God pouring out the Spirit on all flesh in the last days) to interpret the events of Pentecost (Acts 2:17–21) illustrates this conviction well. However, in recognizing the part the Spirit played in charismatic worship we should not overlook the fact that the earliest Christians also thought that such practices took place in 'the body of Christ' (1 Cor. 12:12, 27) and, ultimately, of course, at the instigation of God (1 Cor. 12:6; 12:28; 14:18, 25, 33). We misunderstand the charismatic practices of the first Christians if we fail to note the way that such activities were thought to relate to the broader Christological and theological convictions and experiences of the communities.

Other practices

A number of other practices that can legitimately be called 'religious', and are somewhat harder to characterize, were also undertaken by the earliest churches, or at least some of them. The holy kiss, for example, appears to have been a quite common form of greeting exchanged by members of the first churches (Rom. 16:16; 1 Cor. 16:20; 2 Cor. 13:12; 1 Thess. 5:26; 1 Pet. 5:14). It is difficult to know where the origin of this practice lay (perhaps Jn 20:21–3?) but it was a striking form of behaviour to contemporaries and provided fuel to pagan accusations of Christian immorality (Tertullian, *To His Wife* 2.4). It certainly had a significant role in the construction of group identity among the earliest Christians, symbolically affirming the fictive language of kinship in use among them (see Klassen 1993). The laying on of hands appears to have emerged as an ordination ritual of some kind (Acts 6:6; 13:3; 1 Tim. 4:14) and became in some early traditions closely bound up with the imparting of the Spirit (Acts 8:17). Fasting, a distinctively Jewish practice (Suetonius, *Augustus* 76), seems to have had a place, if a contested one, in the lives of some early communities (Mt 6:16ff.; Acts 13:2; 14:23; cf. Mt 9:14–15; Mk 2:18–20; Lk 5:33–5) as did anointing the sick with oil, mentioned in Mark 6:13; James 5:14; and *Didache* 10:7 – 11:1. The collection for the relief of the poor in the Jerusalem church, which so preoccupied Paul (Rom. 15:15–32; 1 Cor. 16:1–4; 2 Cor. 8 and 9; Gal. 2:10), should also be mentioned as a religious practice (as should the giving of alms generally; Mt 5:42; 19:21; Mk 10:21; Lk 6:30, 38; 18:22; Acts 10:4; 20:35; Gal. 6:9; Jas 1:27; Heb. 13:16; 1 Jn 3:17; Garrison 1993) even though it might not be understood as such by many moderns and even though it can legitimately be interpreted in a number of rather more mundane ways (as, e.g., an expression of early Christian economic mutualism; Meggitt 1998). In the Johannine community the unusual practice of ritual footwashing (Jn 13:15) appears to have been instituted.

Most of these practices, where we can determine anything substantially about them, seem to have been rooted in the story of Christ and its consequences for the believer. This is evident, for example, in Paul's use of the narrative of Jesus' descent ('for your sake he became poor') to encourage participation in the collection (2 Cor. 8:9) but can also be seen elsewhere (Johannine footwashing, e.g., was obviously carried out in imitation of Jesus' own actions).

Distinctive absences from Christian worship

Finally, before we end our survey we should be aware that it is not just what the early Christians *did* when they came together to worship that is important but what they *did not do*. The absence of sacrifice in the early churches (though, as we have noted, some took part in non-Christian sacrifices outside the community) is particularly unusual as it was a central feature of virtually all other forms of religious life in the Empire during the period, including most forms of Judaism before 70 CE (Sanders 1992; Burkert 1985; Beard et al. 1998a, 1998b). The absence of a temple, priesthood or festivals would also have seemed strange to most neighbours of the new movement as all three loomed large in the lives of non-Jews and Jews (even diaspora Jews, before and after its destruction, remained concerned with the Jerusalem temple and publicly celebrated many of the key festivals such as Passover, Tabernacles and the Day of Atonement; Barclay 1996). The single initiation rite of baptism would also have appeared striking, at least to pagans, who were familiar with the concept of multiple initiation (Apuleius, *Apology* 55.8). Participation in Christian worship, at least for preventing a person from taking part in the rites of other groups (e.g. 1 Cor. 10:21), although echoing in some sense the exclusivity of Jewish (and Samaritan) worship (Ex. 20:3; Deut. 5:7), would also have appeared rather unusual to most inhabitants of the first-century world for whom such ideas were antisocial and inimical to the healthy religious life of the Empire.

A number of explanations can be given for the elements missing from early Christian worship. However, belief in the uniqueness and finality of Jesus' death (Moule 1956), which is common to the diverse traditions in the New Testament, is probably the best (although there is some diversity in the articulation of this conviction). For example, in Hebrews, it is made clear that priesthood and sacrifice are at an end because Christ has been appointed eternal High Priest (Hebrews 5ff.) after the order of Melchizedek (Gen. 14:17–20; Ps. 110:4) rather than Aaron, and he is also the eternal sacrifice (Heb. 9:12) rendering all others unnecessary. Other traditions employ a slightly different logic to arrive at the same conclusion: the death of Jesus is both the consummate sacrifice (e.g. Rom. 3:25; Eph. 5:2; 1 Jn 4:10; 1 Pet. 1:2, 19) and also something that makes all Christians priests, all equally capable of offering superior spiritual sacrifices (1 Pet. 2:4–10; Rev. 1:5–6; cf. also Rom. 12:1ff.). There was no longer a need for temples because, at least for some, Jesus was himself the Temple (Jn 2:19–21; cf. also Rev. 21:22), or the body of Christ, the new community, was now the Temple (1 Cor. 3:16; 6:19; Eph. 2:21). Likewise, the need for festivals was considered at an end because of the completeness of the work done by Christ (1 Cor. 5:6–8; Col. 2:8–19).

CONCLUSIONS

The religious practices of the early Christians were diverse, as were the meanings attached to them. But despite this diversity we should recognize that there was, to a large degree, an essential unity of experience that was assumed to underlie them all. This is evident in the language used by the worshippers themselves to explain what they were doing when they prayed, sang hymns, consumed the Lord's Supper, or undertook any other worship activity. And it was from this common experience – which seems to have been understood as the believer's participation in the narrative of Jesus' earthly and heavenly life, and its consequences, in particular the gift of the Spirit that the new identity of the believer, and ultimately the new religion of Christianity, was forged. If we overlook this fundamental experiential feature, deeply and actively entwined with the unique soteriological story of the community, we miss the essence of early Christian worship.

BIBLIOGRAPHY

Barclay, John M. (1996) *Jews in the Mediterranean Diaspora: From Alexander to Trajan (323 BCE–117 CE)*. Edinburgh: T&T Clark.

Barrett, C. K. (1991) 'Attitudes to the Temple in the Acts of the Apostles.' *Templum Amicitiae: Essays on the Second Temple Presented to Ernst Bammel*. Ed. W. Horbury. Sheffield: Sheffield Academic Press, 345–67.

Barth, Markus (1974) *Ephesians 1–3*. Garden City: Doubleday.

Beard, M., J. North and S. Price (1998a) *Religions of Rome: A History*. Cambridge: Cambridge University Press.

——— (1998b) *Religions of Rome: A Sourcebook*. Cambridge: Cambridge University Press.

Beasley-Murray, G. R. (1962) *Baptism in the New Testament*. London: Macmillan.

Beckwith, Roger (ed.) (1995) *Sacrifice in the Bible*. Carlisle: Paternoster.

Benko, Stephen (1985) *Pagan Rome and the Early Christians*. London: B. T. Batsford.

Boismard, M. E. (1957/1958) 'Une liturgie baptismale dans la Prima Petri.' *Revue biblique* 63: 182–208 and 64: 161–83.

Bokser, Baruch (1984) *The Origins of the Seder*. Berkeley: University of California Press.

Bornkamm, G. (1969) *Early Christian Experience*. London: SCM.

Bradshaw, Paul (1996) *Early Christian Worship: A Basic Introduction to Ideas and Practice*. London: SPCK.

Bradshaw, Paul F. and L. Hoffman (1991) *The Making of Jewish and Christian Worship*. London: University of Notre Dame Press.

Bremmer, J. M. (1981) 'Greek Hymns.' *Faith, Hope and Worship: Aspects of Religious Worship in the Ancient World*. Ed. H. S. Versnel. Leiden: E. J. Brill, 193–215.

Burkert, W. (1985) *Greek Religion*. Oxford: Basil Blackwell.

Chazon, E. and M. Bernstein (1997) 'An Introduction to Prayer at Qumran.' *Prayer from Alexander to Constantine: A Critical Anthology*. Ed. M. Kiley. London: Routledge, 9–13.

Collins, A. Y. (1989) 'The Origin of Christian Baptism.' *Studia liturgica*, 19: 28–46.

Cross, F. L. (1954) *1 Peter: A Paschal Liturgy*. London: Mowbray.

Cullmann, O. (1953) *Early Christian Worship*. London: SCM.

—— (1995) *Prayer in the New Testament*. London: SCM.

Cuming, G. J. (1975) 'Service Endings in the Epistles.' *New Testament Studies*, 22: 110–13.

Davies, W. D. and Dale C. Allison (1988) *The Gospel According to St Matthew*, Vol. 1. Edinburgh: T&T Clark.

Dujarier, M. (1979) *A History of the Catechumenate: The First Six Centuries*. New York: Sadlier.

Dunn, J. D. G. (1970) *Baptism in the Holy Spirit*. London: SCM.

—— (1975) *Jesus and the Spirit: A Study of the Religious Experience of Jesus and the First Christians as Reflected in the New Testament*. London: SCM.

—— (1977) *Unity and Diversity in the New Testament*. London: SCM.

Edwards, M. J. (1992) 'Some Early Christian Immoralities.' *Ancient Society*, 23: 71–82.

Falk, Daniel (1995) 'Jewish Prayer Literature and the Jerusalem Church in Acts.' *The Book of Acts in its First Century Setting. Vol 4: Palestinian Setting*. Ed. R. Bauckham. Grand Rapids: Eerdmans, 267–301.

Fantham, E. (1996) *Roman Literary Culture*. Baltimore: The Johns Hopkins University Press.

Fee, G. (1987) *The First Epistle to the Corinthians*. Grand Rapids: Eerdmans.

Forbes, C. (1997) *Prophecy and Inspired Speech in Early Christianity and its Hellenistic Environment*. Peabody: Hendrickson.

Garnsey, Peter (1984) 'Religious Toleration in Classical Antiquity.' *Persecution and Toleration*. Ed. W. J. Shiels. Oxford: Basil Blackwell, 1–28.

—— (1999) *Food and Society in Classical Antiquity*. Cambridge: Cambridge University Press.

Garrison, Roman (1993) *Redemptive Almsgiving in Early Christianity*. Sheffield: Sheffield Academic Press.

Grant, Robert (1981) 'Charges of "Immorality" Against Various Religious Groups in Antiquity.' *Essays on Gnosticism and Hellenistic Religions*. Eds. R. van den Broek and M. J. Vermaseren. Leiden: E. J. Brill, 160–70.

Hanson, A. T. (1983) *The Living Utterances of God*. London: Darton, Longman & Todd.

Hartman, L. (1997) *'Into the Name of the Lord Jesus': Baptism in the Early Church*. Edinburgh: T&T Clark.

Hilton, M. (1994) *The Christian Effect on Jewish Life*. London: SCM.

Horrell, D. (1999) *Social-Scientific Approach to New Testament Interpretation*. Edinburgh: T&T Clark.

Horst, P. W. van der (1994) 'Silent Prayer in Antiquity.' *Numen*, 41: 1–25.

Jeremias, J. (1964) *The Eucharistic Words of Jesus*. London: SCM.

Jewett, R. (1993) 'Tenement Churches and Communal Meals.' *Biblical Research*, 38: 23–43.

Johnson, Luke T. (1997) *Religious Experience in Earliest Christianity: A Neglected Factor in New Testament Study*. Minneapolis: Ausburg Fortress.

Karris, Robert J. (1996) *A Symphony of New Testament Hymns*. Collegeville: The Liturgical Press.

Kiley, M. (1997) *Prayer from Alexander to Constantine*. London: Routledge.

Klassen, W. (1993) 'The Sacred Kiss in the New Testament: An Example of a Social Boundary Line.' *New Testament Studies*, 39: 122–35.

Leitzmann, H. (1979) *Mass and the Lord's Supper: A Study in the History of the Liturgy*. Leiden: E. J. Brill.

Levine, L. I. (1987) *The Synagogue in Late Antiquity*. Philadelphia: ASOR.

Maccoby, H. (1991) *Paul and Hellenism*. London: SCM.

Marshall, I. (1980) *Last Supper and Lord's Supper*. Exeter: Paternoster.

Martin, R. P. (1964) *Worship in the Early Church*. London: Marshall, Morgan & Scott.

Meeks, Wayne (1983) *The First Urban Christians*. New Haven: Yale University Press.

Meggitt, J. J. (1998) *Paul, Poverty and Survival*. Edinburgh: T&T Clark.

Moule, C. F. D. (1956) *The Sacrifice of Christ*. London: Hodder & Stoughton.

—— (1961) *Worship in the New Testament*. London: Lutterworth.

Neyrey, Jerome H. (1990) *Paul in Other Words: A Cultural Reading of His Letters*. Louisville: Westminster John Knox.

Pals, Daniel L. (1996) *Seven Theories of Religion*. Oxford: Oxford University Press.

Rowland, Christopher (1985) *Christian Origins*. London: SPCK.

Sanders, E. P. (1992) *Judaism: Practice and Belief 63 BCE – 66 CE*. London: SCM.

Sandmel, Samuel (1962) 'Parallelomania.' *Journal of Biblical Literature*, 81: 3–13.

Schüssler, Fiorenza, E. (1996) *In Memory of Her: A Feminist Reconstruction of Christian Origins*. London: SCM.

Sigal, P. (1984) 'Early Christian and Rabbinic Liturgical Affinities: Exploring Liturgical Acculturation.' *New Testament Studies*, 30: 63–90.

Slater, W. J. (ed.) (1991) *Dining in a Classical Context*. Ann Arbor: University of Michigan Press.

Smith, Jonathan Z. (1990) *Drudgery Divine: On the Comparison of Early Christianities and the Religions of Antiquity*. London: School of Oriental and African Studies, University of London.

Stauffer, Ethelbert (1955) *New Testament Theology* London: SCM.

Wainwright, G. (1971) *Eucharist and Eschatology*. London: Epworth.

Wedderburn, A. J. M. (1987) *Baptism and Resurrection: Studies in Pauline Theology Against its Graeco-Roman Background*. Tübingen: J. C. B. Mohr.

White, L. M. (1996) *The Social Origins of Christian Architecture. Building God's House in the Roman World: Architectural Adaptation among Pagans, Jews and Christians*. Valley Forge: Trinity Press International.

—— (1997) *The Social Origins of Christian Architecture: Texts and Monuments for the Christian Domus Ecclesiae in its Environment*. Valley Forge: Trinity Press International.

Wiles, G. P. (1974) *Paul's Intercessionary Prayers*. Cambridge: Cambridge University Press.

Williamson, R. (1975) 'The Eucharist and the Epistle to the Hebrews.' *New Testament Studies*, 21: 300–12.

PART VI

BIBLICAL FIGURES

CHAPTER THIRTY-SEVEN

ISRAEL'S ANCESTORS
The patriarchs and matriarchs

—·◆·—

George W. Ramsey

According to Jewish tradition, the patriarchs of Israel are three in number: Abraham, his son Isaac, and his grandson Jacob (Ber. 16b; cf. the frequent mention of these throughout the book of Deuteronomy [e.g., 1:8; 6:10; 9:5; 29:13]; 4 Macc. 7:19). The matriarchs, in turn, are four: Abraham's wife Sarah, Isaac's wife Rebekah, and Jacob's wives, Leah and Rachel. It is the story of the three generations represented by these Ancestors that is recounted in Genesis 12–50, as the horizon of the biblical narrative narrows abruptly from the whole of humankind (Gen. 1–11) to focus on this one family.

It is not clear from the Bible when the storytellers thought of the patriarchs and matriarchs as having lived. The stories purport to describe these Ancestors as living centuries before the time of Moses, whose lifetime most historians would date in the thirteenth century BCE, but the chronological data concerning the Ancestors are inconsistent.[1] Using a combination of chronological information in the Bible and evidence about conditions in the ancient Near East, scholars have located 'the patriarchal era' at various periods from the late third millennium to the late second millennium BCE (Dever 1977: 92–96; Gottwald 1985: 165–66).

Scholars have long debated whether the stories in Genesis 12–50 were based to some degree on actual historical persons and events, or whether the stories are fictitious legends. Most of the stories in Genesis 12–50 are not reports of the sort that the historian could ever verify. These are mostly family stories, with almost no mention of people or events that would find their way into the kinds of written records that have survived from the ancient Near East.

The artifices of the storyteller are evident in a number of ways in these tales of the Ancestors. Many of the tales have to do with private experiences, and the reader is invited to accept that the all-knowing narrator could have access to scenes and situations to which no real external observer would be privy (e.g., Abram and Sarai *en route* to Egypt, Gen. 12:11–13; Abraham and Isaac climbing Mount Moriah, Gen. 22:6–8; Laban and Rachel in her tent as she conceals the stolen idols, Gen. 31:33–5; Jacob wrestling with an angel, Gen. 32:22–32).

The Ancestral stories exemplify a number of popular folk motifs such as the barren wife (Gen. 16), the success of the younger (Jacob, Joseph), the deceiver deceived (Jacob deceives Isaac, Gen. 27, and subsequently, Laban deceives Jacob, Gen.

29:4–30), and the spurned seductress (Gen. 39:7–17). The employment of motifs such as these makes one suspect that, rather than accounts based on actual people and events, we are dealing with tales and tale elements borrowed from a broad array of folk lore (cf. Irvin 1977).

Mythical, legendary, or unrealistic features such as the following also suggest the presence of imaginative fictionalizing: the excessively lengthy lifespans of the patriarchs and matriarchs (cf. Gen. 23:1; 25:7; 35:28; 47:28), a ninety-year old woman bearing a child (Gen. 17:17), a human being changed into a pillar of salt (Gen. 19:17, 24–6), magical prenatal conditioning (Gen. 30:37–43), angel appearances (16:7–14; 18:1–33), and characters of different lands being able to understand and converse readily with one another (Gen. 12:10–20; 20:1–16).

It is not uncommon that the stories in Genesis 12–50 are interpreted as 'political allegory' (Alter 1996: 143; cf. Rosenberg 1986) or as 'typology' (Brettler 1996: 55–9). Many a character in Genesis 12–50 functions as an eponym, that is, the supposed ancestor of a group that bears the name of the individual. Genesis 25:23 makes it very plain that Jacob and Esau were understood as eponymous ancestors of Israel and Edom, respectively (cf. also Mal. 1:2–5). The twelve sons of Jacob represent the twelve tribes of Israel (cf. Gen. 49, esp. v. 28a).[2] Certain of the narratives and poems in Genesis, which ostensibly refer to individuals such as Jacob/Israel and his sons, are interpreted as encapsulations of tribal experiences – tribal movements, occupations, changes in status (Eissfeldt 1965: 40–1). Some of the genealogical narratives and lists found in various Old Testament books apparently contain, under the guise of individual kinship relationships, fragments of information about changing relationships between tribal and clan groups (e.g., a marriage would represent the union of two groups, concubinage a relationship of unequal groups; see Clark 1977: 126; Wilson 1977; Gottwald 1985: 161–2).

The overarching theme of Genesis 12–50 is the promise to the patriarchs of abundant progeny, blessing, and possession of the land of Canaan (Westermann 1980: 95–163; Emerton 1982). The integration of the assorted stories via this theme (sometimes introducing the theme into contexts where it seems to be intrusive, as Gen. 13:14–17; 15:13–16; 26:2–5) reflects the activity of a compiler bringing diverse materials and tales artificially into association with one another (von Rad 1962: 167–71; see further on the promise theme below).

Such factors as the above have led virtually all scholars to acknowledge the presence in Genesis 12–50 of imaginative elements that evolved over time. The debate continues today among those who believe the stories of the Ancestors to be purely fictitious in nature, composed to serve the ideological purposes of later generations of Israelites (e.g., Garbini 1988; Davies 1992), and those who, while admitting that the stories contain legendary and ideological elements, nonetheless maintain that the stories exhibit features which indicate great age and likely contain recollections of actual people and events (Hendel 1995; Kitchen 1995; McCarter 1999).

An influential school of American scholars has maintained that features in the stories in Genesis 12–50 such as the personal names, social customs, and the Ancestors' mode of life fit better with the evidence of nonbiblical documents from the early second millennium BCE than in any later age (cf. especially Bright 1981: 77–87). Thus it has been argued that the stories in Genesis 12–50, while not verifiable in detail, nonetheless have an air of verisimilitude about them, indicating that there was at least a nucleus of historical fact underlying the accounts.

The personal names found in the patriarchal stories (e.g., Abram/Abraham, Jacob, Nahor, Terah) were said to fit more readily into the nomenclature of the population of northwest Mesopotamia of the early second millennium BCE than into that of any later period (Bright 1981: 78). That is the geographical region to which the traditions trace the patriarchal origins (see Gen. 11:31) and the period of ancient history in which the traditions seem to date them.

The most tenacious of the arguments used to substantiate the Ancestral narratives derived from the similarities detected between certain behavior recounted in the patriarchal stories and social customs or legal procedures attested in documents from second-millennium Mesopotamian cultures. Very simply, the argument is that some of the cultural customs and legal practices reflected in the narratives, such as (1) the wife–sister relationship indicated in Genesis 20:12, (2) the 'adoption' of Jacob by Laban, which some interpreters discern in Genesis 29–31, (3) the prices cited for slaves (Gen. 37:28) or (4) the covenant forms reflected in Genesis 21:23–33; 26:28–30; 31:51–4, match up best with customs and laws that prevailed in Mesopotamian cultures of the second millennium – and that comparable parallels are *not* to be found anywhere else (cf. Bright 1981: 78–80; Ramsey 1981: 29–33; Kitchen 1995: 52–6).

Since the 1970s these and similar arguments seeking to locate an exclusive historical context into which the Ancestral narratives 'fit' have suffered crippling attacks. Critics have contended that those who argued in this fashion have (1) seen parallels where none exist, (2) reconstructed either the biblical story or the extrabiblical material or both in order to insert details necessary to create a parallel, or (3) neglected to consider extrabiblical documents from later periods, which provide equally good, if not better, parallels to the practices in the patriarchal stories (see, most notably, Thompson 1974 and Van Seters 1975; cf. Ramsey 1981: 29–40; Hendel 1995: 56).

As discussed further below, it has long been recognized that the Genesis stories were written much later than the times they describe and thus inevitably contain some late elements incorporated by redactors and editors from their own historical circumstances, which were considerably later than the era of the Ancestors.

For example, a number of ethnic relationships reported in Genesis could not have been conceived before the late second or early first millennium (cf. Thompson 1974: 298–308). The association of Abraham's origins with the Chaldeans (Gen. 11:28–29, 31; 15:7) can only have originated after the appearance of this people in the early first millennium (cf. De Vaux 1978: 187–8). The Arameans, among whom wives for Isaac and Jacob are sought (Gen. 24; 29) and among whom Jacob finds asylum from his brother's wrath (Gen. 28–31), did not appear with certainty in Mesopotamian texts until almost 1100 BCE (Van Seters 1975: 29–34). The Philistines (cf. Gen. 21:32–4; 26:1–22) did not arrive in Canaan until shortly after 1200 BCE, that is, not only after the supposed time of the Ancestors, but even after the time of Moses (cf. De Vaux 1978: 503–10).

Occasional references are made to the use of camels (e.g., Gen. 12:16; 24:10–20; 31:17; 37:25), but it is unlikely that the camel was domesticated for use as a burden-carrying animal until at least the very late second millennium BCE (cf. Sarna 1970: 105, 173; Van Seters 1975: 17).

Elements in the 'promise' to the patriarchs that refer to the growth of Abraham's family into a 'great nation' (e.g., Gen. 12:2; 18:18; cf. also 17:5, 6, 16; 35:11) are believed by most biblical scholars to presuppose the development of Israel into a major power (Westermann 1976: 692). Further, those parts of the Jacob cycle that have as their theme the subjection of Edom (Esau) to Israel (Jacob) (Gen. 25:23; 27:27–9, 39–40) likely reflect a period subsequent to David's subjecting Edom (cf. Wagner 1972: 129–30).

On the other hand, there are not lacking some features within the biblical story which suggest that historical memories of earlier periods are indeed preserved in the stories of the Ancestors and that the narratives therefore were not created *de novo* and *in toto* by writers centuries removed from the time purportedly described.[3]

For instance, the Pentateuchal traditions exhibit a consciousness of a distinction between the religion of the patriarchs and the religion of Israel in later times (Westermann 1985: 575–6; Moberly 1990: 113–14; Hendel 1992: 938). The two versions of Moses' call (Exod. 3:13–17, considered a passage in the 'E' source, and Exod. 6:2–3, the 'P' source) imply that the religion of the pre-Mosaic era was different from that of the religion of Moses and that only with Moses was the divine name 'Yahweh' used. There are other indications that the worship of the patriarchs was directed to deities other than Yahweh: there are frequent references in Genesis to 'the god of my/your/his father,' or to 'the god of Abraham/Isaac/Jacob,' and these references have long been taken to reflect the worship of clan deities who revealed themselves first to the eponymous ancestors of the respective clans (Alt 1966: 1–77; Cross 1973: chs 1–3; Fohrer 1974: 35–42, 60–5). The god traveled with the clan and was considered related to the clan (cf. De Vaux 1978: 272–3).[4]

In addition, the Genesis traditions indicate that the individuals depicted there worshipped various manifestations of the Canaanite high god El after their migration into the land of Canaan (Gen. 16:13; 17:1; 21:33; 31:13; 46:3: the English word 'God' in these verses represents the Hebrew word *'el*). Several scholars believe that the form of the El religion which influenced the patriarchal traditions was an earlier form of that religion than is depicted in the fourteenth-century Canaanite texts from the site of ancient Ugarit (Cross 1973: 13–75; De Vaux 1978: 274–9).

Common sense suggests that if the Genesis narratives were purely the product of later centuries, it would have been more natural to ascribe to that earlier era the form of religion the authors themselves practiced. If first-millennium writers were creating the ancestral legends afresh and 'read back' into the patriarchal period their own relations with Arameans and Chaldeans and customs they themselves followed, why should they not also have imposed on the picture of the Ancestors the religion they themselves practiced?

The kinship association of the Israelites with the Arameans reflected in the patriarchal narratives is held by some scholars to be artificial and of late origin (Thompson 1974: 298–308 and Van Seters 1975: 29–34). It is, however, difficult to understand how and why this notion would have arisen and been given credence at a time when Israel was so often engaged in hostilities with the Arameans. The Arameans are not portrayed simply as peripheral acquaintances; the wives of Jacob (and therefore the very mothers of the Israelite tribes) are said to have been Arameans (cf. also Deut. 26:5). If there was in fact nothing in the background of the people of Israel to link them ethnically and geographically to northwest Mesopotamia, why would they trace their origins to that region populated in the first millennium by a hated people?[5]

Several texts from the monarchical period of Israel's history exhibit condemnatory attitudes toward the sanctuary at Bethel (1 Kgs 12: 25–33; 13:1–5; Amos 3:14; 5:4–5; Hos. 4:15; 10:5). The significant role which Bethel plays in the Ancestral narratives (Gen. 12:8; 13:3; 28:11–21; 31:13; 35:1–15) seems likely a tradition inherited from a time before Bethel acquired such an ignominious reputation (Sarna 1970: 192).

An inscription of the tenth-century Pharaoh Sheshonk I of Egypt, in detailing various places the king of Egypt seized on an expedition into Canaan, mentions a site in southern Canaan the name of which seems to be 'field of Abram' or 'fort of Abram.' Several scholars have proposed that such a place-name in southern Canaan likely derives from the prominence of a figure by the name of Abram in earlier times in that area, which is the region where the Genesis narratives locate Abraham (Clements 1967: 45n.; Hendel 1995: 55–9; McCarter 1999: 23–24).

On the theory that the stories of the twelve sons of Jacob are political allegory disguising movements and experiences of the tribes bearing the names of the eponymic Ancestors it is noteworthy that Jacob's eldest sons, Reuben and Simeon, represent tribes that play a very meagre role after the emergence of Israel in Canaan. It is argued that the tradition of their seniority must go back to an era when these tribes were in fact preeminent (Noth 1960: 70–1; Sarna 1970: 199; Bright 1981: 135–6).

There is general agreement among Old Testament specialists that, however old the traditions underlying the Ancestral stories might be, the stories in Genesis were not set down in *writing* until the *first* millennium BCE. For the past century the prevailing theory concerning the composition of Genesis has been that the book is a composite work, consisting of at least three different strands, strata, or redactions. The three major strands are commonly labeled J, E, and P, with J being considered the earliest of these and P the latest.[6] During most of the twentieth century the common dating for 'J' has been in the tenth century, around the time of the monarchy of David and Solomon (Driver 1956: 125; Wolff 1966; Richards 1985: 1152). However, it is held by a growing minority of scholars that the Yahwist (J) material (while still the earliest of the major strands) was not composed until the *sixth* century BCE (Thompson 1974; Van Seters 1975; Whybray 1987; for discussion, see Lemche 1985: 357–66; Nicholson 1991[7]).

Even if the more conservative dating of the Yahwist is assumed (tenth century BCE) and the Ancestral era should be dated as late as the mid- to late second millennium (this latter a view held by very few scholars), there is still a gap of at least several hundred years separating the era of the Ancestors from the writing of their stories. Whether historical recollections can be maintained with accuracy, via oral transmission, for more than about three generations is debated (for differing opinions see Van Seters 1975: 159; De Vaux 1978: 181–5; Kitchen 1978: 66–8; Kirkpatrick 1988: 113–14; Hendel 1995: 70).

In searching for the most likely date for the origin of the stories, scholars attempt to identify an era that would have motivated the themes found in these narratives. For what audience would it be especially critical, for instance, to hear the assurance God gives to Abraham that his descendants will possess the land of Canaan? Some have proposed that traditions about promises such as this originated among clans in the premonarchical era who wished to acquire a holding of arable land (Noth 1972: 55). Others (e.g., Clements 1967: 58–9) have maintained that the unconditional nature of the promise to Abraham of an extensive empire made it an important theologumenon to a writer in the time of the Davidic monarchy, helping to secure divine authority for the Davidic monarchy and the great state over which that king presided. Still others argue that the stories were not at all written with the intention of giving a true representation of the early period, but rather to assure Judeans exiled in Babylon in the sixth century that their rightful place was in Canaan and that their absence from that land was but temporary.[8]

The further one distances the compilation of the Ancestral narratives from the era they purport to describe the more tenuous is the correlation that can be expected between the narratives and historical reality. All biblical critics dealing with Genesis reckon *at least* three to four centuries between 'the patriarchal era' and the earliest written narrative of that era. If we should take the biblical chronological data at face value, we would be facing a gap of about a millennium to a millennium and a half. Given such a gap, one can only assume that, if the stories in Genesis 12–50 are indeed derived eventually from traditions that reach back into the time before the settlement of Israelite tribes in Canaan, the original traditions have been extensively altered in the history of transmission (see, e.g., Clements 1967: chs 3, 4; Noth 1972: 54–8; De Vaux 1978: 165–77; Garbini 1988: 80–2)

Critical research has concluded that the traditions of the several patriarchs developed independently of one another. Originally separate traditions about these patriarchs have, in the opinion of many scholars, been joined together by redactors at a secondary stage of transmission. The stories of Abraham and Jacob, in particular, are concerned with different *themes* (concern for posterity in the Abraham cycle, concern for land in the Jacob cycle; see Och 1993: 168). The narratives of the two men are centered around separate *geographical areas*, where they likely circulated at one time independent of each other (Anderson 1986: 171–2). The *styles* of the separate traditions differ in that the Abraham traditions consist mostly of individual episodes only loosely related to one another, whereas there is a greater connectedness in the Jacob stories, and the material dealing with Joseph and the other children of Jacob constitutes a well-crafted novella (Noth 1972: 208–13; Humphreys 1988). The Abraham and Jacob traditions include frequent theophanies and divine interventions, but there is a distinct absence of such in the Joseph story.

Consequently it is widely held among Old Testament scholars that the arrangement of Abraham, Isaac, Jacob, and the twelve sons of Jacob in a genealogical chain is an artificial connection made at a relatively late stage in the growth of the Genesis traditions (see De Vaux 1978: 165–77; Garbini 1988: 81–2). The notion of the twelve tribal fathers being sons of a single man named 'Israel' (Jacob) is held to be a fiction that grew up in the period of the judges or later. The various groups that eventually constituted Israel acquired their respective homelands in Palestine at different periods of time and in various ways and from diverse backgrounds.[9] The sense of unity among these assorted groups evolved on Palestinian soil certainly no earlier than the period of the judges.

The quest to establish the historicity of these Ancestors – to whatever degree it proves successful – seems certain to arrive only at figures quite different from those portrayed in the Genesis narratives. For example, it is widely conceded that the figure of Jacob (1) was not originally linked to Abraham and Isaac in a genealogical chain; (2) was not originally associated with the twelve sons assigned to him in the present form of the biblical narrative; (3) was not really a brother of Edom's ancestor; and (4) was originally a separate figure from 'Israel' (see Noth 1972: 54–8, 79–101; De Vaux 1978: 165–77). To speak of a 'historical Jacob' whose experiences lay behind the stories in Genesis, but to acknowledge that the associations just mentioned are all secondary developments in the growth of the Jacob cycle, is to speak of a 'historical Jacob' quite different from the biblical Jacob. The fact that the stripped-down Jacob was an 'actual historical person' would mean little. It is the *storied* Jacob who has served the Jewish and Christian communities through the years as a paradigmatic figure.

At present the argument between scholars who believe the Genesis stories to be pure fabrication constructed in the interests of ideology and those who believe that there are old elements in the stories seems to be at a stalemate. With biblical scholars having reached an impasse with regard to the quest to recover historical traces of the Ancestors,[10] we may turn our attention more fruitfully to the significance and understanding of the patriarchs and the matriarchs that have emerged within the faith traditions and among interpreters of the Hebrew Scriptures. What meaning or values do readers find in the figures of Abraham and Sarah, Isaac and Rebekah, Jacob and his wives and his children?

Biblical Abraham[11] may be characterized as '*the* father' (the Hebrew element *'ab* in the names Abram and Abraham means 'father'). It is from him and his wife Sarah that the nation of the Hebrews, whose story constitutes the Old Testament, will issue. The story can move forward only when Isaac is born to the couple as they are at or near the century mark in age. Abraham is the original recipient of God's covenant with the Hebrew people (cf. Gen. 17). He is depicted in Genesis as a rather well-to-do seminomad living often near and in relationship to urban centers; he has a retinue of servants and many possessions (Gen. 12:5, 16; 13:2–7). He is able to assemble an army to deal with invading foreign kings (Gen. 14). Abraham deals gracefully with his nephew Lot in a difficult situation (Gen. 13), and he comes to Lot's defense on two occasions (Gen. 14:11–16; 18:16–33). Abraham is hospitable to three visitors who turn out to be messengers of God (Gen. 18), who will bring destruction upon Sodom and Gomorrah.

The story of Abraham stretches in effect between two divine imperatives: the command in Genesis 12:1 that Abram should 'Go . . . to the land that I will show you' and the command in Genesis 22:2 that Abraham should take his beloved son Isaac and 'Go to . . . one of the mountains that I shall show you' to offer Isaac as a sacrifice. Abraham's unquestioning responses to these commands (cf. the simple report in Gen. 12:4 in a single Hebrew word, *wylk*, 'and-he-went') characterize him as a model of faith and obedience (cf. Gross 1989). However, in several stories Abraham shows himself a man of uncertain faith: twice, in order to save his own life, he pretends that his wife is his sister (Gen. 12:11–13; 20:2–13).[12] Abraham becomes anxious about his lack of an heir, despite God's promise (Gen. 15:2–3); amidst his anxiety, Abraham heeds his wife's suggestion to lie with the Egyptian maid Hagar (Gen. 16) in an effort by the couple to secure a son by a means of their own devising.[13] Abraham laughs in disbelief when God announces the imminent pregnancy of ninety-year-old Sarah (Gen. 17:15–19). Notably, however, in contrast to the first – anxious – recorded words of Abraham to God (Gen. 15:2, 8), the last utterance recorded of Abraham (Gen. 24:7) expresses absolute confidence that the Lord will keep his promise (Sarna 1970: 171).

Figure 37.1 Rembrandt, *Abraham and Isaac*. In this etching from 1645, Rembrandt has depicted Abraham's dilemma as he and Isaac might have conversed about the imminent sacrifice: with one hand the father grips his heart and with the other he points towards the heavens, whose will he is constrained to obey. Isaac appears to comprehend little. Copyright The Pierpont Morgan Library, New York. B.34.

Not only is Abraham commonly represented, especially in Christianity,[14] as a paradigm of faith in God (cf. Rom. 4; Gal. 3:6–9; Heb. 11:8–12); his obedient responses to God's commands have also qualified him as a paragon of faithfulness (cf. Gen. 26:5; *Test. Benj.* 10:2–5). The rabbis often spoke of Abraham's faithfulness such that his merits were sufficient to have salvific effect for his descendants (cf. Moberly 1990). Jewish and Muslim writings credit Abraham with rejection of idolatry (*Jub.* 11–12, 15; *Apoc. Abr.* 1:1 – 9:6; 29:1–8; Qur'an 2:135; 6:74; 19:41–50) and obedience to the Torah even in the centuries before the Law was given to Moses (*Gen. R.* 64:4; *Ned.* 32a; *Yoma* 28b).

No event in the Abraham story has been more significant in later religious history than the story of the Binding of Isaac (Gen. 22), frequently referred to as the 'Akedah' (after the Hebrew term for 'binding'). The costliness of the sacrifice that Abraham is bidden to make is stressed by the Lord's instruction, 'Take your son – your only son – the beloved – Isaac' (Gen. 22:2). As the command to leave his homeland (Gen. 12:1) had bidden him to break with his past, so this command to offer up the heir to the promise bids him to break with his future.[15] New Testament writers utilized several themes of this story: Hebrews 11:17–20 cites Abraham as one of the principal exemplars of faith; James 2:21–3 affirms the faithfulness of Abraham to illustrate the teaching that works accompany faith; the language of Paul in Romans 8:32, referring to God's not witholding his son Jesus, seems to reflect the Septuagint language of Genesis 22:16; some recent studies have perceived the influence of Genesis 22:2 on the report of the utterance from heaven at Jesus' baptism and transfiguration (Daly 1977).

In the biblical account of the second generation of Ancestors, Isaac proves to be a rather pale and passive character. After his long-awaited birth, the first episode involving him is the Akedah passage, in which his is a passive role. When it is time to secure a wife for Isaac, a servant is dispatched by Abraham to accomplish this (Gen. 24). The last episode in which we see Isaac is one in which he cannot see (Gen. 27), and the focus is more on his son Jacob securing a blessing by deception. The only episode in which Isaac holds anything like the center of the stage is the episode recounted in Genesis 26 of his sojourn in Gerar – and here he seems to mimic behavior of his father (cf. Gen. 12, 20), in passing off his wife as a sister.

In the course of later Jewish interpretation of the Akedah the emphasis on the character of Isaac was expanded. Stress was put on the *willingness* of Isaac's near-sacrifice (e.g., 4 Macc. 13:12; cf. Daly 1977 and references there; also Qur'an 37:103). Some interpreters reckoned him to be a man at the age of thirty-seven giving voluntary consent, exhibiting filial piety and devotion to God.[16] According to many rabbinic interpreters the merits of Isaac's offering himself up assured redemptive benefits for his descendants.[17] During times of Jewish struggles against Rome, Isaac perhaps served as a model to inspire voluntary martyrdom (Davies and Chilton 1978: 522, 529).

The narratives about Jacob/Israel constitute a national self-portrait: this is the man whom the Israelites claimed as their eponym – he was their 'Uncle Sam,' their 'John Bull.' In effect they were saying, 'Jacob is who we are.' The candor of the Israelite storytellers is striking, for of all the Ancestors Jacob/Israel is the most morally ambiguous. In portraying Jacob the Israelites acknowledged that they themselves, with all of their keen abilities and their election by God, proved to be calculating, greedy, and deceitful.

Jacob is from birth designated by the Lord as the preeminent of the twins born to Rebekah (Gen. 25:23). According to the blessing by his father, Jacob will be lord over his brothers (Gen. 27:29). But he gains superiority over his twin Esau by greedy and devious means (Gen. 25:29–34; 27:1–40), and he has to flee the promised land to escape Esau's wrath. Jacob does not impress one as an upstanding, God-fearing paragon of faith; the only reference Jacob makes to God in his early career occurs when he takes the Lord's name in vain to deceive his blind father (Gen. 27:20). Jacob's calculating nature is displayed in his carefulness to ensure that his acquisition of the birthright of his elder brother is airtight (Gen. 25:31–3), in his hesitancy to enact Rebekah's plan to deceive Isaac (27:11–12), in his bargaining attitude to God at Bethel (28:20–2), in his careful approach to the reunion with Esau (32:3–8), and in his avoidance of settling in close to Esau (33:12–17) (cf. Alter 1996: 150). Nevertheless the biblical story affirms that the divine word of assurance supports Jacob at nearly every crucial point in the story (Gen. 25:23; 28:13–15; 31:3; 32:28; 35:9–12).

After leaving the promised land to flee from the wrath of his brother and spending twenty years in the employ of his equally devious uncle Laban, whose two daughters become Jacob's wives (Genesis 29–31), Jacob does seem to have matured and changed. He credits his success in Laban's home as the work of the Lord (Gen. 31:5–9, 42), and in his prayer to God on the eve of encountering his brother Esau he acknowledges his unworthiness and his need for deliverance by the Lord rather than by his own craftiness (Gen. 32:10–13 [English 9–12]). In recognition of this maturing, his name is changed to Israel (Gen. 32:28 [English 29]; cf. 35:10).[18] Nonetheless there is ambiguity even after this point. After the name change there are still signs of mistrust. Jacob declines to accept Esau's invitation to visit (Gen. 33:12–18). He does not seem to act nobly in the incident of the rape of his daughter Dinah (Gen. 34:5, 30). In Genesis 37–50, which constitutes the latter part of the Jacob story in tracing the history of his twelve sons and one daughter, we witness Jacob behaving unwisely in the treatment of his children – clutching Joseph and Benjamin in a favoritism that threatens the family's unity. Rather noticeably, the narrator continues to refer to him by the name 'Jacob' as often as by the name 'Israel' (e.g., Gen. 33:1, 18; 34:5; 37:1; 42:1; 47:7), suggesting that there is still at least some of the old devious, calculating, acquisitive character present.

Even though there are few evaluative comments about Jacob's behavior in the biblical text, it would seem that the storyteller intends the reader to infer from the subsequent difficult experiences of Jacob that his devious ways are to be adjudged negatively (Berger 1987: 55–7). He himself is more than once the victim of deception (cf. Gen. 27:1–40; 37:23–35).[19] He suffers many years under the false impression that his beloved son Joseph was killed by a wild animal. And in Genesis 47:9 Jacob himself notes that 'few and evil have been the days of the years of my life' (cf. Sarna 1970: 183–4; Lockwood 1995: 105n). Whatever the estimate of Jacob's character by narrator or reader, it seems that the biblical storyteller delights in showing the nation's eponym get his 'comeuppance' as the deceiver is deceived, as the younger sibling who supplanted his firstborn brother learns via a painful lesson from his father-in-law that this reversal of primogeniture cannot always be the case; and this Jacob who was destined to be 'lord' becomes a servant to Laban (Gen. 29:15–20) and, ironically, to Esau (Gen. 32:5–6, 19 [English 4–5, 18]).

Allusions to Jacob in later Old Testament texts (Hos. 12:3–5 [English 2–4]; Jer. 9:3 [English 4]; Isa. 43:27; Mal. 3:6ff.) suggest that the tradition construed Jacob as a cheat and deceiver (but cf. Gese 1995: 40–3 for a different interpretation of the prophetic texts). On the other hand, Malachi 1:2–3 makes it clear that Jacob was beloved by God, and Paul picks this up in Romans 9:13.

The exile from and return to the promised land by Jacob must surely have functioned as a paradigm and a presage for the experience of the Jewish exiles in the sixth century BCE (Schreiner 1989; Walters 1992: 607), at which time the stories were probably being redacted (and, according to some scholars, initially composed).

The stories of the Ancestors reflect a society that was patriarchal, often treating women's value as deriving primarily from their usefulness to male ends. The stories in Genesis 12–50 generally give the voice and the viewpoint of the female figures short shrift (cf. Fuchs 1985: 120–1, 132). The matriarchs are given scant mention in the Bible outside of the book of Genesis (in the Old Testament, only Jer. 31:15; Isa. 51:2; Ruth 4:11). The patriarchal complexion of the Ancestral narratives may be seen, for instance, in Genesis 12, where Sarah, who is to be the mother of the 'great nation,' is repeatedly 'taken' (voicelessly) in verses 5, 15, and 19 (cf. Exum 1985: 75). Most strikingly Sarah is denied any voice in the story of Isaac's near-sacrifice (Gen. 22). The women in the stories of Genesis 12–50 are present primarily to ensure that the line of the promise is kept legitimate, for there are certain parameters within which any man who bears the promise is to marry (cf. Gen. 24:3–6; 28:1–2), and the woman's role is incomplete unless she fulfills the function of giving birth to perpetuate the patriarch's line. As they seek to play this societally prescribed role, the women are often thrust into circumstances of competition and jealousy (Fuchs 1985: 131–2; Yee 1992).

Nonetheless, female characters in these Ancestral tales play pivotal roles and model noteworthy qualities (Exum 1985: 75–6). The wives of the patriarchs show themselves to be capable of shrewdness and initiative, sometimes exhibiting more resourcefulness than the males in the family: for example, Sarah: Genesis 16:1–2 (Abram 'obeys' Sarai); Rebekah: Genesis 24:57–8; 27:5–17;[20] 27:46; Rachel: Genesis 30:14–16; 31:19, 34–5.

Sarah, like Abraham, is the recipient of God's blessing (Gen. 17:15–16; 21:1). Sarah becomes the vehicle of the promise even when her human capacities are most unpromising. She conceives a son after she is the age of 90 and 'dried up' (18:12; cf. Exum 1993: 144) and her husband is 100. By taking the initiative in the expulsion of Hagar (Gen. 21:9–14), it is Sarah who ensures Isaac's inheritance, and God endorses Sarah's proposal (Exum 1985: 77). Rabbinic interpreters extolled the beauty and the hospitality of Sarah (*B. Bat.* 58a; *Sanh.* 39b; *Gen. R.* 40:4; 60:16), and they perceived Sarah's being taken into the Pharaoh's harem (Gen. 12:15) as a foreshadowing of the Israelites' being held in Egypt (note even the plagues that come upon Egypt, 12:17).[21] In the New Testament, Hebrews 11:11 celebrates Sarah's faith alongside that of Abraham.

Hagar is not commonly reckoned among the matriarchs of Israel, but in a discussion of the women in Genesis she deserves mention. The (mis)treatment Hagar receives at the hand of Abraham and Sarah (16:6; 21:9–14) and the Lord's subsequent care for her make her story a fit vehicle to communicate God's concern for the oppressed – of whatever race (Schwantes 1988). She is a non-Israelite whose character exhibits some of the same traits as Abraham: God engages in a dialogue with Hagar (the only female in Genesis thus blessed) *twice* (Gen. 16:7–14; 21:17–19)[22] and makes a promise to her regarding her son (Gen. 16:10–12; 21:18);[23] she responds with faith (16:13); God provides for her when hope seems lost (21:15–21) (Gordon 1985).

Isaac's wife Rebekah is a more interesting and more active participant in mediation of the promise to the next generation than is her husband. Rebekah is one of the most appealing women in the Old Testament. She demonstrates hospitality in the first scene where she appears (Gen. 24:18–27). In a fashion reminiscent of Abraham, when she is bidden to leave her family to go to Canaan, she responds, 'I will go' (again one word in Hebrew: *'lk*). She is able to help fill the void left in Isaac's life by the death of his mother Sarah (Gen. 24:67; *Gen. R.* 60:16; cf. Frettlöh 1994). Rebekah shares with Abraham's wife Sarah and Jacob's wife Rachel the condition of barrenness, but, unlike the other two, she does not resort to a surrogate wife to secure children during twenty years of barrenness (and therefore avoids the jealous competition with another woman, which engaged Sarah and Hagar, and Rachel and Leah). It is Rebekah rather than Isaac who receives word of God's plan for their sons (Gen. 25:23).[24]

Commentators have differed in their estimate of Rebekah's decisive role in the deception (Gen. 27) of ageing blind Isaac by her favorite son Jacob, the divinely intended heir to the promise: is she heartless and cruel to her blind husband, or is she the faithful and resourceful instrument whereby God's intent is achieved (cf. Turner 1985)? Rabbinic commentators were usually generous in their estimate of Rebekah (*Lev. R.* 23:1; *Gen. R.* 65:15). Paul speaks affirmatively of her in Romans 9:10–13. A good many interpreters, however, have tended to be judgmental, characterizing her as scheming, duplicitous, and self-seeking (cf. Vawter 1977: 299; Davidson 1979: 137; Steinberg 1984: 180–1; Walters 1992: 601–2); other recent studies have advanced a positive assessment of her, recognizing in her one who is willing to put herself in jeopardy (cf. Gen. 27:11–13) for the sake of her son and fulfillment of God's will (Allen 1979; Turner 1985).

Leah and Rachel, daughters of Laban the Aramean (and therefore nieces of Rebekah), engage in a sibling rivalry that mirrors the rivalry between Jacob and his brother Esau. As noted above, their rivalry in the narrative is engendered by the need each feels to provide children for Jacob; in an ironic twist on the patriarchal system, Jacob becomes manipulated by his two wives during the course of their 'competition' (Gen. 30:3–4, 14–16; cf. Pardes 1994: 32; Brenner 1997: 209–10).[25]

Leah, though the less favored wife of Jacob, does manage to produce three times as many sons as Rachel. The storyteller's use of irony is especially effective as the deceitfulness of Laban, whereby Jacob acquired Leah as his first wife, leads eventually to the birth of six sons by this woman to whom Jacob would not have intentionally become betrothed: and among these six sons are the eponymous

Figure 37.2 Tintoretto, *Joseph and Potiphar's Wife.* Copyright Museo del Prado, Madrid.

ancestors of the priestly and the royal tribes of Levi and Judah (whence would eventually come such noteworthy Israelite figures as Moses, Aaron, and David . . . and Jesus). Leah was privileged to be entombed with Jacob and his ancestors, whereas Rachel was buried on the way to the Judahite town of Ephrath, or Bethlehem (Gen. 35:19). Rabbinic interpreters develop Leah's character more positively than does the Old Testament: for instance, her 'weak' eyes (Gen. 29:17) are explained by her weeping that she might have to wed the wicked Esau; and the rabbis taught that Leah implored God on Rachel's behalf so that Joseph, who was to have been Leah's son, was born to Rachel (Dresner 1989: 155).

Rachel likewise is treated more positively by later Jewish interpreters (Dresner 1989: 157). It was her anguished silence on Jacob's wedding night that allowed the substitution of Leah for herself to occur; the rabbis taught that when 'God remembered Rachel . . . and opened her womb' (Gen. 30:22), it was that silence which God recalled (*Gen. R.* 73:1–4). Rachel's theft of her father's gods (Gen. 31:19) represented an effort on her part to wean him away from idolatry. Her burial place on the way to Judah was to be a site whence she could comfort the Jewish captives centuries later on their way to Babylonian exile (cf. Jer. 31:15).[26]

The election of this family to be God's chosen ones has always been a motif laden with mystery (cf. Deut. 7:6–8; 9:4–5). The family of the Ancestors seems at times almost dysfunctional, and even the most noble figures among the patriarchs and matriarchs exhibit unappealing behavior. Yet the story of the generation following Jacob, Rachel, and Leah shows the theme of the divine promises developing steadfastly towards fulfillment. By the end of the book of Genesis the family has grown significantly (Gen. 46:26–7), and the family has prospered and has been a medium of prosperity for others (cf. Gen. 30:25–30; 41; 47:27). The only part of the threefold promise for which the fulfillment seems uncertain is the assurance that Abraham's family would possess the land of Canaan: at the end of Genesis the family, seventy in number, is settled comfortably in Egypt. The stage is set for the birth of the Israelite nation out of the experiences of the exodus from Egypt, the covenant at Sinai, and the resettlement in the promised land, events described in the Old Testament books of Exodus through Joshua.

NOTES

1 For example, Gen. 15:13 relates that Abraham's descendants will sojourn in Egypt for 400 years (Exod. 12:40–1 gives a slightly different time span). But Gen. 15:16 indicates that the period in Egypt will last but four generations, and Exod. 6:16–20 indicates a four-generation sequence from Levi (one of Jacob's twelve sons) to Moses.

2 Some of the individuals (e.g., Judah, Ephraim, Naphtali) bear names that probably were originally geographical terms (Noth 1966: 55–6; De Vaux 1978: 547, 665), presumably deriving from the areas where certain clans resided.

3 Even the scholars who wish to date the Genesis narratives quite late (period of the Babylonian exile, viz., mid-sixth century BCE) usually acknowledge that those late writers had some prior traditions to work with, which they expanded (Van Seters 1975: 313; Garbini 1988: 80). These scholars do not give a clear indication of how much earlier than the exile they would date the origin of those traditions.

4 Note also the distinction made in Josh. 24:2, 14–15, between Yahweh and the gods of the fathers. Herrmann 1975: 48 comments, 'The absence of any such title as "the God of Moses" may already be taken as an indication that in the case of Yahweh we are dealing with a different type of deity from the Gods of the fathers.'

5 Garbini 1988: 77–8 suggests a possible answer in proposing that it was an effort on the part of Jewish exiles to ingratiate themselves with the ruling powers of Mesopotamia.

6 Evidence for the existence of multiple sources (cf. Driver 1956: 8–13; Eissfeldt 1965: 182–8) include such items as different names used for God and for certain sites, multiple occurrences of the same tale motif (e.g., Gen. 12 // 20 // 26; the naming of Bethel in Gen. 28:19 and also in 35:15), diverse writing styles, awkwardnesses or inconsistencies in the narrative (e.g., although Gen. 16:16 and 17:1–21 indicate that Ishmael would have been a teenager by the time of the episode in ch. 21, 21:8–21 implies that Ishmael was but an infant). Differing opinions have been expressed as to whether these sources were separate strands or 'threads' – even documents – or whether the later strata were simply *supplements* to the earlier. See Knight 1985 for discussion.

7 One consideration in the arguments of this latter group is the virtual silence concerning the Ancestors in traditions outside of Genesis prior to the eighth century BCE. If the Ancestral stories were known in Israel from the time of the settlement in Canaan, why is there virtually no allusion to them prior to the eighth-century prophet Hosea (Hos. 12:2–6)? There is no mention of *Abraham* before the time of Isaiah (29:22) unless 1 Kgs 18:36 is a genuine recollection of the ninth-century Elijah. *Isaac* is mentioned in two texts in Amos (7:9, 16), but the term is used there as a synonym for the corporate entity Israel. The few allusions to *Jacob* will be discussed below, but none is older than the mid-eighth century. It would seem that the Israelite prophets would have made more numerous references to well-established traditions. Even the rather frequent references to 'Abraham, Isaac, and Jacob' in the book of Deuteronomy (commonly dated in the seventh century) have been challenged as late additions (Van Seters 1972 and Römer 1990 argue that Deuteronomic references to 'the fathers' originally had in mind the exodus generation, not the pre-exodus patriarchs).

8 Lemche 1996: 32; Van Seters concedes a bit of the tradition to be early, but he asserts, among other points, that literacy was not at a high enough level in the time of the United Monarchy to expect a product such as the Yahwist's work (1992: 38–42, 332).

9 This issue is related to the problem of the process of emergence of the 'Israelites' in Palestine – whether as invaders from outside the land, peaceful infiltrators, indigenous peasant groups rebelling against urban power structures, or resettlement of urban folk in rural areas because of climatic changes – or some combination of these. Cf. Ramsey 1981: 65–98; Dever 1992; Halpern 1992; Lemche 1992.

10 Some have been wondering out loud if it is even possible to write a history of Israel prior to the eighth century BCE (Davies 1992; Brettler 1995: 3; Dever 1996: 22*). Most recent histories of Israel decline to begin the 'history' prior to about 1200 BCE, beginning with the people whom we know as the Israelites settled in the land of Palestine (see Ahlström 1993). Soggin 1984 begins ca. 1000 BCE with David and Solomon; likewise Miller and Hayes 1986. In the absence of contemporary extrabiblical evidence, such historians are now averse to simply paraphrasing the account in Genesis to 2 Samuel and ascribing validity to this record of the Hebrews in the years prior to a time when monuments outside the Bible attest their existence; according to these historians, the story in the Bible should not be used as a primary source for the writing of earliest Israelite history.

11 Although the name Abram is used for him until the name change in Gen. 17:5, for convenience he will customarily be referred to throughout this chapter as Abraham. Likewise with Sarah (originally Sarai).

12 Although Gen. 20:12 (where we have only the word of Abraham to guide us) indicates that this was not a complete lie, the use of the ruse by Isaac – where it is a lie – in Gen. 26:7 as well as its use, Gen. 12 and 20 prompts us to regard it as a lie in Gen. 12 and 20. Moreover, Gen. 11:31 identifies Sarah as the daughter-*in-law* of Terah, Abraham's father.

13 Berg 1982 points out certain similarities to the forbidden fruit story (Gen. 3) which suggest that the action of Abraham and Sarah is to be understood not as an act of admirable resourcefulness, but of faithless lack of trust in the word of the Lord: for example, the wife 'takes' and 'gives to her husband' in an act that seems quite reasonable; punishment follows (in the maid's belittlement – v. 4 – of Sarah); and as in Gen. 3, there is a shifting of blame, v. 5.

14 *Encyclopedia Judaica* (Roth 1971), 2:119, points out that, among Old Testament characters, Abraham is second only to Moses in the number of times mentioned in the New Testament. Philo describes Abraham as 'renowned,' and this is borne out by frequent reference to him in Greek literature, where he is treated positively even by writers who commonly were critical of the Jews (Bowley 1994: 221–32).

15 Cf. Trible 1991:173 and references there. Trible interprets the story as one which elucidates Abraham's characteristic of nonattachment. She argues that throughout the narrative cycle Abraham is portrayed as one who is nonattached (to homeland, to the wife whom he is willing to swap away for his own life, to Canaan, which he is ready to let Lot have, to Ishmael, whom he is willing to send away), and that it is in fact *Sarah* who has the unique tie with Isaac and for whom, according to the logic of the story, the test in Gen. 22 would be more appropriate. However, the poignancy of the narrative in Gen. 22, esp. v. 2, belies any suggestion that the command did not test Abraham's attachment to Isaac. Yahweh's declaration in 22:12 moreover indicates that this was a severe test for Abraham.

16 Based on Sarah's age of 90 at his birth and assuming that the Binding occurred shortly before her death at age 127 recorded in Gen. 23:1; cf. *Gen. R.* 56:8.

17 There is debate among scholars as to whether the rabbinic tradition concerning the expiatory effects of Isaac's action predated and influenced the New Testament theology of Christ's atoning sacrifice, or vice versa. For differing views see Daly 1977; Davies and Chilton 1978; Hayward 1990. An example of the use of Isaac as a type of Christ may be seen in Clement of Alexandria's *Paedagogus* I,5: 'He is Isaac (for the narrative may be interpreted otherwise), who is a type of the Lord, a child as a son; for he was the son of Abraham, as Christ the Son of God, and a sacrifice as the Lord, but he was not immolated as the Lord. Isaac only bore the wood of the sacrifice, as the Lord the wood of the cross. And he laughed mystically, prophesying that the Lord should fill us with joy, who have been redeemed from corruption by the blood of the Lord. Isaac did everything but suffer, as was right, yielding the precedence in suffering to the Word. Furthermore, there is an intimation of the divinity of the Lord in His not being slain. For Jesus rose again after His burial, having suffered no harm, like Isaac released from sacrifice.'

18 Sarna, 206: 'The struggle with the angel may . . . imply the final purging of those unsavory qualities of character that marked his past career.'

19 One midrash (*Gen. R.* 70:19; 71:2) expands the story of his wedding night by imagining that as he cried out 'Rachel! Rachel!' through the night Leah always answered, much as Jacob had passed himself off as Esau to his blind father (cf. Dresner 1989: 155).

20 Note how Rebekah is the subject of the verbs in vv. 14–17 and how Jacob is told to 'obey' her voice (27:8, 13, 43).
21 Cf. Brettler 1995: 51–5. One writer (van Dijk-Hemmes 1997: 230–2) proposes that in Gen. 12:17 the Hebrew phrase *dabar saray* might best be understood not simply as 'because of Sarai' but should be seen as referring to an outcry (a 'word') of Sarah, which elicits God's response. This would imply 'that YHWH is the only one towards whom Sarai does not remain speechless' and one might even venture to say that 'YHWH now reveals himself as Sarai's covenant partner' (232). This would constitute another parallel to Israelite slaves, whose cry the Lord heard (Exod. 3:7).
22 The 'angel of the LORD' is to be understood as a manifestation of God, not a separate being; note Gen. 16:13.
23 Hagar's son Ishmael was to become recognized as the ancestor of the Arabs and a key figure in the Muslim religion, where it is traditional to regard him rather than Isaac as the one who was nearly sacrificed on Mount Moriah. According to the Muslims, it was Ishmael along with his father Abraham who built the Ka'aba, the most sacred shrine of that faith (Qur'an, 2.125; but cf. Guillaume 1956: 61–2).
24 Whether Rebekah received the word directly from God or through some cultic mediator is not clear. Cf. Sarna 1970: 182. Gen. 25:22 states that 'she went to inquire (Heb. *darash*) of YHWH,' and the language is very similar to passages such as 2 Kgs 1:2; 22:13; Jer. 37:7, where inquiry is made through a religious intermediary.
25 The pathos of the sibling struggle is signified in that it manifests itself in the naming of several of the women's sons (e.g., Gen. 29:32–3; 30:8).
26 Useful summaries of the treatment of the patriarchs and matriarchs in the later Jewish traditions may be found in the individual articles on each of the Ancestors in the *Encyclopedia Judaica* (Roth 1971).

BIBLIOGRAPHY

Ahlström, G. W. (1993) *The History of Ancient Palestine*, Minneapolis: Fortress.
Allen, C. G. (1979) 'On me be the curse, my son,' in M. Buss (ed.), *Encounter with the Text*, Philadelphia: Fortress, 159–72.
Alt, A. (1966) 'The God of the Fathers,' in *Essays on Old Testament History and Religion*, trans. R. A. Wilson, Oxford: Basil Blackwell, 1–77.
Alter, R. (1996) *Genesis: Translation and Commentary*, New York: Norton.
Anderson, B. W. (1986) *Understanding the Old Testament*, 4th edn, Englewood Cliffs, N.J.: Prentice-Hall.
Beck, A. B. (1992a) 'Rachel,' in D. N. Freedman (ed.) *The Anchor Bible Dictionary*, New York: Doubleday, Vol. 5, 605–8.
—— (1992b) 'Rebekah,' in D. N. Freedman (ed.) *The Anchor Bible Dictionary*, New York: Doubleday, Vol. 5, 629–30.
Berg, W. (1982) 'Der Sündenfall Abrahams und Saras nach Gen 16:1–6,' *Biblische Notizen* 19:7–14.
Berger, D. (1987) 'On the Morality of the Patriarchs in Jewish Polemic and Exegesis,' in C. Thoma and M. Wyschograd (eds) *Understanding Scripture: Explorations of Jewish and Christian Traditions of Interpretation*, New York: Paulist Press, 49–62.
Bowley, J. E. (1994) 'The Compositions of Abraham,' in J. C. Reeves (ed.) *Tracing the Threads*, Atlanta: Scholars Press, 215–38.
Brenner, A. (1997) 'Female Social Behavior: Two Descriptive Patterns within the "Birth of the Hero" Paradigm,' in A. Brenner (ed.) *A Feminist Companion to Genesis*, Sheffield: Sheffield Academic Press, 204–21.
Brettler, M. (1995) *The Creation of History in Ancient Israel*, London: Routledge.
Bright, J. (1981) *A History of Israel*, 3rd edn, Philadelphia: Westminster.
Clark, M. (1977) 'The Patriarchal Traditions,' in J. H. Hayes and J. M. Miller (eds) *Israelite and Judean History*, Philadelphia: Fortress, 120–48.

Clements, R. E. (1967) *Abraham and David*, London: SCM.

Cross, F. L. (1973) *Canaanite Myth and Hebrew Epic*, Cambridge, Mass.: Harvard University Press.

Daly, R. J. (1977) 'The Soteriological Significance of the Sacrifice of Isaac,' *Catholic Biblical Quarterly* 39: 45–75.

Davidson, R. (1979) *Genesis 12–50*, New York: Cambridge University Press.

Davies, P. R. (1992) *In Search of 'Ancient Israel'*, Sheffield: Sheffield Academic Press.

Davies, P. R. and Chilton, B. D. (1978) 'The Aqedah: A Revised Tradition History,' *Catholic Biblical Quarterly* 40: 514–46.

De Vaux, R. (1978) *The Early History of Israel*, trans. D. Smith, Philadelphia: Westminster.

Dever, W. G. (1977) 'The Patriarchal Traditions,' in J. H. Hayes and J. M. Miller (eds) *Israelite and Judean History*, Philadelphia: Fortress, 70–120.

—— (1992) 'Israel, History of (Archaeology and the "Conquest"),' in D. N. Freedman (ed.) *The Anchor Bible Dictionary*, New York: Doubleday, Vol. 3, 545–58.

—— (1996) 'Archaeology and the Current Crisis in Israelite Historiography,' *Eretz-Israel* 25:18*–27*.

Dijk-Hemmes, F. van (1997) 'Sarai's Exile: A Gender-Motivated Reading of Genesis 12.10–13.2,' in A. Brenner (ed.) *A Feminist Companion to Genesis*, Sheffield: Sheffield Academic Press, 222–34.

Dresner, S. H. (1989) 'Rachel and Leah,' *Judaism* 38: 151–9.

Driver, G. R. (1956) (1957) *An Introduction to the Old Testament*, New York: Meridian.

Eissfeldt, O. (1965) *The Old Testament: An Introduction*, trans. P. R. Ackroyd, New York: Harper & Row.

Emerton, J. A. (1982) 'The Origin of the Promises to the Patriarchs in the Older Sources of the Book of Genesis,' *Vetus Testamentum* 32: 14–32.

Exum, C. (1985) 'Mother in Israel: A Familiar Figure Reconsidered,' in L. M. Russell (ed.) *Feminist Interpretation of the Bible*, Philadelphia: Westminster, 73–85.

—— (1993) 'The (M)other's Place,' in J. C. Exum, *Fragmented Women: Feminist (Sub)versions of Biblical Narratives*, Valley Forge: Trinity, 94–147.

Fohrer, G. (1974) *History of Israelite Religion*, trans. D. E. Green, Nashville: Abingdon.

Fokkelman, J. (1975) *Narrative Art in Genesis*, Assen: Van Gorcum.

Frettlöh, M. L. (1994) 'Isaak und seine Mütter,' *Evangelische Theologie*, 54: 427–52.

Fuchs, E. (1985) 'The Literary Characterization of Mothers and Sexual Politics in the Hebrew Bible,' in A. Collins (ed.) *Feminist Perspectives on Biblical Scholarship*, Chico: Scholars Press, 117–36.

Garbini, G. (1988) *History and Ideology in Ancient Israel*, trans. J. Bowden, New York: Crossroad.

Gese, H. (1995) 'Jakob, der Berträger?' in M. Weippert and S. Tumm (eds) *Meilenstein*, Wiesbaden: Harassowitz, 33–43.

Gordon, C. (1985) 'Hagar: A Throw-away Character among the Matriarchs?' *SBL Seminar Papers* 24: 271–7.

Gottwald, N. G. (1985) *The Hebrew Bible – A Socio-Literary Introduction*, Philadelphia: Fortress.

Gross, H. (1989) 'Zur theologischen Bedeutung von *halak* (gehen) in den Abraham-Geschichten (Gen 12–25),' in A. R. Müller and M. Görg (eds) *Die Väter Israels: Beiträge der Patriarchenüberlieferungen im Alten Testament*, Stuttgart: Verlag Katholisches Bibelwerk, 73–82.

Guillame, A. (1956) *Islam*, Baltimore: Penguin.

Halpern, B. (1992) 'Settlement of Canaan,' in D. N. Freedman (ed.) *The Anchor Bible Dictionary*, New York: Doubleday, Vol. 5, 1120–43.

Hayward, C. T. R. (1990) 'The Sacrifice of Isaac and Jewish Polemic Against Christianity,' *Catholic Biblical Quarterly* 52: 292–306.

Hendel, R. S. (1992) 'Genesis, Book of,' in D. N. Freedman (ed.) *The Anchor Bible Dictionary*, New York: Doubleday, Vol. 2, 933–41.

—— (1995) 'Finding Historical Memories in the Patriarchal Narratives,' *Biblical Archaeology Review* 21/4: 53–9, 70–1.

Herrman, S. (1975) *A History of Israel in Old Testament Times*, trans. J. Bowden, Philadelphia: Fortress.

Humphreys, W. L. (1988) *Joseph and His Family*, Columbia: University of South Carolina Press.

Irvin, D. (1977) 'The Joseph and Moses Narratives,' in J. H. Hayes and J. M. Miller (eds) *Israelite and Judean History*, Philadelphia: Fortress, 180–203.

Jeansome, S. P. (1989) 'Images of Rebekah: From Modern Interpretations to Biblical Portrayal,' *Biblical Research* 34: 33–52.

Kirkpatrick, P. G. (1988) *The Old Testament and Folklore Study*, Sheffield: Sheffield Academic Press.

Kitchen, K. A. (1978) *The Bible in Its World: The Bible and Archaeology Today*, Downers Grove: InterVarsity Press.

—— (1995) 'The Patriarchal Age: Myth or History?' *Biblical Archaeology Review* 21/2: 48–57, 88–95.

Knight, D. A. (1985) 'The Pentateuch,' in D. A. Knight and G. M. Tucker, *The Hebrew Bible and Its Modern Interpreters*, Philadelphia: Fortress, 263–96.

Lemche, N. P. (1985) *Early Israel: Anthropological and Historical Studies on the Israelite Society Before the Monarchy*, Leiden: Brill.

—— (1992) 'Israel, History of (Premonarchic Period)', in D. N. Freedman (ed.) *The Anchor Bible Dictionary*, New York: Doubleday, Vol. 3, 526–45.

—— (1996) *Die Vorgeschichte Israels: Von den Anfängen bis zum Ausgang des 13. Jahrhunderts v. Chr.*, Stuttgart: Kohlhammer.

Lockwood, P. F. (1995) 'Jacob's Other Twin: Reading the Rape of Dinah in Context,' *Lutheran Theological Journal* 29: 98–105.

McCarter, P. K. (1999) 'The Patriarchal Age,' in H. Shanks (ed.) *Ancient Israel: from Abraham to the Roman Destruction of the Temple*, Washington: Biblical Archaeology Society, 1–31, 299–304.

Miller, J. M. and Hayes, J. H. (1986) *A History of Ancient Israel and Judah*, Philadelphia: Westminster.

Moberly, R. W. L. (1990) 'Abraham's Righteousness (Genesis xv 6), in J. A. Emerton (ed.) *Studies in the Pentateuch*, Leiden: Brill, 103–30.

Nicholson, E. W. (1991) 'The Pentateuch in Recent Research: A Time for Caution,' in J. A. Emerton (ed.) *Congress Volume: Leuven, 1989*, Leiden: Brill, 10–21.

Noth, M. (1960) *The History of Israel*, trans. P. R. Ackroyd, New York: Harper & Brothers.

—— (1966) *The Old Testament World*, trans. V. I. Gruhn, Philadelphia: Fortress.

—— (1972) *A History of Pentateuchal Traditions*, trans. B. W. Anderson, Englewood Cliffs, N.J.: Prentice-Hall.

Och, B. (1993) 'Jacob at Bethel and Penuel,' *Judaism* 42: 164–76.

Pardes, I. (1994) 'Rachel's Dream of Grandeur,' in C. Bachman and C. Spiegel (eds) *Out of the Garden: Women Writers on the Bible*, New York: Fawcett Columbine, 27–40, 336–7.

Rad, G. von (1962) *Old Testament Theology*, Vol. 1, trans. D. M. G. Stalker, New York: Harper & Brothers.

Ramsey, G. W. (1981) *The Quest for the Historical Israel*, Atlanta: John Knox.

Richards, K. H. (1985) 'Yahwist,' in P. J. Achtemeier (ed.) *Harper's Bible Dictionary*, San Francisco: Harper & Row, 1152.

Römer, T. (1990) *Israels Väter: Untersuchungen zur Väterthematik im Deuteronomium und in der deuteronomistischen Tradition*, Göttingen: Vandenhoeck & Ruprecht.

Rosenberg, J. (1986) *King and Kin: Political Allegory in the Hebrew Bible*, Bloomington: Indiana University Press.

Roth, C. (ed). (1971) *Encyclopaedia Judaica*, 16 vols, Jerusalem: Keter.

Sarna, N. M. (1970) *Understanding Genesis: The Heritage of Biblical Israel*, New York: Schocken.

Schreiner, J. (1989) 'Das Gebet Jakobs (Gen 32,10–13),' in A. R. Müller and M. Görg (eds) *Die Väter Israels: Beiträge der Patriarchenüberlieferungen im Alten Testament*, Stuttgart: Verlag Katholisches Bibelwerk, 287–303.

Schwantes, M. (1988) 'Hagar and Sarah,' in D. Kirkpatrick (ed.) *Faith Born in the Struggle for Life*, trans. L. McCoy, Grand Rapids: Eerdmans, 76–83.

Soggin, J. A. (1984) *A History of Israel: From the Beginnings to the Bar Kochba Revolt, A.D. 135*, London: SCM.

Steinberg, N. (1984) 'Gender Roles in the Rebekah Cycle,' *Union Seminary Quarterly Review* 39: 175–88.

Thompson, T. L. (1974) *The Historicity of the Patriarchal Narratives*, Berlin: de Gruyter.

Trible, P. (1991) 'Genesis 22: The Sacrifice of Sarah,' in J. P. Rosenblatt and J. C. Sitterson, Jr (eds) *Not in Heaven*, Bloomington: Indiana University Press, 170–91, 249–53.

Turner, M. D. (1985) 'Rebekah: Ancestor of Faith,' *Lexington Theological Quarterly* 20: 42–50.

Van Seters, J. (1972) 'Confessional Reformulation in the Exilic Period,' *Vetus Testamentum* 22: 448–59.

—— (1975) *Abraham in History and Tradition*, New Haven: Yale University Press.

—— (1992) *Prologue to History*, Louisville: Westminster John Knox.

Vawter, B. (1977) *On Genesis: A New Reading*, Garden City, N.Y.: Doubleday.

Wagner (1972) 'Abraham and David,' in J. W. Wevers and D. B. Redford (eds) *Studies on the Ancient Palestinian World*, Toronto: University of Toronto Press, 117–40.

Walters, S. D. (1992) 'Jacob Narrative,' in D. N. Freedman (ed.) *The Anchor Bible Dictionary*, New York: Doubleday, Vol. 3, 599–608.

Westermann, C. (1976) 'Promises to the Patriarchs,' *The Interpreter's Dictionary of the Bible*, Supplementary Volume, Nashville: Abingdon, 690–3.

—— (1980) *The Promises to the Fathers*, trans. D. E. Green, Philadelphia: Fortress.

—— (1985) *Genesis 12–36: A Commentary*, trans. J. J. Scullion, Minneapolis: Augsburg.

Whybray, R. N. (1987) *The Making of the Pentateuch: A Methodological Study*, Sheffield: Sheffield Academic Press.

Wilson, R. R. (1977) *Genealogy and History in the Biblical World*, New Haven: Yale University Press.

Wolff, H. W. (1966) 'The Kerygma of the Yahwist,' *Interpretation* 20: 131–58.

Yee, G. (1992) 'Sarah,' in D. N. Freedman (ed.) *The Anchor Bible Dictionary*, New York: Doubleday, Vol. 5, 981–2.

CHAPTER THIRTY-EIGHT

MOSES

—— ·◆· ——

John Van Seters

THE HISTORICITY OF MOSES

The life and career of Moses is presented to us in the Hebrew Bible within the Pentateuch, spanning virtually the whole of Exodus to Deuteronomy. Reminiscences of his role in the deliverance of his people from Egypt and in his giving of the law are recalled in the historical books and in the Psalms (1 Sam. 12.6, 8; 1 Kgs 8.9, 53, 56; 2 Kgs 18.4; Pss 77.21 [20]; 99.6; 105.26; 106.16, 23, 32; in addition to the numerous references to the law or commands of Moses). He becomes the most revered figure in Judaism, and yet all that we know about him, apart from some later legends, comes to us from the biblical sources.

Since the beginning of the common era Moses was regarded as the author of the Pentateuch, with the possible exception of the account of his death in Deuteronomy 34, both by Jews and Christians so that the Bible was thought to contain an autobiography of his life and career (although most of it in Exodus to Numbers was written in third person style). This opinion held firm until the Enlightenment and the rise of the historical-critical method, which called into question Moses' authorship of the Pentateuch and substituted in his place the work of several authors from a much later period in Israel's history. The events of Moses' life were increasingly viewed as legendary with little hope of getting back to the actual history of Moses and his times.

A major change of scholarly attitude and perspective, however, came about with the recovery and decipherment of the vast quantity of historical documents and monuments of ancient Egypt. These, it was hoped, would allow the historian to sort out from the biblical record just what remained of the historical Moses. The results of intensive investigation over the last 150 years, however, have been both meager and controversial. There are no extant records from Egypt that make any reference to Moses or to the events associated with the liberation from Egypt. The Bible is also very vague about supplying any historical details that would connect Moses with a particular period of Egyptian history. It refers to the kings of Egypt only by the title of 'pharaoh,' without ever giving any names.

In spite of these obstacles, scholars have attempted to use a variety of clues from the account of the Egyptian sojourn and exodus in Exodus 1–15 to try to reconstruct the circumstances that the biblical story portrays and to establish Moses' place in history. There seems to be fairly strong agreement that Moses has an Egyptian name, derived from the Egyptian verb *msy* (to give birth) and found in such well-known names as Thutmose, Ptahmose, Ramesses, where the verb *msy* is compounded with the name of a deity. The form *mošeh* (Hebrew) would represent the popular shortened form of such names and names of this type occur over a long period of time. However, none can be identified with the biblical Moses. The fact that Moses bears an Egyptian name makes it appropriate to the background of the exodus story, but it can tell us little more. There are a few other Egyptian names among the priests and Levites, notably Hophni and Phinehas, but such names may only be survivals from the time of Egyptian control of Canaan in the Late Bronze Age.

A name by itself does not make a historical personality nor guarantee the historicity of events ascribed to him by the Bible. These events would need to have taken place several centuries before the rise of the monarchy. The Bible itself dates the exodus to 480 years before the time of Solomon's construction of the temple, ca 960 BCE (1 Kgs 6:1), which would place it ca 1440 BCE, during the reign of Thutmose III at the height of the Egyptian empire and political control of Canaan. Scholars have generally found this period inappropriate and rejected the figure of 480 years as an artificial construction of twelve generations of 40 years each.

What has been regarded as a safer clue to the historical period is the reference in Exodus 1.11 to the Israelites building the store-cities of Pithom and Rameses. The latter name is identified with the great capital Piramesse, built by Ramesses II, and this fits the events of Exodus into his reign and that of his son Merneptah. Yet this proof-text is not without problems. The reference to Pithom (Tell el-Maskhuta) is anachronistic for such an early date because recent excavations make it quite certain that Pithom was not built until the end of the seventh century BCE. Furthermore, the biblical name Rameses is a late form of the name that survived long after the demise of the Twentieth Dynasty and its capital so that even the Joseph story anachronistically refers to the region as 'the land of Rameses.'

The attempt to fit the portrayal of events in Exodus within the history of the Eighteenth and Nineteenth Dynasties (1550–1200 BCE) has not been any more successful. The pharaohs of this period campaigned actively in Syria–Palestine and took prisoners of war from many different peoples and social classes as slaves, and these were dispersed throughout Egypt to serve in many different capacities on private estates, in temple corporations, in the military, in royal estates, throughout almost the entire workforce. In time many Asiatics became free persons within Egyptian society with varying rank and status in construction projects, in the military, in the royal administration and in the priesthood. The time of Ramesses II, in particular, was one of great assimilation of Asiatic religion and culture in Egypt. Commerce and diplomatic exchange between Egypt and the Levant were very active throughout the period, as well as the need for some military 'security' operations in Canaan in the wake of conquest and the threat to their control there from more distant powers like the Hittites. None of this is reflected in Exodus.

One of the groups from whom captives were taken into Egypt were called the Ḥabiru (Egyptian ʿapiru), and some scholars have been eager to identify them with the 'Hebrews' (ʿibrîm), the term often used in Exodus for the Israelites in Egypt

(Exod. 1.15–22; 2.6–7, 13; 3.18; 5.3; 7.16; 9.1, 13; 10.3). The mere similarity of names, however, does not establish their identity and much speaks against it. The Ḥabiru were a social class of freebooters, often used as mercenaries, and were widely scattered throughout the Near East during much of the second millennium BCE. They were not a specific ethnic group and were not necessarily kept apart in Egypt from others as a distinct group in an isolated location.

The reason given in the Bible for the enslavement of the Israelites was the vast increase in their numbers that made them a security risk, especially in the event of a possible invasion from Asia. However, since Egypt controlled Canaan during the Eighteenth and Nineteenth Dynasties, there was no threat from that direction. Furthermore, Egypt continued to acquire new foreign slaves through conquest, many of whom were quickly assimilated so there was no threat from that quarter either. At the same time, Bedouin from southern Palestine and the Sinai were allowed grazing rights in the eastern Delta and there is no indication that they were made to serve as corvée labor in return. There is no evidence of any acts of genocide against any distinct group or any forced labor of foreigners for particular building projects.

If we understand the story as reflecting the time of the author living in the sixth century BCE (see below), then many of the story's details make much more sense. In terms of geography, the focus is entirely upon the northeastern Delta region of Egypt. The name 'Goshen,' as the region where the Israelites were said to reside, is known only from late geographic texts and corresponds to the Twentieth or Arabia nome on the eastern border of the Egyptian Delta. It lay east of the Pelusiac branch of the Nile and extended at its southern end into the Wadi Tumilat. At its northern end was the 'land of Rameses' and at the eastern end in the Wadi Tumilat was the Eighth nome, the region of Sukkoth with its principal city, Pithom. From Goshen there were two routes out of Egypt, the northern, which would be in the direction of Gaza, 'the way of the land of the Philistines,' and the southern route, 'the way of the desert,' which leads through the Wadi Tumilat past Sukkoth-Pithom towards Lake Timsah, 'the sea' (Exod. 12.37; 13.17–18, 20).

In the time of the exilic author, Egypt had experienced invasion and subjugation by the Assyrians in the seventh century BCE and was under threat from the Babylonians in the sixth century. The building of Pithom as a large fortification and storage depot by Necho II was meant to protect the southern route against this latter threat. Whether foreigners from Palestine were used in this enterprise is difficult to say, although the eastern Delta was a region that harbored increasing numbers of Israelite refugees from the wars of their homeland. While the author is familiar with that part of Egypt that lies closest to Palestine, there is nothing that shows any detailed knowledge of Egyptian life and history. The effort to correlate Moses with Egyptian history is a futile exercise. He now belongs only to legend.

MOSES AS THE FOUNDER OF ISRAELITE RELIGION

Many scholars believe that Moses is the founder of Israel's religion by inaugurating the worship of Yahweh alone, which ultimately led to the rise of monotheism. It has been tempting for some to try to establish a connection between Moses and the pharaoh Akhenaten on the basis of their common advocacy of monotheism, a view made popular by Freud (in *Moses and Monotheism*, 1939). Some have argued that Moses grew up under Akhenaten and was a devotee of his monotheistic cult. When this form of religion was suppressed by the rival priests of Amon, Moses preserved it among an oppressed group and upon their subsequent departure from Egypt it became their religion. All such schemes attempting to make a connection between Moses and Akhenaten are without any serious historical merit.

Within the biblical tradition the first and second commandments of the Decalogue decree the exclusive worship of Yahweh and an imageless cult. Those who attribute the Decalogue to Moses use it as a basis for their view that Moses was the founder of monotheism. However, it is unlikely that these laws predate the seventh century BCE. Archeological evidence has uncovered inscriptions of the eighth century BCE that contain references to Yahweh being worshipped together with a female consort, Ashera. The first commandment may be viewed as a later protest against such a consort being placed or named 'beside' Yahweh, and this exclusive worship of Yahweh eventually led to monotheism. But the rise of monotheism in Israel did not take place until the exile, eight centuries later than Akhenaten and it was of an entirely different character.

A more modest proposal is to consider Moses as the one to inaugurate the worship of Yahweh among the Israelites. Within the call narrative of Exodus 3 one biblical source (vv. 1–6) describes Moses as having a remarkable religious experience on a sacred mountain, Sinai, in Midian. During this experience Moses receives a revelation concerning the divine name Yahweh and its meaning that he is to communicate to the Israelites in Egypt. Yet the story assumes that the deity's name is already known to them and what is being revealed is a new understanding of the name and the character of Yahweh and his relationship with his people. This piece of dialogue has the character of theological speculation and the concerns of the author's own time and little to do with Moses' introduction of a new cult among the Israelites.

A later version of this call narrative in Exodus 6.2–3, in the so-called Priestly source, states that the name Yahweh was not known to the Israelites and their ancestors (in contradiction to what one finds in Gen. 15), but was being revealed to Moses for the first time. This would support the notion of Moses' innovation of the worship of Yahweh. Yet this version of the story is late and postexilic in date and it supports this writer's scheme of the periodization of divine revelation. There is little reason to view it as historical or based on ancient tradition.

A quite different approach, the so-called Midianite hypothesis, suggests that it was while Moses was temporarily in Midian to escape the threat on his life by Pharaoh that he learned of the new religion from Jethro, the priest of Midian and his father-in-law. This view is also supported by references to the god Yahweh in Egyptian texts of the late second millennium BCE that associate this deity with the southern region of Edom and Seir. And some early poetry in the Hebrew Bible seems to point to this same southern association (e.g., Judg. 5.4–5; Deut. 33.2; Hab. 3.3; Ps. 68.8, 18). The connection is tantalizing but too weak to support any reconstruction of the origins of Israelite religion. Nothing in the account of Moses' dealing with Jethro ever indicates that Moses learned of Yahweh from him. Jethro only acknowledges Yahweh's greatness after Moses speaks to him about Yahweh's deliverance of Israel from Egypt (Exod. 18). Moses' temporary respite in a foreign region before he returns to deliver his people is a common folktale motif and therefore tells us nothing about the origins of Yahweh religion.

There are others who would see in the Sinai covenant Moses' achievement in creating a unique politico-religious union centered upon commitment to Yahweh and a new social order among his fellow Israelites. These scholars point to the Hittite suzerainty treaty model of the Late Bronze Age, which demands absolute loyalty to the great king based upon past favors and complete obedience to a series of stipulations regulating relations between king and vassal as well as between vassal states. It is suggested that the Sinai covenant of Yahweh's kingship over his people and their relationship with one another is based upon this model. The force of the argument lies in the attempt to establish parallels between this model and the giving of the law and covenant ratification at Sinai in Exodus 19–24, as well as the fact that the conjectured time of Moses and the time of the Hittite empire are relatively close. The theory, however, has come under criticism because the parallels are too forced to be convincing; the treaty form is not restricted in time to the late second millennium BCE, and the greatest correspondence to such a treaty–covenant form is to be found in Deuteronomy – very likely written shortly after Judah had experienced such vassalage to Assyria. There is, today, an increasing tendency to regard the notion of such a Sinai/Horeb covenant between Yahweh and his people as no older than Deuteronomy and therefore it cannot be traced back to Moses.

A variation on this scheme is to view the origins of Israel not so much as a distinct people who came from Egypt and conquered the land of Canaan, but rather as a peasant revolt from within Canaanite society, using a Marxist sociological model. These peasants withdrew their services and migrated to the hill country from the city states of the lowlands and coast. At the same time a group of slaves under the leadership of Moses escaped from Egypt, attributed their liberation to Yahweh and joined those in Canaan who escaped from a similar oppression of the Canaanite overlords. The liberation religion of Yahweh thus provided the means of creating a cohesion and identity for this motley collection. The chief problem with such an approach, however, is that it imposes a sociological scheme on the tradition and the historical data with complete disregard for any critical evaluation of the texts. We have no direct historical witness to any of the events so described, only a fanciful reconstruction. The scheme radically alters the tradition to make it fit and the tradition thus altered supports the scheme.

THE LITERARY TRADITION

The traditions about Moses are contained in the Pentateuch from Exodus to Deuteronomy and all other biblical references to Moses are dependent upon these, unless the unnamed deliverer in Hosea 12.13 is an allusion to Moses. The view of most critical scholars is that none of the Pentateuch's presentation of Moses is derived from Moses himself or contemporary with him, but is the work of multiple authors developing the tradition over a long period of time. At the risk of serious oversimplification, I shall briefly try to indicate the nature of this discussion. One literary theory that has long held sway is that the Pentateuch is the combination of at least four sources, known as the Yahwist (J), the Elohist (E), Deuteronomy (D), and the Priestly writer (P), and composed in that order. A modification of this view disputes the existence of E (at best very fragmentary) as a work separate from J, and treats J and E as a single corpus, JE. The usual dating for these sources places them in a range from the tenth to the fifth centuries BCE.

A more recent view that is gaining wide acceptance is to view the process as accumulative with a proto-Pentateuchal author (J or JE) in Genesis to Numbers compiling the earliest comprehensive story of Moses, with a Priestly writer (P) expanding this work. Deuteronomy (D) is regarded as originally separate from the rest of the Pentateuch and part of a history that extended from Deuteronomy to 2 Kings. In this scheme D is the oldest of these literary works, dating to the late seventh and early sixth centuries BCE with J (or JE) as exilic and P as postexilic. This late dating of the literary presentation would account for the fact that so little is made of the Moses tradition in any sources before the exilic period outside the Pentateuch. It is also this view that in my opinion best fits with the Egyptian background to Exodus 1–15 as sketched above.

This literary-critical study of the Moses tradition, however, is at best only preliminary to a number of different, sometimes competing, concerns. One such interest is in understanding the literary and tradition-transmission process in order to uncover the origins of the Moses tradition and of Israelite culture and religion, even if one is skeptical about obtaining any help from Egyptian historical materials. The history of the preliterary tradition has occupied a lot of attention but with few convincing results because it is so difficult to control any reconstruction of the various stages of oral tradition about Moses from their present literary forms.

Another approach is to eschew the quest for oral origins as too speculative and to focus on the literary works that make up the tradition in order to unravel and explicate their ideological and theological use of the Moses tradition within their historical contexts. The major obstacle to this research is to get complete agreement on the precise limits of the particular 'documents,' their relationship to each other and the dating of the sources relative to each other and to the history of Israel.

Yet a third method is to take the text as it is, in spite of its complex history of development, either as the product of a 'canonical process' that yields a theological unity and meaning, or as an autonomous literary work in the postmodernist sense. This also is not without its problems. On the one hand, the formation of the canon was a historical process whose investigation cannot be divorced from the literary history that preceded it. On the other hand, a literary work cannot be investigated until its limits and context are established and the present biblical divisions of chapters and books have long been proved inadequate. For a comprehensive treatment of the Moses tradition, there is no escape from the diachronic investigation of the literary works that make up this corpus.

BIBLICAL PORTRAITS OF MOSES

In what follows I shall try to set out the literary presentation of Moses' roles as deliverer, leader, lawgiver and prophet to his people. In doing so I shall make use of the insights of literary criticism, making reference where appropriate to the different literary levels in the tradition, using the simplified scheme in which J represents the older version of the Moses tradition in Exodus to Numbers, P the later expansion of this version and D the portrayal of Moses within Deuteronomy. Nevertheless, my primary concern here is an examination of the traditions about Moses in their final literary forms within the larger context of the Hebrew Bible.

Moses as deliverer of his people

The general background for the role of Moses as deliverer is the tradition of a period in the past when Israel experienced oppression and enslavement in Egypt from which Yahweh, their God, 'redeemed' them. This is often mentioned in the Hebrew Bible without any reference to Moses (note, e.g., Ezek. 20). The Pentateuch continues to stress the theme of God as redeemer but now makes Moses the human agent.

The J writer in Exodus 1 sets out the account of how the enslavement of the Israelites arose out of a kind of xenophobia that ultimately deteriorated to attempted genocide, which then provides the context for the story of Moses' birth and his rescue from the Nile by the daughter of pharaoh (Exod. 2:1–10). Once this story of the child's rescue is told, then the genocide theme disappears, and the issue again becomes that of slavery and hard labor. The story of Moses as a threatened child rescued and reared under the very nose of the pharaoh to become deliverer of his people is paralleled by similar folktales that were told about Sargon of Akkad and Cyrus the Persian. It is a common motif used in the heroic presentation of great kings and leaders. However, Moses' initial attempt at deliverance, whereby he kills an Egyptian for beating a Hebrew, is antiheroic because it ends in failure and leads only to flight to the land of Midian, where he becomes a shepherd (Exod. 2.11–22; 3.1). This prepares the way for the author (J) to present Moses as a leader totally dependent on a divine word from Yahweh for each action he takes, quite different from a military hero.

In Moses' first confrontation with Pharaoh, he is presented more in the role of a labor negotiator seeking to get time off for religious holidays than as a menacing protagonist, and even in this effort he fails and disappoints his fellows. In the plague narrative that follows it is the series of plagues brought by God and merely announced by Moses that turns the tide and forces Pharaoh's hand. In the expansion of the tradition by P, he introduces the theme of a contest between Aaron and the magicians of Egypt (7.8–12). Nevertheless, throughout the plague stories the emphasis is upon the greatness and power of Yahweh to deliver his people.

The climax of the deliverance is at the Red Sea (Exod. 13.17 – 14.31), and here again Moses' role is merely to encourage the people to believe in the divine deliverance. In the J account Moses and Israel do nothing but witness the divine rescue, while in the P version Moses, at God's command, splits the sea with his rod to create a path for the Israelites and, again at the divine command, makes the sea come back upon their pursuers. The effect is that the people fear Yahweh and believe in him and in his servant Moses. It is noteworthy that except for one late addition to Deuteronomy (11.4) there are no references to the sea event in D, even though the exodus is mentioned many times. This suggests that the Red Sea episode is really secondary to the divine deliverance tradition. In its present form in J it constitutes a transition to the wilderness themes and to Moses' direct leadership of his people.

Moses as leader

Apart from an initial contact with Israel's elders in Egypt, which did not turn out very well (Exod. 5.15–21), Moses' direct leadership of the people begins only when they depart from Egypt. Some have tried to construe this role as modeled on that of a king in which Moses is presented as the royal prototype for later Israelite kings. But Moses' leadership in the wilderness bears little resemblance in the biblical tradition to that of a monarch. As their leader Moses is the one to whom the people complain about their hardships in the wilderness. But it is always God who meets their needs, with manna from heaven or water from the rock (Exod. 16.1–36; 17.1–7). In the case of complaints that result in open rebellion of Moses' leadership, it is God who comes to Moses' defense with divine judgment and Moses must plead with God to mitigate the severity of the punishment (Exod. 32; Num. 11; 13–14; 16; 21.4–9). In all of this Moses has no party of supporters, no court, no bodyguard. He is primarily a spiritual leader with no royal trappings to maintain control and no form of royal legitimation.

Moses is the supreme judge and head of the administrative functions of the wilderness community. As such the tradition tells of two occasions in which Moses sets up civil institutions – the one, a system of courts for the purpose of sharing the judicial responsibility of the people (Exod. 18), and the other a council of seventy elders for the general governance of the community (Num. 11.16–30; Deut. 1.9–18). These stories represent etiologies of later Israelite institutions. The basis of all such authority is charisma, the endowment of the spirit. The council of seventy elders, however, was never an institution of the monarchy, and neither J nor P say anything about a future king for the people. Only in D is a limited monarchy envisaged as a future possibility (Deut. 17.14–20) and it is certainly not modeled on Moses in this source.

On a few occasions the Israelites are involved in military encounters, but Moses' role in these is quite limited. In their fight against the Amalekites (Exod. 17.8–16) Joshua is the military captain, while Moses raises his hands as if to petition for divine aid. When Moses sends spies to survey the land of Canaan, it is Joshua and Caleb who play the major role in support of a military campaign and against the negative report of the other spies (Num. 13–14; Deut. 1.19–46). When the people finally attempt a southern assault, Moses does not go with them, and they are defeated. In the campaign against Sihon and Og (Num. 21.21–35; Deut. 2.24 – 3:11) in Transjordan Moses leads the forces in the D account, but in J he recedes into the background. In the campaign against the Midianites in P (Num. 31) it is Phinehas, the priest, who takes charge of the army while Moses remains in the camp. When Moses finally climbs Mount Nebo to die, he is buried in an unmarked grave and receives no posthumous veneration. Moses is not a military hero nor a royal figure in these traditions.

Moses as lawgiver

The theme of Moses as lawgiver is closely associated with the theophany at Sinai/Horeb and with Israel's prolonged stay at the mountain of God, during which the law was given to Israel through Moses. Many scholars have argued that the giving of the law at Sinai originated as a separate tradition. They argue that it reflects a detour on the way from Egypt to Canaan, and that an older tradition of lawgiving is to be associated with Kadesh. These are matters that are debated within discussions on the tradition-history of the Pentateuch and remain unresolved.

Nevertheless, in the popular mind and even among some scholars Moses has been viewed as the author of the Ten Commandments, at the very least. But the two versions of the Decalogue, in Deuteronomy 5 and Exodus 20, are in the sources D and P respectively, and their language is so characteristic of the D source that there seems little reason to believe that they are any older than the seventh century BCE. The P version in Exodus 20 makes use of the D version but with some modification on the law of the sabbath to include P's theology of creation as reflected in Genesis 1. Even in these two sources the 'ten words' are said to have been given to the people directly without the mediation of Moses and only later written by the finger of God upon the two tables of stone. Furthermore, J does not regard the Ten Commandments as a distinct series and has quite a different set of laws and instructions written on the two tables of stone (Exod. 34).

The J corpus of laws in Exodus 20.22–23.33, referred to as the 'Book of the Covenant' in Exodus 24.7, is a mixture of many types of law, religious and civil regulations, principles of religion and ethics, legal procedures and humanitarian recommendations. These are all given through Moses at one time on Sinai and constitute the basis of the covenant between the people and God (Exod. 24.3–8). Portions of the civil laws are generally regarded as quite old in origin and were perhaps taken over from earlier Canaanite society, but this corpus of laws in its present form derives from the exilic period. The Deuteronomic code (Deut. 12–26) is a body of instructions given to Moses after the Ten Commandments were proclaimed. The D code was delivered to the people in written form in the land of Moab as preparation for their entry into the Promised Land. In fact, the code represents a cultic reform of worship in the time of Josiah (ca 625 BCE). The Priestly code is primarily concerned with setting out an elaborate program of cultic regulations to form the basis for worship during the Second Temple period. Its view of Judean society is strongly theocratic, with the high priest as the real head of state – hence the elevation of Aaron alongside of Moses. The P writer has much of this code revealed to Moses at Sinai (Exod. 25–31, 35–40; Leviticus; Num. 1–10), but some instructions are given during the remaining part of the wilderness journey. In P, Moses' role as revealer and instructor in divine law is the most dominant.

Moses as prophet

The one role directly and unequivocally ascribed to Moses is that of prophet, and this, in fact, shapes and modifies all the others given to him. Perhaps the earliest allusion to Moses in the prophetic corpus speaks of Yahweh's deliverance from Egypt 'by a prophet' (Hos. 12.13). When Moses is called by God to lead the people out of Egypt, his role is to be that of a divine spokesman and prophet, announcing to the people God's revelation to him of their deliverance and God's demand to pharaoh to release his people. The objections to the task that Moses raises are similar to those in the call narrative of Jeremiah (Jer. 1.4–10), and much of Moses' role as prophet is modeled on the biography of Jeremiah. Throughout his encounter with Pharaoh, Moses uses the standard prophetic formula 'Thus says Yahweh . . .' The sole basis of his authority is as the bearer of the divine word.

Another important aspect of the prophetic role that is drawn from the Jeremiah tradition is that of Moses' function as intercessor on behalf of his people (Jer. 7.11; 11.14; 14.11; 18.20; 37.3; 42.2, 20). When Pharaoh increases the burdens of the people after Moses' first audience, Moses prays to God about their hardships and this brings the divine response of the plagues. When Pharaoh begs Moses to end a plague, Moses intercedes with God on his behalf (Exod. 8.4–5 [ET 8–9], 24–6 [ET 28–30]; 9.28; 10.17–18). Throughout the wilderness experience in the murmuring stories, when the people face hardships because of a lack of food or water, Moses petitions God for divine relief. When the people are rebellious or sin and are punished by God, Moses begs for mercy and pardon on their behalf (Exod. 15.25; 17.4; 32.11–13, 30–32; Num. 11.2; 14.13–19; 21.7). The construing of the religious leadership of the community as prophetic is a major shaping of the Moses tradition and belongs to both the J and D portrayals of Moses.

In addition to this prophetic shaping of all Moses' activities, there is the explicit identification of Moses as a prophet – indeed the greatest of all the prophets. In a narrative in Numbers 12 in which Miriam and Aaron question Moses' special authority, an oracle makes it quite clear that Moses is unique among prophets in receiving his divine revelation 'mouth to mouth, clearly and not in dark speech' (RSV, v. 8). And Deuteronomy 34.10 proclaims that 'there has not arisen a prophet since in Israel like Moses, whom the LORD knew face to face' (RSV), and goes on to attribute all the signs and wonders he did in Egypt as related to his prophetic role.

Finally, in Moses' capacity as lawgiver, this prophetic role likewise comes to the fore. In the common Near Eastern background the giving of the law by the god is usually associated with a king, as it is in the case of Hammurabi of Babylon, but that is not the case for the Moses tradition. In the two presentations of the Sinai/Horeb theophany in J and D (Exod. 19–20; Deut. 5), the people are so terrified in witnessing the direct revelation and utterance of God that they beg Moses to serve as an intermediary to receive the words of God that they will then accept and obey. This serves as both an explanation of Moses' prophetic role and as a way of subsuming the whole of the legal tradition under prophecy and divine sanction. All of Moses' legal pronouncements become prophetic. At the same time it suggests that the law of Moses is the most complete prophetic revelation and that the later prophets are primarily commentary on the law.

It is, therefore, remarkable that so few direct references are made to Moses in the prophetic literature (Isa. 63.11–12; Jer. 15.1; Hos. 12.13; Mic. 6:4; Mal. 3.22), and all but one of these (Hos. 12.13) are late texts. The classical prophets of the period of the monarchy do not seem to base their moral or religious authority upon the Moses tradition. This led the great biblical scholar of the last century Julius Wellhausen to assert that in Israel's religious history the prophets came before Moses and the law, and not Moses before the prophets.

For all the biblical writers of the Pentateuch the wilderness period was the constitutional age, the time of Israel's beginning. Whatever was most fundamental to

Israelite society was deemed to have arisen in this period. And Moses as deliverer, leader, lawgiver and prophet, was regarded as the one through whom all this came about. In this sense he was the founder of the people of Israel. Modern criticism, however, has made the Moses tradition problematic by identifying its anachronisms and dating its materials to later ages. While some scholars have tried to find some elements of the tradition that may go back to Moses, there are those who dispute that any of it derives from Moses or the wilderness period.

MOSES IN POSTBIBLICAL JUDAISM

The great diversity within the religion of Judaism in the centuries that followed the Hebrew Bible does not allow one to generalize about the development of the Moses tradition in this period. But some common features are shared, even if understood somewhat differently, and may be set down as follows: (1) The legend of Moses continues to develop in the direction of the heroic, with many additional exploits about his youth and life in the Egyptian court. (2) The Law of Moses, the Torah, is gradually understood as encompassing the whole of the Pentateuch, so that Moses is author not just of the laws but also of the history from creation to the time of his own death. (3) Moses as the greatest prophet includes both his mediation of the law and the revelation of past history, including the origins of the world and the mysteries of the universe. (4) Moses' role as intercessor on Israel's behalf is expanded to reach beyond the limits of his death in the mitigation of divine punishment for the people's sins. Within the scope of these shared features are a number of special developments of the Moses tradition that may be briefly considered.

Moses in Hellenistic Judaism

During the period from 200 BCE to 100 CE Hellenistic Judaism took on a strongly apologetic character in response to a number of pagan writings that vilified Judaism and its founder Moses. In order to counteract this, Jewish writers presented their history and scriptures in ways that would appeal to Gentile audiences to win approval, or at least tolerance, for their religion and way of life. Moses was portrayed as a great inventor of the arts of civilization, including writing, philosophy, statesmanship, and religion. Moses' early life was modeled after the Hellenistic biography of the divine man, with prophecies about his birth and greatness, accounts of his beauty and royal upbringing, and his great military exploits on behalf of the pharaoh. All these embellishments were in answer to pagan attacks on the dubious character of Hebrew origins.

Flavius Josephus, a Jewish historian living in Rome at the end of the first century CE, wrote his history of the Jewish people in the manner of Greco-Roman historiography. In it he greatly expands the early life and career of Moses with legends not found in the biblical tradition. For the rest, Moses as the Hebrew 'man of God' is assimilated to the Hellenistic 'divine man' and thus presented as legislator and founder of the ideal constitution – a theocracy. In this he is prior to, and exceeds in greatness, even Solon and Lycurgus among the Greeks (*Jewish Antiquities* 1.18–26; *Against Apion* 2.145–56, 164–6).

Philo Judaeus of Alexandria, who also lived in the first century CE, interpreted the Pentateuch according to Greek philosophical traditions and Jewish mystical religion. In his work *Life of Moses* Moses is presented as the ideal king of Hellenistic philosophy. This includes notions of the king as divine man, the embodiment of law and the chief priest of the nation. Moses' special qualities as divine man, his royal upbringing and his life as a shepherd prepare him to become the king of Israel in the wilderness period. Moses' role as legislator is presented as a royal function. According to Philo Moses is also a royal chief priest in his establishment of the institutions of worship and in his role as intercessor. Moses is likewise the greatest of the prophets, not only through his mediation of the law but in the character of his inspiration, which is a mystical experience of the divine and direct intuition of the truth. In some of his more philosophical and allegorical works, Philo describes Moses as the greatest of the philosophers (*On the Creation of the World*, 8–10) or as a hierophant with the Law as a guide to the divine mysteries (*On the Decalogue* 18; *Allegorical Interpretation* 3.173).

The apocalyptic tradition

In two apocalyptic works, the *Assumption of Moses* and *Jubilees*, Moses receives special and secret knowledge about both past and future events as well as heaven and hell, with special attention given to the events of the Last Days. Great emphasis is also placed on Moses' role as intercessor, not just in his lifetime, but beyond his death on Israel's behalf throughout their history up to the Last Judgment (*Jub.* 1.18–26; *Asm. Mos.* 1.14–18, 11.9–19).

Rabbinic view of Moses

The rabbinic tradition represents a vast array of sources from the second century CE to the Middle Ages, containing a wide spectrum of belief and opinion. In this it was heir to many of the impulses and developments in the Moses tradition noted above.

In the legal tradition (*halakhah*) Moses is the great 'teacher' who instructed Israel in the Law. This includes not only all the laws of the Pentateuch but all oral Torah, which was thought to have been handed down from Moses to Joshua and in succession ultimately to the rabbis. Thus all students of the law are really disciples of Moses.

The homiletic tradition (*aggadah*) highlighted other aspects of the Moses tradition that were a part of Jewish piety. It continued to embellish the legendary Moses as the 'man of God,' but also his role as the 'servant of God' in the people's liberation from slavery and guidance to the Promised Land. Moses' role as intercessor links him closely with his people, thereby ensuring their salvation in the final resurrection. Also as supreme prophet of the divine revelation he inaugurates the great succession of prophets.

MOSES IN THE NEW TESTAMENT

Throughout the New Testament Moses is viewed as the author of the Pentateuch ('Law': Mt 8.4, Mk 7.10; Jn 1.17), which serves not only as the definitive authority for the Jewish religion, but also as prophetic prediction for the rise of Christianity (Lk 24.25–7). At the same time the Law of Moses becomes increasingly associated with those forms of Judaism with which early Christianity came into conflict, so that the new revelation mediated through Jesus supersedes that of Moses.

In the Gospels, elements in the life of Jesus are modeled on the legends of Moses. In Matthew's infancy narrative (ch. 2), these include the predictions to the 'father' and warnings to the king, the slaughter of the innocents, the recognition of Jesus' royalty, and the flight into exile until the king's death.

Jesus forty days of fasting in the wilderness is parallel to Moses' fast on Mount Sinai (Mt 4.1–2; Lk 4.1–3; cf. Deut. 9.9) as well as Israel's forty years of trials in the wilderness. Jesus' feeding of the five thousand (Mt 14.13–21; Mk 6.32–44; Lk 9.10–17; Jn 6.1–14) is interpreted in John's Gospel as parallel to Moses giving manna in the wilderness (6.25–34). Jesus appearance with Moses and Elijah on the mount of transfiguration is reminiscent of the theophany at Sinai (Mt 17.1–8; Mk 9.2–8; Lk 9.28–36). Even the account of Jesus' ascension from the Mount of Olives has similarities with the legend of Moses' assumption on Mount Nebo (Lk 24.51; Acts 1.9–11).

The ministry of Jesus is likewise compared with that of Moses. In Matthew, the setting for the Sermon on the Mount is parallel to Moses expounding the law at Sinai. In Luke, Jesus is a prophet like Moses who redeems his people. For John, 'The law was given through Moses but grace and truth came through Jesus Christ' (REB, 1.17). In John's polemic against Judaism, Jesus is superior to Moses and supplants him as the divine revelation.

The apostle Paul, using the allegorical methods of Hellenistic Jewish exegesis, interprets the event at the Red Sea as a baptism 'into Moses' comparable to the Christian baptism 'into Christ' and the wilderness journey as a spiritual experience and therefore a model for the Christian life (1 Cor. 10:1–11). A similar instance of allegorical interpretation has to do with Moses' reception of the law and especially the veil that was used to cover the splendor of his face when he descended Mount Sinai (2 Cor. 3.7–18; cf. Exod. 34:29–35). Here the typology is intended to argue for the superiority of the manifested glory of the Christian gospel over the veiled religion of the Law of Moses in Judaism.

Likewise, the letter to the Hebrews draws comparisons between Jesus and Moses in order to argue that Jesus is superior. In the household of God, Moses as the servant of God is inferior to Jesus, who is the son of God (3.2–6; cf. Num. 12.7). Moses instituted the earthly sanctuary, which is only a copy and a shadow of the heavenly, and in this sanctuary the levitical priesthood ministers according to the law. But Jesus is the eternal high priest who ministers in the heavenly sanctuary by interceding for the faithful (8.1–6). In the same way Moses is the author of the old covenant, but this was only a preparation to be replaced by the new covenant through Jesus (8.7–10.18).

BIBLIOGRAPHY

Among the older standard works on the scholarly study of the Moses tradition are the following:

Auerbach, Elias, *Moses*, Detroit: Wayne State University Press, 1975 (trans. and ed. from the 1953 German edn by R. A. Barclay and I. O. Lehman).
Buber, Martin, *Moses: The Revelation and the Covenant*, New York: Harper, 1958. A repr. of the 1946 edn.
Gressmann, Hugo, *Mose und seine Zeit: Ein Kommentar zu den Mose-sagen*. Göttingen: Vandenhoeck & Ruprecht, 1913.

Two more recent literary-critical studies are

Coats, George, *Moses: Heroic Man, Man of God*, JSOT Supplement 57, Sheffield: JSOT Press, 1988.
Van Seters, John, *The Life of Moses: The Yahwist as Historian in Exodus–Numbers*, Louisville: Westminster John Knox, 1994.

On the historical problems of the Moses tradition, one may consult

Rainer, Albertz, *A History of Israelite Religion in the Old Testament Period*, 1: 40–66, Old Testament Library, Louisville: Westminster John Knox, 1992.
Herrmann, Siegfried, *Israel in Egypt*, Studies in Biblical Theology, Second Series 27, London: SCM, 1973.
Redford, Donald B., 'An Egyptological Perspective on the Exodus Narrative', in A. F. Rainey, ed., *Egypt, Israel, Sinai: Archaeological and Historical Relationships in the Biblical Period*, 137–61, Tel Aviv: Tel Aviv University Press, 1987.
Soggin, J. Alberto, *An Introduction to the History of Israel and Judah*, London: SCM, 1993. This work contains an extensive up-to-date bibliography.

Books that are especially helpful for the treatment of Moses in Judaism and Christianity are

A collection of essays under the title *Moïse, l'homme de l'alliance*, Paris: Desclée, 1955.
Ginzberg, Louis, *The Legends of the Bible*, New York: Jewish Publication Society, 1956 (an abridgement of the earlier work *The Legends of the Jews*, 7 vols. 1908–37).

CHAPTER THIRTY-NINE

DAVID AND SOLOMON

———•◆•———

Gwilym H. Jones

David and Solomon were the only kings who 'reigned over all Israel and Judah' (2 Sam 5:5). The kingdom of their predecessor Saul was essentially formed by the tribes of Ephraim, Benjamin and Gilead, with other tribes or areas associating themselves loosely and temporarily with them. It was less extensive territorially than the 'empire' of David and Solomon, and lacked the administrative and institutional framework established by them. But the united kingdom of David and Solomon did not survive beyond the death of Solomon, for when Rehoboam took the throne, the Israelites seceded and made Jeroboam king over them, creating two kingdoms, Judah in the south and Israel in the north (1 Kgs 12:20). Reconstructions of biblical chronology place the death of Solomon at various points between 922 and 932 BCE, and because biblical records quote the round figure of forty years for the kingship of both David and Solomon, exact dates cannot be determined. Their period was the early part of the tenth century BCE.

SOURCES

For this period the main sources are the books of Samuel and Kings; the approach of the books of Chronicles is thematic rather than chronological and corroborative evidence from external sources is scarce and fragmentary. The nature of historiography in these works needs definition. Undoubtedly the biblical books depended on basic source material, as is seen from a consideration of two extensive complexes. In 1 Samuel 16–2 Samuel 5, eight narratives about the rise of David to power form a heterogeneous collection with many duplicates and parallels. Narratives that must at one time have existed independently have been brought together by an editor whose primary aim was to prove that David was the only legitimate successor of Saul. The thrust of the section is clearly theological: David was manifestly endowed with divine blessing, which had been withdrawn from Saul and transferred to his only true successor. Although it contains much material that interests the historian, it is undoubtedly a particular kind of history, a 'theological history'.

Another complex, generally known as 'the succession narrative' (2 Sam 9–20; 1 Kgs 1–2) because of its concern with succession to David's throne, has won acclamation as a reliable historical account that has emerged from David's court and has been described as the 'oldest specimen of ancient Israelite historical writing' (von Rad 1966). But doubts have been raised about the term 'historical writing'. Although much of the material is of interest to the historian, several of its most prominent features tell against the appropriateness of the term. Reports of private scenes, interest in the personal rather than political implications, lack of chronology and a distinctly pro-Solomonic *Tendenz* suggest a different kind of writing, which has been variously classified as historical novel, national epic or political propaganda. These complexes, used as source material for the period of David and Solomon, have a special character and are not 'history' in the strict sense of the word.

By now these traditions have been incorporated in a larger work known as the 'Deuteronomistic History' giving an account of Israelite history from the death of Moses in Deuteronomy 34 to the exile at the end of 2 Kings, a period of 1,200 years. The dominant influence of Deuteronomy has given it its name and the history of the period is presented according to one line of interpretation. There are but few instances in which the Deuteronomists have undertaken extensive editorial reworking of the material in the two major complexes mentioned. But it is the Deuteronomists who have determined the general structure for presenting the material. In the case of David it is simply 'David under the blessing – David under the curse'; the same structure is used for Saul and Solomon (Carlson 1964). To uphold this scheme some chronological modifications were necessary.

DAVID'S RISE

David is presented as a charismatic person, and that is why he succeeded Saul. Two contrasting royal ideologies, charismatic kingship and hereditary dynasty, are seen in Israel's early traditions. Saul intended to establish a dynasty, with Jonathan as legitimate successor (1 Sam 20:31), but David and Jonathan did not subscribe to the hereditary dynasty principle (1 Sam 18:3; 20:13). However, when David was king he established a dynasty and was succeeded by Solomon. The dynasty survived among the southern tribes until the exile, but the northern tribes, immediately after Solomon's death, reverted to the charismatic ideal. There is evidence that on more than one occasion an attempt at founding a hereditary dynasty in the north floundered; this is the reason for the revolts against Nadab and Elah (1 Kgs 15:25–32; 16:8–14) and for Jehu's *coup d'état* and the fall of the house of Omri (2 Kgs 9:1 – 10:36) (see Alt 1968).

Traditions about David's introduction to Saul's court and his rise to power are dominated by one theme – the advance of David under divine guidance. The theme is supported by its counterpart, that Saul had lost divine favour and was no longer competent to rule. The main thrust of these intermingled traditions is that David was the legitimate successor. Different accounts of his introduction to court are concerned with legitimization. His anointing at Bethlehem by Samuel is strikingly similar to Saul's election: both were chosen (1 Sam 10:24; 16:8–10); one came from the smallest clan, the other was the youngest son; both were chosen through a process of elimination; both had to be sought and brought from elsewhere for the election. Although this narrative is probably secondary, having been deliberately constructed on the model of Saul's election, it makes the point that Saul was rejected and abandoned to a malevolent spirit, while Yahweh's spirit was transferred to David (1 Sam 16:13). Another account of his admission to court reports how his skill in playing won him a place as armour-bearer (1 Sam 16:14–23), but it refers also to David's other attributes – his military prowess, good judgement, intellect and presence, all of which provide proof of divine blessing. By coming to court he gained training and experience and was thus able to replace Saul, despite the love–hate relationship between them (Gunn 1978, 1980). The third narrative, David's slaughter of Goliath (1 Sam 17:1–58), bears the marks of popular legendary material. It may originally have been connected with Elhanan before it became attached to David, and there is a glaring contradiction between verses 12–16 and 16:14–23. The narrative's aim is clear: it shows that God was with David, the youngster who refused armour and depended on a shepherd's sling. By conquering the Philistine he stood in the tradition of Israel's divinely endowed warriors. Whatever the origin of these often contradictory narratives, they have been placed together to support the theme that David, endowed with divine charisma, was Saul's legitimate successor.

Other sections of the narrative confirm that he was destined for the throne. Once in the court he was generally acclaimed by the populace and courtiers, and was elevated by Saul (1 Sam 18:1–5). Saul was torn between respect and hatred, but nevertheless gave David his daughter Michal to be his wife. It is shown that Saul, troubled by an evil spirit, was thwarted in all his plans, but that David was led by God to outstanding successes (1 Sam 18:14, 30). Particular significance is attached to Jonathan's friendship with David; the biblical words for their attachment, 'love' and 'covenant', signify some kind of political liaison (Thompson 1974). The pact sealed by them had political implications, and the handing over of Jonathan's clothes and armour to David was a symbolic transfer of the right of succession. Jonathan obviously recognized David as heir-apparent (Mettinger 1976).

Another important aspect of the theme is that David gained the throne lawfully and rejected all pressures and opportunities to usurp it. He respected Saul's position of 'the LORD's anointed', and twice spared his life (1 Sam 24:1–22; 26:1–25). He refused the opportunity in the cave in Engedi to take vengeance on Saul. Proof that he could have taken his life was his possession of a piece of his skirt. On another occasion his possession of Saul's spear and water jug (1 Sam 26:11, 16), one denoting his royal office and the other his life, showed that Saul's kingdom and life were in his hands. David restrained himself, and was careful not to be guilty for the death of Saul (1 Sam 29:1–11), Abner (2 Sam 3:28–39) or Ishbaal (2 Sam 4:9–12). The unmistakable inference of the biblical texts is that there are no grounds for taking David as an opportunist engaged in guerrilla warfare against Saul and a leader of bands of malcontents aiming at usurping the throne (as argued by Ishida 1977).

MILITARY SUCCESSES

David's popularity and rise to power is to a great measure attributed to his military prowess. His meeting with Goliath emphasized two important points: firstly, that David met the challenge not because of arrogance or a spirit of adventure but because he was chosen by God; secondly, that he stood in the tradition of Israel's great warriors and, like Saul, triumphed over the Philistines. Despite Saul's endeavours to be rid of David by placing him in situations where he could easily fall into Philistine hands (1 Sam 18: 13, 17, 25), he survived. Eventually he had no option but to leave the court and escape, but it was not out of disloyalty: even as an outlaw, he was careful not to undermine Saul's status as God's anointed.

Nevertheless, during his absence from court David took steps, some of them morally questionable, to consolidate his own position. He secured the support of the priesthood at Nob (1 Sam 21:1–15; 22:6–23), although it was obtained through deception. The slaughter of the entire priesthood of Nob by Doeg the Edomite, who was in charge of Saul's servants, lost for Saul the service of the priesthood. But David had access to Yahweh through Abiathar, the only priest who escaped and then attached himself to David (1 Sam 23:6–13). Another act of deception obtained for David Goliath's sword, the possession of which had symbolic significance: it was a reminder of his success in battle, was an omen of future successes and possibly signified that power was transferred from the sanctuary to God's elect (Edelman 1991).

David's liberation of Keilah in Philistine territory further strengthened his position (1 Sam 23:1–29) and his activity in the wilderness of Maon led to an important acquisition of territory. Abigail intervened and prevented him from annihilating Nabal in retaliation for his refusal to give him provision and accepting his offer of peace and friendship. But it was through marrying Abigail after Nabal's death that he gained his Calebite territory, including Hebron, which became an important power base (2 Sam 2:1–4). He gained some territory too when he married Ahinoam of Jezreel (1 Sam 25:43).

During his sojourn of a year and four months with the Philistines at Gath David was engaged in morally indefensible activity (1 Sam 27:1–12). After escaping from Saul, he defected to the Philistines and after a period in the royal city with Achish he was given Ziklag, possibly as a reward for military assistance. Whether Ziklag is to be identified with Tell el-Khuweilfeh north of Beersheba or with Tell esh-Sherî'ah south-east of Gaza, it gave David a base that remained as crown-property of Judaean kings.

From his base at Ziklag David made a series of attacks on Israel's enemies, the Geshurites, the Girzites and the Amalekites (1 Sam 27:8–12), who were on the route from Telam to Egypt. Giving Achish the impression that he was fighting enemies of the Philistines, David totally annihilated them leaving no trace of evidence to the contrary. An issue is not made of David's dishonesty; it is accepted that by conquering prospective enemies and amassing booty he was preparing for his kingship. Later David had to avenge Ziklag, the Negeb of the Cherethites, the Negeb of Caleb and some Judaean territory. The most powerful town in the area was Hebron, and it was there that the people of Judah acclaimed him as their king (2 Sam 5:1–3).

Even when there was civil war between north and south, David had some support in the north. Two of his marriages, to Ahinoam of Jezreel and to Maacah daughter of Talmai of Geshur, were probably marriage alliances through which he gained support. He had also after the death of Saul made overtures to the men of Jabesh-gilead (2 Sam 5:46–7). Furthermore, a pact with Abner secured an understanding that Israelite territories would be transferred to David on condition that Saul's daughter Michal would return to him (2 Sam 3:6–21); he was obviously staking a claim to Saul's throne. When Ishbaal died David took the throne without opposition and was acclaimed by 'the elders of Israel'. Following this there were further clashes with the Philistines (2 Sam 5:17–25), although the account has been chronologically misplaced in the Old Testament. On two occasions the Philistines came to the Valley of Rephaim to the south-west of Jerusalem. The first time David launched his attack from 'the stronghold' (probably Adullam) and defeated them at Baal-perazim. The second time he won a decisive victory and struck them from Geba (or better, following the LXX, Gibbeon, 6 miles north-west of Jerusalem) back to their border at Gezer.

A catalogue of David's victories in 2 Samuel 8:1–14 has probably been compiled from ancient fragments but has been arranged thematically rather than chronologically. Head of the list is his defeat of the Philistines, and despite a difficulty in identifying Metheg-ammah the implication is that he was in total control of Philistine territory. Moab was subjugated with great cruelty. In the north he faced a threat from Aram-zobah, which was expanding under Hadadezer, the leader of a strong coalition including Damascus and Hamath. David defeated Hadadezer, took prisoners and mutilated horses. The Aramaeans were conquered, and Hamath immediately sought an alliance with David. He also conquered Edom and placed garrisons there. This list indicates that David had taken control of Palestine from the Philistines, had placed garrisons in Moab, Edom and Ammon (corresponding to modern Jordan) and had conquered Aramaean states in the north (corresponding to modern Syria and eastern Lebanon). In view of these phenomenal successes, David was in control of what can be justifiably called an empire (Malamat 1958).

CAPITAL AND COURT

A significant conquest was the capture of Jerusalem (2 Sam 5:6–9). Its name has been preserved in Egyptian execration texts of the nineteenth and eighteenth centuries BCE as well as in the Amarna texts of the fourteenth century BCE. The Israelites had not taken it when they entered Canaan (Josh 15:63; Judg 1:21), and it had remained an independent foreign enclave inhabited by Jebusites. David took a wise move by making it his capital: it was a strong fortress away from the main north–south routes, and it had a measure of independence because of its previous occupation by the Jebusites and its position more or less on the border between Israel and Judah.

The Jebusites were so confident in the strength of the city that they boasted that even handicapped people ('the blind and the lame') could defend it. When David took it he made the point that its defenders were indeed like handicapped people. The city was taken by making use of a vertical shaft from the city to the Spring of Gihon; David's men stopped the flow of water, either to enable them to climb the shaft into the city or to force the city into submission by cutting off the water supply. David took possession of the fortress on the hill in the south-eastern corner called 'the stronghold' or Ophel and renamed it 'the city of David'. He also strengthened the fortifications by building 'from the Millo inward'; the Millo was an earth-fill forming a rampart or a platform, which may have been a terracing on the eastern slope (Kenyon 1974).

Bringing the ark to Jerusalem added to the capital's stature. 2 Samuel 6:1–23 continues the story of the ark in 1 Samuel 4:1 – 7:1, but modern studies tend to discount the theory that they are to be read together as a continuous piece (Miller and Roberts 1977). Whatever its origin the narrative fits well in this particular context; it was after a decisive defeat of the Philistines that David was able to bring the ark to the city. Following Uzzah's cultic aberration, the ark was housed temporarily with Obed-edom, but after proof that it was a source of blessing David brought it to his capital. The cultic significance of the event is unmistakable: there were accompanying sacrifices; David wore a linen ephod, a priestly garment; a ram's horn summoned the people to the celebrations; a tent was constructed to house the ark. Ultimately the ark was placed in Solomon's Temple, and it is possible that the ark narratives served as sanctuary legends for the Jerusalem Temple (Timm 1966; Campbell 1975).

David set up a court in Jerusalem, and two variant lists of his officials have been preserved (2 Sam 8:15–18; 20:23–6); such lists were probably taken from archives. The first person named in both lists is Joab, commander of the army, who had been some time with David. Other officials common to both lists are Benaiah, who was in charge of the Cherethites and Pelethites, the royal bodyguard; Zadok and Abiathar, who shared the priesthood until David's death; Jehoshaphat, bearing the title 'recorder', sometimes translated 'herald', denoting the person responsible for communication between king and country (Mettinger 1971); Seraiah, secretary, possibly responsible for court annals or acting in a managerial capacity as Secretary of State. The second list names Adoram in charge of forced labour, a post probably created towards the end of David's reign. Another difference is that the reference to David's sons as priests has been replaced by the mention of Ira the Jairite. David had established a government in which a number of officials had responsibility for designated areas. It marks a shift from the informal arrangement of Saul to a more developed system of court officials under Solomon. Jerusalem had been established as a capital city with a royal court and a royal sanctuary.

SUCCESSION TO THE THRONE

An important issue in the biblical narrative is succession to David's throne. One section of Nathan's oracle (2 Sam 7:8–16) declares that God was going to found a dynasty (a 'house') for David and the eternity of his kingdom is asserted (Jones 1990). This is the main theme of 2 Samuel 9–20 and 1 Kings 1–2, reaching a climax with the statement that 'the kingdom was established in the hand of Solomon' (2 Kgs 2:46). Lack of references to cultic matters, together with the absence of theological assertions about God's involvement in the events, have been taken as an indication that the succession narrative was a secular piece of writing. Nevertheless the point that Solomon was God's choice as successor is brought out clearly by a master of narrative art in action and dialogue rather than in explicit theological statements (Conroy 1978).

The editor may have seen in David's kindness to Mephibosheth, the last remaining son of Jonathan (2 Sam 9:1–13), some contribution to the theme of succession. Events surrounding Amnon's love for Tamar have a more direct bearing on the theme. Absalom's vengeance resulted in the death of Amnon and eventually of Absalom himself, thus removing two of Solomon's older brothers. Both private affairs (2 Sam 13–14) and more public events (2 Sam 15–19), skilfully recorded without elaborating the point that Solomon was destined for the throne, were of great historical significance for the kingdom. Absalom's responsibility for the death of Amnon led to his exile from court, but after some time he was allowed to return to Jerusalem. Once reinstated he became a contender for the throne, moved by a desire for revenge for the wrong suffered by Tamar. However, despite the narrative's favourable attitude to David, other motives cannot be concealed; deficiencies in the administration of justice under David are noted (2 Sam 15:2–6), and there was possibly unease about his expansionist policy, his ruthless military activities and the development of state bureaucracy. Absalom had a following when he decided to stage his rebellion from Hebron, and when David withdrew from Jerusalem he took the city and arrogantly staked his claim to the throne by possessing his father's harem (2 Sam 16:21; Tsevat 1958). It was a short-lived rebellion. Absalom rejected Ahithophel's advice to follow a well-proven military strategy of launching a night attack, with a swift and successful action, and took Hushai's advice to take time to muster all Israel and to go himself to battle, a delay that gave David an opportunity to muster his troops. His men prevented David from going to battle, but Absalom was killed by Joab, who acted contrary to David's instructions to his commanders to deal gently with the rebel (2 Sam 18:5). By making this point and emphasizing that David had not gone to battle, it is shown that David could not be implicated in Absalom's death. Another point made is that David could rely on the assistance of past supporters of the house of Saul (2 Sam 17:27).

After a prolonged mourning for Absalom, David was persuaded to turn his attention to state matters. The dissatisfied elements who had supported Absalom were willing, after his death, to transfer their allegiance to David; what they found lacking in internal management was probably compensated by his success against the Philistines. David was prevented from immediate acceptance of Israelite overtures by Judah's tardiness in declaring its support. When that was obtained after approaches through the priests Zadok and Abiathar, Judah moved quickly and went to Gilgal to protect David's crossing of the Jordan. The spectacle of Judah leading the king to Jerusalem gave the Israelites a feeling of isolation and led to a conflict (2 Sam 19:41–3); this conflict between north and south was to lead to another rebellion (2 Sam 20) and ultimately to the division of the kingdom (1 Kgs 12).

Only two candidates for the throne remained, Adonijah and Solomon. When David showed signs of senility, Adonijah, the elder, set himself up as king with the support of Joab, commander of David's army, and Abiathar the priest (1 Kgs 1:6). An opposing party had the support of Zadok the priest, Benaiah, commander of David's bodyguards, Nathan the prophet, two unknown persons, Shimei and Rei, and some professional soldiers. On the one hand were representatives of the military and religious institutions of Hebron and the pre-Jerusalemite tradition; on the other were representatives of a new pattern emerging in Jerusalem with the monarchy. In answer to Adonijah's move, Bathsheba and Nathan organized a successful *coup d'état*, with Bathsheba probably taking a more active part in the plot than is attributed to her. By alluding to a fabricated oath, they obtained from David the designation of Solomon as his successor and arrangements were made for his immediate anointing

(1 Kgs 1:29–40). Initially Solomon acted as co-regent; after his acclamation Adonijah's contention collapsed, and when David died he progressed to the throne. Although Solomon granted amnesty to his rival, Adonijah took a false step by requesting Abishag the Shunammite as his wife; because it was interpreted as a claim to the throne Solomon was justified in putting him to death. Solomon further consolidated his position by removing Abiathar the priest to Anathoth and ordering the slaughter of Joab and Shimei. These narratives concerned with succession are suitably concluded with 1 Kings 2:46.

DAVID'S CHARACTER

The account of David's reign from the hands of the Deuteronomistic historians brings out their interest in a number of issues. David is represented as God's elect, who gained popularity and notable military successes. In his progress to the throne he showed remarkable restraint and did not seize it. Among his achievements were an extension of territory to reach the semblance of an empire; the establishment of the capital Jerusalem as cultic and administrative centre; the formation of a court structure with officials responsible for specific areas; an ultimate settlement of the succession issue by securing the throne for an offspring and thus fulfilling the prophecy that a house of David would be founded. However, the editors did not gloss over David's weaknesses and failures. His dishonesty on more than one occasion is frankly reported (1 Sam 21:1–6; 27:8–12), and no attempt has been made to hide acts of cruelty and atrocity (1 Sam 31:17; 2 Sam 8; 10:18). Although the succession issue was resolved, several incidents testify to David's weakness in his dealings with his own family: he failed to deal with Amnon and was unable to establish an effective relationship with Absalom. There is full coverage of his affair with Bathsheba and his despicable treatment of Uriah (2 Sam 11–12), and no attempt has been made to explain his behaviour, whether he acted from love, or lust, or because he wanted to reassert his flagging manhood (Cohen 1965). The story even admits that David's personal weaknesses were not without effect on the affairs of the kingdom (2 Sam 12:10–12).

SOLOMON

Solomon was Bathsheba's son, and it was with her assistance that he came to the throne. Although it has been argued that he was her firstborn, an illegitimate child, who had been given his name because he was a 'replacement' for Uriah her dead husband (Veijola 1979), it is more likely that he was her second son by David, a 'replacement' for the illegitimate firstborn who had died (2 Sam 12:24–5). His succession to David's throne as the result of a *coup d'état* called for the swift and decisive actions he took to consolidate his kingship. It also called for the legitimation of his kingship. The account of his visit to the sanctuary at Gibeon serves to declare that he was endowed with divine charisma. A parallel to this legitimization of royalty is found in the Egyptian 'royal novel' (*Königsnovelle*), such as the text on the Sphinx Stele recording a dream revelation to Thuthmosis IV (1421–1413 BCE). The salient features were: leaving the capital to sacrifice in a sanctuary; a dream-vision; sacrificing and communicating the contents of the vision to members of the court (Herrmann 1953). The inclusion of this visit immediately after Solomon's accession suggests that his kingship needed justification.

WISDOM

According to the Gibeon narrative Solomon's charisma was 'wisdom', which has become a leading motif in the chapters covering his reign because it was probably the dominant theme of their source, 'the book of the acts of Solomon' (Liver 1967). His request for 'an understanding mind' was granted, and the theme recurs in 1 Kings 3:16 – 4:34 and again in 1 Kings 10:1–10, 13, 23–4. His original quest was for 'an understanding mind *to govern* your people', and although the Hebrew *šāpaṭ* translated 'to govern' basically means 'to judge', it must not be given a narrow juridical meaning; Solomon was asking for the ability to decide between right and wrong in governing the people (Mettinger 1971). In its treatment of wisdom the narrative brings out the juridical connotation by placing 1 Kings 3:16–28 immediately after the Gibeon visit. Because of the numerous parallels to this particular section, some from as far as East Asia and India, it seems to be popular folk tradition, and may have come to the Jerusalem court circle and was attached to the Solomonic tradition after suitable modification. Its inclusion has given a narrow interpretation to Solomon's ability to govern.

A different definition of wisdom is that it is the possession of a 'breadth of understanding' surpassing the understanding of all other people (1 Kgs 4:29–34). The addition of verses 31–3 gives it a narrower interpretation – the ability to compose proverbs and poetry and also to produce scientific lists of natural phenomena or nature-wisdom. Many have cast doubt on the reliability of this tradition, and these three verses, together with 1 Kings 10:1–10, 13, 23–4, have been labelled as late and legendary. These arguments, however, are not conclusive. It is not improbable that Solomon's court developed a wisdom tradition on a model already established in Egypt. Indeed wisdom schools were known in Babylon, Egypt and Ugarit, and it is not unlikely that a similar school was established in Jerusalem (Mettinger 1971); the connection with Solomon may have been imposed later on a tradition that belonged to his court circle.

The wisdom theme reaches its climax with the visit of the queen of Sheba (1 Kgs 10:1–10, 13, 23–4), which originated from popular, legendary material similar to that extensively used in the Middle East and elsewhere (Ullendorf 1962–3; 1974). Two aspects of Solomon's wisdom are brought together – the wisdom of his administration and his ability to answer hard questions. Originally the visit was a trade mission, but became attached later to the wisdom tradition. Because of the great distance from the South Arabian kingdom of Sheba, which controlled the trade route between India, East Africa and the Mediterranean, and the lack of direct evidence that the country had been governed by a queen, it is more probable that the visitor came from the land of the Sabeans in North Arabia. It was not too distant from Jerusalem and is frequently mentioned in the royal annals of Tiglath-pileser III (*ANET* 283–6). Because the Sabeans were in control of the northern sections of the trade routes from South Arabia, this visit was unquestionably a trade mission.

Both the similarity between Solomon's Gibeon visit and the Egyptian *Königsnovelle* and the many subsequent references to his wisdom point to Egyptian influence on his court. Solomon seems to have deliberately modelled aspects of the Hebrew monarchy on Egyptian protocol.

INTERNATIONAL RELATIONS

Pronounced Egyptian influence on the Jerusalem court was due to Solomon's marriage alliance with Pharaoh, king of Egypt, an alliance probably contracted early in his reign and possibly initiated by David. Marriage between a pharaoh's daughter and a foreigner was rare and even prohibited in early times; according to Amenophis III 'no daughter of the king of Egypt is given to others' (Schulman 1979). But because of the close friendship between Egypt and the Davidic–Solomonic empire a marriage alliance would not be unlikely (Malamat 1958); the pharaoh in question would probably be one of the last of the Twenty-first Dynasty, either Siamun (978–959 BCE) or Psusennes II (959–945 BCE).

Alliance with Egypt brought with it commercial advantages, as is obvious from the short business memorandum preserved in 1 Kings 10:28–9. Several interpretations of this difficult text have been proposed (Tadmor 1961), but with some reinterpretation it becomes obvious that Solomon had control of the trade passing through his land and derived financial benefits from it. Cilicia was the source of the best horses and the Egyptians built the best chariots; Solomon obtained horses from Cilicia (Kue in v. 29, and deleting 'Egypt') for 150 shekels and chariots from Egypt for four times the price. His merchants controlled the trade between Syria and Egypt, supplying horses to Egypt and chariots to Syria at a standard rate of four horses for one chariot. Such transactions brought financial benefits.

Another advantageous alliance promoted by Solomon was with Hiram King of Tyre, who is not to be confused with the Tyrian craftsman of the same name (1 Kgs 7:13, 40). The political alliance between the two countries since the time of David was beneficial for both. Israel, being on a bridge between north and south, could take advantage of a maritime power like Phoenicia. It was in Tyre's interest to be in alliance with Israel because it controlled the King's Highway through Transjordan and could protect Tyre's hinterland to the east (Fensham 1969). In response to Hiram's initiative, Solomon made his request for cedars from Lebanon to be cut by the Sidonians (1 Kgs 5:6); they had great experience in the craft as is testified by the Palmero Stone inscription referring to a delivery of timber to Egypt 400 years previously (Ap-Thomas 1973). When accepting the proposal, Hiram made two important modifications: firstly, Hiram would take full responsibility for lumbering and transporting the timber to the coast of Palestine, thus preventing Solomon's men from entering Phoenicia and participating in the sea operations; secondly, instead of paying wages to Hiram's men and therefore exercising some control over them, Solomon was to make a block payment to Hiram by supplying food for his household.

A closer co-operation between Hiram's men and Solomon's men is envisaged in their trading activities from Ezion-geber. The two references to trade with Ophir are to be taken together (1 Kgs 9:26–8; 10:11–12). Ezion-geber is to be identified with harbour installations in the bay of Gazirat al-Far'un on the Gulf of Aqaba. By co-operating with Solomon the Phoenicians had the advantage of a trading port with Ophir and were also given an opportunity to break Egypt's monopoly of transit trade (Yeivin 1959–60). Solomon had assistance from the Phoenicians in building and sailing ships, and he had an important trading port to make up for his lack of a port on the Mediterranean. Solomon acquired wealth from these trading enterprises. Taxation on the merchandise was paid to him as controller of trade routes (1 Kgs 10:15). The 'kings of Arabia', who also contributed to his income, were probably merchant princes or sheiks. More wealth was obtained from ships trading from port to port; 'ships of Tarshish' were probably large seagoing vessels and not a fleet connected with any particular place (Hoenig 1979). A list in 1 Kings 10:22 may suggest that they went up the coast as far as India.

Other marriages were contracted by Solomon. A reference to them in a thoroughly Deuteronomistic passage sees foreign alliances as an evil influence, inclining Solomon's heart to follow their gods (1 Kgs 11:1–4). The original notice was probably very brief and listed political marriages with Solomon's immediate neighbours, beginning with three in the east (Moab, Ammon, Edom), three on the coast to the north-west (Sidonians or Phoenicians) and finally the inhabitants of Syria in the north-east (the Hittites). Marriages contracted by kings must be seen against the background of negotiations and treaties with other foreign powers (Malamat 1965). Solomon consolidated the empire by pursuing diplomatic relations with neighbouring powers and reaped benefits from trade and commerce.

BUILDING PROJECTS

Peace in his time gave Solomon an opportunity to undertake large building enterprises. Solomon's Temple and its furnishings are described in detail (1 Kgs 6; 7:13–51; 8). But it has to be admitted that some later modifications to the shrine, including repairs and renovations have found their way into the report. Nevertheless, its plan is clear: it had a tripartite structure, with an entrance hall, a nave and an inner shrine. Similar structures have been found in Egypt, Assyria and Philistia (Busink 1970), but similar Syro-Phoenician temples are more likely to have provided Solomon with a model, for it was from there that he hired his craftsmen. A replica, with an entrance hall, two pillars in front, a cella and a raised shrine, is found in a ninth-century temple at Tell Ta'inat in northern Syria, but it has different dimensions. Another parallel is the temple of Tell-chuera in north-east Syria. However, some features of Solomon's Temple have parallels in the Canaanite cities excavated at Shechem, Megiddo and Hazor. It seems likely that Solomon had taken over an old Jebusite shrine on the site, and in renovating it introduced some Phoenician elements (Rupprecht 1977). The details of structure, masonry, timber, bronze and gold furnishings in the text can be pursued with the aid of a commentary. Although annexed to the palace complex, and smaller than some of these buildings, the Temple was more than a private royal chapel, but was built primarily to house the ark and to be a centre of worship for all Israel.

Details of Solomon's private and secular buildings are more scant, and no exact information is given about their relationship to one another or their location (1 Kgs

7:1–12). It is assumed that, like the Temple, they were situated on the eastern hill and stood to the south of the Temple itself; they may have been more extensive than the biblical list suggests, since palace complexes in the ancient East, as is testified in Mari, covered a vast area. The House of the Forest of Lebanon, so named because of the use of cedar inside the building, was larger than the Temple and had three storeys and chambers. It was probably an armoury for keeping shields and weapons (see 1 Kgs 10:17; Is 22:8), but the exact form of the building is difficult to envisage. Because the length of the Hall of Pillars corresponded to the breadth of the House of the Forest of Lebanon, the Hall may have formed a portico for the House, and possibly there stood a vestibule with pillars and cornice in front of the portico (1 Kgs 7:6). Another building within the complex was the Hall of the Throne, which is also called the Hall of Judgment; it was reserved for the royal throne, for the king was the dispenser of justice (Whitelam 1979). Public buildings were separate from the royal apartments; the former were probably to the east of the Hall of the Throne and the latter to the west behind the throne. The private apartments were 'his own house where he was to dwell' and the house made for Pharaoh's daughter, which may have been built on an Egyptian model with a covered hall rather than an open courtyard.

Building lists were common in the ancient East, and several have been found among royal inscriptions. Probably, therefore, an old archival list lies behind the note about the cities fortified by Solomon (1 Kgs 9:15–19). After mentioning the Millo in Jerusalem, which is most difficult to identify or locate, these verses list six towns that form a line running from north to south. Archaeological excavations have shown that his building works outside Jerusalem were more important than the impression given in the Bible. Evidence of Solomon's rebuilding of Canaanite towns is available in the complex city-gate and elaborate system of casemate city walls at Megiddo, and again in similar gates at Beth-shemesh, Debir, Hazor, Gezer, Dan and Beersheba (Kenyon 1971). Another building not mentioned in the biblical list was the Solomonic temple at Arad (Aharoni 1968). The list at the end becomes more general and refers to store-cities, depots for keeping provisions, and cities for chariots and horsemen, which were military bases.

ADMINISTRATION

The queen of Sheba was impressed by Solomon's administration (1 Kgs 10:9). Court officials and their dependants constituted a significant element in the population of Judah. It has been reckoned that the royal family, court officials and other ancillary staff numbered 1,600, and that the household members of court personnel added another 4,000 to the total (Ishida 1977). The list of court officials (1 Kgs 4:1–6), as would be expected, shows some continuity with the list of David's officials. Azariah had by now succeeded his father Zadok as priest; the mention of Zadok and Abiathar in verse 4 is unnecessary and is probably an erroneous continuation from the Davidic lists. A development from the Davidic period is the mention of two secretaries, one possibly managing internal business and the other dealing with foreign correspondence. Two sons of Nathan are listed: Azariah, in charge of district prefects, a post that was Solomon's innovation; Zabud, 'king's friend' or counsellor. Another office appearing for the first time was held by Ahishar, who was 'in charge of the palace', a post that gave him authority over royal property (Mettinger 1976). The last name on the list is Adoniram in charge of 'forced labour', a post first mentioned in the time of David.

To provide food for the royal household Solomon divided the land into twelve administrative districts under the supervision of a prefect or district governor; each district was to provide food for the royal household for one month each year (1 Kgs 4:7–19). Although the list is more interested in giving the name of each prefect than in defining exactly the geographical boundaries of the districts, there must have been a connection between the districts and the old Israelite tribal system. The geographical extent of some districts and the retention of their former names proves a dependance on the earlier system. But it was also modified, and the names of Canaanite towns have been given in some regions (vv. 9–14). Modification was necessary because Canaanite regions had been added to the kingdom of David (Aharoni 1966). The list belongs to the second half of Solomon's reign, after the transfer of cities in the plain of Acco to Hiram of Tyre (1 Kgs 9:11–13), and confirms that Solomon followed the common practice of establishing a fiscal system. Similar lists based on a division of the population have been found in Ras Shamra, among Neo-Babylonian and Persian cuneiform inscriptions and in the list of towns and officials providing for Sheshonk I of Egypt (Dougherty 1925; Redford 1972).

In addition to financial provision, Solomon's building projects depended on a strong body of labourers. Forced labour is known from Mesopotamia and Egypt as well as Syria–Palestine. An Amarna letter from Megiddo and the Alalakh letters refer to the wages of corvée men and use a linguistically related word to the Hebrew *mas* – 'forced labour' (Mendelsohn 1962). There is an apparent discrepancy in the biblical record: whereas 1 Kings 5:13 states that he 'conscripted forced labour out of all Israel', 1 Kings 9:20–2 suggests that only non-Israelites were conscripted. The contradiction can be resolved if two different kinds of forced labour are envisaged. The 'forced levy of slaves' (1 Kgs 9:20–2) refers to a permanent corvée involving serfdom to the state to which the Canaanites were subjected; they were mainly engaged on Solomon's fortifications. But the 'forced labour' of 1 Kings 5:13–16 was a temporary conscription not involving serfdom and was imposed on Israelites, that is, the northern tribes; they gave a service of three months a year to assist Solomon more specifically with the Temple and the palace. Although the high numbers of Solomon's labourers quoted in 1 Kings 5:15–16 are unrealistically exaggerated, there is no doubt that Solomon's building projects called for great administrative skill to raise finances and to secure a labour force.

ACHIEVEMENTS

Solomon's reign was not beleaguered by the demands of military action, as had been the case in David's time. He was thus able to enter into a peaceful relationship with neighbouring powers. A period of calm made it possible for him to launch major building projects, and gave his court an opportunity to take an interest in wisdom, learning and historical writing, an interest that is sometimes called 'the Solomonic enlightenment'.

However, it was not a period of unsullied success. Solomon's fiscal and labour policies laid heavy burdens on the people. He was unable to pay Hiram of Tyre for labour and material, and had to offer him territories and twenty towns in Galilee between Haifa and Acco in payment of his debt (1 Kgs 9:10–14). Dissatisfaction in the northern districts of Syria acquired by David led to a strike for independence under the leadership of Rezon (1 Kgs 11:23–5). Forced labour was not acceptable to the Israelites in the north (1 Kgs 12:4), and because of unwillingness to address the problem the kingdom was divided after Solomon's death.

According to 1 Kings 11 one result of Solomon's marriage alliances was syncretism. For the Deuteronomists this was an unpardonable evil and a reason for tearing away the kingdom from him. Although this is a highly theological verdict on Solomon, it cannot be doubted that some of his actions did alienate the population. In the construction of the Temple there was a clash between Solomon and the old tribal tradition of Israel. The ark, which symbolized God's presence and was of utmost importance for the faith of the Israelite tribes, was brought to the Temple by 'the elders of Israel' (1 Kgs 8:1–13). Apparently Solomon's part in this action was minimal, for he was more interested in the cherubim, an old Canaanite symbol. Such syncretistic tendencies fuelled discontent, and no doubt contributed to the disruption of the monarchy.

BIBLIOGRAPHY

Aharoni, Y. (1966) *The Land of the Bible: A Historical Geography*, London.

—— (1968) 'Arad: Its Inscriptions and Temple', *Biblical Archaeologist* 31: 2–32.

Alt, A. (1968) *Essays on Old Testament History and Religion*, trans. R. A. Wilson, New York.

Ap-Thomas, D. R. (1973) 'The Phoenicians', *Peoples of Old Testament Times*, ed. D. J. Wiseman, Oxford, 259–86.

Busink, T. A. (1970) *Der Tempel von Jerusalem von Salomo bis Herodes*, 2 vols, Leiden.

Campbell, A. F. (1975) *The Ark Narrative (1 Sam 4–6, 2 Sam 6): Form-Critical and Traditio-Historical Study*, Society of Biblical Literature Dissertation Series 16, Missoula.

Carlson, R. A. (1964) *David, the Chosen King: A Traditio-Historical Approach to the Second Book of Samuel*, Uppsala.

Cohen, H. H. (1965) 'David and Bathsheba', *Journal of Bible and Religion* 33: 124–8.

Conroy, C. C. (1978) *Absalom Absalom! Narrative and Language in 2 Sam 13–20*, Analecta biblica 81, Rome.

Dougherty, R. P. (1925) 'Cuneiform Parallels to Solomon's Provisioning System', *Annual of the American Schools of Oriental Research* 5:23–65.

Edelman, D. V. (1991) *King Saul and the Historiography of Judah*, Journal for the Study of the Old Testament Supplement Series 121, Sheffield.

Fensham, F. C. (1969) 'The Treaty between the Israelites and Tyrians', *Supplements to Vetus Testamentum* 17: 71–87.

Gunn, D. M. (1978) *The Story of King David: Genre and Interpretation*, Journal for the Study of the Old Testament Supplement Series 6, Sheffield.

—— (1980) *The Fate of King Saul*, Journal for the Study of the Old Testament Supplement Series 14, Sheffield.

Herrmann, S. (1953) 'Die Königsnovelle in Ägypten und in Israel', *Wissenschaftliche Zeitschrift Karl-Marx-Universität Leipzig* 3: 51–62.

Hoenig, S. B. (1979) 'Tarshish', *Jewish Quarterly Review* 69: 181–2.

Ishida, T. (1977) *The Royal Dynasties in Ancient Israel: A Study on the Formation and Development of Royal-Dynastic Ideologies*. Beihefte zur Zeitschrift für die Alttestamentliche Wissenschaft 142, Berlin.

Jones, G. H. (1990) *The Nathan Narratives*, Journal for the Study of the Old Testament Supplement Series 80, Sheffield.

Kenyon, K. M. (1971) *Royal Cities of the Old Testament*, London.

—— (1974) *Digging Up Jerusalem*, London.

Liver, J. (1967) 'The Book of the Acts of Solomon', *Biblica* 48: 75–101.

Malamat, A. (1958) 'The Kingdom of David and Solomon in its Contact with Egypt and Aram Naharaim', *Biblical Archaeologist* 21: 96–102.

—— (1965) 'Organs of Statecraft in the Israelite Monarchy', *Biblical Archaeologist* 28: 34–65.

Mendelsohn, I. (1962) 'On Corvée Labor in Ancient Canaan and Israel', *Bulletin of the American School of Oriental Research* 167: 31–5.

Mettinger, T. N. D. (1971) *Solomonic State Officials: A Study of the Civil Government Officials of the Israelite Monarchy*, Coniectanea biblica, Old Testament Series 5, Lund.

—— (1976) *King and Messiah: The Civil and Sacral Legitimation of the Israelite Kings*, Coniectanea biblica, Old Testament Series 8, Lund.

Miller, P. D. and Roberts, J. M. M. (1977) *The Hand of the Lord: A Reassessment of the 'Ark Narrative' of 1 Samuel*, Baltimore.

Rad, G. von (1966) 'The Beginnings of Historical Writing in Ancient Israel', *The Problem of the Hexateuch and Other Essays*, 166–204, Edinburgh.

Redford, D. B. (1972) 'Studies in Relations between Palestine and Egypt during the First Mellennium BC: I The Taxation Systems of Solomon', *Studies in the Ancient Palestinian World*, Festschrift Winnett, 141–56, Toronto.

Rupprecht, K. (1977) *Der Tempel von Jerusalem: Gründung Salomos oder jebusitische Erbe?* Beihefte zur Zeitschrift für die Alttestamentliche Wissenschaft 144, Berlin.

Tadmor, H. (1961) 'Que and Musri', *Israel Exploration Journal* 11: 143–50.

Thompson, J. A. (1974) 'The Significance of the Verb "Love" in the David–Jonathan Narratives in 1 Samuel', *Vetus Testamentum* 24: 334–8.

Timm, H. (1966) 'Die Ladeerzählung (1 Sam 4–6; 2 Sam 6) und das kerygma des deuteronomistischen Geschichtswerk', *Evangelische Theologie* 26: 509–26.

Tsevat, M. (1958) 'Marriage and Monarchial Legitimacy in Ugarit and Israel', *Journal of Semitic Studies* 3: 237–43.

Ullendorf, E. (1962–3) 'The Queen of Sheba', *Bulletin of the John Rylands Library* 45: 486–504.

—— (1974) 'The Queen of Sheba in Ethiopian Tradition', *Solomon and Sheba*, ed. J. B. Pritchard, 104–14, London.

Veijola, T. (1979) 'Salomo – der Erstgeborene Bathsebas', *Studies in the Historical Books of the Old Testament*. ed. J. A. Emerton, Supplements to Vetus Testamentum 30: 230–50.

Whitelam, K. W. (1979) *The Just King: Monarchial Judicial Authority in Ancient Israel*. Journal for the Study of the Old Testament Supplement Series 12, Sheffield.

Yeivin, S. (1959–60) 'Did the Kingdoms of Israel have a Maritime Policy?' *Jewish Quarterly Review* 50: 193–228.

CHAPTER FORTY

JESUS

————•◆•————

Robert Morgan

INTRODUCTION

The phrase 'biblical world' suggests the geographical, social, and cultural settings of Israelite and Jewish history over more than a thousand years and points back behind the conquest of Canaan into the mists of undocumented time. That *historical* reference draws into the field of vision neighbouring states and world powers that came into contact, usually unfriendly, with this ancient people. But the phrase also refers to a stranger, less definable 'world' evoked by the biblical texts. Even if they did not constitute the Christian canon(s) of scripture and include that of the parent religion, these texts would generate a *symbolic* world in which human life finds its meaning in a context that transcends the historical world. The canonical status of this *religious* classic only reinforces the concerns that are prominent in the composition, transmission, and reception of the Bible. Treating this literature purely as ancient history is therefore unlikely to yield adequate interpretations. Historical research is indispensable in the modern critical discussion of any ancient literature, but the gulf between a purely historical interest and what these sources are aiming at needs to be acknowledged at the outset.

The oddities and limitations of the biblical sources pose obvious problems for the historian of the earlier periods. Prior to Saul and David the scanty data consist more of myth, saga and legend than historically reliable traditions. More surprisingly, there are similar problems in knowing about Jesus, even though the sources stand at no great distance from their subject matter. Not until Paul do we have primary sources about Christian origins. The public activity and execution of Jesus were barely two or three generations past when the New Testament gospels were written and his words, deeds, and destiny were remembered and re-enacted in the circles where the gospels took shape. Nevertheless, these four narratives pose special difficulties for modern readers sensitive to the gulf between the biblical world and their own intellectual and cultural contexts.

The novel second-century description of the relevant texts as 'gospels' hints at the difficulty of classifying them generically. It was not merely the curious circumstances of the birth of Jesus as related by two of them, nor even the more mysterious events said to have followed his death, that made these narratives different and special to those who composed them and to the communities that treasured them. It was what generated these peculiar testimonies that led their authors to write no ordinary 'lives' or histories, and their readers finally to settle on the new generic label 'gospel': the unique religious status of the character they render.

If the extraordinary fact of the early Christians' religious veneration of Jesus has led to the production of some not easily classifiable texts, the subsequent history of that religious movement has further conditioned their reception. Both the triumphant expansion of Christianity and its relative decline in the modern and pluralistic West have decisively affected how these texts have been read. People's images of Jesus have varied accordingly.

Christian readers and hearers have typically taken the gospel story at its face value, unconsciously synthesizing and harmonizing the four accounts, and mostly disregarding any elements that fitted badly into their own religious world-views. Until recently they have come to the gospels with faith-pictures of the earthly Jesus set in a doctrinal framework drawn mainly from Paul and John as interpreted by the subsequent Christian tradition and refracting the colours of their own non-Jewish contexts. Today Jesus remains a cultural icon reaching far beyond the circles that find in him the revelation of God. A typical outline of Jesus as generally remembered would be based mainly on Matthew and Luke, reinforced by Christian art. The gospel story encapsulated in that sketch includes the Christmas story and the baptism of Jesus by John; his temptations in the wilderness; his ministry of preaching and teaching (especially in parables) and healing; his choice of twelve disciples and sending them out on a mission; perhaps some nature miracles and a transfiguration; his prophecies of his own sufferings, death, and resurrection, and future coming as Son of Man at the end of the age; his dramatic entry into Jerusalem and cleansing of the Temple; controversies with scribes and Pharisees; his last supper with his disciples, prayer in Gethsemane, betrayal, arrest, trials, crucifixion, resurrection, and ascension. Its beginning and end have long been widely admitted to contain more symbolic than historical elements, and some of the miracle stories are similarly interpreted, but this gospel story is still widely accepted as broadly historical as well as containing and communicating religious and moral truth.

This modern picture is more recognizably human than the subtly dogmatic vision of Christ's glory projected by the gospel according to St John, and that is partly the effect of a two to three hundred years' project to investigate Jesus of Nazareth by the same methods and with the same assumptions that historians approach other documented portions of the human past. In the eighteenth century a few enlightened thinkers in Europe opened the door to modern historical study of the Bible by challenging the doctrinal assumptions, Protestant and Roman Catholic, that had guided the study of scripture for centuries. Their liberation from the incredible beliefs of an intolerant religious culture has been adopted by many twentieth-century readers of the Bible, both inside and outside the churches. This project of 'free investigation' has proved sufficiently persuasive to control the presentation that follows. But history alone has never been more than a minority interest among attentive listeners and serious students of the Bible. Alternative perspectives that do better justice to its religious power are also appropriate.

The New Testament portraits of Jesus reflect and communicate how he was understood in the decades following his death. Dr Williams discusses that in chapter 44 of this volume. The focus of the present chapter is the man himself, but the religious evaluations later summed up in the doctrinal definition 'truly God, truly a human' have put some pressure on enquirers to position themselves with respect to this man and the community of his followers who make such an imposing claim. Whether or not one shares their belief it is hard to avoid its influence.

The tangle of historical, cultural, and religious interests surrounding the modern study of Jesus can be initially sorted by reviewing the modern historical questioning that continues to define the issues. Retracing the arguments and recapturing the pressures exerted on traditional Christianity by modern critical rationality throws light on the perplexities thoughtful readers of the gospels often experience. It will in addition introduce the methods by which scholars have reached their own conclusions about Jesus. They have lifted information about him out of its interpretative frameworks in the gospel sources and interpreted it afresh. Historians and historically sensitive theologians have established points of general agreement and areas of uncertainty and disagreement. Some knowledge of this debate may also suggest limitations to this way of entering the biblical world and so invite attention to other perspectives from which the gospels and their elusive subject matter may be pondered, including the Bible's own theological perspectives.

FROM REIMARUS TO BORNKAMM

It has become conventional to follow Albert Schweitzer in making H. S. Reimarus (1694–1768) the start of the modern historical study of Jesus and to follow the English translation (1910) of Schweitzer's survey *Von Reimarus zu Wrede* (1906) in calling it 'The quest of the historical Jesus'. Reimarus had learned much from the English Deists' criticism of revealed religion but was the first to offer a coherent historical explanation 'concerning the intentions of Jesus and his disciples' (Talbert 1970).

That was the title of the seventh 'Fragment of an unnamed author', which Lessing excerpted from a copy of the complete manuscript and published in 1778, evading the censor and concealing its authorship. He had already dared to publish Reimarus's section 'On the Resurrection Narratives' the previous year. This sixth fragment (Talbert 1970: 153–200) exposed some of the contradictions in the gospel accounts and undermined belief in their historicity, casting doubt on Matthew's improbable story of the guard at the tomb. The more important suggestion of the seventh and final fragment (the censor then intervened) was that the intentions of the apostles were quite different from those of Jesus. The latter had been a political Messiah or worldly deliverer (and also an enlightened moral teacher) who had evidently meant by his undefined phrase 'the kingdom of God' what his Jewish hearers would have understood by it. He remained entirely within Judaism and celebrated his final Passover in the hope of coming again soon in clouds of glory (122). The command to disciple all gentiles and baptize them in the threefold name (Mt 28.19) is not historical, argued Reimarus. When Jesus failed and was executed, the disciples faced ridicule and danger. Their solution was to steal the body, claiming God had raised him from the dead, and to rewrite his teachings, making him claim to be a spiritual Messiah who must die to obtain forgiveness for humanity and then be raised

(151). They also twisted Old Testament texts to support their case with arguments from prophecy, and they claimed that the world would soon end and that anyone who failed to accept their preaching would be damned. However, their rewrite was not fully consistent, and there 'peeps out a worldly deliverer' (147). The end of the world did not come and the modern rationalist critic can see how the evangelists misinterpreted their old scriptures and concocted new ones. The way is thus now open for a modern, scientific, non-miraculous account of Jesus and Christian origins.

Reimarus's fraud hypothesis gains some initial plausibility from the surely fictitious story of the Roman guard at the tomb, but loses this when it is recognized that Matthew's gospel was not written soon after the crucifixion or by one of the apostles. The actual historical reconstruction of Reimarus has therefore found few followers, though many have subsequently doubted the historical reliability of particular resurrection traditions. That justifiable scepticism does not require the fraud hypothesis and is compatible with Christians' accepting these stories' witness to God's having vindicated Jesus. But in almost every other respect Reimarus may be said to have anticipated twentieth-century gospel criticism. A hundred and fifty years later Schweitzer admired him for recognizing the importance of eschatology, or sayings about the end of the world in the gospels – even though he thought that Reimarus was mistaken in attributing to Jesus political aspirations. Schweitzer attributed to Jesus himself the expectation of an imminent end to the world, an expectation Reimarus thought the disciples had concocted after Jesus' death.

Today opinion remains divided and many would agree with Reimarus in attributing the expectation of an imminent end of the world to the early church, not to Jesus. However, they would attribute it to the disciples' conviction about Jesus' vindication by God and the activity of God's Spirit among them rather than to any cynical and self-serving fraudulence. But even more important than Reimarus's eschatology was his recognition that the historical truth about Jesus must be gleaned from between the lines of gospels that tell a rather different story. However wrong Reimarus may have been in associating Jesus with attempted liberation from the Romans he was entirely right to see him in the social and political context of first-century Palestinian Judaism, and to distinguish that from the early church's theological frame of reference projected by the gospels. The historian must interpret the phrases 'Son of God' and 'kingdom of God' from within that Jewish context, not in the light of later credal formulations, and must consider how far the gospel records have already been coloured by post-resurrection beliefs about Jesus.

Lessing's *Fragments of an Unnamed Author* caused a stir among intellectuals without greatly disturbing church or society. That larger shock, which gospel criticism had in store for Christian Europe, was administered by a 27-year old Tübingen tutor: David Friedrich Strauss whose *Life of Jesus* appeared in 1835, marking an epoch in biblical studies and in European religious thought (ET by George Eliot, 1846).

It was not in fact a life of Jesus, and it contained little that was entirely new. It was rather a criticism of the gospel narratives designed to show that they are largely unhistorical, and its impact was cumulative and inescapable. As Reimarus had drawn attention to the contradictions in the resurrection narratives and denied their historicity, so Strauss worked methodically through the whole gospel story from the annunciation to the ascension, remorselessly exposing the contradictions between the four accounts and the implausibility of harmonizations and the inadequacy of previous modes of explanation. He was frank about his incredulity, as a modern man who knew about laws of nature, when confronted with narratives of miracles, or angels, demons, voices from heaven or anything else supernatural. And he was scathing about the absurdities of scholars who tried to preserve a historical core to all these individual stories while discarding their supernatural elements. He had an alternative explanation, which was to recognize the entirely 'mythical' character of many of the stories in the gospels. They are not accurate or even inaccurate reporting by eyewitnesses but the product of the mythopoetic imagination of the first followers of Jesus passed on orally in the early church. Convinced that he was the Messiah, and persuaded by visions that God had vindicated him, they naturally told stories about him based on Old Testament prototypes, notably Moses, Elijah, and Elisha.

A brilliant introduction explained 'the development of the mythical point of view in relation to the gospel histories' from Greek allegorizers to modern rationalists, and also the application of the mythical mode of interpretation first to the Old Testament and to the beginning and end of the gospel story. Strauss showed how the new approach stems from a knowledge of and comparison with cultures other than one's own, and how it is compatible with a proper understanding of religion as the perception of truth, not in the form of an idea, which is the philosophical perception, but invested with imagery (80). Finally his introduction offered 'criteria by which to distinguish the unhistorical in the gospel narrative' (88) by analogy with one's own experience, and by noting contradictions, poetical form, and mythical or doctrinal content – difficult though it admittedly is to draw the boundaries with precision.

Strauss labelled many of the individual stories in the gospels 'myth'. These interpreted Jesus as at once human and divine, and are not a historical record. He excluded from the realm of historical causation everything miraculous or supernatural, while accepting that Jesus no doubt performed (faith) healings. He judged the synoptic picture generally more historical than the Johannine, reversing the traditional preference for John, which had still been maintained by Schleiermacher in 1821 and remained dominant much longer in England. Although Strauss did not write a proper life of Jesus until 1864 his earlier judgments concerning what is probably historical imply a picture of the 'historical Jesus' not very different from what many scholars and popularizers would accept today.

This powerful historical criticism of the gospels echoed and shaped a growing consensus, whereas Strauss's ultra-Hegelian reinterpretation of Christianity in terms of the 'idea' of the unity of the divine and the human in the human race (rather than in the person of the Incarnate Son), which the mythic stories were intended to express, found almost no support. Christians were generally clear that their faith referred to Jesus himself as the revelation of God, and Strauss's attack on the gospels as historical sources led to the more rigorous 'quest for the historical Jesus' that followed. It was hoped that identification by source criticism of the earlier strata of the synoptic gospels (early Mark and the hypothetical collection of sayings apparently used by Matthew and Luke, later called 'Q') would yield a reliable account of Jesus' ministry, his teaching and death (Holtzmann 1863). Strauss himself continued to think Matthew the oldest gospel, but as the material it contains includes both

Mark and 'Q' his *Life of Jesus for the German People* (1864) was not very different from the flood of liberal lives of Jesus built from those earlier sources. The most popular of these were E. Renan's *Life of Jesus* (1863), brilliantly lampooned in Schweitzer's *Quest*, and Harnack's lectures on the essence of Christianity (1900), which celebrated the gospel *of* (not *about*) Jesus concerning the fatherhood of God, the brotherhood of man, and the unique value of each human soul.

But the axe was already at the root of all these modernizing reconstructions. A theological critique of the quest of the 'so-called historical Jesus' had been ignited by Martin Kähler in 1892 and would explode a generation later. More visibly, and also in 1892, Johannes Weiss had claimed in *Jesus' Proclamation of the Kingdom of God* that Jesus did not mean by that phrase what theologians impressed by Kant had thought. Influenced by some Jewish apocalypses (especially the book of *Enoch*), which had been rediscovered in the nineteenth century, Weiss argued that the kingdom of God was for Jesus not an ethical ideal to be brought about by human effort, but an apocalyptic–eschatological transformation soon to be brought about by God. In 'moments of prophetic vision' Jesus even 'perceived the opposing kingdom of Satan as already overcome and broken' and 'at such moments as these he declared with daring faith that the Kingdom of God had actually already dawned' (129).

A less nuanced presentation of Jesus as an apocalyptic visionary (or deluded fanatic) was sketched by Albert Schweitzer in 1901 and argued for in the *Quest* (1906) through a scintillating critique of his predecessors. This Jesus was very different from Harnack's moral and religious teacher, but at least Schweitzer agreed that Jesus could be correctly and adequately understood by historical research. His German title, on the other hand, and a climactic chapter contrasting Wrede's 'thoroughgoing scepticism' with his own 'thoroughgoing eschatology', signal the development of subsequent scholarship that was to undercut both his own and the liberal portraits. Kähler (1892) could be ignored in 1906; Wrede's *Messianic Secret* could not. Schweitzer tried to force a choice between his own eschatological Jesus and Wrede's scepticism about the historical reliability of the gospel traditions. Twentieth-century scholars were to learn from both.

Wrede's dense monograph gave a further twist to Reimarus's claim that Jesus himself was very different from early Christian belief about him, but whereas Reimarus saw Jesus as a political Messiah Wrede doubted the messianic character of the ministry. Led partly by Romans 1.4 and Acts 2.36 and especially Mark 9.9 ('tell no-one until the Son of Man rises from the dead') he suggested that belief in Jesus as Messiah dated from the resurrection. Mark's reports of Jesus' injunctions to silence are sometimes implausible. Wrede saw these and the reported blindness of the disciples, and the improbable theory about parables (4.10–12), as all the product of a tension between the Jesus of history and early Christian belief. The theory has been much modified and sometimes rejected, but Wrede's history of traditions' method, with its strong sense of the gulf between the gospels and Jesus, came to dominate twentieth-century research. The gospels contain biographical material but are also religious propaganda and advocate views probably not made explicit (or perhaps not even shared) by Jesus himself.

This new interest in the shaping of the traditions of Jesus' sayings and doings prior to the composition of the gospels led to the 'form criticism' (or history of the literary forms in which the record was preserved) of Dibelius (1919) and Bultmann (1921). Like Strauss's classic on the gospel traditions (1835) Bultmann's *History of the Synoptic Tradition* (i.e. prehistory of the first three gospels) posited dramatic developments during the period of oral transmission of the tradition. The book owed much of its impact to its success in synthesizing the previous generation's probings: Jülicher on the parables, J. Weiss on eschatology and on form criticism, Wrede on the possibly non-messianic ministry of Jesus, Wellhausen's dissection of the gospel traditions, Bousset on the early Hellenistic church, K. L. Schmidt's dissolution of the framework of the gospels (1919), history of religions parallels from Judaism and paganism, are all presented in Bultmann's methodical analysis of the synoptic material. Form criticism soon dominated German research and by the 1960s was more widely accepted, including by a revitalized Roman Catholic scholarship. The history of traditions approach had undermined the older 'lives of Jesus', but broad agreement about earlier and later strata, and about the criteria for distinguishing more and less reliable traditions had reduced the area of scholarly disagreement to manageable proportions.

How much of the gospel material can be traced back to Jesus remains arguable because all such explorations are uncertain and to some extent circular. We ask what 'coheres' with other material provisionally accepted as authentic, and about the historical continuities between Jesus and his Judaism, and between Jesus and his followers. These are only partly visible and judgments about what distinguished Jesus from his contemporaries are largely intuitive. Bultmann's crisp summaries of Jesus' teaching and preaching (1926, 1948, 1949) represent a consensus that the phrase 'the kingdom of God' contains the key to Jesus' proclamation and ministry, but there has been less agreement about what exactly Jesus meant by this phrase. J. Weiss has been generally followed in his insistence that it refers to what God (rather than humans) would do or was already doing in the 'end time' that was near. But how Jesus understood these impending changes has remained elusive and the conviction of Weiss and Bultmann (and Schweitzer) that the apocalyptic literature of early Judaism and Christianity justifies understanding the kingdom of God as implying an imminent end of the world has been widely disputed. Schweitzer's consistently futurist eschatology was challenged by R. Otto (1934), and by C. H. Dodd's claim (1935) that Jesus saw God's decisive intervention already happening in his own ministry. Dodd labelled this 'realized eschatology' and later accepted Jeremias's modification 'eschatology in the process of being realized', but he was challenging the whole emphasis on an imminent end of the world. It is possible to see Jesus' message as all about God's rule and to insist that a vision of the future is intrinsic to that, while doubting whether he speculated about cosmic upheavals.

Many critics have doubted that much of the 'little apocalypse' in Mark 13.5–27 goes back to Jesus, in which case some end of the world ideas have been later attributed to him (cf. Rev 2.25; 3.11; 22.20). Some of the early church's expectations may have been stimulated by the disciples' conviction that God had vindicated Jesus. But most critics as late as Bornkamm (1956) assumed that Jesus spoke of the Son of Man coming on the clouds, echoing Daniel 7.13, whether he referred this to himself or to someone else. When the authenticity of even the key passage Mark 8.38 (cf. Lk 12.8) became widely disputed, 'end of the world' interpretations of

Jesus' kingdom language became less secure and opened a door to recent American attempts to remove eschatology from Jesus' teaching, as some older liberals had done.

Alongside disagreements about how Jesus' kingdom language is best to be understood the twentieth century has been marked by disagreement about how much this matters to Christian faith today. Harnack and the older liberals thought their conclusions about Jesus should be decisive for modern Christianity. Bultmann, by contrast, thought the message of Jesus merely a presupposition and found the truth of the gospel unfolded in the theologies of Paul and John. This reaction against liberalism, and also the need of a confessional theology during the German political crisis were more responsible than the sceptical thrust of form criticism for the relative decline of German contributions to the 'Quest' from 1920 to the 1950s.

Dibelius wrote a popular work (1939), and Jeremias and Stauffer (1957) continued to see Jesus research as central to theology, as did T. W. Manson (1931) and many lesser figures in England and America. It was, however, neither these nor the advocates of 'salvation history' who revitalized historical study of Jesus in the post-war generation. What came to be labelled 'the new quest of the historical Jesus' (cf. J. M. Robinson 1959), was the work of Bultmann's pupils, all form critics and theologians of 'the Word'. Käsemann (1954) fired an opening salvo; Bornkamm (1956) produced the classic; Conzelmann (1959), Fuchs, Ebeling and others made valuable contributions. All agreed with the common sense of modern theology that somehow historical knowledge of Jesus must be theologically relevant – and also a rational possibility. It cannot yield the object of Christian faith, which is God in Christ confronting people today, but the continuities between this and the historical origins of Christianity are part of the story, and an important aspect of theological claims that the Christian story about God's revelation in history is in some sense true.

Like other gospel critics Bultmann (1921) had made some judgments about which sayings could be traced back to Jesus and noted the criteria (or rules of thumb) employed in making such uncertain decisions (205). In 1926 he summarized what he considered the earliest and most reliable traditions under three headings: the coming of the kingdom of God; the will of God; God remote and near. A generation later his pupil Bornkamm (1956) agreed that Jesus' message was 'about the reality of God, his kingdom and his will' (62) but wrote of the *person* who called followers into discipleship and who travelled to Jerusalem and death, rather than limiting himself with Bultmann to the *Word* that Jesus *brought*. Conzelmann (1959) again considered the self-consciousness of Jesus and gave priority to his faith in God (1968). Like Käsemann (1954) and others Bornkamm shifted the accents in 'the kingdom of God' to the presence of salvation in Jesus who confronted his hearers with the immediacy and nearness of a gracious God. The man from Nazareth brought good news, unlike John the Baptist who preached repentance in the face of imminent doom. Even before Easter, according to this group, Jesus was in essential agreement with Paul (e.g. Jüngel 1962). Käsemann spoke for them all when he saw in 'the connection and tension between the preaching of Jesus and that of his community' (47) the point of their questions about the historical Jesus.

All that reflects the strong theological interests that have been present in most historical research on Jesus from Strauss to the present day. But the ethos of some New Testament scholarship has changed in recent years, and nowhere is this clearer than in the explosion of writing on Jesus in North America. It is misleading to distinguish different *quests* of the historical Jesus, but there are different *phases* in the history of research, and the final quarter of the twentieth century has brought some significant contributions from the literary and social scientific disciplines. It has also witnessed unprecedented media interest, thanks to R. W. Funk's 'Jesus seminar', justly criticized by L. T. Johnson (1995). This group may lack the weight of a Brown (1994) or a Meier (1991, 1994) but Funk echoes the eighteenth-century idea that the modern world needs, and modern criticism can supply, a new narrative of Jesus that has little but the name in common with traditional Christianity. This latest phase is often now called 'Jesus research' to emphasize its secular character, and to avoid the romantic and religious echoes of the word 'quest'. Christians and non-Christians can agree about the cultural significance of this enigmatic historical figure and the appropriate methods by which he may be investigated without bias, and perhaps without religious presuppositions. How much this can achieve remains to be seen.

QUEST AND RESEARCH CONTINUE

The most striking feature of New Testament scholarship in Europe and North America following the Holocaust and the discovery of the Dead Sea Scrolls at Qumran from 1947, and their slow publication, is the flourishing of research into the Jewish context of Jesus and his first followers. The new trend was signalled by the publication in 1973 of *Jesus the Jew* by the Jewish specialist on the Dead Sea Scrolls, Geza Vermes. He sees Jesus as a Galilean charismatic, or holy man, 'heir of an age-old prophetic religious line' (69). He also revived a surprisingly rarely advocated solution to the most vexed question of what Jesus meant by calling himself the Son of Man: simply a human being. The expression is not a title and the passages directly or indirectly referring to Daniel 7.13 are secondary (176).

Standing outside the mainstream of New Testament scholarship Vermes ignores the wider discussion of how the tradition developed, but his emphasis upon the Jewishness of Jesus and his attempt to locate a context and analogies in the complex history of first-century Palestine have become typical. Scarcely any scholar doubts that apart from chance encounters Jesus restricted his activity to his own people and to Palestine. That he was a Galilean, a teacher, healer, and charismatic leader of his disciples, and that he saw himself as a prophet, are widely agreed. Controversies with some of his contemporaries are well documented, but how close he stood to any particular group is uncertain. It is likely that the negative depiction of the Pharisees in the gospels partly reflects later controversies between church and synagogue, and yet Jesus' 'programme' was different from theirs, as it was from that of the Essenes (unmentioned in the gospels) and of the later Zealots. His distance from the Sadducean high-priestly aristocracy – who probably handed him over to Pilate – was surely even greater.

Comparisons with other individuals and groups, including the scribes of his day and later rabbis, have not resulted in any new consensus about Jesus. On the contrary, a better picture of the diversity within Palestinian Judaism during the Second Temple period, and scholarly disagreement about the nature and extent of resistance to Rome prior to the great revolt (66–70 CE), have made room for several possible constructions of the 'Jewish Jesus'. Some, like those of Reimarus and Brandon (1967), are more political and this-worldly in orientation; others envision a more dramatic change to the whole cosmos. Whether and how God's intervention, which Jesus seems to have thought he was inaugurating, would involve a restoration or renewal of Judaism remains uncertain. The different possibilitiees may be illustrated by his dramatic action in the Temple (Mk 11.15). Was this an acted prophecy of its destruction (cf. Mk 13.2), and possibly its rebuilding by God (Cf. Mk 14.58; 15.29; Jn 2.19; Sanders 1985), or a protest about current practice, or even an attempt to change that and make sacrifices purer (Chilton 1992)?

What any historian makes of this incident, or how any saying judged original is interpreted, depends partly on a total view of Jesus' aims and activity. But that construction in turn depends on a large number of individual judgments that seem arbitrary if isolated from the larger web. We can rarely know the original context of Jesus' sayings, and that may have been decisive for their original meaning. Likely contexts can be suggested for particular parables and sayings, where Jesus answers criticisms of his ministry (Jeremias 1962), but these remain hypothetical.

Most of our evidence about Jesus consists in his sayings and parables, but uncertainty about their authenticity and meaning led the most impressive American historian of Jesus and (early) Judaism, E. P. Sanders (1985: 4f.), to rely less on these and more on the facts that provide a reasonably certain external framework of his life. The few certain historical facts, such as Jesus' baptism by John and his crucifixion under Pontius Pilate seem promising. Both these events were embarrassing for the early church and would never have been invented. But our knowledge of the Baptist is limited too, and Jesus both agreed and disagreed with him. Asking why Jesus was executed is a natural second step, but it is Christian theology not history that affirms the unity of his life and death. If his execution was a miscarriage of justice his aims and intentions can hardly be read out of this. So E. P. Sanders begins instead with the event in the Temple and moves on to Jewish expectations of a new Temple, proposing a hypothesis about Jesus' 'restoration eschatology'. This is historical detection at its best, but it remains one guess among others. The evidence remains open to different constructions.

Another way into the evidence is to ask what it was about Jesus that might help account for the emergence and character of Christianity. Sanders appeals to early Christian expectations of the end to support his view that Jesus expected that too. But Jesus might well have differed in substance as well as in style from his disciples' post-resurrection Spirit-filled enthusiasm, and there was more to early Christianity than its eschatology. Jesus apparently convinced his followers that the nearness of the rule of the God whom they could address as Father implied transformed personal and social relationships, in the present, without reference to the future of the world.

In trying to reconstruct the aims and activity of Jesus, or painting a historical portrait of him, gospel data have to be correlated both with the early church and with the historical possibilities suggested by the Palestinian context. Knowledge of his environment is fragmentary, but deciding what can be traced back to Jesus from among the memories and practices of the first-generation church is most uncertain on account of our insufficient knowledge of the post-resurrection Palestinian Jesus movement. That makes it hard to say what began there and what goes back to Jesus. The Acts of the Apostles is a disappointment to the historian of early Jewish Christianity. Some evidence for this early period is no doubt embedded in the synoptic tradition itself, but what in these Greek documents goes back to Jesus, and what only to the Aramaic-speaking church is uncertain. There is a dark tunnel between our sources (the gospels) and the historical reality of Jesus.

Form criticism aimed to illuminate that tunnel period by discovering what had happened to the traditions during their forty years inside it. The literary forms identifiable in the synoptic gospels would perhaps suggest in what social contexts these different forms took shape. This optimism about detecting their 'Sitz im Leben' or 'settings in the life' (of the early church) has proved ill-founded, and it is not even clear how much of the history of the tradition was oral and how much written, or that 'laws' of oral transmission can be traced over so short a period (see Güttgemanns 1970; Kelber 1983). However, Gerd Theissen (1978, 1992) and others have successfully reopened the sociological line of enquiry implicit in form criticism, and even the older source criticism allowed the form critics to see something of how the tradition had developed. They accepted the source-critical hypothesis that Mark (or something very similar to our Mark) was independently used by the later synoptic evangelists. This has been confirmed by 'redaction criticism' of Matthew and Luke, that is, study of their editorial work on Mark, based on that hypothesis of Markan priority. Despite some opposition it is therefore possible to say with confidence how *some* of the tradition developed at those late points. That the evangelists used other sources is also plain, even if one central claim of the Q hypothesis, that Luke could not have known Matthew (or vice versa) is unproven and perhaps unlikely (see Sanders and Davies 1989). These 200 odd verses of 'double tradition', sayings material used (sometimes in different Greek versions) by Matthew and Luke (but absent from Mark), probably lead us back to the early Palestinian Jesus movement that preserved them, and also beyond that to original teaching of Jesus (see Catchpole 1993; Tuckett 1996).

Attempts to distinguish different layers within the hypothetical document Q are altogether more speculative (e.g. Kloppenborg 1987; Mack 1993). It may be wishful thinking that finds an earlier stratum free of eschatology in it. A Jesus altogether free of eschatology might seem more relevant to contemporary social concerns than the eschatological prophet more usually found in the synoptic tradition, and that has perhaps contributed to portrayals of Jesus as an itinerant Greek philosopher engaged in social criticism (Downing 1987; Mack 1988).

This dubious development in gospel study was encouraged by the discovery in 1945 at Nag Hammadi in Upper Egypt of a library of Gnostic documents, including the probably second-century *Gospel of Thomas*, which previously had been known only in fragments. That text consisting of 114 sayings and parables of Jesus overlaps with the synoptic tradition, and some think it is independent of the synoptic gospels (Crossan 1985; Koester 1990). The *Gospel of Thomas* itself is later than these, and plainly heretical by the standards of the emerging catholic orthodoxy, but it contains earlier material, and possibly more original versions of some of Jesus' teaching. It at least helps us to understand how the tradition of his parables and aphorisms developed. However, the heavy reliance placed on this new material by a few scholars, notably J. D. Crossan (1991), may be influenced by the kind of 'historical Jesus' it yields.

These attempts to deny Jesus' eschatology illustrate how wide a range of reconstructions is possible, and even if unpersuasive they identify a problem with one-sided emphases on eschatology. Jesus' moral and wisdom teaching is surely important (Borg 1984, 1987) and not easily combined with some eschatological scenarios. This has led some to emphasize his engagement with his own social context. The description of Jesus as a 'social prophet' (Horsley 1987, 1989) rather than an eschatological prophet leaves room for an eschatological hope in God's future intervention, but places the weight of Jesus' activity on his proposals for local community life. Alternatively, it remains possible to recognize the eschatological dimension of Jesus' teaching but to see this as a necessary aspect of his talk of God.

In short, the historical investigation of Jesus flourishes today as never before, and a scholarly consensus looks less likely than ever. The most interesting advances of the past few years can be summarized under two heads already noted: literary and social scientific.

The most important shift within biblical – especially Old Testament – studies over the past generation has been the application of modern literary approaches to this literature. That has naturally affected the study of the gospel *narratives*, but what is more surprising is its impact on the *historical* study of Jesus. He was a poet (Burney 1925; Jeremias 1971) and teller of stories (Breech 1983), and it is surely significant that he sometimes spoke of God's rule in parables. This figurative language that engages the hearer's *will*, no less than the intellect, is also difficult to reproduce at second-hand. The historian's attempts to describe Jesus' talk of God objectively are likely to distort it: we murder to dissect. Literary analysis of these metaphorical narratives has sharpened critics' antennae for the very *voice* of Jesus, whether or not the very *words* of his poetry and aphorisms can be reconstructed (Via 1967; Wilder 1982; Scott 1989). A new sense of his imaginative and forceful use of language illuminates his understanding of God and religion (Tannehill 1975). The elusiveness of these sources stems from their non-objectifiable subject matter, but the near certainty that Jesus spoke of God's rule in *parables*, that is, indirectly and in a way that 'teases the hearer into active thought' (Dodd 1935), says something about its character.

The interpretation of literature depends in part on the responses it evokes, and a literary or religious sensitivity is more help here than a positivistic demand for the facts. If talk of God is necessarily self-involving and subjective, part of the historian's difficulties in describing Jesus' teaching may actually stem from the attempt to be objective. Bultmann (1926) tried to surmount this difficulty by an existentialist theory of history writing. He wanted to lead his readers to a highly personal *encounter* with history by providing information about his own encounter with history. But what he offers is a literary theory based on his encounter with the *texts*. Most historians have insisted that much can be said about Jesus regardless of one's own commitments, and have left Bultmann's hermeneutics to others. But in doing so they may have surrendered the key to interpreting Jesus' talk of God. And that is surely the key to what Jesus said and did, as his followers claimed.

234

If literary approaches yield a surprising enrichment of historical research, the use of methods and perspectives from the social sciences was a more predictable development. Religion in Second Temple Judaism was inseparable from politics and society, and the social history of Galilee and Judaea in this period has been the subject of further exploration (Hengel 1973; Freyne 1980, 1988). Archaeology, the new written sources, and new questions to old data (e.g. in some parables prevailing social arrangements are reflected) have yielded fresh insights. The task is still historical, but models drawn from cross-cultural studies in sociology and social anthropology have provided new hypotheses to be tested by the fragmentary data. Disciplinary boundaries have melted as these resources are drawn upon to help interpret the symbols adopted, adapted, or generated by Jesus himself.

This does not allow historically verified judgments about the 'inner life of Jesus'. Anything that coincides with post-resurrection belief about Jesus, such as his status, the way he fulfilled the scriptures, or the meaning of his death, might have been influenced by what happened and has to be set aside until its coherence with a critically assured minimum can be ascertained. But even when much of the data has been bracketed as 'doubtful' there is plenty of material to consider. Jesus emerges from the responses of his followers and opponents as a credible historical figure. The disappointment and frustration for would-be biographers is that the trail becomes unclear or uncertain just where our historical questions are most urgent: What did he mean by 'the kingdom of God'? Or 'the Son of Man'? Did he think about himself as a 'messiah', and if so of what kind? Did he expect God to intervene in this world's history soon, and if so what did he expect would follow? The questions that persuaded Schweitzer to return him to the museum of history are again wide open. The witness of the texts invites other forms of judgment, as Schweitzer also recognized.

But historians continue their trade, making their best guesses where certainty is impossible and probability the guide of life, including academic life. The range of possible reconstructions is a school for sceptics but also a constant source of stimulus and a reminder of the real humanity of the person whom believers call master and Lord. Far from leading students and followers of Jesus to give up in despair, the many possibilities are a challenge to exercise the critical judgment that is nowhere more needed than in religion.

Two of the heroes of this great debate, William Wrede (1971: 281–3) and Albert Schweitzer (1910: 137–60) shared a surprising admiration for a friend and teacher of Karl Marx: Bruno Bauer, who later denied the historical existence of Jesus. He was mistaken, but saw more clearly than most the problems in the gospels that had subverted Jesus research. A historical report on Jesus still needs to register the difficulties and admit how tentative anything beyond a bare outline must be. But critical analysis of the sources and attempts at hypothetical reconstructions will continue for as long as the historical figure of Jesus looks important or interesting, and the sources themselves worth sifting. Some proposals seem to have been refuted but the task of interpreting an influential historical figure is never finished. The task of interpreting such literary and religious texts as the gospels also continues, and most theologians continue to welcome the contribution of critical historians.

FROM MARY TO PILATE

The Apostles' and Nicene Creeds refer to the historical context of the first-century Jew that they confess Messiah, Lord, and Son of God, by naming two other historical figures: his mother and the Roman official who was in charge of occupied Judaea from 26 to 36 CE and responsible for Jesus' crucifixion. Like most of the other characters in the gospel story Mary is unknown to world history except through the New Testament and later Christian imagination. Luke's lengthy annunciation and birth narratives evoke an atmosphere of pious Israel awaiting its Saviour Messiah, but add little trustworthy historical information to what can be gleaned from the earlier gospel tradition. Traces of slander concerning Jesus' birth (Jn 8.41) and a later legend about Mary's adultery with a soldier called Panthera (Chadwick 1953) add nothing to our knowledge of Jesus' origins.

If Matthew is correct in associating the birth of Jesus with a story about Herod the Great who ruled Palestine from 37–4 BCE (cf. also Lk 1.5), then Jesus was born a few years before our calendars imply. The reference in Luke 2.1 to the census that took place in 6/7 CE cannot be accurate and was probably drawn into the story to support Christian belief that as Messiah, Jesus of Nazareth must have been born in Bethlehem (cf. Mic 5.2 quoted at Mt 2.6; see also Jn 7.41f.). Luke 3.23 claims that he was about thirty when he began his ministry and this is usually accepted, even though John 8.57 might imply that he was older. John the Baptist is at best an imprecise guide to the beginning of Jesus' ministry, and no help at all on the date of his birth – the legends of Luke 1–2 are structured to clarify the theological relationship of the two men, not their ages or biological kinship.

The genealogies of Matthew and Luke both claim that Jesus was a descendent of David (see also the earlier tradition preserved by Paul at Rom 1.3). Some dispute about this may be reflected in Mark 12.35–7 (as later in the *Epistle of Barnabas*), and perhaps at John 7.27 too. But Christian use of the title 'Son of David' may have grown out of subsequent belief in Jesus' messiahship rather than from reliable information.

Jesus was no doubt brought up in Nazareth in Galilee, a carpenter or builder, whose mother Mary and brothers James, Joses, Judas, and Simon, and unnamed sisters were known (Mk 6.3). There is no mention here of a father, and it may be assumed that Joseph, named Jesus' father at John 1.46 and 6.42 and as his putative father in the birth narratives and genealogies, was already dead when Jesus began his ministry. Some have argued that Jesus' 'brothers' were actually cousins or half-brothers.

It seems that Jesus' family appeared during his ministry 'seeking him' – and were rebuffed (Mk 3.31–5). Several of his sayings indicate that the demands of the kingdom take priority over family ties (Mt 8.21 par. Lk 9.59) and that discipleship might bring divisions within families (Mk 13.12 par. Mt 10.21; Lk 21.16; Lk 14.29). The marginal position of the family of Jesus in the synoptic tradition is hard to reconcile with James' leadership of the Jerusalem church by the late 40s. This may imply rapid promotion – or it may reflect Markan hostility to the Jerusalem church. The importance of James in Jerusalem is clear from Paul (Gal 2), Acts, and Josephus (*Antiquities* 20.200), and the family's role in Jewish Christianity is apparent from fragments of Hegesippus preserved by Eusebius (Louth 1989) and from other echoes, but historical detective-work in this area rapidly becomes speculation (Eisenman 1997).

The historical picture becomes clearer with the activity of John the Baptist, not least because the Jewish historian Josephus who published his *Antiquities* in Rome in 93 CE gives a brief but independent account of John's ministry and his death at the hands of Herod Antipas. This 'good man was telling the Jews to practise virtue and justice towards one another and piety towards God, and to join together for baptism . . .' (*Antiquities* 18.116–19). Josephus's apologia for Judaism was written on an imperial pension, and naturally suppresses John's politically dangerous eschatological message, but it complements what the four gospels say and gives a more plausible account of his murder at the fort Machaerus than the gory legend of Mark 6, summarized in Matthew 14.

Baptism following repentance hardly seemed appropriate to Christian belief in Jesus as the sinless Son of God, and it also suggested Jesus' subordination to John (Mt 3.14f.), and the embarrassment of the early church confirms the historicity of the event, though not of the supernatural details. Jesus associated himself with this movement and that provides a possible key to his own understanding of his mission. It is possible that initially he himself baptized (Jn 3.22, despite 4.2) and quite probable that some of his followers began as disciples of John (so Jn 1.35–7; see also Acts 19.1–7). On the other hand Jesus could contrast his mission and lifestyle with John's; he was himself not a wilderness ascetic: 'For John came neither eating nor drinking and they say "He has a demon"; the Son of Man came eating and drinking and they say "Behold, a glutton and a drunkard, a friend of tax-collectors and sinners!"' (Mt 11.18f. = Lk 7.33f.).

It is this combination of agreement and disagreement with John that offers a key to Jesus' own understanding of his mission. He saw John as a prophet, more than a prophet, none greater, and a marker in what was now happening in his own activity relating to God's rule (Mt 11.9, 11–13). But this key proves difficult to turn. What the gospels tell us about John is coloured by later Christian assumptions about his relationship as forerunner (cf. Mal. 3.1; 4.5) to what God was doing in Jesus (cf. Mt 11.3 par. Lk 7.19). It is possible to distinguish between more and less reliable traditions, and also to reconstruct much of the social and religious context, but rash to suppose that we fully understand John's own expectations or precisely where Jesus agreed and disagreed with him. It is also conceivable that some of John's preaching of judgment has been attributed to Jesus (Lk 13.1–5?).

John in the wilderness called on the nation to repent in the face of God's impending judgment, echoing the religious and moral demands of the biblical prophets, but unlike them offering baptism as a sign of cleansing in response to God's demand. Whether he spoke of God's rule coming, as the editorial Matthew 3.2 claims, is impossible to say.

The Qumran community was also appealing to Isaiah 40.3 and preparing in the wilderness a path for God, studying the law and practising daily ritual lustrations. Luke 1 claims priestly descent for John and a connexion with Qumran is quite possible, but for him as for Jesus withdrawal was the prelude to a public activity that could be considered a threat to political stability (cf. Jn 11.48).

The relationship of Jesus to John the Baptist is important, but leaves us with more questions than answers. At the other end of the gospel story stands another historical character whose decision to crucify Jesus should, if it were just, throw light on the ministry. The crucifixion is the hardest fact in the gospel record, amply attested by Paul who both persecuted and joined the church within three years of the event (cf. Gal 1–2; 1 Cor 15.1–11). This Roman punishment for slaves and rebels at once poses the question whether Jesus was a rebel or revolutionary. Reimarus supposed that he was, and plausibly connected that question to the meaning of Jesus' political metaphor, the kingdom of God.

Unfortunately there is no direct path from the manner of Jesus' death to the manner of his life, because his death was probably a miscarriage of justice. One can understand the nervousness and the hostility of the Temple authorities. Anyone who attracted a following was a threat to civil order in Roman-occupied Palestine, and the death of the Baptist shows how little was needed for precautionary measures to seem appropriate. The response of Caiaphas (according to Jn 11.50) to the fear that Jesus' religious activity and its acceptance could lead the Romans to destroy 'our place and our nation' was entirely reasonable, if not entirely just. But there is nothing in the teaching of Jesus to support the political charge on which according to the probably authentic superscription on the cross ('king of the Jews'), he was executed.

It is important to recognize that Pilate, not the Jews, killed Jesus, even if at Caiaphas' instigation, and to consider whether any aspects of his ministry were deemed politically dangerous, as the superscription on the cross implies. The revealing fact here is that initially only Jesus was executed. That his followers (unlike those of other messianic prophets) were not rounded up suggests that he was not seen as leading a political revolt, and John 6.15 depicts a flight from any such suggestion. Passover was a particularly sensitive time, with large numbers of pilgrims in Jerusalem celebrating a festival that recalled a past political liberation and included future hopes and expectations. Pilate executed Jesus; and the gospels' claim that he found him innocent is hard to credit. The high-priestly aristocracy probably handed him over to Pilate, and the motivation attributed to Caiaphas at John 11.48 is credible. The implication of Mark 3.6 that some Pharisees plotted with some 'Herodians' to destroy him because they opposed his liberal attitude to the law is not credible. We may discount the Johannine placement (Jn 2) of the incident in the Temple and suppose that this finally provoked the high priest's decision. It is hard to doubt that one of Jesus' inner group of disciples, Judas Iscariot, then facilitated his arrest. This was too embarrassing to have been invented by the early church.

The historicity of the details of the passion narratives can be challenged at almost every point (Crossan 1995; but contrast Brown 1994), even though the four gospels agree more closely here than elsewhere and the short time-span dictates the general shape of events. It is clear that the early church's conviction that the death of Jesus took place 'according to the scriptures' (1 Cor 15.3) has influenced its telling and retelling of the story. Psalm 22 in particular has surely supplied some details, including the cry of dereliction (Mk 15.34), which John and Luke have replaced. Mark's 'myrrh' becomes 'gall' at Matthew 27.34 in order to correspond to Psalm 69.22 (Septuagint 68.22). John and the synoptics disagree about whether the Friday on which Jesus was crucified was the 14 or 15 Nisan. Against Jeremias (1963), John's earlier dating is more credible, in which case the Last Supper was not a Passover meal.

What Jesus said and did at that meal, probably like others an anticipation of the future messianic banquet but including a symbolic reference to his impending violent death through bread being broken and wine outpoured, and a word about God's kingdom and his own future vindication in God's kingdom, became the foundation of the Christian liturgy. The three independent records in 1 Corinthians 11, Mark 14 (modified slightly in Mt 26), and Luke 22 do not allow the historian to say precisely what Jesus had in mind. The kingdom sounds other-worldly here and suggestions that Jesus expected an imminent divine intervention are speculative. He more likely expected his imminent arrest (above p. 229).

The Markan account of Jesus' arrest is broadly reliable, even if the improbable story of the ear injury grew out of a scriptural echo of Zechariah 13.7; cf. 14.13. The idea that the disciples were carrying offensive weapons has fuelled modern speculations about armed revolution. The preceding account of Jesus' prayer in Gethsemane (Mk 14.32–42, followed by Matthew and Luke) shows signs of later Christian reflection, and it becomes even harder to vouch for the details of what followed. In Crossan's opinion 'those who cared did not know and those who knew did not care' (1995: 219). Much of what is recorded, such as Peter's denial, is plausible, but could equally reflect a post-resurrection interest in encouraging Christians. Some claims, such as the release of Barabbas, are implausible, and legendary traits appear in Matthew 27 with Pilate's hand-washing and his wife's dream. The apologetic intent of the story of the guard at the tomb is clear (Matthew 28.15), as is the theological interest in the resurrection of saints at Matthew 27.51b-3. The veil of the Temple being rent (Mk 15.38 and parallels) is almost certainly symbolic, as is the darkness over the land, rationalized by Luke into an eclipse – but that is contradicted by astronomy. (Passover falls close to the full moon; a solar eclipse only at a new moon.) The scriptural detail (Ex 12.46; Zech 12.10) that illuminates John's account of the death of Jesus is equally unlikely to be historical.

The trial before the Sanhedrin (Mk 14.55–65) is highly suspect as it stands, and John's account (18.13f.) of an informal hearing before Annas and Caiaphas more likely. Mark's account is not entirely coherent (what *was* Jesus' blasphemy?), and it reaches a climax in the evangelist's Christology, but it is quite likely that the Temple was at issue when Jesus came before the Jewish authorities (so Mk 14.58) and that they brought a political charge against him in order to secure from Pilate the death penalty that they (probably) could not themselves enforce (Jn 18.31).

Modern scholars are rightly concerned that unhistorical details in the passion narratives, such as the crowd's involvement in the crucifixion of Jesus, above all the horrendous cry of Matthew 27.25, have fostered anti-Semitism. Torture and mockery by the soldiers is credible, by the Sanhedrin not. The tendency of the gospels and later Christian tradition to exonerate Pilate does not fit what is known of that brutal governor, and the drama of John's dialogue between him and Jesus is drama not history. It is even possible to suspect that all the trial accounts, including one before Herod in Luke (perhaps inspired by Ps 2.1f; cf. Acts 4.25f.) are fictional, as are probably the various words of Jesus from the cross (different in each gospel), and the Gentile centurion's confession (Mk 15.39), which again echoes Mark's Christology (and Luke's apologetic: 23.47). Simon of Cyrene, by contrast, the father of Alexander and Rufus (Mk 15.21), is surely historical, despite John 19.17.

At many points the argument about historicity can be made either way. Is the young man who flees naked at Mark 14.51 an eyewitness (even the evangelist, as some have imagined), or based on Amos 2.16, or a symbol of the risen Lord leaving his 'garment' (cf. 15.46) behind? More importantly, is the highly illegal sword drawn at Gethsemane (Mk 14.47) historical (and a pointer to insurrection), or does it result from a misunderstanding of an earlier tradition alluding to Zechariah 13.7? (That Old Testament verse is important a little earlier, at Mk 14.28.) The further development of this sword tradition at Luke 22.35–8 is unhelpful and presumably unhistorical, however illustrative of Luke's theology.

Ever since Reimarus, the historicity of the empty tomb has been questioned by sceptics and there cannot be much doubt that many of the contradictory traditions are secondary. But Easter is part of the *Christian* story of Jesus and that goes beyond *historians'* reconstructions of his life and death. Even when we ask how his followers became convinced of his resurrection, and suspect that this might throw light on the man himself, that question concerns his *influence* and offers only indirect support for our reconstructions. The truth or falsity of the mystery or God-event metaphorically called the resurrection of Jesus, which most Christians consider foundational to their faith, is a different kind of question. Its religious answers do not depend on the *historical* question about the reliability of the Easter traditions. These *are* related to the further historical question of how the disciples' Easter faith emerged and some accounts of this might erode or (in the case of Reimarus) falsify Christian faith. But in practice the evidence is too weak either to support or to discredit the disciples' conviction that God had vindicated Jesus.

In contrast to the wealth of detail provided for Jesus' final hours on earth the narratives of his ministry between his baptism and the Last Supper provide a rough framework rather than an accurate outline. Each evangelist has structured the story in order to communicate the message rather than to provide a chronology of the ministry, and the material is sometimes arranged according to subject matter, and sometimes to assist hearers' memory. It is impossible to be sure how long Jesus' ministry lasted (perhaps little over a year, discounting John's extra Passover), or how often he went to Jerusalem prior to his final pilgrimage and what the gospels present as a messianic entry into the city. The gospels' framework can be enriched by what is now known of first-century Palestine and, in the light of this, details can be challenged as implausible (such as the Pharisees who appear in the cornfields on the sabbath at Mk 2.24). Form criticism has taught us to regard the narrative frameworks of these individual incidents as less reliable than the sayings of Jesus, which form their kernels. His teaching will accordingly be the heart of our historical matter, even though it is not the heart of the Christian and biblical story of Jesus.

Particular narratives such as the transfiguration and some miracle-stories have been questioned by historians on account of their heavy overlay of post-resurrection belief, or the difficulty in imagining what might actually have happened. Wrede doubts the reliability of Peter's messianic confession and Jesus' response at Caesarea Philippi (Mk 8.29) whereas some scholars' whole reconstruction of the ministry have hinged on this. They have thought that Jesus must have thought himself the Messiah, but that he needed to reinterpret the title to avoid any national political connotations. But this is already to go to the heart of historical research about Jesus and to try to make sense of his teaching, and with it his own understanding of his message. Before turning to that, the most important and well-attested aspect of his ministry must be underlined: Jesus was a healer and exorcist.

Exorcism can be interpreted negatively, as it was by some of his opponents (Mk 3.22) or positively, as by his disciples, the evangelists, and subsequent Christian believers (Mt 11.5 = Lk 7.22; Mt 12.28 = Lk 11.20; etc.). The witness of opponents is strong evidence for some historical basis, and Jesus' replies are also revealing. He both argues rationally (Mk 3.23–6) and speaks in a parable or metaphor of the strong man being bound and his house plundered (v. 27). He evidently saw the powers of evil being stemmed by his healing activity. He can compare himself with other exorcists, without any claim to uniqueness (Mt 12.27), but he also interprets his exorcisms as showing that the kingdom of God is breaking in (Mt 12.28 = Lk 11.20). The Fourth Gospel selects (20.30) no exorcisms to report, perhaps because its presentation of the transcendent glory of Jesus precludes any hint of a struggle with evil. Mark, however, summarizes (1.32, 39; 3.10f.; 6.56) and reports several.

The category of 'miracle' poses problems for modern historians because it implies an interpretation of an alleged event, which they do not typically entertain. But few historians would doubt or deny that Jesus was a healer and engaged in what some people then and now interpreted as exorcisms. Some would argue that this even more than his teaching is what attracted the crowds to follow him (Smith 1978).

At almost every point it is possible to challenge the historicity of individual narratives, and in the systematic analysis of a Strauss this builds up an impression that very little can be known about Jesus. But that has always been contradicted by the impression of many readers of the gospels that when all allowance is made for the peculiarities of the tradition this Galilean charismatic can be known surprisingly well. Apart from the context and the extraordinary impact of his life, a picture of the man emerges in his relationships with friends and followers, enquirers and opponents. How illuminating this might be was once shown by Cadbury (1947) and now by Theissen (1996) in a co-authored book suggestive of the new climate of 'post-minimalism', an expression applied by J. Barton in Jesus research. How well we can ever know another human being, especially one from a distant time and culture, may still be questioned. Historians and biographers bring much of their own expectations and experience to their narrative task, and there is always room for conflicting interpretations of the data. And some will continue to doubt whether that frame of reference can ever be adequate for interpreting a religious master who became an exclusive focus for so much later religious devotion.

POLITICS, ESCHATOLOGY, ETHICS

The gospels name two Caesars, four Herods, two high priests, and Pontius Pilate, all known also to Roman and/or Jewish historians. This helps modern historians to do what Luke did at 2.1f., 3.1f.: locate Jesus and Christian origins on the map of world history. But everything that is reasonably certain about Jesus comes from Christian sources, in particular the four New Testament gospels. St Paul in the 50s (quoting very early traditions) recalls the Last Supper 'in the night in which he was betrayed' (1 Cor 11.23–6) and his death on a cross, and the second-century *Gospel of Thomas* (above p. 233) contains sayings and parables that overlap and call for comparison with the synoptic gospels. The surviving fragments of other apocryphal gospels are interesting, but historically worthless. Non-Christian sources yield even less, and are dependent on Christian informants. Josephus's account of Jesus as Messiah and risen (*Antiquities* 18.163f.) consists entirely or in part of Christian interpolation, and the Talmud's references to Jesus have probably inserted his name into stories of other outsiders. When all these sources are assessed (Theissen 1996, 17–89) almost all our trustworthy information still stems from the four gospels, sifted and compared. The challenge they pose is that this is part of a story quite unlike what modern historians aim to provide. The latter want credible facts and historical interpretations of this first-century figure, not theological interpretations. The gospels' religious message about Israel's God engaging with the world to put it right through the life, death, and resurrection of God's Messiah, by contrast, is intended to challenge and instruct, not merely inform. The gospels interpret and retell the story of Jesus with religious intent to build up Christian character and community.

This does not make historical research impossible. The evangelists' purposes and perspectives led them to provide some historical information about the Jesus of Nazareth they called Messiah and Son of God. These narratives contain more or less of what Jesus probably said and did and suffered. Even their post-resurrection standpoint and retrojection into the ministry of some later beliefs about Jesus may throw some light on this remarkable man and the mission that somehow led to the formation of a church. The disciples' dawning perceptions of a decisive revelation of God in Jesus can hardly be unrelated to how he behaved and what he taught. These Christian witnesses are likely to reveal something about the man they now see in a new light. It is possible that what attracted his followers was a political programme, but it is more probable that the sources are correct and that Jesus was less directly concerned with the deteriorating political situation in Palestine than some of his contemporaries could have wished. He can scarcely have avoided the political aspects of Jewish life at the time, even if his message was addressed more to individuals (Mt 10.5) than to the nation as a whole. But there is no direct evidence of a political aim or intention. The saying 'render unto Caesar the things that are Caesar's and unto God the things that are God's' is hardly a call to arms, and at 23.2 Luke presents the political charge as a deliberate fabrication, no doubt correctly, even though he himself introduced the dangerous word 'king' at 19.38 (cf. Jn 1.50; 6.15; 12.13; 18.33–9; 19.12–21).

The political metaphor of kingship may, but need not, imply a political programme. The Jewish Prayer of Eighteen Benedictions from around this time includes 'Restore our judges as before . . . and be king over us, you alone'. That leaves no room for Roman rule in Palestine and corresponds to the ideal of the Zealots in the Jewish War. It probably lay behind the question to Jesus about paying taxes to Caesar, but if so Jesus declined the suggestion. The promise to the twelve of 'sitting on twelve thrones, judging the twelve tribes of Israel' (Mt 19.28; cf. Lk 22.30) might originally have referred to political restoration and rule on earth (cf. Ps 122.5) rather than to heaven (cf. Rev 3.21) and the last judgment, but its language of 'rebirth' is so unlike other synoptic sayings of Jesus that its authenticity may be doubted on grounds of coherence (above p. 229). The reference to the eschatological

Son of Man is dubious on other grounds (below p. 252). The saying may reflect the expectations of early Jewish disciples rather than Jesus himself (cf. Mk 10.37).

Some Jews at this time expected a restoration of Israel under a Davidic king, and Luke 1.32f. has a reliable witness (Gabriel) echo that expectation, even though the evangelist knows it was not fulfilled in the way expected (Lk 24.21; Acts 1.6) and needed reinterpreting. The Davidic messianic status of Jesus was a very early Christian belief, as Romans 1.3f. looks like a quotation from an even earlier Christian creed. Both Matthew and Luke emphasize Jesus' descent from David, and Luke the fulfilment of the promise to David (2 Sam 7.14), but Matthew reinterprets the royal title 'Son of David' in the light of the historical reality of Jesus' healing ministry, and there is no good evidence that Jesus cared for it. If Mark 12.35–7 were authentic it would imply the contrary. Jesus' entry into Jerusalem was construed as royal and messianic, whether at the time or later, but there is a trace of Jesus resisting kingship (Jn 6.15). Peter's confession of Jesus as Messiah at Mark 8.27–31 shows too many signs of editorial activity to provide secure information about Jesus' understanding of his mission. If reliable this too would tell against Jesus having political ambitions. The possibility was rightly raised by Reimarus, but has rightly been laid to rest. Jesus' proclamation of the kingdom of God calls for more plausible interpretations.

The strongest indicator of possible political involvement by Jesus is his execution by Pilate with the inscription on the cross, 'the king of the Jews'. But like John the Baptist's execution by Herod Antipas this tells us more about the authorities' caution than about Jesus' intentions (see above, p. 238). To try to discover these we are driven back to the records of what he said and did, placing a question mark against material that shows most signs of a post-resurrection perspective, especially the Johannine discourses, Christological claims, and alleged fulfilments of scripture. That still leaves plenty of material, but also ambiguities in detail and scope for very different total portraits.

The usual scholarly trail has concentrated on Jesus' sayings and parables, recognizing that these will have been more exactly remembered than their contexts or framework. Hardly anyone now attempts to reconstruct a chronology of the ministry. K. L. Schmidt (1919) showed the secondary character of the gospel framework and form criticism that the sayings provide the kernel of the most reliable stories. Uncertainty about the authenticity and precise meaning of these sayings (in Greek translation) and about their original contexts led E. P. Sanders (1985) to take an alternative route (above p. 232) and begin with Jesus' action in the Temple. But this approach founders on the ambiguity of even that near-certain event and Sanders abandoned it in his later book (1993). The most reliable sayings of Jesus must provide the keys to our understanding of his understanding of his mission.

One saying already noted links the most prominent aspect of his activity with what was remembered as the main theme of his teaching. 'If I by the Spirit (Lk: finger) of God cast out demons then indeed the kingdom of God has come upon you' (Mt 12.28; Lk 11.20). Mark summarizes Jesus' proclamation (1.15) as including the claim that 'the kingdom of God has drawn near', and all three synoptic gospels confirm the prominence of the phrase 'the kingdom of God' (usually varied by Matthew to 'the kingdom of heaven' to avoid naming God, but with the same meaning). The phrase also occurs in Acts and in Paul's letters but it is not central to post-resurrection preaching and so is unlikely to have been read back on to Jesus' lips from that.

There is every reason to believe that for Jesus himself it encapsulated his ministry and his message. But what does it mean and in what sense has it 'drawn near'? The verb is ambiguous: if something has drawn near it may be here or near. But the larger question is what 'it' is — if indeed it is an 'it'. What was Jesus referring to that he summed up in the phrase 'the kingdom of God'?

As we have seen (above p. 229), differences of opinion about the meaning of this phrase have generated different accounts of Jesus from Reimarus to the present range of possibilities.

There is general agreement that behind the Greek *basileia* (kingdom or kingly rule) stands the Hebrew *malkut* and Aramaic *malkuta'* usually meaning 'rule' rather than 'realm', 'kingship' rather than 'kingdom', even though Jesus' verb 'to enter' it suggests a place where God rules more readily than the situation of God ruling. The one implies the other, but the primary meaning of the phrase is God's sovereign rule. Jesus is speaking of *God*, and using a common metaphor to express God's supremacy over all the world. Interpretations that refer the phrase to a this-worldly community constructed by human effort do less than justice to Jesus' first-century Jewish understanding of God, even though both human moral effort and this-worldly community were also important in early Judaism.

Interpreting the metaphors, parables and poetry in which Jesus spoke of God involves more than invoking background and parallels. Historical research can clarify some issues and is surely indispensable, but interpreters may also reveal their own prior understandings of God-talk here, and that may account for some of their differences in emphasis.

Some occurrences of 'the kingdom' in Matthew and Luke seem to be editorial, to judge from the parallel passages in Mark, but generally there is no reason to doubt that the Greek of the gospels represent much of what Jesus said in Aramaic. He did not explain his phrase and presumably expected (some of) his hearers to understand him. The underlying assumption is that God rules. According to the Jewish scriptures the Creator is sovereign and all-powerful. Though not common in Jesus' scriptures the metaphor of kingship is found at Psalms 93.1, 96.10, 97.1, 99.1 and elsewhere, and part of what the metaphor *means* for those who acknowledge God as Lord and King is, 'O come let us worship and fall down; let us kneel before the Lord our Maker' (Ps 95.6).

Religious talk of God in general, and Jesus' Jewish tradition in particular has implications for those who use it. In Judah God is known (Ps 76.1) as the one who made a covenant with this people. They are committed to accepting God's rule by obeying God's law. Some rabbis later called the individual's acceptance of this life under God's rule 'taking upon oneself the yoke of the kingdom' (cf. Mt 11.29f.). Many Israelites saw their enemies as God's enemies, people who do not acknowledge God's rule. The present age or world in which the righteous suffer is out of joint, and God seems far off. But things will change, because God is coming to judge the earth and all its peoples with righteousness (Pss 96.13; 98.9). A hope for the future is intrinsic to confidence in a just God in an unjust world. God's promises to Israel,

kept alive by the prophets and in worship, and in the synagogue where the scriptures were paraphrased in Aramaic, could lead to heightened expectations at times
of particular misery.

This active sense of God ruling the world is the background of Jesus' use of the
phrase 'the kingdom (or rule) of God'. When he teaches his disciples to pray for its
coming (Mt 6.10 = Lk 11.2) he echoes the hope for the future that is a vital component of trust in God. The roughly contemporary Jewish Kaddish prayer uses similar
language: 'Magnified and sanctified (hallowed) be His great name in the world . . .
may his kingdom be established during your life and during your days and
during the life of the whole house of Israel, even speedily and at a near time'. The
hope of imminence underlines its urgency, without necessarily expecting immediate
fulfilment.

When Jesus says that the kingdom of God 'has drawn near', on the other hand,
or that it has 'come upon' those who witnessed his exorcisms (Mt 12.28 = Lk 11.20)
this seems to imply that God's coming to rule the earth is imminent or present.
Many interpreters since Weiss (1892) and Schweitzer (1906) have therefore concluded
that Jesus was mistaken. The evidence, however, is weak.

There is no clear eidence that Jesus expected the imminent *destruction of the world*
and the creation of a new heaven and new earth, as some apocalypses did. At Mark
13.32 (Mt 24.36) he denies all knowledge of God's eschatological timetable. Neither
Matthew 10.23 nor much of Mark 13.5–27 is likely to be reliable. The strongest
reason for attributing to Jesus an expectation of the imminent end of the world is
the saying in Mark 13.30 that 'this generation will not pass away before all these
things take place'. The reference in verse 28 to the harvest (a metaphor for the
last judgment) being near rings true, but how much of what precedes this goes back
to Jesus, and therefore what 'all these things' in 13.30 might cover, is unclear. The
verse's time-reference (within this generation) is widely disputed as not cohering
with the rest of Jesus' message. It contains no reference to the kingdom of God, and
its variant form at Mark 9.1, reinterpreted by Matthew at 16.28, is presumably
secondary. Jesus' saying about 'drinking the fruit of the vine new in the (future)
kingdom of God' probably implies the imminence of his arrest, not the imminence
of the kingdom. He is confident of sharing in the eschatological banquet with them
in God's kingdom after his death, but only God knows when (or where, or how)
that will be. Jesus had an eschatology but his proclamation of God's rule should not
be translated into an expectation of an imminent end of this world nor even its
imminent transformation. He will have shared with many of his contemporaries a
passionate hope and expectation that God would establish God's just rule on earth.
Anything less would lack trust in the all-powerful and all-loving Creator in a
palpably unjust world. There is no teleological religion without eschatology. But
how he envisaged the eschatological 'day of the Lord' and the judgment of which
the biblical prophets and psalmists had spoken is probably not the key to his phrase
'the kingdom of God'.

It is clear that some in the early church, notably Paul, did think that the end of
this present evil age was very near, because the new age had already broken in with
the resurrection of Jesus (1 Cor 15.20). That belief is not far from what Jesus himself
thought was happening in his own activity (Mt 12.28 again). Neither Jesus nor Paul

had any illusions about the present time of tribulations, yet both thought God was near enough to be responded to in faith and confident hope, and both encouraged their hearers with this belief (Mt 5.3–9; 1 Thess 4.13–17; 1 Cor 15.58; Rom 8.18–39). Paul thought that he was interpreting Jesus correctly when he said (1 Thess 4.15) that 'we who are alive and survive to the *parousia* of the Lord' will not precede believers who have died. But this does not look like a saying of Jesus. It might be Paul's own inference from the source of Mark 13.30, though it could depend on a 'word of the Lord' by an early Christian prophet (cf. Rev 22.20). That might even be the origin of Mark 13.30, encouraging persecuted followers of Jesus to hold on (cf. Mk 13.13).

When Paul does echo a saying of the earthly Jesus about the day of the Lord coming 'like a thief in the night' (1 Thess 5.2f.; cf. Mt 24.43; Lk 12.39) there is no timetable attached, and that is the point of the simile. Everyone must therefore be prepared. Paul inferred imminence, and that is true to the temporal reference in Mark 13.28, but the concern of both Paul and Jesus is to communicate urgency in view of the nearness of God and the shortness of time, not to predict *how* short the time is. Even Paul can be vague about that (Rom 13.11; Phil 4.5). All this eschatological material has its function in warning or encouraging individuals and groups by reference to the nearness of God. Translating such prophetic and pastoral admonitions into doctrines and predictions about the end of the world perhaps distorts them. Apocalyptic discourse about God and the world need not even be intended or understood literally (Caird 1980; Wright 1996).

It was natural for the early church to interpret Jesus' words and also such scriptures as Daniel 7 in the light of their experience of the resurrection and the Spirit, and to infer that he would shortly return. Paul uses traditional apocalyptic imagery to express his beliefs, and his concern with present relationships and behaviour in this world is set in that context. Those who wrote apocalypses were also guided more by this-worldly political and pastoral purposes than by speculative interests. But Jesus did not write apocalypses and there is little evidence of how he imagined the future apart from his confidence in God's present providence and ultimate victory over evil. The future eschatological aspect of Jesus' uncommon phrase 'the kingdom of God' (the metaphor is scarcely to be found outside Daniel in apocalypses) is better coordinated with his understanding of God than translated into convictions about the future of the world. Unlike some modern social thinkers, his focus was on God and so this world, rather than this world and so its need of transformation. His thinking was theocentric, with all the actions that implied on behalf of the neighbour.

The evidence allows the historian to doubt whether Jesus ever made his expectations about the future very clear, or was himself particularly concerned about this. Schweitzer's appeal to Matthew 10.23 is now generally rejected and Bultmann was driven to the apocalypses (while admitting how slender the evidence is for saying that Jesus expected the end of the world) only because he was sure that Jesus was not guided by any hope of 'the restitution of the idealised ancient kingdom of David' (1921: 4). E. P. Sanders (1985) on the other hand argues that this 'Jewish restoration eschatology' (rather than cosmic apocalypse) is the key to Jesus' activity and preaching, whereas B. D. Chilton (1979, 1984; Chilton and Evans 1995) thinks 'the kingdom of God' means the present revelation of God in strength. Belief in the nearness of God may or may not be eschatological and can be combined with an assumption that life on earth will continue; almost everything that Jesus can be known to have said presupposes that continuation. In that case what *was* his eschatology?

Jesus takes for granted the expectation of a future resurrection and shares it with the Pharisees and most other Jews of his day (Mk 12.25). He occasionally speaks of the (last) judgment, but without any suggestion that it is imminent (Mt 11.21–4 = Lk 10.13–5; Mt 12.41f. = Lk 11.31f.). Those who fail to respond to his mission will ultimately be judged, but unlike John the Baptist Jesus emphasizes the joy and privilege of the present offer of salvation (Mt 13.16f. = Lk 10.23f.). Even the call to repent is rarely explicit, again in contrast to John, and contrary to Luke's special emphasis. It is surely implicit in Jesus' talk of God, as in all Jewish and Christian talk of God, but Jesus seems to have spread less doom and gloom than his predecessor and some of his followers, including Matthew.

Certainly he thought there would be change in the future, vindication by God for the poor and hungry, the persecuted and the bereft (Mt 5.3–10; Lk 6.20–2), and presumably he thought this eschatological reversal would be bad news for others, as Luke implies at 6.24–6. Matthew is especially emphatic about God's judgment, repeating the formula about 'weeping and gnashing of teeth' six times. But that eschatological sanction reflects Matthew's particular concern with Christian behaviour (cf. 28.20), and may not entirely catch the flavour of Jesus' message. Most of what Jesus was rightly remembered to have said concerns human behaviour, or rather human life, but it seems remarkably free of moralism, and not particularly interested in punishment. His authentic references to reward and punishment are quite conventional and it is hard to see here any key to his message.

On the other hand it is hard to doubt that when Matthew understands Jesus' phrase 'the kingdom of God (heaven)' to have a strong moral dimension he is in tune with Jesus' teaching as a whole, with its strong insistence on doing the will of God. Matthew's addition to the Lord's Prayer, 'Thy will be done, on earth as it is in heaven' (6.10, absent from Lk 11.20), sums up much of Jesus' teaching. The only question is how accurately it interprets 'the kingdom of God' and its coming. How are ethics related to eschatology in the teaching of Jesus?

Matthew seems to subordinate eschatology to ethics, making his emphasis on the last judgment serve to underline the seriousness of Jesus' moral teaching, or 'doing the will of my Father who is in heaven' (7.21; 12.50; 21.30) and 'keeping all things whatsoever I commanded you' (28.20). 'The kingdom of heaven' is Matthew's central theological idea, as it was Jesus' (4.17), but Matthew underlines its moral aspect by associating it with 'righteousness', the behaviour that God expects of God's people: 'Seek ye first (God's) kingdom and righteousness (6.33; Lk 12.20 lacks Matthew's editorial 'righteousness'); 'blessed are those who hunger and thirst after righteousness . . . who are persecuted for the sake of righteousness' (5.6, 10; contrast Lk 6.21f.). John the Baptist, who Matthew makes also a preacher of the kingdom (3.2), 'came to you in the way of righteousness' (21.32), and a higher righteousness is required of those entering the kingdom of heaven (5.20). Matthew rightly understands Jesus to mean that God rules, and that to be a disciple is to respond to God and live under God's rule. He therefore interprets 'the kingdom of God' along those lines as a present possibility and a future hope. 'Theirs *is* the kingdom of heaven' (5.3, 10). The Beatitudes, like the antitheses (5.21–48) that illustrate the higher righteousness (5.20), describe discipleship. The ten parables, which Matthew introduces with a formula about what 'the kingdom of heaven is like', show how it is to choose and live under God's rule, and Matthew himself as a Christian 'scribe discipled for the kingdom' (13.52) draws on the tradition of Jesus' teaching, to teach what Christian discipleship involves.

This is not far from the usage of those rabbis who spoke of 'taking upon oneself the yoke of the Torah' and living according to God's will. It does justice to an important aspect of Jesus' teaching without replicating Jesus' own (probable) accentuation of the phrase 'the kingdom of God'. For Jesus the phrase signifies *God* before it signifies ethics (the will of God), though to speak of God at once involves attention to God's will, and it is not surprising that how to live is a central thrust of Jesus' teaching.

The phrase also signifies *God* before it signifies eschatology, even though to speak of God also at once involves speaking confidently of the future, and God's ultimate triumph over evil. It is *God* who rules and will rule, and Jesus' prayer is a better guide to how he thought of God than are some of his contemporaries' visions of the future destruction of the world, whether imminent or not. The nearness of God, which Jesus proclaimed (Mk 1.15) and promised (Mk 12.34), carries its own urgency and implies its own warning regardless of threats. John the Baptist may have wielded a stick, like other prophets of future judgment. Jesus celebrated what God was now doing (e.g. Mk 2.19; Mt 11.5 = Lk 7.22). John the evangelist was no doubt theologically right to conclude that the coming of the light implies judgment on those who prefer darkness because their deeds are evil (Jn 3.16–21), but the shadows that fall across Jesus' ministry stem from his opponents, not from his teaching or actions. His table-fellowship with his disciples, with outcasts, and even with his critics anticipates the messianic banquet and while some of God's people exclude themselves (Mt 8.11f.) there is no hint of vengeance or holy war against God's enemies, as at Qumran.

In prayer Jesus addressed God as 'Abba', that is, Father (Mk 14.36), and taught his disciples to do the same (Mt 6.9 = Lk 11.2; cf. Gal 4.6; Rom 8.15). Matthew sees Jesus underlining God's fatherly providence (classically expressed in Ps 103). There is no need to be anxious (Mt 6.25–34; Lk 12.22–31). God's children can ask for their bread each day confident that God loves and cares for them more than any earthly father (Mt 7.7–11 = Lk 11.9–13). Your heavenly Father feeds the birds of the air and clothes the lilies of the field; are not you worth much more? (Mt 6.26–30).

Both versions of the Lord's Prayer and a powerful parable (Mt 18.23–35) highlight our need for God's forgiveness and the correlative importance of forgiving others – repeatedly (Mt 18.22; Lk 6.37; 17.4). Like the Beatitudes (Mt 5.3–12; Lk 6.20–2) the prayer of Jesus can be accented ethically (Manson 1931; Dodd 1970; Luz 1989) or eschatologically (Meier 1994). Both aspects are present, and both are rooted in the identity and character of God who is active in the world now, even though God's rule is at present hidden, like a seed growing secretly (Mk 4.26–32; Mt 13.24–33).

Against Matthew's tendency to moralize Jesus' proclamation of God's rule (and so subordinate eschatology to ethics), and against Schweitzer's implausible subordination of ethics to an imminent eschatological expectation (making ethics a short-term instruction for the 'meantime', an *Interimsethik*), it seems best to explain both these aspects of Jesus' teaching as arising out of his overwhelming experience of the reality and nearness of God. He shared some common Jewish beliefs and expectations about God's future dealings with the world but saw God's future impinging on the present. He perhaps explained his own celibacy by reference to his dedication to the kingdom (cf. Mt 19.12), rather than as anticipating the time when marriage would be no more (Mk 12.25). Unlike Paul in 1 Corinthians 7.29–31 he seems not to have based his argument on the imminent passing away of the form of this world. Like the Qumran covenanters (CD 4.21; 11Q Temple 57.17) he was critical of the current practice of easy divorce, perhaps because it was often for the sake of remarriage (cf. Mt 5.32f.; Lk 16.18), but this was apparently based on his clear conviction about marriage and the will of God in creation (Mk 10.2–12; Mt 19.3–9) rather than the principle that the eschatological time will be like the primal time, or any abstract theory of indissolubility.

Jesus' severe warnings about the dangers of wealth (Mk 10.23–5; Lk 6.24; 12.13–21; 16.19–31), stem from its capacity to distract people from God's rule. For some this involves the call to discipleship (Mk 10.21), and that involves renunciation (Mk 10.28). This will be rewarded (v. 29). It also involves suffering, perhaps even martyrdom (Mk 8.34–6), and vindication (Mk 13.9–13). Not everyone is called to total renunciation (Lk 19.8f.), but total generosity is required from all. It follows from the character of God (Mt 5.42–5; Lk 6.30–8).

Teaching about discipleship is naturally very common in all four gospels, since Jesus both called and taught his disciples and these preserved his memory and teachings, and used them to instruct subsequent followers who had never known Jesus in the flesh. The cost of discipleship is stressed (Lk 14.28–33), including sometimes divisions within families (Mt 10.35f.; Lk 12.52f.; 14.26), perhaps reflecting his own experience (Mk 3.32f.). Renunciation of status is also characteristic of discipleship (Mk 9.34f.; 10.35–45) and this led Matthew's church to draw conclusions about Christian ministry (23.8–12), reflecting also on Jesus' sayings about status reversal (see also 18.4; Lk 14.11; 18.14).

Like Hillel, Jesus could sum up his moral teaching in the golden rule (Mt 7.12), and like other Jewish writings (*Testament of Issachar* 5.2) in the twofold commandment to love (Mk 12.30f., quoting Deut 6.5 and Lev 19.18). He broadens love of neighbour to include love of enemies (Mt 5.43f. = Lk 6.27f.), and the identification of the neighbour in the parable of the Good Samaritan (Lk 10.29–37) is unforgettable. Again, such merciful behaviour, reflected in reports of Jesus' own compassion (Mk 1.41; 6.34; 8.2; Mt 20.34; Lk 7.13) is motivated and shown to be self-evidently right by reference to the character of God (cf. the parables of Lk 15). The authentic stance of humans before God is humility (Mk 10.15; Mt 18.4; 25.12) and Matthew (like Paul) saw Jesus himself as an example (11.29).

For any Jew the revelation and measure of God's will was of course the law. Mark represents Jesus as sitting loose to cultic demands, to the improbable point even of abandoning the food laws (7.19b), or at least (in tune with Paul) implying that the love commandment fulfils the law (12.31, 33). Matthew, on the other hand, is careful to avoid any suggestion that the written law is abrogated (5.17f.; 12.1–8; 15.11–20), even though he too recognizes that Jesus was critical of unwritten traditions (15.2–9). Matthew is surely correct about Jesus' saying that 'it is not what goes into the mouth but what comes out from the mouth) [i.e. from the heart] that defiles a person' (v. 11). This implies not abolition but that morals are more important than ritual purity (cf. also the priest and Levite who do not risk impurity by contact with a dead body in the parable of the Good Samaritan). Matthew's quotation of Hosea 6.6, 'I desire mercy and not [i.e. more than] sacrifice', at 9.13 and 12.7 is surely appropriate, if not original. Whether Matthew 23.23 (cf. Lk 11.42), 'these things [tithing] you ought to have done, without neglecting the others [the weightier matters of the law: justice, mercy and faith]', originated with Jesus or with some of his more legalistic followers there can be no doubt that Jesus took the law of Moses for granted (cf. Mk 1.44).

Mark's observation that Jesus 'taught them with authority and not as the scribes' (1.22; cf. Mt 7.29), however, rings true to the immediacy of Jesus' 'but I say unto you'. The freshness of his parables confirms this confident independence in saying how things are. They are no more easily reduced to teaching illustrations than those of the later rabbis. His rigorous teaching on divorce relativizes Deuteronomy 24 on appeal to the message of the Torah in Genesis, and his demand for total honesty (Mt 5.33–7) makes oaths redundant, but none of this sharpening of the law should be taken as a fundamental criticism of it. Even the liberal saying that 'the sabbath was made for man, not man for the sabbath' (Mk 2.27, omitted by Matthew and Luke) can be read as repeating the humane justification for the fourth commandment given at Deuteronomy 5.14 (unlike Ex 20.11): your servants need a rest as well as you. The startling injunction to 'let the dead bury their own dead' (Mt 8.22 = Lk 9.60) gives priority to discipleship, but is not intended to abrogate the fifth commandment, which is defended at Mark 7.9–13.

Much of Jesus' moral teaching must have been *ad hoc*, in response to questions and problems. As a charismatic teacher and eschatological prophet Jesus stated God's will in absolute terms, sometimes shocking his hearers into attention by his use of hyperbole. When Matthew in particular repeats and reapplies this teaching as guidance for his Christian community a change of texture becomes apparent. The legislator needs to be practical as the prophet does not. And yet Jesus' teaching does strike the reader as generally practical, even common sense. It was not intended to be an impossible ethic, persuading pietists of their need for grace by setting an unrealistic moral standard. 'Be ye perfect, as your Father in heaven is perfect' (Mt 5.48; contrast Lk 6.36: merciful) sounds like moral perfectionism, but the Aramaic behind the Greek (cf. also Mt 19.21) probably means 'whole' or undivided, having integrity.

The original contexts of Jesus' teaching may explain in part why he did not develop a social or political ethic. When his injunction to resist not evil (Mt 5.39) is made the basis of Christian pacifism a major extension has been made in its application, whether or not legitimately. The advice to turn the other cheek gains its wider Christian application from the whole story of Jesus, culminating in his crucifixion, not from the saying in isolation. Attempts have been made to credit Jesus with a social programme (most recently Horsley 1987) and to discuss 'the politics of Jesus' (Yoder 1972) and these contain important insights. If the emergence of Christianity is considered valid, new applications of Jesus' teachings are also valid. But Jesus himself addressed individuals, even in crowds, whatever his possible programme for Israel. Religious faith (see Jeremias 1971: 159–66, on what Jesus taught about faith) is inescapably individual: nobody can do it for you.

Faith also has social implications, and God's covenant with his people comes first in Judaism. How far Jesus emphasized this is disputed. His attitude to the Temple, the real and symbolic centre of Judaism in his day, is not entirely clear, as the different suggestions of E. P. Sanders and B. D. Chilton (above p. 246–7) show. Like Meyer (1979) and Horsley (1987) these scholars think he had a clearly defined programme. Others are not so sure. H. J. Cadbury (1937: ch. 6) observed that we are prone to impose our expectations of clear goals on Jesus. His obedience to God's will need not have been so specific. He spelled out the social implications of faith only at the level of interpersonal relations, not in a theory about Israel. Too much has perhaps been read into his undoubtedly significant choice of twelve disciples.

Perhaps an appeal to the nation as such may be implicit in his decision to go up to Jerusalem shortly before Passover? He must have known the risk and probably expected to die as a prophet (Mk 6.4) in Jerusalem (Lk 13.33) – and to be vindicated by God (Mk 8.31; etc.). If like the Baptist he was going to be silenced anyway, why not make his last stand at the centre, even in the Temple precincts? Just as his sense of the shortness of time, in sending the twelve on a mission, might have stemmed from his expectation of imminent arrest, so too here. The urgency of the invitation and the necessity of responding are expressed also in the parable of the Great Supper (Matthew 22.2–10; Luke 14.16–24) and explain the eschatological imagery at Matthew 9.37, 10.15 = Lk 10.12. At the Last Supper he probably anticipated imminent arrest or death (in the next twenty-four hours, before he could celebrate the Passover with them), rather than (as is often claimed) an imminent end of the world. To speak of the God of Israel is to speak of the end as well as the creation of the world, but the focus of Jesus' preaching and activity was the present moment in which men and women are confronted with God who is gracious. That is why it could later be described by Mark as good news from God, good news about God, the good news that is God (Mk 1.14f.).

HOPES AND MEMORIES

In *The Genius of Shakespeare* (1997) Jonathan Bate recognizes how very little we know directly about the bard, and yet contrives to reconstruct a historical picture by drawing on what is known of his setting or 'pre-history' (the Elizabethan stage), and what can be inferred from his 'after-life', the history of his influence. The New Testament, constantly echoing the Old Testament and so generating a 'biblical world', has much to say about the 'after-life' of Jesus that is without historical analogy. But its hymnic and credal claims that Jesus is now 'first-begotten from the dead' (Col. 1.18), 'risen on the third day according to the scriptures' (1 Cor 15.3; cf. v. 20), super-exalted Lord (Phil 2.9–11), are part of his 'after-life' in the historian Bate's sense as well as having Christian theological meanings.

It is not the task of this presentation to assess what Christians confess, the mystery of God's having vindicated Jesus. However, whether truth or illusion, the subsequent convictions and activities of his followers do echo Jesus and so contribute to a larger picture of Jesus in history, as well as (more significantly) to the theological portraits, and they are clearly a part of the biblical world. The history of Jesus, tentatively reconstructed from the records of his followers who became worshippers, would not be complete without mention of the transition from an earthly life and death to the emergence and development of a new form of Judaism focused on this Messiah.

Throughout the preceding discussion this transition has been the major factor in assessing the sources and the main reason for reluctance to rely on what they say where the record most clearly reflects the interests of the later community: in claims that the scriptures are being fulfilled in Jesus, especially in his passion (cf. 1 Cor 15.3), and in Christological titles and formulations.

That caution might seem excessive when it leads to scepticism about some passages which see Jesus as the Son of Man. It is hard to doubt (but it has occasionally been doubted) that Jesus spoke of himself using this Aramaic and Hebrew phrase, but it is also hard to believe that he used it in all the different ways the gospels suggest. The gospels naturally see Jesus as the Son of Man in his earthly activity, his passion and resurrection, and his eschatological coming on the clouds, but this combination of meanings is more understandable from the perspective of the early church than on the lips of Jesus. Most critics have felt it necessary to choose between Jesus calling himself 'son of man' in a simple earthly sense (Mt 8.20 = Lk 9.57; Mt 11.19 = Lk 7.34) and his referring to the heavenly Son of Man of Daniel 7.13 (Mk 13.26; 14.62 and other less explicit passages). A generation ago many scholars accepted some of the latter (Mk 8.38; Lk 12.8) whether holding that Jesus referred to himself or to someone else; now many prefer the former option and explain the latter as post-resurrection reflection of Jesus in the light of the Daniel stories of suffering and vindication. We know the early church looked forward to Jesus returning in glory to carry out God's judgment and vindicate his persecuted followers. Jesus' own expectations are impossible to pin down with any certainty, though he must have been confident that God would vindicate his cause somehow (Barrett 1967) and the eschatological language of resurrection was available to him in his Jewish tradition.

Jesus spoke of others rising and being raised in the judgment (Mt 11.41f.), and may also have spoken of his own vindication in these terms (cf. Mk 8.31; 9.31; 10.33), even if the time specification (after three days, on the third day) reflects the Easter experience. His followers were clear (after some initial doubt) that God had already vindicated Jesus, and that the new age which was breaking into the old in his activity had now dawned, even though its visible manifestation was still to come. They themselves lived in the 'meanwhile', waiting and remembering, living by the norms of the new age in the experience of the Spirit, and sharing their memories and hopes with other Jews, and soon with Gentiles too.

They searched their scriptures, trying to make sense of what they had experienced by interpreting it in the light of that tradition of God's word in prophecy and promise to Israel, and also with the help of current eschatological expectations. Whether or not he called himself 'the Messiah' he certainly saw himself as a prophet with a decisive mission to the lost sheep of the house of Israel (Mt 10.5), and his followers soon called him God's Messiah or 'anointed one', a title with various connotations, which in Greek rapidly became a name: Christ. The inscription on the cross 'king of the Jews' was not a title adopted by the early church, but Jesus' execution as a messianic (political) figure could have encouraged that equation after his vindication (cf. Acts 2.36). The expectation of a 'Son of David' or Davidic Messiah was also one of the roots of the title Son of God (cf. 2 Sam 7.14; Ps 2.7). Its early application to Jesus was perhaps reinforced by the memory of his intimacy with God in prayer.

Within a few decades (in 112 CE) we hear of Pliny, a Roman governor in Bithynia (northern Turkey), reporting to his emperor Trajan that groups of Christians 'assembled before daylight to recite a form of words [or sing a hymn?] to Christ as a god and bound themselves *sacramento* to moral behaviour' (*Epistles* 10.96). Of course he executed those who would not desist, but the question for historians is how this elevation of Jesus came about.

The cultic context specified by Pliny was certainly important (Bousset, 1970), as the early Aramaic phrase quoted by Paul at 1 Corinthians 16.22 and the Christ hymn at Philippians 2.6–11 indicate. The experience of the Spirit was vital, and sometimes the distinction between the risen Christ and the Spirit is unclear (Rom 8.9–11; 2 Cor 3.17). But the identification of Jesus as Lord (Rom 10.9; 1 Cor 12.3), and the eucharistic *anamnesis* (remembrance, 1 Cor 11.24f.) of the passion, involved the early church's *memory* of Jesus. It was these memories that a generation or two later were stabilized in the New Testament gospels and it is natural to scan them too for anything about Jesus that might help explain the emergence (or continuation) of the Jesus movement after his shameful death. It is not plausible to credit all that followed to the account of the disciples' conviction of his resurrection. What mattered to them was the *person* whom God had vindicated or exalted, not that event in isolation.

The *authority* of Jesus is a recurring feature of the synoptic record of Jesus' ministry, universalized by Matthew at 28.18. Perhaps it was this that led a few Galileans who were more prosperous than some to 'leave all and follow' him (Mk 10.28). The loyalty that he inspired survived the shock of his arrest and initial dispersal of his disciples (Mk 14.50) and presumably tells something of his character. It may also say something of the character of their response and help to explain the persistence of that loyalty. But the particular mix of hopes and aspirations, economic circumstances, and the impact of a charismatic personality, is impossible to analyse on the basis of such fragmentary sources. The historian is reduced to informed guesswork. Possible factors can and must be assembled, but any construction will be tentative. Jesus was clearly a wise teacher and may have been soon seen as child or envoy of wisdom (Lk 7.35; Mt 23.37–9 = Lk 13.34f.). Was this how he came to be seen (Col 1.15; Heb 1.2f., cf. Jn 1.1–18) as the wisdom of God incarnate (Mt 23.34; cf. Lk 11.49; Mt 11.28–30; cf. Sir 51.23–6)?

The opposition Jesus evoked is another source of possible insight. The historian can only regret that these opponents did not leave contemporary records. They inhabit the biblical world as negative shadows, leaving it to the historian's imagination to do justice to their positive efforts to maintain an uneasy peace and sustain the traditional religion in times that were difficult enough without a Galilean charismatic exciting this volatile people.

Jesus belongs to *history*, the history of first-century Galilee and Judaea, the history of his followers over two thousand years, and the history of the cultures that have been shaped or influenced by the memories preserved in the gospels and by the countless lives inspired by these records. His impact on history, however, has been mediated mainly through the gospels, read mostly in religious contexts. These four familiar versions combine in fresh configurations as the kaleidoscope fragments are mirrored afresh in the minds of new readers. Even his influence on the wider culture stems from this *literature*.

The literary phenomenon one might call the 'biblical Jesus' or 'Jesus of the gospels' would not have emerged without that extraordinary historical person named Jesus. But this first-century Jewish teacher and healer is significant today, for Christians and for many non-Christians, only because he was taken up into the symbolic world of his followers and others influenced by them. Most of what he said might have been said by many wisdom teachers and neither Paul nor John, the two greatest theological minds of the New Testament, seem concerned to preserve it accurately. What he did and suffered is not without precedent either. He was (like every human being) unique, and doubtless more original and independent than most, but what matters finally is that his words and deeds and sufferings have been taken up into a story of God's engagement with the world, retold four times in the New Testament and endlessly outside it.

The Fourth Evangelist spoke for later followers when he insisted that the Jewish Messiah Jesus, who came from the Father and returned to the Father, is the definitive revelation of God: No-one has ever seen God (1.18), but to know Jesus is to know God (8.19), to have seen Jesus is to have seen the Father (14.9) and to reject him is to turn from the light (3.19; cf. 12.44–50). Where 'biblical' refers to the *Christian* scriptures, the central subject of the 'biblical world' of symbols is this contingent historical figure. Whether the historian's honest efforts provide a ladder into that world or a barrier against it remains an open question. The expectations of some critics and advocates of Christianity alike have proved overoptimistic and misplaced. But their efforts and those of many sober historians have provided some clarifications. Those who think of the past in modern historical terms have found that helpful.

BIBLIOGRAPHY

Bammel, E. and Moule, C. F. D. eds (1984) *Jesus and the Politics of His Day*, Cambridge.
Barrett, C. K. (1967) *Jesus and the Gospel Tradition*, London.
Borg, M. (1984) *Conflict, Holiness and Politics in the Teaching of Jesus*, Toronto.
—— (1987) *Jesus: A New Vision*, San Francisco.
—— (1994) *Jesus in Contemporary Scholarship*, Valley Forge.
Bornkamm, G. ([1956] 1960) *Jesus of Nazareth*, London.
Bousset, W. ([1913, 1921²] 1970) *Kyrios Christos*, ET Nashville.
Brandon, S. G. F. (1967) *Jesus and the Zealots*, Manchester.
Breech, J. (1983) *The Silence of Jesus*, Philadelphia.
Brown, R. ([1977] 1993) *The Birth of the Messiah*, London.
—— (1994) *The Death of the Messiah*, London.
Bultmann, R. ([1921, 1931²] 1995) *The History of the Synoptic Tradition*, Oxford.

—— ([1926] 1958) *Jesus and the Word*, New York.
—— ([1948] 1952) *Theology of the New Testament*, Vol. 1, London.
—— ([1949] 1960) *Primitive Christianity*, London.
Burney, C. F. (1925) *The Poetry of Our Lord*, Oxford.
Cadbury, H. J. ([1937] 1962) *The Perils of Modernizing Jesus*, London.
—— ([1947] 1962) *Jesus: What Manner of Man?*, London.
Caird, G. B. (1980) *The Language and Imagery of the Bible*, London.
Catchpole, D. R. (1993) *The Quest for Q*, Edinburgh.
Chadwick, H. ed. (1953) *Origen: Contra Celsum*, Cambridge.
Charlesworth, J. H. ed. (1983–5) *The Old Testament Pseudepigrapha*, London.
—— (1992) *The Messiah*, Philadelphia.
Chilton, B. D. ([1979] 1987) *God in Strength*, Sheffield.
—— ed. (1984) *The Kingdom of God in the Teaching of Jesus*, Philadelphia.
—— (1992) *The Temple of Jesus*, Leiden.
—— (1995) *Pure Kingdom: Jesus' Vision of God*, Grand Rapids.
Chilton, B. D. and Evans, C. A. (1993) *Studying the Historical Jesus*, Leiden.
Conzelmann, H. ([1959] 1973) *Jesus*, ET Philadelphia.
—— ([1968] 1969) *An Outline of the Theology of the New Testament*, London.
Crossan, J. D. (1985) *Four Other Gospels*, Minneapolis.
—— (1991) *The Historical Jesus*, San Francisco.
—— (1995) *Who Killed Jesus?*, San Francisco.
Dibelius, M. ([1919] 1934) *From Tradition to Gospel*, London.
—— ([1939] 1963) *Jesus*, London.
Dodd, C. H. ([1935] 1961) *The Parables of the Kingdom*, London.
—— ([1970] 1971) *The Founder of Christianity*, London.
Downing, F. G. (1987) *Jesus and the Threat of Freedom*, London.
Dunn, J. D. G. (1975) *Jesus and the Spirit*, London.
Eisenman, R. (1997) *James the Brother of Jesus*, London.
Evans, C. A. (1989) *Life of Jesus Research: An Annotated Bibliography*, Leiden.
Freyne, S. (1980) *Galilee from Alexander the Great to Hadrian*, Wilmington.
—— (1988) *Galilee, Jesus and the Gospels*, Philadelphia.
Funk, R. W. and Hoover, R. W. (1993) *The Five Gospels*, New York.
E. Güttgemanns ([1970] 1979) *Candid Questions to Form Criticism*, Pittsburgh.
Harnack, A. ([1900] 1901) *What Is Christianity?*, London.
Harvey, A. E. (1982) *Jesus and the Constraints of History*, London.
—— (1990) *Strenuous Commands: The Ethic of Jesus*, London.
Hengel, M. ([1968] 1981) *The Charismatic Leader and His Followers*, Edinburgh.
—— ([1973] 1974) *Judaism and Hellenism*, London.
Hennecke, E., Schneemelcher, W. and Wilson, R. McL. ([1959–64] 1991–3) *New Testament Apocrypha*, Louisville.
Holtzmann, H. J. (1863) *Die synoptischen Evangelien*, Leipzig.
Horsley, R. (1987) *Jesus and the Spiral of Violence*, San Francisco.
—— (1989) *Sociology and the Jesus Movement*, New York.
Jeremias, J. ([1947] 1963) *The Parables of Jesus*, London.
—— (1971) *New Testament Theology*. Vol. 1: *The Proclamation of Jesus*, London.
Johnson, L. T. (1995) *The Real Jesus*, San Francisco.
Jüngel, E. (1962) *Paulus und Jesus*, Tübingen.
Kähler, M. ([1892] 1964) *The So-Called Historical Jesus and the Historic Biblical Christ*, Philadelphia.
Käsemann, E. ([1954] 1964) *Essays on New Testament Themes*, London.
Keck, L. E. (2000) *Who Is Jesus?*, South Carolina.

Kelber, W. H. (1983) *The Oral and Written Gospel*, Philadelphia.

Kloppenborg, J. S. (1987) *The Formation of Q*, Philadelphia.

Koester, H. (1990) *Ancient Christian Gospels*, London.

Leivestad, R. (1987) *Jesus in His own Perspective*, Minneapolis.

Lindars, B. (1983) *Jesus, Son of Man*, London.

Louth, A. (1989) ed. *Eusebius: The History of the Church*, London.

Luz, U. (1985) *Matthew 1–7: A Commentary*, Edinburgh.

Mack, B. (1988) *A Myth of Innocence: Mark and Christian Origins*, San Francisco.

—— (1993) *The Lost Gospel: The Book of Q and Christian Origins*, Philadelphia.

Manson, T. W. (1931) *The Teaching of Jesus*, Cambridge.

Meier, J. P. (1991, 1994) *A Marginal Jew*, Vols 1, 2, New York.

Meyer, B. F. (1979) *The Aims of Jesus*, London.

Moule, C. F. D. (1977) *The Origin of Christology*, Cambridge.

Otto, R. ([1934] 1957) *The Kingdom of God and the Son of Man*, Grand Rapids.

Perrin, N. (1967) *Rediscovering the Teaching of Jesus*, London.

Powell, M. A. (1998) *Jesus as a Figure in History*, Louisville.

Reimarus, H. S. ([1774–8] 1972) *Fragmente*, ed. Lessing = parts of *Apologie oder Schutzschrift für die vernünftigen Verehrer Gottes*, Frankfurt. See also Talbert (1970).

Renan, E. ([1863] 1864) *The Life of Jesus*, London.

Riches, J. (1980) *Jesus and the Transformation of Judaism*, London.

Rowland, C. C. (1985) *Christian Origins*, London.

Sanders, E. P. (1985) *Jesus and Judaism*, London.

—— (1990) *Judaism: Practice and Belief 63 BCE – 66 CE*, London.

—— (1993) *The Historical Figure of Jesus*, London.

Sanders, E. P. and Davies, M. (1989) *Studying the Synoptic Gospels*, London.

Schillebeeckx, E. ([1974] 1979) *Jesus: An Experiment in Christology*, London.

Schleiermacher, F. D. E. ([1799], 1958) *On Religion*, New York.

Schmidt, K. L. ([1919] 1964) *Der Rahmen der Geschichte Jesu*, Darmstadt.

Schürmann, H. (1994) *Jesus: Gestalt und Geheimnis*, Paderborn.

Schweitzer, A. (1906) *Von Reimarus zu Wrede* (enlarged 1913); ET 1910 *The Quest of the Historical Jesus*, London. Revised and enlarged edition (2000) London.

Scott, B. B. (1983) *Jesus, Symbol-Maker for the Kingdom*, Minneapolis.

Scott, B. B. (1989) *Hear Then the Parable*, Minneapolis.

Smith, M. (1978) *Jesus the Magician*, London.

Stanton, G. N. (1989) *The Gospels and Jesus*, Oxford.

Stauffer, E. ([1957] 1960) *Jesus and His Story*, London.

Strauss, D. F. ([1835] 1973) *The Life of Jesus Critically Examined*, ET 1846; P. Hodgson ed. London.

Talbert, C. H. (1970) *Reimarus: Fragments*, Philadelphia.

Tannehill, R. C. (1975) *The Sword of His Mouth*, Philadelphia.

Theissen, G. ([1977] 1978) *The First Followers of Jesus*, London.

—— ([1986] 1987) *The Shadow of the Galilean*, London.

—— (1992) *Social Reality and the Early Christians*, Edinburgh.

Theissen, G. and Merz, A. ([1996] 1998) *The Historical Jesus*, London.

Tuckett, C. M. (1986) *Nag Hammadi and the Gospel Tradition*, Edinburgh.

Tuckett, C. M. ed. (1996) *Q and the History of Early Christianity*, Edinburgh.

Vermes, G. (1973) *Jesus the Jew*, London.

Vermes, G. ed ([1960] 1997) *The Dead Sea Scrolls in English*, London.

Via, D. (1967) *The Parables: Their Literary and Existential Dimension*, Philadelphia.

Webb, R. L. (1991) *John the Baptizer and Prophet*, Sheffield.

Weiss, J. ([1892] 1971) *Jesus' Proclamation of the Kingdom of God*, London.

Wilder, A. N. (1982) *Jesus' Parables and the War of Myths*, Philadelphia.
Winter, P. (1961) *On the Trial of Jesus*, Berlin.
Witherington III, B. (1994) *Jesus the Sage*, Minneapolis.
Wrede, W. ([1901] 1971) *The Messianic Secret*, Cambridge.
Wright, N. T. (1996) *Jesus and the Victory of God*, London.
Yoder, J. (1972) *The Politics of Jesus*, Grand Rapids.

CHAPTER FORTY-ONE

PAUL

——— •◆• ———

David G. Horrell

INTRODUCTION

Paul is a man of enormous influence, a religious genius whose capacity for creative thought and original writing has made him a mountain[1] on the landscape of Christian history. He has been hailed as 'the real founder of Christianity' (Nietzsche),[2] though whether that is a title of acclamation or condemnation depends on the standpoint of the one who labels Paul thus. For some, Paul is responsible for perverting the religion of Jesus the Jew into a Hellenistic salvation-religion that Jesus would hardly have recognized, let alone approved.[3] For others, Paul is the one who most clearly perceived the meaning of the death and resurrection of Christ and most energetically spread the gospel message among the non-Jewish inhabitants of the Roman empire. For some, Paul is the bearer of a message of grace and liberation; for others, he is at least partly responsible for a history of anti-Semitism and for keeping the downtrodden firmly in their place. But even if Paul was not the founder of Christianity – and there are many reasons for rejecting that tendentious claim – the immensity of his influence cannot be denied.

During his lifetime, however, Paul was not as prominent as the verdict of history might lead us to assume. Positions of greater eminence and authority were held by the 'pillars' of the Jerusalem church, the apostles Peter, James and John, who had been disciples of Jesus (cf. Gal. 2:2, 9; Holmberg 1978: 14–34). And in the early years of his missionary activity, Paul was almost certainly acting under the auspices and commission of the church at Antioch, possibly 'as assistant to Barnabas' (Murphy-O'Connor 1996: 96; cf. Taylor 1992: 87–95; Acts 11:26 – 15:40). Yet it is Paul, and none of these other characters, who warrants a chapter in this book. The reason for this is not hard to discern: Paul's enduring influence is primarily due to his weighty theological letters that are preserved in the New Testament (cf. 2 Cor. 10:10). There are thirteen such letters attributed to Paul, but just one of them – his letter to the Romans – far surpasses in influence that of the New Testament epistles attributed to Peter, James and John combined.

Those epistles written by Paul are obviously the most important source for understanding him. There is a large scholarly majority in favour of the view that Paul did not write the so-called Pastoral Epistles (1–2 Timothy, Titus), nor Ephesians;

arguments for and against Paul's authorship of Colossians and 2 Thessalonians are more finely balanced, though many doubt that they are Paul's own work. That leaves us with Romans, 1 and 2 Corinthians, Galatians, Philippians, 1 Thessalonians and Philemon as the primary sources for the study of Paul. The book of Acts, written by the same author as the Gospel of Luke, probably twenty to thirty years after Paul's death, is also an important source for the study of Paul's life and work, though its reliability is much debated. Undoubtedly the author of Acts, whom I shall call Luke, has theological tendencies that shape the picture he presents, but the historical value of his work should not be ignored. The evidence of Acts must nevertheless be used with due circumspection.

Also important for understanding Paul are the numerous and varied sources that can further our understanding of the social, cultural and religious context in which Paul lived and worked. Jewish sources are vital to understanding the varieties of Judaism that existed at the time of Paul and the particular sect of Judaism to which Paul originally belonged; other sources enable us to appreciate something of the wider political and philosophical context for Paul's Christian mission.

PAUL'S CONTEXT: RELIGIOUS, CULTURAL, SOCIAL AND POLITICAL

Paul was first and foremost a Jew; or, in his own words, 'of the people of Israel, of the tribe of Benjamin, a Hebrew of Hebrews' (Phil. 3:5; cf. Rom. 11:1; 2 Cor. 11:22). More specifically, Paul tells us that he was a Pharisee (Phil. 3:5), a member of a grouping within first-century Judaism whose members sought to practise holiness by careful adherence to both written and oral Torah (see Schürer 1979: 388–403; Saldarini 1992). This Pharisaic identity almost certainly confirms Luke's information that Paul was educated in Jerusalem, since Pharisaic training seems to have taken place only in that city (Acts 22:3; 23:6; 26:4–5; Hengel 1991: 27; Lüdemann 1989: 240). But whether Paul went to Jerusalem in his early childhood, adolescence or early adulthood is open to debate (see Hengel 1991: 2–3, 18–39; Murphy-O'Connor 1996: 46–51). It is also uncertain whether Paul was widowed, divorced, or had always remained single (the first of these is perhaps most likely – see Jeremias 1926, 1929; Murphy-O'Connor 1996: 62–5). However, it is clear that he was 'unattached' when he wrote his letters (1 Cor. 7:7–8; 9:5).

One thing about Paul that we learn only from Acts is that he was from Tarsus, the capital city of Cilicia (Acts 9:11; 21:39; 22:3; see Figure 41.1), though this detail about Paul's life is hardly ever doubted (Hengel 1991: 1). Being born and probably educated, at least initially, in Tarsus, Paul was thus a member of the Jewish diaspora, educated in Greek and specifically in the Greek version of the Hebrew scriptures, the Septuagint (LXX; see chapter 12 above), even though his Pharisaic training also ties him closely into Palestinian Judaism. Moreover, like other Jews of his day, Paul was influenced by popular philosophical discussion from a range of sources, as well as by his specifically Jewish heritage (see e.g. Malherbe 1989; Deming 1995; Downing 1998). If Luke is right that Paul was a Roman citizen (Acts 22:25–2) – again, this is not something Paul ever mentions, and it is doubted by some (e.g. Stegemann 1987; Roetzel 1998: 19–22) – this was probably inherited

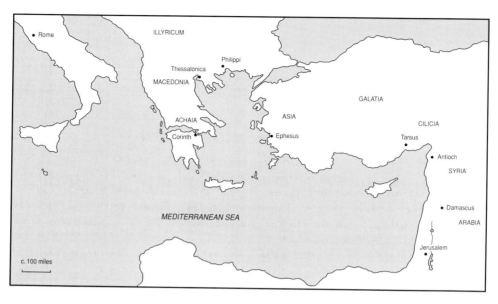

Figure 41.1   Map showing places and areas mentioned in the text.

through his family, granted perhaps to his father or grandfather on release from slavery (see Hengel 1991: 4–15; Rapske 1994: 71–112; Riesner 1998: 147–56). The name Paul uses in his letters is his Latin *cognomen* Paulus, and he does not himself mention his Jewish name 'Saul' (Hebrew: *Sha'ul*; Greek: *Saoul/Saulos*), which appears frequently in the first half of Acts (e.g. 7:58; 8:1; 12:25; note 13:9).

These last details remind us that Paul was a citizen, or at least an inhabitant, of the Roman empire, and the structure of empire was the dominant social and political *datum* for both Jews and Christians, indeed all inhabitants of the Mediterranean region, at the time. The impact of this socio-political reality can be seen in Paul's references to imprisonments and beatings (Rom. 16:7; 2 Cor. 11:23; Phil. 1:7–17; Phlmn 1, 9, 23; he also received lashes as synagogue discipline on several occasions; see 2 Cor. 11:24), as well as in his advice to his converts on issues like slavery (1 Cor. 7:21–4) and their attitudes to the imperial authorities (Rom. 13:1–7). In the end, the cost of his work as a Christian missionary in the Roman empire was his life, since he was almost certainly executed in Rome, perhaps along with Peter, towards the end of Nero's reign (c. 60–7 CE; cf. *1 Clem.* 5.2–7; Eusebius, *HE* 2.25.5).

FROM JESUS TO PAUL: PRE-PAULINE CHRISTIANITY

Despite his polemical insistence that he received his gospel by divine revelation and not from any human being (Gal. 1:11–12), and despite the personal nature of his encounter with the risen Christ, it is clear that Paul owed much to those who were believers in Christ before him (cf. 1 Cor. 15.3–9). He himself tells us of a visit to

Jerusalem to 'get acquainted with Peter'[4] when, we may be sure, he learnt something about the historical Jesus and about the gospel as Peter understood it. Paul also spent some time at Antioch (in Syria), operating as a missionary with Antioch as his base. He did not found the church at Antioch and must have learnt substantially from the teaching and practice already established there. For these reasons, and to show that Paul was not 'the founder of Christianity', it is important very briefly to sketch the progress of Christianity in its earliest period, before Paul's 'conversion' and well before his letters, although this period spans only a few years.[5]

After the death and resurrection of Jesus – and whatever 'happened' at the resurrection, it is clear that early Christianity is based on the *belief* in its occurrence – some of his disciples, including leading figures such as Peter, James and John, remained in Jerusalem, where they met regularly with fellow believers in Jesus as Messiah/Christ. At this point in time, however, such believers were all Jews and loyally continued their Jewish religious practice (Acts 2:46; 3:1). While the details of the events that followed are much debated, Luke's account in Acts indicates that there were divisions and differences within this earliest Christian community, notably between the 'Hebrews' and the 'Hellenists' (Acts 6:1) and that, due to persecution, at least some of the believers were dispersed from Jerusalem (Acts 8:1–4; 11:19). Many believe that it was primarily the so-called Hellenists who were persecuted and dispersed, and who held a theology more critical of Jewish law and temple than the so-called Hebrews,[6] though the tidiness of this division has been sharply questioned by Craig Hill (1992).[7] Whatever the details, with the scattering of Christians from Jerusalem, within a few years the gospel began to be shared with non-Jews (Acts 11:20–6).[8] Moreover, in at least some places these Gentile converts (often already Jewish sympathizers or 'godfearers') were not expected to become Jewish, that is, to adopt all the marks of Jewish identity and obedience to the Jewish law (circumcision, food laws, sabbath observance, etc.). This development was absolutely crucial for the future character of Christianity, and was the cause of heated debate (in which Paul looms large) for decades, even centuries, afterwards.[9]

Antioch was certainly one place where the gatherings of Christians included both Jews and Gentiles, without the latter being expected to become Jews, and it is not insignificant that a few years after his conversion Paul was based at Antioch for some time as a Christian missionary. How far this development had taken place prior to Paul's joining the community at Antioch and how far Paul may have been involved in it elsewhere is difficult to say, since we know so little about the earliest church at Antioch and about Paul's activities between his conversion and the first of his letters, a period of some years (see below). However, it is clear that the spread of the gospel from Jerusalem to Antioch and elsewhere, and the inclusion of Gentiles as well as Jews within the company of Christians, took place independently of Paul, and well before he wrote any of his letters (see further Riesner 1998: 108–24).

Nevertheless, Paul's commitment specifically to the task of evangelizing the Gentiles and the arguments he formulated to justify their inclusion within the Christian movement without their becoming Jews were of decisive significance for the long-term development and identity of Christianity. Paul and Barnabas were sent as representatives of the Antioch church to the gathering in Jerusalem to discuss precisely the issue of Gentile converts (Acts 15:1–29; Gal. 2:1–10[10]), and when disagreement later flared at Antioch itself, Paul argued vigorously for the acceptance of Gentiles without their obedience to the demands of Jewish law (Gal. 2:11–21).[11] Although Paul may have lost the argument at Antioch, he presented it once more, at greater length and with considerable heat and passion, in his letter to the Galatians, and, indeed, at even greater length but without so much heat, in Romans.

It is important to bear in mind, however, that while Paul turned out to be a pivotal person in these crucial debates, formulating in detail the arguments on which the Gentiles' acceptance *as Gentiles* was based, he was not a solitary or unique figure. Paul owed much to his predecessors, from and with whom he learnt much about the nature of belief in Christ. Furthermore, though it is often forgotten, Paul operated within a wide circle of co-workers (see Rom. 16:3, 9, 21; 2 Cor. 8:23; Phil. 2:25; 4:3; etc.), some of whom are named as co-authors in some of the epistles we tend to think of solely as Paul's (see 1 Cor. 1:1; 2 Cor. 1:1; Gal. 1:2; Phil. 1:1; 1 Thess. 1:1; Phlmn 1).

PAUL'S CALL TO APOSTLESHIP AND MISSIONARY ACTIVITY

How did Paul come to be arguing about the place of Gentile converts in the church in the first place? He had not known or followed Jesus during his lifetime, nor, as far as we know, was he converted directly by hearing the message announced by early Christian preachers. In the earliest years of the Christian movement, Paul tells us, he was a zealous persecutor of the church (Gal. 1:13, 23; 1 Cor. 15:9; Phil. 3:6). Precisely how and why a Pharisee engaged in such persecution is not altogether clear,[12] but what is indisputable is that a zealous persecutor became an equally zealous proponent of the gospel of Christ. Paul never recounts in detail the nature of the experience that caused this volte-face (contrast the lengthy accounts in Acts 9:1–30; 22:3–21; 26:9–23) but he does make clear that it was a revelation, a 'seeing', of the risen Christ that was the foundation of his call to be an apostle of Christ to the Gentiles (1 Cor. 9:1; 15:8; Gal. 1:12–16), and that this experience took place near Damascus, as Luke more famously reports (Gal. 1:17; cf. 2 Cor. 11:32). Paul describes this call in a manner reminiscent of the calling of Jeremiah and of the 'servant' of deutero-Isaiah (Jer. 1:5; Isa. 49:1–6; cf. Gal. 1:15–16); in this sense he is not 'converted' at all, but rather commissioned to a new task by the God whom he has served all his life (cf. Stendahl 1976: 7–23). On the other hand, however, although Paul certainly sees his Christian faith as a continuation of the biblical story of God's dealings with Israel and the world, the radical change in perspective and the consequent reinterpretation and re-valuation make the term 'conversion' apposite (cf. Phil. 3:4–14).[13]

Paul understood this conversion experience, which probably took place around 33 CE, a few years after the crucifixion of Jesus,[14] not only as a revelation of Christ to him, but also, at least in retrospect, as his own commission specifically to be apostle to the Gentiles, a role he later affirms in conjunction with Peter's different commission as apostle to the Jews (Gal. 1:15–16; 2:7–8). In the years immediately after his conversion, then, years about which we know so very little,[15] it seems likely that Paul was involved in spreading the message about Christ and making converts

(Murphy-O'Connor 1996: 82), though on what basis is debatable.[16] For about three years he was in Arabia and Damascus (Gal. 1:17). Then he went up to Jerusalem for his first meeting with Peter (Gal. 1:18; c.37 CE). The next nine years were probably spent in activity as a missionary based in Antioch, alongside, or perhaps even under the direction of, Barnabas (Murphy-O'Connor 1996: 96). From around 46 CE, on Murphy-O'Connor's reckoning, Paul became an independent missionary, and began an extensive journey that took him through Galatia, Macedonia, and to Corinth (see Figure 41.1). Fourteen years after his first visit to Jerusalem, in about 51 CE, he returned there again, this time for the 'conference' called to discuss the issue of Gentile converts and the requirements to be placed upon them (see above; Gal. 2:1–10). After this conference Paul undertook another extensive tour, returning first to Antioch, then moving on to Ephesus, Macedonia, Illyricum and Corinth, before returning once more to Jerusalem with the proceeds of his long-standing collection project – money raised from the Pauline congregations for the 'poor among the saints in Jerusalem' (Rom. 15:25–6).[17] After that he undertook a somewhat less voluntary journey, as a prisoner, to Rome, where he may have remained for some time before being executed under Nero some time in the 60s CE. Whether he made his hoped-for visit to Spain (Rom. 15:24) between his first arrival in Rome and his later execution there is possible but seems unlikely, for there is no direct evidence of such a visit.[18]

Whatever the details of his travels and their dates – and the conventional picture of Paul's three missionary journeys is, as John Knox has pointed out, based upon the evidence of Acts more than on that of the epistles (Knox 1987: 25–6) – Paul travelled many thousands of miles, enduring all the dangers of travel: shipwreck, robbery, lack of sleep, hunger and thirst, not to mention punishments by both Roman and Jewish authorities (2 Cor 11:24–9). He did so because he believed he had a crucial role to play – and one he was divinely compelled to play (1 Cor. 9:16–17) – in making the gospel known among the Gentiles (Rom. 15:18–24), so fulfilling his part in the divinely orchestrated drama that was reaching its final culmination. Once the full number of the Gentiles had come in, Paul believed, Israel would then be saved, and God's plan of mercy for humanity could finally be brought to fruition (Rom. 11:25–32), the last enemy of God destroyed (1 Cor. 15:24–6), and the renewed creation liberated to share in the glorious freedom of God's redeemed children (Rom. 8:19–25). And all this, Paul was convinced, lay just around the corner.

These theological convictions motivated Paul and undergirded what he sought to achieve as apostle to the Gentiles. To understand him, therefore, we must attempt to understand his theology, and the message he announced as he travelled round the cities of the Roman empire.[19]

THE HEART OF PAUL'S THEOLOGY:
CENTRAL THEMES

One of the difficulties inhibiting the quest for the heart of Pauline theology is that Paul never wrote a summary either of his theology or of his missionary message. His letters are all, including Romans,[20] shaped by the contingent circumstances of the communities he is addressing and hence are enormously varied. For some the differences lead to the conclusion that Paul was not consistent (Räisänen 1983), while others posit development in his thought over time (Dodd 1934; Hübner 1984). Many, however, consider that Paul was a coherent thinker, even though his expression varies according to situation (Beker 1980, 1990) and even if he reasons 'backwards', from 'solution to plight' (E. P. Sanders 1977: 442–7, 474–51; see below).

It is not easy, then, to express concisely what lies at the centre of Paul's theology. Much of the modern debate revolves around two opposing poles. The first, which finds its roots primarily in Martin Luther's interpretation of Paul, claims that the idea of 'justification by faith' is the key to Paul's gospel. The guilty and undeserving sinner finds unexpected forgiveness from a gracious God. The dominant imagery is juristic or legal: the acquittal of the guilty. The second pole, whose most famous modern exponent is Albert Schweitzer, is the notion of participation in Christ. Schweitzer argued, contrary to Luther, that the mystical notion of 'being-in-Christ' was the key to understanding Pauline teaching: 'once grasped it gives the clue to the whole' (1953: 3). For Schweitzer, in a way 'incomprehensible' to modern people, Paul 'speaks of living men [*sic*] as having already died and risen again with Christ' (1953: 18). These two alternatives remain prominent in much recent discussion, although proponents of either view seek more nuanced ways of expressing their ideas – such as Morna Hooker's notion of 'interchange' (Hooker 1990). E. P. Sanders, for example, insists that 'the "participationist" way of thinking brings us closer to the heart of Paul's thought than the juristic', though he rightly maintains that the two 'sets of terminology' serve to 'interpret' and 'correct' each other (1977: 520; cf. 502–8; 1991: 74). The language of sacrifice and acquital is certainly present in Paul (Rom. 3:23–6; 4:24–5; 5:6–9; 1 Cor. 5:7; 15:3) – so this theme should not be denied – but Sanders is right, I think, to emphasize the centrality for Paul of the language of identification, or participation, 'with' or 'in' Christ (e.g. Rom. 6:1–11; 1 Cor. 15:22; 2 Cor. 5:14–21; Gal. 2:19–20). It is by dying with Christ that the believer is freed from the dominion of sin, and by living in Christ that she or he begins anew as a person with a new identity, a new creation (see further below).

One attempt to circumvent the often polarized debate is that of J. C. Beker (1980; 1990), who argues that at root Paul is an 'apocalyptic theologian' whose thought revolves around the conviction that in Christ God has acted decisively and in a way that demonstrates that the end of time is near. For Beker, 'the real center of Paul's gospel lies in the lordship of Christ as it anticipates the final triumph of God' (1990: 92). According to Beker, neither mystical nor juristic language can rightly be elevated as more fundamental than the other; rather, Paul uses various symbols and themes according to context, which are 'analogous to the coherent field of interlocking circles on the Olympic logo' (Beker 1990: 114).

Certainly Beker has valuably drawn attention to the fact that Paul is a *theocentric* theologian (1980: 362–7; 1990: 21–4, 115). Although his gospel is focused on the death and resurrection of Christ, Paul is always clear that this is the work of *God*, that God is the one whose saving purposes for creation are being worked out and brought to fruition. One need only read, say, Romans 3:21–31, or 1 Corinthians 15:27–8, to see how clearly God is the author of all that Paul describes. And this God is, of course, the God of Abraham and Moses, the God whose dealings with

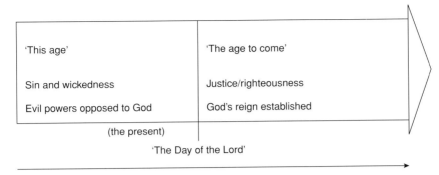

Figure 41.2 Jewish eschatology. Adapted from Davis 1995: 18 by permission of The Edwin Mellen Press. (Cf. further Davis 1995: 16–24.)

his people Israel are recorded in the Hebrew Bible. Paul is quite convinced that it is the promises of God to Abraham – the 'father' of God's people the Jews – which have been fulfilled in Christ, even if he sometimes uses some rather clever exegesis to establish this (e.g. Gal. 3:16; cf. Gen. 12:2–3; 13:15–16; 15:3–6; 17:4–8). The act of God in raising Christ from death, then, is the decisive act of Israel's God, which demonstrates that the end is near. Thus Paul's thought is fundamentally eschatological – orientated towards 'the last things'. The structure of Jewish eschatological hope can be broadly summarized in terms of a contrast between 'this (evil) age' (cf. Gal. 1:4) and 'the age to come', with the day of the Lord expected to mark the establishment of the latter (see e.g. Joel 2; Mal. 4:1–6; *4 Ezra* 7:113; 8:52; Matt. 12:32; Mark 10:30; Figure 41.2). This structure was adopted and altered by Paul and the early Christians, who believed that Christ's coming, and specifically his resurrection, marked the 'beginning of the end': somehow, the decisive and long-awaited intervention of God had happened, but had not yet happened! For believers in Christ, who had died to sin and begun a new life in the power of the Spirit, who were already new creations, the present was a time of tension, an interim time 'between the ages' (see Figure 41.3; cf. Dunn 1998a: 462–6). The time of tension, of groaning, suffering and waiting, was, however, expected to be short; for the day of the Lord would soon come, when the return of Christ would signal the final victory of God and salvation for his people.

We may then attempt to summarize Paul's gospel briefly, though virtually every phrase could be, and often has been, the subject of extended and intricate discussion. The one true God, the God of the Hebrew Bible, has fulfilled his promise to Abraham – to bless all the nations of the earth through him (Gen. 12:3) – in Jesus Christ, who was sent by God as a human being, to die for the sins of humanity. God raised him from death and exalted him as Lord, the firstborn of a new creation, that, in him, all who have faith might also die to sin, to their former lives, and live as holy people in the power of the Spirit, which is given to all who believe. The completion of the process of salvation is near, when the mysterious plan of God to show mercy to all and to restore the whole creation will finally come to fruition, and when believers will live with the Lord forever.

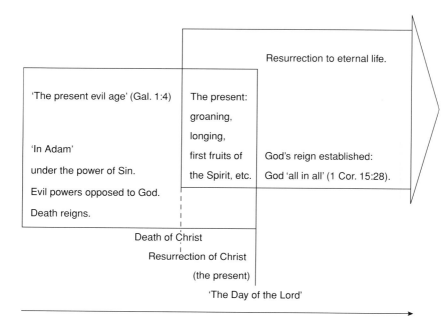

The content of the figure:

Resurrection to eternal life.

'The present evil age' (Gal. 1:4)

'In Adam' under the power of Sin.

Evil powers opposed to God.

Death reigns.

The present: groaning, longing, first fruits of the Spirit, etc.

God's reign established: God 'all in all' (1 Cor. 15:28).

Death of Christ

Resurrection of Christ

(the present)

'The Day of the Lord'

Figure 41.3 Pauline eschatology. Adapted from Davis 1995: 24 by permission of The Edwin Mellen Press. (Cf. further Davis 1995: 16–24.)

To understand this somewhat compact summary, and to appreciate some of the tensions and debates it conceals, it is necessary to examine various areas of Paul's theology in more depth. We begin with what from Paul's own writing can clearly be seen to be central: Christ (cf. Phil. 3:7–11).

Christology

While it is God who is the author of all Paul describes, and God who will ultimately be all in all (1 Cor. 15:28), the focus of Paul's devotion and proclamation is Christ, and specifically his death and resurrection. Paul clearly shares and repeats the early Christian creed: Christ died for us (*hyper hēmōn*) and was raised from the dead (cf. 1 Cor. 15:3–4). Here again the debate concerning the 'heart' of Paul's theology looms large: Did Paul understand the significance of Christ's death primarily in sacrificial or in participationist terms? Paul certainly presents the view that Christ died as a means of atonement for the transgressions of others (Rom. 3:22–5; 4:24–5; 5:6–9; 1 Cor. 15:3), a view he seems most likely to have inherited from his predecessors, and is happy to repeat. But his own thought is arguably more focused on the participatory idea of dying *with* Christ: 'the prime significance which the death of Christ has for Paul is not that it provides atonement for past transgressions (although he holds the common Christian view that it does so), but that, by *sharing* in Christ's death, one dies to the *power* of sin or to the old aeon, with the result that one *belongs to God* . . . The transfer takes place by *participation* in Christ's death' (E. P. Sanders 1977: 467–8, citing Rom. 6:3–11; 7:4; Gal. 2:19–20; 5:24; Phil. 3:10–11, etc.). In the death of Christ God has not only dealt with past transgressions, but has provided the way in which believers in Christ can be liberated from the dominion of sin, by dying with Christ; in the resurrection of Christ God has not only vindicated Christ and exalted him as Lord, but has also made him the firstborn of a resurrected new humanity (cf. 1 Cor. 15:20). Those who live in Christ look forward confidently to their own attainment of resurrection from the dead (Phil. 3:11).

The appellation 'Christ', so frequent in Paul, is itself a declaration of faith, an affirmation about who Jesus is: the Greek word *Christos* is a translation of the Hebrew *Mashiah*, Messiah, anointed one. Thus Paul's primary conviction about Jesus is that he is the expected Messiah, the anointed one of God, sent to save and restore God's people. Equally fundamental for Paul, and also frequent in his letters, is the affirmation that Jesus is Lord, this affirmation being the touchstone of Christian confession (Rom. 10:9; 1 Cor. 12:3). Somewhat less frequently attested, though nevertheless significant, is the description of Jesus as Son of God (Rom. 1:4; 8:3; 1 Cor. 1:9; 2 Cor. 1:19; Gal. 2:20; 4:4; 1 Thess. 1:10; etc.). Each of these 'titles' – Christ, Lord, Son of God – has roots in the Jewish scriptures, though the latter two

Figure 41.4 One of many Roman coins naming Octavian as CAESAR DIVI F[ilius]. (Octavian, who was later to become Augustus and first emperor, had been adopted as the son of Julius Caesar, deified after his death.) The drawing shows the reverse of the coin, minted about 31–29 BCE, with Victory standing on a globe holding a wreath and palm. For a plate of the coin see Sutherland (1974: pl. 213). For many other examples see Mattingley (1965: pl. 15, etc.).

also have resonances in the wider world of the Roman empire, where the emperors adopted or were given various titles, including *kyrios* (Lord) and *divi filius* (son of the divine; see Figure 41.4).[21] None of these terms in themselves *necessarily* implies that Jesus is divine, nor that he is 'God the Son' in the later sense of the trinitarian confession. Indeed, there has been considerable debate as to whether Paul actually thought of Jesus as divine and pre-existent or not.

In an important but controversial book, *Christology in the Making* (1980, 1989[2]), James Dunn argues that Paul did not view Jesus as a pre-existent divine figure who became 'incarnate' at his birth. On the contrary, Dunn argues, Paul's Jesus was a man in whom God's 'wisdom' and power are embodied, and who, through his obedience to the call and commission of God, was raised and exalted to become Lord. A particularly crucial passage is Philippians 2:5–11, most likely a pre-existing hymn to Christ, which Paul adapts for his purposes in that letter (see Martin 1983). According to Dunn, the hymn is best read in the light of its parallels with the story of Adam in Genesis 1–3: both Adam and Jesus were made in God's image, yet while Adam reached out to become like God (Gen. 3:5, 22), Jesus willingly took the role of humble obedience, even to the point of death on the cross. Because of his obedience, he accomplished the restoration of what Adam had ruined, and was exalted by God to the position of Lord, from where he will receive the acclamation due to God himself (cf. Isa. 45:23; Dunn 1980: 114–21; 1998a: 281–8).

Without needing to deny the parallels with the Adam story here and elsewhere in Paul, it seems to me more compelling to follow those who consider that Philippians 2:5–11 does encapsulate a belief in Christ's pre-existence (e.g. Casey 1991: 112–13; Fee 1995: 203 n. 41; Bockmuehl 1997). Such pre-existence is also hinted at in 1 Corinthians 8:6 and probably 2 Corinthians 8:9 (which Dunn interprets as referring to the moment of Christ's death, rather than his becoming human; Dunn 1980: 122).[22] It is notable, however, that Paul avoids stating that Jesus *was* God (note Phil. 2:6, 11). Within the framework of Jewish monotheism at the time, Paul and the early Christians could affirm Jesus' pre-existence with God from the beginning of time and his exalted position as God's supreme agent, since there were parallels in Jewish scripture and tradition, notably in the personification of wisdom as God's agent in creation (see esp. Prov. 8:22–31; Wisd. 7:22–8:1; Sir. 24:2–22).[23] Indeed, the wisdom tradition seems likely to have influenced Paul's Christological language at some points (1 Cor. 1:21–30; 8:6), and certainly influenced the follower of Paul who wrote Colossians (Col. 1:15–20). Precisely because he was a Jew and thus a monotheist, however, Paul not only avoids calling Jesus God, but also retains a clear and careful distinction between God (the Father) and Christ (the Lord), in places clearly implying the subordination of Christ to God (see esp. 1 Cor. 3:23; 11:3; 15:28; cf. also 8:6; Phil. 2:11, etc.).[24]

One of the characteristics of Paul's Christology is what has been termed his 'corporate Christology'. In this area of his thinking, the parallels with Adam are particularly significant. Paul refers to Adam as a 'type' of Christ (Rom. 5:14); indeed, he explicitly speaks of 'the first Adam' and 'the last Adam', contrasting their identities and roles (1 Cor. 15:45–9; cf. Barrett 1962; Scroggs 1966). In Romans 5:12–21 the nature and scope of Christ's redemption are described by contrast with Adam: through the disobedience of one man (Adam), sin and death came into the world and affected all humanity, but through the obedience of one man (Christ) came grace, righteousness and eternal life. The life of humanity under the power of sin and death can be described as life 'in Adam' (1 Cor. 15:22); similarly, the life of those who with Christ have died to this realm of sin and death (see Rom. 6:1–11) is described as life 'in Christ', a phrase Adolf Deissmann long ago emphasized as frequent and significant in Paul.[25] Christians live, individually (2 Cor. 5:17; 12:2) and corporately (1 Cor. 12:12–27; Gal. 3:26–8), 'in Christ'; indeed, they *are* the body of Christ (1 Cor. 12:27). This body-image is one of Paul's most profound and memorable descriptions of 'the church' – a rather anachronistic term for the local gatherings of Christians, which Paul called *ekklēsiai*, the usual term for the gathering of citizens in a Greek city, and frequently used in the LXX of the 'assembly' of Israel (*ekklēsia* translating the Hebrew *qāhāl*).[26]

The Spirit, ethics and the Christian community

Paul writes to his fellow followers of Christ as members of a local *ekklēsia*, a body of people who together are citizens of heaven (Phil. 3:20), and who eagerly await the return of Christ to announce God's final triumph. The rite of initiation into this new movement was baptism, administered in the name of Christ Jesus, which symbolized believers' participation in the death of Christ, and their taking on a new identity, clothed with Christ, dead to the old, alive to the new (Rom. 6:1–11; 1 Cor. 1:13–15; Gal. 3:26–9). At the regular gatherings for worship and instruction, the Christians shared a meal together that recalled the fundamental narrative of their faith – about 'the Lord Jesus, on the night when he was betrayed' (1 Cor. 11:23) – and demonstrated their integration into one body in Christ (1 Cor. 10:16–17).[27] They are addressed by Paul as 'holy ones' (*hagioi*), brothers and sisters (*adelphoi*), fellow members of the body of Christ.

As such, Paul's Christian converts are clearly expected to live in a particular way, to be distinctive, set apart ('holy') from the 'evil age' in which they live. A number of times in his letters, Paul paints in stark colours the contrasts between his converts' former and present lives, between evil things and good things (Rom. 13:11–14; 1 Cor. 6:9–11; Gal. 5:19–23). Yet these 'lists' of vices and virtues can apparently be both a description of a change that has taken place and a warning, or exhortation, about the ways in which people must live if they are to inherit God's kingdom. Indeed, one of the puzzles in Pauline ethics is to comprehend the relationship between what is generally labelled the 'indicative' and the 'imperative'.[28] As we have already seen, Paul describes believers as people who have died with Christ; they have died to sin and are new creations. These are indicative statements about their new identity. Yet living in a way 'appropriate' (in Paul's view) to being a new person in Christ clearly did not simply come automatically. Indeed, Paul was sometimes scandalized at the conduct of some of his converts (1 Cor. 5:1–13). He had to urge them to act rightly, to live in a holy manner; and so, along with the indicatives, we find imperatives (cf. e.g. Rom. 6:2–10 with 6:11–14; see also 1 Cor. 10:14; 1 Thess. 4:9–12). The relation between indicative and imperative in Pauline ethics has often been summarized in the phrase 'Be what you are!' For Paul it is profoundly true to say that a believer *has* already died with Christ and is already a new person; yet in the in-between times, the (short) time between the resurrection of Christ and his final return, there is also a sense in which this dying and rising has not yet occurred (hence another popular epitome of Pauline eschatology: 'already but not yet'). The final act in the drama, the defeat of death itself and the day of resurrection, lies in the future, and so the completion of the process of redemption, the redemption of the body (Rom. 8:23), is still awaited. While dying with Christ can be spoken of as having already happened, resurrection for the believer remains for Paul a future hope (see Rom. 6:4–5; 8:22–5; E. P. Sanders 1977: 449–50, 468; Beker 1990: 73, 85; contrast Col. 2:12; 3:1). In the here and now, Christians must make a commitment; they must 'set their minds' one way and not the other, must live in the power of the Spirit and not allow sin to reign over them (Rom. 8:5–13). They must anticipate what will soon be complete. To this extent Pauline ethics is eschatologically orientated, though the imminence of Christ's return is not, in my view, as controlling a theme as some have suggested (J. T. Sanders 1975). Rather, it is their identity 'in Christ' that for Paul lies at the foundation of believers' conduct, and specifically the fact that they are brothers and sisters, co-members of the one body of Christ. On these grounds, and in fulfilment of a commandment of the Jewish scriptures (the command to love one's neighbour; see Lev. 19:18; Rom. 13:9; Gal. 5:14), Christians are urged to be pure and holy, to love one another, to imitate Christ in looking to the interests of the other (e.g. Phil. 2:1–16).

While the theological underpinning of Pauline ethics consists primarily in believers' identity in Christ, and in the need for them to live holy lives in the power of the Spirit, the substance of Pauline ethics is derived from various sources. Already mentioned immediately above are the Jewish scriptures and the example of Christ. Also to be considered are the various parallels between Paul's ethics and various Graeco-Roman sources, especially those of the Stoics and Cynics (Malherbe 1989; Deming 1995; Downing 1998), though the extent of such influence on Paul is debated. Paul certainly cites and alludes to the Jewish scriptures in his ethical exhortations (see e.g. Rosner 1994) and is deeply shaped by his Jewish heritage – for example, in his aversion to idolatry and sexual immorality (cf. Rom. 1:18–31 and Wisd. 13–15). However, he makes very little clear reference to the teaching of Jesus. The number of echoes and allusions to that teaching is much disputed, but most scholars are agreed that there are at most only a handful of *explicit* references (1 Cor. 7:10–11; 9:14; 11:23–5; perhaps Rom. 14:14; 1 Thess. 4:15–17).[29] Moreover, some of these teachings may have come to Paul mediated as Christian teaching or liturgy, so he may not cite them specifically as *Jesus'* words (e.g. 1 Cor. 11:23–5; 1 Thess. 4:15–17), and in one case, he refers to Jesus' teaching, only to state that he does not follow it (1 Cor. 9:14–15; Horrell 1997a). More important, perhaps, is Paul's emphasis on Jesus as an example, with the pattern of Christ's self-giving serving as a paradigm for Christian morality (Rom. 15:2–3; Phil. 2:3–8; 1 Cor. 11:1; see Horrell 1997b: 105–9; Dunn 1994: 168–73).

The power to live a holy life in the in-between time before the return of Christ, is, for Paul, given by the Spirit (Rom. 8:1–17) – 'God's empowering presence', active in the world and in the lives of God's people (Fee 1994). Just as there is a basic contrast in Paul's thought between life 'in Adam' and life 'in Christ', so another clear dichotomy is between life *kata sarka* (according to the flesh) and life *kata pneuma* (according to the Spirit). The former produces deeds of wickedness that lead to destruction, whereas the latter produces the fruit of love, joy, peace, patience, and so on (Gal. 5:16–26). More fundamentally than this even, the Spirit is the essential mark of someone's being a true Christian (Rom. 8:9; 1 Cor. 12:3). The Spirit affirms their adoption as God's children (Rom. 8:14–29; Gal. 3:26; 4:4–7; see Scott 1992), gives diverse gifts for the good of the whole community (1 Cor. 12:4–11), produces the fruit of holy living (Gal. 5:22–3), and groans and prays with the believer in their present time of suffering and yearning for redemption (Rom. 8:26–7). How Paul conceives of the consummation of this process of redemption we shall consider further below.

Israel and the Law

Thus far we have focused on Paul's commitment to Christ, and on how he understands the implications of what God has done in Christ for those who now live as Christians. Yet throughout it is obvious that Paul's gospel is a thoroughly Jewish message, rooted in the Jewish scriptures and in a claim about how the God of Israel has acted in fulfilment of his covenant promises to Abraham. But although the very notion of messianic hope is also entirely Jewish, Paul's insistence that these promises of God have been fulfilled in *Christ* – beside whom all his Jewish credentials are nothing but 'crap'[30] – distances him from his fellow (non-Christian) Jews. For them, there is simply no reason to believe that this crucified messianic leader, despatched by the Romans like so many other deluded characters, marks the pivotal and long-awaited intervention of their God. For Paul, on the other hand, convinced of Christ's resurrection and lordship through his vision, his christophany, Christ is the one in whom God has manifested his saving righteousness and through whom all the nations will come to join Israel in worshipping God, just as the prophets foresaw (Isa. 2:1–5; Micah 4:1–5). One of the most prominent areas of recent discussion in Pauline studies, then, and one with considerable implications for Christian theology and Jewish–Christian dialogue, concerns Paul's Christian view of the law, which he had as a Pharisee so zealously sought to uphold, and of God's people Israel. Only a very brief sketch of the issues and of recent discussion can be given here.

In seeking to present his gospel as the fulfilment of God's promises to Israel, as the culmination of Israel's hopes, yet at the same time insisting that salvation is to be found, for both Jew and Gentile, only in *Christ,* Paul is caught in a profound tension. He would never take the route later taken by Marcion, denying that the 'Old Testament' God had anything to do with the God who had acted in Jesus Christ. Paul is insistent that the same God was at work throughout Israel's history and in Christ, and that Israel's law and scriptures, given by God, testify faithfully to God's purposes now fulfilled in Christ. On the other hand, however, since Paul is convinced that salvation is found only in Christ, he has to maintain that Israel's law – the basis of her identity and covenant relationship with God – cannot 'save', for else Christ died in vain (cf. Gal. 2:21).

In short, Paul has to maintain that God gave the law, but that salvation is now found in Christ. He cannot therefore condemn the law, for that would be to deny its God-given nature or to impugn God, but neither can he portray it as sufficient to create a righteous people, for then Christ came to no purpose. Hence we find in Paul both negative and positive comments about the Jewish law (positive statements include Rom. 7:12, 22; 13:8–10; Gal. 5:14; negative ones are 1 Cor. 15:56; 2 Cor. 3:6–11; Gal. 3:10–13; etc.).

The problem over which scholars continue to wrestle, with little apparent agreement, is how to make coherent sense of Paul's view of the law, if indeed coherent sense can be made of his varied and contrasting statements (for overviews of recent discussion see Thielman 1994; Roetzel 1995; Kruse 1997). Discussion of this issue has been decisively influenced by the publication of a book often credited with opening up a whole new perspective on Paul (see Dunn 1983), E. P. Sanders' *Paul and Palestinian Judaism* (1977). Sanders showed how New Testament scholars, often influenced by a Lutheran understanding of Paul's gospel, had presented a negative caricature of Judaism, portraying it as a religion of 'legalistic works-righteousness', a religion in which people sought to earn their salvation by notching up a sufficient quantity of 'good works'. Through an exhaustive study of relevant Jewish texts, Sanders sought to demonstrate that this portrayal of Judaism was completely inaccurate. He proposed instead that Judaism's 'pattern of religion' could be epitomized in the term 'covenantal nomism': the basic foundation of Judaism was the covenant, made through the gracious and generous initiative of God, and the appropriate response on the part of those who were members of the covenant people was to live in obedience to the way of life, the *Torah* or law (Greek: *nomos*) given by God. Obedience to this law did not earn one's place in the covenant people; it served to sustain and confirm it (E. P. Sanders 1977: 419–28).

Sanders' book has given rise to considerable discussion, and books and articles on Paul and the law abound. But whether they agree or disagree partly or profoundly with Sanders, scholars have certainly been forced to consider Judaism at the time of Paul on its own terms, and not rest content with Christian caricatures. In the light of Sanders' work, however, the question remains as to how then to understand Paul's criticisms of the law. Was Paul not attacking 'legalism', and if he was not, what was he criticizing and why?

Sanders' own answer is essentially that Paul is reasoning from a new perspective: since he is now convinced that God has acted in Christ to save all, both Jew and Gentile, Paul reasons backwards to the conclusion that all must have needed saving. Paul as a pre-Christian Jew did not feel himself to be labouring under a heavy conscience, under the weight of impossible legal commands; on the contrary, he evidences a robust view of his (previous) status under the law (Phil. 3:6; Stendahl 1976: 78–96). But having become convinced that Christ is indeed God's chosen way to save all people, Paul's perspective on his Jewish past radically alters. 'In short', Sanders argues, *'this is what Paul finds wrong in Judaism: it is not Christianity'* (1977: 552, his emphasis). The apparent inconsistency in Paul's statements about the law can be resolved, Sanders suggests, by observing that Paul gives different answers to different questions (E. P. Sanders 1983). To the question 'How does someone enter the people of God' Paul's answer is emphatically, 'Not by works of law but by faith in Christ' (Rom. 3:28; Gal. 2:16). But on the question of what behaviour is appropriate for those who are 'in' God's people, and wish to remain 'in', the answer is that the law's demands must be fulfilled, not in all its particular requirements (specifically circumcision, food laws and sabbath observance), but in its basic demand of love for one's neighbour (Rom. 8:4; 13:8–10; Gal. 5:14; E. P. Sanders 1983: 93–135).

Inevitably, some scholars have not found Sanders' reconstructed Paul convincing, and other attempts to make sense of Paul's view of the law abound. Heikki Räisänen, for example, argues that Paul's statements on the law are more contradictory and inconsistent than Sanders allows and that they simply cannot be reconciled or brought into a coherent schema (Räisänen 1983). Going further than those who have suggested that Paul's views change between different letters, especially between Galatians and Romans (Hübner 1984; cf. Drane 1975), Räisänen maintains that even within one and the same letter, Paul's statements about the Jewish law do not reveal a consistent perspective.

At the other end of the spectrum are scholars who insist that Paul is rather more consistent than scholars like Räisänen allow, but who nevertheless are unsatisfied with Sanders' Paul. Some, while taking Sanders seriously, have argued with renewed conviction the case for a largely 'traditional' understanding of Paul's criticism of the law and his doctrine of justification by faith (e.g Westerholm 1988; 1991: 57–74; 1997). Others have sought to develop a 'new perspective' on Paul, indebted to, yet differing from, Sanders. James Dunn, for example, regards Sanders' picture of Paul as unsatisfactory, presenting a Paul who simply and arbitrarily jumps from one system of religion to another, without there being any real reason or sense in his critique of Judaism (Dunn 1990: 186–7). Dunn accepts Sanders' presentation of the Judaism contemporary with Paul, and thus agrees that Paul cannot have been attacking legalism *per se*, nor the idea that doing good works could lead to salvation, since Jews did not believe this anyway. Rather, Dunn argues, Paul attacks the way in which the Jews of his time regarded the works of the law as a boundary marker demarcating who is and who is not 'in' the people of God; he attacks their narrow, racially, ethnically, and geographically defined notion of God's people and, in its place, sets out a more 'open', inclusive, form of Judaism (based on faith in Christ). Thus, 'Paul's criticism of Judaism was, more accurately described, a criticism of the xenophobic strand of Judaism, to which Paul himself had previously belonged . . . Paul was in effect converting from a closed Judaism to an open Judaism' (Dunn 1998b: 261; cf. 271; 1998a: 137–50, 349–66, 514–19).

However, despite his clear advocacy of a 'new perspective' on Paul, Dunn's Paul is perhaps not as different from the Lutheran Paul as Dunn himself suggests (Campbell 1998: 99–101; Matlock 1998: 86). Instead of criticizing his fellow Jews for their legalism, Paul now criticizes them for their xenophobia, or ethnocentric separatism, but the basic structure remains the same: there really was a 'problem' with Judaism and Christ really was the answer! That formulation should highlight how theologically loaded Dunn's perspective is; nothing wrong with that, of course, as long as we make clear that this is Paul's *Christian* perspective on Judaism.[31] Moreover, what Dunn sees as an 'open' form of Judaism is of course a Judaism (if the term can still be appropriately claimed) based on belief in Christ, with its own forms of particularism and exclusivism (see Barclay 1997). While Dunn is right that *Paul* did not see himself as in any way betraying his Jewish heritage, his evangelistic message to the Gentiles was entirely based on the conviction that it is in the crucified and risen Christ that God has fulfilled his promises to Israel. His argument only makes sense from that perspective – here I think Sanders is right – and while Paul is utterly convinced of its truth it is equally understandable that most of his Jewish contemporaries were not.

Paul reasons from a 'Christian' perspective. From that viewpoint, a decisive moment has occurred in the death and resurrection of Christ, and a new era has begun. Whereas people previously lived under law, as human beings 'in Adam', enslaved to the power of sin, now they can live in Christ, dead to the old era, alive in the Spirit, by whose power they 'walk in newness of life' (Rom. 6:4). The law belongs to the old era, so even though its righteous requirements will be fulfilled by those who live in Christ (Rom. 8:4; 13:8–10; Gal. 5:14), Christians, whether they be Jew or Gentile, no longer live 'under law' (*hypo nomon*) but live 'in Christ', in the power of the Spirit (Rom. 6:14–15; 1 Cor. 9:20; Gal. 2:14–21). To a considerable extent Paul's dispute with his fellow Jews, and specifically with his Jewish-Christian opponents, concerns a fundamental question of boundaries and *identity*: from a Jewish perspective it is living in obedience to Torah that defines the identity of the people of God called Israel; Paul argues that the people of God – the 'true' Israel, as he sees it – find their identity in Christ alone.

Even that summary, contentious though it doubtless is, raises a further question: Why then did God give the law, if it was inadequate for the task of creating a righteous people? Paul recognizes the force of this question, and attempts a number of answers to it, even though, again, scholars disagree as to how exactly to interpret those answers. Clearly Paul regards the law as given for a time, a time now ended, since Christ has come (Rom. 10:4; Gal. 4:4–5) and God's children have come of age (Gal. 4:1–7). In Galatians 3:19–25, Paul gives the law a temporary and subsidiary role in the purposes of God (cf. Ziesler 1992: 44–9): it was given 'because of transgressions'[32] (that is, probably, to provide a means of reckoning, limiting, and dealing with sin) and came 'through angels by a mediator' (Gal. 3:19), a description that relativizes the status of the law *vis-à-vis* the promise made to Abraham (cf. Gal. 3:15–18). The law acted as a tutor, or guardian (*paidagōgos*; Gal. 3:24), until Christ came, in whom people are redeemed from 'the curse of the law' (Gal. 3:13). In Romans 7, where Paul is a good deal less angry and confrontational than in Galatians, he is more concerned to defend the law's status. The bondage of humankind under sin is not the law's fault. On the contrary, the law itself is 'holy, just and good' (Rom. 7:12); the fault lies with sin (portrayed as an almost personified 'power'). In two similar yet different attempts to elucidate this situation, Paul first portrays sin as stealing in to take advantage of the opportunity the law offered (Rom. 7:7–12) and secondly describes a divided self in which the inner self delights in the law of God and wishes to do right, while the outer self is subject to the law of sin (7:13–25; see further E. P. Sanders 1983: 65–91). The deliverance from this anguished situation comes through the Spirit-empowered new life in Christ (Rom. 7:24 – 8:4). The law, then, was given to show what was right and to keep track of sin, but was powerless to liberate humanity from the power of sin, under which all in Adam are enslaved.

A further pressing question underlies all this: What has become of Israel's special status as God's people? Crucial questions concerning God's faithfulness and reliability are at stake here (cf. Meeks 1991): Does God make promises but then break them, or try plan A but abandon it for a new plan if it fails? Here again Paul was aware of the questions, but once more was caught in an awkward tension by the very nature of the gospel he proclaimed. Especially in Romans, Paul tries to hold together on the one hand the assertion that both Jew and Gentile are equally in need of salvation and are dealt with on the same basis by an impartial God (Rom. 1:16; 2:9–11; 3:20, 29–30; 10:12–13), and on the other hand the insistence that Israel does indeed have a special status and that God's gift and call to her are irrevocable (3:1; 9:4–5; 11:29).[33] This awkward tension is clearly visible, for example, in Romans 3:1–9. To the rhetorical question 'What advantage, then, has the Jew?' Paul replies, 'much in every way' (3:1–2). Yet only a few verses later Paul refutes any claim to special confidence or defence on the part of the Jews, since 'all, both Jews and Greeks, are under sin' (3:9b).[34]

However, it is in Romans 9–11 that Paul turns to face these issues head on. These chapters are among the most dense and difficult in the Pauline corpus, as Paul wrestles to make sense of God's purposes and their implications for the people of Israel. Paul's anguish over the matter is clear (9:1–3) and his need to explain Israel's lack of faith (in Christ) pressing. Various reasons are given in this profound yet complex argument, as it progresses (and progress it does) through the three chapters. 'Not all Israelites are true Israelites', is one argument (9:6–13); 'God is sovereign and can do as he likes', is another (9:14–29).[35] 'Only a remnant of Israel is faithful, as at other times in her history', is a further explanation (11:1–6). Finally, Paul sees a divine purpose in the faithlessness of Israel, and in the faith found among the Gentiles: just as Israel's rejection meant the offer of salvation to the Gentiles, so in turn the salvation of the Gentiles will make Israel jealous and in the end 'all Israel will be saved' (11:7–27; cf. 9:30 – 10:21; Bell 1994). This is indeed, Paul exclaims, as well he might, a 'mystery' (11:25–6), and he does not answer the questions that immediately crop up in our minds: What does he mean by *all* Israel? Does he mean every individual Israelite who has ever lived, or only the 'true' Israelites he referred to earlier? And will Israel be saved when she finally comes to have faith in Christ, or simply as Israel – since God's gifts and call are irrevocable?[36] Yet even the mystery of Israel's final salvation is only a part, albeit a central one, in the wider mystery with which chapter 11 ends. That is the mystery of God's plan to have mercy on all people, Jews and Gentiles (11:30–2), a marvellous yet mysterious plan to which Paul can only respond with words of wonder and praise (11:33–6). Here too Paul hardly answers all the questions about which we would like to have heard his views: Does he mean *all* people? And if he does, how does he hold together the need for people to turn in faith from wickedness to Christ with his conviction that God's sovereign plan of salvation will ultimately be unstoppable? Without formulating it in so many words, Paul is of course caught on the horns of a well-known theological dilemma: how to hold together both human responsibility and the sovereignty of God. And without denying either side of the tension, it is important to do justice to the theme of God's universal mercy in Paul, to Paul's vision of the redemption not only of all humanity but also of the whole creation (Rom. 8:21), not least because these have all too often been ignored. That leads us on to consideration of one final theme: Paul's hopes for the future, his vision of the eschaton.

The goal of salvation: Paul's view of the eschaton

In his earliest letter, 1 Thessalonians, Paul describes the Thessalonian Christians as having 'turned to God from idols . . . to wait for his Son from heaven' (1 Thess. 1:9–10). Later in the same letter he deals with the apparent worries caused to some of the Thessalonians by the fact that some of their number had died before this expected return of God's Son (4:13 – 5:11). The message they had heard from Paul had clearly led them to expect an imminent return of Christ, and an imminent end to the process of their salvation. Paul's response to their worries indicates that he still envisages Christ's return as very near (4:15), and as an apocalyptic event when those in Christ, both dead and living, will be caught up to meet the Lord in the air, to be with him for ever. The precise time is unknown, but the day will come suddenly, 'like a thief in the night' (1 Thess. 5:2; cf. Matt. 24:43; Luke 12:39).

By the time of 1 Corinthians it may be that more of the first generation of Christians have died (1 Cor. 15:51; cf. Lüdemann 1984: 239–41) and because of the specific problem Paul is dealing with at Corinth he focuses primarily on the future resurrection of all believers. But the general picture is similar to that in 1 Thessalonians: the final day of victory and resurrection will soon come, following in order from the event of Christ's resurrection, for he is 'the first-fruits of those who have fallen asleep' (15:20). On this final day, announced by the sound of the trumpet (15:51; 1 Thess. 4:16), not only will the dead in Christ rise and be clothed with immortality, but death and sin will finally be destroyed; God will complete the task of subjecting all such powers to Christ, and so Christ will be subjected to God, who will be 'all in all' – almost a panentheistic vision of the final consummation of the saving work of God in Christ (see 15:20–8, 35–50; Héring 1962: 169).

Perhaps through the experiences of near-death suffering and imprisonment (Dodd 1934; Harvey 1996), Paul comes in later letters to reflect more on the possibility of his own death, and on the confidence with which he faces death. In 2 Corinthians 5:1–5, for example, he describes the transition from earthly life to heavenly life in terms of an unclothing and reclothing: he will one day leave his earthly tent (a metaphor for the body) and put on a heavenly dwelling (cf. also Phil. 1:20–4, written from prison). Whether or not Paul is anxious about the time of disembodiment he might face between death and the final resurrection is not altogether clear,[37] but it is clear that his reflections on death are framed by his belief in the final day of judgment (5:10) and his hope for resurrection (4:14; Phil. 3:11). In Romans 8:18–39 the contrast between the sufferings of the present and the far greater glory to come is powerfully portrayed. Paul is confident that no suffering or hardship – absolutely nothing (see 8:35–9) – can separate Christians from the love of God in Christ, while they await the completion of the process of redemption already begun and anticipated on earth (8:23). Unique to Romans 8 in Paul's writings is the vision of the whole creation yearning for the completion of God's saving work, yearning for the liberation that will come when God's children are revealed (8:20–3).

Although the most extensive discussions of the final day of victory and resurrection are found in Paul's earlier letters, whereas reflections on the prospect of death occur in later letters, the evidence does not really support the idea of a change in Paul's mind, as has sometimes been suggested (Dodd 1934). Changes in emphasis there may be, caused by Paul's own experiences of suffering and imprisonment and by the delay of the Lord's return, but the expectant hope for the final day of salvation is a constant feature throughout (Rom. 13:11–13; Phil. 3:11, 20–1; 4:5). Paul's theology is eschatologically orientated: he is constantly looking forward amid the sufferings and pressures of the present to the completion of the process of redemption, the salvation of Israel and of all humanity (Rom. 11:25–32), the liberation of creation, and the resurrection and immortality of God's children. These are the future visions towards which Paul's life and work as apostle of Jesus Christ are orientated; these are the goals that drove him on with resolute determination: 'One thing I do: forgetting what lies behind and straining forward to what lies ahead, I press on toward the goal for the prize of the heavenly call of God in Christ Jesus' (Phil. 3:13–14 NRSV)

PAUL'S LEGACY IN THE NEW TESTAMENT AND BEYOND

Because of the debate about Paul's authorship of some of the letters attributed to him, it is difficult to say where Paul ends and the interpretation of Paul begins. If we accept only the seven letters listed above as authentically from Paul, then the appropriation and reinterpretation of Paul's theology begins in 2 Thessalonians, Colossians and Ephesians (see Beker 1992). In these letters we find characteristic Pauline themes and phrases, yet also significant theological developments, such as the more realized eschatology of Colossians (2:12; 3:1), together with its more exalted Christology (1:15–20; 2:9–10) and more conservative social teaching (3:18 – 4:1). The Pastoral Epistles stand at an even clearer distance from Paul, with new themes and phraseology reflecting the demands of a different time and context. With the apostle long since dead, and the perceived threat of heretics and false teachers pressing, a prime concern is to preserve and guard what is seen as sound teaching (1 Tim. 1:10; 6:3; etc.), the 'deposit' of the apostolic generation (1 Tim. 6:20; 2 Tim. 1:14). This deposit, however, appears only in concise credal formulae (e.g. 1 Tim. 3:16) and the theological themes characteristic of Paul are hardly developed at all; instead we find an emphasis on the need for behaviour that is decent and respectable (e.g. 1 Tim. 3:1–13; 6:1–2; Titus 2:1–10; cf. Verner 1983: 147–60).

It is certainly clear, even within the New Testament itself, that Paul's legacy rapidly became subject to varied and disputed interpretations. The complexity of his letters, and their extended arguments, may well have contributed to the diversity of appropriations of Paul (2 Pet. 3:15–16) and to the tendency to focus on Paul as a heroic apostolic figure rather than on the substance of his teaching (see further Lindemann 1979; Babcock 1990). Paul was as popular – perhaps more popular – with versions of Christianity that were eventually deemed to be 'heretical' as in what we might call 'orthodox' circles, as can be seen from some of the apocryphal literature (e.g. the Acts of Paul) and from the use of Paul's writings by the Gnostics (see Pagels 1975), not to mention his centrality for Marcion. Indeed it can be claimed with some justification that Paul's theology was more frequently ignored or misinterpreted than understood in the subsequent history of the Church.

Paul's writings have, however, played an enormously important role in the thinking of some of the great and most influential figures in Church history. The names of Augustine and Luther are most frequently mentioned. Whether they redis-covered or distorted the apostle's teaching – or perhaps, inevitably, to some degree both – may be open to dispute, but the power and influence of their interpretations cannot be denied. Paul was not 'the founder of Christianity', nor hardly even 'the second founder of Christianity', but his thought and letters were of enormous signifi-cance in the construction of Christian, as distinct from Jewish, identity. Paul's letters continue both to inspire and to irritate, to challenge and to confuse, not only within the Christian Church. He remains a mountain on the landscape of Christian history and an enormous influence on all subsequent Christian theology.[38]

NOTES

1 For this image, see the marvellous poem entitled 'Paul' by R. S. Thomas (172–3 in *Later Poems*, London: Macmillan, 1983).
2 Quoted by Beker 1990: 62.
3 A view represented by Maccoby 1991. Wilson 1997 also makes much of the influence of non-Jewish religions on Paul; note the critique in Wright 1997: 167–78.
4 The precise sense of the Greek *historēsai Kēphan* (Gal. 1:18) has been much discussed; see e.g. Dunn 1990: 110–13, 126–8.
5 For a brief overview of this period from the perspective of the 'Jewish Christianity' repre-sented by James, Peter, etc., see Horrell 2000: 138–41.
6 See esp. Hengel 1983: 1–29, 53–8; also Wedderburn 1989a; Räisänen 1992: 149–202.
7 For criticisms of Hill, see Esler 1995.
8 Hengel and Schwemer (1997: xi) date the beginning of the mission of the 'Hellenists' in Antioch to c. 36/37. They stress the importance of the Hellenists to the early Christian mission, but also emphasize both that this Gentile mission is not strictly *pre*-Pauline (see 31–4, 208, 281, etc.), since Paul was converted in c. 33 CE, and that Paul was crucial in establishing and justifying theologically the Gentile mission (309).
9 See e.g. Justin's comments on those within the Church who practise the Jewish way of life (*Dial.* 46–7). On Jewish Christianity and its eventual exclusion from 'orthodox Christianity', see Horrell 2000.
10 I take it that these two accounts describe the same occasion, though that is not universally agreed.
11 There has been extensive discussion of the 'incident at Antioch' and the issues surrounding it; see e.g. Dunn 1990: 129–82; Esler 1987: 71–109; 1998: 93–116; E. P. Sanders 1990.
12 See discussion in Murphy-O'Connor 1996: 65–70; Hengel 1991: 63–86; Elliott 1994: 143–80.
13 See Segal 1990, e.g. 6: 'Paul was both converted and called.' For an overview of the consid-erable discussion on this subject, see Hurtado 1993.
14 Working out the chronology of Paul's life is difficult, not least because of the paucity of rele-vant data and the problems involved in correlating the more detailed information in Acts with the primary data in the epistles. On all of what follows in this paragraph, see Murphy-O'Connor 1996: 1–31; Jewett 1979; Lüdemann 1984; Riesner 1998.
15 On this period, see Murphy-O'Connor 1996: 71–101, and esp. the massive studies of Hengel and Schwemer 1997; Riesner 1998.
16 It is debated whether Paul's 'law-free' gospel for the Gentiles goes back to his conversion (so e.g. Kim 1982: 56–66, 269–311), or whether he initially required full obedience to Jewish law (cf. Gal. 5:11), or whether indeed he initially preached to Jews rather than Gentiles (so e.g. Watson 1986: 28–31).
17 For the details of this itinerary see Murphy-O'Connor 1996: 24–31; Jewett 1979:162–5. On Paul's collection see Horrell 1995 and other literature mentioned there.

18 Cf. Koester 1982: 144–5. For a discussion of this last period of Paul's life see Murphy-O'Connor 1996: 341–71, who draws evidence from the Pastoral Epistles (especially 2 Timothy, which he regards as authentic) for a rather overimaginative reconstruction of this phase of Paul's activity, including the idea of a visit to Spain.

19 Mention should be made of the massive recent study of Paul's theology by Dunn (1998a).

20 See Wedderburn 1988; Donfried 1991. It is now widely accepted that Romans is not a systematic compendium of Paul's theology, but is shaped by the circumstances both of Paul himself and of the Roman churches.

21 See further Wright 1997: 56–7, 88; Horsley 1997. On the use of the title *kyrios* in the eastern empire see Deissmann 1910: 353–64, and on the deification of Roman emperors, Kreitzer 1996: 69–98.

22 Other passages subject to such debate include Rom. 1:3–4; 8:3; Gal. 4:4.

23 See further discussion in Dunn 1980: 163–212; Hurtado 1988. Hurtado explores the Jewish evidence for 'divine agency speculation' – that is, concerning 'heavenly figures who are described as participating in some way in God's rule of the world and his redemption of the elect . . . as occupying a position second only to God and acting on God's behalf in some major capacity' (1988: 17). Hurtado distinguishes three types of such speculation: divine attributes and powers (such as wisdom); exalted patriarchs (such as Moses and Enoch); and principal angels.

24 A different view is taken by Wright 1991: 120–36; 1997: 65–75, who argues that Paul has redefined Jewish monotheism, weaving Christ (and the Spirit) into the very being of God, in a trinitarian manner.

25 Deissmann 1926: 140. According to Deissmann, the phrase 'in Christ' (or 'in the Lord') occurs 164 times in Paul's epistles.

26 See e.g. Deut. 23:2–9; 1 Kgs 18:14, 22, 55. However, *synagōgē* appears somewhat more frequently in the LXX than *ekklēsia*.

27 On these ritual dimensions of life in the Pauline churches, see Meeks 1983: 140–63; Horrell 1996: 80–8.

28 See Furnish 1968; and the essays by Bultmann and Parsons in Rosner 1995: 195–247.

29 See Horrell 1997a: 588–90; Wenham 1995: 3–4. Wenham provides the most detailed recent discussion of this whole area of debate. See also Wedderburn 1989b.

30 This is the translation of *skybala* (Phil. 3:8) suggested by Hays 1989: 122. Whether this is the best rendering has been disputed (see Fee 1995: 319) but the word is certainly a vulgarity referring to filth, dirt, excrement, etc.

31 Matlock is therefore right, in my view, to insist that 'Paul's Christian theology of the law has an irreducibly solution-to-plight character that Dunn would avoid' (1998: 78).

32 The meaning of the phrase is much discussed in the commentaries; see e.g. Dunn 1993: 188–90.

33 The argument of Stowers (1994) that Paul is addressing Gentiles only in Romans has been refuted by Hays 1996.

34 The translation of Rom. 3:9a, it should be noted, is notoriously difficult and open to various possibilities; see Dunn 1988: 146–8.

35 Famously regarded by Dodd (1959: 171) as 'the weakest point in the whole epistle': 'man is not a pot; he *will* ask, "Why did you make me like this?" [9:20] and he will not be bludgeoned into silence'.

36 See further discussion in Longenecker 1989; Hvalvik 1990; Donaldson 1993.

37 The nuances and ambiguities here are discussed in the commentaries; see e.g. Thrall 1994: 356–85; Barnett 1997: 255–67.

38 I am very grateful to David Catchpole for his comments on a draft of this chapter, and to Fern Clarke for help in compiling the bibliography. However, I alone am responsible for the opinions, and any errors there may be.

BIBLIOGRAPHY

Babcock, W. S. (ed.) (1990) *Paul and the Legacies of Paul*. Dallas: Southern Methodist University Press.

Barclay, John M. G. (1997) 'Universalism and Particularism: Twin Components of Both Judaism and Early Christianity', in Markus Bockmuehl and Michael B. Thompson (eds) *A Vision for the Church*. Edinburgh: T&T Clark, 207–24.

Barnett, Paul (1997) *The Second Epistle to the Corinthians*. Grand Rapids: Eerdmans.

Barrett, C. K. (1962) *From First Adam to Last: A Study in Pauline Theology*. London: A&C Black.

Beker, J. Christiaan (1980) *Paul the Apostle: The Triumph of God in Life and Thought*. Edinburgh: T&T Clark.

—— (1990) *The Triumph of God: The Essence of Paul's Thought*. Minneapolis: Fortress.

—— (1992) *Heirs of Paul: Paul's Legacy in the New Testament and in the Church Today*. Edinburgh: T&T Clark.

Bell, Richard H. (1994) *Provoked to Jealousy: The Origin and Purpose of the Jealousy Motif in Romans 9–11*. WUNT 2nd series, 63. Tübingen: Mohr.

Bockmuehl, Markus N. A. (1997) '"The Form of God" (Phil. 2:6). Variations on a Theme of Jewish Mysticism', *JTS* 48: 1–23.

Campbell, Douglas A. (1998) 'The ΔΙΑΘΗΚΗ from Durham: Professor Dunn's *The Theology of Paul the Apostle*', *JSNT* 72: 91–111.

Casey, P. Maurice (1991) *From Jewish Prophet to Gentile God: The Origins and Development of New Testament Christology*. Cambridge: James Clarke.

Davis, Christopher A. (1995) *The Structure of Paul's Theology: 'The Truth Which Is the Gospel'*. Lampeter: Mellen.

Deissmann, G. Adolf (1910) *Light From the Ancient East: The New Testament Illustrated by Recently Discovered Texts of the Graeco-Roman World*. London: Hodder & Stoughton.

—— (1926) *Paul: A Study in Social and Religious History*. 2nd edn. London: Hodder & Stoughton.

Deming, Will (1995) *Paul on Marriage and Celibacy: The Hellenistic Background of 1 Corinthians 7*. SNTSMS 83. Cambridge: CUP.

Dodd, C. H. ([1934] 1953) 'The Mind of Paul: II', in idem, *New Testament Studies*. Manchester: Manchester University Press, 83–128.

—— (1959) *The Epistle to the Romans*. London: Fontana.

Donaldson, Terence L. (1993) '"Riches for the Gentiles" (Rom 11:12): Israel's Rejection and Paul's Gentile Mission', *JBL* 112: 81–98.

Donfried, Karl P. (ed.) (1991) *The Romans Debate*. Rev. and expanded edn. Edinburgh: T&T Clark.

Downing, F. Gerald (1998) *Cynics, Paul and the Pauline Churches*. London: Routledge.

Drane, John W. (1975) *Paul: Libertine or Legalist?* London: SPCK.

Dunn, James D. G. (1980) *Christology in the Making*. 2nd edn 1989. London: SCM.

—— (1983) 'The New Perspective on Paul', *BJRL* 65: 95–122; now in Dunn 1990: 183–214.

—— (1988) *Romans*. 2 vols; WBC 38. Waco: Word.

—— (1990) *Jesus, Paul and the Law: Studies in Mark and Galatians*. London: SPCK.

—— (1993) *The Epistle to the Galatians*. London: A&C Black.

—— (1994) 'Jesus Tradition in Paul', in B. Chilton and C. A. Evans (eds) *Studying the Historical Jesus*. Leiden: Brill, 155–78.

—— (1998a) *The Theology of Paul the Apostle*. Edinburgh: T&T Clark.

—— (1998b) 'Paul: Apostate or Apostle of Israel?' *ZNW* 89: 256–71.

Elliott, Neil (1994) *Liberating Paul: The Justice of God and the Politics of the Apostle*. Maryknoll: Orbis.

Esler, Philip F. (1987) *Community and Gospel in Luke–Acts: The Social and Political Motivations of Lucan Theology*. SNTSMS 57. Cambridge: CUP.

—— (1995) 'Review of Hill 1992', *BibInt* 3: 119–23.

—— (1998) *Galatians*. London: Routledge.

Fee, Gordon D. (1994) *God's Empowering Presence: The Holy Spirit in the Letters of Paul*. Peabody: Hendrickson.

—— (1995) *Paul's Letter to the Philippians*. Grand Rapids: Eerdmans.

Furnish, V. P. (1968) *Theology and Ethics in Paul*. Nashville: Abingdon.

Harvey, Anthony E. (1996) *Renewal Through Suffering: A Study of 2 Corinthians*. SNTW. Edinburgh: T&T Clark.

Hays, Richard B. (1989) *Echoes of Scripture in the Letters of Paul*. New Haven: Yale University Press.

—— (1996) '"The Gospel Is the Power of God for Salvation to Gentiles Only"? A Critique of Stanley Stowers' *A Rereading of Romans*', *CRBR* 9: 27–44.

Hengel, Martin (1983) *Between Jesus and Paul: Studies in the History of Earliest Christianity*. London: SCM.

—— (1991) *The Pre-Christian Paul*. London: SCM.

Hengel, Martin and Schwemer, Anna Maria (1997) *Paul Between Damascus and Antioch*. London: SCM.

Héring, Jean (1962) *The First Epistle of Saint Paul to the Corinthians*. London: Epworth.

Hill, Craig C. (1992) *Hellenists and Hebrews: Reappraising Division within the Earliest Church*. Minneapolis: Fortress.

Holmberg, Bengt (1978) *Paul and Power: The Structure of Authority in the Primitive Church as Reflected in the Pauline Epistles*. Lund: CWK Gleerup.

Hooker, Morna D. (1990) *From Adam to Christ: Essays on Paul*. Cambridge: CUP.

Horrell, David G. (1995) 'Paul's Collection: Resources for a Materialist Theology', *Epworth Review* 22/2: 74–83.

—— (1996) *The Social Ethos of the Corinthian Correspondence: Interests and Ideology from 1 Corinthians to 1 Clement*. SNTW. Edinburgh: T&T Clark.

—— (1997a) '"The Lord commanded . . . But I have not used . . .": Exegetical and Hermeneutical Reflections on 1 Cor 9.14–15', *NTS* 43: 587–603.

—— (1997b) 'Theological Principle or Christological Praxis? Pauline Ethics in 1 Corinthians 8.1–11.1', *JSNT* 67: 83–114.

—— (2000) 'Early Jewish Christianity', in Philip F. Esler (ed.) *The Early Christian World*. London: Routledge, 136–67.

Horsley, Richard A. (ed.) (1997) *Paul and Empire: Religion and Power in Roman Imperial Society*. Harrisburg: Trinity Press International.

Hübner, Hans (1984) *Law in Paul's Thought*. Trans. James C. G. Greig. SNTW. Edinburgh: T&T Clark.

Hurtado, Larry W. (1988) *One God, One Lord: Early Christian Devotion and Ancient Jewish Monotheism*. London: SCM.

—— (1993) 'Convert, Apostate or Apostle to the Nations: The "Conversion" of Paul in Recent Scholarship', *SR* 22: 273–84.

Hvalvik, Reidar (1990) 'A "Sonderweg" for Israel: A Critical Examination of a Current Interpretation of Romans 11:25–27', *JSNT* 38: 87–107.

Jeremias, Joachim (1926) 'War Paulus Witwer?' *ZNW* 25: 310–12.

—— (1929) 'Noch einmals: war Paulus Witwer?' *ZNW* 28: 321–3.

Jewett, Robert (1979) *Dating Paul's Life*. London: SCM.

Kim, Seyoon (1982) *The Origin of Paul's Gospel*. Grand Rapids: Eerdmans.

Knox, John (1987) *Chapters in a Life of Paul*. Rev. edn; London: SCM.

Koester, Helmut (1982) *Introduction to the New Testament*, Vol 2. Philadelphia: Fortress.

Kreitzer, Larry J. (1996) *Striking New Images: Roman Imperial Coinage and the New Testament World*. JSNTSup 134. Sheffield: Sheffield Academic Press.

Kruse, Colin (1997) *Paul, the Law and Justification*. Peabody: Hendrickson.

Lindemann, Andreas (1979) *Paulus im ältesten Christentum: Das bild des Apostels und die Reception der paulinischen Theologie in der frühchristlichen Literatur bis Marcion*. Tübingen: Mohr.

Longenecker, Bruce W. (1989) 'Different Answers to Different Issues: Israel, the Gentiles and Salvation History in Romans 9–11', *JSNT* 36: 95–123.

Lüdemann, Gerd (1984) *Paul, Apostle to the Gentiles: Studies in Chronology*. London: SCM.

—— (1989) *Early Christianity According to the Traditions in Acts*. London: SCM.

Maccoby, Hyam (1991) *Paul and Hellenism*. London: SCM.

Malherbe, Abraham (1989) *Paul and the Popular Philosophers*. Minneapolis: Fortress.

Martin, Ralph P. (1983) *Carmen Christi: Philippians ii.5–11 in Recent Interpretation and in the Setting of Early Christian Worship*. Grand Rapids: Eerdmans.

Matlock, R. Barry (1998) 'Sins of the Flesh and Suspicious Minds: Dunn's New Theology of Paul', *JSNT* 72: 67–90.

Mattingley, Harold (1965) *Coins of the Roman Empire in the British Museum*. Vol. 1: *Augustus to Vitellius*. London: Trustees of the British Museum.

Meeks, Wayne A. (1983) *The First Urban Christians*. New Haven: Yale University Press.

—— (1991) 'On Trusting an Unpredictable God: A Hermeneutical Meditation on Romans 9–11', in *Faith and History: Essays in Honor of Paul W. Meyer*, John T. Carroll, Charles H. Cosgrove, E. Elizabeth Johnson (eds) Atlanta: Scholars Press: 105–24.

Murphy-O'Connor, Jerome (1996) *Paul: A Critical Life*. Oxford: OUP.

Pagels, Elaine H. (1975) *The Gnostic Paul: Gnostic Exegesis of the Pauline Letters*. Philadelphia: Fortress.

Räisänen, Heikki (1983) *Paul and the Law*. Tübingen: Mohr.

—— (1992) *Jesus, Paul and Torah: Collected Essays*. JSNTSup 43, trans. David E. Orton. Sheffield: JSOT Press.

Rapske, Brian (1994) *The Book of Acts and Paul in Roman Custody*. Grand Rapids: Eerdmans.

Riesner, Rainer (1998) *Paul's Early Period: Chronology, Mission Strategy, Theology*. Grand Rapids; Cambridge, UK: Eerdmans.

Roetzel, Calvin J. (1995) 'Paul and the Law: Whence and Whither?' *CurBS* 3: 249–75.

—— (1998) *Paul: The Man and the Myth*, Columbia, S.C.: University of South Carolina Press.

Rosner, Brian S. (1994) *Paul, Scripture and Ethics: A Study of 1 Corinthians 5–7*. Leiden: Brill.

Rosner, Brian S. (ed.) (1995) *Understanding Paul's Ethics: Twentieth-Century Approaches*. Grand Rapids: Eerdmans.

Saldarini, Anthony J. (1992) 'Pharisees', in David N. Freedman (ed.) *Anchor Bible Dictionary*, Vol. 5. New York: Doubleday, 289–303.

Sanders, E. P. (1977) *Paul and Palestinian Judaism*. London: SCM.

—— (1983) *Paul, the Law and the Jewish People*. London: SCM.

—— (1990) 'Jewish Association with Gentiles and Galatians 2:11–14', in Robert T. Fortna and Beverly R. Gaventa (eds) *The Conversation Continues: Studies in Paul and John in Honour of J. Louis Martyn*. Nashville: Abingdon, 170–88.

—— (1991) *Paul*. Oxford: OUP.

Sanders, Jack T. (1975) *Ethics in the New Testament: Change and Development*. London: SCM.

Schürer, Emil (1979) *The History of the Jewish People in the Age of Jesus Christ (175 B.C. – A.D. 135)*, Vol. 2; rev. and ed. Geza Vermes, Fergus Millar, Matthew Black. Edinburgh: T&T Clark.

Schweitzer, Albert (1953) *The Mysticism of Paul the Apostle*. Trans. William Montgomery, 2nd edn. London: A&C Black.

Scott, James M. (1992) *Adoption as Sons of God: An Exegetical Investigation into the Background of HUIOTHESIA in the Pauline Corpus*. WUNT 2nd series, 48. Tübingen: Mohr.

Scroggs, Robin (1966) *The Last Adam*. Oxford: Basil Blackwell.

Segal, Alan F. (1990) *Paul the Convert: The Apostolate and Apostasy of Saul the Pharisee*. New Haven: Yale University Press.

Stegemann, Wolfgang (1987) 'War der Apostel Paulus ein römischer Bürger?' *ZNW* 78: 200–29.

Stendahl, Krister (1976) *Paul Among Jews and Gentiles and Other Essays*. Philadelphia: Fortress.

Stowers, Stanley (1994) *A Rereading of Romans: Justice, Jews, and Gentiles*. New Haven: Yale University Press.

Sutherland, C. H. V. (1974) *Roman Coins*. London: Barrie & Jenkins.

Taylor, Nicholas H. (1992) *Paul, Antioch and Jerusalem: A Study in Relationships and Authority in Earliest Christianity*. JSNTSup 66. Sheffield: JSOT Press.

Thielman, Frank (1994) *Paul and the Law: A Contextual Approach*. Downers Grove: IVP.

Thrall, Margaret E. (1994) *A Critical and Exegetical Commentary on the Second Epistle to the Corinthians*, Vol. 1. Edinburgh: T&T Clark.

Verner, David C. (1983) *The Household of God: The Social World of the Pastoral Epistles*. SBLDS 71. Chico: Scholars Press.

Watson, Francis (1986) *Paul, Judaism and the Gentiles: A Sociological Approach*. SNTSMS 56. Cambridge: CUP.

Wedderburn, Alexander J. M. (1988) *The Reasons for Romans*. SNTW. Edinburgh: T&T Clark.

—— (1989a) 'Paul and Jesus: Similarity and Continuity', in Wedderburn (ed.) 1989b: 117–43.

Wedderburn, Alexander J. M. (ed.) (1989b) *Paul and Jesus: Collected Essays*. JSNTSup 37. Sheffield: JSOT Press.

Wenham, David (1995) *Paul: Follower of Jesus or Founder of Christianity?* Grand Rapids: Eerdmans.

Westerholm, Stephen (1988) *Israel's Law and the Church's Faith: Paul and His Recent Interpreters*. Grand Rapids: Eerdmans.

—— (1991) 'Law, Grace and the "Soteriology" of Judaism', in Peter Richardson, Stephen Westerholm et al., *Law in Religious Communities in the Roman Period: The Debate over Torah and Nomos in Post-Biblical Judaism and Early Christianity*. Ontario: Wilfred Laurier University Press, 57–74.

—— (1997) *Preface to the Study of Paul*. Grand Rapids: Eerdmans.

Wilson, A. N. (1997) *Paul: The Mind of the Apostle*. London: Sinclair-Stevenson.

Wright, N. T. (1991) *The Climax of the Covenant: Christ and the Law in Pauline Theology*. Edinburgh: T&T Clark.

—— (1997) *What Saint Paul Really Said: Was Saul of Tarsus the Real Founder of Christianity?* Oxford: Lion.

Ziesler, John (1992) *The Epistle to the Galatians*. London: Epworth.

PART VII

RELIGIOUS IDEAS

CHAPTER FORTY-TWO

SALVATION IN JEWISH THOUGHT

——— •◆• ———

Dan Cohn-Sherbok

In the Hebrew Bible, the Apocrypha and the Pseudepigrapha, the salvation of the Jewish nation is understood in terms of Messianic deliverance. While the Jewish people were promised a future reward for the observance of the commandments, the Messianic Age holds the promise of ultimate salvation and redemption.

THE BIBLICAL MESSIAH

In the book of Samuel the notion of the salvation of the Jewish nation through a divinely appointed agent is explicitly expressed. Here Scripture asserts that the Lord has chosen David and his descendants to reign over Israel to the end of time. Thus 2 Samuel 23 proclaims:

> Now these are the last words of David:
> The oracle of David, the son of Jesse,
>   . . . the anointed of the God of Jacob . . .
> The God of Israel has spoken,
>   the Rock of Israel has said to me:
> When one rules justly over men,
>   ruling in the fear of God . . .
> Yea, does not my house stand so with God?
> For he has made with me an everlasting covenant,
>   ordered in all things and secure. (2 Samuel 23:1, 3, 5)

In this passage David is depicted as the anointed in the sense that he is consecrated for a divine purpose.

Of similar significance are the verses in 2 Samuel and 1 Chronicles where Nathan the prophet assures the king that his throne will be established for all time and that his throne will be secure forever. Speaking to David about the construction of the Temple, he declares:

> Thus says the Lord of hosts, I took you from the pasture, from following
> the sheep, that you should be prince over my people Israel; and I have been

with you wherever you went, and have cut off all your enemies from before you; and I will make for you a great name, like the name of the great ones of the earth. And I will appoint a place for my people Israel, and will plant them, that they may dwell in their own place. (2 Samuel 7:8–10)

This early biblical doctrine assumes that David's position will endure through his lifetime and be inherited by a series of successors who will carry out God's providential plan of deliverance. With the fall of the Davidic empire after the death of King Solomon, there arose the view that the house of David would eventually rule over the two divided kingdoms as well as neighbouring peoples. Yet, despite such a hopeful vision of Israel's future, the pre-exilic prophets were convinced that the nation would be punished for its iniquity. Warning the people of impending disaster, Amos speaks of the Day of the Lord when God will unleash his fury against those who have rebelled against him. This will not be a time of deliverance, but of destruction: 'Woe to you who desire the day of the Lord!' he declared. 'Why would you have the day of the Lord? It is darkness, and not light' (Amos 5:18). Here the prophet portrays such a day in the most negative terms:

> Therefore thus says the Lord, the God of hosts, the Lord:
> 'In all the squares there shall be wailing;
> and in all the streets they shall say, "Alas! alas!"
> They shall call the farmers to mourning
> and to wailing those who are skilled in lamentation,
> and in all vineyards there shall be wailing;
> for I will pass through the midst of you.' (Amos 5:16–17)

For Amos the Day of the Lord will be bitter – feasts will be turned into mourning and songs to lamentation (Amos 8:10). Those who are secure in Samaria will go into captivity, and Israel will be driven into exile (Amos 6:7; 7:17).

For Amos then, the Day of the Lord is the necessary result of sin; this fearful prediction serves as the backdrop to deliverance. Before Israel can be saved, the nation is to suffer exile, destruction and slaughter. Only after such terrible events will the house of David be restored to its former glory and the kings of the house of David rule over the ten tribes. At the time of salvation there will be an ingathering of the exiles and Israel will rule over all foreign powers.

Like Amos, Hosea believes that God will punish his people for their sinfulness. Such suffering, however, is to serve as the means to moral reform. Israel is to endure the pangs of childbirth before salvation can come (Hosea 13:13). Such chastisement is to bring about repentance and dedication to the covenant. Then the Lord will have mercy on his chosen people and exalt them among the nations.

There is thus a direct link between destruction and salvation. According to Hosea, although the people shall be deprived of their king this situation will change once the Israelites mend their ways and return to the Lord:

> For the children of Israel shall dwell many days without king or prince,
> without sacrifice or pillar, without ephod or teraphim. Afterward the

children of Israel shall return and seek the Lord their God, and David their king; and they shall come in fear to the Lord and to his goodness in the latter days. (Hosea 3:4–5)

Echoing Amos, Hosea predicts that the Day of the Lord will be great and abundant. It will result in earthly prosperity and bliss:

I will be as the dew to Israel;
he shall blossom as the lily,
he shall strike root as the poplar;
his shoots shall spread out;
his beauty shall be like the olive,
and his fragrance like Lebanon.
They shall return and dwell beneath my shadow,
they shall flourish as a garden. (Hosea 14:5–7)

The captives and the exiles shall return to their own land, and in another passage Hosea prophesies that the order of nature will be fundamentally altered: 'And I will make for you a covenant on that day with the beasts of the field, the birds of the air, and the creeping things of the ground; and I will abolish the bow, the sword, and war from the land; and I will make you lie down in safety' (Hosea 2:18). Here in embryonic form is the concept of perfect salvation in the end of days. Drawing faith from the closing chapters in the history of northern Israel, both Amos and Hosea predict a future age in which the glories of the Lord will be manifest in the land.

FROM ISAIAH TO THE DESTRUCTION OF JUDAH

The book of Isaiah begins by explaining that what follows is an account of the prophecies of Isaiah concerning Judah and Jerusalem. In the first prophetic oracle the prophet presents God as disappointed with his people because of their iniquity. Nonetheless, he predicts the eventual salvation of the nation:

It shall come to pass in the latter days
that the mountain of the house of the Lord
shall be established as the highest of the mountains,
and shall be raised above the hills;
and all the nations shall flow to it,
and many peoples shall come and say:
'Come, let us go up to the mountain of the Lord,
to the house of the God of Jacob;
that he may teach us his ways
and that we may walk in his paths.'
For out of Zion shall go forth the law,
and the word of the Lord from Jerusalem.

He shall judge between the nations,
and shall decide for many peoples;
and they shall beat their swords into ploughshares,
and their spears into pruning hooks;
nation shall not lift up sword against nation,
neither shall they learn war any more. (Isaiah 2:2–4)

This future vision of the salvation of the Jewish people, however, is overshadowed by calamity. In chapter 2 Isaiah levels criticism against idolatry, foretelling that such rebellion against God will bring about the destruction of the Temple. After discussing the place of Assyria in God's providential plan of devastation, Isaiah returns to the promise of salvation. A child will be born, he states, who will be the Prince of Peace, yet this promise is placed into the context of God's dissatisfaction with his people. According to the prophet, God will use Assyria as an instrument of punishment. Only a faithful remnant will remain, from which a redeemer will issue forth to bring about a new epoch in the nation's history:

There shall come forth a shoot from the stump of Jesse,
and a branch shall grow out of his roots.
And the Spirit of the Lord shall rest upon him . . .
He shall not judge by what his eyes see,
or decide by what his ears hear;
but with righteousness he shall judge the poor,
and decide with equity for the meek of the earth . . .
The wolf shall dwell with the lamb,
and the leopard shall lie down with the kid,
and the calf and the lion and the fatling together.

(Isaiah 11:1–2, 3–4, 6)

In another passage, the prophet presents a song of praise that is to be sung on the day of Israel's salvation:

In that day this song will be sung in the land of Judah:
'We have a strong city;
he sets up salvation
as walls and bulwarks.
Open the gates,
that the righteous nation which keeps faith
    may enter in.
Thou dost keep him in perfect peace,
whose mind is stayed on thee . . .
Trust in the Lord for ever,
for the Lord God is an everlasting rock.' (Isaiah 26:1–4)

A contemporary of Isaiah, the prophet Micah prophesied in the southern Kingdom from 750 to 686 BCE. Condemning both Samaria and Judah for their wickedness, he declares that God will bring about judgement of the people: Samaria will be reunited and the places of idolatry destroyed. Yet despite this dire prediction, the prophet wishes to reassure the nation that it will not be utterly cut off. God, he states, has a purpose for its people in the future:

> I will surely gather all of you, O Jacob,
> I will gather the remnant of Israel;
> I will set them together
>   like sheep in a fold,
> like a flock in its pasture,
> a noisy multitude of men. (Micah 2:12)

Confident in the restoration of the people, he looks forward to an age of prosperity and fulfilment. Like Isaiah he predicts a time of salvation for the Jewish nation. All nations, he declares, will go to the mountain of the Lord and dwell together in peace; in those days swords will be turned into ploughshares and each man will sit under his vine and fig tree:

> For out of Zion shall go forth the law,
> and the word of the Lord from Jerusalem.
> He shall judge between many peoples,
> and shall decide for strong nations afar off;
> and they shall beat their swords into ploughshares,
> and their spears into pruning hooks;
> nation shall not lift up sword against nation,
> neither shall they learn war any more;
> but they shall sit every man under his vine and under his fig tree,
> and none shall make them afraid. (Micah 4:2–4)

The prophet Zephaniah was active in Judah during the reign of Josiah in about 625 BCE. Like the prophetic figures who preceded him, he warns against the nation's unfaithfulness: in his view, impending destruction would be the result of sinfulness. The great Day of the Lord is at hand, the prophet announces – it will be a time not of fulfilment but of calamity:

> a day of distress and anguish
> a day of ruin and devastation,
> a day of darkness and gloom,
> a day of clouds and thick darkness,
> a day of trumpet blast and battle cry
>   against fortified cities
> and against lofty battlements. (Zephaniah 1:15–16)

Nothing will be able to prevent this outpouring of God's wrath; nonetheless, such devastation will not totally overwhelm the people. In the final part of his book, Zephaniah calls on the Israelites to wait for God's salvation: he will gather the nations and pour out the heat of his anger. But at that time he will change the speech of all nations so that they will call on the name of the Lord and serve him with one accord. Knowing that their chastening is over, the people can exult. Certain of God's lovingkindess, the nation can look forward to restoration and renewal: 'Sing aloud, O daughter of Zion', he declares. 'Shout, O Israel! Rejoice and exult with all your heart, O daughter of Jerusalem' (Zephaniah 3:14). Confident of the future, the prophet declares in God's name:

> 'Behold at the time I will deal
>   with all your oppressors.
> And I will save the lame
>   and gather the outcast,
> and I will change their shame into praise
>   and renown in all the earth.
> At that time I will bring you home,
> at the time when I gather you together;
> yea, I will make you renowned and praised
>   among the peoples of the earth,
> when I restore your fortunes
>   before your eyes,' says the Lord. (Zephaniah 3:19–20)

In 626 BCE Jeremiah was commissioned as a prophet during the reign of Josiah – his ministry continued until the destruction of Judah. Jeremiah's earliest prophecies date from the time of Josiah: Judah, he states, has forsaken God and in consequence will be punished. What is now required is repentance: if the inhabitants refuse, God will send forth an invader to subdue the country:

> Flee for safety, O people of Benjamin,
> from the midst of Jerusalem!
> Blow the trumpet in Tekoa
>   and raise a signal on Beth-haccherem;
> for evil looms out of the north. (Jeremiah 6:1)

Although persuaded that the country is doomed, Jeremiah is certain that the Lord will not completely destroy his people: a remnant will return with a new king at its head:

> Behold the days are coming, says the Lord, when I will raise up for David a righteous Branch, and he shall reign as king and deal wisely, and shall execute justice and righteousness in the land. In his days Judah will be saved, and Israel will dwell securely. (Jeremiah 23:5–6)

In his view, this new redemption resulting in the salvation of Israel will bring a new spiritual life for the nation. The Lord will create a new heart for his people and pour out a new spirit upon them:

> Behold the days are coming, says the Lord, when I will make a new covenant
> with the house of Israel and the house of Judah, not like the covenant which
> I made with their fathers when I took them by the hand to bring them out
> of the land of Egypt, my covenant which they broke, though I was their
> husband, says the Lord. But this is the covenant which I will make with
> the house of Israel after those days, says the Lord: I will put my law within
> them, and I will write it upon their hearts; and I will be their God, and
> they shall be my people. (Jeremiah 31:31–3)

For Jeremiah, in this blissful time a noble king filled with fear of the Lord will
rule over the people:

> Behold, the days are coming, says the Lord, when I will fulfil the promise
> I made to the house of Israel and the house of Judah. In those days and at
> that time I will cause a righteous Branch to spring forth for David; and he
> shall execute justice and righteousness in the land. In those days Judah will
> be saved and Jerusalem will dwell securely. And this is the name by which
> it will be called: 'The Lord is our righteousness.' (Jeremiah 33:14–16)

POST-EXILIC PROPHECY

Dwelling in Babylon, the prophet Ezekiel begins his ministry seven years before the
conquest of Jerusalem. Like the earlier prophets, he castigates the Jewish people for
their iniquity – because they have turned away from God further punishment will
be inflicted upon them. Yet, despite the departure of God's glory from the Temple,
Ezekiel reassures the nation that it will not be abandoned: 'Thus says the Lord God:
I will gather you from the peoples, and assemble you out of the countries where you
have been scattered, and I will give you the land of Israel' (Ezekiel 11:17)

In this spirit the prophet offers words of comfort and hope after the fall of Judah.
In his view, God takes no pleasure in the death of sinners; what he requires instead
is a contrite heart. Using the image of a shepherd and his flock, Ezekiel reassuringly
declares that God will gather his people from exile and return them to the Promised
Land:

> For thus says the Lord God: Behold I, I myself will search for my sheep,
> and will seek them out. As a shepherd seeks out his flock when some of his
> sheep have been scattered abroad, so will I seek out my sheep; and I will
> rescue them from all places where they have been scattered on a day of
> clouds and thick darkness. (Ezekiel 34:11–12)

This prophecy is followed by a further vision of restoration – the Lord promises
that cities will be reinhabited and their ruins rebuilt. Such national restoration, the
prophet continues, will be accompanied by personal dedication to the law. This reassurance is reinforced by Ezekiel's vision of dry bones: although the nation has been
devastated, it will be renewed in a further deliverance:

As I prophesied, there was a noise, and behold, a rattling; and the bones came together, bone to its bone. And as I looked, there were sinews on them, and flesh had come upon them, and skin had covered them . . . Then he said to me, 'Son of man, these bones are the whole house of Israel. Behold, they say, "Our bones are dried up, and our hope is lost; we are clean cut off." Therefore prophesy, and say to them, "Thus says the Lord God: Behold, I will open your graves, and raise you from your graves, O my people; and I will bring you home into the land of Israel . . . And I will put my Spirit within you, and you shall live, and I will place you in your own land."'
(Ezekiel 37:7–8, 11, 14)

This vision is followed by a description of a future king who will rule over his people. Under his dominion Jerusalem will benefit from the promises of the covenant:

My servant David shall be king over them; and they shall all have one shepherd. They shall follow my ordinances and be careful to observe my statutes. They shall dwell in the land where your fathers dwelt that I gave to my servant Jacob; they and their children and their children's children shall dwell there for ever; and David my servant shall be their prince for ever.
(Ezekiel 37:24–5)

Like Ezekiel, Second Isaiah is anxious to offer words of consolation to those who have experienced the destruction of Judah. In place of oracles of denunciation, the prophet offers the promise of restoration. According to Second Isaiah, the Lord will return in triumph to Jerusalem as a shepherd leading his flock: 'He will feed his flock like a shepherd, he will gather the lambs in his arms, he will carry them in his bosom, and gently lead those that are with young' (Isaiah 40:11). All the world will witness this act of salvation and declare that the God of Israel is Lord.

In chapter 49 the prophet depicts the servant of the Lord through whom salvation will be brought to the ends of the earth – he will be mocked and despised. This theme is further developed in chapter 53:

He was despised and rejected by men;
a man of sorrows, and acquainted with grief;
and as one from whom men hide their faces
    he was despised, and we esteemed him not.
Surely he has borne our griefs
    and carried our sorrows;
yet we esteemed him stricken,
smitten by God, and afflicted.
But he was wounded for our transgressions,
he was bruised for our iniquities;
upon him was the chastisement that made us whole
    and with his stripes we are healed. (Isaiah 53:3–5)

Second Isaiah concludes with a vision of the future glory of Zion: God will be reunited with his people, and all will be fulfilled.

Echoing the predictions about the restoration of Zion in Second Isaiah, Third Isaiah emphasizes the role of the Jewish people in God's providential plan. Through Israel's salvation all nations will be blessed, and the Temple become a focus of worship for all peoples. Chapter 60 continues with a description of the glory of Zion. Jerusalem will be honoured throughout the world because of God's greatness. This theme is developed in the next chapter, which speaks of a figure on whom the Spirit of God will rest; he will liberate all captives, bring tidings to the afflicted, and rebuild Zion:

> The Spirit of the Lord is upon me,
> because the Lord has anointed me
>   to bring good tidings to the afflicted;
> he has sent me to bind up the broken hearted,
> to proclaim liberty to the captives,
> and the opening of the prison to those who are bound . . .
> They shall build up the ancient ruins,
> they shall raise up the former devastations,
> they shall repair the ruined cities,
> the devastations of many generations. (Isaiah 6:1, 4)

At this time Jerusalem will be acknowledged as the place where the Lord's redeemed dwell. Although God will judge those who have been unfaithful, the promise of salvation is offered to all who are loyal to him. Here Third Isaiah speaks of a new heaven and a new earth that will be created at the end of days:

> 'For behold, I create new heavens
>   and a new earth;
> and the former things shall not be remembered
>   or come into mind.
> But be glad and rejoice for ever
>   in that which I create;
> for behold, I create Jerusalem a rejoicing,
> and her people a joy . . .
> The wolf and the lamb shall feed together,
> the lion shall eat straw like the ox;
> and dust shall be the serpent's food.
> They shall not hurt or destroy
>   in all my holy mountain. (Isaiah 65:17–18, 25)

The prophet Haggai together with Zerubbabel engaged in the rebuilding of the Temple. In a series of discourses Haggai describes the glories of the rebuilt Temple. God, he declares, is with his people. No longer is he determined that they will be punished because of their iniquities as he was when he used the Assyrians and

Babylonians to accomplish his purposes. God, he states, will be victorious over Israel's enemies. In this context, he emphasizes that the Lord has chosen Zerubbabel as his servant – he is to be God's signet ring:

> The word of the Lord came a second time to Haggai on the twenty-fourth day of the month, 'Speak to Zerubbabel, governor of Judah, saying, I am about to shake the heavens and the earth, and to overthrow the thrones of kingdoms: I am about to destroy the strength of the kingdoms of the nations, and overthrow the chariots and their riders; and the horses and their riders shall go down, every one by the sword of his fellow. On that day, says the Lord of hosts, I will take you, O Zerubbabel my servant, the son of Shealtiel, says the Lord, and make you like a signet ring; for I have chosen you, says the Lord of hosts.' (Haggai 2:20–3)

Zechariah, a contemporary of Haggai, also focuses on the importance of rebuilding the Temple. Although the Lord has punished Judah by sending its inhabitants into exile for seventy years, the nation has suffered sufficiently. Now God's mercies will be made known to his chosen people – the land will prosper and God's dwelling will be established in Jerusalem. Prophesying about such a glorious future, Zechariah foretells that a king will come who will reign over the people. In a vision of hope, the prophet describes this Messianic figure who will be a descendant of David. He shall enter the city in triumph riding upon an ass: 'Rejoice greatly, O daughter of Zion! Shout aloud, O daughter of Jerusalem! Lo, your king comes to you; triumphant and victorious is he, humble and riding on an ass, on a colt the foal of an ass' (Zechariah 9:9). According to Zechariah, God will redeem his people – he will strengthen them and bring them back to Zion; the inhabitants of Jerusalem shall be as though they had never been rejected.

Like Haggai and Zechariah, the prophet Malachi was a post-exilic prophet active after the exiles returned from Babylonia. In his view, Israel's sinfulness caused the Lord great distress. In order to remedy such transgression, God prophesied to send his messenger to prepare the way for the Lord's entry into his Temple: 'Behold I send my messenger to prepare the way before me, and the Lord whom you seek will suddenly come to his Temple; the messenger of the covenant in whom you delight; behold he is coming, says the Lord of hosts' (Malachi 3:1). However, because of their iniquity the people will not be able to deal with such a message – the coming of the Lord will thus not bring about Israel's salvation. Rather, it will be like a refiner's fire that will purify the nation.

The prophet insists that the promise of God's forgiveness and restoration will be fulfilled. Even though Israel has been iniquitous, God will return to his people if they seek him. In the final section of the book, Malachi describes the day of the Lord: it will be a time of destruction for the wicked and reward for those who fear his name. In conclusion Malachi announces that God will send the prophet Elijah before the day of the Lord so that the nation will be reconciled:

> Behold, I will send you Elijah the prophet before the great and terrible day of the Lord comes. And he will turn the hearts of the fathers to their children

and the hearts of children to their fathers, lest I come and smite the land with a curse. (Malachi 4:5–6)

THE PSALMS AND DANIEL

In addition to predictions about a future salvation of Israel found in the prophetic writings, the book of Psalms contains numerous references to divine deliverance. The first of the Messianic psalms begins with tumult. The world is in agitation – kings and princes have rebelled against God and his anointed. Yet, the Lord will prevail:

> He who sits in the heavens laughs;
> the Lord has them in derision.
> Then he will speak to them in his wrath,
> and terrify them in his fury, saying,
> 'I have set my king
>   on Zion, my holy hill.'
> I will tell of the decree of the Lord:
> He said to me, 'You are my son,
> today I have begotten you.
> Ask of me, and I will make the nations your heritage,
> and the ends of the earth your possession.' (Psalm 2:4–8)

The allusion to the enthronement of the king is echoed in Psalm 110; here there is the same promise of victory over the enemies of the Lord:

> The Lord says to my lord:
> 'Sit at my right hand,
> till I make your enemies your footstool.'
> The Lord sends forth from Zion
>   your mighty sceptre.
> Rule in the midst of your foes! (Psalm 110:1–2)

The subsequent verses promise defeat of Israel's enemies:

> He will execute judgment among the nations,
> filling them with corpses;
> he will shatter chiefs
>   over the wide earth. (Psalm 110:6)

Other psalms, traditionally attributed to King Solomon, present a different picture of this future king: he is the righteous ruler and the guarantee of the nation's prosperity:

> Give the king thy justice, O God,
> and thy righteousness to the royal son!
> May he judge the people with righteousness,

and thy poor with justice!
Let the mountains bear prosperity for the people,
and the hills, in righteousness!
May he defend the cause of the poor of the people,
give deliverance to the needy,
and crush the oppressor! (Psalm 72:1–4)

For the psalmist there is a fundamental link between the righteousness of the
king and the fruitfulness of the land. Repeatedly the moral character of his rule is
expressed:

For he delivers the needy when he calls,
the poor and him who has no helper.
He has pity on the weak and the needy,
and saves the lives of the needy.
From oppression and violence he redeems their life;
and precious is their blood in his sight. (Psalm 72:12–14)

Continuing the theme of kingly rule, Psalm 21 states that the king is God's
beloved whom he has given long life, victory, glory and majesty:

Thou hast given him his heart's desire,
and has not withheld the request of his lips.
For thou dost meet him with goodly blessings;
thou dost set a crown of fine gold upon his head.
He asked life of thee; thou gavest it to him,
length of days for ever and ever.
His glory is great through thy help;
splendour and majesty thou dost bestow upon him.
Yea, thou dost make him most blessed for ever;
thou dost make him glad with the joy of thy presence. (Psalm 21:2–6)

Connected with this notion of kingly rule, Psalm 132 contains God's promise to
David that a scion of his dynasty will always reign in Israel:

The Lord swore to David a sure oath
    from which he will not turn back:
'One of the sons of your body
    I will set on your throne.
If your sons keep my covenant
    and my testimonies which I shall teach them,
their sons also for ever
    shall sit upon your throne.' (Psalm 132:11–12)

In summary, then, the book of Psalms depicts the king as the Anointed of the
Lord; he is placed by the Lord on his throne, proclaimed as his son, and appointed

to maintain righteousness and justice throughout the land. Through his actions he conveys divine blessing to his people, fertility to the soil, and victory over foreign powers. Ruling over the entire world, his throne is established for all time.

Turning from the Psalms to the book of Daniel, a different picture is given of such a divinely anointed deliverer. According to tradition, Daniel lived in Babylonia in the sixth century BCE during the final days of the Babylonian empire; most scholars, however, contend that the book was written in the second century BCE. Chapters 7 to 12 consist of a series of dreams foretelling future events. The first is a vision of beasts – a lion, bear, leopard and another creature terrifying in appearance. Each of these beasts symbolizes an empire: the lion corresponds to Babylonia; the bear the Medo-Persian empire; the leopard that of Alexander the Great; the fourth creature Rome. The theme is that Babylonia will be succeeded by these other empires until God's everlasting reign will be established. Here Daniel refers to one like a Son of Man who will be given dominion over all the earth:

> I saw in the night visions,
> and behold, with the clouds of heaven
>   there came one like a son of man,
> and he came to the Ancient of Days
>   and was presented before him.
> And to him was given dominion
>   and glory and kingdom,
> that all peoples, nations, and languages
>   should serve him;
> his dominion is an everlasting dominion,
> which shall not pass away,
> and his kingdom one
>   that shall not be destroyed. (Daniel 7:13–14)

In the next vision a ram representing the Medo-Perisan kings is succeeded by a goat – this denotes the king of the empire established by Alexander the Great. According to some scholars Daniel 8:23–5 refers to the coming of the Syrian King Antiochus IV, an enemy of the Jews:

> And at the latter end of their rule, when the transgressors have reached their full measure, a king of bold countenance, one who understands riddles, shall arise. His power shall be great, and he shall cause fearful destruction, and shall succeed in what he does, and destroy mighty men and the people of the saints.

These visions are followed by Daniel's prayer for deliverance despite the Israelites' sinfulness. Here Daniel appeals to God's mercy to deliver his people from their plight. In a response, Daniel is assured concerning the future of Jerusalem and the coming of the Anointed One:

> Seventy weeks of years are decreed concerning your people and your holy city, to finish the transgression, to put an end to sin, and to atone for iniquity,

to bring in everlasting righteousness, to seal both vision and prophet, and to anoint a most holy place. Know therefore and understand that from the going forth of the word to restore and build Jerusalem to the coming of an anointed one, a prince, there shall be seven weeks. (Daniel 9:24–5)

This supplication is followed in chapter 10 by a vision of the last days. On the fourth day of the first month, a man clothed in linen whose loins were girded with rich gold of Uphaz appeared on the Tigris. In a series of speeches, he strengthened and encouraged Daniel, revealing to him later kings who would reign during the period of Greek rule. This passage is followed by prophecies concerning an unknown king, and a final assurance that the Lord will remain faithful to his people:

And there shall be a time of trouble, such as never has been since there was a nation till that time; but at that time your people shall be delivered, every one whose name shall be found written in the book. And many of those who sleep in the dust shall awake, some to everlasting life, and some to shame and everlasting contempt. And those who are wise shall shine like the brightness of the firmament; and those who turn many to righteousness, like the stars for ever and ever. (Daniel 12:1–3)

THE APOCRYPHA

Throughout Ben Sira (c. 190–170 BCE) the love of Israel is manifest; in the author's view, Israel is pre-eminent among the nations. Such dedication is manifest even when he is discussing abstract ideas. Hence in chapter 35, while discussing the plight of the oppressed, he turns to God's chosen people:

Yea, the Lord will not tarry
And the mighty One will not refrain himself
Till he smite the loins of the merciless,
And requite vengeance (to the arrogant);
Till he dispossess the sceptre of pride,
And the staff of wickedness utterly cut down;
Till he redeem to man his due,
And recompense people according to their devising,
Till he plead the cause of his people,
And rejoice them with salvation. (Ben Sira 35:22–5)

The next chapter makes it clear that this vision is of the Age to Come. This prayer of hope is filled with Messianic expectation:

Save us, O God of all,
And cast thy fear upon all the nations.
Shake thy hand against the strange people,
And let them see thy power.
 As thou has sanctified thyself in us before them,
So glorify thyself in them before us;

That they may know, as we also know,
That there is none other God but thee.
Renew the signs, and repeat the wonders,
Make Hand and Right Arm glorious.
Waken indignation and pour out wrath,
Subdue the foe and expel the enemy.
Hasten the 'end' and ordain 'the appointed time'...
Gather all the tribes of Jacob,
That they may receive their inheritance as in the days of old.
Compassionate the people that is called by thy name.
Israel, whom thou didst surname Firstborn.
Compassionate thy holy city,
Jerusalem, the place of thy dwelling.
Fill Sion with thy majesty,
And thy temple with thy glory ...
That all the ends of the earth may know
That thou art the eternal God. (36:1–22)

This passage outlines the various stages of Messianic anticipation – the destruction of Israel's enemies, the sanctification of God's name by elevating the Jewish nation, the performance of miracles, the ingathering of the exiles, the glorification of Jerusalem and the Temple, reward for the righteous and punishment for the wicked, and the fulfilment of prophetic expectations.

Although Ben Sira does not specify that salvation will come through Davidic rule or an individual Messiah, the author does specify that the house of David will be preserved. As a reward for his accomplishments, God gave him the decree of the kingdom and established his throne over Jerusalem (Ben Sira 47:11). Later in the same chapter he adds:

Nevertheless God did not forsake his mercy,
Nor did he suffer any of his words to fall to the ground.
He will not cut off the posterity of his chosen,
Nor will he destroy the offspring of them that love him.
And he will give to Jacob a remnant,
And to the house of David a root from him. (Ben Sira 47:22)

Just as the kingdom of David will last for ever, so will the priesthood of Aaron:

And he exalted a holy one (like unto him),
Even Aaron of the tribe of Levi.
And he made him an eternal ordinance,
And bestowed upon him his majesty. (Ben Sira 45:6–7)

Thus, not only does he believe in the continuation of the house of David, but also in the perpetuity of the priesthood of Aaron. In another passage, both of these institutions are coupled together:

Therefore for him, too, he established an ordinance,
A covenant of peace to maintain the sanctuary:
that to him and to his seed should appertain
The High-Priesthood for ever.
Also his covenant was with David,
The son of Jesse, of the tribe of Judah;
The inheritance of the king is his son's alone,
While the inheritance of Aaron (belongs) to him and to his seed.

(Ben Sira 45:24–5)

In Ben Sira there is a further future expectation – the coming of Elijah in the Messianic Age. After describing the mighty deeds of the prophet, he adds:

Who art ready for the time, as it is written,
To still wrath before the fierce anger of God,
To turn the heart of the fathers unto the children,
And to restore the tribes of Israel. (Ben Sira 48:10)

For Ben Sira, not only will the Jewish people endure for all time, but they will be a light to the gentiles. Speaking of Abraham and his descendants, the author declares:

Therefore with an oath he promised him
To bless the nations in his seed,
To multiply him 'as the dust of the earth',
And to exalt his seed 'as the stars';
To cause them to inherit 'from sea to sea
And from the River to the ends of the earth'. (Ben Sira 44:21)

Turning to the apocryphal Baruch (early part c. 130 BCE; later part c. 90 BCE), in the first part of this work there is a reference to the idea that God will bring about the return of the exiles to the land of their fathers once they have turned from their evil ways (Baruch 2:24–35). Later in the book the author describes Jerusalem which is to be renewed:

O Jerusalem, look about thee toward the east,
And behold the joy that cometh unto thee from God.
Lo, thy sons come, whom thou sentest away,
They come gathered together from the east to the west (at
    the word of the Holy One),
Rejoicing in the glory of God.
Put off, O Jerusalem, the garment of thy mourning and affliction,
And put on the comeliness of the glory that cometh from God
    for ever.
Cast about thee the robe of the righteousness which cometh
    from God;
Set a diadem on thine head of the glory of the Everlasting.

For God will show thy brightness unto every region under heaven.
For thy name shall be called of God for ever
The peace of righteousness, and the glory of godliness.
(Baruch 4:36 – 5:4)

The book continues with a description of the return of the exiles:

Arise, O Jerusalem, and stand upon the height,
And look about thee toward the east,
And behold thy children gathered from the going down of the
    sun unto the rising thereof (at the word of the Holy One),
Rejoicing that God hath remembered them.
For they went from thee on foot,
Being led away of their enemies:
But God bringeth them in unto thee
Borne on high with glory, as on a royal throne.
For God hath appointed that every high mountain, and the
    everlasting hills, should be made low,
That Israel may go safely in the glory of God.
Moreover the woods and every sweet-smelling tree have
    overshadowed Israel (by the commandment of God).
For God shall lead Israel with joy in the light of his glory
With the mercy and righteousness that cometh from him. (Baruch 5:5–9)

Alluding to Second Isaiah's vision of the ingathering of the exiles, the author depicts the re-establishment of Zion in glowing terms.

Unlike earlier apocryphal works that predict the transformation of earthly life, 2 Maccabees (c. 70 BCE) speculates about the nature of eternal life. Here the author emphasizes that reward and punishment are to be meted out in a future world. Of particular importance is a passage, presumably critical of Sadducean doctrine, stating that Judas Maccabaeus was 'bearing in mind the resurrection – for if he had not expected the fallen to rise again, it would have been superfluous and silly to pray for the dead' (2 Maccabees 12:43–4). Here the resurrection of the dead is conceived in bodily terms. Elsewhere the author contends that only the righteous will be restored to life; for sinners like Antiochus Epiphanes there is no deliverance from death.

Finally like 2 Maccabees, the Wisdom of Solomon is preoccupied with the World to Come, eternal life, and divine retribution. Thus in chapter 3 the author describes the reward for the righteous:

But the souls of the righteous are in the hand of God,
and no torment shall touch them.
In the eyes of fools they seemed to die;
And their departure was accounted to be their hurt,
And their going from us to be their ruin:
But they are in peace.
For though in the sight of men they be punished,
Their hope is full of immortality. (Wisdom of Solomon 3:1–4)

Turning to the destruction of the wicked, he describes the future Day of the Lord:

> He shall sharpen stern wrath for a sword:
> And the world shall go forth with him to fight against
>   his insensate foes,
> Shafts of lightning shall fly with true aim,
> And from the clouds, as from a well drawn bow, shall
>   they leap to the mark.
> And as from an engine of war shall be hurled hailstones
>   full of wrath;
> The water of the sea shall rage against them,
> And rivers shall sternly overwhelm them;
> A mighty blast shall encounter them,
> And as a tempest shall it winnow them away:
> So shall lawlessness make all the land desolate,
> And their evil-doing shall overturn the thrones of princes.
>   (*Wisdom of Solomon* 5:20–3)

THE ETHIOPIC *BOOK OF ENOCH*

Although the early parts of the Ethiopic *Book of Enoch* date from c. 110 BCE, its later parts were in all probability composed after the destruction of the Temple. Here the author presents a variety of reflections about the Messianic Age beginning with the Day of Judgement. During this period the Day of the Lord was identified with the 'birth pangs of the Messiah' – this did not refer to any suffering of the Messiah himself, but to the tribulations of the Messianic Age. In the *Book of Enoch* these events are portrayed in dramatic terms. The Holy Lord will come forth from his dwelling, appear from the highest of heavens and tread on Mount Sinai. As a consequence people will be overcome with fear and anguish will spread through the world. The mountains will be shaken, the high hills made low, and the earth sink; everyone will then undergo judgement. The righteous will be rewarded, whereas the wicked will be punished for their deeds (*Enoch* 1:3–9).

Not only will the wicked be chastised; so too will Satan and the angels who have corrupted the earth be brought to judgement. In addition, evil spirits, demons and devils will be condemned. The righteous, however, will prosper:

> Then shall they rejoice with joy and be glad,
> And into the holy place shall they enter;
> And its fragrance shall be in their bones,
> And they shall live a long life on earth,
> Such as their fathers lived:
> And in their days shall no sorrow or plague
> Or torment of calamity touch them. (*Enoch* 25:6)

In other passages the destruction to be visited upon the world is described in detail: severe affliction will come upon the world: the destitute will abandon their children, pregnant women will miscarry, and mothers will cast sucklings away:

In those days the nations shall be stirred up,
And the families of the nations shall arise on the day of destruction.
And in those days the destitute shall go forth and carry off their children,
And they shall abandon them, so that their children shall
    perish through them:
Yea, they shall abandon their children (that are still)
    sucklings, and not return to them,
And shall have no pity on their beloved ones. (*Enoch* 99:4–5)

On those days fathers and sons will be slain in one place; and brothers will fall together:

And in those days in one place the fathers together with their
    sons shall be smitten
And brothers one with another shall fall in death
Till the streams flow with their blood. (*Enoch* 100:1)

As far as the Messianic Age is concerned, the *Book of Enoch* states that only the elect will be worthy of entering the divine realm. They will live and never sin again, and there will be light and knowledge for the worthy:

And then there shall be bestowed upon the elect wisdom,
And they shall all live and never again sin . . .
And they shall not again transgress,
Nor shall they sin all the days of their life,
Nor shall they die of (the divine) anger or wrath,
But they shall complete the number of the days of their life.
                                  (*Enoch* 5:8–9)

As far as the terrestrial Messianic expectations are concerned, at the end of days the righteous will be delivered, beget a thousand children, and complete all their days in peace. The whole earth will be filled with righteousness and the fields will prosper. Along with such material prosperity, the *Book of Enoch* describes the spiritual renewal that will take place during the Days of the Messiah. The Lord will open the storehouses of heavenly blessing, which he will pour out upon the faithful:

And in those days I will open the store chambers of blessing which are in the heaven, so as to spread them down upon the earth over the work and labour of the children of men. And truth and peace shall be associated together throughout all the days of the world and throughout all the generations of men. (*Enoch* 11:1–2)

In the historical section of the book, the author presents the history of the world and the Jewish people to the present day – all of this is a prelude to the Days of the Messiah. Like the author of the book of Daniel, historical characters take the form of various creatures. After surveying the rise and fall of empires, the author goes on to describe the Day of Judgement, which is followed by the Days of the Messiah. The Messiah, he states, is a 'white bull with large horns', and all the beasts of the field and birds of the air fear and make supplications to him.

Added to this conception of the Messianic Age is a detailed description of the Messiah in chapters 37–71. Here it is asserted that the Messiah existed before the creation of the world. His dwelling-place is under the wings of the God of Spirits where the elect shall pass before him:

> And in that place mine eyes saw the Elect One of righteousness and of
>   faith,
> And I saw his dwelling-place under the wings of the Lord of Spirits.
> And righteousness shall prevail in his days,
> And the righteous and elect shall be without number before him for ever
>   and ever.
> And all the righteous and elect before him shall be strong as fiery lights,
> And their mouth shall be full of blessing. (*Enoch* 39:6–7)

On that day the Elect One will sit on the throne of glory and choose the occupations of men and their dwelling-places; their spirits will grow strong when they see the Messiah, and heaven and earth will be transformed. The elect will then dwell in a new and blessed earth upon which sinners and evildoers will not set foot:

> On that day Mine Elect One shall sit on the throne of glory
> And shall try their works,
> And their places of rest shall be innumerable.
> And their souls shall glory strong within them when they see
>   Mine Elect ones,
> And those who have called upon My glorious name:
> Then will I cause Mine Elect One to dwell among them.
> And I will transform the heavens and make it an eternal
>   blessing and light:
> And I will transform the earth and make it a blessing:
> And I will cause Mine Elect ones to dwell upon it:
> But the sinners and evil-doers shall not set foot thereon.
>   (*Enoch* 45:3–5)

The next chapter begins with imagery drawn from the book of Daniel:

> And I asked the angel who went with me and showed me all the hidden things, concerning that Son of Man, who he was, and whence he was, (and) why he went with the Head of Days? And he answered and said unto me:

> This is the Son of Man who hath righteousness,
> With whom dwelleth righteousness,
> and who revealeth all the treasures of that which is hidden,

Because the Lord of Spirits hath chosen him,
And whose lot hath the pre-eminence before the Lord of Spirits
    in uprightness for ever.
And this Son of Man whom thou hast seen
Shall raise up the kings and the mighty from their seats
(And the strong from their thrones)
And shall loosen the reins of the strong,
And break the teeth of the sinners. (*Enoch* 46:2–4)

In chapter 47 the Ancient of Days is depicted on the throne of glory where the books of the living will be opened before him:

In those days I saw the Head of Days when he seated himself upon
    the throne of his glory,
and the books of the living were opened before him:
And all his host which is in heaven above and his counsellors
    stood before him,
And the hearts of the holy were filled with joy. (*Enoch* 47:3)

In the next sections the importance of the Messiah is emphasized. He will be a staff to the righteous and holy, and a light to the gentiles. All who dwell on earth will worship and bless him and praise the God of Spirits. During the Days of the Messiah wisdom will be like the waters that cover the sea, and the glory of the Lord will be revealed. At this time drastic changes will take place in nature. The earth will bring to life those who have died and the Messiah will choose from among those who have risen righteous and holy: he will sit upon his throne and reveal secret knowledge:

And in those days the earth shall also give back that which has
    been entrusted to it,
And Sheol also shall give back that which it has received,
And hell shall give back that which it owes.
For in those days the Elect One shall arise,
And he shall choose the righteous and holy from among them:
For the day has drawn nigh that they should be saved.
                          (*Enoch* 51:1–2)

The latter part of the book adds new features to the presentation of the Messiah and his relation to the righteous. All the heavenly powers praise the Elect One; he will be seated on the throne of glory as he judges the deeds of the holy:

And the Lord of Spirits placed the Elect One on the throne of glory.
And he shall judge all the works of the holy above in the heaven,
and in the balance shall their deeds be weighed. (*Enoch* 61:8)

Then God commands the mighty kings and exalted rulers to recognize the Elect One as they see him seated on the throne with the spirit of righteousness poured out upon him:

> And he will summon all the host of the heavens, and all the holy ones above, and the host of God, the Cherubim, Seraphim and Ophannim, and all the angels of power, and all the angels of principalities, and the Elect One, and the other powers on the earth (and) over the water. On that day they shall raise one voice, and bless and glorify and exalt in the spirit of faith, and in the spirit of wisdom, and in the spirit of patience, and in the spirit of mercy, and in the spirit of judgment and of peace, and in the spirit of goodness, and shall all say with one voice: 'Blessed is he, and may the name of the Lord of Spirits be blessed for ever and ever.' (*Enoch* 61:10–11)

On this day the righteous and elect will be saved; the God of Spirits will abide over them and with the Son of Man they will eat and lie down and rise up forever:

> And the Lord of Spirits will abide over them.
> And with that Son of Man shall they eat
> And lie down and rise up for ever and ever.
> And they shall have been clothed with garments of glory,
> And these shall be the garments of life from the Lord of Spirits:
> and your garments shall not grow old,
> Nor your glory pass away before the Lord of Spirits. (*Enoch* 62:15–16)

JUBILEES, TESTAMENT OF THE TWELVE PATRIARCHS, AND PSALMS OF SOLOMON

Written in c. 100–90 BCE, the *Book of Jubilees* does not refer to a King–Messiah – in all likelihood this omission was due to the fact that at the time of its composition there existed an anointed king and priest of the house of Levi. Nonetheless, the book does contain Messianic ideas similar to those found in the Apocrypha. Because of the nation's sinfulness, the people will be punished; this will be followed by repentance, and only then will Israel will be redeemed. The Lord will build his sanctuary in their midst and dwell among them: 'And I will build my sanctuary in their midst, and I will dwell with them, and I will be their God and they shall be my people in truth and righteousness' (*Jubilees* 1:18).

Then a new world will be made: heaven and earth and all creatures will be renewed and the sanctuary of the Lord will be manifest in Jerusalem on Mount Zion.

In Chapter 23 the process of salvation is described in detail. After fearful punishment, there will be complete repentance and then divine redemption:

> And all their days they shall complete and live in peace
>   and joy,
> And there shall be no Satan nor any evil destroyer;
> For all their days shall be days of blessing and healing.

And at that time the Lord will heal his servants,
And they shall rise up and see great peace,
And drive out their adversaries.
And the righteous will see and be thankful,
And rejoice with joy for ever and ever,
And shall see all their judgments and their curses on their
     enemies. (*Jubilees* 23:29–30)

The *Testament of the Twelve Patriarchs* (c. 110–70 BCE) consists of ethical injunctions preceded by stories about the tribal patriarchs. In the last section of the *Testament of Simeon* there is a lofty Messianic oracle. Here Simeon encourages his sons to remove their envy and stiff-neckedness. Then, he states:

As a rose shall my bones flourish in Israel,
And as a lily my flesh in Jacob,
And my odour shall be as the odour of Libanus;
And as cedars shall holy ones be multiplied from me for ever,
    and their branches shall stretch afar off.
Then shall perish the seed of Canaan,
And a remnant shall not be unto Amalek,
And all the Cappadocians shall perish,
And all the Hittites shall be utterly destroyed.
Then shall fail the land of Ham
And all the people shall perish.
Then shall all the earth rest from trouble
And all the world under heaven from war.
Then the Mighty One of Israel shall glorify Shem,
For the Lord God shall appear on earth,
And Himself save men. (*Testament of the Twelve Patriarchs* 6:2–5)

Again, in the *Testament of Levi*, there is a depiction of divine redemption. After punishment has come from the Lord, he will raise up to the priestly office a new priest to whom all the words of God will be revealed; he will then execute judgement upon the earth:

Then shall the Lord raise up a new priest.
And to him all the words of the Lord shall be revealed;
And he shall execute a righteous judgment upon the earth
    for a multitude of days
And his star shall arise in heaven as of a king.
Lighting up the light of knowledge as the sun the day.
And he shall be magnified in the world.
He shall shine forth as the sun on the earth,
And shall remove all darkness from under heaven,
And there shall be peace in all the earth.
The heavens shall exult in his days,

And the earth shall be glad
And the clouds shall rejoice;
(And the knowledge of the Lord shall be poured upon the
earth, as the waters of the seas)
And the angels of the glory of the presence of the Lord shall be
  glad in him.
The heavens shall be opened,
And from the temple of glory shall come upon him sanctification.

(Testament of the Twelve Patriarchs 18:2–6)

The *Testament of Judah* also contains a vivid description of Messianic redemption. The star of peace will arise and walk in meekness among men. The heavens will be opened and pour out their blessings. The spirit of truth will come upon the children of Judah. A shoot will come forth from the stock of Judah and the rod of righteousness will be in his hand to judge and save all those who call upon him. All the tribes will become one people and have one language. Those who died in grief will arise and awake to everlasting life. The hungry will be satisfied, the poor made rich, and the weak become strong:

And ye shall be the people of the Lord, and have one tongue;
And there shall be no spirit of deceit of Beliar,
For he shall be cast into the fire for ever.
And they who have died in grief shall arise in joy,
And they who were poor for the Lord's sake shall be made rich,
And they who are put to death for the Lord's sake shall awake to life.

(Testament of the Twelve Patriarchs 25:3–4)

The *Psalms of Solomon* is a later book, written in c. 45 BCE, which enlarges on the personality of the Messiah. According to the author, the Hasmonean kings have acted wickedly; therefore it is a mistake to regard them as Messiahs. Turning to God, he prays for redemption, which he connects with the ingathering of the exiles:

Turn, O God, thy mercy upon us, and have pity upon us;
Gather together the dispersed of Israel, with mercy and goodness;
For thy faithfulness is with us.
And (though) we have stiffened our neck, yet thou art our chastener;
Overlook us not, O our God, lest the nations swallow us up, as
  though there were none to deliver. (*Psalms of Solomon* 8:33–6)

Such Messianic predictions continue in *Psalms of Solomon* 11:

Blow ye in Zion on the trumpet to summon the saints,
Cause ye to be heard in Jerusalem the voice of him that
  bringeth good tidings;
For God hath had pity on Israel in visiting them.
Stand on the height, O Jerusalem, and behold thy children,
From the East and the West, gathered together by the Lord;
From the North they come in the gladness of their God,

From the isles afar off God hath gathered them.
High mountains hath he abased into a plain for them;
The hills fled at their entrance . . .
Put on, O Jerusalem, thy glorious garments;
Make ready thy holy robe;
For God hath spoken good concerning Israel, for ever and ever.

(Psalms of Solomon 11:1–6, 8)

Continuing this Messianic theme, *Psalms of Solomon* 17 contains an accusation against the Hasmonean dynasty followed by a depiction of the redeemer of Israel:

Behold, O Lord, and raise up unto them their king, the son of
  David,
At the time in the which thou seest, O God, that he may reign over
  Israel thy servant.
And gird him with strength, that he may shatter unrighteous
  rulers,
And that he may purge Jerusalem from nations that trample (her)
  down to destruction . . .
And he shall gather together a holy people, whom he shall lead
  in righteousness,
And he shall judge the tribes of the people that has been sanctified
  by the Lord his God . . .
And he shall have the heathen nations to serve him under
  his yoke:
And he shall glorify the Lord in a place to be seen of all the
  earth;
And he shall purge Jerusalem, making it holy as of old:
So that nations shall come from the ends of the earth to see
  his glory,
Bringing as gifts her sons who had fainted,
And to see the glory of the Lord, wherewith God hath glorified her.
And he (shall be) a righteous king, taught of God, over them,
And there shall be no unrighteousness in his days in their midst,
For all shall be holy and their king the anointed of the Lord . . .
(He will be) shepherding the flock of the Lord faithfully and
  righteously,
And will suffer none among them to stumble in their pasture.
He will lead them aright,
And there will be no pride among them that any among them should
  be oppressed.
This (will be) the majesty of the king of Israel whom
  God knoweth;
He will raise him up over the house of Israel to correct him.
His words (shall be) more refined than costly gold, the choicest;
In the assemblies he will judge the peoples, the tribes of the
  sanctified.

His words (shall be) like the words of the holy ones in the midst
  of sanctified peoples.
Blessed be they that shall be in those days,
In that they shall see the good fortune of Israel which God shall
  bring to pass in the gathering together of the tribes.

(Psalms of Solomon 17:23–4; 28; 32–6; 45–50)

ASSUMPTION OF MOSES, SYRIAC BOOK OF BARUCH, 4 EZRA, AND THE SIBYLLINE ORACLES

Dating from c. 4–6 CE the *Assumption of Moses* does not contain an account of the Messiah; nonetheless in chapter 10 there is a depiction of the Day of the Lord. According to the author, Israel will triumph over her enemies, and there will be bliss and freedom in the Age to Come:

And then his kingdom shall appear throughout all his creation,
And then Satan shall be no more,
And sorrow shall depart with him.
Then the hands of the angel shall be filled
Who has been appointed chief,
And he shall forthwith avenge them of their enemies.
For the Heavenly One will arise from his royal throne,
And he will go forth from his holy habitation
With indignation and wrath on account of his sons . . .
For the Most High will arise, the Eternal God alone,
And he will appear to punish the Gentiles,
And he will destroy all their idols.
Then thou, O Israel, shalt be happy,
And thou shalt mount upon the neck and wings of the eagle,
And they shall be ended.
And God will exalt thee,
And he will cause thee to approach to the heaven of the stars,
In the place of their habitation.
And thou shalt look from on high and shalt see thy enemies
  in (Gehenna).
And thou shalt recognize them and rejoice,
And thou shalt give thanks and confess thy Creator.

(Assumption of Moses 10:1–3; 7–10)

Dating from c. 70–80 CE the *Syriac Book of Baruch* contains numerous Messianic expectations beginning with the birth pangs of the Messiah. The appointed time is coming – it will be a period of affliction:

Behold! the days come
And it shall be when the time of the age has ripened,
And the harvest of the seed of the good and the evil has come,

That the Mighty One will bring upon the earth,
And upon its inhabitants and its rulers,
Perturbation of spirit and anxiety of mind.
And they shall hate one another,
And provoke one another to fight;
And the mean shall rule over the honorable,
And those of low degree shall be extolled above the famous.
And the many shall be delivered into the hands of few,
And those who were nothing shall rule over the strong;
And the poor shall have control over the rich,
And the impious shall exalt themselves above the heroic.
And the wise shall be silent,
And the foolish shall speak. (*Syriac Book of Baruch* 48:53–4)

These events are to be followed by the coming the Messiah. After the signs have appeared, the Messiah will appear and he shall rule in peace and glory:

And then healing shall descend in dew,
And disease shall withdraw,
And anxiety and anguish and lamentation pass from amongst men,
And gladness proceed through the whole earth;
And no one shall again die untimely,
Nor shall any adversity suddenly befall.
And judgments and revilings and contentions and revenges,
And blood and passions and envy and hatred,
And whatsoever things are like these
Shall go into condemnation and be removed . . .
And wild beasts shall come from the forest
     and minister unto men,
And asps and vipers shall come forth from their holes
     to submit themselves to a little child;
And women shall no longer then
     have pain when they bear,
Nor shall they suffer torment
     when they yield the fruit of the womb . . .
For that time is the end of that which is corruptible,
And the beginning of that which is not corruptible.
Therefore those things which were predicted
     shall belong to it;
Therefore it is far away from evildoers,
And near to those who do not die.
                         (*Syriac Book of Baruch* 73:1 – 74:3)

Central to the *Syriac Book of Baruch* is the notion of a new world that is different from the Messianic Age. This is the World to Come, a new era in which there is no end and the righteous will receive a great light:

And the hour comes which abides forever,
And the new world, which does not turn to corruption
    those who enter into its blessedness,
And has no mercy on those who depart to torment,
And leads not to perdition those who live in it. (*Syriac Book of Baruch*
    44:12)

Fourth Ezra, which dates from c. 90–100 CE, contains numerous Messianic expectations along similar lines. Here, too, are descriptions of the birth pangs of the Messiah. According to *4 Ezra*, the signs that will precede the coming of the Messiah include great confusion and desolation. Responding to the question when such signs will take place, Ezra receives new signs indicating that the end is near:

When in the world there shall appear
quakings of lands
tumult of peoples,
schemings of nations,
confusion of leaders,
disquietude of princes,
then shalt thou understand that is of these things the Most High has spoken
since the days that were aforetime from the beginning. For just as with
respect to all that has happened in the world, it has a beginning in the
word (of God at creation) and a manifest end, so also are the times of the
Most High: the beginnings are revealed in portents and powers, and the
end in deed and in signs. (*4 Ezra* 8:62 – 9:6)

These occurrences are followed by the Messianic Age and the Day of Judgement. After the signs of the Messiah:

My Son the Messiah shall be revealed, together with those who are with
him (the righteous), and the survivors shall rejoice for four hundred years.
And it shall be, after these years, that My Son the Messiah shall die, and
all in whom there is human breath. Then shall the world be turned into
the primeval silence seven days, like as at the first beginnings, so that no
man is left. And it shall be after seven days that the age which is now asleep
shall be roused, and that which is corruptible (the age of corruption) shall
perish. And the earth shall restore those that sleep in her, and the dust those
that are at rest therein; and the chambers shall restore those that were
committed unto them. (*4 Ezra* 7:26–32)

The end of the world and the beginning of the World to Come is initiated by
the Day of Judgement. Then

the Most High shall be revealed
    on the throne of judgment,

and then cometh the End.
And compassion shall pass away,
    and long suffering be withdrawn;
But judgment alone shall remain,
    truth shall stand,
    and faithfulness triumph.
And recompense shall follow,
    and reward be made manifest;
Deeds of righteousness shall away,
    and deeds of iniquity shall not be repeated.
Then shall the pit of torment appear,
    and over against it the place of refreshment;
The furnace of Gehenna shall be made manifest,
    and over against it the Paradise of delight. (*4 Ezra* 7:33–6)

In a series of Messianic visions, the personality and work of the Messiah are depicted. From before the creation of the world he existed, and he is being kept with God until the time for him to be revealed. He is as strong as a lion and swift as an eagle, able to dominate all those who seek to wage war against him.

Finally, the *Sibylline Oracles* whose contents date from c. 140 BCE to 130 CE, contain a variety of Messianic ideas. Book 3 describes the confrontation between God and the anti-Messiah Beliar; here the Lord is victorious, bringing about the transformation of nature:

> Now from the Sebastenes shall Beliar come, and he shall move the high mountains, still the sea, make the great blazing sun and the bright moon stand still, raise the dead, and do many signs among men; but his signs shall not be effective in him. Yet he leads many astray, and shall deceive many faithful and elect of the Hebrews, and lawless men besides, who never have hearkened to God's word. But when the threatened vengeance of the Almighty God draws near, and a fiery power comes through the deep to land and burns up Beliar and all men of pride, even all that put their trust in him – then shall the world be ruled beneath a woman's hand and obey her in all things. And when a widow rules over the whole world, and casts gold and silver into the deep sea with the bronze and iron of short-lived mortals, then shall all the elements of the world be as one widowed, when God that dwelleth in the heavens shall roll up the sky as a book is rolled up. And the whole firmament with its many signs shall fall upon the earth and the sea; and then shall flow a ceaseless torrent of liquid fire, and shall burn up the earth and burn up the sea; and the firmament of heaven and the stars and creation it shall melt into one molten mass and clean dissolve. (*Sibylline Oracles*, Book 3, 63–87)

Reversing the order of other works, the *Sibylline Oracles* depicts the war with Gog and Magog after the advent of the Messianic Age. Then the children of Israel will dwell on their own soil with the King Messiah ruling over them. He will put an end to all wars on the earth and make a covenant with the righteous. After the war, all the sons of God will live quietly around the Temple, rejoicing in their salvation. Then all the peoples will see God's mercies and turn to him. They will acknowledge the rightness of the commandments and forsake their idols. Then humanity will live in peace:

> When this destined day is fully come . . . the fertile earth shall yield her best fruit of corn and wine and oil and sweet honey from heaven for drink, treats bearing fruit after their kind, flocks of sheep, oxen, lambs, and kids of the goats . . . No war nor drought shall afflict the land, no dearth nor hail to spoil the crops, but deep peace over all the earth. (*Sibylline Oracles*, Book 3, 741–55)

Then all the earth will be filled with knowledge of God; famine will cease, wars will be ended, and one system of law will prevail for all.

BIBLIOGRAPHY

Anderson, B. W., *The Eighth-Century Prophets*, London, 1979.

Ben-Sasson, H. H., *A History of the Jewish People*, Cambridge, 1976.

Bright, J., *A History of Israel*, London, 1972.

Charles, R. H., *The Apocrypha and Pseudepigrapha of the Old Testament in English*, vol. 2, Oxford, 1913.

Cohn-Sherbok, D. *The Jewish Messiah*, Edinburgh, 1997.

Grant, M., *The History of Ancient Israel*, New York, 1984.

Jacobs, L., *A Jewish Theology*, New York, 1973.

Klausner, J., *The Messianic Idea in History*, London, 1956.

Lindblom, J. *Prophecy in Ancient Israel*, Oxford, 1962.

Seltzer, R., *Jewish People, Jewish Thought*, London, 1980.

Silver, A. H., *A History of Messianic Speculation in Israel*, Gloucester, Mass., 1978.

CHAPTER FORTY-THREE

SALVATION IN CHRISTIAN THOUGHT

—·◆·—

Andrew Chester

Salvation is a central emphasis in early Christian thought from the earliest stages. Fundamental to this is the fact that the death of Jesus is seen as a saving event. The most profound and best-known exposition is that of Paul. His basic position can be summed up quite simply: the death of Christ potentially brings about salvation for all. This is worked out in a number of different ways, using a variety of metaphors, and involves several difficult questions. The central theme, that Christ's death has final, saving effect, is found not only in Paul (Williams 1975) but in most of the rest of the New Testament as well (Grayston 1990). It is therefore important to do justice, as far as possible within the constraints here, to this theme, its different facets, implications and problems, and to the distinctive emphasis of the different writings. Along with this, and indeed as preliminary to it, it is worth asking whether what we find in much of the New Testament is true to what Jesus himself understood about his own death and its significance.

First, however, it needs to be made clear that the use of the term and concept 'salvation' is in itself something quite remarkable in a first-century context. It is perhaps above all because Paul's position has become so important and influential that it may appear to us completely obvious that salvation should be set at the heart of Christianity, and should perhaps indeed be seen as central to any major religious system. Yet the fact is that both Paul and Jesus, whatever else they were, were Jews of the first century, and for these 'salvation' (in the sense it acquires in developed Christian theology) would seem strange (Sanders 1977; Loewe 1981). The focus of Jewish usage would be much more obviously on deliverance and release, and being brought back to health and safety. Hence the sense 'salvation' takes on in the New Testament is itself notable; whether it is a justifiable and coherent development is something we need to investigate.

JESUS

We come, then, in the light of this, to Jesus. The question that obviously arises, in view of the very early and emphatic interpretation of his death as a saving event, is whether he himself points in this direction as well. There does not, at least at first sight, appear to be much evidence for this. If such evidence is lacking, it does not of course necessarily mean that it is invalid for Paul and others to interpret his death as they do and make it central to their theology. But clearly it would raise the question of whether there is genuine continuity and consistency between what Jesus sets in motion and what Paul and others are responsible for developing as a movement, and as an understanding of the movement's founding figure.

The most obvious, and famous, place in the gospels where Jesus does have a 'Pauline' view of his death is Mark 10.45 (and parallels): 'The Son of Man came not to be served but to serve, and to give his life as a ransom for many' (and 'many' here is best understood as Semitic usage for 'all'). This looks clear and impressive (Jeremias 1971; Stuhlmacher 1986). To many scholars, however, it looks too good (or too close to Paul) to be true. That is, its authenticity has been strongly questioned (Bultmann 1965; Sanders 1985); it is seen as a form of words, set on Jesus' lips, to conform to the main view held in the early church and to show Jesus anticipating his death and making sense in advance of this horrendous event. Hence it would be dangerous to base too much, initially at least, on this verse; if a case is to be made for Jesus interpreting his death in a redemptive sense, it will be important to establish a different and wider basis.

There are certainly arguments and evidence that can be used to make this kind of case (Wenham 1995), although inevitably some will find them more convincing than others. It is quite plausible that Jesus predicted his own death (Bayer 1986). In Palestine in the first century, the Roman and Jewish authorities were quick to put to death leaders of popular movements (whether or not they were threatening violence), and figures such as John the Baptist who were openly critical of the authorities. Hence Jesus would easily have seen it as probable that he would be put to death, especially in view of his own confrontation with the authorities and the offence he caused them. He could even have seen his death as inevitable and as part of the divine plan: that is, as necessary to fulfil scripture and to help bring in the kingdom. So, for example, at the Last Supper (Mark 14.22–6 and parallels), Jesus appears to see his death as imminent (and it was, of course, immediately following the Last Supper that he was arrested and put on trial), and the final realization of the kingdom as bound up with and lying just beyond it (cf. Luke 22.15–16). The Last Supper was in all probability celebrated as a Passover meal (Jeremias 1966); hence Jesus could be pointing to his death as helping to bring about a new Exodus or final deliverance. According to one tradition (Luke 22.20; cf. 1 Cor. 11.25), he understood his broken body and outpoured blood as helping bring in the 'new covenant', that is, the new and fully and finally transformed relationship (Jer. 31.31–4). In Mark 14.24 he speaks of his blood being poured out 'for many'. This calls to mind not only Mark 10.45, but also Isaiah 53.12. Hence Jesus could be pointing (as also in the Mark 10.45 tradition) to his death as that of the righteous, innocent, Suffering Servant of Isaiah (thus Hengel 1981, in contrast to Hooker 1959; Barrett 1967). There was by the first century a strong Jewish tradition of vicarious martyr's death and redemptive suffering (e.g. 2 Macc. 7; 4 Macc. 17). Jesus may then consciously have aligned himself with this, and even seen his death as bound up with the forgiveness he offered openly, indeed offensively, as far as the Jewish authorities were concerned.

All of this is possible, and needs to be reckoned with seriously. It would clearly mean that Mark 10.45 could be understood as consistent with what Jesus says, and acts out, otherwise. Yet there are also strong traditions, which are difficult to explain away, that Jesus was appalled at the prospect of his execution, and looked to God to avert it (Mark 14.32–42; 15.34: Barrett 1967). In this case, he could have expected divine intervention even at the very last moment. The fact remains, in any case, that the real heart of Jesus' message and ministry is liberation from evil, oppression, deformity and being despised. That is, the most striking aspect of the Synoptic Gospels' accounts of Jesus' life and teaching is that he is centrally concerned with providing healing and deliverance from all forces of evil as an integral part of the coming of the Kingdom of God. Above all, these forces of evil are thrown out in Jesus' exorcisms and healings, and the kingdom is already beginning to break in (Jeremias 1971). The thrust of what Jesus says and does is concentrated on the kingdom, with its enormously positive force and liberating potential, and Jesus himself is instrumental in bringing it in, or at least to the threshold of arrival. What is not clear, however, is that Jesus sees his own death as a necessary or even an integral part of this happening, or as having any saving or liberating effect in and of itself. His death at the hands of the authorities may seem inevitable, but it does not appear to be required for or causally connected with the coming of the kingdom. And it is the kingdom, imminently expected, where the truly liberating message and force of Jesus is to be found.

The Synoptic Gospels certainly have their own distinctive interpretations of Jesus' death (Hooker 1994). Thus for Mark it represents the beginning of a new people, covenant and Passover, and the pattern for a discipleship of taking up the cross. For Matthew, Jesus' death and resurrection constitute a cosmic event that brings about the resurrection of God's people. In Luke–Acts, Jesus *has* to die, and his death makes forgiveness available to all. Salvation pervades the whole of Jesus' ministry and the apostolic proclamation, and the church and new community owe their existence to Jesus' death. These are striking emphases, but the central focus for Jesus in the Synoptics is still, decisively, the kingdom. The most that Mark 10.45 or the account of the Last Supper may do is to suggest that Jesus' death can have symbolic significance within this wider context and in relation to this central theme (i.e. the kingdom and what it implies). It cannot, however, prove that Jesus' death in this manner is the core of God's salvific intervention and decisive act of deliverance, which is what Paul (and not only Paul, of course) makes Jesus' death to be. Jesus saw the future kingdom as the culmination of what had begun in his ministry. He also saw the salvation of Israel in a quite specific, down-to-earth sense, involving the overthrow of Israel's enemies and the restoration of divine sovereignty. His vision of this is certainly remarkable: it will not be brought about by violent means, but the disciples are promised a share in the rule of this kingdom, and outcasts and outsiders will share prominently in it as well. It is, then, a ministry of healing, casting out of evil, forgiveness and reconciliation, but there is no conclusive evidence that Jesus set his own violent death as necessary for this, still less as being the main focus.

PAUL

For Paul, by contrast, the main focus for salvation is the death of Christ. But we need then to ask what exactly is Paul's understanding of salvation. There are several major aspects that have to be taken into account (Scott 1927). In one sense, this understanding can be seen as both *negative and positive*: that is, both what people are saved *from*, and also what they are saved *for*, as a new experience and way of life. Negatively, then, salvation for Paul means deliverance from death, from sin, from the curse and constraints of the law, and from an evil and immoral way of life. It also denotes deliverance from divine wrath, judgement and condemnation. Hence it can be said that salvation in Paul is to be understood as liberation from all forces and powers of evil, and thus overlaps considerably with the Gospels' portrayal of Jesus; but in fact the main emphasis in each case only coincides to a limited extent. Positively, salvation leads to a completely new way of life, characterized by being in Christ and filled with the Spirit. It is a way of life that involves a profoundly new relationship with God, characterized by peace, freedom and holiness.

Salvation also has both an *individual* and a *collective focus* in Paul's writings. It is true that Paul has often appeared to be simply individual in emphasis, and that can indeed be seen as his primary emphasis. So much is clear, for example, from the importance he attaches to *faith*.. There is no merit in believing, but each individual has to respond in faith in order for the gift of salvation to take effect. In certain respects, then, there is a contrast here with Judaism, where all belong (by definition) within the covenant relationship (Sanders 1977). Yet there is also a collective aspect: Paul speaks in prospect of the Gentiles being saved and, famously, affirms that 'All Israel will be saved!' (Rom. 11.26). And in Romans 5.12–21 Paul speaks of 'acquittal and life for all', 'the grace of God and the free gift in the grace of the one man Jesus Christ abounding for many', and 'many being made righteous' (where 'many' in both cases probably means 'all'). Here and in a few other places it appears that Paul's understanding of salvation is actually universalist. In fact, however, the most plausible interpretation of what Paul says is that salvation is *potentially* universalist in scope, but has to be *actualized* for each individual in order to be effective. Underlying this, of course, is the question of God's nature, as well as the scope and effect of Christ's death. That is, does God's love and mercy encompass all and apply to all with saving effect, whether or not there is specific human response? Or does failure to respond to, or wilful rejection of, the gospel put individuals (or, indeed, whole *groups* of people) outside the scope of God's saving work in Christ?

In a few places, the scope of salvation in Paul appears to be not only universal, but *cosmic* as well. Indeed, these overlap. The statement 'God was in Christ, reconciling the world to himself' belongs to a context (2 Cor. 5.18–21) where the scope of salvation seems potentially all-embracing. Yet the reference here is not cosmic in any full sense: the 'world' has to be understood primarily in terms of the people in it. Romans 8.18–25 clearly goes further: the main focus in this passage is the whole created order, where it is said that it 'waits with eager longing for the revealing of the sons of God'. Equally striking are Colossians 1.19–20: 'For in him all the fulness of God was pleased to dwell, and through him to reconcile all things to himself, whether on earth or in heaven, making peace by the blood of his cross', and Ephesians 1.9–10: 'according to (God's) purpose which he set forth in Christ as a plan for the fulness of time, to bring together all things in him, things in heaven and things on earth'.

All three of these passages represent a vision of the consummation of God's plan in cosmic terms. They are closely related to a strong Jewish visionary, or apocalyptic, tradition. But the Pauline authorship of Colossians and Ephesians is disputed (especially so for Ephesians, which is very probably dependent on Colossians). That only leaves Romans 8 as a definitely Pauline vision of cosmic redemption. It portrays the whole created order being delivered from the forces of evil that have held it captive, and becoming part of God's domain again. Rhetorically it is impressive, but the detail is vague, and again it cannot be said that all *people* are set free, except *potentially* so. Notably, Romans 8 begins (8.1): 'There is now no condemnation for those in Christ'. Thus Paul's vision of salvation is individual, corporate and cosmic in scope, but the individual emphasis predominates, and responding by faith and being 'in Christ' are primary, indeed essential, elements of Paul's understanding.

Paul's concept of salvation also ranges over *past, present* and *future*. It is firmly rooted in the *past*: Christ's death is the saving event, which has already happened, is once-for-all and unrepeatable, and has inaugurated the final, eschatological age (so, e.g., Rom. 4.25; 5.6–8; 8.32). Not only the fact, but also the effect, of Christ's death can also be spoken of as in the past. 'Since then we have been justified by faith . . .' (Rom. 5.1); 'while we were enemies, we were reconciled to God by the death of his Son' (Rom. 5.10); 'in this hope we were saved' (Rom. 8.24). Clearly Paul sees those who respond in faith to God's saving act in Christ as already saved. Yet Paul also speaks of 'being saved' as though it is a continuing process in the *present* (e.g. 1 Cor. 1.18; 2 Cor. 2.15, especially in contrast to those who 'are perishing'; cf. 1 Cor. 15.2). Nor is that all. Salvation is also set firmly in the *future*, as for example at Romans 5.9–10: 'we shall be saved by him from the wrath of God . . . we shall be saved by his life' (cf., e.g., 1 Cor. 15.2). This all seems confusing, if not indeed contradictory. In some cases those whose salvation is set in the future have not yet responded in faith, and so it is clear why there should be a distinction. But in Romans 5.9–11 there is a constant shifting between past and future in relation to the same group of people: they both have been saved and will be saved. And this is by no means an isolated instance in Paul.

How then is this apparent contradiction to be resolved? Romans 8.24 ('for we were saved in hope') may provide a clue. Where salvation is spoken of as something lying in the past it also has, implicitly, a future aspect as well. Paul's perspective, for his concept of salvation as much as for the rest of his life and thought, is above all *eschatological* (Pate 1995). One aspect of this is that Paul lives in expectation of the imminent final judgement. It is part of his Jewish heritage, but it is equally something he reckons with very seriously and not as a mere formality, both for himself and for his churches. So the future aspect of being saved refers at least, and perhaps primarily, to being delivered from condemnation and divine wrath in the final judgement. This does not mean that the past experience of being saved is emptied of meaning. Nor does it imply that the status of salvation is merely arbitrary and easily forfeited. But there is a real cutting edge to the final judgement, and Paul implies at least that some of those in the communities (e.g. at Corinth), who assume that they are saved, may find that in the end they are not. Hence we are faced with the paradox that Paul on the one hand gives absolute assurance of salvation, while on the other he seems to leave this still open to question. The contradiction, for Paul, is apparent, not real. He sees the response of faith as giving rise to a new life, filled with the Spirit and characterized by the fruits of the Spirit.

Hence, despite the fact that he stands in awe of the final judgement, he can see final deliverance as already assured.

Thus salvation for Paul is not something static. Nor is it something that simply happens at one point in the past, as though with magical effect. There is, of course, a decisive moment when the good news of salvation is accepted. But being saved is itself a continuing process; hence it is that Paul can speak of 'we who are being saved' (1 Cor. 1.18). And salvation is not an abstract idea for Paul. It is an urgent and pressing issue for everyone. The end is imminent, and the only important thing for each person is to make sure that they are within the sphere of God's saving grace. The present aspect of salvation is also caught up with this urgent emphasis: '*Now* is the time of salvation' (2 Cor. 6.2). The 'now' is both urgently present and also eschatological; the two are bound up together. Paul does not at any point work with an extended time-scale; hence past, present and future all stand much closer together than we might assume. 'Our salvation is nearer now than when we first believed' (Rom. 13.11), but it was never very far distant. And, as we have seen, living in the light of salvation means, for Paul, living in Christ, filled with the Spirit and being made a 'new creation'. It means, in short, living in a manner fit for the messianic age. Paul's very different statements about salvation cannot simply be collapsed into each other, but they are much less unconnected than might at first appear.

From this vantage point we may also be able to understand another apparently strange aspect of what Paul says. The major thrust of his position on salvation is that it is entirely God's gracious initiative and act of love; the human response of faith is necessary, but that is all. Ephesians 2.8–9 was probably written by a follower of Paul, not Paul himself, but it sums up his position very clearly: 'By grace you have been saved by faith; and this is not your own doing, it is a gift of God. It is not because of works, lest anyone should boast.' In view of this, some of Paul's statements are quite startling, even scandalous: 'Work out your own salvation with fear and trembling!' he tells the Philippians (Phil. 2.12). And at Colossians 1.24 we are confronted by the following (from Paul or someone very close to him): 'Now I rejoice in my sufferings for your sake, and I in my flesh make up what is lacking in Christ's afflictions for the sake of his body, that is, the church.' All this seems quite extraordinary. Is it not fundamental for Paul that Christ's death is the once-for-all, sole and sufficient source of salvation? What can possibly be *lacking* in Christ's suffering on the cross? And what part can humans possibly play in effecting their own salvation?

What Colossians 1.24 says, in apparently blasphemous fashion, is in fact echoed in part in other Pauline passages which speak of suffering for or on behalf of Christ. Paul clearly sees the afflictions and sufferings of believers as representing active participation in Christ's own suffering and death, and as belonging to the important and inevitable sufferings of the messianic age, which is now set in motion and that will culminate in the Kingdom of God. Such suffering can be understood, in one sense at least, as having redemptive significance; that is, it has a place within the overall redemptive plan of God, which is now coming to its climax. The primary place in this redemptive schema belongs of course to Christ and his death, and the suffering of Christians can only take on significance when it is set in relation to that, but Paul assigns to it at least indirect salvific purpose. Philippians 2.12 is very difficult to explain. The idea that humans could 'work out' or 'bring about' their own salvation does indeed seem to go against all that Paul says otherwise. But from what immediately follows (2.14–16), it is clear that Paul is exhorting the Philippians to live transformed lives, pure and holy, fit for the new and final age. This is consistent with what we have seen already, and is an integral part of Paul's urgent eschatological message. It is precisely because the final days are now approaching that it is necessary to live holy lives. It is also precisely because of this sense of urgency that Paul can stress the importance of human agency in salvation. So he speaks of himself as 'saving' people (Rom. 11.14; 1 Cor. 9.22): he does so in the sense that he acts as the agent of divine salvation. The saving work is always God's, but human involvement is always present, in preaching the gospel, which enables people to respond, in the response in faith, and (as here) in ensuring that salvation is consistently worked out and taken hold of.

There are thus tensions (at times apparently bordering on contradictions) in Paul's understanding of salvation. Not all of these can easily be resolved, and at least to that extent it is not possible to give a fully coherent account. And Paul is writing letters (if very unusual letters!) for contingent and urgent circumstances (Beker 1980). So he nowhere sets out to present a systematic account of his thought (not even in Romans). Much of what we have considered, however (e.g. the past, present and future, individual and corporate reference of salvation), shows that Paul's thought is not monochrome, but is subtle and multifaceted. This is also reflected in the variety of impressive metaphors he uses to describe God's saving work in Christ (Scott 1927; Dunn 1998).

The most famous of these metaphors is that of *justification by faith* (Stuhlmacher 1986; Seifrid 1992). Justification represents essentially the language of the law-court: the point, then, is that God accounts as just or righteous those who in themselves have no righteousness. But Paul uses it in a strongly eschatological sense: this anticipates the verdict God will give at the final judgement. He reckons them righteous because they accept through faith what he has brought about in the death of Christ, which satisfies the just requirements of the law. Paul stresses that righteousness can come only thus, and not by observing the law (as he once held), or by human merit. For humans, being righteous depends entirely on God's grace. Paul thus transforms the legal categories. Justification is not a legal fiction (calling just what is not), but opens up a new relationship with God, which fulfils the covenant relationship and shows God to be true to his covenantal, righteous character (Ziesler 1972).

Where Paul speaks of *redemption* (e.g. Gal. 4.5; Rom. 3.24; 1 Cor. 6.2; 7.23: Gibbs 1971; Marshall 1990), God is pictured as buying back those who really belong to him already. The main focus of the metaphor is release from slavery. In Jewish tradition it denotes above all liberation from captivity at the Exodus, and hence deliverance from oppression in the final age. This is fundamental for Paul as well: what God has brought about in the death of Christ is deliverance, in the final age, from captivity to sin, law and death, and liberation from a condemned form of existence.

Occasionally Paul hints at Christ being a *sacrifice* (e.g. 1 Cor. 5, 7; 15.20, 23; Rom. 8.3, 32: Davies 1981; Dunn 1998), although only later (e.g. Eph. 5.2) is there a clear statement of Christ's death being a sacrifice or offering. The difficult and disputed Rom. 3.25 is also best understood in a sacrificial sense, although the idea of Christ's death being a propitiatory sacrifice (Morris 1965), used by God to appease his own anger, is certainly to be rejected (Dodd 1935; Hooker 1994).

Paul uses the metaphor of *reconciliation* sparingly, but it comes at central points of his argument at 2 Corinthians 5.18–21 and Romans 5.10–11 (Martin 1981). It represents a powerful expression of his understanding of God's saving work in Christ. The imagery is that of mending a broken relationship. Paul emphasizes that Christ's death has broken down the barriers caused by sin and restored a right relationship with God. The usage is, then, above all personal and relational. Here (2 Cor. 5.21) it is said that Christ became sin (just as he became a 'curse', Gal. 3.13); that is, Christ shared the human condition of sin, death and alienation, so that humans could share in his overcoming of these (Hooker 1990).

None of these (or the other) metaphors that Paul uses is fully adequate to express his understanding of salvation, or what is involved in his conception of the scope of the divine action, the effect of this, and the nature of the human response. They can be seen for the most part as mutually complementary and expressing different and important aspects of what is involved and how it can best be articulated. But what is not always immediately obvious from them is Paul's profoundly *relational* sense of salvation. It is most evident with 'reconciliation', that is, the overcoming of the fragile nature of the human relationship with God, and the bringing together of those for whom normal relationships have seriously broken down. It is at least implied in the others, and is especially evident in the characteristic Pauline expression being 'in Christ' (as also the correlative theme of the Spirit dwelling in the believer), used to denote the new sphere of life that has now been entered into (Schweitzer 1931; Moule 1977). Finally, the importance of the *resurrection* for Paul's understanding of salvation should not be overlooked (Grayston 1990; Hooker 1994). It is of course the death of Christ that for Paul has final, salvific effect; but it is Christ's resurrection that is central and a prerequisite for his whole concept of salvation, and of the new way of life that this denotes.

The Pastoral Epistles (1 and 2 Timothy, Titus), reflecting a development of Pauline tradition at least a generation beyond Paul's death, contain Pauline-sounding summaries of the salvation brought about through Christ (e.g. Tit. 3.4–7), and strong emphasis otherwise on salvation and final judgement (1 Tim. 1.14–15; 3.16; 2 Tim. 1.9–10; Tit. 2.14). Notably, both Jesus and God are specifically designated as Saviour (1 Tim. 4.10; Tit. 1.4), but statements otherwise about salvation are curious (or worse: 1 Tim. 2.15), and generally lack Paul's profound and urgent probing of the issues.

HEBREWS

Hebrews, like Paul, portrays Jesus' death as a saving event. In contrast to Paul, however, its terms of reference are strongly and consistently those of Jewish cult and sacrifice. More precisely, Hebrews draws an absolute contrast between what Jesus' death achieves and what the Jewish priesthood and sacrificial system fail to. Thus while Paul says that Jesus' death effects what the law could not do, Hebrews stresses, again and again, that what Jesus' death achieves perfectly, the priests and sacrifices could only ever do imperfectly (7.23–8; 9.6–14).

As far as salvation is concerned, Jesus' death is the perfect, final sacrifice that atones for sin fully, once and for all (7.27; 10.10, 12: Chester 1991; Lindars 1991a, 1991b). He is the eternal, perfect, unique and sinless High Priest, who has passed through the heavenly world and gives direct access to the presence of God (1.3; 4.14; 6.19–20; 8.1). All this stands in deliberate and stark contrast to the Jewish cult. There, the same sacrifices have constantly to be repeated, and are completely ineffectual and unable to deal with sin; the priests are human, impermanent, tainted by sin and limited to the earthly world (7.23; 9.6, 25; 10.1–4, 11). So Jesus' saving death renders the Jewish priestly and sacrificial system obsolete: it no longer has a place in providing salvation. One main reason for this absolute contrast, and harsh, negative judgement lies in the context for the writing of the letter. Those addressed – Jews who now formed a 'Christian' community – were apparently being tempted back to observance of Jewish cultic practice. Partly this was because they were faced with the problem of sins they had committed, and for which there seemed no means of atonement (10.27–8). They had cut themselves off, for example, from the provisions of the Day of Atonement, and now felt themselves drawn back to it, as also to other tangible forms of divine presence and forgiveness.

In the face of this, Hebrews draws its absolute contrast, and argues that Christ's sacrifice surpasses the limitations of the Jewish system of sacrifice and atonement. The Day of Atonement deals only with sins of ignorance; Jesus' death deals with all sins for all time (Gordon 1991). On the Day of Atonement, the High Priest enters the Holy of Holies only briefly; Jesus has entered it permanently (Lindars 1991b). Indeed, Christ's death achieves its full, saving power in the *heavenly* sanctuary, not in the earthly world.

It is important for Hebrews' argument that Christ belongs fully in the true, heavenly world and that the salvation his death brings is fully effective there. Yet along with this very elevated picture, Hebrews also stresses that Jesus voluntarily takes on himself human nature, weakness and a shameful form of death (2.14–18; 4.15). As with Philippians 2.5–11, so also Hebrews maintains that what makes Christ's saving activity truly distinctive is his stooping so low and sharing fully the human condition. Thus overall, while Paul has the most profound and prolific treatment of salvation in the whole of the New Testament, that in Hebrews is the most concentrated and powerfully intense.

1 PETER

Although it lacks a sustained argument, 1 Peter presents a constant stress on salvation throughout. There is strong emphasis especially on the death of Christ as central to salvation. The clearest and most vivid summary statement is provided in 3.18 and, in what it says, it stands very close to the main Pauline themes. That is, humans are in themselves unrighteous, but the death of Jesus, the righteous one, allows them access to God and enables them to be accepted by him, and so have new life in the Spirit (cf. Paul, e.g. Rom. 5.2). Similarly, 1.18–19 speaks of those it addresses as being 'ransomed . . . with the precious blood of Christ', which is reminiscent of both Paul and Hebrews, while the reference to 'sprinkling with his blood' (1.2) recalls Hebrews 9.13, 15–20 and, as there, sets salvation specifically in relation to the covenant.

References to Christ's suffering are frequent (e.g. 4.1: 'suffered in the flesh'), but the most outstanding aspect, as indeed of 1 Peter's whole portrayal of salvation, is the way Jesus is presented as the Suffering Servant of Isaiah 53. This may be implicit in 1.19 ('a lamb without blemish or spot'), but is in any case made completely explicit in 2.21–5, with its virtual citation of Isaiah 53. Here Christ's wounds, suffering and death are given salvific value, on the pattern of the Suffering Servant.

It is notable as well that Christ's suffering is seen as an *example* for believers' suffering (2.21), and that the suffering of believers also appears to have a role in the schema of salvation. This emerges, for example, from 4.13–14, and again is close to what we have already seen in Paul. The necessity of suffering and prospect of persecution, both for individuals and also for the community, are strongly stressed throughout the letter, and have clear ethical implications. There is also a prominent eschatological emphasis, which is closely related to both suffering and salvation. Thus 4.7 is unequivocal about the imminent nature of the end, while 1.5–9 speaks of being protected by the power of God through faith for a salvation ready to be revealed in the last time, but the *genuineness* of the faith is to be tested by fire, that is, the 'trials' of 1.6. The passage as a whole concludes (1.9): 'As the outcome of your faith you obtain the salvation of your souls.' Clearly this will be 'at the revelation of Jesus Christ', that is, at the end; but the obvious implication is that this depends on their faith withstanding the testing.

Thus salvation is, in an important sense, provisional. The final judgement is still awaited, and the result of this cannot be taken for granted. Faith is essential, but needs to be proved in the severe and final testing. So salvation is not something already fully assured. Much of this is close to what we find in Paul, although there appears in 1 Peter to be less assurance of salvation, and the concept of faith stands rather closer to that in Hebrews. Certainly 1 Peter is reminiscent of Paul in its stress on the need for holy living, obedience to the gospel and new life in the Spirit. In showing how God's saving act takes effect, however, 1 Peter uses the unusual metaphor of being born again, or born anew. This is found otherwise in the New Testament only in John 3. The way this 'rebirth' is expressed, in both 1.3 and 1.23, is vivid (and the latter especially has obvious affinities with Gnostic ideas). But in 1 Peter, a corollary of the being 'born anew' appears to be that they begin again as infants, and need careful tending and nourishment (e.g. 2.2). That is, salvation involves a process of maturing. Here 1 Peter goes beyond what we have found otherwise.

There is a further remarkable, indeed unique, aspect of 1 Peter's view of salvation. This is the idea (3.19–20; 4.6) that Christ went and preached to the formerly disobedient 'spirits in prison' and that 'the gospel was preached to the dead' (Reicke 1946; Dalton 1965). The idea, then, is that Christ descended to the underworld and proclaimed the gospel there; the idea of *descent*, at least, is found also in Ephesians 4.9. The point of this is to allow universal repentance and salvation; so at least it would appear from the reason given in 4.6 ('For this is why the gospel was preached even to the dead, that though judged in the flesh like men, they might live in the spirit like God'). But if this is curious, still more so is the sequel in 3.20–1, the account of Christ's preaching to the departed, where baptism is apparently portrayed as a (or the?) means of salvation. The force of this is presumably that the purification that baptism entails and symbolizes is essential for salvation, and the implication can of course be that it is baptism that gives rise to life in the Spirit. At any rate, the guarantee of salvation here, effectively, is not baptism but Christ's resurrection and heavenly authority.

The understanding of salvation in 1 Peter thus has much in common with what we find in Paul and Hebrews. Jesus' death represents God's supreme saving act. It has final, eschatological significance and all the urgency that this implies. Salvation is an act of God's mercy and grace. It effects a transfer from darkness to light, from a state of non-existence to a state of true existence. All this implies the need for pure and holy living, as the final events come to a climax and eschatological tribulation is endured. The final judgement is still in the future, and only in the light of that can salvation be secure. Along with these points held in common, however, several aspects of salvation in 1 Peter are altogether distinctive.

GOSPEL AND EPISTLES OF JOHN

In John's Gospel (Dodd 1953) Jesus is sent by God, in order to die and to save the world. He is himself a fully willing and conscious participant in this; his death is set as part of the divine plan from the beginning, and Jesus is completely in control of his part in this. He chooses to lay down his life (it cannot be taken from him until the right moment in the divine plan of salvation), and is in control of his own trial (7.30; 13.1; 19.11). His death is represented as a triumph, not a tragedy, and as the fulfilment of the divine plan (19.28, 30). The manner of his death, with blood and water flowing from him, symbolizes life and salvation (19.34). He speaks of himself being 'lifted up', in a deliberately double sense: being lifted up on the cross, to be put to death, and being lifted up in glory (3.14; 8.28; 12.32: there is indeed a third sense, which overlaps with this, of being lifted up in the resurrection). Hence, astoundingly, his death represents not only life and salvation, but the glory of God as well.

Jesus can therefore be spoken of as the Saviour of the World: he comes to save the world, not to judge it (3.17; 4.42). Nevertheless, judgement and condemnation are inexorably written into the equation. A sharp dualism hovers over the whole of the Gospel: between death and life, salvation and judgement (or condemnation), above and below, believers and the world (or the Jews), light and darkness. There is indeed a deep ambiguity about the world throughout the Gospel. Jesus has overcome the world, and this would seem to suggest that the world no longer exists as a hostile or alien force. At the same time, however, remaining in the world denotes condemnation. Thus Jesus is in himself the light of the world, the bread of life and the resurrection and the life, but it is only those who believe who share this light and life. The clear implication is that the world outside the community stands in darkness and condemnation (3.36). 'Life' in John is interpreted as 'eternal life' and this becomes the supreme designation in this Gospel for salvation. It is what the Gospel otherwise speaks of as 'life to the very full' (10.10). Both the Father and the Son 'give life', but again it is necessary to believe or be 'born anew' (3.3) in order to share in this. Jesus dies for the 'whole people', just as he comes to save 'the world', but again the potentially universal scope of this is sharply limited by the terms the Gospel uses to demarcate the different categories it speaks of.

The fate of the individual has already been decided by the response that has been made to Jesus. The final judgement, and the eschatological battle and triumph over evil, are only briefly alluded to. Each individual has already settled the decisive issue, and their final destiny, for themselves. The resurrection life, as also the state of condemnation, has already been anticipated (and it is the Paraclete, or Spirit, who now mediates this life, and the presence of Jesus). It is in the end knowledge of Jesus that brings life. This is not an esoteric saving knowledge, as in Gnostic systems, though these can obviously represent an easy and early development from this Johannine tradition.

There is substantial affinity between the Gospel and what we find in the Epistles (especially 1 John). Here it is said that God sent his only Son into the world, to give eternal life (4.9). Jesus lays down his own life (3.16). To abide in Jesus, and to *know* him, is to have life, which means *eternal* life; not to know him means not to have this (2.3–6, 24–5). Again there is a stark contrast drawn. Along with these themes, however, there are also others. Jesus is sent to be the expiation (or propitiation) for sin (4.10). He is just and faithful, and acts as advocate in the heavenly world, so that those who belong to him can have confidence in the final judgement (2.1). Jesus' death purifies and cleanses from sin (1.7). There is, however, no automatic state of perfection for believers, and the writer stresses the need for repentance and forgiveness (1.9). Specifically, there is the repeated demand for them to keep the commandments of Jesus. Above all, this means the commandment of love (2.7–8; 3.11). Jesus' death is portrayed as an expression of God's love, and it should result in an expression of reciprocal love between members of the community (4.11). The salvation, or eternal life, Jesus brings, thus has a much more emphatically ethical dimension here than it does in the Gospel.

REVELATION

The most striking aspect of Revelation is its portrayal of Jesus as the Lamb who has been slain (5.6–12; 13.8; cf. John 1.29). Thus it presents Jesus as the Passover Lamb (as well as Suffering Servant), who brings redemption and liberation in the new Exodus (15.2–4). Yet he is also the Davidic Messiah (5.5; 22.16), who has won the decisive victory, in the eschatological battle, against all the forces of evil, political as well as spiritual (11.15–18; 16.14–16; Schüssler Fiorenza 1985; Bauckham 1993). His victory, however, has been brought about not by military might but through his sacrificial death (5.6–14; 12.11). The victory over evil powers (including Rome) is final, but has still to be brought to completion, and the chosen, who already belong to the Lamb, have a vital part to play in this. Just as Jesus conquered by his death, as a faithful witness or martyr (3.14), so do they (6.9–11; 7.4–14; 12.11). Their martyrdom has potentially universal effect, in bringing about the faith and repentance of all nations (11.1–13; 14.14–20; 15.3–4), and thus in establishing God's kingdom on earth (11.15; 12.10). Judgement still poses a threat for those outside the elect (chs 15–19), but the positive fulfilment of God's purpose, and of the Lamb's sacrificial death and witness, will finally be found in the consummation of this kingdom. Thus the work comes to its climax with the superb portrayal of the new Jerusalem, new heaven and new earth that will appear at Christ's Parousia

(21.1 – 22.5). Revelation makes passing reference to salvation from sin (1.5), but the book as a whole is characterized above all by a focus on the deliverance and reward already assured for the faithful community, and by the most powerful vision in the whole of the New Testament of a world that is redeemed and restored.

CONCLUSION

From all of this, it is clear that there is no single view of salvation in earliest Christianity. There are real differences in conception as well as expression. The Pauline version is in many respects the most profound and powerful, and has become overwhelmingly predominant. It is worth remembering, however, that there are other accounts of salvation within the New Testament, some highly distinctive and original, others quite discordant. Thus James has nothing of the death of Christ, and justification is by works, not faith alone (2.14–26). Nevertheless, the main thrust in most of the New Testament is deliverance from sin and death and liberation from evil and oppressive forces, and being brought into a new sphere of existence and a new relationship with God. It is the death of Christ that is central throughout, as that which effects salvation and inaugurates the new age that the believer now belongs to. In all the varied tradition of the New Testament, however, it is not only Christ's death but also his resurrection that belong together at the heart of the Christian understanding of salvation. It is Christ's resurrection that marks the defeat of death and opens up the possibility of new life. Salvation, that is, effects a transfer from a state of death to a state of life, from being in darkness to living in the light, from the old age to the new age. These categories are set in completely contrasting, polarized terms because the new age that has been brought about is also the final age. It is therefore urgent and essential, in the face of the final judgement that is about to come, to be found in the true community of those who are saved, and to live a transformed life. The concept of being saved belongs to an overriding eschatological perspective. The death of Christ is seen throughout to have final effect, and salvation is set at the centre of Christian proclamation and Christian theology from the very start.

REFERENCES AND FURTHER READING

Banks, R. (ed.) 1974 *Reconciliation and Hope*, Exeter: Paternoster Press.

Barrett, C. K. 1967 *Jesus and the Gospel Tradition*, London: SPCK.

Barth, M. 1961 *Was Christ's Death a Sacrifice?*, Edinburgh: Oliver & Boyd.

Bauckham, R. J. 1993 *The Theology of the Book of Revelation*, London: SPCK.

Bayer, H. F. 1986 *Jesus' Predictions of Vindication and Resurrection* (WUNT 2.20), Tübingen: J. C. B. Mohr.

Becker, J. 1993 *Paul: Apostle to the Gentiles*, Louisville: Westminster.

Beker, J. C. 1980 *Paul the Apostle: The Triumph of God in Life and Thought*, Philadelphia: Fortress Press.

Bouttier, M. 1966 *Christianity according to Paul*, London: SCM Press.

Bultmann, R. 1965 *Theology of the New Testament*, 2 vols, London: SCM Press.

Caird, G. B. 1994 *New Testament Theology* (ed. L. D. Hurst), Oxford: Clarendon Press.

Carroll, J. H. and Green, J. B. 1995 *The Death of Jesus in Early Christianity*, Peabody: Hendrickson.

Cerfaux, L. 1959 *Christ in the Theology of St Paul*, Freiburg: Herder.

Chester, A. 1991 'Hebrews: The Final Sacrifice' in S. W. Sykes (ed.) *Sacrifice and Redemption: Durham Essays in Theology*, Cambridge: Cambridge University Press, 57–72.

Chester, A. and Martin, R. P. 1994 *The Theology of the Letters of James, Peter and Jude*, Cambridge: Cambridge University Press.

Conzelmann, H. 1969 *An Outline of the Theology of the New Testament*, London: SCM Press.

Cousar, C. B. 1990 *A Theology of the Cross: The Death of Jesus in the Pauline Letters*, Minneapolis: Fortress Press.

Dahl, N. A. 1977 *Studies in Paul: Theology for the Early Christian Mission*, Minneapolis: Augsburg.

Dalton, W. J. 1965 *Christ's Proclamation to the Spirits: A Study of 1 Peter 3.18–4.6*, Rome: Pontifical Biblical Institute.

Davies, W. D. 1981 *Paul and Rabbinic Judaism*, 4th edn, London: SPCK.

Dodd, C. H. 1935 *The Bible and the Greeks*, London: Hodder & Stoughton.

—— 1953 *The Interpretation of the Fourth Gospel*, London: Cambridge University Press.

Dunn, J. D. G. 1998 *The Theology of Paul the Apostle*, Edinburgh: T&T Clark.

Gibbs, J. G. 1971 *Creation and Redemption: A Study in Pauline Theology*, Leiden: E. J. Brill.

Gordon, R. P. 1991 'Better Promises: Two Passages in Hebrews against the Background of the Old Testament Cultus' in W. Horbury (ed.) *Templum Amicitiae*, Sheffield: JSOT Press, 434–49.

Grayston, K. 1990 *Dying We Live: A New Inquiry into the Death of Christ in the New Testament*, London: Darton, Longman & Todd.

Green, E. M. B. 1965 *The Meaning of Salvation*, London: Hodder & Stoughton.

Green, J. B. 1988 *The Death of Jesus: Tradition and Interpretation in the Passion Narrative* (WUNT 2.33), Tübingen: J. C. B. Mohr.

Hanson, A. T. 1987 *The Paradox of the Cross in the Thought of St Paul*, Sheffield: JSOT Press.

Hengel, M. 1981 *The Atonement: A Study of the Origins of the Doctrine in the New Testament*, London: SCM Press.

Hill, D. 1967 *Greek Words and Hebrew Meanings: Studies in the Semantics of Soteriological Terms*, London: Cambridge University Press.

Hooker, M. D. 1959 *Jesus and the Servant: The Influence of the Servant Concept of Deutero-Isaiah in the New Testament*, London: SPCK.

—— 1990 *From Adam to Christ: Essays on Paul*, Cambridge: Cambridge University Press.

—— 1994 *Not Ashamed of the Gospel: New Testament Interpretations of the Death of Christ*, Carlisle: Paternoster Press.

Hultgren, A. J. 1987 *Christ and His Benefits: Christology and Redemption in the New Testament*, Philadelphia: Fortress Press.

Jeremias, J. 1966 *The Eucharistic Words of Jesus*, London: SCM Press.

—— 1971 *New Testament Theology*. Part 1: *The Proclamation of Jesus*, London: SCM Press.

Käsemann, E. 1969 *New Testament Questions of Today*, London: SCM Press.

—— 1971 *Perspectives on Paul*, London: SCM Press.

Lindars, B. 1991a *The Theology of the Letter to the Hebrews*, Cambridge: Cambridge University Press.

—— 1991b 'Hebrews and the Second Temple' in W. Horbury (ed.) *Templum Amicitiae*, Sheffield: JSOT Press, 410–33.

Loewe, R. 1981 '"Salvation" Is Not of the Jews', *Journal of Theological Studies* n.s. 32, 341–68.

Lyonnet, S. and Sabourin, L. 1970 *Sin, Redemption and Sacrifice*, Rome: Pontifical Biblical Institute.

Marshall, I. H. 1990 *Jesus the Saviour: Studies in New Testament Theology*, London: SPCK.

Martin, R. P. 1981 *Reconciliation: A Study of Paul's Theology*, London: Marshall, Morgan & Scott.

Moffatt, J. 1931 *Grace in the New Testament*, London: Hodder & Stoughton.

Morris, L. 1965 *The Apostolic Preaching of the Cross*, 3rd edn, Grand Rapids: Eerdmans.

Moule, C. F. D. 1977 *The Origin of Christology*, Cambridge: Cambridge University Press.

Munck, J. 1959 *Paul and the Salvation of Mankind*, London: SCM Press.

Murphy-O'Connor, J. and Charlesworth, J. (ed.) 1990 *Paul and the Dead Sea Scrolls*, New York: Crossroad.

Pate, C. M. 1995 *The End of the Ages Has Come: The Theology of Paul*, Grand Rapids: Zondervan.

Reicke, B. 1946 *The Disobedient Spirits and Christian Baptism: A Study of 1 Peter iii.19 and Its Context*, Copenhagen: Munksgard.

Ridderbos, H. 1975 *Paul: An Outline of His Theology*, Grand Rapids: Eerdmans.

Sanders, E. P. 1977 *Paul and Palestinian Judaism: A Comparison of Patterns of Religion*, London: SCM Press.

—— 1983 *Paul, the Law and the Jewish People*, Philadelphia: Fortress Press.

—— 1985 *Jesus and Judaism*, London: SCM Press.

Schüssler, Fiorenza, E. 1985 *The Book of Revelation: Justice and Judgement*, Philadelphia: Fortress Press.

Schweitzer, A. 1931 *The Mysticism of Paul the Apostle*, London: A&C Black.

Scott, C. A. A. 1927 *Christianity According to St Paul*, Cambridge: Cambridge University Press.

Seeley, D. 1990 *The Noble Death: Graeco-Roman Martyrology and Paul's Concept of Salvation*, Sheffield: JSOT Press.

Seifrid, M. A. 1992 *Justification by Faith: The Origin and Development of a Central Pauline Theme*, Leiden: E. J. Brill.

Stendahl, K. 1977 *Paul Among Jews and Gentiles*, London: SCM Press.

Stuhlmacher, P. 1986 *Reconciliation, Law and Righteousness: Essays in Biblical Theology*, Philadelphia: Fortress Press.

Swetnam, J. 1981 *Jesus and Isaac: A Study of the Epistle to the Hebrews in the Light of the Aqedah*, Rome: Pontifical Biblical Institute.

Tannehill, R. C. 1967 *Dying and Rising with Christ: A Study in Pauline Theology*, Berlin: Alfred Töpelmann.

Taylor, V. 1946 *Forgiveness and Reconciliation*, (2nd edn), London: Macmillan.

—— 1958 *The Atonement in New Testament Teaching*, 3rd edn, London: Epworth Press.

Vanhoye, A. 1989 *Structure and Message of the Epistle to the Hebrews*, Rome: Pontifical Biblical Institute.

Wenham, D. 1995 *Paul: Follower of Jesus or Founder of Christianity?*, Grand Rapids: Eerdmans.

Whiteley, D. E. H. 1964 *The Theology of St Paul*, Oxford: Basil Blackwell.

Williams, S. K. 1975 *Jesus' Death as Saving Event: The Background and Origin of a Concept*, Missoula: Scholars Press.

Young, F. M. 1975 *Sacrifice and the Death of Christ*, London: SPCK.

Ziesler, J. A. 1972 *The Meaning of Righteousness in Paul*, Cambridge: Cambridge University Press.

—— 1990 *Pauline Christianity*, 2nd edn, Oxford: Oxford University Press.

CHAPTER FORTY-FOUR

INTERPRETATIONS OF THE IDENTITY AND ROLE OF JESUS

———·◆·———

Catrin H. Williams

It is something of a commonplace in studies of New Testament interpretations of Jesus ('New Testament christology') to draw attention to a question that, according to Gospel traditions, Jesus posed to his disciples: 'Who do people say that I am?' (Mark 8:27; cf. Matt. 16:13; Luke 9:18). They report that people view him as John the Baptist, Elijah or as one of the prophets, while the disciples' own evaluation of Jesus is expressed by Peter: 'You are the Christ' (Mark 8:29). It is the variety rather than the content of the responses offered in this scene that merits attention at this point, because it serves as an illustration of the diverse ways in which the New Testament writers sought to express their understanding of the identity and role of Jesus. Before examining the christological beliefs attested in individual New Testament texts, some attempts at delineating the origins and early development of christology will be considered.

MAPPING OUT EARLY CHRISTOLOGY

The study of New Testament christology during the early decades of the twentieth century was dominated by scholars belonging to 'the history-of-religions school', who argued that many early Christian beliefs and practices were drawn from ideas current in the cultural environment of the Graeco-Roman world. In an influential study entitled *Kyrios Christos* (1913) Wilhelm Bousset offered a historical sketch of the development of early christology, giving particular attention to the period between Jesus and Paul. The beliefs of the Palestinian community in the earliest post-Easter period centred on the confession of Jesus as the 'Son of Man' whose imminent return (*parousia*) as heavenly Messiah was eagerly awaited. A decisive turning point occurred when Christianity entered the Gentile communities of Antioch, Tarsus and Damascus. The eschatological hope characteristic of the congregations in Judaea was now replaced by the cultic veneration of Jesus as the exalted Lord present with the community in worship and sacrament. The title 'Lord' (*kyrios*) was first applied to Jesus by Gentile believers, and arose as a result of its use to address pagan deities in Syria and Egypt, as well as Roman emperors in the ruler-cult – a development viewed by Bousset as inconceivable within the monotheistic environment of the Jewish-Christian communities. Paul was deeply influenced by these Gentile churches, and he also developed their beliefs by depicting Christ as a living presence with whom believers enjoyed a mystical relationship.

The impact of Bousset's study on subsequent scholarship cannot be overestimated. It was particularly well received by later proponents of the history-of-religions school, and Rudolf Bultmann commented in the foreword to the fifth edition of *Kyrios Christos* that he viewed it as an indispensable work. Bultmann also developed his own hypotheses with regard to the origins of christology, and argued that the historical Jesus did not claim any titles for himself; nor did he possess what could be termed a messianic self-consciousness (1952, 1: 26–32). Thus the legacy of Bousset and his successors was their assessment of New Testament christology as the product of distinct early Christian communities that did not stand in any real continuity with the self-understanding of Jesus.

Others have argued that the foundations of christology were already laid down in the activity and proclamation of Jesus of Nazareth. Oscar Cullmann, for example, rejected the notion that New Testament christology developed simply by conforming to a conceptual scheme provided by ancient Judaism or Hellenism, since Jesus' self-understanding and the impact of his person and ministry must also be considered (1963: 5). C. F. D. Moule has argued, moreover, that early christological conceptions should not be viewed as the result of an evolutionary process, which implies an ever-increasing distance from Jesus and the introduction of alien factors in response to different cultural environments, but rather as an organic development, in that 'successive descriptions and evaluations of Jesus constituted only new insights into what was there from the beginning' (1977: 22).

Attempts at determining the relationship between the claims of the historical Jesus and the early Christian beliefs about him can be outlined according to the categories of explicit, implicit and evoked christology (Theissen and Merz 1998: 520–553). It is difficult to ascertain whether Jesus embraced an explicit christology by laying claim to one or more titles (a consensus is emerging among scholars that he used the obscure expression 'Son of Man' as a self-designation, though not necessarily as a title). An implicit christology may, nevertheless, be detected in Jesus' consciousness of eschatological authority (his statements introduced by 'Amen', 'but I say to you' or 'I have come'), as well as special intimacy with God in his use of the Aramaic address 'Abba' (Mark 14:36). Jesus' claims relating to the forgiveness of sins (Mark 2:5–11) and his healings and exorcisms also point to a consciousness of his role as one whose words and activity signify the coming of the kingdom of God. In addition, an *evoked christology* denotes expectations that Jesus aroused among people during his lifetime. According to several Gospel traditions, titles drawn from traditional Jewish categories (such as 'Messiah' and 'Son of David') were attached to Jesus by his disciples and followers (Mark 8:29; 10:47–8) and are reflected in the charge that led to his execution as a messianic pretender (Mark 15:2, 26, 32). Such factors imply that the issue of Jesus' messianic identity was already raised during his ministry, while his own response is described as one of reticence rather than outright rejection (Mark 8:30; Matt. 26:64). Even without explicitly claiming the title 'Messiah', the ministry and self-understanding of Jesus could be termed 'messianic' in view of the eschatological character of his proclamation of the kingdom of God, which in turn led to further reflection among his followers after Easter.

What was the nature of christological reflection during the decisive period between Jesus' death (about 30 CE) and the emergence of the earliest New Testament writing, probably Paul's first letter to the Thessalonians (50 CE)? Because Bousset's outline of two largely unconnected stages of development makes no allowances for probable lines of communication between Jewish-Palestinian-Christian and Gentile-Christian communities, his scheme has been refined to accommodate an intervening stage or pattern described as Hellenistic-Jewish Christianity (Hahn 1969; Fuller 1965). Within the context of a Greek-speaking Hellenistic-Jewish church deeply influenced by the Greek Bible (LXX) and Hellenistic ideas, the eschatological expectation of Jesus' return as 'Son of Man' gave way for the first time to reflection on the heavenly exaltation and divine lordship of the risen Christ. The titles 'Lord' and 'Son of God' were then transformed by Hellenistic-Gentile Christians into expressions of Jesus' status as a pre-existent divine being who became incarnate. Hahn and Fuller stress that this three-stage classification should not be linked too rigidly to specific chronological periods or geographical locations, although the three types of community do correspond, in broad terms, to a movement from Palestine to the Jewish Diaspora to the Gentile world, and from a 'lower' to a 'higher' christology.

The notion of christological development in three stages can certainly allow for some degree of overlap between, and fluidity within, the early Christian communities, but it raises fundamental questions about the nature of the early Church during the obscure years between Jesus and Paul. The nature of the available New Testament evidence means that attempts at reconstructing distinct developments in early christology is dependent on identifying key traditions in texts that evidently belong to a later period. It has also been asked whether the rapid development of christology during the years up to the time of Paul's earliest known letter can really accommodate three different stages, and whether one can speak of a purely Gentile form of Christianity in the period before Paul's mission (Hengel 1983). It is probable that virtually all the missionaries who founded communities in cities like Antioch and Damascus were Jewish Christians, and their preaching would have included Jewish-Christian concepts as well as (Gentile) elements familiar to their new audiences. There are problems also with the proposed distinction between Palestinian-Jewish Christianity and Hellenistic-Jewish Christianity in terms of their geographical and chronological origin, for it has been conclusively demonstrated that Jewish Palestine had for a long time been subjected to Hellenistic influence in a variety of ways (Hengel 1989).

Attention is also paid to what many view as a historically reliable tradition in Acts 6:1 about the presence of 'Hebrews' and 'Hellenists' in the Jerusalem church (Hengel 1983; Marshall 1990). The term 'Hellenists' is interpreted as denoting Greek-speaking Jewish Christians from the Diaspora who now resided in Jerusalem and, from an early date, had formed a community alongside the Aramaic-speaking Jewish Christians ('Hebrews'). Hengel proposes that these Greek-speaking Jewish Christians played a decisive role in the shaping of beliefs about Jesus, and that their missionary activities led to the formation of Christian communities in such important places as Caesarea, Antioch and Damascus (1983: 40–7). They believed that Jesus, the crucified Messiah, would soon return, but they also interpreted his present status in terms of the exaltation of the Son of Man. In this respect the interpretation of Scripture played a significant role in early Jewish-Christian reflection on the titles and functions of the risen Christ, including his Sonship (2 Sam. 7:14; Ps. 2:7), his exaltation as Son of Man (Ps. 8) and his enthronement as Lord at the right hand of God (Ps. 110:1).

Christological reflection on Psalm 110:1, whose Greek version in the LXX includes two occurrences of the designation *kyrios* ('The Lord said to my Lord, "Sit at my right hand . . ."'), also suggests that the use of the title *kyrios* for Jesus is not necessarily to be derived from the influence of pagan cults, but can be traced back to Greek-speaking Jewish Christians. The likelihood that this title was applied to Jesus at an early stage, among members of the Palestinian community, is further strengthened by examples of the title '[the] Lord' as a divine designation in first-century Jewish Palestine. In addition to the use of *kyrios* as a title for God among Greek-speaking Jews (Josephus, *Antiquities* 13:68; 20:90), evidence for its Aramaic counterpart *marê'* has been uncovered in some Qumran texts (Fitzmyer 1979: 124–5). It is thus conceivable that Aramaic-speaking Jewish Christians in the Jerusalem church applied the title *marê'* to Jesus in its role as a divine designation, which was then translated as *kyrios* for or by the Greek-speaking Jewish Christians. The use of *marê'*, though not in its absolute form, also accounts for the distinctive liturgical formula *maranatha* cited by Paul in 1 Corinthans 16:22. Indeed, the fact that this untranslated Aramaic phrase is preserved in a text written in Greek suggests that it originated among members of the Palestinian community, where it served as an eschatological petition for the return of Jesus ('Our Lord, come'), probably within the liturgical context of the eucharistic meal (cf. 1 Cor. 11:26). Both the *maranatha* invocation and the christological appropriation of Psalm 110:1 therefore offer glimpses of significant developments already established by Aramaic- and Greek-speaking Jewish Christians, for to call Jesus 'Lord' was to confer upon him a title with clear divine connotations.

The distinctive use of *maranatha* in 1 Corinthians 16:22 clearly raises important questions about the relationship between the development of christology and the liturgical practices of the early Christians (Hurtado 1998). Devotional practices viewed as indicative of what is described as Christ-devotion (Hurtado) or a cult of Christ (Horbury 1998) also include the singing of hymns in honour and celebration of Christ (1 Cor. 14:26), baptizing in his name or 'into Christ Jesus' (Rom. 6:3; Acts 2:38) and confessing that 'Jesus is Lord' (Rom. 10:9–13; 1 Cor. 12:3; Phil. 2:11). Because these elements are attested in the earliest New Testament writings, the letters of Paul, it has been proposed that a number of devotional practices (as in the case of *maranatha*) could have originated at an earlier stage among Jewish Christians. Not only is it widely agreed that Paul cites already existing formulae in his letters (for example, Rom. 1:3–4; 1 Cor. 15:3–5), but it is also noted that there are no indications in Paul's letters that his views about Christ were unique to him or indeed conflicted with those of other Jewish Christians; his disagreements with the Jerusalem church centred on his mission to the Gentiles (Hengel 1983: 44; Hurtado 1999: 52–4). The liturgical practices reflected in Paul's letters, including the acclamation of Jesus as 'Lord', have therefore been cited as evidence that the exalted Christ became an object of cultic devotion alongside God in early Christian communities. What is noted as striking, in this respect, is that the Jewish Christians did not regard their Christ-devotion as a threat to the uniqueness of God, but as an affirmation of his glory and sovereignty (cf. Phil. 2:11). The accommodation of the exalted Christ into the worship of the one God attests 'the use of monotheistic language as a christological category' (Rainbow 1991: 84), finding its clearest expression in 1 Corinthians 8:6: 'Yet for us there is one God, the Father, from whom are all things and for whom we exist, and one Lord, Jesus Christ, through whom are all things and through whom we exist.' In other words, Jewish Christians like Paul viewed themselves as loyal to the Jewish monotheistic faith in their worship of 'one God', but their conviction that the crucified Jesus had been exalted to heavenly glory led to the veneration of Christ as 'one Lord'.

The central chapters of Hurtado's important study examine the ways in which ancient Judaism provided a conceptual framework, broadly labelled as 'divine agency', which enabled Jewish Christians to explain the exaltation of Jesus to God's right hand without compromising their commitment to the one God. A number of Jewish texts, from Palestine and the Diaspora, depict God as appointing a particular figure to act as his chief agent (Hurtado 1998: 17–92; also Davis 1994). The category of divine agency manifests itself in various forms, since a chief agent can be a divine attribute (Wisdom or the Logos), an exalted patriarch (Moses or Enoch) or a principal angel like Michael (Dan. 10:13–21), Yahoel (*Apocalypse of Abraham* 10–11) or Melchizedek (in a fragmentary Qumran text known as 11QMelchizedek). The nature of the role exercised by God's principal agent also varies, for Wisdom is depicted as participating in creation (Wisdom 7:22), Melchizedek as active in eschatological redemption, while Michael and Yahoel exercise power in their role as the grand vizier of God. The chief agent is therefore portrayed in these Jewish texts as having a highly exalted and unique status, second only to God in terms of authority and significance. In some cases, the chief agent possesses special divine attributes and powers, as in the depiction of Yahoel as one who bears the Divine Name (cf. Exod. 23:21) and whose appearance is described in language reminiscent of theophanies (*Apocalypse of Abraham* 10:3, 8; 11:2–3).

None of these chief agent traditions, according to Hurtado, compromises Jewish monotheism. Wisdom and the Logos are metaphorical descriptions of God's active involvement in the world rather than semi-independent beings or hypostases (1998: 36–7, 46–8; also Dunn 1989: 163–76, 213–30), whereas depictions of the exalted status of patriarchs like Moses are intended to validate Jewish religious tradition and foreshadow the reward of the elect ones. Even principal angels remain distinct from, and subordinate to, God, since their authority and status are derived from the one whose majesty they serve to magnify. Above all, Hurtado emphasizes that, although the honour accorded to these figures may have included such phenomena as the application of venerative language to angels (Stuckenbruck 1995), there is no convincing evidence that any of them became the object of formal corporate worship in a Jewish cultic context.

Since 'in the exclusive monotheism of the Jewish religious tradition . . . it was worship which was the real test of monotheistic faith in religious practice' (Bauckham 1993b: 118), Hurtado claims that the inclusion of the risen Christ with God as the recipient of cultic veneration produced an innovation or 'mutation' of Jewish monotheism, unparalleled in Jewish traditions of God's chief agent. In other words, monotheistic piety was redefined in order to accommodate a binitarian devotion to Jesus alongside God. This modification is viewed by Hurtado as resulting primarily from the post-Easter religious experiences of the early Christians (1998: 117–22), especially their visionary experiences of the risen Christ as exalted and participating fully in the glory and power of God (cf. Acts 7:55–6; 2 Cor. 3:16–18).

Two quite different assessments of the material examined by Hurtado can be noted. First, his view that Christ-devotion marked a significant development in relation to Jewish monotheism is shared by others (Dunn 1989; Casey 1991), although they contend that truly binitarian patterns of belief in the divinity or incarnation of Jesus only occurred during the last decades of the first century CE (particularly in John's Gospel). Secondly, others argue that there are Jewish precedents for the binitarian elements in early christology, in that several of the traditions about principal angels demonstrate that ancient Jewish monotheism could accommodate a second divine being alongside God (Rowland 1982; Fossum 1985). Rowland argues that there is evidence in certain Jewish texts of a separation of divinity involving God and his personified glory, with the latter acting as a quasi-angelic mediator (Ezek. 1:26–8; 8:2–4; Dan. 10:5–9), as also attested and further developed in the description of Yahoel in the *Apocalypse of Abraham* (1982: 94–113). The depiction of Yahoel in this text as one who bears the Divine Name (10:3, 8) is interpreted by Fossum as indicating that a principal angel could be regarded as the personification of the Name, thus sharing God's nature of mode of being (1985: 318–20), whereas according to Hurtado the Name is rather the medium of his power. What becomes apparent from these different assessments of principal angel traditions is that there is clear disagreement as to whether the exalted status attributed to such figures as Yahoel should be understood in functional terms alone or points to a belief in their divine nature.

Hurtado's proposal that the visionary experiences of the early Christians were the major impetus for their cultic veneration of Jesus requires a degree of caution due to the nature of the New Testament evidence. It is a particularly difficult task to determine the relationship between subsequent reflections on such experiences, as in Paul's claim to have seen the risen Lord (1 Cor. 9:1; 15:8; cf. Gal. 1:15–16), and the actual content and nature of those experiences. Moreover, it is debated whether one can speak of visionary experiences of the risen Christ as actually generating christological convictions (for example, Christ as a heavenly divine figure) or should view these experiences as having been shaped by already existing categories provided, in particular, by Jewish traditions and patterns of belief. William Horbury has recently proposed that the worship of Christ in fact finds its origins in Jewish messianism (1998: 127–40): it was the recognition and praise of Jesus as messianic king, beginning during his ministry and developed in the early Christian communities, that led to the acclamations, hymns and titles offered to Christ and are preserved in the writings of the New Testament.

The debate among scholars on the origins of New Testament christology continues to be vigorous and illuminating. The publication of important sources, particularly the Dead Sea Scrolls, has led to a much clearer understanding of the diversity in ancient Judaism and to a greater appreciation of the importance of intermediary figures in Jewish traditions. And although it is difficult to offer a detailed picture of the development of christology during this early period, recent scholarship has made a decisive contribution to our understanding of the earliest Christian beliefs about Jesus as well as the factors that helped to shape them. Strong arguments have been offered in several studies for viewing the devotion to Christ as a divine figure alongside God as a characteristic of the devotional practices of early Jewish Christians rather than as a later innovation attributable to Gentile believers. This was, moreover, a period marked by deep christological reflection on the Scriptures, thus enabling early Christians to express their conviction that the crucified and risen Christ had been exalted as Lord to a heavenly position at the right hand of God. These were the foundations upon which the authors of the individual writings in the New Testament developed their own interpretations of the identity and role of Jesus.

INTERPRETATIONS OF JESUS IN NEW TESTAMENT WRITINGS

Until recently the study of New Testament christology has largely been approached through an analysis of individual titles applied to Jesus, giving particular attention to their conceptual background and usage. The limitations of this procedure are now widely recognized (see Keck 1986: 368–70). This approach not only tends to isolate the christological titles from their context, particularly their narrative contexts in the case of the Gospels, but it can overlook other, equally significant, christological passages. This is not to deny that the New Testament authors sought to interpret Jesus in the light of already existing titles or expressions, but this is only one of many forms of christological expression adopted in the writings. A selection of New Testament texts exhibiting various emphases and a wide range of interpretations of Jesus will therefore now be examined.

The letters of Paul

Paul expresses his understanding of Jesus Christ in seven letters generally acknowledged to have been written by him between 50 and about 60 CE (1 Thessalonians, Galatians, Philippians, 1 and 2 Corinthians, Romans and Philemon). Ephesians, 2 Thessalonians and the Pastoral letters are certainly post-Pauline compositions, but the stronger case for the Pauline authorship of Colossians justifies its inclusion for consideration with the seven undisputed letters. Nearly every passage in Paul's writings discloses one aspect or other of his views about Christ, but his letters were not written for the purpose of offering a systematized discussion of christology. In each case Paul is responding to specific situations arising in individual communities, and his presentation of christological themes can take forms and include emphases relevant to the circumstances of those whom he addresses. For example, Paul's extended discussion of his conviction that the risen Christ will return (1 Thess. 4:13 – 5:11) arises from the concern voiced by members of the community at Thessalonica about the fate of those who had already died before the *parousia*. But while due regard must be given to the context and concerns reflected in each letter, there is also an underlying consistency in Paul's expressions of his christological convictions.

What may appear remarkable is that Paul offers very few indications in his letters of the extent of his knowledge about Jesus of Nazareth. Limited references to the earthly life of Jesus include declarations about his birth of a woman under the Jewish law (Gal. 4:4) and his descent from the line of David (Rom. 1:3). The paucity of such statements should not, however, be interpreted as implying that Paul displays no interest in the events of Jesus' life and ministry. The citation of formulaic traditions (cf. Rom. 1:3–4), together with several subtle allusions to the teaching of Jesus (cf. Rom. 12:14; 13:7–10; 1 Cor. 7:10–11; 11:23–5), suggest that Paul takes for granted that the recipients of his letters are already familiar with traditions about Jesus due to the earlier preaching activity carried out in their midst by Paul or other early Christian missionaries.

The central events for Paul are the passion, death and resurrection of Christ, as demonstrated when he appeals to the tradition he has received and handed on to the Corinthians: 'that Christ died for our sins in accordance with the scriptures, and that he was buried, and that he was raised on the third day in accordance with the scriptures (1 Cor. 15:3–4). The salvific death and resurrection of Jesus are presented here as the core of the Christian message, as Paul himself had experienced when the risen Christ 'last of all . . . appeared also to me' (15:8). Thus, on the few occasions that Paul does make explicit reference to his own call or conversion, he emphasizes that this was due to a revelation of the risen Lord (Gal. 1:12, 15–16). This christophany experience resulted in a decisive shift in Paul's understanding of the significance of Jesus; it was an event that led him to accept the claim of the first believers that the crucified Christ had been raised from the dead, and it was an experience that, according to several scholars, brought about many key aspects of Paul's christology (Kim 1984; Longenecker 1997).

The centrality of Jesus' death and resurrection in the gospel preached by Paul also means that his reflections on christology and on the salvific effects of the Christ-event are closely intertwined in his letters. This is particularly apparent in two passages where Paul sets up an explicit contrast between Christ and Adam, understood as representative figures of humankind from creation to death (Adam) and of eschatological humankind from death to life (Christ) (see Dunn 1998: 241). In Romans 5:12–21 the disobedience of Adam, which resulted in death and condemnation for all, is contrasted with the obedience of Christ, resulting in grace and the gift of righteousness (5:17–18). In an earlier letter (1 Cor. 15:20–2, 45–9) Paul's interest in the Adam/Christ motif centres on the resurrection of Jesus as the beginning (15:20: 'the first fruits') of those who have died. All who are 'in Adam' die, but those who are 'in Christ' shall be made alive (15:21–2). This line of argumentation is resumed in 15:45–9, and Christ is now described as 'the last Adam' who has become a life-giving spirit; he is the beginning of a new humanity and his image will be borne by those who belong to him.

It is true that a study of the titles used by an author like Paul cannot provide a comprehensive picture of his views about Jesus, but the importance he attaches to Jesus' identity as 'Messiah (Christ)', 'Son of God' and 'Lord' certainly calls for comment. It is interesting that Paul uses the designation 'Christ' more as a second name for Jesus ('Jesus Christ' or 'Christ Jesus') than as a title. This apparent lack of attention to the fulfilment of messianic hopes in Jesus results from the fact that *christos* as a title would have little meaning for Gentile readers, because to them it was a word that simply meant 'anointed or smeared with oil'. The titular use of *christos* to describe Jesus as the promised Messiah does occur in a few passages, especially Romans 9:3–5 where Paul describes the privileges received by the Jews from whom the Messiah comes.

Particularly significant are those rarer occasions where Paul speaks of Jesus as 'Son of God' (Rom. 1:4; 2 Cor. 1:19; Gal. 2:20) or 'Son' (Rom. 8:3, 29; 1 Cor. 1:9; Gal. 4:4), even describing Jesus' divine sonship as the content of the gospel (cf. Gal. 1:15–16). These declarations are more likely to have been influenced by ancient Jewish traditions than pagan religious concepts, particularly as sonship terminology occurs frequently in the Scriptures to denote Israel (Exod. 4:22; Hos. 11:1), the Davidic king (2 Sam. 7:14; Ps. 2:7) and, in some Qumran texts, the Davidic Messiah (4QFlorilegium 1:10–13). Assessing the Pauline evidence against a Jewish background therefore leads Hurtado to propose, 'Paul did not employ the language of divine sonship primarily to claim that Jesus was divine. Essentially Paul's references to Jesus as God's "Son" communicate Jesus' unique status and intimate relationship to God. But the contexts of these references supply several additional and more particular nuances to the term' (Hurtado 1993: 900). The actual context of the Pauline sonship language is important in such cases as the kerygmatic formula cited by Paul in Romans 1:3–4, a formula with which his readers were probably already acquainted: 'the gospel concerning his Son, who was descended from David according to the flesh, and was appointed (NRSV: declared) to be Son of God in power according to the spirit of holiness by resurrection from the dead, Jesus Christ our Lord'. In this two-part declaration Jesus' earthly status as 'Son of David' is juxtaposed with his installation as 'Son of God' in power by virtue of his resurrection. Scholars have long pondered whether the second part declares that divine sonship was first conferred upon Jesus at his resurrection, leading some to propose that Paul added the words 'in power' in order to tone down its 'adoptionist' ring (Barrett 1962: 20). The role of this formulaic tradition as a twofold affirmation of Jesus' divine sonship, with probable echoes of Davidic traditions (2 Sam. 7:12–14; see Hengel 1976: 62), is confirmed by the way Paul prefaces the whole citation with the clause 'the gospel concerning his Son'. Another declaration in the same letter stresses that Jesus' sonship expresses his unique relationship with God, for Jesus' salvific death is described in terms of God not withholding his own Son 'but gave him up for all of us' (8:32; cf. 5:10; Gal. 2:20; 4:4–5).

It is the title 'Lord' that receives most prominence in the Pauline writings. To speak of the risen Christ in terms of lordship is to define his relationship with all believers, and so Paul stresses that the central confession of their faith is that 'Jesus is Lord' (Rom. 10:9; 1 Cor. 12:3). Paul displays awareness of the use of *kyrios* as a designation for the 'many lords' honoured in pagan cults (1 Cor. 8:5), but he probably inherited this title from Jewish Christians, as indicated above. Paul uses the title *kyrios* for God in several scriptural citations (for example, Rom. 4:8; 1 Cor. 3:20), but in other places he applies *kyrios*-texts to Christ himself. One of the most striking examples occurs in Romans 10:9–13, for the confession of Jesus as Lord leads to the declaration, 'The same Lord is Lord of all and is generous to all who call on him. For, "Everyone who calls on the name of the Lord shall be saved"'

(Joel 2:32). Similarly in the second part of Philippians 2:6–11, one of the best-known New Testament christological passages, the exaltation of Jesus is described in the loftiest of terms: God has greatly exalted him and bestowed upon him the name above every name, so that every knee should bow and every tongue confess that Jesus Christ is Lord, to the glory of God the Father. The universal acclamation that 'Jesus is Lord' means that the exalted Christ is proclaimed worthy of the honour usually reserved for God, whereas the name given to him is probably God's own name (*kyrios*–YHWH) since the scriptural passage cited in 2:10 refers to God in its original context (Isa. 45:23; cf. Rom. 14:11).

This distinctive appropriation to Jesus of a text like Isaiah 45:23, which contains one of the most unequivocal declarations of monotheism in the Hebrew Scriptures, signifies that Paul directly, and quite boldly, associates Christ with God. Depicting Jesus in such exalted terms does not, however, conflict with the emphasis in Philippians 2:9–11 on the sovereignty of God, for the bestowal of the Name indicates a unique status conferred upon the exalted Christ by God himself (2:9), while those who confess Jesus as 'Lord' do so to the glory of the Father. The inclusion of Christ in expressions of commitment to the one God is graphically attested in 1 Corinthians 8:6, viewed by many commentators as an adaptation of the *Shema*, the traditional monotheistic formula recited daily by the Jews (Deut. 6:4: 'Hear, O Israel: The Lord our God is one Lord'). Emphasis on 'one God, the Father' is combined with a confession of the uniqueness of Christ's lordship, for there is 'one Lord, Jesus Christ, through whom are all things and through whom we exist' (1 Cor. 8:6). Once again, to describe Jesus as 'one Lord' is not viewed by Paul as impinging on his belief in the one true God. 'All things are *from*, that is originating in, deriving out of, the Father, but *through* the Son, that is by his agency' (Ziesler 1990: 35).

If Paul can speak of Christ in such exalted terms, even as the mediator of creation, does he envisage that Christ also existed before his earthly manifestation? There is vigorous debate over this issue, particularly as statements about God having sent his Son (Gal. 4:4; Rom. 8:3) could imply a sending from another mode of existence or, alternatively, a commissioning reminiscent of the sending of the prophets. Scholars are primarily interested in a cluster of passages where epithets and functions traditionally associated with divine Wisdom are now applied to Christ. His depiction as 'the image of the invisible God' (Col. 1:15) echoes the description of Wisdom as 'the image of his goodness' (Wisdom 7:26), whereas declarations attributing to Christ a role in creation (1 Cor. 8:6; Col. 1:16) also possess analogies in ancient Jewish reflection on Wisdom as instrumental with God in the work of creation (cf. Prov. 8:30; Wisdom 7:22). What are the christological implications of such associations? Dunn argues that they point to a Pauline conception of Christ's pre-existence in ideal rather than personal terms, particulary as Jewish Wisdom traditions seek, with the aid of metaphorical language, to bridge the gap between the transcendent God and his immanent activity in the world. When Paul drew upon these traditions, his claim was that pre-existent Wisdom – God's creative plan and power – is now revealed and realized in Jesus (1998: 267–77). But even if Jewish traditions do present Wisdom as a personification of God's activity rather than as a personal figure, it does not necessarily follow that Paul's attribution of the functions and epithets of Wisdom to Christ amounts to an unmodified transference of a fixed or readymade model (see Schüssler Fiorenza 1975). Indeed, it is made clear in the relevant Pauline passages that their subject is not a divine attribute or function, but the concrete historical figure whose personal relationship with God is highlighted by his naming as 'Lord, Jesus Christ' (1 Cor. 8:6) and 'Son' (Col. 1:13).

Even more decisive is the opening line of the poetic passage in Philippians 2:6–11, where Christ Jesus is depicted as existing 'in the form of God'. The opinion of most scholars is that this declaration expresses Christ's divine and sovereign status before his earthly existence; he did not count his equality with God as something he could use to his own advantage (*harpagmos*), but rather, by becoming human and assuming the status of a slave, he humbled himself and was obedient unto death (2:6–8). Again, Dunn seeks to demonstrate that this passage does not attribute pre-existence to Christ, but establishes an implied contrast between Adam and Jesus (1989: 114–21; 1998: 281–8). During his earthly life Christ, like Adam, bore the image of God (Gen. 1:27), but, different from Adam, he was obedient and did not seek to snatch equality with God (Gen. 3:5; with a different interpretation of *harpagmos*). The earthly Adam failed in his quest to be like God, but Christ embraced the fate of humankind by accepting death (the consequence of Adam's disobedience) and was consequently exalted (cf. Ps. 8:6). Those who favour the traditionally accepted interpretation contend, however, that the language of the first half of this passage is most naturally read as one of movement from Christ's pre-incarnate state to his human existence and death (2:6–8), and not of Jesus' earthly life and death as a two-stage contrast with Adam's state before and after his choice in the garden. Possibly more problematic for Dunn's interpretation is the lack of clear Adamic allusions in Philippians 2:6–11, and his view that 'form' (*morphē* in 2:6) is interchangeable with 'image' (*eikōn* – Gen. 1:27: LXX) does not adequately account for the repetition of the word in 2:7 where it cannot refer to image ('taking the form of a servant').

What must be acknowledged when attempting to determine whether Paul believed in the heavenly pre-existence of Christ is that he never seeks to explain or discuss at any length the nature of this pre-existent state. Indeed, to enquire about the precise nature of Christ's role as the one 'through whom are all things' (1 Cor. 8:6) or his ontological status 'in the form of God' (Phil. 2:6) and as 'Son' (Gal. 4:4) is to seek answers from Paul to questions that characterized the christological controversies of later centuries.

The Gospel of Mark

The Gospel of Mark, the earliest of the four canonical Gospels, was written during the turbulent years leading up to, or possibly shortly after, the destruction of the Temple in 70 CE. At least fifteen years therefore separate the later undisputed letters of Paul from the first Gospel account of Jesus' ministry, death and resurrection. The importance of Mark's role as a compiler or editor of existing traditions about Jesus is indisputable, but the distinctive character of his christology becomes evident in the way he shapes and structures his material. Recurrent themes and motifs can certainly be detected, and declarations or episodes of particular christological import are strategically placed at key points in the narrative. The significance of the introductory declaration about 'the gospel of Jesus Christ (or the Messiah), the Son of

God' (1:1) is in fact disclosed in events located at the beginning, middle and end of the Gospel (1:11; 8:29; 9:7; 14:61–2; 15:39, although it should be noted that some important textual witnesses do not include the title 'Son of God' in 1:1). The unfolding of Jesus' identity through the flow of the narrative, especially in Jesus' responses to the way others view him, leads to the description of Mark's christology as a 'narrative christology' (Tannehill 1979; Matera 1999: 5–26).

The first major section of Mark's Gospel describes Jesus' public ministry in Galilee (1:16–8:26). His declaration that 'the time is fulfilled, and the kingdom of God is at hand' (1:15) finds confirmation in his activity as authoritative teacher (cf. 1:21; 6:2), powerful healer (5:25–43; 7:31–7) and exorcist (1:23–7; 5:1–20). People marvel at Jesus' authority and power, but they only gain a partial understanding of his identity and mission. Even the disciples, to whom has been revealed the mystery of the kingdom of God (4:11), fail to grasp his true significance. Their response, after Jesus stills the storm, is to ask, 'Who then is this, that even the wind and the sea obey him?' (4:41), and, despite the feeding of the multitude and the epiphanic character of Jesus' act of walking on the sea, the disciples are rebuked for their lack of faith (8:17–21; cf. 6:52). Jesus' unique status is, nevertheless, recognized by the demons, whose acclamation that he is the 'Son of God' (3:11; cf. 1:24; 5:7) echoes the baptism scene where Jesus alone hears the divine voice declare, 'You are my Son, the Beloved; with you I am well pleased' (1:11, with words drawn from Ps. 2:7 and Isa. 42:1). But the demons' open acknowledgement of Jesus' divine sonship is followed by his command for them to be silent, a command that forms a key component of the Markan secrecy motif, known as the 'messianic secret' (see Tuckett 1983).

A command to silence features prominently in the account of Peter's confession at Caesarea Philippi, a scene that marks an important turning point in Mark's Gospel (8:27–30). When Jesus asks his disciples, 'Who do you say that I am?' Peter acts as their representative and, in the light of Jesus' miracles and teaching ministry, responds, 'You are the Messiah (or: the Christ).' This declaration of Jesus' messianic status, the first time for it to be mentioned since the introduction (1:1), is curiously followed by Jesus' command for them 'not to tell anyone about him' (8:30). This response does not amount to a rejection of Peter's confession, although Jesus immediately qualifies it by openly predicting that he, the 'Son of Man', must suffer, be rejected by the authorities, killed and then rise again (8:31; cf. 9:31; 10:32–4). In other words, Jesus emphasizes that the true meaning of his messiahship cannot be understood in isolation from his suffering, death and resurrection. Peter is clearly unable to reconcile his own concept of messiahship (presumably based on certain traditional Jewish expectations) with the theme of suffering (8:32–3), while Jesus will later stress that the significance of his messianic identity cannot be restricted to such categories as 'Son of David' (12:35–7; Marcus 1993: 130–52). On the occasion of the transfiguration, after the divine voice declares, 'This is my Son, the Beloved' (9:7), the disciples are again commanded to say nothing of this revelation of Jesus' glory until after the resurrection (9:9). Only in the light of Jesus' death can his divine sonship be openly acknowledged by others.

Jesus' arrival in Jerusalem brings about the fulfilment of his earlier predictions. Since the shadow of his death clearly looms over the narrative, the Markan secrecy motif now gives way to openness and disclosure. When the high priest questions

Jesus about his identity during his trial before the Sanhedrin, he brings together the two titles which have hitherto been kept separate (apart from 1:1): 'Are you the Messiah, the Son of the Blessed one?' (14:61, 'the Blessed one' is a circumlocution for 'God'). Jesus, for the first and only time in Mark's Gospel, unequivocally affirms his identity ('I am'), and continues by speaking of his future vindication as the Son of Man enthroned at God's right hand and who will return in glory (14:62; cf. Ps. 110:1; Dan. 7:13). It is at this point in the narrative, with Jesus' fate now sealed as he is charged with blasphemy (14:64), that he can publicly declare his true identity. Jesus' divine sonship is consequently acclaimed at the moment of his death on the cross, not by a supernatural being or one of the disciples, but by a Roman centurion: 'Truly this man was God's Son' (15:39). This marks the climax of Mark's narrative christology.

The Gospel of Matthew

Mark's Gospel was employed by Matthew and Luke, who, independently of each other, also made use of another source consisting of Jesus' sayings (known as Q, from the German word *Quelle* = source) as well as their own special material. Both Matthew and Luke, whose Gospels were composed sometime during the final quarter of the first century CE, essentially follow the general outline of the Markan narrative after their infancy narratives. Identifying the distinctive christological features of the Gospels of Matthew and Luke certainly involves studying how they have modified and interpreted their sources, but it is the interweaving of christological themes in their narratives that discloses the true depth of the Matthean and Lukan presentations of Jesus.

Several of the key christological motifs in Matthew's Gospel are already set out in the four opening chapters (the infancy, baptism and temptation narratives). The first theme highlighted by Matthew in his infancy narrative is Jesus' status as the Messiah who is the fulfilment of Israel's hopes. His messianic identity as 'Son of David' is explicated in an account of his genealogy (1:1–17), while Jesus' Davidic descent is legitimized in a narrative stressing his adoption and naming by Joseph (1:18–25). His role as the long-awaited Messiah of Israel is confirmed by the various scriptural prophecies fulfilled in the events of his birth to a virgin (1:23) in Bethlehem (2:6), his return from Egypt (2:15) and Herod's slaughter (2:18). Jesus' public ministry in Galilee is described, moreover, in terms of his mission to the lost sheep of Israel (9:36; 15:24), and, after he is presented as the supreme interpreter of the Torah through his Sermon on the Mount (Matt. 5–7), the narratives about his healings are said to offer further confirmation that he is the one in whom scriptural prophecies find their fulfilment: 'He took our infirmities and bore our diseases' (8:17; citing Isa. 53:4). However, the growing hostility of the Jewish religious leaders towards Jesus leads him to end the parable of the wicked husbandmen with the words, 'The kingdom of God will be taken away from you and given to a people that produces the fruits of the kingdom' (21:43). The disciples form the nucleus of this 'new people' (Stanton 1992: 10–12), while the inclusion of Gentiles is described as the fulfilment of Scripture (4:15–16; 12:18–21) and as the core of the commission received by the disciples after Jesus' resurrection (28:19–20). This unmistakable focus on mission to the Gentiles, brought about by Israel's rejection of Jesus as the Messiah, is integral to what has been described as Matthew's 'inclusive story' (Luz 1995: 9), for it mirrors the situation of the first recipients of this Gospel, who probably no longer remained within the synagogue and for whom the Gentile mission was a major concern.

A study of Matthean christology cannot overlook the centrality of Jesus' divine sonship in this Gospel. The Markan secrecy motif in relation to the 'Son of God' title is not sustained by Matthew, and his redactional activity includes the modification of the disciples' response at the end of the sea-walking narrative (Matt. 14:33: 'Truly you are the Son of God'; cf. Mark 6:52), thus preparing for Peter's confession at Caesarea Philippi: 'You are the Messiah (or the Christ), the Son of the living God' (16:16). The divine origin of Jesus' sonship is of course established by Matthew in his infancy narrative, since the virgin birth prophesied in Isaiah 7:14 (LXX) occurs through the power of the Holy Spirit. How, then, does Matthew envisage and elaborate upon the significance of Jesus as the 'Son of God'? Jesus' sonship certainly expresses his unique relationship with God, both in terms of his sovereign authority (14:33) and their mutual knowledge (11:27). But Matthew places particular emphasis on the obedience of Jesus as Son. By means of his baptism he 'fulfils all righteousness' (3:15), as confirmed by God (3:17: 'This is my Son, the Beloved'), and during his testing by Satan (4:3, 6: 'If you are the Son of God . . .') Jesus refuses to use his power for any purpose other than to accomplish God's will. His path of obedience is also a path of suffering that leads to the pouring out of his blood for the forgiveness of sins (26:28), thereby echoing the earlier interpretative explanation of the name 'Jesus' (1:21: 'he will save his people from their sins'). Jesus remains obedient unto death and refuses to succumb to testing by the crowds and chief priests, who mockingly challenge him to descend from the cross (27:38–44).

Matthew, like so many New Testament writers, emphasizes that God ultimately vindicates his Son by raising him from the dead. The first words of the risen Jesus to his disciples as he appears to them on the mountain is that all authority in heaven and on earth has been given to him (28:18), reminiscent of his earlier predictions of future judgement and glorious return as the Son of Man. What is even more striking is that the Gospel ends on a christological note already encountered in the first chapter, since the prophecy of Isaiah 7:14 is fulfilled both in the virginal conception of Jesus and in his naming as 'Emmanuel', meaning 'God is with us' (1:23). Matthew accordingly stresses from the outset that Jesus is in fact God's presence with his people (cf. 18:20), a theme that resonates in the final declaration of the risen Jesus to his disciples: 'I am with you always, to the end of the age' (28:20).

The Gospel of Luke and the Acts of the Apostles

The Gospel of Luke and the Acts of the Apostles form a two-volume composition by an author who emphasizes the continuation between the life and teaching of Jesus and the mission of his followers. Indeed, an important theological theme for an understanding of Lukan christology is the sustained focus in Luke–Acts on Jesus' life and ministry and the establishment of the church as the realization of the salvific purpose of God (Squires 1993; Green 1995). This theme is expressed in a variety of ways, including the use of vocabulary relating to God's plan or design (*boulē*; cf. Luke 7:30; Acts 2:23; 20:27) and the Lukan emphasis on the necessity of events (cf. Luke 9:22; 24:7; Acts 3:21; 17:3) as predetermined by God (Luke 22:22; Acts 10:42). Central to the divine plan is the fulfilment in Jesus of God's ancient promises, a theme firmly established in the Lukan birth and infancy narratives. The story begins in the Temple, where the message that salvation comes through the Lord's Messiah (2:26) is received by those like Simeon and Anna who long for Israel's consolation and redemption (cf. 2:25, 30–2, 38). Thus Zechariah blesses the God of Israel who has raised 'the horn of salvation' within the house of David (1:69), and the angel of the Lord announces the birth of a saviour in the city of David 'who is the Messiah, the Lord' (2:11). It is the language of royal messianic hopes that also characterizes Gabriel's announcement of Jesus' birth to Mary: 'he will be called the Son of the Most High, and the Lord God will give to him the throne of his ancestor David' (1:32). The acclamation 'Son of the Most High' draws from traditions about the Davidic king (Ps. 2:7; 2 Sam. 7:12–16) and the Davidic descent of Joseph is noted (1:27; 2:4; 3:31), but there is no doubt that Luke, like Matthew, is eager to stress that Jesus' divine sonship is unique by virtue of his conception by the Holy Spirit (1:35).

The theme of Jesus' unique relationship with the Father is also adopted by Luke from his sources, and the emphasis on the Son's obedience serves to reinforce the Lukan interest in the saving plan of God. The activity of the Holy Spirit, again indicative of divine purpose and guidance, features prominently in the prelude to Jesus' Galilean ministry (3:22; 4:1, 14) and in the opening scene of that ministry set in Nazareth. Jesus here announces to his synagogue audience that the passage from Isaiah (Isa. 61:1–2, conflated with 58:6) is fulfilled in their presence (4:21). Hence Luke presents this Isaianic text ('The Spirit of the Lord is upon me, because he has anointed me to bring good news to the poor . . .') as an expression of the purpose and significance of Jesus' ministry. He has been anointed with the Holy Spirit to carry out a ministry of proclamation to the poor (cf. 6:20; 18:22), a message of release to the oppressed, including lepers (5:12–16), women (13:10–17) and tax collectors (5:27–32; 19:1–10). And although Jesus himself has little contact with Gentiles during his earthly ministry (cf. 7:1–10), his mission of removing those barriers that divide people prepares the way for the Gentile mission of the apostles (24:47), described by Luke in his second volume (Green 1995: 47–8, 126).

Luke also stresses, to a far greater extent than the other Gospels, that Jesus engages in a prophetic ministry. His rejection by the people of Nazareth leads him to draw a parallel between his own situation and the activity of the prophets Elijah and Elisha (4:24–7), while, on a more positive note, the people of Nain glorify God after Jesus has raised the widow's son and declare, 'A great prophet has risen among us' (7:16; cf. 24:19; Acts 2:22). Towards the end of the Galilean ministry, after Peter's confession that Jesus is 'the Messiah of God' (9:20) and Jesus predicts his suffering and rejection (9:22), the Lukan transfiguration scene includes an unparalleled reference to Moses and Elijah speaking of the 'departure' (*exodos*) that Jesus was about to accomplish in Jerusalem (9:31). The term *exodos* not only implies an understanding of Jesus as the Prophet like Moses (Deut. 18:15–18; cf. Acts 3:22–3; 7:37), but it may point to his departure through death and resurrection as a 'new exodus' (Tuckett 1996: 84).

A distinctive aspect of Luke's Gospel is the extended narrative of Jesus' journey towards Jerusalem (9:51 – 19:44), whose importance is indicated by its introduction: 'When the days drew near for him to be taken up, he set his face to go to Jerusalem.' This statement expresses Jesus' resolve to reach the city where his mission and destiny will be fulfilled through his passion, death, resurrection and ascension (his 'taking up'; cf. Acts 1:2, 11, 22). During this journey Jesus declares that he must (*dei*) be on his way, 'because it is impossible for a prophet to be killed away from Jerusalem' (13:33). After the resurrection Jesus tells the two disciples on the road to Emmaus that it was necessary (*dei*) for the Messiah to suffer such things in order to enter into his glory, as written in Moses and the prophets (24:26–7). And when he appears to the eleven disciples in Jerusalem, he again draws attention to the fulfilment of what Moses, the prophets and the psalms had written about him, namely 'that the Messiah is to suffer and to rise from the dead on the third day (24:44–6). In the same way as the infancy narrative announces that Israel's long-awaited salvation is realized in Jesus, the final chapter highlights the theme that Jesus, the Messiah who suffered and is vindicated through resurrection, is indeed the fulfilment of God's promises. Before his ascension Jesus commissions the disciples to act as his witnesses that 'repentance and forgiveness of sins is to be proclaimed in his name to all nations, beginning from Jerusalem' (24:47–8). This commission prepares for the disciples' mission after their empowerment by the Holy Spirit, a mission narrated in the Acts of the Apostles.

Luke's favoured vehicle for his christological message in the first half of Acts is a series of speeches, delivered by Peter on such occasions as the outpouring of the Holy Spirit on the day of Pentecost (2:14–39), after the healing of the lame man in Solomon's Portico (3:12–26), in the presence of the Sanhedrin (4:8–12) and Jewish leaders (5:29–32), and his missionary speech to Cornelius and his household in Caesarea (10:34–43). To these one may add the address delivered by Paul to Jews and Godfearers in the synagogue of Pisidian Antioch (13:16–41). The elements that feature prominently in the speeches are kerygmatic summaries of the events of Jesus' life, death, resurrection and exaltation, a demonstration that these events fulfil Scripture, and an appeal for repentance (see Bauckham 1996). Consistency of language and style, as well as variations in actual content and sequence, are evident in these speeches, prompting much debate among interpreters as to whether Luke has made use of earlier sources or that the speeches should be viewed as purely Lukan compositions.

While interest in Jesus' earthly life is displayed in some of the kerygmatic summaries (Acts 2:22; 10:37–9), it is his death, resurrection and exaltation that are of central concern. The suffering and death of Jesus the Messiah are depicted as events that accord with 'the definite plan and foreknowledge of God' (2:23; cf. 4:28) or as foretold in Scripture (3:18; cf. 17:2–3; 26:22–3), recalling Jesus' words after his resurrection. A recurring motif in these speeches is the contrast between the conduct of those responsible for Jesus' death and the way God reverses their actions through his powerful act of raising him from the dead. This motif appears in its most concise form in Peter's speech before the Sanhedrin, where he tells the Jews that the healing of the lame man was 'by the name of Jesus Christ of Nazareth, whom you crucified, whom God raised from the dead' (4:10), before describing this act of reversal in terms of the rejected stone that becomes the cornerstone (4:11, citing Ps. 118:22). Some of the speeches delivered by Peter and Paul therefore demonstrate the centrality of Jesus' resurrection in the saving purpose of God by appealing to the Scriptures now fulfilled (2:25–32 [Ps. 16:8–11]; 13:32–7 [Pss 2:7; 16:10]) and confirmed by the apostles in their role as witnesses to the risen Christ (2:32; 3:15; 5:32; 10:41; 13:31).

As a result of his resurrection and ascension, Jesus as been exalted to the right hand of God (2:34–5, citing Ps. 110:1) who 'has made him both Lord and Messiah' (2:36). This declaration could imply that the titles *kyrios* and *christos* were first conferred upon Jesus by virtue of his resurrection, although the Lukan emphasis is possibly on divine confirmation rather than installation. Several other christological titles or designations, some unparalleled, occur in Acts, especially in Peter's speech after the healing of the lame man: Jesus is the Servant glorified by God (3:13, 26), the Holy and Righteous One (3:14; cf. 7:52; 22:14), the Founder of Life (3:15; 5:31), the Prophet like Moses (3:22–5). The Jews of Jerusalem would presumably be able to appreciate the theological force of these titles, but they find no place in Peter's speech at Caesarea where the emphasis lies on the universal significance of Jesus as 'Lord of all' (10:36). He is the one whose resurrection and ascension serve as a guarantee for his future role as 'judge of the living and the dead' (10:42).

The repeated call for repentance in the speeches of Peter and Paul highlights the Lukan presentation of Jesus as the divine agent of salvation (2:38–9; 3:19; 5:31; 13:38–9). The final words of Joel 3:1–5, the scriptural passage with which Paul opens his Pentecost speech, announces that 'everyone who calls upon the name of the Lord shall be saved'. These words are clearly appropriated to Jesus as 'Lord', for Peter declares to the Sanhedrin that there is salvation in no one else, since there is no other name 'by which we must be saved' (4:12). The invocation of Jesus' name signifies his continuing power to effect salvation, and it is for this reason that the proclamation of the Christ-event in the speeches is accompanied by a call for repentance. The forgiveness of sins proclaimed by the earthly Jesus (Luke 5:20, 32; 7:47–50) is once more offered by the apostles to those who repent and turn to him as their Saviour (Acts 5:31).

The letter to the Hebrews

The letter to the Hebrews offers one of the most distinctive interpretations of Jesus in the New Testament, although the identity of its author, as well as the circumstances and location of its recipients, are shrouded in mystery. What does become clear is that this letter's christology is integrally linked to the author's pastoral concerns, for he exhorts his readers to hold on to their faith during a time of crisis for the community. Appeal is therefore made in the prologue (1:1–4) to the confession of faith shared by the author and his readers (Isaacs 1992: 186–8), beginning with the definitive character of God's revelation in Jesus, his Son, as compared with the 'many and various ways' God spoke through the prophets. Jesus' divine sonship, a major christological theme in this letter, is presented in all-embracing and cosmic terms: the one whom God has appointed heir of all things (cf. Ps. 2:8) is the one 'through whom he also created the worlds' (1:2). Echoes of Jewish traditions relating to the role of divine Wisdom can be detected in this description of the Son as active in creation (cf. 1 Cor. 8:6; Col. 1:16; John 1:3), and especially in the claim that 'he is the reflection of God's glory' (1:3; cf. Wisdom 7:26). But it is upon two further aspects of the Son's activity as outlined in the prologue that the letter will focus, namely that Christ in his atoning death has made purification for sins and has accordingly been exalted to the right hand of God (1:3). The allusion to Psalm 110:1 prepares the way for an intricately developed christology steeped in citations of and allusions to Scripture, while the universal sovereignty granted to the Son by means of his exaltation affirms his superiority to the angels (1:4).

The author proceeds to establish the Son's unique status over against the angels with the aid of seven proof-texts (1:5–14). Among the passages cited are two royal Davidic traditions (Ps. 2:7; 2 Sam. 7:14) whose influence on the shaping of early christological reflection is attested in many of the New Testament writings already considered. Due to the Son's incomparable status and his eternal rule as one designated *theos* (1:8, citing Ps. 45:6) and *kyrios* (1:10, citing Ps. 102:25), the angels are to worship him (1:6) and act as ministering servants (1:14). The Son alone is enthroned at the right hand of God, as confirmed by a seventh scriptural citation to which the prologue has already alluded (1:13, citing Ps. 110:1). The highlighting of Jesus' supremacy over the angels continues in 2:5–9, this time to emphasize that God intends to subject all things to humankind. An exposition based on Psalm 8:4–6 leads the author to explain that Jesus was for a little while made lower than the angels, but he is now crowned with glory and honour because of the suffering and death he endured for all (cf. 1:3; 10:12). Christ is also the 'pioneer of their salvation' (2:10; cf. 5:9), for people will be brought to glory as a result of his death and exaltation. It was necessary for him to be made perfect through sufferings (2:10; cf. 5:8) and live in solidarity with the rest of humankind, because only one who is fully human can be a 'merciful and faithful high priest' making a sacrifice of atonement for the sins of the people (2:14–18).

Having announced that Jesus is high priest (2:17), this christological theme is taken up again in the description of the Son of God as a 'great high priest who has passed through the heavens' (4:14), a theme explored in detail in subsequent chapters (5:1–10; 7:1 – 10:18). Christ qualifies for the high priestly role because of his genuine capacity to sympathize with human weaknesses, yet himself without sin (4:15; cf. 7:26–7). The divine appointment of Jesus to the office of high priest is confirmed by Scripture (5:5–6), with the author appealing for the second time to Psalm 2:7, and to another royal psalm repeatedly cited by him in connection with Jesus' exaltation, this time in relation to his priesthood: 'You are a priest for ever, according to the order of Melchizedek' (110:4). The implications of this high priestly designation for Jesus, unparalleled in other New Testament writings, are explained in an exposition of the only other passage in Scripture to mention the king–priest Melchizedek (Gen. 14:18–20). It is argued that this high priestly order is eternal since the Genesis passage fails to mention the father, mother or genealogy of Melchizedek (7:3), and, because he received tithes from Abraham and blessed him, Melchizedek must have been greater than the patriarch and the descendants of Levi who came from Abraham (7:4–10). Thus the high priesthood of Jesus 'in the order of Melchizedek' is superior to the Levitical priesthood and is permanently effective (7:23–5); Christ, due to his resurrection and ascension rather than physical descent, is eternally high priest by 'the power of an indestructible life' (7:16), interceding on behalf of those who draw near to God through him (7:25).

Unlike the repeated offerings presented by the Levitical priests, Jesus did this 'once for all' when he offered himself as the atoning sacrifice (7:26–7; cf. 9:14, 24–6). This is followed by a detailed demonstration of the effectiveness of the sacrifice made by the eternal high priest who now ministers in the heavenly sanctuary. Jesus has become the mediator of a new and better covenant (8:6; 9:15; 12:24). The high priest of the old order entered the Holy of Holies once a year to make a sacrifice of atonement for sins (9:7), but Jesus, by means of his sacrificial death, has entered once for all into 'the Holy Place', the very presence of God (9:12; cf. 10:12). The message communicated by the author of Hebrews is that Jesus has made the heavenly sanctuary accessible to all, for his death has opened up the way to enable those who accompany him to enter heaven itself (10:19–21). For this reason, those presently in danger of losing hope are urged by the author to stand firm in their faith and to approach the throne of grace with confidence (4:16). In Jesus they find not only their forerunner (6:20), but the pioneer and perfecter of their faith (12:1–4), for his supreme example of endurance and faithfulness offers encouragement to believers in their present trials (12:5–13).

The book of Revelation

Those addressed as 'the seven churches in Asia' (1:4) are the recipients of a letter introduced by the author as 'the revelation (*apokalypsis*) of Jesus Christ, which God gave him to show his servants what must soon take place' (1:1). This New Testament writing is therefore presented as a record of the divine revelation given to Jesus Christ, the one whose decisive role in the unfolding of 'what is and what is to take place' (1:19) is demonstrated in a series of heavenly visions. John, nevertheless, experiences his first vision on the island of Patmos (1:9–20), where he encounters 'one like a son of man' who commands him to write down messages for the seven churches. This christophany depicts Jesus as a glorious heavenly being (1:12–16), one whose angelic and divine attributes are described in language drawn from biblical angelophanies and theophanies (cf. Dan. 7:9–14; 10:5–6; Ezek. 1:24; 9:2). This exalted portrayal of Jesus continues when he identifies himself to the seer: 'I am the first and the last, and the living one. I was dead, and see, I am alive for ever and ever' (1:17–18). The second part of this declaration confirms that the heavenly figure is the crucified and risen Christ, whereas the initial self-designation (cf. 2:8; 22:13) resembles God's own self-declaration (1:8; 21:6) and especially his claim to sovereignty in Deutero-Isaiah (44:6; 48:12; cf. 41:4). For the author of Revelation to describe Christ as 'the first and the last', and as 'the origin of God's creation' (3:14; cf. Col. 1:15), is to associate him with God in the closest possible terms (see Bauckham 1993a: 54–8).

It is in the vision of the heavenly throne-room (Rev. 4–5) that the close connection between God and Christ is made most apparent. It describes the worship offered by the heavenly host to God, 'the one seated on the throne' (4:8–11), in whose hand is a scroll with seven seals (5:1). John is told that the only one worthy to open the scroll is 'the Lion of the tribe of Judah, the Root of David' (5:5), a figure described with the aid of Jewish messianic designations (cf. Gen. 49:9; Isa. 11:1, 10). But what John actually sees is a Lamb standing as though it had been slain (5:6). The appearance of the Lamb marks the introduction of a central christological image in Revelation, for the Lamb-Messiah is the crucified Christ who has conquered by means of his redemptive death. In celebration of his victory, the four living creatures and the twenty-four elders sing a new song, declaring that the Lamb is worthy to open the scroll because he has by his blood ransomed people for God from all the nations, and 'made them to be a kingdom and priests serving our God' (5:9–10; cf. 1:5–6).

A second hymn of praise to the Lamb sung by myriads of angels (5:11–12) closely resembles the honouring of God the Creator as worthy to receive glory and honour and power (4:11). In fact the third hymn sung by the whole creation is addressed to them both: 'To the one seated on the throne and to the Lamb be blessing and honour and glory and might for ever and ever', and the elders fall down and worship (5:13–14). This scene signifies that the Lamb, having taken the scroll, becomes the object of heavenly worship alongside God, while Christ elsewhere states that he has 'sat down with my Father on his throne' (3:21; cf. 7:17; 22:1, 3). This is all the more significant in view of the references to an angel refusing obeisance from John, declaring, 'Worship God!' (19:10; 22:8–9). There are indications, however, that the inclusion of Christ as the object of worship is not viewed by the author of Revelation as a compromise of monotheistic belief (cf. 15:3–4). It has, for example, recently been noted that formulaic expressions such as 'before the throne and before the Lamb' (7:9; cf. 6:16) and 'the kingdom of our Lord and of his Messiah' (11:15; cf. 12:10; 20:6) certainly express the close relationship between God and the Lamb, yet at the same time they retain the distinction between them (Stuckenbruck 1995: 261–2).

Following the scene of heavenly worship, the Lamb begins to open the seals in order to reveal the contents of the scroll, thereby initiating the plan that will lead to the establishment of God's kingdom on earth. The involvement of the Lamb in this plan of judgement and salvation, in the struggle between good and evil, means that he brings wrath upon the wicked (cf. 6:16) but leads his people to springs of living water (7:17); he stands on Mount Zion in triumph with those who have been redeemed from the earth (14:1–5). Revelation repeatedly emphasizes the nearness of the end, and Christ himself declares, 'I am coming soon' (3:11; 22:7, 12, 20). And while the Lamb has already conquered by his sacrificial death (3:21; 5:5; cf. 12:11), he will conquer again at the *parousia*. And so John receives a vision of Christ appearing as a rider on a white horse with the armies of heaven (19:11–16). He is called 'Faithful and True' (19:11), 'the Word of God' (19:13), 'King of kings and Lord of lords' (19:16; cf. 17:14), and with a sharp sword coming from his mouth he strikes the nations (cf. Isa. 11:4). The final victory over the powers of evil will result in the new creation, and John sees a holy city, the new Jerusalem, coming down from heaven (21:1–2). The appearance of heaven on earth thus signifies the fulfilment of God's plan to establish his universal kingdom, for his presence fills the new Jerusalem whose temple is 'the Lord God the Almighty and the Lamb' (21:22).

The Gospel of John and the letters of John

The Gospel of John offers the following summary statement in its originally intended conclusion: 'But these [the signs] are written so that you may believe that Jesus is the Messiah, the Son of God, and that through believing you may have life in his name' (20:31). The two titles selected as expressions of the christological belief that will lead to life figure prominently in the other Gospels, and certainly provide the key to the Markan portrayal of Jesus. Behind this Johannine statement, however, there lies a distinctive christology that not only introduces new dimensions of meaning and significance to the titles 'Messiah' and particularly 'Son of God', but offers a presentation of Jesus that cannot be contained in the two titles. Christological claims are the focus of John's Gospel from beginning to end; its narratives and discourses are explicitly concerned with Jesus' true identity and, in a manner unparalleled in the Synoptic Gospels, with his revelatory and salvific role. The Johannine Jesus speaks openly about his origin and identity, discusses his relationship with the Father and offers the gift of eternal life to all who believe in him. A particular characteristic of the Fourth Gospel is that Jesus is often depicted as defending his christological assertions in confrontation with 'the Jews', a designation used primarily for the Jewish religious authorities who even accuse Jesus of making himself equal to God (5:18–19; 10:33). As it is now widely accepted that John's Gospel presents a two-level drama centred on the historical Jesus and the situation of the evangelist and his community (Martyn 1979), christology was at the heart of the controversies that led to the synagogue expulsion of those who confessed Jesus to be the Messiah (cf. 9:22; 12:42; 16:2). Exalted claims about Jesus were either the cause (Brown 1979) or the result (Martyn 1979) of the separation of believers forming 'the Johannine community', while the Gospel itself developed over a period of time before reaching its present form around 85–95 CE.

John's christological assertions begin in the prologue (1:1–18), where Jesus is identified with the Word (*logos*) of God. To state that the Word was 'in the beginning' before creation (1:1) amounts to a declaration of timeless existence, one to which Jesus lays claim during his earthly ministry (cf. 8:58; 17:5), whereas to describe the Word as the agent of creation (1:3) echoes those Wisdom traditions appropriated by other writers (cf. Col. 1:16; Heb. 1:2). The opening verse clearly seeks to express the relationship between the Word and God ('the Word was with God'), followed by the affirmation that 'the Word was God'. The precise meaning of the latter declaration continues to be the subject of considerable debate, with many scholars noting the subtleties of the Greek text; the definite article is included before 'God' in the declaration 'the Word was with God' (*ho theos*), but not in the clause 'the Word was God (*theos*)'. This variation is then interpreted to mean that, while the prologue identifies the Word as God (*theos*), 'it avoids any suggestion of personal identification of the Word with the Father' (Brown 1966, 1: 24). Even if the verse does preserve a distinction between the Word and God without separating them, it is significant that Jesus is also called *theos* in 1:18 (if one accepts the reading 'God, the only Son') and in the confession of Thomas (20:28: 'My Lord and my God'). This is not a title claimed by the earthly Jesus, but its attribution to Christ at key points in the Gospel expresses the conviction that he is the authentic and definitive revelation of God. As the vehicle of God's self-revelation in the world, the Word becomes flesh and reveals his glory (1:14). And since 'no one has ever seen God' (1:18; cf. Exod. 33:20), the revelation communicated by the Son is superior to that received in the past, for he alone is in direct communion with the Father.

It is through the Son, the Word incarnate, that humankind receives the perfect revelation of life (1:4), light (1:4–5), grace and truth (1:14) and God (1:18).

Scholars who attempt to identify different christological strands in the Fourth Gospel usually attribute the prologue to a later stage of development, although there is no doubt that this Logos christology determines the overall Johannine presentation of Jesus in the Gospel in its present form. The Logos title does not appear again, but the Father–Son language (1:14–18) is sustained throughout and serves as a key concept to express the significance of Jesus as the one who reveals God. To express his intimate relationship with God, Jesus is described as the 'only Son' (1:14; 3:16, 18) who is loved by the Father (cf. 5:20; 10:17) and to whom he has 'placed all things in his hands' (3:35). The one sent into the world (3:17; 10:36) also expresses consciousness of his eternal status as Son, for when Jesus states, 'I declare what I have seen in the Father's presence' (8:38), he is testifying to what he, and he alone, has seen and heard in heaven before he was sent into the world. Even the words and works of the Son are not his own, but those of the Father (cf. 5:36; 8:28; 12:49–50; 14:10).

During his earthly life the Son speaks and acts in perfect unity with the Father (10:30: 'The Father and I are one'); to see him is to see the Father (12:45; 14:9), and whoever knows him knows the Father (8:19; 14:7). Because belief in Jesus leads to eternal life, the Son can declare that he, like the Father, has the power to give life (5:21). But he has also been given authority to execute judgement (5:27), for all who encounter Jesus are obliged to respond to him; those who believe enter the light and gain life, but those who reject him remain in darkness and face death. The coming of Jesus therefore amounts to the judgement of this world (12:31), even though the purpose of his mission was in order that 'the world might be saved through him' (3:17). From the early days of his ministry Jesus commits himself to the will of the Father: 'My food is to do the will of him who sent me and to complete his work' (4:34). It is in obedience to the Father's plan that he follows the path of the cross, but as one who is in full control (cf. 13:27; 18:4–8; 19:30), for 'no one takes my life from me, but I lay it down of my own accord' (10:18). Jesus' death is therefore depicted in John's Gospel as the fulfilment of his mission to reveal the Father and as the completion of his salvific work: 'It is finished' (19:30). It is the fulfilment of Jesus' prediction that he must be lifted up on the cross so that whoever believes in him may receive eternal life (3:14–15). The 'lifting up' of Jesus, linked specifically to his identity as the Son of Man, points to this salvific death as exaltation, for the evangelist takes advantage of the double meaning of a Greek verb (*hypsoō*) that can connote both the lifting up of Jesus on the cross as well as his exaltation (3:14; 8:28; 12:32–4). Moreover, it signifies the arrival of Jesus' hour of glorification (12:23; 13:31), for his passion is the supreme revelation of divine glory, as well as the means whereby the Son returns to the Father and ascends to the glory which was his before creation (17:5).

The significance of Jesus as the revelatory and salvific presence of God also finds expression in the Johannine 'I am' declarations. On seven occasions Jesus' use of 'I am' (*egō eimi*) is combined with an image drawn primarily from scriptural promises of divine salvation. When Jesus declares that he is the bread of life (6:35), the light of the world (8:12) or the true vine (15:1), such evocative images serve to demonstrate that he is the source and giver of eternal life. However, certain pronouncements are attributed to Jesus in which *egō eimi* possesses no predicate or antecedent. He declares to his opponents, 'You will die in your sins unless you believe that I am (he)' (8:24; cf. 8:28, 58), and, when Jesus predicts his imminent betrayal, he informs the disciples, 'I tell you this now, before it occurs, so that when it does occur, you may believe that I am (he)' (13:19). To these may be added the occurrences of *egō eimi* where a predicate is implied (4:26; 18:5, 8; cf. 6:20), although its use by Jesus as he walks on the sea (6:20) and the dramatic response of the arresting party in the garden (18:6) suggest that it serves here as more than a form of self-identification, especially in view of the fourth evangelist's fondness for words or expressions with double meanings. The key that appears to unlock the christological significance of these 'absolute' statements is the distinctive use of *egō eimi* in the Greek versions of Isaiah (41:4; 43:10; 46:4; 52:6) and the Song of Moses (Deut. 32:39) to render Yahweh's claim to unique sovereignty (Hebrew: *anî hû'*). Indeed the presentation and function of *egō eimi* as uttered by Jesus in the Fourth Gospel bears striking resemblance to its setting and purpose in these biblical traditions. Jesus, like Yahweh, pronounces *egō eimi* to convey his role as revealer and saviour; he exists from eternity (8:58), is able to foretell and control events (13:19; 18:5), offers salvation to those who believe in him (6:20; 8:28; 18:8), while those who reject him face condemnation (8:24). The Johannine Jesus can declare *egō eimi* in this manner because he is the eternal Word incarnate, the Son who speaks and acts in unity with the Father, the unique revelation of God.

However, one factor that led to the composition of the Johannine letters, particularly the first and second, was a crisis caused by those who, as a result of their christological views, had recently left the community. The root of this controversy seems to be that certain believers deviated from the teaching of the Johannine community by embracing a kind of 'docetic' christology that cast doubt on the reality of Jesus' humanity and sufferings; his divine glory was emphasized to such an extent that the significance of his earthly life and the salvific effects of his death were disputed. The response expressed in the first two letters of John is to reaffirm the confession that 'Jesus Christ has come in the flesh' (1 John 4:2–3; 2 John 7) and that he 'came by water and blood' (1 John 5:6). Believers are also exhorted to walk in the light, for Jesus' blood cleanses from all sin (1:7; cf. 2:1–2; 3:5: 4:10). Other pronouncements certainly resemble the christology of John's Gospel, a writing known in its present or earlier form to the author(s) of the Johannine letters. For to state that Jesus was the Son sent by God 'so that we might live through him' (1 John 4:9) firmly echoes the Gospel's pivotal declaration that 'God so loved the world that he gave his only Son, so that everyone who believes in him may not perish but may have eternal life' (3:16). In this respect both the Gospel and letters of John attest the central christological conviction expressed in all the writings of the New Testament, namely that Jesus, the Christ and unique Son of God, is the key to divine salvation.

BIBLIOGRAPHY

Barrett, C. K., *A Commentary on the Epistle to the Romans*, BNTC, London: A & C Black, 1962.

Bauckham, R., *The Theology of the Book of Revelation*, Cambridge: Cambridge University Press, 1993a.

—— 'The Worship of Jesus', *The Climax of Prophecy: Studies on the Book of Revelation*, Edinburgh: T & T Clark, 1993b, 118–49.

—— 'Kerygmatic Summaries in the Speeches of Acts', *History, Literature, and Society in the Book of Acts*, ed. B. Witherington III, Cambridge: Cambridge University Press, 1996, 185–217.

Bousset, W., *Kyrios Christos: A History of the Belief in Christ from the Beginnings of Christianity to Irenaeus*, ET Nashville: Abingdon, 1970.

Brown, R. E., *The Gospel according to John*, The Anchor Bible Commentary, 2 vols, New York: Doubleday, 1966; London: Geoffrey Chapman, 1971.

—— *The Community of the Beloved Disciple: The Life, Loves, and Hates of an Individual Church in New Testament Times*, New York: Paulist Press, 1979.

Bultmann, R., *Theology of the New Testament*, 2 vols, ET London: SCM, 1952, 1955.

Casey, P. M. *From Jewish Prophet to Gentile God: The Origins and Development of New Testament Christology*, Cadbury Lectures at the University of Birmingham, 1985–6 and Cambridge: James Clarke; Louisville: Westminster, John Knox Press, 1991.

Cullmann, O., *The Christology of the New Testament*, ET London: SCM, 1963[2].

Davis, P. G., 'Divine Agents, Mediators and New Testament Christology', *JTS* 45, 1994, 479–503.

De Jonge, M., *Christology in Context: The Earliest Christian Responses to Jesus*, Philadelphia: Westminster, 1988.

Dunn, J. D. G., *Christology in the Making: A New Testament Inquiry into the Origins of the Doctrine of the Incarnation*, London: SCM, 1989[2].

—— *The Theology of Paul the Apostle*, Edinburgh: T & T Clark, 1998.

Fitzmyer, J. A., 'The Semitic Background of the New Testament *Kyrios*-Title', *A Wandering Aramean: Collected Aramaic Essays*, Missoula: Scholars Press, 1979, 115–42.

Fossum, J., *The Name of God and the Angel of the Lord: Samaritan and Jewish Concepts of Intermediation and the Origins of Gnosticism*, WUNT 1:36, Tübingen: J. C. B. Mohr (Paul Siebeck), 1985.

Fuller, R. H., *The Foundations of New Testament Christology*, London: Lutterworth, 1965.

Green, J. B., *The Theology of the Gospel of Luke*, Cambridge: Cambridge University Press, 1995.

Hahn, F., *The Titles of Jesus in Christology: Their History in Early Christianity*, ET London: Lutterworth, 1969.

Hengel. M., *The Son of God*, London: SCM, 1976.

—— 'Christology and New Testament Chronology: A Problem in the History of Earliest Christianity', *Between Jesus and Paul: Studies in the Earliest History of Christianity*, ET London: SCM, 1983, 30–47.

—— *The 'Hellenization' of Judaea in the First Century after Christ*, London: SCM, 1989.

—— *Studies in Early Christology*, Edinburgh: T & T Clark, 1995.

Horbury, W., *Jewish Messianism and the Cult of Christ*, London: SCM, 1998.

Hurtado, L. W., 'Son of God', *Dictionary of Paul and His Letters*, eds G. F. Hawthorne and R. P. Martin, Leicester: InterVarsity Press, 1993, 900–6.

—— *One God, One Lord: Early Christian Devotion and Ancient Jewish Monotheism*, Edinburgh: T & T Clark, 1998[2].

—— 'Pre-70 CE Jewish Opposition to Christ-Devotion', *JTS* 50, 1999, 35–58.

Isaacs, M. E., *Sacred Space: An Approach to the Theology of the Epistle to the Hebrews*, Sheffield: JSOT, 1992.

Keck, L. E., 'Toward the Renewal of New Testament Christology', *NTS* 32, 1986, 362–77.

Kim, S., *The Origin of Paul's Gospel*, WUNT 2:4, Tübingen: J. C. B. Mohr (Paul Siebeck), 1984[2].

Longenecker, R. N., 'A Realized Hope, a New Commitment, and a Developed Proclamation: Paul and Jesus', *The Road from Damascus: The Impact of Paul's Conversion on his Life, Thought, and Ministry*, ed. R. N. Longenecker, Grand Rapids: Eerdmans, 1997, 18–42.

Luz, U., *The Theology of the Gospel of Matthew*, Cambridge: Cambridge University Press, 1995.

Marcus, J., *The Way of the Lord: Christological Exegesis of the Old Testament in the Gospel of Mark*, Edinburgh: T & T Clark, 1993.

Marshall, I. H., *The Origins of New Testament Christology*, Leicester: Apollos, 1990[2].

Martyn, J. L., *History and Theology in the Fourth Gospel*, Nashville: Abingdon, 1979[2].

Matera, F. J., *New Testament Christology*, Louisville: Westminster John Knox, 1999.

Moule, C. F. D., *The Origin of Christology*, Cambridge: Cambridge University Press, 1977.

Rainbow, P. A., 'Jewish Monotheism as the Matrix for New Testament Christology: A Review Article', *NovT* 33, 1991, 78–91.

Rowland, C., *The Open Heaven: A Study of Apocalyptic in Judaism and Early Christianity*, London: SPCK, 1982.

Schüssler Fiorenza, E., 'Wisdom Mythology and the Christological Hymns of the New Testament', *Aspects of Wisdom in Judaism and Early Christianity*, ed. R. L. Wilken, Notre Dame: University of Notre Dame Press, 1975, 17–41.

Squires, J. T., *The Plan of God in Luke–Acts*, SNTSMS 76, Cambridge: Cambridge University Press, 1993.

Stanton, G. N., *A Gospel for a New People: Studies in Matthew*, Edinburgh: T & T Clark, 1992.

Stuckenbruck, L. T., *Angel Veneration and Christology: A Study in Early Judaism and in the Christology of the Apocalypse of John*, WUNT 2:70, Tübingen: J. C. B. Mohr (Paul Siebeck), 1995.

Tannehill, R. C., 'The Gospel of Mark as Narrative Christology', *Semeia* 16, 1979, 57–95.

Theissen, G. and Merz, A., *The Historical Jesus: A Comprehensive Guide*, ET London: SCM, 1998.

Tuckett, C. M., *Luke*, NTG, Sheffield: Sheffield Academic Press, 1996.

Tuckett, C. M. (ed.), *The Messianic Secret*, London: SPCK, 1983.

Ziesler, J., *Pauline Christianity*, Oxford: Oxford University Press, 1990[2].

CHAPTER FORTY-FIVE

DEATH AND AFTERLIFE

———— •◆• ————

John J. Collins

'If Christ has not been raised,' says St Paul, 'your faith is futile . . . If for this life only we have hoped in Christ, we are of all people most to be pitied' (1 Cor 15: 17, 19). The belief in resurrection is so fundamental to Christianity that Christians are often surprised to discover how alien it was to the religion of ancient Israel. The belief in a significant, differentiated, life after death only gained currency in Judaism in the Hellenistic period, and was not universally accepted even then. Without these new developments in Judaism in the Hellenistic age, however, the Christian belief in resurrection would have been unintelligible.

DEATH IN THE ANCIENT NEW EAST

In the ancient Near East, Egypt was exceptional in having a widespread belief in immortality,[1] but Egyptian ideas on this subject leave no verifiable trace in the Hebrew Bible. The attitude of the Semitic cultures is perhaps best summed up in the futile quest of Gilgamesh, who, though two-thirds divine, is told both by the God Shamash and by Siduri the ale-wife that he will not find the (eternal) life that he seeks, for 'when the gods created mankind they appointed death for mankind and kept life for themselves.'[2] The lot of humankind is vividly expressed in the death-dream of Enkidu, where he is driven down 'to the house which those who enter cannot leave, on the road where travelling is one way only, to the house where those who stay are deprived of light, where dust is their food, and clay their bread. They are clothed, like birds, with feathers, and they see no light, and they dwell in darkness.'[3] In Akkadian the Netherworld is *māt la târi*, the land of no return. A very similar account of the Netherworld is found in the myth of *Ishtar's Descent to the Netherworld*.[4] There is some variation in the Akkadian accounts of the Netherworld. In some cases it is gloomy and melancholic, but serene, while in others it is terrifying. In the neo-Assyrian *Vision of the Netherworld*, a crown-prince called Kummaya (possibly a pseudonym for Asshurbanipal) is hauled before Nergal, god of the Netherworld, who is attended by an entourage of deities in hybrid form: 'The nether world was filled with terror . . . when [I] saw him, my legs trembled as his brilliance overwhelmed me.'[5] Only exceptional individuals, like the flood-hero Utnapishtim, are allowed to escape it and be as gods.[6] Even Adapa, in the myth that bears his name, refuses the bread and water of life when they are offered to him and is sent back to earth.

The culture of Canaan, which provided the immediate context of early Israel, is known to us mainly from the Ugaritic texts. There Death is portrayed as a god, Mot, who is an adversary of Baal. At one point in the myth Baal is given into his power and Mot swallows him: 'One lip to earth, one lip to the heavens; he will stretch his tongue to the stars. Baal must enter inside him; he must go down into his mouth, like an olive cake, the earth's produce, the fruit of the trees.'[7] Baal is eventually rescued from Death by the goddess Anat, and so may be said to be a dying and rising god. Whether any human beings can hope for beatific afterlife, however, is disputed. The main issue here concerns figures called Rephaim, and the institution of the *marzēaḥ*. The Rephaim have been identified as gods, shades of the dead, and/or living persons.[8] The identification as gods has few adherents. The identification both with the shades and with people (giants, warriors, or vaguely defined ethnic groups) can be supported by analogy from the Hebrew Bible.[9] Some scholars argue that they were originally kings and heroes, who were deified after death.[10] Recently Brian Schmidt has argued strenuously that they were legendary heroes and earthly warriors. But even Schmidt allows that 'the ancient Rephaim' (*rp'im qdmym*) were associated with the Netherworld.[11] These ancient Rephaim, and some dead kings, are invoked in *KTU* 1.161, which appears to reflect a funerary ritual. Other texts speak of the Rephaim coming to a feast, without making clear whether the reference is to dead or living beings.[12] Some scholars hold that the *marzēaḥ* entailed such a feast for and with the dead ancestors, or *Rephaim*.[13] The *marzēaḥ* is widely attested over a period of more than a thousand years. It was an institution that had a banquet hall, had a designated leader and patron deity or deities, and was associated especially with drinking.[14] The evidence that it was a funerary institution consists mainly of a Nabatean text that refers to 'the *marzēaḥ* of Obodas the god'[15] (Obodas was a historical king) and Jeremiah 16:5, where Jeremiah is told not to enter the *bêt marzēaḥ* to lament or grieve. Whether it was always or necessarily associated with funerary practices, or was an occasion for communion with the dead, remains uncertain.[16] This issue underlies the debate as to whether the kings of Ugarit were thought to enjoy life with the gods in the hereafter. In the Aramaic Panammu inscription from the eighth century, King Panammu expresses the hope that the son who succeeds him will offer sacrifice to Hadad and 'mention the name of Panammu, saying: "May the soul of Panammu eat with Hadad, and may the soul of Panammu drink with Ha[d]ad."'[17] None of these texts, however, implies that the dead kings or Rephaim live permanently with the gods, even on a maximal interpretation, only that they are allowed to feast with the gods on occasion. Their usual abode after death is still the Netherworld.

The idea that a human being could attain eternal life with the gods is proposed in the story of Aqhat, where the goddess Ishtar says to Aqhat: 'Ask for life, O hero Aqhat, ask for life and I will give it to you, immortality and I will bestow it upon you. I will let you count with Baal the years, with the sons of El you will count the months.'[18] But Aqhat replies: 'Don't lie to me, Virgin, for with a hero your lies are wasted. A mortal – what does he get in the end? what does a mortal finally get? plaster poured on his head, lime on top of his skull. As every man dies, I will die;

yes, I too will surely die.'[19] Aqhat is no different from Gilgamesh, in this respect. Even if we accept that the dead kings, the ancient Rephaim, might dine with the gods, the common fate was a gloomy existence in the Netherworld.

DEATH IN THE HEBREW BIBLE

According to Genesis 2–3, Adam and Eve are not initially forbidden to eat of the tree of life, but are prevented from doing so after they have transgressed the command relating to the tree of knowledge. Henceforth Adam must eat his bread by the sweat of his brow, 'until you return to the ground, for out of it you were taken; you are dust, and to dust you shall return' (Gen 3:19). The sin of Adam, however, is never invoked to explain the human situation in the Hebrew Bible. Ben Sira, writing in the first quarter of the second century BCE, puts the blame on Eve: 'from a woman sin had its beginning, and because of her we all die' (Sir 25:24). But elsewhere the same writer implies that mortality is simply the divine pleasure: 'The Lord created human beings out of earth and makes them return to it again' (Sir 17:1); 'this is the Lord's decree for all flesh' (41:4). Beginning with Ben Sira, we find increasing speculation about the opening chapters of Genesis, but it is only in texts from the first century CE (St Paul, *4 Ezra*) that the sin of Adam is well established as the cause of human mortality. The story in Genesis 2–3 has remarkably little influence in the world of the Hebrew Bible.

While there was an obvious sense in which the dead returned to the earth, other ways of describing the fate of the departed are more typical of the biblical texts. Those who die a peaceful death are typically said to be gathered to their ancestors; for example Abraham died 'in a good old age, an old man and full of years, and was gathered to his people' (Gen 25:8). The idiom here reflects the burial customs of ancient Israel. Family members were buried together in underground caves; Abraham was buried with Sarah in the Cave of Machpelah. Tombs of the Iron Age were often characterized by waist-high benches around three sides of the chamber. The use of caves declined as the bench-tombs grew in popularity. Often, the area under one of the benches was hollowed out to serve as a repository for secondary burial. Bodies were laid on the benches until they had decomposed and then the bones were gathered into the repository. Bench-tombs were the predominant form of burial in Judah from the late eighth to early sixth centuries BCE.[20]

In a more mythological vein, the dead are said to descend to Sheol. 'Those that go down to Sheol do not come up' (Job 7:9). Other designations for the Netherworld include ארץ (land), and בור or שחת (pit), sometimes modified by תחתית or תחתיות (nether; lowest).[21] Gates of Sheol are mentioned several times (Isa 38:10; Ps 9:14; Job 38:17). Gates and gate-keepers also figure prominently in Mesopotamian and Egyptian accounts of the Netherworld. Sheol is a place of darkness (Job 17:13; 18:18) and dust (Job 17:16; 21:26; Ps 7:6) and of silence (Pss 31:17–18; 94:17; 115:17; Isa 47:5). Those who go down to Sheol cannot praise God (Pss 30:9; 88:10–12). It is sometimes personified, as Death (*Mot*) is too. It has an insatiable appetite (Isa 5:14; Hab 2:5; Prov 27:20; 30:15b–16) and is said to swallow its victims (Isa 25:8), like Mot in the Ugaritic myth. This mythology is continuous with concepts of the Netherworld in Canaan and Mesopotamia. Sheol is not associated with terror in the Hebrew Bible, however. The biblical Sheol is not yet a Hell, but merely a gloomy Limbo.

Most scholars assume that everyone in the Hebrew Bible goes to Sheol after death, with the exception of extraordinary individuals such as Enoch and Elijah. Some, however, dispute this view, and argue for a difference between the peaceful death of those who are gathered to their fathers and the evil (violent or premature) death of those who go down to Sheol.[22] On this line of interpretation, the psalmist who asks God not to let him go down to Sheol is praying for deliverance from premature death, and to be allowed to live out his life. He was surely not asking for immortality. Similarly Jacob's declaration that 'I shall go down to Sheol to my son mourning' (Gen 37:35) may be taken to mean that he would die prematurely, just as Joseph supposedly had. There are some problems with the distinction, however. Josiah is told that he would be gathered to his ancestors in peace before disaster befell Jerusalem (2 Kgs 22:20) although he would die a violent death. David tells Solomon that he must not let the grey head of Joab 'go down to Sheol in peace' (2 Kgs 2:6), which implies that one might in principle die a peaceful death and go to Sheol. Centuries later, Ben Sira insists that 'whether life is for ten or a hundred or a thousand years, there is no inquiry about it in Hades' (Sir 41:4). In short, neither the fullness of life nor virtue makes a difference as to one's ultimate destination. Similarly the psalmist asks: 'Who can live and never see death? Who can escape the power of Sheol?' (Ps 89:49). It seems likely then that Sheol is the final abode of all mortals, although biblical authors sometimes speak euphemistically about people being gathered to their ancestors in order to avoid the negative associations of Sheol.

The degree to which a cult of the dead was practiced in ancient Israel is controversial. Throughout the period of the monarchy, bowls for food, jars for liquid and sometimes a lamp for light were placed in tombs. Two tombs have been found where a bowl containing sheep bones was covered with another inverted bowl, as if to keep the food warm, while a knife was also provided. Jewelry and amulets were commonly placed in tombs.[23] Various figurines and statuettes are also found. The most common figurines were female pillar figurines with solid or hollow bodies and prominent breasts, emphasized by the arms supporting them.[24] These figurines are peculiar to Judean tombs, although they are also found in domestic contexts in Israel. They are found from the eleventh century onward, and are very common by the eighth and seventh centuries. They most probably represent a goddess, possibly Asherah. The prominence of the breasts suggests a concern for fertility. The precise function of such figurines is unclear, but they probably represent some kind of sympathetic magic, or possibly reflect the hope that the dead can intercede on behalf of the living.

Deuteronomy forbids offering tithed food to the dead (Deut 26:14), but does not prohibit other offerings. It also forbids the consulting of ghosts or spirits, or seeking oracles from the dead (18:11) and self-laceration in mourning (14:1). Consultation of the dead is also noted in Isaiah 8:19–23, 19:3 and possibly 29:4. Second Kings notes that Manasseh consulted mediums and wizards (21:6), and that Josiah put them away (23:24). The most famous story about the consultation of the dead, however, concerns Saul and the witch of Endor in 1 Samuel 28:

They came to the woman by night. And he said, 'Consult a spirit for me, and bring up for me the one whom I name to you . . .' Then the woman said, 'Whom shall I bring up for you?' He answered, 'Bring up Samuel for me' . . . The woman said to Saul 'I see a divine being (אלהים) coming up out of the ground' (28:8–13).

The larger context of this story shows signs of Deuteronomic influence. Saul anticipates Deuteronomy by banning mediums and wizards from the land. The fact that a story about necromancy is nonetheless told is taken by some scholars as an indication that the incident must have been famous.[25] Schmidt, however, has argued that it is a late, post-Deuteronomic invention, and that necromancy was an innovation in Judah, adopted from the Assyrians during the reign of Manasseh.[26] The references to necromancy in Isaiah and in Deuteronomic literature are compatible with this view. It is also supported by the absence of clear evidence of the practice in Syria or Palestine prior to that time. We cannot safely infer that the necromancy was known in Israel before the Assyrian period, but the story gives a vivid impression of religious practice during the late monarchy.

BEATIFIC AFTERLIFE IN THE HEBREW BIBLE?

In view of the evidence reviewed thus far, it should be clear that there was little hope for a beatific afterlife in the ancient Near East outside of Egypt. A few biblical texts, however, have been adduced as evidence for belief in a beatific afterlife. These texts are of two kinds, one found especially in the Psalms, describing the presence of God in transcendent terms, and the other found in prophetic texts, using the language of resurrection in connection with the restoration of Israel.[27]

The key passages in the Psalms are found in Psalms 16: 9–10, 49:16 and 73:23–6. Psalm 16:9–10 ('Therefore my heart is glad and my soul rejoices; my body also rests secure. For you do not give me up to Sheol, or let your faithful one see the Pit') can be interpreted most simply in terms of protection from premature death. A stronger case can be made for Psalm 49:16 ('but God will ransom my soul from the power of Sheol, for he will take me'). The use of the verb 'take' (לקח) here recalls the fate of Enoch, who 'walked with God; then he was no more for God took him' (Gen 5:24). The context in Psalm 49 is a reassurance that one need not fear those who trust in their wealth, for 'like sheep they are appointed for Sheol; Death shall be their shepherd' (Ps 49:15). There is no ransom that one can give to God for one's life, so as to live forever (49:8–10). But the psalmist also affirms that the wise die, together with the fool and the dolt (Ps 49:11), and twice declares that 'humankind shall not live in glory; they perish like the beasts' (49:13, 21). In view of this emphatic refrain, the psalmist's confidence that God will make an exception for him is puzzling.

The verb 'to take' (לקח) is used in a similar way in Psalm 73: 'Nevertheless I am continually with you; you hold my right hand. You guide me with your counsel, and afterward you will receive (תקחני) with honor . . . My flesh and my heart may fail, but God is the strength of my heart and my portion forever' (Ps 73:23–6). Here again there is a contrast with the wicked, who are said to be 'destroyed in a moment, swept away utterly by terrors' (Ps 73:19). The psalmist perceives the contrasting fates of righteous and wicked when he goes into the sanctuary (73:17). The cultic context raises the possibility that what is at issue here is the sense of the presence of God as an experience that transcends time: 'For a day in your courts is better than a thousand elsewhere' (Ps 84:10). In poetic language, 'forever' may only mean that no end is in view. We might compare the assertion of Canticles 8:6 that 'love is as strong as death.'

'Life' and 'death' are often used in this qualitative sense, especially in the wisdom literature.[28] In Proverbs 8:36–6 Wisdom declares that 'whoever finds me finds life . . . all who hate me love death.' Most scholars regard such statements as affirmations of the transcendent value of wisdom. Some, however, believe that the author of Proverbs affirms a beatific afterlife for the just: 'for the wise the path of the life leads upward, in order to avoid Sheol below' (Prov 15:24). Proverbs 12:28 claims that 'in the path of righteousness there is life, in walking its path there is no death.' Whether such statements should be taken literally is debatable.[29] It they are so taken, they are highly exceptional in the world of the Hebrew Bible. The strongest cases are those of Psalms 49 and 73, which may envisage the hope that the psalmist will be granted an exception to the common fate, as was granted to Enoch or Elijah. A case can also be made that the king was sometimes thought to be immortal. Psalm 21:4–5 says: 'He asked you for life; you gave it to him – length of days forever and ever.'[30] This formulation recalls the offer of Anat to Aqhat in the Ugaritic myth. Anat's promise is not fulfilled, but the psalm claims that the request of the king for similar blessings is granted. But this, again, is an exceptional passage, and there is little evidence to suggest that the immortality of the king was commonly accepted in Israel.

Two other famous texts are commonly adduced as evidence for immortality in exceptional cases. The NRSV translates Job 19:25–6 as follows: 'For I know that my Redeemer lives, and that at the last he will stand upon the earth; and after my skin has been thus destroyed, then in my flesh I shall see God.' The text, however, is notoriously corrupt and difficult. In view of Job's frequent expressions of pessimism on the subject of death (e.g. 14:12: 'if mortals die, will they live again?'), it is likely that he is expressing hope for vindication in this life rather than in the hereafter.

The poem about the Servant of the Lord in Isaiah 52:13 – 53:12 is also problematic. The servant is allegedly cut off from the land of the living, and given a grave among the wicked (53:8–9). Yet, though his life is made an offering for sin, 'he shall see his offspring and shall prolong his days' (53:10). It is possible, then, to read this poem in terms of death and resurrection, and in fact it was often so read in ancient Judaism. The Servant does not necessarily die, however. It may suffice that he has been condemned to death and submitted to his fate. Moreover, it is not at all clear that the poem has an individual person in mind. While the interpretation is endlessly disputed, the most probable interpretation remains the collective one, whereby the Servant represents either Israel or the righteous remnant.[31] In that case the language of death and resurrection is metaphorical, and this passage should be considered in conjunction with passages such as Ezekiel 37, which envision the resurrection of Israel as a people.

The most vivid example of resurrection language as a metaphor for the restoration of Israel is found in Ezekiel's vision of a valley full of dry bones. The vision implies familiarity with the concept of resurrection. In Zoroastrianism the bodies of the dead are exposed to be picked clean by the vultures, and this custom may have suggested the vision of dry bones.[32] Ezekiel, however, is explicit in his interpretation: 'these bones are the whole house of Israel.' There is no question here of the resurrection of individuals. Hosea 6:2 ('After two days he will revive us; on the third day he will raise us up, that we may live before him') is also clearly in the context of national restoration.[33] The speakers are stricken but not dead. A more difficult case is provided by Isaiah 26:19: 'Thy dead shall live, their bodies shall rise. O dwellers in the dust, awake and sing for joy!' Many scholars understand this passage as an affirmation of the resurrection of individuals, in the context of national restoration.[34] The context, however, is entirely concerned with the restoration of the people. 'Thy dead' are contrasted with 'other lords' who have ruled over Israel. They are dead and shall not live; shades (*Rephaim*) do not rise. In contrast, the Lord has increased the nation and enlarged the borders of the land (26:14–15). The passage, then, should most probably be interpreted as analogous to Ezekiel 37. Its language, however, would have a profound influence on the subsequent development of belief in resurrection.[35]

Isaiah 26 is part of the so-called 'Apocalypse of Isaiah' (Isaiah 24–7), written early in the Second Temple period. It contains one other passage that is relevant to our discussion of death and afterlife. In Isaiah 25:6–10 we are told that God will make a great feast 'on this mountain' (Zion) and that 'he will swallow up death forever.' The language evokes the old Canaanite myth, where Mot (Death) swallows Baal. The figure of Death here is a powerful symbol for 'the shroud that is cast over all peoples.' The promise is that life will be transformed and Death will be no more. The removal of the threat of death does not require that the dead be raised, but it does imply a hope for an immortal state in the future. This hope, however, should not be pressed in too literal a fashion in the context of the early Second Temple period. Another passage in the book of Isaiah, from roughly the same period, envisions a new heaven and a new earth. In this new creation there will no longer be 'an infant who lives but a few days or an old man who does not live out a lifetime; for one who dies at a hundred years will be considered a youth and one who falls short of a hundred will be considered cursed' (Isa 65:20). In the new creation people will still be mortal, even if the length of life is greatly expanded.

THE EARLY APOCALYPSES

The first clear evidence of belief in a differentiated life after death in Jewish sources appears in the apocalyptic literature of the Hellenistic period. The Book of the Watchers (*1 Enoch* 1–36) tells the story of the fallen angels. Enoch ascends to heaven to intercede for them, and then he is given a tour of the ends of the earth. In chapter 22 he is shown 'a large and high mountain, and a hard rock and four beautiful places, and inside it was deep and wide and very smooth' (22:2). The angel Raphael informs him that 'these beautiful places are intended for this, that the spirits, the souls of the dead, might be gathered into them,' to await the judgement. The text is unfortunately corrupt, and subsequently speaks of three places rather than four. The souls of the righteous are kept apart, with a spring of water on which there is light (22:9). 'Likewise, a place has been created for sinners when they die and are buried in the earth and judgement has not come upon them during their life.' The third place is prepared for the souls of those who complain and give information about their destruction, when they were killed in the days of the sinners. Finally, another place is prepared for sinners 'accomplished in wrongdoing' (22:13). We are told that 'their souls will not be killed on the day of judgment nor will they rise from there.'

This is the oldest passage in Jewish literature that attempts to distinguish the lot of righteous and wicked in the afterlife. It is a rather eccentric passage. Its views are never repeated in other Jewish literature. It seems to be influenced by various traditions.[36] The location of these chambers inside a mountain recalls the Epic of Gilgamesh, where Gilgamesh has to enter the base of a mountain to reach the Netherworld. The spring of water with a light on it is an Orphic motif. Both the Greeks and the Persians, the main cultures that the Jews encountered in the Second Temple period, had well-developed mythologies of life after death, as had the Egyptians.[37] It is not surprising that such beliefs also appealed to the Jews as a solution to the problem of theodicy, or the gap between divine justice and the flagrant injustice on earth.

Other formulations of the belief in judgment of the dead appear in other sections of *1 Enoch*.[38] In some cases, resurrection comes as a public event at the climax of history. The Animal Apocalypse (*1 Enoch* 85–90) promises that at the judgment at the end of history all those who have been destroyed and scattered will be gathered in (90: 33). The Epistle of Enoch says that 'the righteous will rise from sleep and wisdom will rise and will be given to them' (91:10). In other cases, the emphasis is on the transformation of the individual, and the place in the historical sequence is less important. *1 Enoch* 104, also in the Epistle tells the righteous to be hopeful, because: 'you will shine like the lights of heaven and will be seen, and the gate of heaven will be opened to you ... be hopeful, and do not abandon your hope, for you will have great joy like the angels of heaven ... for you shall be associates of the host of heaven.'[39] A very similar concept is found in Daniel 12, as the climax of a historical sequence:

> At that time your people will be delivered, everyone who is found written in the book. Many of those who sleep in the dusty earth will awake, some to everlasting life and some to reproach and everlasting disgrace. The wise will shine like the splendor of the firmament and those who lead the common people to righteousness like the stars forever and ever.

As is clear from the parallel in *1 Enoch*, to shine like the stars is to become a companion of the host of heaven.[40] The language, however, carries overtones of the idea of astral immortality that was widespread in the Greco-Roman world.[41]

As we have seen, prior to the Hellenistic age only exceptional individuals were believed to be elevated to the angelic or heavenly realm. The notion that such a destiny could be attained by the righteous as a group was novel in this period. In the book of Daniel this belief is brought to bear directly on the problem of theodicy. The wise (מַשְׂכִּילִים) are the leaders of the spiritual resistance to the persecution of Antiochus Epiphanes. (They do not seem to have supported the military resistance of the Maccabees.) Some of them, we are told, fall (die), 'to refine and purify and make them white, until the time of the end' (Dan 11:35). But in the resurrection they are vindicated, when they are elevated to shine like the stars. The deaths of the martyrs in the time of persecution must have created a situation of considerable cognitive dissonance in ancient Judaism. Traditionally, people were supposed to be rewarded for keeping the law, and the reward was long life and seeing one's children's children. During the persecution, however, those who kept the law were killed, while violators prospered. The book of Daniel addressed that situation by assuring its readers that this life is not the end. The faithful could afford to lose their lives in this world if they believed that they would be elevated to join the angels in heaven. In the Epistle of Enoch the dynamic is similar although the situation envisaged is not one of persecution, but simply of social injustice. The injustice of the present will be set right in the judgment. Interestingly enough, this is also the situation envisioned in Psalms 49 and 73: 'Why should I fear in times of trouble when the iniquity of my persecutors surrounds me, those who trust in their wealth and boast of the abundance of their riches?' (Ps 49:5–6).

While the belief in reward and punishment after death was obviously relevant to times of persecution, it did not necessarily arise as a response to such situations. The Book of the Watchers, arguably the oldest section of *1 Enoch*, does not envision a persecution, although it does depict a situation where the world is out of joint, because of the excesses of the fallen angels and their offspring: 'and the world was changed, and there was great impiety and much fornication and they went astray and all their ways became corrupt' (*1 Enoch* 8:2). Many scholars think that the changes wrought by the watchers serve as an allegory for the changes brought about by Hellenistic culture in the Near East. The author of the Book of the Watchers recoils from these changes in horror. The clash in value systems is vividly expressed when Enoch ascends to heaven to present the petition of the Watchers. The petition is rebuffed:

> Go say to the Watchers of heaven who sent you to petition on their behalf, you ought to petition on behalf of men, not men on behalf of you. Why have you left the high, holy and eternal heaven, and lain with the women and became unclean with the daughters of men and taken wives for yourselves and done as the sons of the earth and begotten giant sons? And you were spiritual, holy, living an eternal life, but you became unclean upon the women . . . as they do who die and are destroyed. And for this reason I gave them wives, namely that they might sow seed in them and that children might be born by them and thus deeds might be done on earth. But you formerly were spiritual, living an eternal immortal life for all the generations of the world. For this reason I did not arrange wives for you because the dwelling of the spiritual ones is in heaven. (*1 Enoch* 15:2–7)

What is at issue here is the contrast between the spiritual, heavenly, imperishable world and the world of corruption and death. The Watchers sinned because they abandoned the spiritual world for the attractions of flesh. Conversely, Enoch becomes the paradigmatic human being by ascending to heaven and becoming like the angels. His transformation is inchoate in the Book of the Watchers but is developed at length in later tradition. In the Similitudes of Enoch, which were probably written in the early first century CE, Enoch ascends to heaven and is greeted by an angel who tells him: 'you are the son of man who has righteousness,' thereby assimilating him to the heavenly Son of Man who sits on a throne of glory (*1 Enoch* 71:14).[42] In *2 Enoch*, he is transformed into an angel (*2 Enoch* 22:10). His glorification reaches its zenith in *3 Enoch* (*Sefer Hekalot*) where he is identified as Metatron, the lesser YHWH (*3 Enoch* 4; 9–12).[43] The exaltation of Enoch then takes on an exceptional character. But even in the Similitudes, he is representative of the righteous, who have 'their dwelling with the angels and their resting places with the holy ones' (*1 Enoch* 39:5). In Daniel, too, the goal of the righteous is to become like the angels, who are Daniel's constant interlocutors throughout his visions.

It has often been claimed that Jewish eschatology is distinguished from Greek by its emphasis on the resurrection of the body in contrast to the immortality of the soul, an emphasis that has obvious implications for the value attached to bodily activities, including sex. This distinction, however, is far too simple and fails to do justice to the kind of belief that emerges in the books of Daniel and *Enoch*. While this is not the Greek idea of immortality of the soul, neither is it resurrection of the body.[44] It might better be described as resurrection of the spirit, the exaltation of the *nepeš* from the Netherworld to the heavenly regions. In the formulation of *Jubilees* 23: 'their bodies shall rest in the earth and their spirits shall have much joy.' The spiritual nature of the afterlife is underlined in the Book of the Watchers, in contrast to the earthly life of corruptible flesh and sexuality. While Jewish tradition generally had a robust appreciation of earthly life, including marriage, the Levitical tradition associated bodily functions, including sex, with impurity. We find here the elements of a spirituality vastly different from that expressed in Deuteronomy or the biblical wisdom books. The ultimate goal of life has been changed from prosperity in the land and the succession of generations to a spiritual form of existence beyond the grave.

The idea of bodily resurrection is also attested in Judaism, beginning in the second century BCE. The brothers in 2 Maccabees 7 taunt their torturers, in full confidence that their limbs will be restored in the resurrection. (It should be noted that 2 Maccabees was written in Greek, adapted from the work of a Diaspora Jew, Jason of Cyrene.) The *Pseudo-Ezekiel* text from Qumran (4Q385) interprets Ezekiel's vision of the dry bones in terms of actual resurrection, which is, accordingly, physical in nature. Ezekiel 37 also underlies a prophecy of bodily resurrection in *Sibylline Oracles* 4, another Greek text from the Diaspora. Bodily resurrection was one of several ways in which the afterlife might be imagined. It was in no sense normative or standard in ancient Judaism.

The apocalyptic idea of resurrection that we have seen in the books of Daniel and *Enoch* was adapted in various ways in other bodies of literature.

The Dead Sea Scrolls

The people who wrote the Dead Sea Scrolls were certainly familiar with the idea of resurrection. They preserved multiple copies of the books of Daniel and *Enoch*. There are also clear references to resurrection in 4Q385 (*Pseudo-Ezekiel*), in a paraphrase of Ezekiel 37, and in 4Q521 (the so-called *Messianic Apocalypse*), which lists the raising of the dead among the wonderful works of the end-time, and refers to God as 'the one who gives life to the dead of his people.' These texts, however, are not necessarily sectarian products; they may simply be part of the community library like the books of Daniel and *Enoch*. There is a long-standing controversy about the sect's own understanding of resurrection and life after death.[45]

In part this controversy is fueled by conflicting accounts of the beliefs of the Essenes, who are widely believed to be identical with the Dead Sea sect. Josephus, who apparently relied on a Greek ethnographic source, wrote:

> It is a firm belief among them that although bodies are corruptible, and their matter unstable, souls are immortal and endure for ever; that, come from the subtlest ether, they are entwined with the bodies which serve them as prisons, drawn down as they are by some physical spell; but that when they are freed from the bonds of the flesh, liberated, so to speak, from long slavery, then they rejoice and rise up to the heavenly world. Agreeing with the sons of the Greeks, they declare that an abode is reserved beyond the Ocean for the souls of the just; a place oppressed neither by rain nor snow nor torrid heat, but always refreshed by the gentle breeze blowing from the Ocean. But they relegate evil souls to a dark pit shaken by storms, full of unending chastisement. The Greeks, I think, had the same idea when they assigned their valiant ones, whom they call 'heroes' and 'demi-gods,' to the Islands of the Blessed, and the souls of the bad to Hades, the place of the wicked . . .[46]

Josephus, or his source, is clearly at pains to emphasize the similarity between the beliefs of the Essenes and those of the Greeks, but even if we allow for some exaggeration, he paints a clear picture of a belief in immortality that did not require bodily resurrection. A quite different account is given by Hippolytus:

> The doctrine of the resurrection has also derived support among them, for they acknowledge both that the flesh will rise again and that it will be immortal, in the same manner as the soul is already imperishable. They maintain that when the soul has been separated from the body, it is now borne into one place, which is well ventilated and full of light, and there it rests until judgement. This locality the Greeks were acquainted with by hearsay, calling it Isles of the Blessed.[47]

Hippolytus probably drew on the same source as Josephus, not on Josephus directly. His account is sometimes confused or distorted. He identifies the Essenes with the Zealots and he eliminates reference to sun worship. His claim that the Essenes believed in a final conflagration of the universe, however, finds support in

1QH 11:29–36, and some scholars have argued that he also gives the more accurate account of the belief in afterlife. Emile Puech has offered the most thorough defence of the belief in bodily resurrection in the Scrolls,[48] but the evidence remains ambiguous at best.

There is no doubt that the sect firmly believed in reward and punishment after death. According to the *Community Rule*, the visitation of those who walk in the spirit of light 'will be for healing, plentiful peace in a long life, fruitful offspring with all everlasting blessings, eternal enjoyment with endless life, and a crown of glory with majestic raiment in eternal light' (1QS 4:6–8). Conversely, those who walk in the spirit of darkness are destined for 'a glut of punishments at the hands of all the angels of destruction, for eternal damnation for the scorching wrath of the God of revenge, for permanent error and shame without end with the humiliation of destruction by the fire of the dark regions' (1QS 4:11–14).[49] A quite similar formulation is found in the *Damascus Document*, column 2. These passages can be reconciled rather easily with Josephus's account of the Essenes. They do not require a belief in bodily resurrection. The debate about that belief has centered mainly on a couple of texts from the *Hodayot*, or *Thanksgiving Hymns*.

1QH 19:10–14 thanks God 'because you have done wonders with dust, and have acted very mightily with a creature of clay.' The hymn goes on to say:

> for your glory, you have purified man from sin so that he can make himself holy for you from every impure abomination and blameworthy iniquity, to become united with the sons of your truth and in a lot with your holy ones, to raise from the dust the worm of the dead to an [everlasting] community.

The phrase 'worm of dead ones' (תולעת מתים) also occurs in 1QH 14:34: 'Hoist a banner, you who lie in the dust; raise a standard, worm of dead ones.' There is an allusion here to Isaiah 26:19, which refers to those who dwell in the dust, but also to Isaiah 41:14, 'do not fear, worm of Jacob, men of Israel.' (The word for 'men' here is מתי, a rare word that only occurs in the construct and has the same consonants as the word for 'dead ones.') It may be that Isaiah 41 was understood at Qumran to refer to dead ones, and that there is a reference to resurrection here. It is also possible, however, that the phrase refers metaphorically to abject human nature, and that the point is exaltation rather than resurrection.

Another motif in the passage from 1QH 19 just cited is more characteristic of the hope of the Dead Sea Scrolls. The hymnist claims to be raised up 'to become united with the sons of your truth and in a lot with your holy ones.' Similarly in 1QH 3:19–23 he claims to have taken his place with the lot of the holy ones and entered into communion with the congregation of the sons of heaven. The goal here is fellowship with the angels, as it also was in *Enoch* and Daniel. The difference is that the hymnist at Qumran claims to enjoy in the present the fellowship that was promised to the righteous after death in the apocalypses. The members of the community believed that they had already made the essential transition to the angelic life. Consequently, future resurrection was not so important. Josephus certainly distorted this belief when he assimilated it to the Greek idea of immortality, but he was correct in placing the emphasis on immortality rather than on resurrection.

The Qumran community buried its dead in individual graves, with the head to the south and the feet to the north.[50] There were no family tombs, a fact that lends support to the view that the lifestyle was celibate. (Celibacy was alien to rabbinic Judaism, but it is quite intelligible in view of the aspiration to an angelic lifestyle; compare the passage from *1 Enoch* 15 cited above.) J. T. Milik argued that Paradise was believed to be in the north (cf. the importance of Mount Zaphon, the mountain of the north, in the Hebrew Bible, Ps 48:3; Isa 14:13).[51] The Essenes were buried this way so that they would rise facing north and march directly to Paradise. We have no reliable information, however, as to where the Essenes imagined Paradise. In the Book of the Watchers, the abode of the dead is in the west (*1 Enoch* 22), but the Garden of Righteousness is 'far away to the east' (*1 Enoch* 32). Later apocalypses located Paradise in the third heaven. Even if the dead were buried facing towards Paradise, however, this would not necessarily imply a belief in bodily resurrection.

The immortality of the soul

The apocalyptic idea of angelic afterlife was adapted in another way in the Hellenistic Diaspora. The Wisdom of Solomon, written in Alexandria early in the Roman era, is clearly acquainted with apocalyptic judgment scenes.[52] The wicked, who have denied that there is any reward or punishment after death, are astounded when they see the righteous exalted: 'We thought that their lives were madness and that their end was without honor. Why have they been numbered among the children of God? And why is their lot among the holy ones?' (Wis 5:4–5). The 'children of God' and the 'holy ones' are the angels. But while Wisdom uses the apocalyptic judgment scene as a rhetorical device, it actually subscribes to a Greek idea of immortality, informed by the Platonic tradition.[53] God created us for incorruption, and made us in the image of his own eternity (Wis 2:23). The soul, then, is created immortal. In this life, 'a perishable body weighs down the soul' (9:15) but the soul that is devoted to wisdom can gain immortality. There is no question here of resurrection of the body. This essentially Platonic idea of the immortal soul was shared by philosophically sophisticated Jews, such as Philo of Alexandria.[54] It would have enormous influence on Christianity, through the writings of the Church Fathers. It was very much a minority view in ancient Judaism, however, and plays no role in the New Testament. It was, then, a marginal, although ultimately very important, factor in 'the biblical world.'

It should be noted that not all Diaspora Judaism shared the philosophical refinement of Philo and the Wisdom of Solomon. The main collections of Jewish *Sibylline Oracles* from Egypt, Books 3 and 5, do not address the question of afterlife. *Sibylline Oracles* Book 4, which seems to be of different provenance from the other books, predicts resurrection in very physical terms (*Sib Or* 4:181–2). *The Sayings of Pseudo-Phocylides*, which are of uncertain provenance but are usually located in Egypt, caution against disturbing graves:

> for we hope that the remains of the departed will soon come to the light again out of the earth. And afterwards they become gods. For the souls remain unharmed in the deceased. For the spirit is a loan from God to

mortals, and his image. For we have a body out of earth, and when after-wards we are resolved again into earth we are but dust; but the air has received our spirit (lines 103–8).

This passage seems to be a confused combination of ideas of immortality of the soul and resurrection of the body,[55] but may well be more representative of popular belief than Philo or Wisdom.

Beliefs around the turn of the era

It is difficult to say how widely accepted ideas of reward and punishment after death were in Judaism around the turn of the era. The famous skepticism of Qoheleth (Qoh 3:21: 'Who knows whether the human spirit goes upward and the spirit of animals goes downward to the earth?') may already be a reaction to the ideas of immortality presented in the early apocalypses. The Pharisees allegedly accepted belief in resurrection;[56] the Sadducees did not. The evidence of Jewish epitaphs in this period is ambiguous.[57] There are occasional indications of belief in a meaningful afterlife. The epitaph of a woman at Leontopolis in Egypt says that 'her soul flew to the holy ones.' An inscription from Corycos in Cilicia says that God has placed us in the sphere of the planets, a probable allusion to astral immortality. One epitaph almost humorously wishes the deceased 'good luck with your resurrection!' (ευτυχως τη υμων αναστησει). A few centuries later, belief in resurrection is well attested in the epitaphs from Beth Shearim. The majority of epitaphs from the turn of the era, however, wish the dead person peace (שָׁלוֹם, ειρηνη pax). Many of these inscriptions are difficult to date, and it is difficult to know what peace in the hereafter entails.

By the end of the first century there is evidence of more systematic reflection on the fate of the individual after death. In the apocalypse of *4 Ezra*, written towards the end of the first century CE, an angel assures Ezra that after the messianic age the world will be turned back to primeval silence for seven days. Then it will be roused again, and 'that which is corruptible shall perish. And the earth shall give up those who are asleep in it, and the dust those who dwell silently in it; and the chambers shall give up the souls which have been committed to them' (*4 Ezra* 7:30–3). Then follow judgment and recompense. 'Then the pit of torment shall appear, and opposite it shall be the place of rest; and the furnace of hell shall be disclosed, and opposite it the paradise of delight' (7:36). Ezra asks about the interval, 'whether after death, as soon as every one of us yields up his soul, we shall be kept in rest until those times come when thou wilt renew the creation, or whether we shall be tormented at once' (7:75). He is told that the souls of the unrighteous do not immediately enter into habitations, but wander grieving in torments, because they realize the error of their ways. The righteous immediately see the glory of God and rejoice. Their face is to shine like the sun, and they are to be made like the light of the stars. There will no longer be any intercession on the day of judgment, but everyone is judged on his or her own merits.

The roughly contemporary apocalypse of 2 *Baruch* shows similar attention to detail. Here Baruch asks the Lord, 'in what will those live who live in thy day, and what will they look like afterwards?' (2 *Bar* 49:2). He is told:

> the earth will certainly then restore the dead it now receives so as to preserve them: it will make no change in their form, but as it has received them, so it will restore them, and as I delivered them to it, so also will it raise them. for those who are still alive must be shown that the dead have come to life again, and that those who had departed have returned (2 *Bar* 50:2–3).

After the judgment, however, appearances will be changed. 'The appearance of the evil-doers will go from bad to worse, as they suffer torment' (51:2), but the righteous 'will assume a luminous beauty so that they may be able to attain and enter the world which does not die, which has been promised to them' (51:3). 'Time will no longer age them, for in the heights of the world shall they dwell, and they shall be made like the angels and be made equal to the stars' (51:10).

These apocalypses stand in the tradition of Daniel, in so far as there is a general resurrection at the end of history, and the righteous are eventually transformed to shine like the stars. But they have given thought to some of the problems involved. At this point what is envisioned is a bodily resurrection, but the body is then transformed into an angelic state.

Other apocalypses from the same period ignore the general resurrection and take the form of ascents of the visionary through the heavens.[58] In *3 Baruch*, the abode of righteous souls is apparently in the fourth heaven,[59] while sinners, such as those who built the tower of Babel, are punished in the second. *Second Enoch* locates Paradise in the third heaven, but there is also a place of torment in the northern part of the same heaven (chs 8–9). These apocalypses are remarkable for the fact that both Paradise and the places of judgment are located in the heavens. In some apocalypses of this type, however, the location of the place of punishment is not specified (e.g., the *Apocalypse of Zephaniah*). Tours of this sort are very popular in Christian apocalypses from the second century CE onward, and the punishments of the damned become a subject of great fascination.[60]

Belief in reward and punishment after death did not necessarily make death more welcome, even for the righteous. The *Testament of Abraham*, written in Egypt in the late first or early second century CE, says that when it was time for Abraham to die, God dispatched the angel Michael to fetch him. But Michael cannot bring himself to break the news, and when Abraham finally learns it, he is reluctant to go. So Abraham is given a tour of the heavens, and allowed to witness the judgment of the dead. In the end, God sends Death in disguise, but this fails to deceive Abraham. Finally God has to draw out his soul as if in a dream. This text is part tale, part apocalypse, but it is exceptional in the literature of ancient Judaism for its ironic appreciation of human reluctance in face of death.[61]

EARLY CHRISTIANITY

Resurrection and judgment play a much more central role in early Christianity than they had in ancient Judaism. Christianity was based on the conviction that God had raised Jesus from the dead and elevated him to heaven, as Christ (*Messiah*) and Son of God. The earliest discussion of the role of the resurrection in the new faith is that of St Paul in 1 Corinthians 15.

St Paul

This account shows some of the same concerns that we have seen in *4 Ezra* and *2 Baruch* and can only be understood in the context of Jewish apocalypticism as it had developed from the Hellenistic period.[62] Paul begins by affirming the Christian belief that Christ died, was buried, and was raised on the third day, after which he appeared to many people, including Paul himself. Given this belief, asks Paul, 'how can some of you say there is no resurrection of the dead? If there is no resurrection of the dead, then Christ has not been raised' (1 Cor 15:11–13). The denial of the resurrection has been explained in various ways.[63] One possibility is that the Corinthians had a form of realized eschatology, whereby they thought they had already passed from death to life. We have seen such an idea in the Dead Sea Scrolls; it also appears in the Gospel of John and is characteristic of Gnostic writings some centuries later. Alternatively, and perhaps more plausibly, they may have had a 'Hellenistic anthropology' similar to the Wisdom of Solomon's, with a belief in the immortality of the individual soul but not in a general public resurrection at the end of history, which was an idea without precedent in Greek thought. In that case they would have understood the resurrection of Jesus in terms of his exaltation after death. It is probable that there was some misunderstanding between Paul and his addressees and that they did not so much deny the resurrection as understand it differently.

For Paul, the resurrection of an individual (Jesus) is unintelligible apart from the expectation of general resurrection. Christ is 'the first fruits of those who have died' (1 Cor 15:20); if he is risen the general resurrection must be underway. Paul believed that it would be fulfilled within his own generation: 'we will not all die, but we will all be changed' (1 Cor 15:51). He tells the Thessalonians: 'the dead in Christ will rise first. Then we who are alive, who are left until the coming of the Lord, will be caught up in the clouds to meet the Lord in the air' (1 Thess 4:16–17). The imminence of this climactic moment is invoked repeatedly to lend urgency to Paul's message.

Like *2 Baruch*, Paul entertains the question of the kind of body with which the dead are raised (1 Cor 15:35–57). He responds by the analogy of sowing: 'what you sow does not come to life unless it dies . . . you do not sow the body that is to be but a bare seed . . . but God gives it a body . . .' He goes on to explain that there are different kinds of bodies, human and animal, earthly and heavenly. In the case of the resurrection, 'what is sown is perishable, what is raised is imperishable . . . it is sown a physical body, it is raised a spiritual body.' Lest anyone miss the point, he concludes emphatically: 'flesh and blood cannot inherit the kingdom of God, nor does the perishable inherit the imperishable.' Therefore even those who do not die before the Parousia must be changed, 'for this mortal perishable body must put on imperishability, and this mortal body must put on immortality.'

It is clear from this discussion that what Paul envisions is neither resurrection of the body nor immortality of the soul. It is resurrection of the spiritual body, a concept close to what we found in the books of *Enoch* and Daniel, except that Paul elaborates the contrast between fleshly and spiritual, corruptible and incorruptible in a way that has overtones of Greek philosophy. Paul would not have been discomfited to learn that Jesus' skeleton had been found. This would be only the bare seed that was sown. It is clear, then, that his disagreement with the Corinthians was not due to a simple contrast between bodily resurrection and immortality, although Paul's concept of a spiritual body may have been as alien, and incomprehensible, to the Corinthians as physical resurrection.

The empty tomb

St Paul does not mention an empty tomb. Neither were there any stories about empty tombs in the case of the Maccabean martyrs. Whether even the (occupied) tombs of the righteous were the focus of much attention is disputed. In Matthew 23:29 Jesus criticizes the Pharisees for building the tombs of the prophets and adorning the monuments of the righteous. The saying is paralleled in Luke 11:47, and so belongs to the Q source, a relatively early stage of the Gospel tradition. The *Lives of the Prophets*, which gives copious information about the tombs of prophets, has sometimes been thought to reflect popular Jewish piety around the turn of the era,[64] but David Satran has argued strongly that it is a Byzantine Christian composition.[65] Tombs were very important in the cult of Greek heroes.[66] While little attention is paid to the tombs of heroes in the Hebrew Bible or in the literature of Second Temple Judaism, interest in such gravesites may have grown gradually in the Hellenistic and Roman periods.

The story of the discovery of Jesus' empty tomb is told in all four Gospels, but with significant differences in detail.[67] Further elaborations of the story are found in later, apocryphal, gospels. (In *The Gospel of Peter*, the stone rolls itself away.) The basic story may have been invented to explain, in narrative form, how the resurrection must have happened. In Greek tradition there were numerous examples of the translation of human beings to the immortal realm. Such people were sometimes said to 'become invisible,'[68] and Josephus uses this terminology for the translation of Enoch and Elijah.[69] Pausanias tells the story of one Kleomedes, who killed his opponent in a boxing match, and was disqualified. In his anger he further caused the death of some boys. Finally, he fled to a temple and hid in a chest. When his pursuers opened the chest, he had disappeared. An oracle proclaimed that he had become a hero.[70] Herodotus (4.14) tells the story of a poet and wonder-worker named Aristeas who died in a fuller's shop. The fuller shut up the shop and went to notify the relatives, but when they came Aristeas had disappeared. He appeared elsewhere seven years later and made a poem, but then disappeared again.[71] In the early imperial period, there are several reports of sworn testimony that people had seen a dead emperor (Augustus) or member of the imperial household (the mother and sister of Caligula) ascending to heaven.[72] While none of these stories provides a close parallel to the resurrection narratives, they come closer than anything in biblical or Jewish tradition. In short, the stories of the empty tomb should be seen in the context of

Greek and Roman accounts of translation.[73] The declaration of the angel in Mark 14:6 that 'he is not here,' however, would seem to discourage a hero-like cult at the tomb. The Gospel of John provides the most interesting reflections on the resurrection body of Jesus, which is verifiably physical but nonetheless can enter a room where all the doors are closed (John 20:24–9).

The general resurrection

The Gospel of Matthew claims that when Jesus was crucified 'the tombs also were opened and many bodies of the saints who had fallen asleep were raised. After this resurrection they came out of the tombs and entered the holy city and appeared to many' (Matt 28:52–3). We are not told whether their resurrection was final, or only a temporary furlough. In general, in the New Testament, people other than Jesus must wait for the general resurrection. In the book of Revelation, John of Patmos sees under the altar 'the souls of those who had been slaughtered for the word of God and for the testimony they had given.' They cried out to the Lord: 'How long will it be before you avenge our blood on the inhabitants of the earth?' (Rev 6:9–11). While these souls seem not yet to be at rest, a great multitude of others stand before the throne, clothed in white, holding palm branches (7:9; cf. 14:1–5). Revelation, however, also awaits a more public vindication of the elect. 'Those who had been beheaded for their testimony' are singled out for special honor: 'They came to life and reigned with Christ for a thousand years. The rest of the dead did not come to life until the thousand years were ended' (Rev 20:5–6). Then follow the great judgment, and Death and Hades are thrown into the lake of fire.

Not all forms of early Christianity were oriented to the final resurrection to the same degree as the book of Revelation. The Gospel of John proclaims that 'the hour is coming, and is now here, when the dead will hear the voice of the Son of God . . . and will come out – those who have done good, to the resurrection of life, and those who have done evil, to the resurrection of condemnation' (John 5:25–9). It also affirms that the believer 'has already passed from death to life' (5:24). There is an analogy here with the Dead Sea Scrolls, where the community believed that it was already living with the angels. This kind of realized eschatology finds its most developed form in the Gnostic writings from Nag Hammadi, several centuries later. In the words of the *Gospel of Philip*: 'Those who say: "First one will die and (then) rise" are wrong. If men do not first experience the resurrection while they are alive, they will not receive anything when they die.'[74]

The most typical belief about death in early Christianity, however, is that the soul goes to its reward or punishment immediately after death. For philosophically sophisticated Christians like Clement of Alexandria, this was conceived in terms of immortality of the soul. Popular Christianity is probably more accurately reflected in the multitude of apocalypses in the names of Peter, Paul, John, Mary, and so on, that flourish from the second century CE on.[75] Many of these take the form of other-worldly journeys, but even the *Apocalypse of Peter*, which does not describe such a journey, contains an extensive account of the places of punishment and a brief vision of Paradise. There were clear Jewish antecedents for these apocalypses that can be traced back to the Book of the Watchers in *1 Enoch*, but they are also indebted to the Orphic tradition, and are very much a product of Hellenistic–Roman syncretism. The world they imagine is very different from that of the Hebrew Bible, despite their indebtedness to postbiblical Jewish tradition.

NOTES

1　See L. H. Lesko, 'Death and the Afterlife in Ancient Egyptian Thought,' in J. M. Sasson, ed., *Civilizations of the Ancient Near East* (4 vols; New York, 1995), 3: 1763–74; J. Zandee, *Death as an Enemy according to Ancient Egyptian Conceptions* (Leiden, 1960).

2　Epic of Gilgamesh, Old Babylonian Version, tablet X, columns i and iii. S. Dalley, *Myths from Mesopotamia* (Oxford, 1989), 150.

3　Gilgamesh, Standard Version, VII, iv; Dalley, *Myths*, 89.

4　Dalley, *Myths*, 155.

5　'A Vision of the Netherworld,' trans. E. A. Speiser in J. B. Pritchard, ed., *Ancient Near Eastern Texts* (Princeton, 1969), 110. See W. von Soden, 'Die Unterweltsvision eines assyrischen Kronprinzen,' in idem, *Aus Sprache, Geschichte und Religion Babyloniens: Gesammelte Aufsätze* (Naples, 1989), 29–67.

6　There is some evidence for the deification of kings in ancient Sumer, K. Spronk, *Beatific Afterlife in Ancient Israel and in the Ancient Near East* (Kevelaer, 1986), 115.

7　*KTU* 1.5.II. 1–7. M. Coogan, *Stories from Ancient Canaan* (Philadelphia, 1978), 107.

8　B. Schmidt, *Israel's Beneficent Dead* (Tübingen, 1994), 62–7; C. L. L'Heureux, *Rank Among the Canaanite Gods: El, Ba'al and the Repha'im* (Missoula, 1979).

9　M. S. Smith, 'Rephaim,' *Anchor Bible Dictionary* (New York, 1992), 5: 674–6; L'Heureux, *Rank Among the Canaanite Gods*; H. Rouillard, 'Rephaim,' in K. van der Toorn, B. Becking and P. W. van der Horst, eds, *Dictionary of Deities and Demons in the Bible* (Leiden, 1995), 1308–24.

10　J. C. de Moor, 'Rāpi'ūma-Rephaim,' *Zeitschrift für die alttestamentliche Wissenschaft* 88 (1976), 323–45.

11　Schmidt, *Israel's Beneficent Dead*, 91.

12　Spronk, *Beatific Afterlife*, 161–96.

13　M. H. Pope, *Song of Songs* (New York, 1977), 210–29; 'The Cult of the Dead at Ugarit,' in G. D. Young, ed., *Ugarit in Retrospect* (Winona Lake, 1981), 159–79; Spronk, *Beatific Afterlife*, 196–202.

14　T. J. Lewis, *Cults of the Dead in Ancient Israel and Ugarit* (Atlanta, 1989), 80–94; 'Banqueting Hall/House,' *Anchor Bible Dictionary* (New York, 1992), 1: 581–2.

15　Lewis, 'Banqueting Hall/House,' 582.

16　For the negative view, see Schmidt, *Israel's Beneficent Dead*, 62–7.

17　*KAI* 2.220–1. M. S. Smith and E. Bloch-Smith, 'Death and Afterlife in Ugarit and Israel,' *Journal of the American Oriental Society* 108 (1988), 279.

18　*KTU* 1.17.VI. 25–32. Spronk, *Beatific Afterlife*, 77–8.

19　1.17.VI. 33–40. Trans. Coogan, *Stories*, 37.

20　E. Bloch-Smith, *Judahite Burial Practices and Beliefs about the Dead* (Sheffield, 1992), 137.

21　N. J. Tromp, *Primitive Conceptions of Death and the Nether World in the Old Testament* (Rome, 1969), *passim*.

22　R. Rosenberg, 'The Concept of Biblical Sheol within the Context of Ancient Near Eastern Beliefs,' unpublished dissertation, Harvard University, 1980. See T. J. Lewis, 'Dead, Abode of the,' *Anchor Bible Dictionary* (New York, 1992), 2: 101–5.

23　Bloch-Smith, *Judahite Burial Practices*, 141. There was a well-established ritual of feeding and giving drink to the dead (*kispu*) in Mesopotamia. See J. Bottéro, *Mesopotamia: Writing, Reasoning, and the Gods* (Chicago, 1992), 282.

24　Ibid., 96–100.

25　So Lewis, *Cults of the Dead*, 174.

26 Schmidt, *Israel's Beneficent Dead*, 201–45.

27 For a full, recent review see E. Puech, *La Croyance des Esséniens en la Vie Future: Immortalité, Résurrection, Vie Éternelle?* I. *La Résurrection des Morts et le Contexte Scripturaire* (Paris, 1993). See also J. J. Collins, *Daniel* (Minneapolis, 1993), 395–8.

28 G. von Rad, 'Life and Death in the OT,' in G. Kittel, ed., *Theological Dictionary of the New Testament* (Grand Rapids, 1964), 2: 843–9.

29 For the positive assessment see Puech, *La Croyance*, 1:59–66; for the negative, B. Vawter, 'Intimations of Immortality and the Old Testament,' *Journal of Biblical Literature* 91 (1972), 158–71.

30 J. Healey, 'The Immortality of the King: Ugarit and the Psalms,' *Orientalia* 53 (1984), 245–54.

31 J. Blenkinsopp, *A History of Prophecy in Israel* (Philadelphia, 1983), 215–18.

32 B. Lang, 'Street Theater, Raising the Dead, and the Zoroastrian Connection in Ezekiel's Preaching,' in J. Lust, ed., *Ezekiel and his Book* (Leuven, 1986), 297–316.

33 F. I. Andersen and D. N. Freedman, *Hosea* (Anchor Bible 24; New York, 1980), 420–1, argue that Hosea's admittedly metaphorical usage presupposes a belief in resurrection.

34 See Puech, *La Croyance*, 1:66–73.

35 J. Day, 'Resurrection Imagery from Baal to the Book of Daniel,' in J. A. Emerton, ed., *Congress Volume 1995* (Leiden, 1997), 125–34.

36 M. T. Wacker, *Weltordnung und Gericht: Studien zu 1 Henoch 22* (Würzburg, 1982).

37 For Greek views see the classic study of E. Rohde, *Psyche: The Cult of Souls and Belief in Immortality among the Greeks* (New York, 1925), and for recent discoveries F. Graf, 'Dionysian and Orphic Eschatology: New Texts and Old Questions,' in T. H. Carpenter and C. A. Faraone, eds, *Masks of Dionysus* (Ithaca, 1993), 239–58. On Persian eschatology see A. Hultgård, 'Persian Apocalypticism,' in J. J. Collins, B. McGinn and S. Stein, eds, *The Encyclopedia of Apocalypticism* (New York, 1998), 1: 39–83. On Egyptian afterlife mythology see J. G. Griffiths, *The Divine Verdict: A Study of Divine Judgment in the Ancient Religions* (Leiden, 1991), 160–242.

38 J. J. Collins, *The Apocalyptic Imagination* (Grand Rapids, 1998), 43–79.

39 G. W. Nickelsburg, *Resurrection, Immortality, and Eternal Life in Intertestamental Judaism* (Cambridge, Mass., 1972), 112–29.

40 Collins, *Daniel*, 393–4.

41 P. Perkins, *Resurrection* (New York, 1984), 56–9. Already in the fifth century BCE, Aristophanes had joked about 'what people say, that when we die we straightaway turn to stars' (*Peace*, 832–4).

42 See Collins, *The Apocalyptic Imagination*, 187–91.

43 M. Himmelfarb, 'Revelation and Rapture: The Transformation of the Visionary in the Ascent Apocalypses,' in J. J. Collins and J. H. Charlesworth, eds, *Mysteries and Revelations* (Sheffield, 1991), 82–4.

44 G. Stemberger, *Der Leib der Auferstehung* (Rome, 1972), 115–16, insists that the afterlife in Palestinian Jewish texts of this period always has a bodily form, but also that it is not the resuscitation of a corpse.

45 J. J. Collins, *Apocalypticism in the Dead Sea Scrolls* (London, 1997), 110–29.

46 Josephus, *Jewish War* 2.154–6; trans. G. Vermes and M. Goodman, *The Essenes According to the Classical Sources* (Sheffield, 1989), 47.

47 *Refutation of All Heresies*, 27; Vermes and Goodman, 73.

48 Puech, *La Croyance*, vol. 2.

49 Trans. F. García Martínez, *The Dead Sea Scrolls Translated* (Leiden, 1994), 7.

50 On the burials at Qumran see Puech, *La Croyance* 2: 693–702.

51 J. T. Milik, 'Hénoch au pays des aromates (chap XXVII à XXXII): Fragments araméens de a grotte 4 de Qumrân,' *Revue biblique* 65 (1958), 70–7.

52 Nickelsburg, *Resurrection*, 68–92; L. Ruppert, 'Gerechte und Frevler (Gottlose) in Sap 1,1–6,21: Zum Neuverständnis und zur Aktualisierung alttestamentlicher Traditionen in der Sapientia Salomonis,' in H. Hübner, ed., *Die Weisheit Salomos im Horizont Biblischer Theologie* (Neukirchen-Vluyn, 1993), 1–54.

53 J. J. Collins, *Jewish Wisdom in the Hellenistic Age* (Louisville, 1997), 185–7.

54 The Jewish view was not identical to the Platonic. The Jewish authors did not accept the preexistence of the soul.
55 P. W. van der Horst, *The Sayings of Pseudo-Phocylides* (Leiden, 1978), 185–92.
56 Acts 23:8; cf. Acts 4:1, Josephus, *Jewish War* 2.8.14 §§162–5; 3.8.5 §§374–5; *Antiquities* 18.1.3–4 §16; *Against Apion* 2.218 §30.
57 P. W. van der Horst, *Ancient Jewish Epitaphs* (Kampen, 1991), 114–26.
58 A. Yarbro Collins, *Cosmology and Eschatology in Jewish and Christian Apocalypticism* (Leiden, 1996), 21–54.
59 *3 Baruch* 10. The Greek text reads 'third heaven' but this is evidently a mistake or scribal alteration, since Baruch proceeds from there to the fifth heaven.
60 M. Himmelfarb, *Tours of Hell: An Apocalyptic Form in Jewish and Christian Literature* (Philadelphia, 1983).
61 For the text see E. P. Sanders, 'The Testament of Abraham,' in J. H. Charlesworth, ed., *The Old Testament Pseudepigrapha* (New York, 1983), 1:882–902.
62 M. C. de Boer, *The Defeat of Death: Apocalyptic Eschatology in 1 Corinthians 15 and Romans 5* (Sheffield, 1988); J. Holleman, *Resurrection and Parousia: A Traditio-Historical Study of Paul's Eschatology in 1 Corinthians 15:20–23* (Leiden, 1995).
63 Holleman, *Resurrection*, 35–40.
64 J. Jeremias, *Heiligengräber in Jesu Umwelt (Mt 23,29; Lk 11,47): Eine Untersuchung zur Volksreligion der Zeit Jesu* (Göttingen, 1958).
65 D. Satran, *Biblical Prophets in Byzantine Palestine: Reassessing the Lives of the Prophets* (Leiden, 1995).
66 Rohde, *Psyche*, 121: 'The worship of a hero is everywhere connected with the site of his grave.'
67 Perkins, *Resurrection*.
68 G. Lohfink, *Die Himmelfahrt Jesu* (Munich, 1971), 41.
69 *Antiquities* 9.28. C. Begg, '"Josephus's Portrayal of the Disappearances of Enoch, Elijah and Moses": Some Observations,' *Journal of Biblical Literature* 109 (1990), 691–3.
70 Pausanias, 6.9.6–7. Rohde, *Psyche*, 129–30.
71 A. S. Pease, 'Some Aspects of Invisibility,' *Harvard Studies in Classical Philology* 53 (1942), 29.
72 Pease, 'Some Aspects,' 17.
73 A. Yarbro Collins, *The Beginning of the Gospel: Probings of Mark in Context* (Minneapolis, 1992), 141.
74 K. Rudolph, *Gnosis* (San Francisco, 1977), 191.
75 A. Yarbro Collins, 'The Early Christian Apocalypses,' *Semeia* 14 (1979), 61–121.

SELECT BIBLIOGRAPHY

Bailey, L. R. *Biblical Perspectives on Death* (Philadelphia, 1979).
Bloch-Smith, E. *Judahite Burial Practices and Beliefs about the Dead* (Sheffield, 1992).
Collins, J. J. *Apocalypticism in the Dead Sea Scrolls* (London, 1997).
——— *The Apocalyptic Imagination.* 2nd edn (Grand Rapids, 1998).
Lewis, T. J. *Cults of the Dead in Ancient Israel and Ugarit* (Atlanta, 1989).
Nickelsburg, G. W. *Resurrection, Immortality, and Eternal Life in Interestamental Judaism* (Cambridge, Mass., 1972).
Puech, E. *La Croyance des Esséniens en la Vie Future: Immortalité Résurrection, Vie Éternelle?* (Paris, 1993).
Schmidt, B. *Israel's Beneficent Dead* (Tübingen, 1994).
Spronk, K. *Beatific Afterlife in Ancient Israel and in the Ancient Near East* (Kevelaer and Neukirchen-Vluyn, 1986).
Tromp, N. J. *Primitive Conceptions of Death and the Nether World in the Old Testament* (Rome, 1969).

PURITY

—— •*• ——

Gordon Wenham

INTRODUCTION

Concepts such as holiness, purity and uncleanness are unfamiliar to modern Western readers of the Bible. We may sometimes use these terms, but we invest them with a quite different set of meanings from what they had in biblical culture. Our notions of purity tend to be based on scientific and medical understandings of the idea, whereas in the Bible these concepts are intensely theological and served to place powerful constraints on people's actions by setting boundaries of permissible behaviour.

The rules about purity and cleanness are clearly set out in the Old Testament, but penetrating the rationale behind them has proved much more difficult. However the introduction of anthropological methods of enquiry has shed much light on the biblical notions, for similar ideas of purity and uncleanness are found in many traditional societies and serve to define hierarchies, acceptable and unacceptable modes of behaviour, and even the boundaries of society itself. Societies of course have different sets of purity rules, so we cannot simply equate biblical ideas with those of other cultures, but the type of sociological analysis applied to tribal societies has proved very fruitful in understanding the Bible. Indeed it has highlighted some of its fundamental convictions about God, Israel, and ethics in the Old Testament, and clarified the social definition of the church in the New Testament.

In this chapter I shall review first the data from the Old Testament and then discuss the rationale behind these regulations. Then I shall do the same for early Jewish texts and the New Testament. Inevitably there are differences about the interpretation of these texts, to which attention will be drawn, but I shall focus on the most likely approach endorsed by a majority of scholars.

ANCIENT NEAR EASTERN PARALLELS

Israel's neighbours, from Babylon in the East to Egypt and the Hittites in the West, had their own ideas about purity and uncleanness, about the people who might approach the gods and under what circumstances. Like Israel they had holy places and holy people, and were aware that sin and uncleanness were obstacles to worship. In Egypt purity was an indispensable prerequisite for worship. The temple, its vessels, and the priests all had to be pure. Washing with water was the main means of purification. Pictures of coronations show water being poured over the king to endue him with new life. In Mesopotamia purity and holiness were also closely associated. Cult personnel and cultic objects are often described as pure, and again water is commonly used for purification. These provide interesting parallels to biblical ideas. However our knowledge of the practices of Israel's ancient neighbours is too limited to help much with understanding the Old Testament. No other ancient society's rules have been preserved as comprehensively as those found in the Pentateuch, and they must be treated as a coherent entity in themselves.

THE OLD TESTAMENT PICTURE

The Old Testament seems to envisage the distinction between clean and unclean being known from primeval times, for Noah was told to take into the ark seven pairs of every type of clean animal and one pair of each unclean animal. (Genesis 7:2–3). But the detailed regulations about purity are nearly all contained in the book of Leviticus, part of the laws given to Moses at Sinai (c. 1300 BC). Scholars generally hold that these laws were drafted in their present form by priests in post-exilic times (c. 500 BC) without necessarily supposing that they were invented then. Texts dealing with the time of David (1000 BC) seem to show awareness of the purity rules (e.g. 2 Samuel 11) as do some prophetic passages, and divine holiness is a key idea in both the Psalms and Isaiah. It is therefore very difficult to be dogmatic about the origin and date of these concepts. However it is clear that the Old Testament rules are much less developed than they became in later Judaism: one-sixth of the Mishnah (c. AD 200) is devoted to explaining the rules of cleanness. Happily for an understanding of the biblical purity system its date of origin is relatively unimportant.

The Old Testament purity system

According to Leviticus 10:10–11 it is the duty of the priests 'to distinguish between the holy and the common, between the clean and the unclean' and to teach the people about the differences. These fundamental categories of biblical thought are then expounded in the following chapters of Leviticus.

The key principle is that God is the supremely holy being, and anyone who wishes to come into his presence must be holy too. But uncleanness is a bar to holiness: indeed if any unholy person comes into contact with the holy, he will die, as Uzzah did when he touched the ark of the covenant (e.g. 2 Samuel 6: 6–7). Numbers 4 is concerned that if the Levites just see the ark, they may die. It is therefore of vital importance to know what constitutes uncleanness, which has a variety of causes and different degrees of severity. The basic idea is that the clean may enter God's presence in worship, but the unclean must not. Domesticated clean animals may be sacrificed, but others may not. Only 'clean' people, that is, those unpolluted by discharges or other problems, should enter the sanctuary to offer sacrifice. Leviticus 11–22 gives a full treatment of these issues.

Leviticus 11 classifies living creatures into clean and unclean. Clean may be eaten, and some of the clean creatures may be sacrificed, but unclean may not. Cud-chewing animals with split hooves (e.g. cattle, sheep), are clean and may be eaten, but others (e.g. pigs, camels, rock badgers) are unclean. All birds are clean and edible apart from a list of twenty, whose identity is not always clear: as far as can be determined all these birds are birds of prey or were thought to live on carrion. Ordinary fishes with fins and scales are also clean, but other aquatic creatures, such as shellfish, are unclean. Locusts may also be eaten, but not other winged insects. 'Swarming things' such as mice or lizards are also unclean.

This sort of uncleanness is quite benign. It just means these creatures may not be eaten. Unclean creatures do not pollute unless they are dead. You do not become unclean by touching a live camel, for example. But all animals, whether clean or unclean when alive, when dead will make those who touch them unclean (Leviticus 11:28, 31, 39) Even more polluting are human corpses. So holy people like priests and Nazirites are forbidden to mourn for the dead, lest they make themselves unclean (Leviticus 21:1–12; Numbers 6:1–12). Laity who become unclean by touching a corpse remain so for a week and must undergo a special decontamination rite as prescribed in Numbers 19: failure to do so may lead to being 'cut off', that is, premature death.

Some bodily discharges also make people unclean. Mothers are polluted by the puerperal discharge for forty days after giving birth to a son, and for eighty days after bearing a daughter (Leviticus 12). Sexual intercourse pollutes both parties for a day, and menstruation makes a woman unclean for a week (Leviticus 15:18–19). Long-term discharges from the sexual organs make people unclean for as long as the discharge continues.

Skin diseases may also make a person unclean. Skin disease has often been mistranslated as leprosy. This cannot be what is meant, for leprosy (Hansen's disease) did not reach the Middle East till about the Christian era, nor is it spontaneously cured as some of these conditions are. Psoriasis or eczema could produce the symptoms described in Leviticus 13. It is the symptoms that determine whether a skin complaint is clean or not: active, sore, peeling conditions make a person unclean, whereas stable conditions, such as baldness or leukoderma, are classed as clean. Similar principles are applied to determine whether moulds or fungi (again called in Hebrew 'skin disease') affecting garments or houses are serious: if the mould is deep and spreading, it is unclean and the whole garment or house must be destroyed, but if it is static and superficial, it is pronounced clean and the garment or building is spared (Leviticus 13: 47–59; 14: 33–57). Anyone suffering from a polluting skin condition remains unclean until it clears up. In general short-term human uncleanness may be cleared by waiting a day and washing in water. When a condition causing long-term uncleanness, such as skin disease, clears up, the sufferer has also to offer a sacrifice to be ritually clean again (Leviticus 14).

Whereas the above naturally occurring conditions pollute the person involved and anyone he or she comes in contact with, some sins may cause a much more serious pollution: they pollute not just the sinner but the land and even the sanctuary itself. For example Leviticus 18 gives a long list of forbidden sexual relationships including incest, adultery, homosexuality and bestiality, which are said to pollute both those involved and the land (18:24–5). It was these practices that Leviticus says led to the previous inhabitants of Canaan being 'vomited out'. So it warns Israel that if they

Tolerated		Prohibited	
Non-sacrificial	Sacrificial	Unintentional	Intentional
e.g. menstruation	e.g. skin disease	e.g. forgotten cleansing	e.g. homicide, idolatry

Figure 46.1 Tolerated and prohibited moral uncleanness.

do the same, they may be exiled from the land or the offender will be cut off, that is, die by supernatural causes (18:25, 28–9). Idols and idolatry are also polluting. Worship of other gods, consulting the dead or possession of idols makes the perpetrators, the land, and the sanctuary unclean (Leviticus 18:21; 20:2–5; Ezekiel 20:7, 18). Homicide is another sin that pollutes the land (Numbers 35:33–4). The uncleanness caused by these sins is so serious that only the death of the sinner suffices to cleanse it.

These different types of uncleanness may be classified according to the severity of their effects. At the one extreme is the uncleanness that occurs naturally, which needs no cleansing, such as that associated with certain animals. Then come the uncleanness that can be dealt with simply by washing. More serious, but still natural, are the types of uncleanness associated with bodily discharges, which require the offering of sacrifice. Finally at the other extreme is the uncleanness generated by idolatry, homicide or illicit sex, which can only be countered by the death of the offender and the Day of Atonement ceremonies. Often the milder forms of uncleanness are classified as ritual, and the more serious as moral. However it is preferable to see them as forming a continuum (see Figure 46.1).

Purification rituals

The severity of uncleanness varies with the cause and determines what is the appropriate rite of purification. For example touching a live but unclean animal has no effect. Israelites simply have to refrain from eating them. But bodily discharges that are natural but short-term, such as menstruation and seminal emissions, have to be treated by washing and waiting till evening. However longer-term abnormal discharges from the genital organs or long-term skin diseases or the puerperal discharge require recovery from the condition, washing of the body and the person's clothes, and the offering of sacrifices. A layperson who comes into contact with a corpse is similarly unclean for a week, must wash himself twice and his clothes, and be sprinkled with water mixed with the ashes of the red heifer.

These types of uncleanness are tolerated, so long as the appropriate cleansing procedures are followed. But failure to undergo cleansing has grave consequences for the unclean and for the community. In this case the impurity threatens the sanctuary: like a deadly gas it enters the shrine and pollutes it, thus making it uncongenial for God to dwell there. Since the Old Testament views God's presence among Israel as the greatest boon of their status as the chosen people, to drive him away is disastrous and will bring the nation to ruin. Hence it is essential to carry out purification rites, and if they are inadvertently omitted, to offer a purification offering as soon as the fault is realized, for inadvertent sins like this can be atoned for: one function of the purification offering is to cleanse the sanctuary.

More serious still is the uncleanness generated by three types of sin: idolatry, homicide, and illicit sexual acts pollute not only the sanctuary but also the land. The only way of cleansing the sanctuary is through the rituals on the Day of Atonement, which involve taking sacrificial blood into the innermost part of the shrine, the holy of holies, and then transferring the sins and impurities of the nation that have been stored in the sanctuary and carried by the high priest on to the scapegoat. Despatching this goat into the wilderness symbolically removes sin and impurity from the nation.

The purification offering and the Day of Atonement

Leviticus chapter 4 deals with the sacrifice called the purification offering. This illustrates in a vivid way the importance of purity for ancient Israel and how uncleanness can affect the nation if it is not properly treated.

The main part of the ritual is similar to other sacrifices. The worshipper must bring the animal, bull, goat, lamb or pigeon, to the courtyard of the tabernacle. There he must lay his hand on the animal's head as a token of his identification with the animal, kill it, dismember it, and burn part of it on the altar. These features are common to all the sacrifices.

However with the purification offering something unusual is done with the blood. In other sacrifices the victim's blood is splashed on the main altar. In the purification offering the blood is carefully collected and then smeared or sprinkled on different parts of the sanctuary. The blood smearing purifies the item treated. Where the blood is smeared depends on the status of the offerer.

If a layperson has sinned the blood is smeared on the horns of the main courtyard altar, where the sacrifices are burned. (The horns of the altar are shaped like animal horns and attached to the top corners of the altar.) If however the high priest or the congregation of Israel, the assembly of adult males, has sinned, the blood is taken into the holy place. There it is smeared on the horns of the incense altar and sprinkled seven times before the curtain that hides the ark in the holy of holies. This suggests that the pollution generated by laypeople's unwitting sins affects the outer altar, whereas that produced by the high priest or the national assembly defiles the inner shrine.

Once a year on the day of atonement two sin offerings are offered and their blood taken into the holy of holies by the high priest to be sprinkled on and in front of the mercy seat or place of atonement (Leviticus 16). The mercy seat is the holiest place of all, where God himself is pictured as sitting shrouded in fire or smoke on the outstretched wings of two cherubim, which look like winged bulls or lions with human heads. To enter the holy of holies the high priest has to don special white vestments and surround himself with clouds of incense for fear that he might see God and die. That the high priest is expected to take such a risk shows how important it is that the sanctuary (see Figure 46.2) should be cleansed from impurity. If this is not done, it is feared that God will leave his sanctuary, which will entail

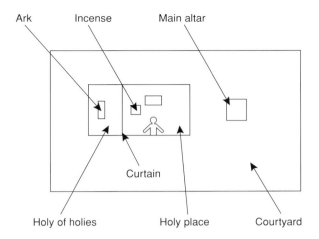

Figure 46.2   The tabernacle, or sanctuary.

disaster befalling the nation. Ezekiel in fact pictures the cloud of God's presence taking off from the temple and this presages the eventual fall of Jerusalem (Ezekiel 8–11).

From these rules about the purification offering and the day of atonement it seems that different categories of offence produce different degrees of uncleanness. Or, more precisely, the more serious the offence the more deeply the impurity penetrates the sanctuary. Inadvertent offences by the laity merely pollute the altar in the outer courtyard. Inadvertent offences by the whole congregation or the high priest defile the holy place, so that to cleanse it the incense altar and curtain must be sprinkled with blood. But deliberate offences penetrate the holy of holies itself and require the mercy seat over the ark to be sprinkled if God is to continue to dwell among his people.

However the blood smearing and sprinkling do more than cleanse the different parts of the sanctuary, they make atonement for the offender so that his or her sin is forgiven. The application of the blood to the altars does not merely make them ritually clean, it secures the forgiveness of the sinner. This is made even clearer on the Day of Atonement, which deals with the most serious sins and the impurities associated with them. On this day the high priest enters the holy of holies and sprinkles blood there, but he also takes a goat, lays both his hands on its head, confesses all the transgressions and sins of the people of Israel, thus symbolically transferring them to the goat. The goat is then driven away into the wilderness to a solitary place to Azazel. This is the ritual of the scapegoat. It is uncertain what Azazel means, possibly 'complete destruction' or the name of a demon responsible for sin, but the fundamental idea is clear: through the Day of Atonement ceremonies the nation is purged of all its sin and associated impurity. Its sins are symbolically despatched to a desolate place so that they will not return to trouble the people.

Holiness

Before trying to clarify the biblical concepts of purity, it is necessary to look at its idea of holiness, for conceptually holiness and uncleanness are opposite ends of a spectrum in which purity comes in the middle. Persons or things are either holy or common, clean or unclean. It is possible to divide 'common' into two subcategories, 'clean' or 'unclean'. This sets up a sequence 'holy' – 'ordinary' – 'clean' or 'unclean'. In their natural state people or things are 'common'/'clean'. When they are given to God they are 'sanctified', that is, they become 'holy'. When they are spoiled in some way, holy things are 'profaned' and clean things 'polluted' (see Figure 46.3).

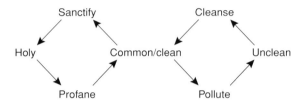

Figure 46.3 'Holy' – 'clean' – 'unclean' sequence.

Things that are intrinsically holy, such as God's name, are *profaned* when abused. Clean things, such as the human body, may be *polluted* by the unclean, for example blood, disease, or death. To reverse the process unclean things may be *cleansed* by waiting, washing, and sometimes offering a sacrifice. To *sanctify* something clean is more difficult: it usually involves an explicit command from God, sacrifice and anointing with oil.

Holiness is intrinsic to God's character and everything that belongs to him. Israel is frequently urged to 'Be holy, for I am holy.' God's name, which expresses his character, is holy, so to swear falsely or to resort to idolatry profanes his name. Anyone or anything given to God becomes holy. Thus the priests' portions of the sacrifices are holy, as are the tabernacle and its equipment. Those dedicated to the service of God, such as priests, Levites and Nazirites (the Old Testament equivalent of monks and nuns) are regarded as holy. In a more general sense the whole nation of Israel is set apart from other nations to serve God and is therefore described as holy.

But does holiness mean anything more than separation to God? What is it about God that makes him holy in himself? This is more difficult to answer. Mary Douglas (1966) suggests that holiness involves wholeness and completeness. This means that holy men like priests have to be free of deformity and physical handicap. Animals offered to God must be free of blemish. Holy behaviour involves moral integrity: thus theft, dishonesty, double-dealing and hypocrisy are all incompatible with holiness.

Though wholeness partially captures what the Old Testament means by holiness, it is more precisely encapsulated in the notion of full and perfect life. God is the source of life, and so holiness virtually equates to the life-giving power of God. The Garden of Eden is not only pictured as the place where God dwelt, but its verdant vegetation, four rivers and the tree of life all strengthen the association between

God, holiness and life. So in the laws about sacrifice and priests, it is not that blemishes and handicaps are somehow abnormal, but their lack of perfect life debars them from being of use in worship. Those who come into the presence of God must demonstrate they have perfect life.

Uncleanness

Once the association between holiness and life has been grasped, it becomes easier to see the principles being expressed through the laws on uncleanness outlined above. Fundamental is the contrast between holiness and uncleanness. God is the perfectly holy, whereas the unclean are those opposed to God, or who fall short of his perfection. Hence idolatry, which involves worshipping another god, is one of the most severe forms of uncleanness: it pollutes the idolater, the land and the sanctuary. But divine holiness does not merely demand total religious and moral commitment; it means life. God himself is full and perfect life, so that death is the very antithesis of holiness. Thus it is not surprising that homicide generates an intense form of uncleanness. Indeed other forms of uncleanness are very often associated with death. The Old Testament thus operates with the following polarities:

$$God \text{——} sin$$
$$life \text{——} death$$
$$holiness \text{——} uncleanness$$

The world and its contents are viewed as revolving around two poles, the holy God of life, and sin/death, the unclean. Israel, the people of God, is called to be holy, 'because I the LORD am holy' (Leviticus 20:26). This means shunning those sins that are the antithesis of holiness, such as idolatry, murder, and sexual immorality. Sexual congress is the most powerful and Godlike of all human powers, in that it enables man to be like God creating beings in his own image, but its misuse is viewed by the Old Testament as gravely as idolatry or homicide – *Corruptio optimi pessima* (the misuse of the best is the worst). But uncleanness also means avoiding the other conditions associated with death.

If the quintessence of uncleanness is death, it becomes clear why corpses are regarded as so polluting. Thus if Nazirites, the holiest laypeople in Israel, come unexpectedly in contact with the dead, their vow is invalidated and they must start the period under the Nazirite vow again (Numbers 6). Whereas the holiness of the Nazirite is temporary, that of the high priest is permanent and he must not even compromise it by going near his dead father or mother. Less serious uncleannesses may similarly be viewed as related to lack of life. Men or women suffering abnormal discharges from their sexual organs cannot generate new life, so they are unclean. This is probably the reason why menstruation and the puerperal discharge in women and seminal emissions in men are regarded as unclean: they are preventing or at least not leading to the procreation of new life. An apparent association with death can also explain why skin disease is viewed negatively. People suffering from serious skin diseases are not enjoying the fullness of life: part of their body seems to be

God				
life				death
holy				unclean
priests	handicapped priests	clean laity	unclean, e.g. skin-diseased	corpses
sacrificial animals	blemished sacrificial animals	clean animals	unclean animals	dead animals

Figure 46.4 Spectrum of conditions from holy to unclean.

rotting away, and they are therefore classified as unclean. Only the pure and clean may approach God. Thus handicapped priests may not officiate at the altar and blemished animals may not be sacrificed there, because they appear to lack perfect life, and therefore they may not enter God's presence. Similarly lay people affected by uncleanness, for example skin disease or discharge, are barred from worship and sometimes forced to live outside the community until they recover (Numbers 5:1–4; 2 Kings 7:3–4).

Thus there are degrees of uncleanness in biblical thinking. So rather than regard holy and unclean, life and death, as mutually exclusive categories, it is better to see a spectrum of conditions ranging from the very holy at one extreme to the very unclean at the other (see Figure 46.4).

Similar spectra may be drawn to show Israel's conception of space: from the holy of holies, God's dwelling place, at the centre of the tabernacle, the tabernacle courtyard, the camp, to the unclean area outside the camp.

These harsh regulations declared very loudly one aspect of God's character: he is life, perfect life, both morally and physically. He is opposed to death: those who willingly or even involuntarily embrace actions that lead to death separate themselves from God.

The food laws

Of the three key principles in the Jewish dietary laws, no consumption of blood, no mixing of meat and milk in the same meal, and the avoidance of certain foods altogether, only the last is spelled out in detail in the Old Testament. The ban on blood is mentioned immediately after the flood in Genesis 9:4, where the consumption of meat is first permitted with the proviso 'Only you shall not eat flesh with its life, that is, its blood.' The later law in Leviticus 17 threatens anyone who does eat blood with 'cutting off', that is, premature death. For Deuteronomy to eat meat from which the blood has not been drained is incompatible with Israel's vocation to be a holy nation.

Once again the tie-up between holiness and life on the one hand and uncleanness and death on the other is apparent in the blood ban. Because blood represents the life of the animal it is sacred; it belongs to God, therefore man should not consume it. Animals that die naturally have their lifeblood still in them, so are banned from consumption by the holy people of Israel. But foreigners who are not in this close relationship with God may eat the flesh of such carcasses.

Three times the law insists, 'You shall not boil a kid in its mother's milk' (Exodus 23:19; 34:26; Deuteronomy 14:21), and this is the basis of the Jewish ban on eating meat and milk products at the same meal. The original circumstances of the ban are obscure. It is often surmised that it was a rejection of a Canaanite religious custom. It may also be relevant that goat's meat cooked in leben (a sort of yoghurt) is still enjoyed in the Middle East today. But neither observation explains why the Old Testament forbids it. It could be that like the blood ban it is inculcating respect for life. A kid should be living on its mother's milk not being cooked in it. Such a dish seems to subvert the natural order, and confuse the realms of life and death in an unacceptable way.

However the other food laws (Leviticus 11; Deuteronomy 14) do not immediately seem to fit this understanding of uncleanness. It is not apparent, for example, why pigs and camels and crabs are unclean, whereas sheep, goats or salmon are classified as clean. The criterion that clean land animals must have cloven hooves and chew the cud is only another way of defining the classes clean and unclean: it does not explain why there should be different classes in the first place. The same may be said about the distinction between fish with scales and fins, which are clean, and other water creatures that are not. When it comes to the birds, Leviticus and Deuteronomy simply give a list of twenty hard-to-identify birds that are unclean and therefore may not be eaten, and declare the others clean.

Over the centuries various theories have been put forward to explain these food laws. The standard Jewish view is that the classification is arbitrary: they test obedience. Will you obey God's commands, even if you cannot understand his reasons? If people are willing to keep rules like this for which they can see no reason, it may be hoped that they will keep the moral law, which is clearly beneficial to society. This altruistic approach to law is commendable, but as an explanation it must be clearly a last resort, for it is an admission that the purpose of the law cannot be understood.

An approach that has been popular since the advance of modern medicine in the nineteenth century is that the food laws were given to promote health: pork, shellfish, and so on, often carry disease. By forbidding Israel to eat such foods God was safeguarding their health. Though this fits well with the Old Testament picture of God as a deity very concerned about human welfare, there is nothing in the text to support this explanation. It is never stated that observing the food laws is good for your health, though motive clauses giving reasons for keeping particular laws are frequent elsewhere in the Pentateuch. At a pragmatic level, if the Israelites had discovered that eating pork might give one tapeworms, might they not also have discovered that thorough cooking kills them? Why are poisonous plants not banned? Indeed closer examination shows that some items classified as unclean are healthy foods, and some that are clean are problematic. A hygienic explanation also causes theological problems, at least for Christians. Why should Jesus according to Mark 7 have suggested the abrogation of the food laws, and the early church have implemented it, if they contributed to health? Would the apostles have wanted church members to have eaten unhealthy foods?

Another scholarly explanation is that some of the unclean animals, for example pigs, were used in pagan worship. Israel was expected to shun any religious acts that smacked of syncretism or compromise. While pig bones apparently used in sacrifice have been found at Canaanite sites, it is certain that the Canaanites most frequently sacrificed sheep, goats and oxen, the same animals as in Israel. In particular the bull, the premier clean sacrificial beast in Israel, was also highly valued in Egyptian and Canaanite religion. This indicates that reaction to foreign practice does not explain these rules.

Anthropological explanations that see these food rules as both symbolic and social have more to commend them. These rules are symbolic, in expressing a society's self-understanding, and social, in that they tend to support the boundaries and hier-archies of that society. Mary Douglas has put forward several possible explanations of this type. In *Purity and Danger* (1966) she argued that wholeness, holiness and cleanness were closely related ideas in biblical thinking. As already noted above this is an important insight. She further observed that the mode of locomotion of different species seemed to be an important factor in whether or not they were classed as clean. Air, land, and sea all have an appropriate mode of motion associated with them. Birds have two wings with which to fly, and two feet for walking; fish have fins and scales with which to swim; land animals have hooves to run with. Animals that conformed to their type were clean and could be eaten, whereas anomalous creatures were classified as unclean. While this could explain some of the distinctions,

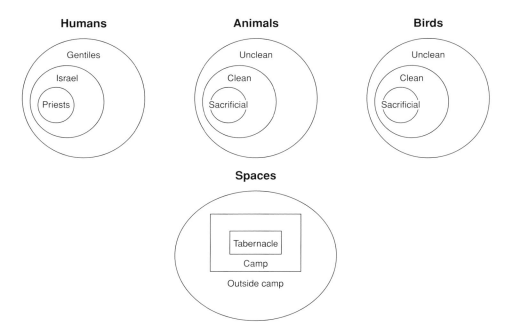

Figure 46.5 Cleanness rules relating to humans, animals and birds.

such as why snakes are unclean (they do not move in the right way for land animals), it hardly explains the finer distinctions, for example between a camel and a goat or between the birds.

She later noted in *Implicit Meanings* (1975) that the cleanness rules structure the human, animal and bird realms in a similar way. Both the realms of birds and beasts contain a mixture of clean and unclean species. The clean may be eaten, the unclean may not. Within the clean group there is a subgroup of animals or birds that may also be sacrificed, such as sheep or pigeons. This threefold division of the bird and animal kingdoms corresponds to the divisions among human beings (see Figure 46.5). Mankind falls into two main groups, Israel and the Gentiles. Within Israel only one group, the priests, may approach the altar to offer sacrifice. This in turn matches the law's understanding of sacred space. Outside the camp is the abode of Gentiles and unclean Israelites. Ordinary Israelites dwell in the camp, but only priests may approach the altar or enter the tabernacle tent.

These distinctions made in the food laws between clean and unclean foods thus match the divisions among Mankind, between Israel the elect nation and the non-elect Gentiles. They serve to remind Israel of her special status as God's chosen people. Just as God has selected just one people to be near him, so Israel has to be selective in her diet. Through this system of symbolic laws the Israelites are reminded at every meal of their redemption to be God's people. Their diet is limited to certain meats in imitation of their God, who has restricted his choice among the nations to Israel. It serves also to bring to mind Israel's responsibilities to be a holy nation. As they distinguish between clean and unclean foods, they are reminded that holiness is more than a matter of meat and drink, but a way of life characterized by purity and integrity.

The oldest Jewish explanation of these laws in the second-century BC *Letter of Aristeas* seems to endorse such a symbolic interpretation. The writer states that humans must behave like the clean birds that eat grain, not like the wild and carnivorous unclean birds. These regulations teach Israel to act 'with discrimination according to the standard of righteousness – more especially because we have been distinctly separated from the rest of mankind'.

These food laws not only reminded Israel of her distinctiveness, they served to enforce it. Jews faithful to these laws would tend to avoid Gentile company, lest they were offered unclean food to eat. This may partially explain the reluctance of Daniel and his friends when exiled in Babylon to eat the food provided by the royal court: they feared they might be defiled, so they insisted on eating only vegetables (cf. Daniel 1:8–16).

But if the general symbolic significance of the food laws has been clarified, can the specific reasons for assigning animals into one category or the other be discovered? Is the classification of pigs and shellfish as unclean purely arbitrary? The list of unclean birds (Leviticus 11:13–19; Deuteronomy 14:11–18) is suggestive. As far as these can be identified they are all birds of prey or were believed to feed on carrion. In other words they ate flesh with blood in, something forbidden to humans in Genesis 9, which insists all blood must be drained out of a creature before it may be eaten. Similarly sheep, goats and cattle are obviously vegetarian as well as being the most valuable possessions of pastoralists. One way of defining what sheep, goats and cattle have in common is to say they all have cloven hooves and chew the cud. Anything that does not fit this definition, such as cats or dogs, donkeys, is unclean. Carnivorous animals obviously fall into this category, as well as some herbivorous ones. So once again blood-consuming animals are banned from human consumption, because they act in a way that humans should not.

It would have been possible to give a list of the commonest clean land animals, corresponding to the list of unclean birds as Deuteronomy 14:5 attempts: instead the Leviticus law prefers to give a definition that can be used to categorize any animal, whether it has cloven hooves and chews the cud. This allows the consumption of many wild animals caught in hunting, such as deer. However, wild animals do not come into the super-clean category of animals or birds that may be sacrificed. Sacrificial victims must fulfil all the criteria for cleanness and also be domesticated: to give an animal caught in a hunt is not allowed, probably for the reason stated by David in 2 Samuel 24:24: 'I will not offer burnt offerings to the LORD which cost me nothing.' This also explains why the world of water creatures simply divides into clean and unclean: there is no sacrificial subset of sacrificial clean fish, because ancient Israel had no fish farms.

These food laws also fit into the broader framework of the uncleanness laws. If God is identified with life and holiness, and uncleanness is associated with death and opposition to God, the food laws symbolize that Israel is God's people called to enjoy his life, while Gentile idolaters are by and large opposed to him and his people and face death. The food laws also underline respect for life directly as well as symbolically. Eating meat is described as a concession in Genesis 9:1–4. And it may only be eaten if the blood is drained out first, 'for the life is . . . the blood' (Leviticus 17:11). Consumption of the life liquid, blood, is thus banned. Furthermore wanton slaughter of living creatures is also discouraged by the limited number of animals classified as clean. In both ways, then, these food laws tended to promote respect for life.

Clean/unclean in the prophets

Outside the Pentateuch the terms 'clean' and 'unclean' are much less common. That is not to say the prophets were not familiar with the ideas, though. The incompatibility of uncleanness with holiness and the danger of entering God's presence in worship if you are not clean is dramatically expressed by Isaiah in his call vision. He hears the seraphim calling, 'Holy, holy, holy is the LORD of hosts', and he responds,' Woe is me! For I am lost; for I am a man of unclean lips, and I dwell in the midst of a people of unclean lips; for my eyes have seen the King, the LORD of hosts!' (Isaiah 6:3–5).

But though the distinction between clean and unclean is well known to the prophets, they focus on the worst types of prohibited uncleanness attributable to human sin, not on tolerated types of uncleanness caused by bodily functions. Thus Hosea 5:3 accuses Israel of contracting uncleanness through unfaithfulness to the LORD, which he calls spiritual harlotry. Hosea 6: 7–10 associates uncleanness with murder and infidelity to the covenant. Isaiah 30:22 and Jeremiah 2:7, 7:30 declare that idolatry defiles the land and the sanctuary.

But it is the priest/prophet Ezekiel, brought up strictly to avoid uncleanness (4:14), who makes most of the concept in his condemnation of Israel. Though he knows the laws on naturally occurring uncleanness (44:25; cf. 22:26 alluding to Leviticus 10:10–11), he repeatedly focuses on the uncleanness caused by Israel's moral and spiritual apostasy, particularly bloodshed and idolatry, which he terms harlotry (e.g. 22:3–4, 11; 23:7; 33:25–6; 36:17–18).

CLEAN/UNCLEAN IN THE FIRST CENTURY

Jewish beliefs

Among first-century Jews purity laws were both important and controversial: different groups had quite different interpretations and applications of the biblical laws. The concern to be ritually clean is shown both by archaeology and the texts relating to this period. More than a sixth of the Mishnah (completed c. AD 200) is concerned with purity regulations, and the New Testament often refers to Jewish beliefs about uncleanness as well as using the terminology of purity and uncleanness in its own way.

Archaeologically the importance of purity is attested by the discovery of numerous Jewish ritual baths or *miqveh*s in Palestine and in the diaspora. The biblical law prescribes that after some kinds of pollution the sufferer must wash himself as part of the cleansing process. This was necessary before he or she could participate in temple worship. By the first century strict Jews were taking daily ritual baths to ensure that they were always ritually clean. To this end many *miqveh*s were constructed. Often these were cut in the rock under buildings or alongside synagogues. They were large tanks (typically 2 m deep and up to 3 m square) with one or two sets of steps for entering and leaving the water. The person to be cleansed walked into the water down one side of the steps, immersed, and then up the other side. The water for a *miqveh* had to flow directly into it, either from a stream or from collected rainwater: a *miqveh* could not be filled from waterpots.

As far as ordinary Jews were concerned, it is assumed that they simply accepted the rules about purity in the Bible. In certain respects first-century practice seems to have become stricter than earlier times. For example, women were expected to bathe after menstruation and childbirth, which is not explicit in Leviticus. Farmers and others involved in the production of priestly food had to be clean when they handled it. Jews outside Palestine often had qualms about eating meat from pagan sources, for it might not have been slaughtered properly to drain all the blood out, or it might have come from a temple where it had been offered to an idol.

But two groups within Judaism, the Qumran community and the Pharisees, interpreted the rules on purity even more strictly. The Qumran community was part of the wider Essene movement that developed in the second century BC and established a monastic community at the northern end of the Dead Sea. This whole community viewed itself as priestly and therefore applied the rules governing priestly purity in the temple to their everyday life. According to Josephus this involved bathing twice a day, before each main meal, and wearing different clothes at table from their working ones. The Essenes rarely if ever drank wine, because priests could not drink before serving in the temple. They also shunned the use of oil on their skin, because it made the skin sticky and therefore more likely to attract dust that could carry pollution. Their desire for permanent cleanness may explain their famed preference for celibacy, for sexual intercourse is seen as defiling in Leviticus 15:18.

If the Essenes were sticklers for ritual purity, they were also very concerned about moral purity. They held like the Old Testament that sin could pollute the sinner. In the Old Testament only idolatry, sexual offences, and bloodshed have this effect, but the Essenes seem to have held that other grave sins defiled people. Thus sinners within the community and outsiders were banned from the community meals lest they defiled the pure members. Then after punishment and repentance the sinner was readmitted, but only after ritual bathing. The Old Testament envisages bathing as part of the process of cleansing but not as part of the atonement for sin but the Essenes seem to have equated the two procedures.

The Pharisees unlike the Essenes were not concerned with the impurity caused by sin, they focused almost entirely on ritual pollution and its antidotes. Quite how strict they were in the first century is a matter of debate, for the most important sources for their beliefs reflect a later era. The general view is that the Pharisees were a group most concerned with food purity, so that their meals were as pure as those of the Jerusalem priests in the temple. For this reason they insisted on washing their hands before meals, cleansing the inside and outside of cooking vessels, and regulating farming practices so that food would be pure. The evidence that the Pharisees saw themselves as imitating the priests is questionable: their practices could be explained as part of a piety that viewed ingesting impurity by eating as more serious than contracting it by touch. Whatever the explanation, food purity was certainly of great concern to them.

The New Testament

The gospels portray Jesus disputing with the Pharisees on various issues, including purity. Matthew 15:1–20 and Mark 7:1–23 recount a heated debate. It is introduced by 'Why do your disciples transgress the tradition of the elders? For they do not wash their hands when they eat.' Jesus concludes that sin which comes from inside a person defiles, not the food that comes from outside. 'For out of the heart come evil thoughts, murder, adultery, fornication, theft, false witness, slander. These are what defile a man; but to eat with unwashed hands does not defile a man.' On another occasion he criticizes the Pharisees for worrying about the cleanliness of the outside of a pot while not caring about their own purity of heart (Matthew 23:25–6; Luke 11:37–47). He was challenged by Pharisees about his habit of eating with sinners, something they would have avoided to prevent themselves being made unclean, and he replied by telling three parables (Luke 15). In his healing ministry he touched lepers, a woman with a long-term discharge, and even corpses (the acme of uncleanness). Though it is not said that he was criticized by the Pharisees for these actions, they fit in with his general attitude to ritual uncleanness.

At one level his teaching and actions may be viewed as a rejection of Pharisaic custom and a reassertion of the seriousness of the uncleanness caused by sin over against the lesser impurity resulting from food, disease and death. More positively if these acts are set within the holiness spectrum of the Old Testament (see Figure 46.4 above), where life, holiness and cleanness are associated with God but uncleanness and sin are associated with death, they suggest a new dimension to Jesus' ministry. In the Old Testament the unclean had to wait for their uncleanness to clear up before they could draw near to God in fullness of life. In Jesus, the life-giving God draws near to the unclean, restoring them to life and fellowship with himself. Whereas the Old Testament portrays God as perfect life to which only those with life could have access, Jesus declares God's forgiveness of sin and cleansing of impurity and demonstrates it by associating with sinners and healing the unclean.

In the Old Testament the food laws reminded Israel of her election, of her status as the chosen people distinct from all the other nations. Commenting on Jesus' remarks that food does not pollute, only sin does, Mark says, 'Thus he declared all foods clean.' If all foods were clean, that could imply all nations were potentially clean, that is, open to God's grace. It is therefore striking that the next episode in Mark (7:24–30) tells of Jesus leaving Jewish Galilee and visiting Tyre, where he heals the son of a Greek woman.

However the implications of these comments and actions were not grasped immediately by the early church. Acts 10 tells of the first Gentile convert to enter the church. Cornelius is a Roman centurion posted to Palestine who sends messengers to Peter to enquire about the new faith. While they are on their way to him, Peter has a dream in which he sees a sheet full of unclean animals and reptiles that no Jew would consider eating. But a voice tells him to kill and eat them. He protests that he has never eaten anything common or unclean. But the voice says again, 'What God has cleansed, you must not call common.' Puzzled by this dream, Peter understands what it means only when Cornelius' men arrives and ask him to go and preach to their master. Next day when he reaches Cornelius, Peter justifies his visit as follows: 'You know how unlawful it is for a Jew to associate with any one of another nation, but God has told me that I should not call any man common or unclean.' His dream suggests that the food laws distinguishing clean and unclean beasts is no longer applicable, and he connects this with the divine permission to evangelize Gentiles as well as Jews. This shows that the symbolic significance of these laws rediscovered in recent times by Mary Douglas was still known in the first century. Jews like Peter realized that they marked Israel's unique status, and that their abrogation signalled a new era in which the kingdom of God was open to believers of all nations.

Such a move was highly contentious among Jewish Christians of a more traditionalist frame of mind and led to a fierce debate at the council of Jerusalem (Acts 15), which is reflected in Paul's epistles. However Peter's inclusivist approach to the Gentiles was endorsed with the proviso that Gentile converts should be advised to abstain from idolatry, unchastity, what is strangled, and blood. In other words they were specially warned about those sins that caused prohibited uncleanness as opposed to the tolerated ritual uncleanness. This is akin to the prophets who tended to emphasize the impurity caused by these sins rather than ritual uncleanness.

The same concerns are apparent in the epistles. Paul's basic position about food is that 'nothing is unclean in itself' (Romans 14:14). However if anyone has qualms about eating something, he should avoid it. This is especially the case if eating meat upsets the faith of others or appears to endorse idolatry. So he tells the Corinthians to avoid meals in pagan temples. (1 Corinthians 8). But they should be prepared to go further: if anyone points out that meat sold in the markets has come from heathen temples, they should avoid eating it (1 Corinthians 10).

Like the prophets and the gospels, the epistles are more concerned with those sins that cause grave uncleanness, namely idolatry, sexual immorality and murder. According to Jesus, 'What comes out of a man ... makes him unclean ... evil thoughts, sexual immorality, theft, murder, adultery, greed', etc. (Mark 7:15, 21–2 NIV). In the epistles uncleanness is sometimes sandwiched between sexual immorality and greed, which is idolatry (e.g. Ephesians 5:3; Colossians 3:5), again reflecting Old Testament thought patterns. However, as in the prophets and Mark 7:21, uncleanness is most often associated with sexual sin (e.g. Romans 1:24; Galatians 5:19), so that impurity is virtually identified with misuse of sex.

In the book of Revelation the oldest meaning of uncleanness is reasserted: it is unfitness to worship in God's temple. So into the new Jerusalem, where God dwells, 'nothing unclean shall enter'. Only those whose clothes have been washed may enter the city. 'Outside are the dogs and sorcerers and fornicators and murderers and idolaters, and everyone who loves and practises falsehood' (Revelation 21:27; 22:14–15). Thus in the last book of the Bible the notions of purity and uncleanness first mooted in Genesis continue to resonate powerfully.

BIBLIOGRAPHY

Douglas, M. *Purity and Danger*, London, Routledge, 1966.
—— *Implicit Meanings*, London, Routledge, 1975.
Houston, W. *Purity and Monotheism*, Sheffield, JSOT Press, 1993.
Jenson, P. P. *Graded Holiness*, Sheffield, JSOT Press, 1992.
Klawans, J. 'The Impurity of Immorality in Ancient Judaism', *Journal of Jewish Studies* 48, 1997, 1–16.
Poirier, J. C. 'Why Did the Pharisees Wash their Hands?' *Journal of Jewish Studies* 47, 1996, 217–33.
Sanders, E. P. *Judaism: Practice and Belief 63 BCE – 66 CE*, London, SCM Press, 1992.
Wenham, G. J. *The Book of Leviticus*, Grand Rapids, Eerdmans, 1979.
Wright, D. P. 'Unclean and Clean (OT)', *Anchor Bible Dictionary*, New York, Doubleday, 1992, 6: 729–41.

PART VIII

THE BIBLE TODAY

CHAPTER FORTY-SEVEN

JEWISH
BIBLE TRANSLATION

————·◆·————

Leonard J. Greenspoon

For at least 2,200 and perhaps as many as 2,500 years, Bible translating has been taking place within the Jewish community. During this long period Jews pioneered, experimented with, and some would say perfected certain types of translation. Although this experience is rich and varied, it is not as well known or well studied among Jews as is the analogous process within the Christian community.

The earliest documentable Bible translation dates from the first half of the third century BCE and is located in the Egyptian capital city and metropolis of Alexandria. As recorded in the *Letter of Aristeas*, which was composed at least a century after the events it purports to narrate from an eyewitness perspective, the second Macedonian/Greek ruler of Egypt, Ptolemy II Philadephus, was persuaded by his librarian that a Greek translation of the Jewish laws, equivalent in extent to the Pentateuch or Torah, should be carried out under royal auspices, with the resulting text to occupy a place of honor at the great Library (see Shutt 1985 for the most recent translation of, and introduction to, the *Letter of Aristeas*; Greenspoon 1989 provides a more popular account). Seventy-two elders (equivalent to six from each of the traditional twelve tribes of Israel), renowned as scholars and of unblemished morality, were brought in from Jerusalem to insure that the translation would accord with the highest standards of both Hellenistic and Jewish scholarship. After the elders arrived and experienced a prolonged and undoubtedly welcomed reception from Ptolemy, they set about their work. In seventy-two days they completed their task, working in subcommittees and consulting with each other much in the same way that modern translators work (though without the palatial surroundings of their ancient counterparts).

Three aspects of Aristeas's narrative are worthy of further consideration, since they point in many ways to issues that recur in the long history of Jewish Bible translating. At the end of his document Aristeas describes the formal ceremony that, according to him, constituted the acceptance by Alexandrian Jewry of the LXX (Septuagint, or Old Greek) text of the Torah as Sacred Writ. In its details this ceremony is consciously modeled on the account of Moses' giving of the Law in the biblical book of Exodus (see especially Orlinsky 1975). So serious is this matter, according to Aristeas, that a curse is uttered against anyone who would alter the wording of this Greek translation.

That a translation could have sanctity and authority equal to the original is evident in the elaborations and embellishments to which the *Letter of Aristeas* was subject in subsequent Jewish and later Christian retellings of this tale of Septuagint origins. There is nothing of the 'miraculous' in Aristeas's narrative, except for the coincidence (noted somewhat apologetically in the letter itself) that seventy-two scholars took exactly seventy-two days to produce their work. As the story evolved, the seventy-two were placed in individual cells (rather than working in a consultative process, as in Aristeas), each producing a text identical in every respect to all the others. Surely, this pointed to the divine inspiration that guided this project, so much so that the first-century CE Jewish philosopher Philo (himself an Alexandrian) spoke of those responsible for the Septuagint as prophets rather than translators (for details, see Shutt 1985).

As noted above, the *Letter of Aristeas* ascribes to the Ptolemaic government the impetus for this translation. This assertion has been challenged as unlikely, with Septuagint origins more often sought within the Jewish community itself, where (it is reasonably argued) the Hebrew language was increasingly displaced in writing and in speech by Greek, thus necessitating a translation of the former into the latter (for accessible bibliography, see Greenspoon 1989).

In assessing these three issues, we look first at the last and then at the first two, which are closely interrelated. In terms of the impetus for this first Bible translation, the matter is typically phrased as either/or; that is, either the call emanated from outside the Jewish community or from within. In fact, these two views are not mutually exclusive, and we can well imagine a convergence of interests and needs that resulted in the Old Greek version of the Pentateuch. That is likely also to be the case with subsequent translations, since the process is typically bound up with a complex of cultural, social, political, and religious factors.

Moreover, it cannot be demonstrated, even if common sense and opinion make it likely (certain?), that Bible translation results directly from the perception that the original language is no longer comprehensible and must be replaced by a vernacular version. The insight to be considered here is that a translation and the original it reflects may coexist for a period of time, with the former functioning initially as an (official) interpretation of the latter. Subsequently, when the language of the original has indeed fallen out of usage, the translation-as-accompaniment becomes the independent-version-as-replacement. This process would also involve, to a greater or lesser extent, changes of nuance and meaning as words originally tied to one language (in this case Hebrew) now circulate freely in another (here, Greek).

When, at the conclusion of his letter, Aristeas portrays the warm, one might say worshipful, reception proffered by the Jewish community to the Greek translation, it is difficult not to discern a note of stridency and urgency in the narrator's voice. It thus becomes clear that questions of textual authority and authenticity reflect practical and not simply theoretical concerns. Already (that is, by the mid-second century BCE), voices were raised in opposition to the high status apparently accorded to the Septuagint. The source of this opposition can probably be located in Jerusalem, but it could have developed elsewhere or in fact anywhere careful readers noted differences between the Greek and Hebrew texts. Today we understand that such differences are as likely (or more likely) to arise from the fact that the Old Greek translators had before them Semitic texts that differed from those gaining ascendancy elsewhere (especially, we can well imagine, in Jerusalem) as they are from conscious interpretive changes on the part of the translators themselves. Ancient observers were undoubtedly less concerned about the reasons for such differences (which they would probably have viewed as discrepancies) than with their existence (for further details, consult Peters 1992).

Accepting the unique authority of the Hebrew text carried with it the necessity of revising the Greek where it differed. Such an attitude was a major motivating factor in the work of Theodotion, Aquila, and Symmachus, to whom Greek texts of the first centuries BCE and CE are attributed. In my opinion, all three were Jewish and motivated, among other factors, by a concern to reconcile the current Greek editions with the then-regnant Hebrew texts. If they and other unnamed individuals carrying out the same sort of revision and retranslation were aware of Aristeas's view, they implicitly rejected or ignored it through their efforts. More explicit in terms of his evaluation of the Septuagint's authority as secondary is the author of Ben Sirach, as he makes clear in his prologue. Aristeas was not without his later supporters within the Jewish community (so Philo, see above), and the attitude he promoted dominated early Christian thought and practice (with the marked exception of Jerome) (Greenspoon 1992, 1993).

Among these Greek speakers we detect no suggestion that Bible translation *per se* was to be avoided as unnecessary (since all educated Jews ought to know Hebrew) or dangerous (since potentially misleading interpretations and new meanings could be introduced into what should be a uniquely immutable and sacred text). Out-and-out opposition to Bible translation does appear in some rabbinic texts, whose dates and provenance are difficult to determine (as is often the case with such material). But there are other rabbinic pronouncements far more favorable to translations of the Bible, some of which hold the Greek version in highest repute. It is likely that the totality of such material accurately reflects deep divisions among rabbinic authorities (and their communities), tied to chronological (e.g., before or after the fall of the Jerusalem Temple in 73 CE), geographical (in the Land or the Diaspora), ideological, and other factors (see several articles in Orlinsky 1974; also Orlinsky and Bratcher 1991: 6–7).

In sum, the *Letter of Aristeas* accurately and rather forcefully presents a case for Septuagintal origins that was being made, I would guess, in at least one mid-second century Jewish community – quite possibly in Alexandria itself. As evidence for what *really* happened a hundred or so years earlier, this document is not unexpectedly far from completely reliable, but (I maintain) equally far from useless in reconstructing the circumstances in which the very first biblical translation arose. We can, I feel, be especially grateful that the author of Aristeas raised almost all of the questions that would continue to both plague and enrich Jewish Bible translating from that point until the present.

There is, however, one matter that received essentially no comment in the letter and was little commented upon explicitly elsewhere in ancient Jewish (and most Christian) sources; namely, what sort of translation was this oldest Greek version of the Torah. Today we can speak of literal and free (with interlinear and paraphrase defining the respective ends of what may be termed the translation continuum).

Or we can use more precise terms such as formal equivalence and dynamic or functional equivalence. Ancient translators certainly knew of these (and other) options even if they differed with respect to terminology.

From almost all perspectives ancient and modern, the Old Greek of the Pentateuch belongs squarely in the literal or functional equivalence realms of translating. We are not able in all cases to (re)construct the Hebrew text or *Vorlage* that lay before these translators, but where we can (and even when we are not sure) it is clear that they generally translated to the best of their abilities what was in front of them. This is not to say that there were no modifications for ideological reasons or for purposes of updating a text that was by then antiquarian and antiquated. However, most changes simply sought to convey to the reader what the translators understood the Hebrew to be saying. In this process the translators could count on a considerable amount of shared linguistic and theological knowledge with their intended audience.

Careful study of the Old Greek of the Pentateuch does allow for generalizations of the type presented in the previous paragraph. And it is accurate to speak of this Greek text as serving as something of a model for many of the later translators responsible for the Old Greek version of the remainder of the Old Testament. But such research also reveals the fact that the five books of the Torah are not the product of one individual or group of individuals. Rather, we can detect at least one translator for each of the five books (with the possibility of more than one for the book of Exodus).

When we move beyond the Pentateuch, the diversity of translation style or technique increases. In the opinion of some, this reflects the lesser or looser degree of sanctity in which books outside of the Torah were regarded by Jews in the Hellenistic period. But this explanation cannot be maintained. First, the approach taken by the Pentateuchal translators, while not unrelated to the sanctity in which they held Holy Writ, is probably more the result of their being pioneers than anything else. For they had no antecedents, no tradition from which they could directly draw. In such circumstances, it made more sense, from a technical as much as a theological perspective, simply to render as clearly and cleanly as possible what appeared in the Hebrew before them.

Moreover, there are a number of other books of the Septuagint that partake of a fairly literal approach as well as those far down on the free or functional scale. This is partly a result of how individual translators or groups of translators approached their task, about which we have no secure evidence outside of the texts themselves, since the translators left no introductions, committee minutes, or notes of any kind. But the varied nature of the Septuagint translations is also the result of the fact that our Septuagint is an artificial construct, containing not only the Old Greek of many books (such as the Pentateuch) but later versions or revisions, as in the case of Daniel and Ecclesiastes. This circumstance arises from the fact that the great Greek uncials, such as Alexandrinus and Vaticanus, contain a mixture of oldest, older, and newer materials, presumably reflecting the practice of the churches in the areas where these codices were produced in the early Christian centuries (for further discussion of these issues and extensive bibliography, see Peters 1992; Tov 1997).

These observations hold true for other Bible translations within Jewish (and other) contexts, in the sense that what we have is not always the oldest, not always the best, not always the most authentic produced. In the happenstance of preservation, transmission, and collation, we have surely lost a lot. But perhaps the greater source of surprise and certainly of satisfaction is that so much has been preserved.

Research into what has been preserved of ancient Jewish Bible translations into Greek yields one further important insight: the tendency among later translators and revisers was toward a more literal representation of the Hebrew. This is true not only in the quantitative changes necessary to bring older Greek texts into conformity with the Hebrew (understood as the original), but also in the numerous qualitative changes, where even the limited lexical and stylistic freedoms indulged in by, say, the Pentateuchal translators were eradicated or leveled through deference to the Hebrew. This led not only to the very readable and generally accurate version identified with Theodotion, but the heavily Hebraized rendering associated with Aquila that would have been difficult if not impossible for most Greek speakers to comprehend without recourse to the Hebrew (see Greenspoon 1992). But Aquila's approach did indeed remain popular among Greek-speaking Jews in spite of our perception of its shortcomings, as is witnessed by the fact that these Jews continued to use and further develop an Aquila-like Greek Bible through the Byzantine Period (so de Lange 1995).

Although it is commonplace (and, I believe, largely correct) to speak of the Septuagint or Old Greek as the earliest Bible translation, it is likely that the process of rendering the Bible into a foreign language has an even earlier origin within the Jewish community. Chapter 9 of the biblical book of Nehemiah describes what is clearly a momentous event in mid-fifth century BCE Jerusalem. The scribe Ezra, having recently arrived from Babylon, was reading to the assembled populace from the Book of the Law (roughly equivalent, I suggest, to our Torah) in Hebrew. As Ezra spoke, so the book of Nehemiah narrates, others provided an explanation of Ezra's words for the benefit of the huge crowd gathered to hear them.

As understood by many scholars (and I tend to agree), the explanation was in the form of translation/interpretation into the Aramaic language, which by then was the lingua franca of the Near East. (Although Hebrew and Aramaic are closely related Semitic languages, knowledge of one did not necessarily lead to competency in the other.) If this understanding of the event pictured in Nehemiah 8 is correct, we can look to this as the initial context for Bible translating. Two factors bear further notice. First, the procedure envisioned at this point is oral, with no indication of scribal activity in Aramaic. Second, the Aramaic translation/interpretation is portrayed as supplementing, rather than supplanting, the Hebrew.

The term 'Targum' (plural 'Targumim' or 'Targums'), from the Aramaic word for translation, is generally used to denote Aramaic texts of the Bible (for extended discussions, with full bibliography, see Alexander 1992; Beattie and McNamara 1994). There are few written Targums from pre-Christian times. As recorded in Jewish tradition, the Torah was the first portion of the Hebrew Bible rendered into Aramaic. This accords well with the procedure followed by those responsible for the Septuagint and also with Jewish beliefs and practices from almost all periods, whereby the Torah is given greatest prominence. Fragments from the Dead Sea Scrolls at Qumran do provide some confirmation for tradition, in that two small fragments from Cave 4 preserve a Targum to the book of Leviticus. It may be only by chance, although perhaps not, that the most extensive remains of a Targum at Qumran are from the book of Job (VanderKam 1994: 32–3).

Far more extensive and very well studied are the Targums from the Christian or common era. There are several important Aramaic texts of the Torah; Targums also exist for the Former Prophets (roughly equivalent to the Historical Books in the Christian tradition), the Latter Prophets, and the Writings (Ketubim, the third section into which Jews divide the Hebrew Bible). They stem from both Palestine and Babylonia, with the latter becoming dominant in subsequent times.

Looked at as a whole and with due allowance for differences in time and locale, the Targums do not support the oft-articulated assertion that they are uniformly periphrastic. Upon closer examination, those responsible for the Targums are seen as carefully representing the thoughts, if not the exact words, that appeared in their *Vorlage.* At the same time, many (although surely not all) Targumists felt free to add extensive and extended narrative and legal material into the text they were translating. Much of this material was in the form of updatings, to conform to beliefs and practices of the communities in which the Targums were produced. Among the techniques thus adopted by the Targumists were circumlocutions for references to the Divine. In a practice parallel to successive revisions of the Greek text, later Aramaic versions tended to admit fewer and fewer periphrastic passages.

It is likely that, if queried, those who prepared the Aramaic version would have responded that their additions and other modifications were in complete accord with Oral Tradition, which was held to be of equal antiquity and authority with the Written Law from Mount Sinai. The Aramaic text that resulted was as a whole quite different in its texture from much of the Greek version we call the Septuagint, in that the latter tended to be more sparing in its acceptance of exegetical interventions on the part of translators (Orlinsky and Bratcher 1991: 4–6). I hasten to add a caveat pertaining to all vast enterprises (the LXX and the Targums emphatically included) that are the results of many people working over an extended period of time: namely, that each book or body of material must be looked at separately; generalizations are to be avoided.

It has long been noted – and more recently discussed with greater linguistic and methodological sophistication – that the writers of the New Testament often cited Scripture in a form identical to the LXX or at least closer to the LXX than to the Masoretic Text (see Archer and Chirichigno 1983; Barr 1994; Lim 1997). This is not at all surprising, given that most of the writers of the New Testament were Greek-speaking Jews, who would have been familiar with their sacred writings in that language as the appropriate means of conveying their beliefs to the world at large. Less frequent, but also demonstrable, is the dependence of some New Testament writers on an Aramaic version of Scripture. These examples combine with the Qumran fragments and with isolated historical allusions in existing Palestinian and Babylonian Targumim to document the reality, if not the scope, of Aramaic translations in pre-Christian times.

The Hebrew Bible (along with what later came to be known as the New Testament) circulated widely in a number of other ancient languages. Among the most prominent were texts in Syriac (Eastern Aramaic) and Latin. By at least the third century CE, most, if not all, of the Old Testament had been rendered into

Syriac, and it is possible that Jews were responsible for some of this translating. But little is known of the process that ultimately led to the Peshitta, as the standard version of the Syriac Bible became known within Eastern churches.

The efforts of Jerome, in the late fourth century, that culminated in the Latin version eventually known as the Vulgate, were not – as is commonly thought – the first to produce a Bible in the reigning language of the Western Roman Empire. Rather, Jerome's mandate, which he fulfilled with extraordinary industry, was to prepare a text that would supplant the many older Latin renderings already in existence. Although it is well known that Jerome learned the Hebrew language and something of Jewish exegetical traditions from contemporary rabbis, there is no sure evidence that any Jews produced a Latin text of the Bible for their own use. We should, however, leave open at least the possibility that in some community or other, perhaps in North Africa (where Christians first translated biblical texts into Latin), Jews followed the lead of their Alexandrian ancestors.

Beginning in the mid-seventh century, Jews resident in the East and in North Africa came under the sway of Muslim rule and the Islamic religion. With these political and religious changes, the Arabic language came to the fore. As was the case with Greek- and Aramaic-speaking Jews in earlier times, the need arose for a Jewish Bible translation into Arabic. Unlike the Septuagint or Targums, however, the version that filled this need was not the product of one or more groups, but rather of a single individual, an extraordinary individual at that, Saadia ben Joseph, who was the Gaon (or head of a rabbinic academy) in early tenth-century Babylonia (for his life, see Malter 1921).

Saadia Gaon, as he is commonly known, was actively involved in the communal affairs of his people and did not shy away from controversy. He, nonetheless, found the time to prepare an Arabic translation of the Hebrew Bible. This text, although in the Arabic language, was probably written with Hebrew characters, making it likely that Saadia's primary audience was his fellow Jews. Saadia sought to present to his contemporaries the unadorned meaning of the Hebrew, as he understood it. In order to accomplish his goal, he was willing to jettison distinctive features of Hebrew grammar and syntax in favor of clear exposition in Arabic. The resultant text achieved a rare balance between elegance and intelligibility (so Margolis 1917: 53–5; Orlinsky and Bratcher 1991: 21–3; Orlinsky 1992: 839). So successful was Saadia that his version, albeit revised several times over the centuries, continues in use among Yemenite Jews to this very day.

For the early modern and modern periods, as for antiquity and the early Middle Ages, my discussion is necessarily selective – reflecting the available evidence, but also my interests and research strengths. This comment arises not so much as an apology, but as an invitation for readers to go beyond the specific examples I provide so as to appreciate more fully the richness of the process I am describing.

Among the European languages we look first at Spanish. Jews, who had fared well on the Iberian Peninsula under Muslim rule, were forced by Christians to leave, culminating in the (in)famous expulsion of 1492. So it was that the most famous and influential Jewish Bible translation into Spanish came not from Spain, but from Italy, specifically the northern city of Ferrara, to which Jews had fled in the late fifteenth and early sixteenth centuries. This Ferrara Bible was first printed in 1553, making use of Hebrew characters (as, e.g., Saadia had done earlier). Its essentially Jewish character is also evident in its close adherence to Hebrew syntax, its transcription of many Hebrew proper names, and its division of the text in accordance with traditional Jewish practice.

But there is more. The Ferrara Bible, which later appeared in Roman script, formed the basis for other Spanish-language Bibles designed for use among the general, that is, non-Jewish populace. It may be thought that certain theologically sensitive passages would require distinctive handling when a Bible originally aimed at a Jewish audience was made widely available to Christians, and vice versa. Indeed, that is frequently the case, as we shall see below. Interestingly enough, such sensitivity does *not* seem to be the reason for there being three different renderings of the Hebrew word *alma* (young woman) at Isaiah 7:14 in various editions of the Ferrara Bible. Although it is tempting to ascribe the rendering 'virgin' to Christian interests and to allocate the translation 'maiden' and the transcription *alma* to Jewish circles, the available evidence simply does not allow for such a neat division (on this and related issues, see Margolis 1917: 62–3; Orlinsky and Bratcher 1991: 122–3; Orlinsky 1992: 839–40).

Jews resided in German-speaking lands from earliest times. Their translation efforts with respect to the Bible can be traced back to the 1200s, when very – one might even say painfully – literal versions appeared, each covering a book or block of the Hebrew Bible. Serviceable at best within the contexts of homes and schools, these texts were devoid of literary merit or charm (for an overview of Jewish translations into German, see Billigheimer 1968).

The efforts of Jacob ben Isaac of Yarnow (in eastern Poland), as published in the mid-1600s, had a far greater impact on subsequent renderings of the biblical text. His work, first known as the *Teutsch Humash*, incorporated an extraordinary amount of extraneous, largely haggadic, material. A single biblical verse of a dozen or so words could be expanded into a creative narrative encompassing dozens of phrases, hundreds of words. The reader of this would naturally come to understand his or her 'Bible' in terms of the augmented picture thus presented. Although we might be reluctant to bestow the title 'translation' on such a paraphrase, this Judeo-German version was not so very different from certain of the freer Aramaic Targums.

Moreover, such embellishments were thought to be especially appropriate for the intended audience of such a work, which is more widely known as the *Tsena Ureena* (a Hebrew phrase from Song of Songs 3:11). This was a 'Women's Bible' (Orlinsky and Bratcher 1991: 125). While this designation may today carry with it feminist overtones, nothing was farther from the minds of those who understood this version, and others, in this manner: men should know the Hebrew Bible in its original language; translations are for women and children, for the home and schools. This understanding of the preferred, if not always actual, audience for Jewish Bible translations persisted well into the twentieth century in some places. By their adopting (and adapting) the practice of Bible translating, virtually all Jewish groups today are united in their recognition of the necessity of this practice – for all segments of their constituencies.

A steady stream of Jewish translations, typically by individual rabbis or printers, continued throughout this period. The foremost accomplishment in German Bible translating, however, came not from Jews, but from the Protestant reformer Martin Luther. His German version of the Old Testament, on which he labored from 1522 to 1534, was a monumental literary, linguistic, and theological achievement, against which all subsequent undertakings would be measured, whether or not they sought such comparisons. Luther's language was forceful; his diction direct. Imbued with a strong sense of the justness of his own (he would have said, the Lord's) cause, he brought the Old, and then the New, Testament to life as a vitalizing force in his efforts to reform Christianity.

When, some two and a half centuries later, the Jewish intellectual Moses Mendelssohn sought to create a new version for his family and for his community, he did not turn his back on all that Luther had accomplished. At the same time, he strongly felt that Jews should not be dependent on Christians and Christological presuppositions. A translation for Jews must be a product of Jews. Something of the same argumentation is evident in the development of English translations, as we shall note shortly.

Mendelssohn had another motive in mind as he crafted his version; namely, that the language and style of his German should conform to the best in general (that is, non-Jewish) German literature of his day. Although others might argue that a simpler form of German was in keeping both with the Semitic original of the Hebrew Bible and with the women and children who required translation in the first place, Mendelssohn viewed such tortured jargon as an impediment to the acceptance of Jews into German society (and to the acceptance of the ideas and ideals of German society by Jews). Among the elites, both Jewish and Christian, to whom Mendelssohn had his greatest appeal, his translation and accompanying commentaries were quite successful. One way to measure this success is by observing that his translation, although for the most part printed in Hebrew characters when first published, soon circulated in German script, with two desirable (from Mendelssohn's perspective) results – German Jews would become more deeply acquainted with the German language, German non-Jews with an 'elevated' version of Judaism (for further details see Margolis 1917: 86–7; Billigheimer 1968).

Throughout the nineteenth century, as successive editions of Mendelssohn appeared, a number of other versions, in German or in Judeo-German, reached what was clearly a growing market. Some of these efforts made extensive use of insights coming out of the new critical schools of biblical interpretation, while at the same time maintaining a distinctively Jewish flavor. Orthodox communities supported versions that adhered to more traditional Jewish sources. As Reform and Orthodox adherents developed rival synagogues and institutions of learning, it seemed natural that the battle would spill over to the Bible, in translated form. Recognizing perhaps in a more positive light than earlier the value of Bible reading and study in the home, several versions were specifically packaged as Family Bibles.

Bible translating by Jews continued up to, and in some cases beyond, the Holocaust. One of the most extraordinary German-language translation projects had its inception in the pre-World War I period and reached completion only in the early 1960s. This version grew out of the very fruitful and original collaboration between two Jewish philosophers, Martin Buber and Franz Rosenzweig. Their philosophy of translation could not be more different from Mendelssohn's. As they worked through the Hebrew Bible, they sought to reflect, to the greatest extent possible for German speakers, its distinctive features in terms of sound, sentence structure, and sensitivity to every nuance of the Original. The result was nothing like nineteenth- or twentieth-century German. It was difficult to read, but worthy of the effort if readers were willing to allow themselves to be transported to another time, to another place, to another culture. If Buber–Rosenzweig sounded foreign, and it did, so much the better, for the (con)text of the Bible was from another, far distant, culture. (The materials collected and translated in Buber–Rosenzweig 1994 provide fascinating insight into the theoretical nature and practical consequences of their approach.)

In this way, readers would be brought to the text (rather than the text to the reader). Buber and Rosenzweig understood this as a singularly Jewish accomplishment, a task to which they wholeheartedly devoted themselves. The society in which Buber and Rosenzweig had begun their work was destroyed, but their legacy remains – not only in reprints of their German version, but in the highly praised English-language Torah recently published by Everett Fox (in the introduction to Fox 1995, Everett Fox explicates his dependence on and independence from his distinguished predecessors; see also Greenstein 1989).

Efforts to interact with mainstream German language, literature, and society were paralleled, if not matched, by the recurrence of versions in Yiddish, intended for those millions of Jews in Europe and North America whose first (or second) language it was. As with Buber–Rosenzweig, perhaps the most notable achievement in this regard came late in the game, as it were. As early as 1910 Solomon Bloomgarden (1870–1927), using the pen name Yehoash, began publishing his version of the Hebrew Bible in Yiddish. Working for the most part in the United States, he continued to perfect his craft and revise his text almost up to the day of his death. Much of his translation was published in serialized form in a Yiddish daily, and it was a decade after his death before his work appeared in its entirety (for Yehoash, see especially Orlinsky 1974: 310–12 and 418–22; also Malachi 1963–4; Orlinsky and Bratcher 1991: 126–7). By that time, of course, what was left of Yiddish-speaking communities in Europe was already destined for destruction. Yehoash's work, thankfully, survives.

Jewish translations of the Bible, as this phrase is commonly and correctly understood, are versions prepared by Jews primarily for the benefit and education of other Jews. We should acknowledge, if only in passing, that some individuals who were born Jews but converted to Christianity prepared translations of the Old Testament to aid in Christian proselytizing of Jews. Thus, there were several Yiddish translations of the Bible – Old and New Testaments – aimed specifically at the Jews of Central and East Europe, as well as those immigrating to the United States (Greenspoon 1998a). In this connection we can also mention Hebrew translations of the New Testament. Those former Jews who took part in such projects, and the Christians who supported them, were undoubtedly motivated by the belief that they were benefiting Jews by making the Good News accessible to them. This view was not, of course, shared by other Jews or by all Christians.

There are many parallels – some deliberate, some by chance – between the history of English- and German-language translations of the Bible by Jews. Jews have lived for a shorter period in the United Kingdom and certainly in North America than in German lands, and their experience in Great Britain has been marked by periods of expulsion and prejudice in addition to eras of acceptance and cooperation. It was during one of the former that the King James or Authorized Version (KJV) of the Bible appeared, in 1611. In many ways, the KJV functions for English speakers as Luther's version does for Germans. It stands not as the first Bible translation into English (as so many people even to this day mistakenly believe), but as the culmination of several centuries of dedicated efforts both in the British Isles and in Europe. Its vocabulary, its turn of phrase, its very format still define for many what the English Bible should look and sound like. Love it or hate it (and indeed emotions about the KJV often run high), no later translator could ignore it.

The influence wielded by the KJV was so great that it influenced Jews as well as Christians. For a century after the mid-1660s, when Jews were again allowed in England, the KJV apparently served their needs on those occasions when they required an English text of the Hebrew Bible. It was not until the late 1770s that the Jews of England had an English Bible of their own – and even here that term may be a bit misleading, since the earliest efforts among Jews consisted of a Hebrew text, facing the KJV, with a sprinkling of notes (in English or in Hebrew) from classical Jewish commentators like Rashi. Soon the Jewish community had access to collections of passages, where the KJV rendering was considered either erroneous or not in keeping with Jewish exegesis. It was not until the 1840s that a complete version of an English Bible by/for Jews appeared (for details on these and later developments, see Hertz 1938 [unfortunately, this article is not widely available]; see also Margolis 1917: 93–105; Orlinsky and Bratcher 1991: 127–44; Orlinsky 1992: 840–2; Greenspoon 1993: 31–8).

The motives leading to these and later developments are complex, and involve factors both internal and external to the Jewish community itself. In this respect, I suggest, activities in England recall (without being identical to) those early efforts in Alexandria with which I began this account of Jewish translations. The Jews of England, with their center in London, were clearly becoming more and more comfortable with the English language in their personal as well as professional lives. There were considerable numbers of Jews from both German (Yiddish)- and Spanish-speaking lands; both groups established extensive synagogue and social structures to serve the needs of their constituents. By the early 1800s prayer books that included at least some English and some sermons in English were regular features of many synagogues throughout London. In this context, editions of the Bible that incorporated both Hebrew and English (even if the English text was virtually identical to the KJV) made sense (Greenspoon forthcoming).

At the same time (i.e., the early 1800s), missionary groups aimed specifically at converting Jews to Christianity (primarily, Protestant Christianity) were founded and quickly gained the financial support and social status associated with 'causes' favored by many of the elite. The London Society for Promoting Christianity Among the Jews, often referred to simply as the London Jews Society, was the most prominent, but certainly not the only example, of such groups. The British and Foreign Bible Society, founded in 1804, was not a missionary enterprise, but did serve the cause of missionaries by making huge numbers of Bibles, including translations into Yiddish and other languages aimed at Jews (see also above), available at low cost

(Greenspoon 1998a). Jewish efforts to produce Bible translations *of their own* were undoubtedly in part a reaction to the often fever-pitched proselytizing they experienced (for some details, see Greenspoon 1998b).

Nonetheless, it took a while, in fact about a half century, before the leadership of English Jewry grasped the potential value of English-language versions of the Bible. By and large, the earlier texts had been produced by those on the periphery of organized Judaism or even in opposition to its leadership. But, by the mid-1800s, this had all changed. Several Jewish versions trumpeted the sanction/approval of the Chief Rabbi himself on their title pages. Interestingly enough, this phenomenon demonstrates that there is something equivalent to 'authorized' versions among at least some Jews – but with a most significant difference *vis-à-vis* Protestant Christianity. Christian Bibles, most prominently the KJV and certain of its successors, were authorized for use in church. The 'authority' bestowed on Jewish translations was specifically located in the home and the classroom. This accords with the phenomenon we observed in connection with German Bibles that emphasized the role of Jewish women and children as primary users of translated Bibles. But, as was also the case among German speakers, the make-up of potential audiences for English Bibles was soon expanded through the designation of some as Family Bibles and the sponsorship of others by prominent community-wide organizations like the Jewish Publication Society of America (to which we turn shortly).

A few further observations are in order concerning these English-language versions. Throughout the nineteenth century and especially during the first decades of the twentieth, we can observe growing dissatisfaction with the KJV on the part of some Christians. Fresh translations, some embodying an appeal to more up-to-date vocabulary and grammar, began to appear, alongside increasingly extensive KJV revisions. By and large, the Jewish community stuck with the basic KJV style and format well into the middle of the twentieth century, which was long after its abandonment by many Christians. Some might attribute this conservatism, if you will, to an effort on the part of Jews to be 'more English than the English,' and indeed the established leadership of British Jewry rarely sought to rock the boat. On the other hand, many of the KJV's distinctive features were the result of careful study of the Hebrew text and of classical Jewish sources, especially David Kimchi. A century earlier, as Luther worked on his German Old Testament, he had access to Rashi. In this way, then, both the KJV and Luther, although clearly not Jewish Bibles, do transmit Jewish exegesis (Margolis 1917 *passim*; Orlinsky 1990; Orlinksy and Bratcher 1991 *passim*; Greenspoon 1993: 26–31).

The figure of Luther or of Jerome, each of whom dominated if they did not entirely translate *their* version, recalls the similar identification of most English- and German-language Jewish translations with an individual or a pair of individuals. This does not suggest, at least not uniformly, a lack of communal support, but does contrast with the translation-by-committee that resulted in the KJV and its successors/revisions (the RV, RSV, NRSV, NASB, among others) and, on the Jewish side, the LXX and Targums, so far as we can reconstruct their origins.

The number of English versions produced in the nineteenth century by America's Jews was considerably smaller than those produced in Great Britain, not surprisingly given the relatively lower number of Jews resident there prior to the great immigrations of the 1880s and following decades. It is perhaps surprising that, despite the smaller numbers (of Jews and of Jewish versions), the most distinctive and distinguished nineteenth-century Jewish translation into English emanates from the United States (for an overview, see Sarna and Sarna 1988; Sarna 1989). This was the work of one individual, Isaac Leeser, who published his Torah in the mid-1840s, followed approximately a decade later by his version of the whole Hebrew Bible, which was frequently republished over the next seven decades and served as *the* English Bible for almost all Jews in North America and many in Europe. Leeser recalls Saadia Gaon, in that he was actively involved in all aspects of contemporary communal affairs. Like Saadia, he was in many ways the leading Jew of his day (in addition to sources cited above, see Sussman 1985). Unlike Saadia, however, whose version garnered almost unanimous praise and is still in use, Leeser's translation, although gaining the support of many, did have its detractors – and a much briefer 'shelf life' than Saadia's.

By the end of the nineteenth century, the Jewish community of the United States had grown in organizational sophistication to the point that it could support an important publishing operation, the Jewish Publication Society (JPS). It was under its aegis that a group gathered in the early 1910s, under the leadership of Max L. Margolis, to prepare what amounted to Leeser's successor. In practice, this committee but lightly revised the Revised Version of 1885, which itself constituted the first major revision of the KJV. Christological interpretations were expunged, and Jewish exegesis found its way into the text. But overall this JPS version, which initially appeared in 1917, looked and sounded very much like the KJV. This especially suited Margolis who, himself an immigrant from Eastern Europe, firmly believed that the stately, if decidedly dated, diction and style associated with the KJV offered to his fellow immigrants the very best possible exemplar for 'proper' English usage. Margolis, who was a superb scholar, clearly knew of the earlier efforts of Mendelssohn, and consciously fashioned himself, and his version, in that mold (see further Margolis 1917: 99–105, 115–6; Greenspoon 1987: 55–75; 1988, 1990; Sarna 1989: 104–16). This also served the purposes of the Jewish establishment that financed and in general supported this JPS effort.

Like Leeser, the JPS 1917 served English-speaking Jews for about half a century. Its place, in turn, has been taken by a new JPS Bible translation, under the general editorship of Harry M. Orlinsky. Begun in the 1950s, the full *TANAKH* (as it is titled) first appeared in the mid-1980s. It has been frequently reprinted and repackaged in a variety of formats and editions. This New Jewish Version marks a distinct departure from almost all earlier English-language versions for Jews, in that it consciously abandons the KJV's more literal approach for the dynamic or functional equivalence also favored by such contemporary non-Jewish projects as the Good News Bible and the Contemporary English Version (on this translation, see several chapters in Orlinsky 1974, 1969; Sarna 1989: 233–47; Greenstein 1990; Orlinsky and Bratcher 1991: 179–91).

Among Christians, especially Protestants, the post-World War II period has seen the proliferation, some might say explosion, of new, often competing English-language Bibles. Moreover, many of these, and in particular the New International Version, offer their text in an almost endless variety of packages aimed at increasingly specific markets (e.g., recent widows, teenaged virgins, recovering alcoholics). The market for Jewish Bible translations is naturally smaller, and parallel developments within it are correspondingly fewer in number and in scope. But it is not clear that, at the end of the twentieth century, there is a dominant Jewish Bible translation in English – as there was at that century's beginning (among recent versions and editions are Kaplan 1981; *TANAKH* 1985; Plaut 1991; Fox 1995; Plaut 1996; *The Tanach* 1996).

There are many factors – theological, literary, social, even fiscal – that promote the production of Bible translations in today's society. The number of factors and of translations and the immediacy and scope of their influence are unprecedented. But the questions they raise and, by and large, the answers that come to mind are at least as old as the oldest Bible translation. What is it that makes a translation Jewish (see Greenstein 1989, 1990)? Can/should a Jewish translation of the Bible ever be conceived as more than a complement to the Hebrew Original? Who in the end, if anyone, can determine which translation is good/better/best for Jews and in what contexts? It is difficult, if not impossible, to predict developments even for the next few decades. The Bible, in its original languages and in translation, has unique potential to unify or to divide. At their best, Jewish Bible translations will – I hope – continue to serve the needs of their communities, whose very nature and make-up they themselves will influence.

ACKNOWLEDGEMENT

Frederick E. Greenspahn (of the University of Denver) very kindly provided me with a prepublication draft of his chapter on Jewish Bible Translations. He also took the time to read through a draft of this chapter. To him I am deeply indebted. Alas, I must take full responsibility for whatever inaccuracies or infelicities my work may still contain.

BIBLIOGRAPHY

Ackroyd, P. R., Lampe G. W. H. and Greenslade, S. L. (eds) (1963–70) *The Cambridge History of the Bible*, Cambridge: Cambridge University Press.

Alexander, P. S. (1992) 'Targum, Targumim,' in Freedman, D. N. (ed.) *Anchor Bible Dictionary*, Vol. 6, Garden City, N.Y.: Doubleday.

Archer, G. L. and Chirichigno, G. (1983) *Old Testament Quotations in the New Testament: A Complete Survey*, Chicago: Moody.

Barr, J. (1994) 'Paul and the LXX: A Note on Some Recent Work,' *Journal of Theological Studies*, 45: 593–601.

Beattie, D. R. G. and McNamara, M. J. (eds) (1994) *The Aramaic Bible: Targums in Their Historical Context*, Sheffield, JSOT Press.

Billigheimer, S. (1968) 'On Jewish Translations of the Bible in Germany,' *Abr-Nahrain*, 7: 1–34.

Buber, M. and Rosenzweig. F. (1994) *Scripture and Translation* (ET), Bloomington: Indiana University Press.

Davies W. D. and Finkelstein, L. (eds) (1984–) *The Cambridge History of Judaism*, Cambridge: Cambridge University Press.

Fox, E. (1995) *The Schocken Bible.* Vol. 1: *The Five Books of Moses. A New Translation with Introductions, Commentary, and Notes,* New York: Schocken [earlier versions of Genesis and Exodus also appeared].

Greenspoon, L. J. (1987) *Max Leopold Margolis: A Scholar's Scholar,* Atlanta: Scholars Press.

—— (1988) 'A Book "Without Blemish": The Jewish Publication Society's Bible Translation of 1917,' *Jewish Quarterly Review,* 79: 1–21.

—— (1989) 'Truth and Legend about the Creation of the Septuagint, the First Bible Translation,' *Bible Review,* 5: 34–41.

—— (1990) 'On the Jewishness of Modern Jewish Bible Scholarship: The Case of Max L. Margolis,' *Judaism,* 39: 82–92.

—— (1992) 'Aquila,' 'Symmachus,' 'Theodotion,' and 'Versions, ancient (Greek),' in Freedman, D. N. (ed.) *Anchor Bible Dictionary,* Vols 1 and 6, Garden City, N.Y.: Doubleday.

—— (1993) 'From the Septuagint to the New Revised Standard Version: A Brief Account of Jewish Involvement in Bible Translating and Translations,' in M. I. Gruber (ed.) *The Solomon Goldman Lectures,* Vol. 6, Chicago: Spertus College of Judaica Press.

—— (1998a) 'Bringing Home the Gospel: Yiddish Bibles, Bible Societies, and the Jews,' in Greenspoon, L. J. (ed.) *Yiddish Language and Culture: Then and Now. Proceedings of the Ninth Annual Symposium of the Philip M. and Ethel Klutznick Chair in Jewish Civilization (October 27–28, 1996),* Omaha: Creighton University Press.

—— (1998b) 'Traditional Text, Contemporary Contexts: English-Language Scriptures for Jews and the History of Bible Translating,' in *Interpretation of the Bible,* Sheffield: Sheffield Academic Press.

—— (forthcoming) 'Jewish Translations of the Bible,' in Brettler, M. and Berlin, A. (eds) *Jewish Study Bible,* New York: Oxford University Press.

Greenstein, E. (1989) *Essays on Biblical Method and Translation,* Atlanta: Scholars Press.

—— (1990) 'What Might Make a Bible Translation Jewish?' in *Translation and Scripture: Proceedings of a Conference at the Annenberg Research Institute May 14–16, 1989,* Philadelphia: Annenberg Research Institute.

Hertz, J. H. (1938) 'Jewish Translations of the Bible in English [the concluding lecture in the series "Translations of the Bible," Toynbee Hall, 1919],' in *Sermons, Addresses and Studies.* Vol. 2: *Addresses,* London: Soncino.

Hertz, J. H. (ed.) (1961) *The Pentateuch and Haftorahs,* London: Soncino.

Kaplan, A. (1981) *The Living Torah: The Five Books of Moses* (2nd edn), New York: Maznaim [subsequent volumes incorporate Kaplan's insights and principles].

Lange, N. de (1995) *Greek Jewish Texts from the Cairo Genizah,* Tübingen, Mohr (Paul Siebeck).

Lim, T. H. (1997) *Holy Scripture in the Qumran Commentaries and Pauline Letters,* Oxford: Oxford University Press.

Malachi, A. R. (1963–4) 'Yiddish Translations of the Bible [in Yiddish],' *Jewish Book Annual,* 21: 22–41.

Malter, H. (1921) *Saadia Gaon, His Life and Works,* Philadelphia: Jewish Publication Society of America.

Margolis, M. L. (1917) *The Story of Bible Translations,* Philadelphia: Jewish Publication Society of America.

Mulder, M. J. (ed.) (1988) *Mikra,* Philadelphia: Fortress.

Orlinsky, H. M. (ed.) (1969) *Notes on the New Translation of the Torah,* Philadelphia: Jewish Publication Society of America.

—— (1974) *Essays in Biblical Culture and Bible Translation,* New York: Ktav.

—— (1975) 'The Septuagint as Sacred Writ and the Philosophy of the Translators,' *Hebrew Union College Annual,* 46: 89–114.

—— (1990) 'The Role of Theology in the Christian Mistranslation of the Hebrew Bible', in *Translation and Scripture: Proceedings of a Conference at the Annenberg Research Institute May 14–16, 1989*, Philadelphia: Annenberg Research Institute.

—— (1992) 'Versions, Jewish,' in Freedman, D. N. (ed.) *Anchor Bible Dictionary*, Vol. 6, Garden City, N.Y. Doubleday.

Orlinsky, H. M. and Bratcher, R. G. (1991) *A History of Bible Translation and the North American Contribution*, Atlanta: Scholars Press.

Peters, M. K. H. (1992) 'Septuagint,' in Freedman, D. N. (ed.) *Anchor Bible Dictionary*, Vol. 5, Garden City, N.Y.: Doubleday.

Plaut, W. G. (ed.) (1991) *The Torah: A Modern Commentary*, New York: Union of American Hebrew Congregations.

—— (ed.) (1996) *The Haftorah Commentary*, New York: Union of American Hebrew Congregations.

Sarna, J. D. (1989) *JPS: The Americanization of Jewish Culture 1888–1988*, Philadelphia: Jewish Publication Society of America.

Sarna, J. D. and Sarna, N. (1988) 'Jewish Bible Scholarship and Translations in the United States,' in Frerichs, E. S. (ed.) *The Bible and Bibles in America*, Atlanta: Scholars Press.

Shutt, R. J. H. (1985) 'Letter of Aristeas (A New Translation and Introduction),' in Charlesworth, J. H. (ed.) *The Old Testament Pseudepigrapha*, Vol. 2, Garden City, N.Y.: Doubleday.

Sussman, L. J. (1985) 'Another Look at Isaac Leeser and the First Jewish Translation of the Bible in the United States,' *Modern Judaism*, 5: 159–90.

TANAKH (1985) *A New Translation of THE HOLY SCRIPTURES According to the Traditional Hebrew Text*, Philadelphia: Jewish Publication Society of America [this is the first edition of the entire text, containing revisions from earlier publications of the Torah, the Prophets, and the Writings].

The Tanach (1996) The ArtScroll Series/Stone Edition, Brooklyn, N.Y.: Mesorah [this text incorporates in revised form earlier editions as well as new material].

Tov, E. (1997) *The Text-Critical Use of the Septuagint in Biblical Research*, Jerusalem: Simor.

VanderKam, J. C. (1994) *The Dead Sea Scrolls Today,* Grand Rapids: Eerdmans.

CHRISTIAN BIBLE TRANSLATION

——·◆·——

Henry Wansbrough

It would be impossible in the short space of this chapter to consider translations into every language. There are still languages into which the Bible is being translated for the first time. Since this book is being published in English the concentration will be on the formation of the English Bible. But the English Bible cannot be understood without a previous consideration of the Latin translation of the Bible that for over a millennium constituted the Bible of western civilization, and which was the basis of all early translations. Secondly, I shall outline early attempts, up to the Renaissance and Reformation, to render the Bible into the vernacular. Thirdly, I shall consider the genesis in the fifteenth century of the first complete vernacular Bibles, to which so much of our culture since then is indebted. Finally, modern English translations of the Bible and the spread of modern translations of the Bible will be surveyed.

THE LATIN VULGATE

From the time of Constantine's acceptance of Christianity (symbolically dated from the Battle of the Milvian Bridge in 313 CE) till the Reformation in the fifteenth century, Christianity, and a Latin Christianity at that, was increasingly the dominant culture of western Europe. Latin was the language of law, science, politics, literature and religion, and in general of all civilized written intercourse. Myriad quotations and allusions throughout this period refer back to the Latin version, which became known as the Vulgate, that is, diffused or common, Bible. The dominant position it had held for many centuries was confirmed by the pronouncement of the Council of Trent in 1546 that it should be considered the authentic version of the Bible. In the Roman Catholic Church it has retained this position. To this day it is still used in the Latin liturgy celebrated on international Church occasions.

    This great version of the Bible was essentially the work of one man, Jerome. Jerome had been born in the Roman province of Dalmatia and had been meticulously trained in the classics, to the extent that he once dreamed that he was being divinely rebuked, 'You are not a Christian but a Ciceronian' (*Letter* 22.30). Before his time a scatter of Latin versions had existed. In 382 CE Pope Damasus commissioned Jerome to work on the text of the gospels, and to decide which of the many versions agreed with the original Greek (*Praef. in Quattuor Evangelia*). The first translations of the Greek Bible into the Latin of the west had been made in Africa and western Europe in the second century. Two centuries later there were 'almost as many forms of the text as there are copies', says Jerome. Jerome now set about revising the gospels. He claims to have revised 'the New Testament', but this revision does not seem to have included the whole of the New Testament. It is doubtful whether the version incorporated in the Vulgate of the Acts, the New Testament letters and the book of Revelation stems from Jerome; he certainly quotes a version of the letter of James that differs widely from the Vulgate version. In his commentaries on several of Paul's letters he criticizes details of the text on which he is commenting, and ascribes it freely to other translators. He rightly predicts that his revision would be greeted with anger by those who preferred the familiar versions, even if they were incorrect. His reply to his critics is characteristically both abusive and exact, pointing out how much superior are the readings he adopts (*Letter* 27).

It was only after the death of his patron Pope Damasus, and Jerome's departure from Rome to take up residence in Bethlehem, that he embarked upon a revision of the Old Testament. At this time the Bible of Christianity was the Greek Septuagint, to the entire neglect of the Hebrew Bible. It did not seem to occur to anyone, even to Jerome himself, that the Hebrew should be consulted. At first Jerome worked on his Greek version of the Bible, following the great Greek biblical scholar Origen. He made a second revision of the Psalter (the first, made at Rome, is entirely lost), basing himself still on the Old Latin version, but also using Origen's text and his own knowledge of Hebrew. This was the version of the Psalms that was to be used throughout the Christian west for over 1,500 years.

Gradually, however, he became more and more aware of the limitations of the Septuagint. The Greek (and Latin versions that depended on it) lacked the literary merit of the original Hebrew. Furthermore, the differences between the various Greek versions made it essential for accuracy to return to what Jerome came to call the 'Hebrew truth'. One very important factor for him seems to have been controversy with the Jews, who scoffed at the inaccuracy of the scriptures used by Christians. He had long ago confronted the task of learning Hebrew ('How often I despaired; how often I gave up and in my eagerness to learn started again', *Letter* 125.12), and also acquired some knowledge of Aramaic and Syriac. Such a return to the Hebrew was nothing short of revolutionary, but Jerome was daunted neither by the unpopularity such a return would inevitably incur in traditionalist circles, nor by the warning of Augustine of Hippo that it would create a split between Latin Christianity and the Greek-speaking east. Augustine warns Jerome that the unfamiliarity of his new translation of Jonah occasioned such a riot at Oea in Tripoli that the bishop felt obliged to appeal to some local Jews for arbitration. And they, 'whether from ignorance or from spite', supported the old translation (Augustine, *Letter* 71:3–5)! Jerome's prefaces to his translations of different books of the Old Testament reflect the controversy and outrage that his return to the Hebrew aroused.

Jerome's methods and the care he devoted to each book differed considerably. He worked on the Old Testament for some 15 years, but he claims to have produced the three books of Proverbs, Ecclesiastes and Song of Songs in three days (*Praefatio in Libr. Sal.*). The short books of Tobit and Judith he considered to be of less importance since they were apocryphal. He co-opted the best scholar of Hebrew and Aramaic he could find, and seems to have been content with an oral running translation, for he says he 'gave to the subject one day's hasty labour, my method being to explain in Latin, with the aid of a secretary, whatever an interpreter expressed to me in Hebrew' (*Prefatio*).

Two general characteristics of this great translation should be noted. Firstly, Jerome is well aware of the need for the translator to tread the tightrope between slavish literalism and paraphrase; several of his letters discuss the problem (e.g. *Letters* 57, 99). In one of his letters he avers that there is a 'mystery' even in the order of the words. By this he means that even the order of words has religious significance. Reverence for the actual words of the sacred text is one of the marks of Jerome's work, and in some books (e.g. the Psalter) the flow of the Latin is undoubtedly sacrificed to a doggedly literal reproduction of the Hebrew words and constructions. The first books translated, Samuel and Kings, are considerably more literal than the final books; in the preface to Samuel and Kings he vigorously defends the literalness of the translation. On the other hand Judges, one of the last books, is not far from being a paraphrase. Secondly, in the matter of style he was perfectly capable of flights of high rhetoric, but in his translation he deliberately avoids them: 'A version made for the use of the Church', he writes, 'even though it may possess a literary charm, ought to disguise it and avoid it so far as possible, in order that it may not speak to the idle schools and few disciples of the philosophers, but may address itself rather to the entire human race' (*Letter* 49.4). The translations are deliberately straightforward, retaining the bone-structure of the original Hebrew. This is the secret of the quiet dignity and lasting quality of his translation and of the distinctively Christian Latin he created.

The Vulgate later came to be regarded as one single book; this was not the case from the beginning. Just as Jerome produced them individually, so the biblical books often circulated independently. Cassiodorus (d. 580) already mentions a collection of all the books of the Bible in Jerome's translation (*Institutiones* 1.12.3), but the earliest manuscript we possess of the collection that became the standard Latin Vulgate is the *Codex Amiatinus*. Jerome's text was brought from Rome to Northumbrian monasteries, the furthest outpost of the Christian world, and transcribed into this Codex in the monasteries of Wearmouth and Jarrow under the direction of Abbot Ceolfrid. This is an immense and valuable book (famously described by one researcher as the weight of a full-grown female Great Dane), and was taken by him to Rome for presentation to Pope Gregory II in 716. It consists of the following books in the 'Vulgate' translation:

1. The books of the Jewish Bible, translated from the Hebrew.
2. The 'Gallican' Psalter, revised from the Old Latin with some use of Hebrew.
3. Tobit and Judith, translated from the Aramaic (which Jerome called 'Chaldean').
4. Wisdom, Ecclesiasticus, 1–2 Maccabees, Baruch, unrevised from the Old Latin.
5. The gospels in Jerome's early revision of the Old Latin.
6. The remainder of the New Testament, by unknown translators.

This was the Bible, largely but not wholly the work of Jerome, universally accepted by western Christianity until the end of the Middle Ages.

MEDIEVAL TRANSLATIONS

Medieval Europe was dominated linguistically by Latin, at any rate for the latter half of the first millennium. Latin was the language of courts, schools, the Church, indeed of civilized intercourse everywhere. King Alfred, as a sign of lack of education in England, instances the inability of the clergy to write in Latin. In his preface to the translation of Gregory's *Cura Pastoralis* he writes that there are few south of the Humber who could translate a letter from Latin into English, and not many beyond the Humber. 'There were so few that I cannot think of a single one south of the Thames when I came to the throne.' Nevertheless it was unthinkable that there should be any sort of official version of the Bible in any language other than Latin, the language of the Church and of all its liturgy. Lack of understanding of the text of the Bible was supplemented by the living voice of Church teaching and by the luxuriant representation of biblical scenes in art, poetry and (later) drama. Translations were either helps for the ignorant or tools of instruction; there was never a suggestion that they should take the place of the official Latin text. It was only at the end of this period that the dominance thus given to the official teaching of the Church was felt to be a stranglehold, and independent access for all to the actual text of the Bible was perceived to be important. This was often associated with a heretical questioning of the Church's official teaching. Only a few illustrations of this, drawn from different parts of Europe, may be offered.

England

The tradition of paraphrase of the text, rather than translation, is enshrined in the poem of Caedmon and *The Dream of the Rood*. Bede recounts (*Hist. Eccl.* 5.24) how Caedmon, an unlettered labourer at the monastery of Whitby, was commanded in a dream to sing of the creation. His nine-line poem, marked by the strong rhythm and alliteration of Old English poetry, is, of course, derived from the account in Genesis; it is not in any sense a translation. The anonymous *Dream of the Rood* is another, longer (some 150 lines), triumphant masterpiece of Old English, in which the tree of the cross sings of its experience in bearing the warrior Saviour, a scintillating application of the Anglo-Saxon heroic tradition to the biblical story.

Besides these there is some mention of genuine translations. Bede on his deathbed in 735 is said to have completed his translation of the gospel of John, though Cuthbert says explicitly only that he translated the first six chapters; in any case none of this survives. William of Malmesbury tells that some two centuries later King Alfred translated the first part of the Psalter. The Anglo-Saxon prose translation of Psalms 1–50 in the *Paris Psalter* may represent his work.

Nevertheless there does not seem to have been any extensive translation of the Bible at this period. It was not until Aelfric of Winchester in 1010 that significant progress was made. In his preface to *Genesis* Aelfric writes of his reluctance to translate because of the danger of misunderstanding by the foolish. Here already is the attitude that for many centuries deprived the unlearned of the biblical text. Aelfric claims to be writing no more than the bare narrative, but his work must in fact have been a paraphrase, for he compressed the whole text of the four 'books of Kings' into one homily. Progress towards a real translation comes in interlinear glosses rather than in independent translations of biblical material: over the marvellous Latin text of the Lindisfarne Gospels (written before 700) a ninth or tenth-century scribe has written the word-for-word equivalent in the Northumbrian dialect. A similar gloss on the gospel of Matthew exists in the Old Mercian dialect. An early copy of this was given to Exeter Cathedral by Bishop Leofric (d. 1072). These may well be the earliest extant exemplars of a translation of the whole gospel into any vernacular language.

The Norman culture was sternly Latinate, without a vernacular culture, so that after the Norman Conquest English as a cultural medium went into a period of decline, from which it did not begin to emerge again until Chaucer gave it renewed literary standing. From the theological point of view the increasing sophistication of theology made theological thinking less and less accessible to laypeople. More and more it became the province of a group of clerical and university experts for whom knowledge of Latin was only one of the entry qualifications. This viewpoint is clear in the continuator of Knighton's *Chronicle* who wrote, soon after Wyclif's death, of 'the gospel that Christ gave to the clergy and doctors of the Church', complaining that by translation 'the pearl of the gospel is scattered abroad and trodden underfoot by swine'. Possession of a copy of a translation of scripture amounted almost to presumption of heresy, though special permission to own a copy was given to some pious laypeople, such as Anne of Bohemia, wife of Richard II, who died in 1394.

In England, particularly, suspicion that translation of the Bible carried the taint of heresy became deeper as a result of Wyclif and Lollardy, and indeed direct reliance on scripture was among the basic presuppositions of Wyclif's efforts to free the people from the tyranny of Church authority. Wyclif does not seem to have been responsible personally for the translations, although Jan Hus maintained that 'it is said that Wyclif translated the whole Bible from Latin into English'. There exists, however, a group of over 100 manuscripts of English translations, in at least five different hands (and showing some variation of dialect) from the late fourteenth and early fifteenth centuries that clearly belong to this movement. The only name mentioned in the text as a translator is that of Nicholas of Hereford, who was certainly a follower of Wyclif, and was condemned with him at Oxford in 1382 (he subsequently recanted, and retired to a Carthusian monastery in 1417).

These translations can be subdivided into two groups, one of which is more literal, the other more free, readable and idiomatic. The latter version has been tentatively attributed to John Purvey (by Henry Hargreaves in Evans, Lampe and Greenslade 1963–70, 2: 410). It is significant that, just as Jerome earlier complained of the variety and corruption of the readings given in the Old Latin version, now the translator (in his *General Prologue*) complains of the need for correction in the common Latin Bibles available to him. The spread of these manuscripts shows that these translations were popular, perhaps as the only English versions available. Despite the prohibition (in the 1407 Constitutions of Oxford) of the translation of scripture into English 'whether in the time of John Wyclif or since' unless it is approved by the diocesan, they survived well into the sixteenth century, thought they were never diffused by the new invention of printing. In 1529 Sir Thomas More may well be referring to these two groups of manuscripts when he differentiates between on the one hand the translation of the 'great arch-heretic Wyclif' who 'purposely corrupted the holy text' and on the other 'Bibles fair and old written in English which have been known and seen by the bishop of the diocese'.

Germany

The situation in England has its parallels also in German-speaking lands. Here translation seems to have occurred first as a means of study. The psalms were the stuff of Christian prayer, sung daily in countless religious communities; it was therefore important that the beginner should understand them. Just as the Psalter was the first part of the Bible translated into Anglo-Saxon, so the monk and teacher Notker Labeo of Sankt Gallen made an interlinear gloss of the Psalter into German about 1000. Other translations of the Psalter in the Benedictine monastic schools were probably associated with the schooling of novices (e.g. as suggested by fragments already from the ninth century in the Abbey of Reichenau). Similarly in the twelfth century such fragmentary translations, whose exact rendering of the Latin words suggests school use, have been found in convents of Dominican sisters and Cistercians. An important new step was taken in the fourteenth century in the great work of Marchwart Biberli (*c.* 1265–1330), the Dominican Lector of Zurich, who translated first the Psalter and then the whole Bible. His work is both exact and poetic, though his aims were primarily devotional and educational. His care was principally for students and religious in Zurich itself, and copies appear only in the Zurich area until 1360. His work never benefited from the new invention of printing, though it was widely diffused by the workshop of Diebolt Laubers from *c.* 1440.

Eastern Europe

Christianity was brought to the Slav countries (more specifically Moravia or, in more recent nomenclature, Poland, Hungary and Czechoslovakia) from Constantinople by the brothers Cyruil and Methodius. They saw the importance of translation into the vernacular. There was as yet no writing or alphabet, and they immediately set about forming the alphabet now called Glagolitic or Cyrillic. In the teeth of opposition from the episcopate to the west of them, in Bavaria, they succeeded in obtaining permission in 869 from Pope Hadrian II to celebrate the liturgy in Slavonic; the scriptural readings were to be proclaimed first in Latin, then in Slavonic. So, while in western Europe Bible translation originated as an educational help, in eastern Europe the origin of translation of the Bible into Slavonic was liturgical.

The *Vita Constantini* (Cyril's original name was Constantine) says that he began to write the gospels down in Slavonic with the first verse of John, but modern opinion (Metzger 1977: p 401) is that this was more probably only a homily on John 1.1. According to the *Vita Methodii* Methodius translated the whole Bible into Slavonic in the six months March to October 884. Again, it is hard to envisage that he completed this vast task in so short a time, and these were probably only liturgical extracts; in any case, the translation is not extant. A century later, however, the *Codex Zographensis* does contain the four gospels in Glagolitic script. The full translation of the Bible into Church Slavonic had to wait for the work of Archbishop Gennadius of Novgorod, shortly before 1500.

RENAISSANCE AND REFORMATION

In the early sixteenth century two new factors became operative, the new learning and the new theology. The rediscovery of the classical languages had gathered pace in Italy during the fifteenth century, and soon spread to northern Europe. This included Hebrew as well as Greek. In Italy Hebrew Bibles had been printed as early as 1480. In Spain a professor of Hebrew had been appointed in 1508, and by 1517 the Complutensian Polyglot Bible (including a Hebrew text and analysis) was published. In 1506 Reuchlin's Hebrew grammar, *De Rudimentis Hebraicis*, was published in Germany. England hung a little behind. When John Fisher founded St John's College, Cambridge, in 1511, he provided that Hebrew as well as Greek should be studied there, and in 1524 a Hebrew lecturer was appointed, in the person of Robert Wakefield. In 1519 Erasmus was writing to the President of Corpus Christi College, Oxford (with typical flattery), that Corpus was *inter praecipua decora Britanniae* on account of its *bibliotheca trilinguis* (1982, *Letter* 990). On the other hand, just how far Oxford was lagging behind shows from the fact that in the 1537 catalogue of the College library, Reuchlin is still the only Hebrew book mentioned.

The study of Greek also proceeded apace, and monastic students of Magdalene College, Cambridge, were embellishing the walls with Greek graffiti before 1500. The enormously significant event was the publication in 1516 of Erasmus's hastily edited first printed edition of the New Testament. In some ecclesiastical circles, for whom the Vulgate provided a sufficient Bible, it was greeted with a puzzled lack of enthusiasm; but this and its extensive revisions would provide a means of significant advance.

The second factor affecting translation of the Bible was the new theology. The provision of a vernacular text of the Bible was seen by the Protestant reformers as a vital factor in the liberation of the Christian message from the thrall of ecclesiastical tyranny. Erasmus (who never committed himself to the reform) wrote in the preface to the first edition of his Greek New Testament, 'I could wish even all women to read the gospel and the epistles of Paul, and that the farmer may sing parts of them at his work, and the weaver may chant them when engaged at his shuttle and the traveller with their stories beguile the weariness of the journey.' About the same time and in the same vein (perhaps even with conscious reminiscence) occurred the famous conversation of William Tyndale, quoted in Foxe's *Book of Martyrs*:

> Master Tyndale happened to be in the company of a certain divine, recounted for a learned man, and in communing and disputing with him he drave him to that issue, that the said great doctor burst out into these blasphemous words, and said, 'We were better to be without God's laws than the pope's.' Master Tyndale, hearing this, full of godly zeal and not bearing that blasphemous saying, replied again and said, 'I defy the pope and all his laws', and further added that, if God spared him life, ere many years he would cause the boy that driveth the plough to know more of scripture than he did.

Germany

Martin Luther had the advantages and impetus of both these factors. He early made use of the advance in classical learning. His lectures on Romans in 1515/16 reflect knowledge of Greek and those on the letter to the Hebrews in 1517/18 knowledge of Hebrew. So already in 1522 he published a New Testament, which he had worked from Erasmus's Greek with the advice of Philipp Melanchthon, one of the most distinguished Greek scholars of the Renaissance, and professor of Greek at Wittenberg. In the following year he made a start on the Old Testament, with the Pentateuch. His Bible was not finished until 1534; its effect was immediate and striking. The desire for such a translation is shown by the whirlwind spread of the work: within three years the New Testament had been translated into Dutch, Danish and Swedish. It has been calculated that by 1533 on average one in every ten German households possessed a copy of his New Testament. The Catholic reaction is also indicative of the grip Luther's work immediately exerted, for in quick succession Catholic translations by Emser (1527), Dietenberger (1527) and Eck (1537) appeared, though in fact they were heavily dependent on Luther's own translation. Now for the first time the Bible became part of the German literary heritage. The cadences, rhythms and vocabulary of Luther's Bible became part not only of German Protestantism but also of the whole linguistic treasury.

England

In England the crucial work of translating the Bible was initiated by William Tyndale. In 1522 he offered his services as a translator to Bishop Tunstall of London but was turned away on the grounds that the bishop had no place for him in his household. Soon afterwards he emigrated to Flanders, and there set about his work of translating. After a mere two years, in 1526 his first New Testament, translated from the Greek (a revised version was published in 1534), arrived in England. As it reached the docks it was seized by the Bishop of London and burnt.

Enough copies got through to make further action necessary, and in 1528 Tunstall commissioned the learned Thomas More, himself a humanist and friend of Erasmus, to counter-attack. This More did in his *Dialogue Concerning Heresies*, which appeared in June 1529. More characterized Tynedale variously as 'a hell-hound in the kennel of the devil' and 'a drowsy drudge drinking deep in the devil's dregs' (Daniell 1994: 277). More's animosity was surely aroused chiefly by Tyndale's theological glosses rather than by the translation itself, for they were polemically Lutheran. On the surface, however, More's objection was to terms used by Tyndale to avoid what he called 'juggled and feigned terms', Latinate terms, which for More represented the hallowed legacy of Christendom. Thus for 'priest' Tyndale read 'elder' (or 'senior'), for 'charity', 'love', for 'grace', 'favour', for 'penance', 'repentance'.

Nothing daunted, Tyndale set about working on the Old Testament too, and in 1530 the first five books were completed. Two elements combined to make this translation the unique work that it is. The first is Tyndale's extraordinary grasp of language and his determination to make the text both readable and intelligible, the second his knowledge and use of Hebrew.

The dominant characteristics of Tyndale's translation are an incomparable freshness and directness, so that the debt of the English language to Tyndale is immense. His achievement cannot be analysed here in detail. The reader can only be encouraged to compare the accounts of the Creation and the Fall in Genesis 1–3 with the Wyclifite version to see its genius. Indeed from many points of view subsequent versions have failed to improve on it at all. Tyndale's rhythms still haunt the language, 'Not unto us, O Lord, not unto us'. There were biblical expressions for which no English equivalent existed. He invented such words as 'scapegoat' and 'passover'. Any number of expressions that have become proverbial were his: 'the powers that be', 'the fat of the land', 'eat, drink and be merry'.

The second element that made Tyndale's translation different, this time the Old Testament, was the use of Hebrew. It was no doubt Tyndale's move to the continent that gave him the necessary contact with Hebrew. He taught himself Hebrew, but also made considerable use of Luther's Bible translated from the Hebrew. He was, however, only about halfway through the Old Testament when he was kidnapped and imprisoned by the Catholic authorities in the Netherlands. Even from his dank prison cell Tyndale was sending letters to the governor, begging for Hebrew Bible, dictionary and grammar. In 1534 he was cruelly garrotted. His work did not die with him. A couple of years later (1537) 'Matthew's Bible' was published in England by Tyndale's friend John Roger. It contained Tyndale's translations but did not use his name; ironically it was licensed by Henry VIII.

Nearly a century later, in 1611, the King James Version, the 'authorized version' of the Bible, and the basis for virtually all modern English versions, was issued – an event that has been described as the coming of age of the Church of England. This also relies heavily on Tyndale – up to 80 per cent in those parts he had translated. In fact this Bible does not seem finally to have been authorized by anyone, but at least it was one of the first acts of King James I to initiate its composition, and he himself played a considerable part in organizing the six panels of translators involved. Nevertheless, it is no exaggeration to say that the achievement of this version is Tyndale's. The nobility, rhythm, freshness and even wit of this translation are his: 'Then said the serpent unto the woman, "Tush, ye shall not die."' Where the King James Version does change Tyndale, it often shies away from his imaginative, daring version; the serpent's enticement fades to 'Ye shall not surely die'. Similarly the lively 'the woman saw it was a good tree to eat of and lusty unto the eyes' is softened to the pedestrian 'the woman saw that the tree was good for food and a tree to be desired'.

The Catholic reaction

The Catholic reaction to this work of translation varied from country to country. It was always inspired by a certain protectiveness, a conviction that the text alone is only part of the story, and that it must be read as part of the living tradition. Thus even today Catholic translations are not authorized without some explanatory notes. The disfavour Bible translation suffered in the predominantly Catholic countries of Europe has meant that in these countries translations of the Bible have had markedly less influence on the formation of the language than in England and Germany.

So in 1551 and again in 1559 the Spanish Inquisition banned any translation of the Bible into 'Castilian or any other vulgar tongue'. Consequently the first translation of the Bible into Spanish, by the ex-religious Cassiodoro da Reyna, was printed not in Spain but in Protestant Basel in 1569, 'so that the common people should not be deprived of the Word of God', as he says in his introduction. When it was revised by Cipriano de Valera, to become the translation standard in Spanish-speaking countries until this century, the New Testament was printed in London in 1596 and the whole Bible in 1602 in Amsterdam. The circulation of translations in Spain was always restricted, dependent largely on the anti-clericalism of the government. The story of George Borrow's travels in Spain to disseminate the Bible in the vernacular is a classic of English literature.

Similarly in Italian the standard Protestant Bible was a translation by Giovanni Deodati, professor of theology at Geneva (1607). A Catholic translation (by A. Martini from the Latin Vulgate) was, however, authorized in 1778. The extreme case is perhaps Ireland, for the first authorized Catholic translation of the Bible into Irish was not published until 1985.

For English-speaking Catholics the counterblast to the classic Protestant translations stemming from Tyndale consisted in the Rheims–Douai version of Gregory Martin. The New Testament was published at Rheims in 1582, the Old Testament at Douai in 1609. Translated from the Vulgate, it was heavily Latinized, a style modernized by Bishop Challoner's revision in 1749–63. This remained the standard Catholic version until it was superseded in America by a short-lived version sponsored by the Confraternity of Christian Doctrine (1941) and in England by the brilliant but quirky version of Ronald A. Knox. This too was translated nominally from the Vulgate, though in 1944 I witnessed Knox using also the Greek and Hebrew texts.

MODERN ENGLISH BIBLES

For over three centuries the English-speaking world seemed to be content more or less with the translations of the sixteenth century, the King James Version and (in Roman Catholic circles) the Rheims-Douai version. This had been completed by Gregory Martin in 1582 and thoroughly revised by Bishop Challoner in 1749–50. Apart from this revision the most important biblical revision was the Revised Version of 1870–85. This was intended to incorporate the advances in textual knowledge and other biblical sciences, but the decision to preserve the language of the King James Version resulted in a wooden and antiquarian translation that failed to win a place in the heart of English readers.

It was only after the Second World War that a proliferation of translations of the Bible into English occurred. Several factors contributed to this explosion. The archaeological, literary and textual studies of the previous century had begun to trickle down beyond the merely academic world. There was a renewed impetus in Christianity not only to expunge the shame felt at the atrocities of war but also to counter the opposition of secularism, atheism and Communism. Popular interest in the origins of Christianity was further aroused by sensationalist claims following the discovery in 1945 of the Nag Hammadi writings and in 1946 of the Dead Sea Scrolls. Among the many available, the profile of four versions will here be sketched.

The first of the new translations to appear was the Revised Standard Version (RSV), commissioned in 1937 and completed in 1952. Despite being the work of American scholars, it has become fully accepted on both sides of the Atlantic as a dignified and accurate translation, being widely used both in public reading and for academic work. A number of archaisms (such as 'saith') and Semitisms (such as 'and it came to pass that') have been eliminated, and 'thou' is retained only for addressing God (not Jesus, which causes some theological problems). A revision, the New Revised Standard Version (NRSV, 1989) has caused controversy, and failed to win acceptance in some circles, by its uncompromising use of inclusive language, to the extent of changing singulars into plurals ('their' avoids 'his/her') and the addition to 'brothers' of 'and sisters'. The storytelling of the Old Testament is often scintillating, and a number of the solutions to translation problems can only be described as brilliant, but there remains a certain staidness about it that betrays it still as a revision of a revision of the King James Version.

The RSV was closely followed by the Roman Catholic Jerusalem Bible in 1966, the first translation into fully modern English, the work of a distinguished literary panel under the editorship of Alexander Jones. The parent *Bible de Jérusalem* was begun in 1946 at the French Catholic Biblical School in Jerusalem, and was intended to incorporate the important advances in Roman Catholic biblical scholarship this century. The books, copiously annotated and introduced, were published first in separate fascicules over ten years. The English Jerusalem Bible, having no basis in a traditional English version, has the freshness of freedom from traditional biblical language. For Catholics it rapidly supplanted the antiquated Rheims–Douai version. Perhaps the most controversial feature was the use of 'Yahweh' for the divine name, which was excoriated as a reversion to a mere local, tribal deity. It was basically a translation from the French *Bible de Jérusalem*, conceived primarily to convey to the English-speaking world the biblical scholarship of this French Bible; the translation of the text was originally no more than a vehicle for the notes. The New Jerusalem Bible, published 1985, was edited by the present writer. The notes and introductions were brought up to date, and the accuracy of the translation considerably improved, some books being translated completely afresh. It was the first complete Bible to make consistent use of inclusive language wherever possible, though without the rigour of the NRSV.

In France, however, the *Bible de Jérusalem* had its own special importance. After centuries of division between Protestants and Catholics over translations of the Bible, following the Second Vatican Council (1962–6), in 1968 agreement was reached between the Vatican and the United Bible Societies over a set of principles for translation. Following these principles the *Bible de Jérusalem* formed the basis for the first French ecumenical version of the Bible, the *Traduction Oecuménique de la Bible*. In Germany also the *Einheitsübersetzung* was launched jointly by a Catholic cardinal and a Protestant bishop in 1980. In the French- and German-speaking countries respectively these two translations now hold the field with little competition. No such agreement has yet been reached in English-speaking lands.

The New English Bible, initiated by the Church of Scotland in 1946 and completed in 1970, was an attempt to break away from the mould of 'biblical English' associated with the tradition stemming from Tyndale. It also deliberately eschewed any effort consistently to translate the same word in the original Greek or Hebrew by the same English word. There is an impressive freshness and modernity about this version that reflects the eagerness of the translators to bring home the meaning of the text to a reader unused to the traditional language of the Bible. Some of the solutions to translation problems are breathtakingly apt, though the avoidance of all Semitic 'biblical' language has sometimes led to accusations of paraphrase rather than translation. It was revised as the Revised English Bible (REB) in 1989, with participation (at least notional) from the Bible Society and most of the mainstream Churches of the British Isles. This united ecclesiastical participation has not, however, enabled it to overcome all competition; indeed the REB is not one of the versions authorized for use in Roman Catholic churches.

Among the most widely used versions is the Good News Bible (completed 1976), sponsored by the American Bible Society, prepared by the United Bible Society and published on both sides of the Atlantic in slightly different versions. The British subtitle, Today's Good News, reflects its purpose accurately, for dignity and literary quality have been sacrificed to the desire to make the Bible accessible to those whose English is less sophisticated. It is a determined effort to move out of the biblical world and culture ('the Covenant Box' replaces 'the Ark of the Covenant'), even to the extent of tabulating or condensing into a few phrases verses judged unimportant (e.g. Numbers 7.12–88). The price paid is a certain loss of richness and imagery, when God's 'right hand' and his 'mighty arm' become simply his 'power'. This version certainly has its uses as a first introduction to the Bible for children and those for whom English is a second language. It is the only major Bible illustrated throughout, richly and aptly, with thoughtful and witty line-drawings, which combine humour with reverence.

NON-EUROPEAN TRANSLATION OF THE BIBLE

The whole situation of translation of the Bible into modern languages changed radically with the advent of the missionary movement of Christianity, first with the sixteenth-century Jesuit missions to the Far East, then with the opening up of North America and of the Indian subcontinent by the East India Companies, and finally with the discovery of sub-Saharan Africa. Translation of the Bible has been an essential element in the missionary movement. There are perhaps two poles of this translation. The first is where the Bible is an instrument of preliminary evangelization. There is no spreading of Christianity without some version of the gospel, though there are today regions (e.g. northern Namibia) where ministers have to provide their own oral rendering, and others (e.g. the southern Philippines) where missionaries are still preparing a first written translation. The other pole is when Christianity has reached sufficient maturity for the indigenous speakers of a language to provide, or at least co-operate in providing, a lasting translation. The problems are made vastly greater than for translation into European languages by the need to move into another thought-world, far removed from the Mediterranean culture that is at the basis of western civilization. Gestures, colours, climatic features, marriage-customs, images may carry entirely different overtones (the spirits have a different function in African religions from that of the Spirit in Judaeo-Christian thought), though certain tribal or nomadic conditions in some areas may also make elements of the Old Testament world far more accessible than they are to modern western peoples.

Catholic stress on the living tradition of teaching, and mistrust of the unsupervised reading of the Bible, meant that less priority was given to biblical translation by Catholic than by Protestant missionaries. Remarkable among the early missions to the Far East were the Jesuit missions to China and Japan, for to them provision of a vernacular Bible was not a priority. Amid considerable production of books and of Christian literature, it simply does not seem to have occurred to them that a Bible should be included. In 1604 the awesome polyglot Plantin edition of the Bible in eight volumes was brought to China in its own packing-case, but Matteo Ricci refused all requests to translate it, on the grounds that special permission would be required from the Pope (Cronin 1955: 216). It is striking that from 1590 to 1610 the Jesuit presses at Kyushu produced a whole series of catechetical and devotional books in Japanese, prayerbooks, Thomas à Kempis, lives of saints, the Exercises of St Ignatius, dictionaries. But neither a Bible nor even a New Testament is listed among the considerable number of books known to have been produced there (Satow 1888), though the Jesuits are said to have produced a complete New Testament (now lost) in Japanese in 1613. Similarly in Africa, though 'Protestant vernacular Bibles had multiplied across the continent before the close of the [nineteen] century, Catholic ones were simply non-existent' (Hastings 1990: 281).

Consequently it is to a Dutch Protestant, and a merchant in the Dutch East India Company, that falls the honour of the first known extended biblical translation into a non-European language: Albert Cornelius Ruyl translated the gospel of Matthew into Malay in 1629. It was similarly a Dutch merchant, Bartholomaus Ziegelbalg, who was responsible for the first translation into Tamil in 1715. The first printed translation into a North American language was John Eliot's for the Mohican Indians of Massachussetts (1663).

The evangelical revival in England at the beginning of the nineteenth century was a particularly potent force for spreading the biblical text around the expanding British Empire. The Baptist missionary William Carey at Seranpur in 1800–33 oversaw the translation of the Bible into Bengali, Mahratta, Tamil and altogether 26 Indian languages. The most powerful manifestation of the evangelical movement, however, was the foundation of the Bible Societies. The first of these, the British and Foreign Bible Society, was formed (1804) at a meeting at the London Tavern in Bishopsgate, strangely enough initially in response to a demand for Bibles in Welsh. The cry was raised that if this was possible in the British Isles, why not to the whole of the British Empire, indeed to the whole world? The Society was deliberately lay and interdenominational, with a committee consisting of 15 Anglican and 15 Free Church laymen, afforced by 6 representatives of European Churches, and pledged to distribute Bibles 'without note or comment'. Within a decade Bible Societies had been formed in Germany, Russia, Greece, the United States and many other countries, as independent offshoots of the parent Society. These societies were instrumental in translating the Bible into the languages to which Christianity was spreading through the burgeoning missionary movement. Thus, to take only two examples, in 1806, Bibles in Spanish were taken to Buenos Aires 'probably for the first time in the history of South America' (Roe 1965: 11). In 1812 Robert Morrison secured the post of interpreter to the East India Company and began the translation of the Bible into Chinese, in the hope that China would soon be opened to Christian missionaries.

This work was carried on with impressive zeal and perseverance. By the time of the Golden Jubilee of the British and Foreign Bible Society in 1854 it was reckoned that 28 million copies of scripture had been distributed in 152 languages and dialects. In 1997 the Bible Society (as it had been renamed) claimed translation of the whole Bible into 349 languages and dialects, and individual books into 2,123 languages. In 1995 they distributed 560 million Bibles or parts of Bibles. They reckoned that there still remained some 4,000 languages without any scripture.

BIBLIOGRAPHY

Ackroyd, P. R. and Evans, C. F. *Cambridge History of the Bible*. Vol. 1: *From the Beginnings to Jerome* (Cambridge University Press, 1970)

Augustine *Confessions and Letters* [Nicene and Post-Nicene Fathers, Vol. 1] (Hendrickson, 1995)

Bruce, F. F. *History of the Bible in English* (Lutterworth, 1979)

Cronin, V. *The Wise Men from the West* (Hart-Davis, 1955)

Daniell, David *William Tyndale* (Yale University Press, 1994)

Erasmus *Collected Works of Erasmus*, Vol. 6 (University of Toronto Press, 1982)

Evans, C. F., Lampe, G. W. H. and Greenslade, S. L. (eds) *Cambridge History of the Bible* (Cambridge University Press, 1963–70)

Forshall, J. and Madden, F. *The Holy Bible . . . in the Earliest English Version Made from the Latin Vulgate by John Wycliffe and his Followers* (Oxford, 1850)

Foxe, John *Acts and Monuments . . .* (William Tegg, 1863)

Greenslade, S. L. *Cambridge History of the Bible*. Vol. 3: *The West from the Reformation to the Present Day* (Cambridge University Press, 1963)

Hargreaves, H. 'From Bede to Wyclif', *BJRL* 48 (1965), 118–40

Hastings, A. *The Church in Africa 1450–1950* (Clarendon Press, 1990)

Jerome *Letters and Selected Works* [Nicene and Post-Nicene Fathers, Vol. 6] (Hendrikson, 1995)

Kamesar, Adam *Jerome, Greek Scholarship and the Hebrew Bible* (Clarendon, 1993)

Kelly, J. N. D. *Jerome* (Duckworth, 1975)

Lampe, G. W. H. *Cambridge History of the Bible*. Vol. 2: *The West from the Fathers to the Reformation* (Cambridge University Press, 1969)

Levi, Peter *The English Bible from Wyclif to William Barnes* (Constable, 1974)

Metzger, Bruce *The Early Versions of the New Testament, Their Origin, Transmission and Limitations* (Oxford University Press, 1977)

Robertson, E. H. *Makers of the English Bible* (Lutterworth, 1990)

Roe, James M. *History of the British and Foreign Bible Society 1905–1954* (British and Foreign Bible Society 1965)

Satow, E. M. *The Jesuit Mission Press in Japan, 1591–1610* (privately printed, 1888)

Skeat, W. W. *The Holy Gospels in Anglo-Saxon etc* (Cambridge University Press, 1871–87)

Tyndale, William *Tyndale's New Testament*, ed. David Daniell (Yale University Press, 1989)

Wallach-Faller, M. *Ein deutscher Psalter aus dem 14. Jahrhundert* (Studia Friburgensia 28, Fribourg, 1981)

Whitelock, D. *Swete's Anglo-Saxon Reader* (Oxford University Press, 1967)

CHAPTER FORTY-NINE

MODERN BIBLICAL INTERPRETATION

—— ·◆· ——

William R. Telford

INTRODUCTION

The nature, scope and complexity of modern biblical interpretation and its subject matter

Modern biblical interpretation is a complex and multifaceted enterprise. Its subject matter, a collection of some sixty-six writings (thirty-nine in the Hebrew Bible, or the Old Testament, as Christians call it, and twenty-seven in the New Testament), displays remarkable variety and diversity. Dating from a millennium before the birth of Christianity's founder to approximately a century and a half after, these writings present us with history, literature and theology, with legends, sagas and stories, with proverbs, songs and poems, with prophecy, apocalyptic and wisdom, with gospels, epistles and apocalypses as well as a host of other historical, literary and theological forms and genres. Created, preserved and transmitted by ancient Near Eastern and Mediterranean societies, and cherished as sacred by Jewish, Christian and Muslim communities, these sixty-six writings have exerted a profound influence on Western culture and civilization. Modern biblical interpretation in all its many forms recognizes this diversity, and its own wide-ranging agenda reflects the complexity of its subject matter and the multifarious levels at which, and the multitudinous ways in which, the Bible itself may be interpreted.

Any biblical text has a variety of contexts within which it may be understood and interpreted, and within which it achieves its meaning and significance (Bauckham 1989: 13–15). It may be examined in relation to its original context and interrogated with respect to the meaning intended by its author(s). It may be investigated in relation to the literary context in which it is found, either in terms of the specific literary unit(s) within which it is placed, or, more broadly, with respect to the general literary tradition within which it stands (its genre). In pursuing the original context, the biblical interpreter may be concerned to illuminate the immediate historical circumstances of the author and his community or readership, or the text may be viewed within the wider social, political, economic, cultural and religious context of the writer's own day. The text may also acquire meaning and significance through its theological context, either with respect to the particular religious tradition or history of ideas which it reflects or engages, or with respect to its place in a unified body of sacred writings (the canon). Biblical texts also have a history of interpretation and reception, and contexts other than the original one(s) have also contributed to their meaning for the reader. Modern biblical interpretation is interested in these secondary contexts also (the text's use in literature, for example, or in liturgy), recognizing that the meaning of a biblical text is influenced by the perspective of the readers who construct meaning from it in line with their own presuppositions or world-view, or within the context of the interpretative communities (church, synagogue, academy) whose exegetical traditions shape its reception.

The aims of the chapter

In this chapter, it will not be my purpose to provide a detailed or even comprehensive introduction to modern biblical interpretation and its many different individual methods and approaches, or to outline the history of biblical interpretation in the past (my definition of the term 'modern' will be restricted for the most part to developments in the last quarter of the twentieth century). The reader should consult some of the standard reference works in this area (Morgan and Barton 1988; Coggins and Houlden 1990; Thiselton 1992). Rather, my aim will be to offer some general reflections (some autobiographical) on the current state of biblical interpretation, on the nature and scope of contemporary biblical hermeneutics and on the major paradigms, and the principal methods and approaches that have been in operation in this period. More specifically, I shall direct my remarks to what may be perceived, especially by those stepping into this field for the first time (though no less so by biblical scholars themselves!), as the bewildering array of such methodological tools and approaches. I shall attempt to offer some definitions of these methods and approaches and try to identify their respective aims and limitations and their varying concerns, perspectives and assumptions. A basic taxonomy of approaches will be proffered, and some key issues engaged. A central one will be whether the methodological pluralism that characterizes modern biblical interpretation betokens refinement, complementarity, confusion or even fragmentation within the discipline of biblical studies. The final section of the chapter will comment on some of the methodological issues in two of the biblical fields with which I myself am most familiar, namely, historical Jesus studies and Markan studies.

Biblical hermeneutics: methods, criticisms, interpretations, approaches and theologies

But first, let me offer some definitions. The term 'hermeneutics' (from the Greek *hermeneuo* meaning 'I understand' or 'I interpret') refers to the science (some prefer to call it an 'art') or theory of interpretation. Scholars and students entering the field of modern biblical interpretation and engaged in the pursuit of meaning encounter a veritable forest of '-ics' (e.g. 'linguistics', 'semantics'), '-isms' (e.g. 'structuralism', 'new historicism') or '-ologies' (e.g. 'etymology', 'philology'), and a formidable host of 'methods' (e.g. 'the historical-critical method'), 'criticisms' (e.g. 'redaction criticism', 'rhetorical criticism', 'canonical criticism'), 'interpretations' (e.g. 'feminist interpretation', 'Marxist interpretation' or 'materialist interpretation'), 'approaches' (e.g. 'allegorical approaches', 'literary approaches', 'sociological approaches), 'theologies' (e.g. 'black theology', 'narrative theology', 'pastoral theology') or even 'exegeses' (e.g. 'Jewish exegesis'). Some of these '-ics', '-isms' or '-ologies' form themselves into cognate areas of investigation within a particular science. Linguistics, for example, the science of language, embraces such divisions as semiotics, a method of enquiry that concerns itself with 'signs' as forms of verbal or non-verbal communication, or semantics, which investigates the meaning of 'words', or (comparative) philology, which seeks to establish the meaning of words within their original or historical context, or etymology, which is concerned with the 'root-meanings' of words, or structuralism, which searches for the permanent 'deep structures' of language itself, the universal grammar and syntax of the communicating mind.

What distinguishes the many 'methods', 'criticisms', 'interpretations', 'approaches', 'theologies' or 'exegeses' are the different questions they address to their subject matter, the different aims they pursue, the different assumptions they make, the different perspectives they share, the different concerns they embrace, and the different methodologies they adopt. 'Methodology' is a key word in modern biblical interpretation. It refers to the rational strategies, method(s) or procedure(s) scholars agree to adopt with respect to the aims and objectives of their chosen field of activity, including the criteria by which they will evaluate their results in the interests of the widest possible consensus. A 'method' can be distinguished to a certain extent from an 'approach' in that it often involves distinct procedures, steps or operations performed on the subject matter for investigation in pursuance of specific aims, whereas an 'approach' is often characterized more by the particular concerns, perspectives or point of view it adopts towards the text (or reader).

Form criticism is a method, for example, that proceeds by first identifying and classifying the 'forms' or stereotypical units of tradition (sayings or narratives) that circulated orally in the community (e.g. parables, miracle stories, etc.) before being incorporated into the written text, then assigning them a 'life-situation' (*Sitz im Leben*) or function within the community (worship, parenesis, catechesis, apologetic, polemic, etc.) and finally making a historical judgement on the origin (or authenticity) of each form in the light of the degree of development it evinces in both the oral and literary traditions. Feminist interpretation, on the other hand, is more of an approach to the biblical text, one sensitive to the representation of women in the Bible, which is concerned to uncover its androcentric or patriarchal bias, which aims to expose derogatory images of women or highlight complimentary ones. In directing itself to the role and status of women in the Bible, feminist interpretation may itself employ a variety of methods, whether traditio-critical (e.g. source, form or redaction criticism) or literary (e.g. rhetorical criticism or narrative criticism), or it may draw upon a variety of other approaches, for example, social-scientific (anthropological or sociological), (socio-)psychological or other culturally informed approaches.

Among the important historical-critical methods utilized by modern biblical scholars, in addition to those already mentioned, are textual criticism, which seeks to establish, by a series of logical procedures, and from a number of variant readings, the original form of a text; or source criticism, which is concerned to discover, on the basis of a number of criteria (e.g. unevenness or incoherence in the text, interruption of the context, repetition or duplication of material, inconsistencies or discrepancies, etc.), whether the author has used sources; or tradition criticism, which concentrates on certain constituent elements of a text (a motif, concept, theme or combination of these), and seeks to establish the tradition history of this element prior to its incorporation into the text.

Among the significant literary methods are composition criticism, which examines the text as a whole to determine how it was composed, what factors or concerns governed or motivated its composition, and what compositional techniques and devices were used by its writer(s); or genre criticism, which seeks to identify, by comparison with other writings with similar traits, the category, type or genre into which the text may be placed (e.g. history, biography, tragedy, romance, letter, apocalypse, etc.) as an aid to the overall determination of its meaning; or reader-response criticism, which investigates the reading process itself, and the ways in which readers construct meaning from a text by paying close attention to the clues or coded signals within a text (gaps, ambiguities, discrepancies, opacity, irony, repetitions, intertextual allusions, unanswered questions, the use of 'reliable commentary', etc.).

'Approaches' may sometimes lack such finely tuned precision but are frequently characterized by their commitment to a particular interpretative framework, a set of general principles or a specific dimension within which the text, they claim, should be viewed. Historical approaches tend to look 'behind' the text, to locate its meaning in the past, to see the clue to its interpretation in its original context, and in the intention of its original author(s). 'Historicism' indeed is '[t]he belief that history holds the keys to human existence and self-understanding originates here' (Morgan 1990: 290). An historical approach like that of the History of Religion(s), for example, which was particularly influential in the first half of the last century, is characterized not only by its strict adherence to historical methodology but more so by its absolute rejection of theological or dogmatic presuppositions, and by its comparative analysis of the external religious matrix (Jewish, Hellenistic and oriental religions and cultures), which is deemed to have influenced biblical religion and to account, in particular, for the evolution of New Testament Christianity. Literary approaches, on the other hand, tend to 'deal with the text in its final form rather than with its genesis, and are concerned with the literary world projected "in front of" the text rather than with the historical world "behind" the text' (Brown and Schneiders 1989: 1160).

Ethical approaches view the biblical text through a moral lens, looking at it with a view to the ethical teaching it presents, or the ethical perspectives it reflects, examining its normative structures, its standards of judgement, its treatment of right and wrong or good and evil and so on. Such approaches also examine the consequences that biblical ethics have had for both past and contemporary society, how they have impinged upon moral choices and shaped individual and social conscience. Ecological approaches, for example, have concentrated upon biblical attitudes to nature, the environment, creation, and on matters of human responsibility flowing therefrom, while moral criticism has not hesitated to apply moral judgements to biblical texts themselves in relation to their effects (e.g. in promoting anti-Semitism, imperialism, exclusivism or sexism).

Ethical approaches overlap with ideological approaches, whose major thrust is to examine the Bible as an ideological system whose informing world-view(s) or nexus of governing ideas also have a relation to social, political and economic realities. Liberationist approaches are characterized by their focus on certain central biblical themes such as 'justice and oppression', 'wealth and poverty', 'freedom and slavery', 'power and weakness', while materialist interpretation seeks to explain such central ideas in relation to the social formations, political structures and economic systems underlying them. The latter draws very heavily on Marxist interpretation with its highlighting of the ways that religious and theological ideas may be used to legitimate these realities.

Ideological approaches overlap in turn with theological approaches whose essential characteristic is their engagement with what they regard as the major subject matter of the biblical text, namely, its communication of 'divine' realities or of 'heavenly things' (John 3.12), and hence its revelatory significance for faith. One particularly extreme but popular form of biblical interpretation is fundamentalism, which is characterized by its dogmatic adherence to the literal meaning of the text, or perhaps, more accurately, its view of biblical inerrancy (Barr 1981; Corner 1990). But there are also more moderate theological approaches, and within this category, too, are to be counted the various confessional and devotional approaches to the Bible, with their interest in 'spirituality' and other existential concerns and their conviction that the Bible is a sacred text not only to be interpreted but also to be appropriated and applied.

Developing out of these theological approaches, and building on some of the methods mentioned above are a number of important 'theologies'. A 'theology' is a 'reflective, analytic, abstract discipline which seeks to formulate a carefully conceptualized account of ultimate truths regarding God and his relationship with the world in the light of the ways of thought which characterize the academic thinking of the day' (Goldingay 1990: 692). Some of these theologies build on historical-critical approaches and methods (e.g. 'historical theology'). Some give priority to the literary study of the Bible, as with 'narrative theology', which focuses on the use of stories as a structuring device in human experience, and employs the methods and results of narrative criticism. Some of these 'theologies' are purely 'descriptive' or 'evaluative', as with 'historical theology', or as with certain forms of 'biblical theology', that is, they see it as their task to identify, analyse, contextualize (historically) and even systematize, as objectively as possible, the theological features of the text, but with no further theological agenda. Other forms of 'biblical theology' are 'actualizing', which means that they see it as 'a discipline involving normative authority, personal commitment, and interpretation for the present day and the modern religious community' (Barr 1999: esp. 6, 9, 15).

This aim to link the concerns of academic biblical scholarship with the needs of the religious community (compare canonical criticism) is seen, for example, in 'pastoral theology' with its interest in the value and use of the Bible in areas of personal growth, or pastoral care, or in teaching and preaching (homiletics). Some 'theologies' that attempt to be both critical and confessional represent or address particular constituencies, such as liberation theology with its concern for oppressed communities, and its interpretation of biblical concepts such as 'sin', 'judgment', 'faith' or 'salvation' in collective or institutional terms rather than personal ones. It is out of this movement that some of the so-called 'people's' or 'grass roots' approaches have come, approaches that emphasize the 'actualization' of biblical interpretation within 'base communities' of the disprivileged, or that promote the value of the Bible in the advancement of a human-rights culture (Mesters 1983; Botha 1996). Other 'theologies' seek to interpret the Bible in relation to specific classes of the 'oppressed', black theology, for example, offering exegesis in the light of the black experience, feminist theology with the needs and aspirations of women in mind.

The major paradigms (historical, literary, theological)

In the face of this plethora of methods, criticisms, interpretations, approaches and theologies, it is very easy to get confused or disoriented. One analytical category that has helped to create some order within the hermeneutical chaos is the concept of the 'paradigm'. A paradigm can be described as 'any idea or set of ideas that provides the framework within which a given set of phenomena is understood' (Robertson 1976: 547). In the field of biblical interpretation, three paradigms can be identified, namely, the historical paradigm, the literary paradigm and the theological paradigm. The Bible, in other words, can be viewed as history, as literature or as theology. From one perspective, the biblical texts are historical documents, which by careful analysis can yield information about the past. From another perspective, they are literary compositions and hence subject to all the possibilities and limitations that written self-expression involves, including multiple interpretations. From yet another perspective, they are religious (or sacred) texts, seeking to express a relation to what is perceived as the divine.

Associated with these three broad perspectives, there is a series of concomitant aims, principles and assumptions, and generated by them are the various hermeneutical tools I have described. Most, if not all, of the above methods and approaches, indeed, can be seen to pursue certain aspects of an agenda appropriate to one or more of these paradigms. According to its practitioners, the historical paradigm, put simply, offers us a window into the past, the literary paradigm a window into the imagination (or the nature of language), and the theological paradigm into the mind of God himself (or herself, if we allow ourselves to be influenced by feminist theology). As a rough guide through the hermeneutical maze, these three paradigms are extremely helpful, although they bring with them certain dangers. There is the obvious danger of oversimplification, for there are overlapping elements in each of these paradigms, as with the methods and approaches deriving from them. There is also the danger of what I might call 'paradigmatic imperialism', the prevailing tendency for followers of any one of these paradigms to subsume the others within its own perspective, or to declare the others illegitimate or obsolete. Examples, perhaps, of the rigorous application of a single perspective might be 'historicism', with respect to the historical paradigm, 'structuralism', with respect to the literary paradigm, and 'fundamentalism', with respect to the theological paradigm.

Modern biblical interpretation in historical perspective

For the majority of the centuries in which biblical interpretation has been practised, the theological paradigm has been most in evidence. For Judaism, Christianity and Islam the Bible has been (and still is) a holy book. Despite the critical (and at times iconoclastic) scholarship permitted in the Judaeo-Christian tradition (though markedly less so in the Muslim tradition of interpretation), it has been regarded as a fountain of revealed truth or divine learning. While the historical or 'literal' meaning was recognized as a dimension in itself by ancient exegetes, contradictions at this 'surface' level were frequently taken as signals pointing to the 'deeper' spiritual or theological significance of the text as revealed to the enlightened by the allegorical approaches then in vogue.

From the eighteenth century onwards, the historical paradigm has been dominant in the field of biblical studies, although there have been signs in the last quarter of the twentieth century that things are changing (Watson 1994). When I first began my own postgraduate work, in Cambridge, in 1972, the historical-critical method was clearly predominant in the field of New Testament studies. Source and form criticism had ruled Gospel studies for generations, and the third member of the traditio-critical trinity, redaction criticism, was coming more and more into vogue. Like many postgraduates of that time, I opted to conduct a traditio-critical investigation into a single Gospel pericope, namely, the Cursing of the Fig-Tree story in Mark 11 and its relation to the Cleansing of the Temple (Telford 1980, 1991). After a survey of the history of interpretation, literary-, form-, source- and redaction-critical work on the Synoptic Gospels, and on Mark in particular, were brought to bear on the pericope. Then certain related motifs pertaining to the story were traced within background material supplied by the Old Testament (or Hebrew Bible), early Judaism and nascent Christianity. In particular, the place of the tree and especially the fig-tree within this material was examined, and their literary, religious and symbolic usage explored. Attention was given especially to the cultic dimension and note taken where fig-tree imagery was linked to temple imagery. The aim was to construct thereby a conceptual pattern or grid of related ideas and associations that would enable a modern reader to place himself or herself within the interpretative frame of reference that might have been adopted by a first-century reader of the Gospel. The approach, then, was a standard traditio-critical one with elements of what we might now describe as intertextuality, motif criticism and (ancient) reader-response criticism, although these terms were not in vogue then.

Throughout the twentieth century, indeed, historical-critical approaches like these have dominated biblical studies in general and the Gospel of Mark, my own special interest, in particular. For the major part of the century the emphasis has focused on the text's component parts and on the complex traditio-historical process that brought it into being. Chief among the now established historical-critical approaches are the interrelated methods of source, form and redaction criticism already mentioned. These methods start with the recognition that, archaeological evidence aside, written texts like the canonical Gospels are our major route to historical knowledge about Jesus, the early Christian communities and the world of early Christianity. As major champions of what Robert Alter has pejoratively termed an 'excavative' approach (Alter 1981: 13–14), source, form and redaction criticism have taught us to start with the evidence before us and to work back from the text (or behind it) to uncover the historical information it is capable of revealing. All three methods attempt to explain, for example, the discrepancies, ambiguities and awkwardnesses apparent on a close reading of the text in terms of the sources, forms and redaction of the literary or oral material drawn upon by the evangelist.

All three methods, in my view, have been and are extremely valuable (Telford 1995a: 30–1). Source criticism has taught us to establish the criteria by which we judge sources to have been used in our texts and to explore the evidence for the use of written sources in our Gospels. Form criticism has taught us to investigate the structured form taken by the traditional material, a form taken to be related to its function within the life and worship of the communities that transmitted it. Redaction criticism has taught us how to analyse the use made by the evangelists of their sources, whether written or oral, and has helped us to appreciate their literary and theological contribution to the developing Jesus tradition.

In the late seventies and early eighties, however, when I was just beginning my teaching career as a Lecturer at the University of Newcastle, the historical-critical method was under considerable fire, and there were dire warnings that it was clearly in decline. This was apparent in two of the fields that have occupied my attention, namely Markan studies and historical Jesus studies. Secular literary criticism and the so-called synchronic approaches (rhetorical criticism, narrative criticism, reader-response criticism, structuralism, etc.) were encouraging a more holistic approach to the text and with it a greater emphasis on textually integrative rather than textually disintegrative features. Criticisms were being directed increasingly against the three principal traditio-critical methods (source criticism, form criticism and redaction criticism) with respect to the tensions that actually exist between them, to their own intrinsic weaknesses or limitations, to the high degree of speculation involved in their putative diachronic reconstructions and to the lack of consensus in their results.

A key issue in Markan studies was whether the process that led from oral tradition to Gospel composition was an inevitable, collective and evolutionary one (as form critics claimed) or whether the non-linear and multidirectional nature of the tradition required us to posit Gospel composition as the consequence of individual authorial intention adopting a specific genre (as literary critics tended to claim) (Telford 1993: 492). There was also confusion in the field of Jesus studies. J. I. H. McDonald, in a penetrating article (1980), had talked about the maze scholars were in with regard to this question. A similar evaluation was given by the Italian scholar G. Ghiberti (1982). In assessing the state of Life of Jesus Research at that time, Ghiberti referred to it as one of relative stagnation. The then-prevailing mood of pessimism, and indeed scepticism, about what might be said about Jesus was attributed to the influence of Rudolf Bultmann (and hence to form criticism) (Telford 1994: 33–74).

In the eighties and nineties, however, the historical-critical method has, I believe, weathered the storm. In Markan studies, despite the criticism levelled against source, form or redaction criticism, a traditio-critical method involving these methods has continued to be practised throughout both decades particularly by European scholars.

In Jesus studies, the revitalization of the quest for the historical Jesus, which has been so distinctive a feature of the eighties and nineties, is due in no small measure to a renewed confidence in the historical-critical method (Telford 1994: 33–74, esp. 49–51). What is new, of course, is not that the historical-critical method has declined but that it must now compete with a whole panoply of new methods and approaches, a number of them operating within the increasingly influential literary paradigm.

The new methods and approaches

I began by drawing attention to what may be perceived, especially by those stepping into this field for the first time (though no less so by biblical scholars themselves!) as the totally confusing and bewildering array of methodological tools and approaches available to present-day researchers. This has been illustrated for me by my work on the Gospel of Mark. Indeed one aspect of this Gospel's importance over the last 150 years has been its important role in the history of biblical interpretation. Very few of the methods developed by biblical scholars have not been applied to Mark, and a number of them have in fact taken Mark as their principal subject (Telford 1990: 424–8).

This is true, for example, of composition criticism, with its focus on the way the evangelist has assembled diverse materials into a meaningful structure whose form reflects his theology (Dowd 1988); or genre criticism, with its aim of identifying the Gospel's literary environment, as well as literary type, and of establishing its place within the history of ancient literature (Collins 1990; Burridge 1992; Bryan 1993); or rhetorical criticism, with its investigation of the structural patterns, rhetorical devices and idioms used by its original author, and its examination of the literary strategies employed by the author to guide, persuade or manipulate the reader engaged in the construction of meaning (Dewey 1980; Thompson 1989; Camery-Hoggatt 1992); or reader-response criticism, with its focus on the reception of the Gospel by its modern or original readership (Fowler 1991); or narrative criticism, with its emphasis on the narrative qualities of the text, its narrative 'world', its point of view, plot, settings and characters (Rhoads and Michie 1982; van Iersel 1989; Marshall 1989); or structuralism, with its complex analysis of the 'deep structures' underlying the text and its abstract investigation of the mechanisms by which texts themselves become meaningful (Malbon 1986).

These new approaches have all been immensely valuable. They have made us aware of how texts operate as texts, of the distinctiveness of textuality and of the restraints imposed upon a writer by virtue of literary factors (such as genre, composition, rhetoric) as well as historical ones (such as sources or traditions). They have highlighted the textually integrative features (such as structure, compositional technique or rhetoric) that have operated on our texts and, where individual textual units are concerned, they have helped us to appreciate the importance of their immediate literary context as well as their prior sociological function.

METHODOLOGICAL PLURALISM IN MODERN BIBLICAL INTERPRETATION

The variety of approaches

After this brief overview, it would be fair to say, in summing up, that, while the traditional methods seem to be still alive and well, what characterizes the present scene, and what constitutes a challenge for the contemporary exegete or researcher at the beginning of the new millennium, is the application of a whole variety of approaches, methods and techniques (including the ever-increasing use of the computer) on the part of biblical scholars, especially those, as I have said, who have produced the recent work on Mark or Jesus. How are we to make sense of all of this? How are we to deal with this methodological pluralism? How do the methods relate to one other? Do we face a situation of complementarity between the methods, or one of confusion? Is the present situation a sign that the discipline of biblical studies is becoming more refined, or simply fragmenting?

To gain a further impression of this diversity, let me tabulate alphabetically, and by no means exhaustively (see Figure 49.1 below), the number of methods and approaches applied in the biblical field, some of which have been mentioned already.

Towards a taxonomy of methods and approaches

In trying to make sense of this hermeneutical cornucopia, and to understand how each of these relates to another, one's first task is to work towards some kind of taxonomy or classification of methods and approaches. One basic division that suggests itself is the paradigmatic one previously referred to, namely, an organization based on the threefold nature of biblical texts, that is, one that classifies the individual methods and approaches in respect of their treatment of the text as history, as literature, or as theology. A number of our methods and approaches can be divided up, therefore, very naturally, though very roughly, into those that address historical questions, those that engage literary issues, and those whose primary concern is in some sense theological.

If this classification is applied, then our lists (with some selection and rearrangement) become something like this (see Figure 49.2 below).

Historical approaches

If we remind ourselves of the various contexts within which a biblical text may be interpreted, then the historical approaches would relate to one another somewhat as follows. Beginning with the establishment of the original text through textual criticism, historical criticism would seek to locate the text in its general historical context. The closely related traditio-critical methods, tradition criticism, source criticism, form criticism and redaction criticism would aim to provide a picture of the prehistory of the text's individual components, investigating the question of their incorporation into connected sources, their pre-literary form, the extent to which they have been edited. The history of religions approach would seek to relate the traditions encountered in the text to comparable ones in the text's religious and cultural environment, and the history of ideas approach would examine in particular the place of certain of its ideational elements within a chosen trajectory. If prehistory or parallel developments are the principal focus of traditio-critical methods and the history of religions approach, then forward trajectories of the text or its constituent elements are the province of the history of interpretation or of reception. The social-scientific approaches, on the other hand, would seek to locate the text within the culture and society that gave rise to it, anthropological approaches seeking to foreground it with respect to cultural relations, sociological approaches employing either social description to illuminate significant features of its social

Allegorical Approaches	Historical Theology	Pastoral Theology
Anthropological Approaches	Historicism	'People's'/'Grass-roots' Approaches
Biblical Theology	History of Ideas	Philology
Black Theology	History of Interpretation	Psychological Approaches
Canonical Criticism	History of Reception	Reader-Response Criticism
Composition Criticism	History of Religions Approach	Redaction Criticism
Confessional Approaches	Holistic Interpretation	Rhetorical Criticism
Contextual Approaches	Ideological Approaches	Semantics
Cultural Criticism	Intertextuality	Semiotics
Cultural Relativism	Intratextuality	Social-Scientific Approaches
Culturally Informed Approaches	Jewish Exegesis	Socio-Cultural Approaches
Deconstruction	Liberationist Approaches	Socio-Historical Approaches
Devotional Approaches	Liberation Theology	Socio-Political Approaches
Ecological Approaches	Linguistics	Socio-Rhetorical Criticism
Ethical Approaches	Literary Approaches	Sociological Approaches
Etymology	Literary Criticism	Source Criticism
Feminist Interpretation	Materialist Interpretation	Structuralism
Feminist Theology	Marxist Interpretation	Textual Criticism
Form Criticism	Moral Criticism	The New Hermeneutic
Fundamentalism	Motif Criticism	The New Historicism
Genre Criticism	Muslim Interpretation	Theological Approaches
Hermeneutics	Narrative Criticism	Tradition Criticism
Historical Criticism	Narrative Theology	

Figure 49.1   Methods and approaches in the biblical field.

HISTORICAL	LITERARY	THEOLOGICAL
Textual Criticism	Linguistics	Biblical Theology
Historical Criticism	Semiotics	Narrative Theology
Tradition Criticism	Semantics	The New Hermeneutic
Source Criticism	Etymology	Canonical Criticism
Form Criticism	Philology	Confessional Approaches
Redaction Criticism	Literary Approaches	Devotional Approaches
History of Religions Approach	Bible as Literature	Pastoral Theology
History of Ideas	Intertextuality	Fundamentalism
History of Interpretation	Bible and Literature	Liberationist Approaches
History of Reception	Literary Criticism	Liberation Theology
Social-Scientific Approaches	Composition Criticism	People s / Grass-roots Approaches
Anthropological Approaches	Genre Criticism	Black Theology
Culturally Informed Approaches	Rhetorical Criticism	Feminist Theology
Cultural Criticism	Narrative Criticism	Ethical Approaches
Cultural Relativism	Reader-Response Criticism	Ecological Approaches
Socio-Cultural Approaches	Structuralism	
Sociological Approaches	Deconstruction	
Socio-Historical Approaches		
Socio-Political Approaches		
Psychological Approaches		

Figure 49.2 A taxonomy of methods and approaches in the biblical field.

matrix, or social theory to explain these. Psychological approaches, by contrast, would serve to illumine aspects of the author's own mindset, predispositions, character traits, and so on, or socio-psychological approaches, corresponding elements relating to his community.

Literary approaches

Following the literary paradigm, the literary approaches would focus on the text as text, as a vehicle of communication. Linguistics, as we have seen, would examine the language of the text, employing its associated disciplines, semiotics, semantics, philology and etymology, to explore its meaning. Broader literary approaches might consider the biblical text as literature, or, overlapping with the history of interpretation, or reception, pursue increasingly popular intertextual studies such as the use of the Bible in literature and film (Telford 1995b). The narrower methods associated with literary criticism or theory, some of which have been referred to already, might be employed to achieve specific aims: composition criticism, for example, to ascertain the arrangement or compositional techniques associated with its surface structure, genre criticism to determine its overall literary antecedents, rhetorical criticism to illumine its mechanisms of persuasion, narrative criticism to explore its plot, settings, characterization, and so on, reader-response criticism to investigate its effect upon the reader, structuralism to examine the elements associated with its deep structure, or even deconstruction to undermine any confidence in the notion of a 'fixed' meaning at all, and to emphasize the indeterminacy of the text.

Theological approaches

Following the theological paradigm, a biblical theology approach would seek to do justice to the distinctive content of the biblical text, namely, its religious or theological ideas, and the relation of such ideas to the rest of the biblical tradition. Narrative theology would focus on such ideas in so far as they were expressed through the literary medium of parable, allegory, story, and so on. With this category of approach could also be cited the 'new hermeneutic' associated with the work of postwar scholars such as E. Fuchs and G. Ebeling, a movement in exegesis that emphasizes the power of the biblical text, and of biblical language, not only to impart historical information but also to raise existential awareness and to promote a new self-understanding on the part of the reader. Both critical and confessional, and operating with the presupposition of the biblical text's place in an authoritative body of scripture, canonical criticism would seek, like other confessional approaches, to express the text's significance for the believing community. Devotional approaches to the text would likewise have the spiritual needs of the individual or the community in mind, as would pastoral theology. Other theological approaches to the biblical text have also been mentioned, in particular the ideological ones: fundamentalism, for example, with its insistence on the divine origin and infallibility of scripture, and on the necessity for the reader to be judged by rather than to judge the text; or the liberationist approaches (liberation theology, 'people's'/'grass roots' approaches, black theology, feminist theology), which seek to relate the text to the needs, aspirations and experience of the oppressed.

Some further categories, qualifications and distinctions

In sum, then, the threefold paradigmatic model goes a considerable way towards supplying us with a rough taxonomy of approaches within which we may make some sense of modern biblical interpretation's burgeoning hermeneutical enterprise. Inevitably, any systematization of a complex area produces some distortion. In this scheme, I have included the social-scientific and psychological approaches with the historical ones, and ideological approaches with the theological ones. Arguably each of these could constitute a category of its own. It would also be possible to argue that theology is a form of ideology, and that our third paradigm could be the ideological one, with theological approaches subsumed under this category along with materialist interpretation or Marxist interpretation, which I have had to leave out. And where should ethical approaches be placed (including moral criticism)? Should these appear likewise with theological (or ideological) approaches, or remain distinct?

Nevertheless, the scheme here proffered serves to reminds us that, despite their diversity, the variety of current methods represents in many ways a hermeneutical toolbox from which the exegete may select different tools for the textual job in hand. The medley of contemporary approaches, likewise, reflects the many divergent or convergent contexts within which biblical texts may be viewed. While it is possible to recognize clear demarcations in many cases between the paradigms and/or methods and approaches subsumed under these categories (some literary approaches, structuralism, for example, are committedly ahistorical, their purpose being to explore how meaning is achieved in a received text without reference to its antecedents or prehistory, and so they can be sharply distinguished from the traditio-historical methods), in other respects this is not the case. Some methods cross the boundary lines. Genre criticism has literary concerns, but in so far as it seeks to place a text in its literary-historical environment, historical ones. Some forms of reader-response criticism are only interested in the 'ideal' reader or the (implied) reader 'in' the text, while other approaches emphasize the reception of the text by its ancient readership, and hence retain a historical interest.

Some approaches are interdisciplinary in that they draw from more than one paradigmatic area or method, or have dual or even multiple concerns. Narrative theology, for example, may draw on the insights of narrative criticism. Redaction criticism is historical in the sense that it attempts to enter the mind of the original author of the text, literary in the sense that it builds upon, among other things, emendations made by the author to his sources, and theological in the sense that an understanding of the author's theology is its ultimate goal. Socio-rhetorical criticism focuses not only on a text's literary techniques and rhetorical devices but also on the relation of these to the text's social world. Some approaches are interdisciplinary, moreover, in the sense that they approach their texts with a combination of two or more distinct methods. In both Markan and Jesus studies, for example, one often sees an approach that combines a literary with a sociological perspective (Freyne 1988; Camery-Hoggatt 1992), hence seeking to do justice to our texts as literary products, on the one hand, but with 'real-world' connections and concerns on the other.

With such qualifications to our paradigms in mind, let me make, therefore, some further hopefully useful distinctions between the various methods and approaches. Certain of these have been touched upon already. An act of literary communication involves an author, a text and a reader, and the production of meaning through a process of interpretation involves due attention to one or more of these aspects. One way of differentiating the various methods and approaches, consequently, is with respect to the relative weight accorded to each of these aspects. Some approaches may be distinguished by their emphasis on the intention of the original author (compare the historical approaches, historical criticism, redaction criticism), others by their location of meaning in the text itself (compare literary approaches such as genre criticism or structuralism), and still others by their claim that it is readers who create meaning (compare literary approaches such as reader-response criticism).

Analyses of the text may be 'diachronic', that is, attuned to the prehistory of its component parts (e.g. tradition criticism, form criticism, source criticism), or 'synchronic', that is, directed to its final form, interrelationships and effects without regard to the process that brought it into being in the first place (e.g. rhetorical criticism, reader-response criticism, structuralism). Within these broad categories, further demarcations can be made. The influence of secular literary studies has led scholars to distinguish between those methods that treat the biblical text 'atomistically', that is, those that 'disintegrate' or 'fragment' the text (e.g. tradition criticism, source criticism, form criticism), and those that treat it 'holistically', that is, as a whole (e.g. redaction criticism, composition criticism, genre criticism, rhetorical criticism, reader-response criticism, structuralism). Holistic interpretation, a 'synchronic' rather than a 'diachronic' form of interpretation, is also one of the distinguishing features of canonical criticism, for example, an individual passage or text being accorded meaning in relation to its place within the entire body of inspired scripture.

A similar way of characterizing the various approaches is to distinguish those that focus on individual passages in a text without reference to the whole, that is, those preoccupied with 'micro-structure' (e.g. form criticism), and those that interpret individual units in light of the whole, that is, those preoccupied with 'macro-structure' (e.g. composition criticism). Methods and approaches may focus on discrete units (e.g. form criticism) or they may involve themselves with wider synchronic or diachronic contexts, the social-scientific approaches, for example, or those seeking to establish trajectories of various kinds (tradition criticism, history of religions, history of ideas, history of interpretation, history of reception).

A further differentiating feature are those methods and approaches that are prepared to invoke extrinsic factors outside of the text in the process of its interpretation (e.g. the historical-critical methods) and those prepared to invoke only intrinsic factors (like many of the literary approaches), or, to put it another way, those that may be deemed to be occupied with the author's 'real world' as opposed to his 'narrative' or 'story world'. The distinction may also be expressed in terms of those approaches that are literary-historical in nature (like source, form and redaction criticism), and those that are literary-aesthetic, that is, which explore the ways the author and/or text achieve their effects (e.g. rhetorical criticism). One of the most common images now employed, indeed, almost to the point of cliché, is the notion of texts as 'windows' (that is, allowing us to get back behind them to the history they reveal) and texts as 'mirrors' (that is, reflecting only their own story world).

Three more related hermeneutical *differentiae* might be mentioned. The first is the distinction to be made between 'intratextual' and 'extratextual' methods and approaches. The former epithet is applied to those methods and approaches, whether social-scientific or literary, which hold that 'experiences and events are only understood with reference to a framework of categories and values developed within a particular culture', or claim that 'the meaning of a religious text is inseparable from the particular language within which it is formed' (Brett 1990: 320). Canonical criticism would be an example of the use of intratextuality in relation to a theological approach. In this context, 'extratextual' would then refer to those methods and approaches that apply an interpretative framework to the data or text that is not intrinsic to either.

The second is the distinction to be made between approaches that are 'contextual' and those that are not. Contextual approaches

> have in common that they include the reader in the definition of the literary work and include the context of reader and/or writer in the process of interpretation. The 'work' is not the text but comes into being when text and reader interact. The text, therefore, is not an 'object' upon which the interpreter performs analytic or investigative procedures (as does a scientist) in order to extract a theoretically univocal intrinsic meaning. Rather, it is a poetic structure that is engaged, from within a concrete situation, by a reader in the process of achieving meaning. (Brown and Schneiders 1989: 1159)

A number of the literary approaches (especially reader-response criticism) would come under this rubric, as would a number of the ideological approaches (e.g. liberation or feminist theology) in so far as they invite interpreters to exercise a 'hermeneutic of suspicion' not only upon the text and its author(s) but also upon themselves.

This brings us to our third *differentia*, one touched upon already, and this is the distinction to be drawn between those methods and approaches that are purely 'descriptive', 'evaluative' or 'analytical', that is, those that aim to be as objective as possible, or attempt to keep a distance between the interpreter and that which is being interpreted (e.g. the historical-critical approaches), and those methods and approaches that are 'actualizing', that is, which challenge or involve the interpreter existentially, or call forth various forms of response or commitment (e.g. the ideological approaches, or the confessional or devotional approaches).

Refinement, complementarity or fragmentation?

Thus far, then, I have reviewed the current state of modern biblical interpretation, commenting on the nature and scope of contemporary biblical hermeneutics, mentioning the three major paradigms in the field, and outlining the principal methods and approaches that have been in operation, especially in the last quarter of the twentieth century. Having proffered a basic taxonomy of these methods and approaches, and offered some qualifications to it as well as some further distinctions, let me now take up the key question introduced at the beginning of this chapter, before finishing with discussion of some methodological issues. My question, you will recall, was whether the methodological pluralism, which so obviously characterizes modern biblical interpretation today, betokens refinement, complementarity, confusion or even fragmentation within the field of biblical studies. Do the methodological developments of the nineteen eighties and nineties represent centripetal or centrifugal tendencies with respect to the discipline?

The case has been argued both ways. A number of the new methods and approaches can be considered as refinements or developments of the older more traditional methods. Socio-rhetorical criticism (Robbins 1996), for example, can clearly be seen to be a development of classic form criticism. Composition criticism, and even some aspects of narrative criticism, can be seen to have emerged or are indistinguishable from redaction criticism in its broader applications. One feature of Markan studies in the late nineteen seventies and eighties was a growing consensus that summary passages, seams, insertions or modifications of pericopae were an inadequate base for developing a full picture of Mark's style and theology. Redaction (or editorial) criticism of the narrower kind began to give way, therefore, to a broader composition criticism (Dowd 1988) or narrative criticism (Marshall 1989) in its search for the Markan fingerprints. One major aspect of the sociological approach, namely, the use of social description to interpret the Bible, has long been a feature of what was called 'Introduction', and, methodologically, little distinguishes this aspect from the traditional approaches.

A case can be made, then, that what we are seeing is the increased sophistication of the biblical hermeneutical enterprise. Texts supply us with contexts within contexts, and the plurality of methods matches the complex nature of the biblical text itself, as I have indicated. The plurality of methods, therefore, is to be welcomed, each supplying a corrective to the other, and the whole offering us a much richer perspective on our sources. This can be seen, for example, in the way that the three principal traditio-critical methods, source, form and redaction criticism, have complemented each other, each separating source material from editorial material, tradition from redaction, with source criticism pursuing evidence of written sources underlying the text, form criticism investigating its oral antecedents, and redaction criticism (at least in its earlier manifestation) engaging the editorial remainder.

This complementarity can be seen to a degree also in the relationship pertaining between redaction criticism, composition criticism, rhetorical criticism and narrative criticism. All are holistic methods, with redaction criticism interfacing with the text's prehistory by highlighting the author's use of the sources, composition criticism analysing the structure and arrangement of the resultant whole in relation to its individual components, rhetorical criticism investigating the text's 'discourse' or patterns of persuasion, and narrative criticism examining the text's 'story' in terms of its plot, settings, characters, point of view, and so on.

Other voices have been raised, however, in favour of the fragmentation view. There have been numerous doomsayers, for example, announcing the end of the traditio-critical methods, whether source criticism (Friedman 1987), or form criticism (Güttgemanns 1979) or redaction criticism (Black 1989). Where source criticism is concerned, there has been an increasing impatience on the part of biblical scholars with the minutiae of atomistic, diachronic, source-critical enquiry, and its allegedly speculative reconstructions, and a corresponding enthusiasm for the holistic and synchronic literary approaches. Where form criticism is concerned, some have questioned the very concept of an original 'form' in respect of the sayings or actions of Jesus transmitted in the oral tradition, or have called for new models for the oral transmission process, and a revised understanding of the differences between orality and textuality (Kelber 1983). Where redaction criticism is concerned, some have argued that the very broadening of the redaction-critical method has brought it into the field of general literary criticism and hence within range of dehistoricizing methods and approaches that undermine its validity as a literary-historical method. In this respect, it could be argued, the method has sown the seeds of its own destruction. Advocates of the theological paradigm have likewise berated historical-critical methodologies for excluding theological concerns from their agenda (Watson 1994). Given that the religious community is still a primary context for the biblical text, and that its interpretation depends to some degree on the interpreter's point of view, then the privileging of historical questions to the detriment of the text's role in promoting theological reflection is to be resisted.

Faultlines within the biblical hermeneutical enterprise, then, are apparent, especially between the historical paradigm and the literary one. It is undoubtedly true that literary criticism has posed a challenge to the historical-critical method, though not, of course uniformly or even inevitably. Literary-critical approaches have certainly come to dominate discussion since the 1970s, but they too have their problems and limitations, and these should be acknowledged if synchronic and diachronic methods are to work in harmony with one another (Telford 1993). Likewise, it would be unfortunate if a legitimate desire to give a renewed accent to the theological dimensions of the biblical text were to undermine the very solid gains made by the historical-critical method in advancing biblical scholarship, illuminating the Bible and its world, and freeing the modern interpreter from hitherto dogmatic or obscurantist views.

Some issues in methodology

What is/are the appropriate interpretative method(s)?

In this final section, I would like to raise some methodological issues, and in particular to discuss three that I have encountered in my own work on Mark and Jesus. One major problem for the contemporary interpreter or exegete, given the extensive hermeneutical toolbox at his or her disposal, is to determine what the appropriate method is for the particular text under scrutiny. Biblical scholars are all familiar with the fact that a particular textual problem may be the subject of a bewildering number of attempted solutions by virtue of the equally bewildering number of different methods applied to it. In the Gospel of Mark, a notorious crux is 14.51–2, the flight of the naked young man. Where different hermeneutical orientations are concerned, few passages in the New Testament are as revealing as this one! At one end of the spectrum are historical-critical or perhaps historical-not-so-critical proposals that would identify this young man as a thinly disguised John Mark of Jerusalem. At the other end are a number of interpretations that would invest the young man with Christological or baptismal significance (by virtue of the 'garment' associated with him, which he then discards in the manner of the Christian initiate). The Old Testament or Hebrew Bible has also often been suggested as the underlying catalyst for this curious datum (cf. e.g. Amos 2.16, 'And he who is stout of heart among the mighty shall flee away naked in that day' or even the Joseph story in Gen. 39.11–12 and 41.39–43 where the flight of Joseph from Potiphar's wife, leaving his garment behind, is taken as an allusion supporting an underlying Christ as second 'Joseph' motif in the text). On the other hand, it has been suggested that these two verses are simply the expurgated residue of a longer passage in what was an earlier 'Secret Gospel of Mark' and that in its fuller version all would have been revealed to the reader. In short, what we witness here is a number of solutions that reflect the application of a variety of different methods deemed appropriate to the text, whether historical criticism, source criticism, literary criticism, motif criticism, intertextuality, or narrative criticism! Interpreters must therefore learn to exercise their discretion in determining which tool is appropriate for the particular textual problem encountered.

A major issue in my work on Mark is the question whether source criticism or literary criticism should be invoked in the treatment or explanation of inconsistencies or ambiguities in the text. Breaks, gaps in the narrative, inconsistencies, ambiguities, duplications or repetitions (all of which abound in Mark) are generally taken by source critics as evidence of the use of sources, and hence of faulty editing, but by literary critics as narrative devices or strategies (opacity, irony, misdirection, emphasis, etc.), and hence as conscious or unconscious signals to the reader involved in the construction of meaning. How do we decide between the two? Decisions on these questions can affect our judgement on certain of the key Markan questions, namely, 'How skilful an author is the evangelist?' 'How coherent a story world has he created?' and 'What is the relationship between the narrator's 'story' world and the author's 'real' world?' Some scholars, therefore, following the literary paradigm, would argue that Mark's ambiguities were deliberately created by him in line with a consistent literary and theological purpose, while others, following the historical paradigm, would maintain that they are the product of the inadequate redaction of his sources. This dispute over creativity in fact lies at the heart of the modern debate about Mark's Gospel. Some scholars, following the stricter form-, source- and redaction-critical model that I have already outlined, tend to see Mark as a conservative redactor or editor, while others, influenced by a wider literary criticism, tend to see Mark almost as a candidate for the Nobel Prize for Literature! The reality is that Mark is a composite text that displays considerable awkwardness at pericope level but considerable sophistication when viewed holistically. That, indeed, is one of its continuing puzzles.

What is/are the appropriate interpretative context(s)?

A second major problem for the contemporary interpreter or exegete is to determine what the appropriate interpretative context is for the data or text under consideration. This is an important point, for example, in contemporary Jesus studies. Which proposed background, especially within Judaism, can be established as the most important interpretative context for the reconstruction of Jesus' teaching and mission: Pharisaism, apocalyptic, the wisdom tradition, Rabbinic Judaism, the prophetic tradition, Essene sectarianism, the charismatic Hasidism of Galilee, the Zealots? All have been suggested (Telford 1994: 33–74, esp. 68). In Markan studies, the debate revolves around a number of connected issues. The first of these is what one might call 'intrinsic versus extrinsic referencing'. In studying the Gospel from a purely literary point of view, can extrinsic factors be kept at bay? All texts point beyond themselves (intertextuality) and so even from a literary point of view, can we ignore the major fact of intertextuality in the case of Mark (or most of the New Testament writings, for that matter), namely, the writer's use of the Old Testament or Hebrew Bible?

A related issue is whether the 'world' of the text and the 'real world' can be kept separate. According to a recent literary study of Markan irony by J. Camery-Hoggatt, 'The reader who ignores the historical and cultural milieu in which the narrative originates will be unable to detect even literary features of the text [e.g. ironic nuances]' (1992: 75). Mark's story world is often interpenetrated with the world of his present community, and literary methods that seek to discount the latter often run into difficulties. A third issue is what one might call 'holistic versus atomistic referencing'. Should one interpret any passage in Mark in the light of the whole (macro-structure), or independently in respect of its component parts (micro-structure)? According to scholars such as H. Räisänen, it is better to make sense of individual passages without constraint than to seek to fit them into Mark's total view (1990: 30). According to others, the total view is indispensable in understanding individual passages (Geddert 1989).

What is the appropriate interpretative sequence?

A third related problem for the contemporary interpreter or exegete is to determine what the appropriate interpretative sequence is for the hermeneutical operation under consideration. If more than one method or approach is to be employed, then what governs the priority or order in which they should be applied? Should synchronic analysis precede diachronic analysis, for example? Should holistic interpretation take precedence over an atomistic approach? Should we begin with a literary approach to our texts and then proceed to a historical one, or vice versa, as most Introductions to the Bible tend to do? Should we invoke extrinsic factors to interpret our texts only when the possibility of intrinsic explanations have been exhausted? The relationship of all these methodologies to one another, therefore, is likely to continue to be a burning hermeneutical issue well into the new millennium!

CONCLUSION

Despite this, it is possible to conclude that the plurality of methods and approaches is a sign of richness and not of disorder in modern biblical interpretation. Biblical texts are complex, as I hope I have demonstrated, and require a variety of competencies on the part of the interpreter. Each of the methods and approaches adumbrated in this chapter have their strengths as well as their weaknesses. Scholars will continue to hold reservations about the use of certain methods and particular approaches. While they may serve to illumine the 'narrative world' of a biblical text, literary approaches can often serve to cast radical doubt on the 'real world' correspondences predicated of it by historical approaches. Modern sociological approaches and theories often raise questions of appropriateness and comparability when pressed into the service of ancient text analysis. Though popular nowadays, a combined literary and sociological approach, critics say, may simply be unwise to bypass the prehistory of the text, or the intention of its author, in the search for historicity. Nevertheless, despite these divisions, the revitalization of biblical studies in our own day has, in considerable measure, been occasioned by the application of these new methods and approaches. The future lies, in my opinion, with the further refinement and fruitful integration of these various methodologies. Biblical interpretation will continue to develop and, if it is not to fragment, the pressure will grow for an inclusive, consensus-building methodology (or methodologies), particularly one(s) that will reconcile the synchronic and diachronic approaches that have in part divided American and European scholarship in recent times. Such a methodology will need to be sophisticated enough to offer criteria, for example, whereby we might assess the textual evidence that leads to divergent literary and source-critical evaluations. Starting from a synchronic literary analysis, for example, it might proceed by asking what are the principles by which we might deconstruct the text in such a way as to establish diachronic theories that might lead to greater consensus. Whatever the eventual methodological solutions, a balance will need to be kept between historical, literary and theological concerns in biblical interpretation, since all three, like the Trinity, represent the threefold nature of its subject matter.

BIBLIOGRAPHY

Alter, R. (1981) *The Art of Biblical Narrative*, New York: Basic.

Barr, J. (1981) *Fundamentalism*, London: SCM.

—— (1999) *The Concept of Biblical Theology: An Old Testament Perspective*, London: SCM.

Bauckham, R. (1989) *The Bible in Politics: How to Read the Bible Politically*, London: SPCK.

Black, C. C. (1989) *The Disciples according to Mark: Markan Redaction in Current Debate* (Journal for the Study of the New Testament Supplement Series, 27), Sheffield: JSOT Press.

Botha, J. (1996) 'The Bible in South African Public Discourse – With Special Reference to the Right to Protest', *Scriptura* 58: 329–43.

Brett, M. G. (1990) 'Intratextuality', in R. J. Coggins and J. L. Houlden (eds) *A Dictionary of Biblical Interpretation*, London: SCM; Philadelphia: Trinity Press International, 320–1.

Brown, R. E. and Schneiders, S. M. (1989) 'Hermeneutics', in R. E. Brown, J. A. Fitzmyer and R. E. Murphy (eds) *The New Jerome Biblical Commentary*, London: G. Chapman, 1146–65.

Bryan, C. (1993) *A Preface to Mark: Notes on the Gospel in Its Literary and Cultural Settings*, New York: Oxford University Press.

Burridge, R. A. (1992) *What Are the Gospels? A Comparison with Graeco-Roman Biography* (Society for New Testament Studies Monograph Series, 70), Cambridge: Cambridge University Press.

Camery-Hoggatt, J. (1992) *Irony in Mark's Gospel* (Society for New Testament Studies Monograph Series, 72), Cambridge: Cambridge University Press.

Coggins, R. J. and Houlden, J. L. (eds) (1990) *A Dictionary of Biblical Interpretation*, London: SCM; Philadelphia: Trinity Press International.

Collins, A. Y. (1990) *Is Mark's Gospel a Life of Jesus? The Question of Genre* (Père Marquette Lecture in Theology, 21), Milwaukee: Marquette University Press.

Corner, M. (1990) 'Fundamentalism', in R. J. Coggins and J. L. Houlden (eds) *A Dictionary of Biblical Interpretation*, London: SCM; Philadelphia: Trinity Press International, 243–7.

Dewey, J. (1980) *Markan Public Debate: Literary Technique, Concentric Structure, and Theology in Mark 2:1–3:6* (Society of Biblical Literature Dissertation Series, 48), Chico: Scholars Press.

Dowd, S. E. (1988) *Prayer, Power and the Problem of Suffering: Mark 11:22–25 in the Context of Markan Theology* (Society of Biblical Literature Dissertation Series, 105), Atlanta: Scholars Press.

Fowler, R. M. (1991) *Let the Reader Understand: Reader-Response Criticism and the Gospel of Mark*, Minneapolis: Fortress.

Freyne, S. (1988) *Galilee, Jesus and the Gospels: Literary Approaches and Historical Investigations*, Dublin: Gill & Macmillan.

Friedman, R. E. (1987) 'The Recession of Biblical Source Criticism', in R. E. Friedman and H. G. M. Williamson (eds), *The Future of Biblical Studies: The Hebrew Scriptures*, Atlanta: Scholars Press, 81–101.

Geddert, T. J. (1989) *Watchwords: Mark 13 in Markan Eschatology* (Journal for the Study of the New Testament Supplement Series, 26), Sheffield: JSOT Press.

Ghiberti, G. (1982) 'Überlegungen zum neueren Stand der Leben-Jesu-Forschung', *Münchener Theologische Zeitschrift* 33: 99–115.

Goldingay, J. (1990) 'Theology (Old Testament)', in R. J. Coggins and J. L. Houlden (eds) *A Dictionary of Biblical Interpretation*, London: SCM; Philadelphia: Trinity Press International, 691–4.

Güttgemanns, E. (1979) *Candid Questions Concerning Gospel Form Criticism: A Methodological Sketch of the Fundamental Problematics of Form and Redaction Criticism* (Pittsburg Theological Monograph Series, 26), Pittsburg: Pickwick.

Iersel, B. van (1989) *Reading Mark*, Edinburgh: T. & T. Clark.

Kelber, W. H. (1983) *The Oral and Written Gospel: The Hermeneutics of Speaking and Writing in the Synoptic Tradition, Mark, Paul and Q*, Philadelphia: Fortress.

Malbon, E. S. (1986) *Narrative Space and Mythic Meaning in Mark* (New Voices in Biblical Studies), San Francisco: Harper & Row.

Marshall, C. D. (1989) *Faith as a Theme in Mark's Narrative* (Society for New Testament Studies Monograph Series, 64), Cambridge: Cambridge University Press.

McDonald, J. I. H. (1980) 'New Quest – Dead End? So What about the Historical Jesus?', in E. A. Livingstone (ed.) *Studia Biblica*. Vol. 2: *Papers on the Gospels, Oxford, 3–7 April, 1978*, Sheffield: JSOT Press, 151–70.

Mesters, C. (1983) 'The Use of the Bible in Christian Communities of the Common People', in N. K. Gottwald (ed.), *The Bible and Liberation: Political and Social Hermeneutics*, Maryknoll: Orbis, 119–33.

Morgan, R. (1990) 'Historicism', in R. J. Coggins and J. L. Houlden (eds) *A Dictionary of Biblical Interpretation*, London: SCM; Philadelphia: Trinity Press International, 290–1.

Morgan, R. and Barton, J. (1988) *Biblical Interpretation* (Oxford Bible Series), Oxford: Oxford University Press.

Räisänen, H. (1990) *The 'Messianic Secret' in Mark* (Studies of the New Testament and its World), Edinburgh: T. & T. Clark.

Rhoads, D. and Michie, D. (1982) *Mark as Story: An Introduction to the Narrative of a Gospel*, Philadelphia: Fortress.

Robbins, V. K. (1996) *Exploring the Texture of Texts: A Guide to Socio-Rhetorical Interpretation*, Harrisburg: Trinity Press International.

Robertson, D. (1976) 'Literature, the Bible as', in K. Crim (ed.) *The Interpreter's Dictionary of the Bible*, Nashville: Abingdon, 547–51.

Telford, W. R. (1980) *The Barren Temple and the Withered Tree: A Redaction-Critical Analysis of the Cursing of the Fig-tree Pericope in Mark's Gospel and its Relation to the Cleansing of the Temple Tradition* (Journal for the Study of the New Testament Supplement Series, 1), Sheffield: JSOT Press.

—— (1990) 'Mark, Gospel of', in R. J. Coggins and J. L. Houlden (eds) *A Dictionary of Biblical Interpretation*, London: SCM; Philadelphia: Trinity Press International, 424–8.

—— (1991) 'More Fruit from the Withered Tree: Temple and Fig-Tree in Mark from a Graeco-Roman Perspective', in W. Horbury (ed.) *Templum Amicitiae: Essays on the Second Temple Presented to Ernst Bammel*, Sheffield: JSOT Press, 264–304.

—— (1993) 'Mark and the Historical-Critical Method: The Challenge of Recent Literary Approaches to the Gospel', in C. Focant (ed.) *The Synoptic Gospels: Source Criticism and the New Literary Criticism*, Leuven: Peeters; Leuven University Press, 491–502.

—— (1994) 'Major Trends and Interpretive Issues in the Study of Jesus', in B. Chilton and C. A. Evans (eds) *Studying the Historical Jesus*, Leiden: E. J. Brill, 33–74.

—— (1995a) *Mark* (New Testament Guides), Sheffield: Sheffield Academic Press.

—— (1995b) 'The New Testament in Fiction and Film: A Biblical Scholar's Perspective', in J. G. Davies, G. Harvey and W. Watson (eds) *Words Remembered, Texts Renewed: Essays in Honour of J. F. A. Sawyer*, Sheffield: Sheffield Academic Press, 360–94.

Thiselton, A. C. (1992) *New Horizons in Hermeneutics: The Theory and Practice of Transforming Biblical Reading*, London: HarperCollins.

Thompson, M. R. (1989) *The Role of Disbelief in Mark: A New Approach to the Second Gospel*, New York: Paulist Press.

van Yerzel, B. (1989) *Reading Mark*, Edinburgh: T. & T. Clark.

Watson, F. (1994) *Text, Church and World: Biblical Interpretation in Theological Perspective*, Edinburgh: T. & T. Clark.

INDEX OF BIBLICAL REFERENCES

OLD TESTAMENT

451

Daniel

1:8–12   II.124
2–7   II.123
2:4–7:28   I.6, II.18
2   I.21
2:31   II.123
2:34   II.123
2:37   I.17
3   I.134, II.65
3:6   II.123
3:23–24   I.22
3:31–33   II.123
4–6   I.152
4   I.134
4:31–32   II.123
5:17–30   II.123
5:31   I.159
6:10   I.134, 429
6:26–28   II.123
7–12   I.152, 153, II.299
7   I.132, 134, 141, II.124
7:1–15   II.123
7:9–14   II.350
7:9   I.131
7:13–14   II.299
7:13   II.229, 252, 344
7:18   II.123
7:27   II.123
8:14   II.124
8:23–25   II.299
9   II.124
9:24–25   II.300
9:27   II.124
10–12   II.124
10   I.134
10:5–9   II.337
10:5–6   II.350
10:13–21   II.336
10:14   I.12
11:14   II.123
11:32–35   II.124
11:35   II.365
12   I.21, II.364
12:1–3   II.300
12:1   II.124
12:2   I.134, II.117, 124
12:3   II.124
12:10   II.124
12:11   II.124
12:12   II.124

Hosea

1:1–2:1   I.101
1:1–2   I.101
1:2   I.101

1:10   II.72
2:2–23   I.101
2:4   II.94
2:23   II.72
2:11–17   II.94
2:11–15   II.94
2:16   I.278
3:1–5   I.101
3:1   I.101
3:4–5   II.289
4:1   I.101
4:11–14   II.92, 94
4:15   II.179
5:3   II.390
5:12–14   II.94
6:2   II.363
6:6   I.175, II.250
6:7–10   II.390
9:7   II.94
10:5   II.179
11:1   II.94, 340
11:5   II.94
11:11   II.94
12:2–6   II.188
12:2–4   II.185
12:13   II.198, 202, 203
13:1–8   II.94
13:13   II.288
14:5–7   II.289

Joel

1:15   I.100
2   II.265
2:28–32   II.168
2:32   I.99, II.340
3:1–5   II.348
3:10   I.100
3:16   I.99, 100
3:18   I.99

Amos

1:2   I.99, 100
1:3   I.509
1:13   I.516
1:14   I.515
1:15   I.515
2:4   II.87
2:6   II.94
2:16   II.240, 444
3:1–2   II.95
3:7   I.429
3:14   II.179
4:13   II.47

471

NEW TESTAMENT

1 Corinthians

INDEX OF MODERN AUTHORS

—◆—

SUBJECT INDEX

————•◦•————

Note: Page references in **bold** type indicate main discussion of a topic; those in *italics* indicate illustrations.

Aaron: and Moses II.200, 202, 203; and priesthood I.9, 426, II.76–7, 301–2
Aaron ben-Asher I.210, 211, 292
Aaron ben-Moses ben-Asher I.211
'Abdu-Heba (king of Jerusalem) I.375, 386
abecedaries I.272, 299, *299*, II.22, *22*
Abiathar (priest) II.211, 214–15, 219
Abraham: and Binding of Isaac II.*182*, *183*; and covenant II.181, 271, 302; descent from Adam I.9; and Hagar I.326, II.186; and historicity I.356, 373, II.175, 177–80, 188 n.7; in *Jubilees* I.324; and significance II.181–3, 265, 274, 359
Absalom (son of David) I.79, 323, II.213–14, 215
Achaemenid period *see* Persia
Achish, king of Gath I.493, 498, II.211
Achish (son of Padi) of Ekron I.495, 497
Actium, battle (31 BC) I.468
Acts of the Apostles: and age of the Church I.177–8; and apocalyptic I.144–5; and authorship I.178; and christology II.347–8; date I.29; as history I.28, 29, 150, 459, II.233, 259; and Luke I.176–8; and Paul I.30, 31, II.259–61; and Roman authorities II.140; texts and versions I.236, 238–45
Acts of John I.178
Acts of Paul and Thecla II.147, 277
Acts of Peter I.31
Acts of Thomas II.166
Adad-nerari III of Assyria I.495, 502, 509, 519, 520
Adam: and Abraham I.9; and death II.359; as type of Christ II.31, 268–9, 339, 342

Adapa: myths of I.50, II.357–8
Adonijah (son of David) II.214–15
adoptionism I.246, II.340
Aelfric of Winchester II.416–17
Aemilius Scaurus, governor of Syria I.267, 461, 462
afterlife: in Apocrypha I.24–5; in early apocalypses II.363–71; in early Christianity II.372–5; in Hebrew Bible II.361–3, *see also* resurrection
Agathachides of Cnidus I.446
agency, divine II.336–7, 352
agriculture: Iron Age I.394–400, 401, 404; and pre-exilic religion II.91–2
Agrippa I I.471, 473–4, **474–6**, II.77, 82
Agrippa II I.474, 477, 480, 483
Ahab, king of Israel: and Aram Damascus I.508, II.41; and Jezebel I.90, II.77, 93–4; and Moab I.517–18; and Phoenicians I.501–2; and prophets I.89, 90; and warfare II.35, 41, 44, 46
Ahab (prophet) I.429
Ahaz, king of Judah I.95, 509
Ahaziah, king of Israel I.91
Ahaziah, king of Judah I.276
Ahmose, Pharaoh I.381, 384
'Ai (et-Tell) I.353, 370, *370*, 371, II.45
Ak(h)enaten (Amenhotep IV), Pharaoh I.382, 385, II.6, 54, 197
Akiba/Akiva, R. I.138, 215, 295
Akkadia: and cuneiform script I.41–2, 44, 56, 374–5, II.3, 6, 22; myths and legends I.42, 47, 49–57, II.357, *see also* Sargon of Agade

507